Introduction to Data Mining with Case Studies

Introduction to Data Mining with Case Studies

THIRD EDITION

G.K. GUPTA
Adjunct Professor of Computer Science
Monash University
Clayton, Australia

PHI Learning Private Limited
Delhi-110092
2024

In fond memory of ***Shri Asoke K. Ghosh*** *(October 1942 – February 2024), Founder Chairman and Managing Director of PHI Learning, whose vision endlessly inspires.*

The Legacy Continues....

Published by Pushpita Ghosh, PHI Learning Private Limited, Rimjhim House, 111, Patparganj Industrial Estate, Delhi-110092 and Printed by Mudrak, C-55, Sector 65, Noida, U.P.-201301

₹895.00

INTRODUCTION TO DATA MINING WITH CASE STUDIES, THIRD EDITION
G.K. Gupta

ISBN-978-81-203-5002-1 (Print Book)
ISBN-978-81-948848-8-0 (e-Book)

The export rights of the book are vested solely with the publisher.

To

the memory of

Professor C.S. Wallace

Foundation Professor and Head

Department of Computer Science

Monash University

26 October 1933–7 August 2004

Contents

Chapter 4 CLASSIFICATION 152–215

Chapter 5 CLUSTER ANALYSIS 216–269

Preface

The third edition of this book is a substantially revised version of the earlier editions. The first chapter has been rewritten and expanded. A new example has been added. Whereas the second chapter is completely new to this edition. It discusses the importance of data preprocessing in data mining. A number of issues are discussed in this chapter. An interesting example is included as an exercise at the end of the chapter. This example may also be used in Chapter 5 on Clustering. Chapter 3 has been revised and a new project has been included. Chapter 4 has been revised and so has been Chapter 5. Minor modifications have been made to Chapter 6. Whereas Chapter 7 has been revised substantially. A new section on Query Data Mining has been added to this chapter. Minor modifications have been made to Chapters 8 and 9. Finally, Chapter 10 has been revised substantially to focus on privacy developments in India.

Please continue to send me feedback about the book at my email address gkgupta@acm.org.

G.K. Gupta
gkgupta@acm.org

Preface to the Second Edition

The second edition of this book preserves the spirit and style of the earlier edition. The changes in the second edition primarily involve the addition of a large number of questions at the end of each chapter. These include Review Questions, Short Answer Questions, Multiple Choice Questions as well as some suggestions for class projects. In addition, some material has been revised to include more recent information. Finally, some errors identified by instructors have been fixed. I shall be grateful to all the readers who would kindly bring to my notice any such missed-out errors, as well as suggestions for improving the book further.

G.K. Gupta
gkgupta@acm.org

Preface to the First Edition

This book is based on a set of notes that were prepared for a course on data mining that I taught at Bond University during 2000–2002 and then at the Monash University School of Computer Science and Software Engineering during 2004. The course was designed for third-year computer science students although many students doing a Masters degree by coursework also took it. The classes at both Bond and Monash were diverse and some of the students did not have a strong mathematical background. My aim in preparing these notes was to ensure that students were exposed to all major data mining techniques without the mathematical rigour that one would prefer to use. Mathematical concepts were not totally avoided but presented in such a way that they could be understood by students without a strong mathematical background. The courses became quite popular and the student feedback for the courses and the way they were presented was very positive.

In recent years there has been an explosive growth in the generation and storage of electronic information as more and more operations of enterprises are computerized. The cost of processing power and storage has been declining for many years. Buying a terabyte of disk would have been unthinkable only 10 years ago but is now affordable.

Major enterprises have been using database management systems for at least 30 years and have accumulated a large amount of information. Some companies, for example major banks and telecommunications companies, now have mountains of data and they have started to realize that the information accumulated over the years is an important strategic asset. There is potential business intelligence hidden in the large volumes of data. What these companies require is techniques that allow them to distil the most valuable information from the accumulated data. The field of data mining provides such techniques.

Data mining or knowledge discovery in databases (KDD) deals with exploration techniques based on advanced analytical methods and tools for handling a large amount of information. It is a collection of techniques that finds novel patterns that can assist an enterprise in understanding its business better. Many data mining techniques are closely related to some of the machine learning techniques that have been developed since the 1960s. Others are related to techniques that have been developed in statistics (sometimes called *Exploratory Data Analysis*). These techniques were developed some time ago and were designed to deal with a limited amount of data. Many techniques have been modified to deal with large amounts of data.

To the Teacher

The book deals with most of the important topics in data mining, yet there are some topics that have not been covered. Most notably the book does not cover neural networks and text mining.

The book includes many examples which I believe are essential in getting students motivated and in helping them understand the material. I have also provided exercises and references. References in the book provide some of the most highly cited papers in data mining.

I have also included a number of case studies that have been published in refereed journals to illustrate how the different techniques are used in practice. The case studies are an essential part of the course. Students should be required to study them, attempt the case studies' exercises given at the end of each chapter and prepare summaries of at least one or two of them.

To the Student

Data mining is an exciting area and I hope you will enjoy the book. The book is written primarily for you. I have provided many examples to help you learn the concepts and the techniques. A large number of references have been provided including a small number specially selected for you since they are easy to read. I appreciate that most students do not have the time to read references other than the prescribed textbooks and lecture notes but these references should be useful if you decide to learn more about the techniques during your studies or after you finish your studies. Some of the references for teachers are the most highly cited references in data mining literature and are therefore highly regarded by data mining researchers.

Exercises have been provided at the end of every chapter. Please make sure that you try to solve all of these to better understand the material in the book.

Each chapter has either one or two case studies associated with it. These case studies have been published in scholarly journals. The case studies show you how the techniques described in the book are used in practice. Study them carefully, try the case study exercises given at the end of each chapter and try to prepare a one-page summary of at least one or two of them to make sure you have understood what was done and how it was done. I am sure you will gain a lot of insight by studying the case studies.

How the Book is Structured

This data mining book is organized differently than other such books. In particular, I decided to defer discussion of data cleaning, data warehousing and OLAP to the end of the book because I have found that students want to get on with learning data mining techniques and find data warehousing and OLAP material not so interesting right at the beginning. Students appreciate this material better once they have a good understanding of the aims and techniques of data mining. Also, by reading the case studies they will realize how important these topics are and how much time they consume in a data mining project.

In any case if a teacher wanted to follow a more conventional sequence of topics and cover data warehousing and OLAP before doing other data mining topics, Chapters 7 and 8 can be done after Chapter 1. Chapters 7 and 8 do not depend on other chapters and the other chapters do not require material from these two chapters.

Chapter 1 is an introductory chapter that explains what data mining is and presents a definition. It also explains the data mining process and briefly discusses the techniques that are covered in this book. An important part of this chapter is the discussion of a number of application areas of data mining. A brief description of a number of case studies from different application areas is presented to show the wide range of applications of data mining. Some information on data mining software and how to select suitable software is also included in this chapter.

In Chapter 2 we present a conceptually simple yet interesting example of analysing supermarket data with the aim of discovering association rules. This is called *association rules mining* or *market basket analysis* and involves searching for interesting customer habits by looking at associations. The classical example is the one where an American store was reported to have discovered that people buying nappies tended also to buy beer. The association rules mining technique has many applications other than market basket analysis including applications in marketing, customer segmentation, medicine, electronic commerce, classification, clustering, Web mining, bioinformatics, and finance.

We explain the classical Apriori algorithm for association rules mining and then present a number of other algorithms that are designed to carry out association rules mining more efficiently.

In Chapter 3 we discuss supervised classification. Classification is a classical problem extensively studied by statisticians and machine learning researchers and is probably one of the most widely used data mining techniques. In classification it is assumed that the classes have been decided apriori and classification then consists of training the system so that when a new object is presented to the trained system the system is able to assign the object to one of the existing classes. This approach is called *supervised classification*. Some techniques are available for unsupervised classification in which the classes are determined based on the given data. These are discussed in Chapter 4 on cluster analysis.

In Chapter 3, the widely used decision tree approach of supervised classification is described. The Naïve Bayes method is also discussed.

In Chapter 4 unsupervised classification or cluster analysis is discussed. Classification and cluster analysis (or clustering) are both important techniques that partition multidimensional data into meaningful disjoint subgroups, members in each subgroup being more similar to each other in the values of their attributes than they are to members of the other groups.

There are major differences between cluster analysis and supervised classification. In supervised classification, the user already knows the classes and training data that is already labelled by their class membership is available to train or build a model. In cluster analysis, the user does not know what classes or clusters exist in the data and the aim is to group the given data into meaningful groups.

There are a large number of cluster analysis methods available; they are often based on diverse underlying principles and they lead to qualitatively different results. In some ways cluster analysis is best used as an exploratory data analysis exercise when the user has no hypothesis to test. We will discuss a number of cluster analysis methods. In the widely used K-means method it is required that the user specify the number of clusters and starting seeds for each cluster. In many applications it might be difficult to specify these without some insight into the data that the user may not have. One possible approach then might be to combine a method like this with a hierarchical method. We will describe two hierarchical methods.

In Chapter 5 the relatively new area of Web mining is discussed. Web mining is the application of data mining techniques to find interesting and potentially useful knowledge from Web data including hyperlink structures of the Web and Web log data. Web mining includes Web content mining which deals with discovering useful information or knowledge from Web page contents. It goes well beyond using keywords in a search engine. Web structure mining deals with modelling the link structure of the Web while Web usage mining deals with understanding user behaviour in interacting with the Web or with a Web site. One of the aims of Web usage mining is to obtain information that may assist Web site reorganization or assist site adaptation to better suit the user.

Chapter 6 deals with another Web-related topic, search engines. Search engines are huge databases of Web pages as well as software packages for indexing and retrieving pages that enable users to find information of interest on the Web. Normally the search engine databases of Web pages are built and updated automatically by Web crawlers. When one searches the Web using one of the search engines, one is not searching the entire Web. Instead one is only searching the database that has been compiled by the search engine. Normally the huge search engine database is searched using an index that has been built. In this chapter we explain how search engines work and how Web pages are ranked.

Chapter 7 is devoted to discussing issues related to an overall enterprise view of the data and data warehousing. It has been reported that several years ago a soft drinks company could not quickly determine how many bottles were produced in a day since the information was distributed in more than 20 different computer systems in different locations. In some cases it may be difficult for an enterprise even to obtain a well maintained list of all the customers or all the suppliers since the customers and suppliers may be spread over more than one system. We explain an approach that involves creation of a separate database that only stores information that is of interest to management. This involves analysing the needs of management staff and identifying the enterprise systems that store some or all of the information. A suitable data model is developed and the information is then extracted, transformed and loaded in the new database. Once that has been done, the new database is then used to answer management queries and the other enterprise systems are not accessed for such queries.

We discuss data warehousing to assist in efficiently computing aggregates and trends. We explain that implementing a data warehouse can be a complex task requiring substantial resources. While it may also involve considerable research regarding requirements, tools available in the market and trial and error, once implemented the benefits can be significant.

In Chapter 8, Online Analytical Processing (OLAP) is discussed. OLAP is perhaps simply explained as using a database like using a spreadsheet. In a spreadsheet, data is provided in a two-dimensional table, and all the summaries of columns and rows are easy to obtain and often very useful. Although a spreadsheet can only be two-dimensional or three-dimensional, OLAP can deal with many dimensions providing management with a variety of summaries and aggregations to assist decision making.

Chapter 9 is devoted to the important issue of information privacy in data mining. During the 1970s and 1980s, most Western societies developed a similar set of privacy principles and most of them enacted legislation to ensure that governments and the private sector were following good privacy principles. These privacy principles developed some 20–30 years ago are not particularly effective in dealing with the privacy concerns that are being raised about data mining. These concerns have been heightened by the dramatically increased use of data mining by governments as a result of the 9/11 terrorist attacks. This chapter briefly discusses these issues.

Writing this book has been a wonderful experience for me. Although some of the material in the book was written some time ago when I taught data mining courses at Bond University, the major effort was during the second half of 2004 when I taught the data mining course at Monash University and the first half of 2005 while I was spending a sabbatical at the International University in Bruchsal in Germany. In some ways, this book has been my companion over the last several months and it has supported me during some difficult times—in particular when my mentor, Chris Wallace, was ill and when he passed away on 7 August 2004. He was a brilliant man who was very gentle with a great sense of humour. I was fortunately able to press on with the book because I knew that this is what Chris would have wanted me to do. I dedicate this book to Chris who was my Ph.D. supervisor, mentor, boss, colleague, and a family friend.

I would like to thank a number of people who have helped in reading, correcting and giving ideas during the writing of this book. The book could not have been completed without the document preparation support of Jeanette Niehus. Joe Incigneri provided much support in editing and improving the readability of the book. He also identified many mistakes in my examples. My family has been very supportive of this endeavour. I also thank the publishers of the case studies who have kindly allowed me to republish the case studies in this book.

Finally, in spite of considerable care taken in editing the book, there are sure to be errors and mistakes in it. I should be grateful if I could be informed of any errors or mistakes discovered and any suggestions readers might have about how the book could be improved for the next edition. My email is gkgupta@acm.org.

G.K. Gupta

CHAPTER 1

Introduction

LEARNING OBJECTIVES

After completing this chapter, you will be able to:

- Develop a basic understanding of data mining, what it is and where it may be useful
- Understand the basic steps of the data mining process and be able to list the steps that the process usually involves
- Understand why data mining has become important
- List and briefly explain some important data mining techniques
- Develop an understanding of some data mining applications
- Provide a list of some important data mining software
- Become familiar with some data mining Web resources and understand how to use the bibliography to find further information

1.1 INTRODUCTION

In 2008, Google found that certain search terms used by people in the Google search engine were good indicators of flu activity. Based on this finding, Google launched a website *Google Flu Trends* to provide timely estimates of flu activity in 28 countries. Since then, a number of researchers have used search terms data to identify other trends.

The Google trends system allows any user to enter a search term and see the trend. This has been quite a useful tool for many researchers. Google has also found ways in which a user may upload his/her own data series and see a list of search terms whose popularity best corresponds with that user's trend data. For example, if real flu data from a country was input in this Google software (the software is called *Correlate*), it may find that people search for terms like cold or flu in a similar pattern to actual flu rates.

A case study described at the end of this chapter studied a US pharmaceutical company called *Medicorp* which is the largest retail pharmaceutical company in the USA. It has 4100 stores in 25 US states. The company maintained an inventory worth almost one billion dollars to ensure that any drug required by a customer had a 95% chance of being available from any outlet of the company. To achieve this goal, the company had a rule of thumb to maintain "three weeks of supply" of every drug. The case study described found that a weekly forecasting model, better suited the company's needs. The study concluded that the company needed to change its rule of thumb of maintaining three weeks supply of drugs and recommended that the three weeks should be reduced for popular drugs and needed to be extended for less popular items, since large selling items can be easily replenished on a weekly basis. The company managed to reduce its inventory by half, resulting in considerable savings.

These are just two examples of data mining applications but there are many others. It has been reported that even Barrack Obama's election team was collecting a lot of data and mining it during the 2012 USA federal election.

Data mining is a new and growing technology that is being taken seriously as the amount of data grows. A recent buzz word, *Big Data*, is being used to describe huge amounts of data that would take too much time and cost too much money to load into a relational database for querying or analysis. The term Big Data is often used when talking about petabytes[1] or exabytes of data that is being generated from social networks like Facebook, SMS and tweets, audio and video messages, billions of emails every day, browsing habits and click streams, smartphone location trails or genomic information. Such huge amount of data is being used by researchers in designing clever data mining techniques to make sense of it all.

Big Data is changing the types of data we have studied in database management courses since it consists of data that extends beyond structured data represented in relational tables. As noted earlier, it includes data of all varieties including text, audio, video, click streams, log files and more. Big Data may be time sensitive and therefore it may have to be used as it is streaming in to the enterprise in order to maximise its value to the business.

Data mining technology is allowing us to see and measure things as never before; much as the microscope allowed scientists to examine the mysteries of life at the cellular level. Some people claim that Big Data will open the door to making smarter decisions in almost every field. It will make modern societies data-driven societies. This also raises serious concerns about surveillance which is discussed in Chapter 10.

CHAPTER OVERVIEW

The next section explains what data mining is and provides a definition of data mining. An example that will be used in various parts of the book is presented. Section 1.3 presents some of the reasons for the increasing use of data mining. Five major reasons are discussed including growth of data and decline in the cost of computer hardware. Section 1.4 describes two somewhat different data

[1] A terabyte is one trillion bytes or 10^{12} bytes. It is roughly equivalent to storing two million books. A petabyte is one thousand terabytes (10^{15} bytes) and an exabyte is one thousand petabytes (10^{18} bytes) and a zetabyte is one thousand exabytes or 10^{21} bytes.

mining processes. The first one is more like the process used in software development while the second one is specifically designed for data mining by a consortium of companies. The next section describes a number of application areas of data mining followed by description of a number of data mining techniques in Section 1.7, Section 1.8 presents a number of case studies in brief. The following section discusses the future of data mining; Section 1.10 presents some guidelines for implementing a data mining project. The remaining sections deal with limitations of data mining and data mining software.

1.2 WHAT IS DATA MINING?

Data mining or *knowledge discovery in databases (KDD)* is a collection of exploration techniques based on advanced analytical methods and tools for handling a large amount of information. The techniques can find novel patterns that may assist an enterprise in understanding the business better and in forecasting. Many data mining techniques are closely related to some of the machine learning techniques that have been developed over the last 50 years. Others are related to techniques that have been developed in statistics, sometimes called exploratory data analysis. These techniques were developed some time ago and were designed to deal with a limited amount of data. The techniques have now been modified to deal with large amounts of data. Yet other techniques are relatively new, for example Web data mining.

Data Mining

Data Mining is a collection of techniques for efficient automated discovery of previously unknown, valid, novel, useful and understandable patterns in large databases. The patterns must be actionable so they may be used in an enterprise's decision making.

As noted earlier, we assume that we are dealing with a large amount of data. Data mining techniques may be used for smaller amounts of data, but the larger the data the better the chance of finding something novel and interesting. Also, if something interesting is discovered, large amount of data provides confidence in the discovery. In other words, we want to ensure that what has been discovered is indeed something interesting about the process underlying the data that is being analysed and not simply a result of some random fluctuations. We want to ensure that the novel pattern that we have discovered is in fact consistent and replicable.

Conventional database systems are often designed for day-to-day running of an organisation and are called Online Transaction Processing (OLTP) systems. These systems are designed to capture business transactions online and are optimised for high throughput, a high level of availability and in some cases high security of information. Since the operation of an enterprise may depend on the running of such operational OLTP systems, high availability is essential. For example, a telecommunication company's accounting system or a bank's ATM OLTP system has got to be available day and night and such a system could not be used for complex queries that a manager might require for gathering intelligence about the business.

Since OLTP systems are performance driven, many enterprises are deciding that another separate database is needed for decision making. Such databases are called *data warehouses*[2]. A data warehouse does not duplicate an OLTP database since the aims of the two database systems are quite

[2] Data warehouses will be discussed in detail in Chapter 8.

different. A data warehouse is designed to have summary information collected from one or more OLTP systems. It is long term storage to allow detection of patterns which have longer time frame. In addition, a data warehouse can support complex queries, report writing and analysis of information. It does not need detailed information about transactions of all customers. A data warehouse need not be updated every minute or even every day, although some updating of information is required to ensure that the information is current.

OLTP systems provide users with query and reporting tools. To some extent, the query and reporting tools can assist in answering questions like "which state did the largest number of students come from last year?" but these tools cannot provide any intelligence about why it happened. Data mining is an attempt at providing some of the intelligence that lets a manager understand his/her business better. In conventional analysis, a manager may have a question or hypothesis or perhaps just a hunch and he/she is interested in proving or disproving it. If the manager had a series of hypotheses, the process of proving or disproving them using OLTP databases is likely to be time consuming and expensive. In data mining, the responsibility of the manager does not disappear entirely, but much of the work is shifted to the data mining software, thereby reducing the analysis effort required of the manager.

Data mining is often a complex process and may require a number of steps before some useful results are obtained. Usually data pre-processing including *data cleaning* may be needed. This is discussed in Chapter 2. In some cases, sampling of data and testing of various hypotheses may be required before data mining can start. Certainly, data mining is neither a simple nor an inexpensive process that anyone with a database can carry out.

We conclude this section by considering the following example. Table 1.1 presents a number of social indicators about all the states in India as well as Delhi NCR. Looking at the table, it is difficult to figure out if there are similarities between some states. Some people say that one of the groups of Indian states is the relatively poor states that some have called BIMARU states (these are: [Bi]har, [Ma]dhya Pradesh, Rajasthan and Uttar Pradesh). It would be nice to know if such a group of states or possibly other groups exist given this data.

Let us briefly describe the data. The first column obviously is the state name. The second column is population divided by the mean population of the states. The third column is each state's GDP divided by average GDP per capita of India. It is necessary to scale all attributes so that no attribute dominates the data. The next column is the percentage of population that lives in their own house. The next two columns are self-explanatory. The next column is the percentage of males that are underweight. Next column is the number of police per crore of the population. HDI is the United Nations Human Development Index and the final column is the population growth rate.

Almost every attribute shows significant variation amongst the states.

We will come back to this example in the later chapters. We will also provide further smaller example data sets that may be used for practical work in the class.

1.3 WHY DATA MINING NOW?

There are a number of reasons for the recent growth of data mining. These include:

1. Growth in data
2. Decline in the cost of processing

Table 1.1 A number of social indicators of the Indian states and Delhi NCR

Name	*Population*	*GDP per capita*	*House Ownership*	*Sex Ratio*	*Literacy*	*Under-weight Males*	*Police per crore*	*HDI*	*Pop. Growth Rate*
Andhra Pradesh	1.694	1.2	0.56	0.99	0.68	2.3	1.06	0.473	1.7
Arunachal Pradesh	0.028	1	0.20	0.92	0.67	3	5.39	NA	2.8
Assam	0.624	0.57	0.20	0.95	0.73	0.31	1.73	0.444	2.3
Bihar	2.076	0.39	0.20	0.92	0.64	2.7	0.65	0.367	3.5
Chhattisgarh	0.51	0.56	0.17	0.99	0.71	3	1.73	0.358	2.6
Goa	0.03	3.2	NA	0.97	0.87	1.5	3.7	0.617	1.5
Gujarat	1.208	1.4	0.73	0.92	0.80	2.6	1.19	0.527	2.3
Haryana	0.508	1.8	0.78	0.88	0.77	2.5	1.99	0.552	2.1
Himachal Pradesh	0.138	1.2	0.52	0.97	0.84	1.8	2.13	0.652	1.7
Jammu & Kashmir	0.258	0.7	0.50	0.88	0.69	1.8	6.12	0.529	1.8
Jharkhand	0.66	1.1	0.28	0.95	0.68	0.31	1.67	0.376	2.8
Karnataka	1.222	1.3	0.55	0.97	0.76	2.4	1.22	0.519	1.8
Kerala	0.668	0.6	0.88	1.08	0.94	1	1.35	0.79	1.7
Madhya Pradesh	1.452	0.77	0.25	0.93	0.71	3.4	1	0.375	3
Maharashtra	2.248	1.6	0.67	0.95	0.80	2.3	1.63	0.572	1.8
Manipur	0.054	0.74	0.25	0.99	0.80	1	8.77	NA	2.6
Meghalaya	0.06	0.95	0.35	0.99	0.76	0.6	3.81	NA	3.5
Mizoram	0.022	0.91	0.23	0.98	0.92	0.4	9.96	NA	2.7
Nagaland	0.04	0.99	0.21	0.93	0.83	0.9	5.05	NA	3.3
Odisha	0.84	0.76	0.32	0.98	0.73	3	1.1	0.362	2.2
Punjab	0.554	1.3	0.77	0.89	0.80	0.2	2.42	0.605	1.7
Rajasthan	1.372	0.8	0.40	0.93	0.67	3.2	1.11	0.434	2.9
Sikkim	0.012	1.5	0.51	0.89	0.82	0.5	7.32	NA	1.8
Tamil Nadu	1.442	1.4	0.59	0.99	0.80	1.7	1.33	0.57	1.7
Tripura	0.074	0.84	0.12	0.96	0.88	3.6	6.61	NA	2
Uttar Pradesh	3.992	0.49	0.27	0.91	0.72	3.1	0.94	0.38	3.3
Uttarakhand	0.202	1.24	0.49	0.96	0.80	2	1.82	0.49	2.1
West Bengal	1.826	0.91	0.60	0.95	0.80	1.2	0.92	0.492	1.7
Delhi	0.336	1.4	NA	0.87	0.85	NA	4.48	0.75	NA

As noted above, some data in this table has been scaled

Note: NA stands for data not available

3. Growth in data storage capacity
4. Competitive environment
5. Availability of data mining software

Now, we discuss these reasons one by one.

1.3.1 Growth in Data

As noted earlier, there has been an explosive growth in the amount of data stored electrically that the world now generates. It is being generated from many sources, for example, transactions, remote devices, websites and user-generated content. It is expected that this growth will continue because enterprises are collecting data with greater granularity and frequency. While writing this section in mid-2013, for example, it was disclosed that the National Security Agency (NSA) of the USA was capturing data about every telephone conversation in the country as well as in other countries every day. NSA was perhaps generating billions of records each day. Furthermore, various social network sites like Facebook are storing billions of photographs and images that individuals are uploading. Not only more and more information is being stored but the nature of information is changing. For example, medical information now includes not just doctors' notes but images like X-Rays and CT scans.

McKinsey Global Institute claims that Big Data is going to improve the productivity of workers as well as managers since it is likely to lead to management innovation. It is claimed that a number of companies around the globe are already using Big Data effectively.

Consider the data generated by a large USA chain of stores like Wal-Mart. It has more than 4000 stores worldwide and has to deal with a database of more than 2.5 petabytes. Wal-Mart handles more than 20 million point-of-sale transactions everyday. With such growth in electronic information, most enterprises have started to realise that there is potential business intelligence hidden in the large volumes of data. This intelligence can be the secret weapon on which success of a business may depend. Given the volume of information and its growth (information is claimed to be doubling every 20 months), not even a small fraction of it could be looked at by a human eye. It is therefore no simple matter to discover business intelligence that might assist decision making. What is required are techniques that allow the enterprise to distil the most valuable information from mountains of accumulated data. The field of data mining attempts to provide such techniques.

The first database systems were implemented in the 1970s. Many enterprises therefore have more than 40 years of experience in using database systems and they have accumulated large amounts of data during that time. Also, as noted earlier, a number of other technological developments have also resulted in dramatic growth in data. For example, growing use of credit cards and mobile phones are important areas of data growth. In India, use of credit cards and debit cards is growing strongly. Table 1.2 shows the total number of credit and debit cards in 10 major countries. The total number of cards in the ten countries in 2010 was over five billion and the number of cards continues to grow. In some countries with strongly growing economies and low use of cards, for example, in Asia-Pacific, Central and Eastern Europe, Middle-East and Africa, the number of cards is growing by up to 40% a year.

The number of mobile phones is also growing dramatically. It has been reported that well over 200 million phones were sold in India in 2010. The worldwide mobile phone market continues to grow and it was reported in January 2014 that the sale of smart phones in 2013 grew 38.4 per cent to touch more than one billion units from 725.3 million units in 2012.

It has been claimed that in addition to data collected by phone companies, millions of mobile phones, across service providers, are under the surveillance of the Central security agencies in India. Such surveillance, like the NSA surveillance, must lead to accumulation of a lot of data[3].

[3]For details, refer to http://in.reuters.com/article/2013/06/20/india-surveillance-idINDEE95J04V20130620

Table 1.2 Estimated numbers of credit/debit cards and mobile phones in 10 major nations

Country	*Population* (millions)	*Total number of cards* (millions)	*Cards per capita*	*Mobile Phones* (millions)	*Mobile Phones* per capita
Brazil	268	424	2.15	1.58	1.00
Canada	34	109	3.21	3.20	0.79
China	1349	1999	1.49	1.48	0.91
France	65	112	1.72	1.72	1.11
India	1220	154	0.13	0.13	0.74
Japan	121	773	6.09	6.39	1.00
Russia	256	129	0.91	0.50	1.00
South Korea	53	162	3.38	3.06	1.00
UK	76	141	2.27	1.86	1.00
USA	328	1174	4.12	3.58	1.00

This data is several years old.

E-commerce developments have also resulted in information about visitors to websites being captured, once again resulting in large amounts of data for some companies. In a recent survey of data growth, about a third of the enterprises listed online data as one of the sources of data growth. According to some news sources, Facebook has attracted more than 82 million monthly active users in India in 2013 and YouTube had 55 million unique users a month. Facebook user numbers have grown by 37.4% in the year 2012-13! Of course there are a number of other popular websites, for example orkut, Google and Yahoo. The search engine market in India has been estimated to be growing by more than 90% annually! Every search engine captures information about user queries identified by the user's computer IP address.

In addition to data generated by the cards and mobile phones, the use of Unique Identification Aadhaar card (UID) in India is likely to generate a vast amount of data. In fact some experts estimate that when Aadhar has all the citizens enrolled, the size of its database may be as large as 10 times the size of Facebook.

1.3.2 Decline in the Cost of Processing

The decline in the cost and increase in the processing power of digital technologies during the 50 years have been quite extraordinary. Moore's law states that the amount of power in a processor doubles approximately every 18 months and this trend is likely to continue.

Not only processor costs but cost of disks has been falling dramatically. Figure 1.1 shows how the price of disks has been falling since 1980. A one gigabyte disk that used to cost almost one million dollars in 1980 is not even available now. Larger disks are currently selling for as low as ₹1 per gigabyte.

Cheaper hardware makes it worthwhile to attempt intensive analysis applications that may not have been possible in the past, although it should be noted that implementing data mining applications can still be expensive.

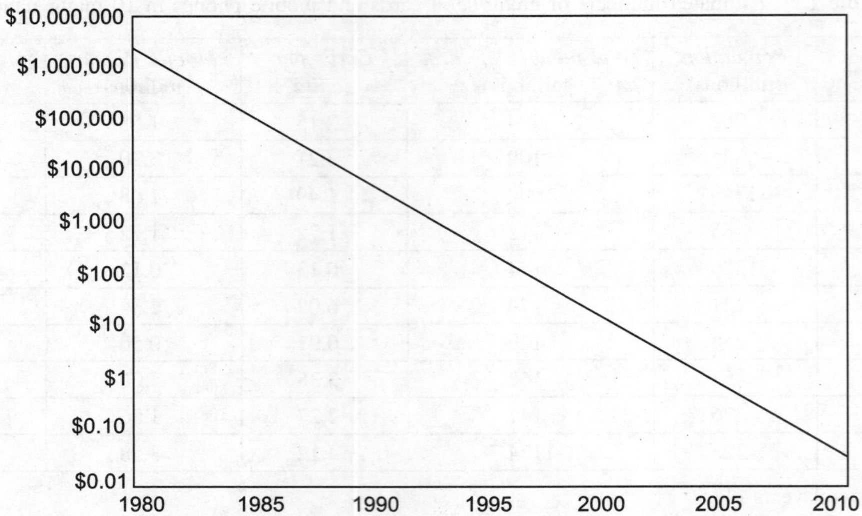

Figure 1.1 Decline in the cost of computer hardware.

1.3.3 Growth in Data Storage Capacity

The growing data has to be stored somewhere. Most enterprises choose a simple solution. They buy and install additional disk storage to store it. Annual disk storage sales have been growing strongly as noted in Figure 1.2. In the last ten years, disk sales have grown by almost a factor

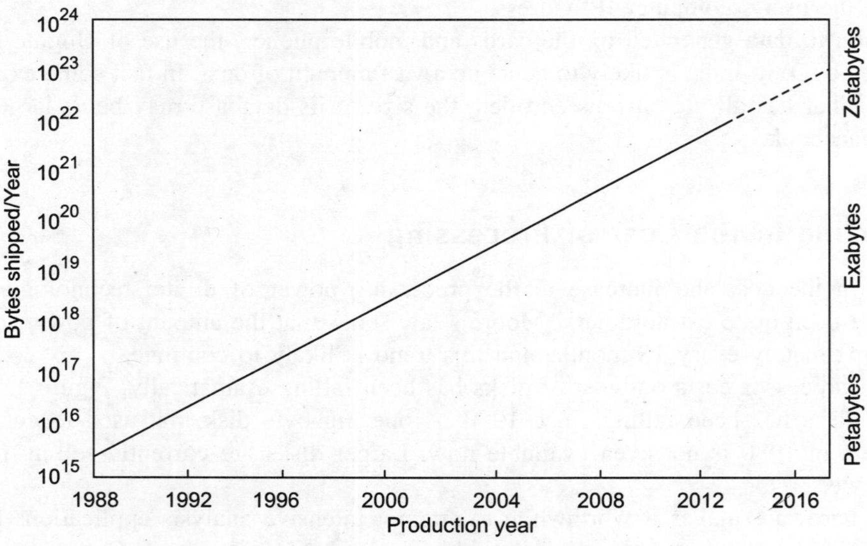

Figure 1.2 Annual disk storage sales.

of one million. The annual disk storage sold is now approaching a zetabyte[4]. This is shown in Figure 1.2. The annual disk sales are now more than 100 gigabytes per person in the world per year! One has to wonder what all this storage capacity is used for! No doubt there is a lot of redundant data stored on the disks.

1.3.4 Competitive Environment

Due to increased globalisation of trade, business environment in most countries has become very competitive. To thrive in today's environment, it's vital for every business to get an edge so that it can grow. Without a doubt, the most efficient way to do this is to make the most of technology including data mining technology. For example, in many countries the telecommunications industry used to be a state monopoly but has now been mostly privatised leading to intense competition. Businesses have to work harder to find new customers and to retain old ones.

In order to be able to survive, grow and be profitable, any profit-seeking organisation must seek a competitive advantage. Each enterprise wishes to create and sustain a competitive advantage because every enterprise wishes not only to survive but also gain advantage against their rivals and earn above average profits.

One of the central bases for achieving advantage is the organisational capability to create new knowledge and transfer it across various levels and parts of the organisation. Because knowledge is central to strategy formulation and implementation, *knowledge management* has become a key strategic task facing managers for achieving success in today's complex and dynamic environment. Therefore the most valuable assets of the 21st century enterprise are its knowledge and knowledge workers.

1.3.5 Availability of Data Mining Software

A number of companies have developed useful data mining software in the last several years. Companies that were already operating in the statistics software market and were familiar with statistical algorithms, for example SAS and SPSS, have entered the data mining field developing data mining software. There are many other software packages available, for example GhostMiner and Quadstone as well as some add-ons to Microsoft Excel. Further details of data mining software are presented at the end of this chapter.

Summary

To summarise, the main reasons for why data mining is becoming increasingly popular for enterprises is that data is growing rapidly and at the same time the cost of storing this data and processing it has been declining dramatically. Therefore, we have the resources to carry out data mining.

How does one plan and implement a data mining project? We discuss two different approaches now. The first approach is an adaptation of the well-known software development process and the second one is CRISP-DM approach.

[4]Note that a kilobyte (KB), a megabyte (MB) and a gigabyte (GB) are 2^{10}, 2^{20} and 2^{30} bytes respectively. 2^{40} is a terabyte, 2^{50} is a petabyte and 2^{60} is an exabyte. Finally 2^{70} bytes is a zetabyte.

1.4 THE DATA MINING PROCESS—SOFTWARE DEVELOPMENT APPROACH

For data mining to be effective, much careful work is needed in defining the aims of the enterprise data mining and then in selection, cleaning, transformation and perhaps separate storage of data that is suitable for data mining. This separate database may be a data warehouse that stores information that is needed by the enterprise's decision makers. Such a database should include not just current data but also historical data.

As noted above, the data mining process involves much hard work. A typical data mining process is likely to include the following six steps. These steps are based on a typical software development process. It should be noted that all such processes are iterative and work done at Step 1 may need to be revised based on some new information or new insight further down in the process.

1.4.1 Step 1: Requirements Analysis

The enterprise decision makers need to formulate goals that the data mining process is expected to achieve. The business problem must be clearly defined. One cannot use data mining without a good idea of what kind of outcomes the enterprise is looking for, since the technique to be used and the data that is required are likely to be different for different goals. Furthermore, if objectives have been clearly defined, it is easier to evaluate the results of the project. A document that describes the result of the requirements analysis should be produced.

1.4.2 Step 2: Data Selection and Collection

Once the data required has been identified, this step may include finding the best source databases for the data that is required for the given requirements. If the enterprise has implemented a data warehouse then most of the data could be available there. If the data is not available in the warehouse or the enterprise does not have a warehouse, source OLTP systems need to be identified and the required information extracted and stored in some temporary system. In some cases at the beginning only a sample of the data available may be sufficient. A document that gives details of the data that is to be used should be produced.

1.4.3 Step 3: Cleaning and Preparing Data

This may not be an onerous task if a data warehouse containing the required data exists, since most of this must have already been done when data was loaded in the warehouse. Otherwise this task can be very resource intensive and sometimes more than 50% of effort of a data mining project is spent in this step. As noted earlier, a data store that integrates data from a number of databases may need to be created. When integrating data, one often encounters problems like identifying data, dealing with missing data, data conflicts and ambiguity. An ETL (extraction, transformation and loading) tool may be used to assist with these problems. ETL is discussed in more detail in Chapter 2. The cleaning and data preparation carried out should be documented in a report.

1.4.4 Step 4: Data mining Exploration and Validation

Once the required data has been collected and cleaned, it is possible to start data mining exploration. Assuming that the user has access to one or more data mining tools, a data mining model may be constructed based on the enterprise's needs. It may be possible to take a sample of data and apply a number of promising techniques. For each technique the results can then be evaluated and their significance interpreted. Again, this is likely to be an iterative process which should lead to selection of one or more techniques that are suitable for further exploration, testing and validation. The details of exploration and the experience gained should be described in a report.

1.4.5 Step 5: Implementing, Evaluating and Monitoring

Once a model has been selected and validated, the decision makers can implement the model for use. This may involve software development for generating reports or explanation for managers. It may be that more than one technique is suitable for the given data mining task. It is then important to evaluate the results and choose the best technique. Evaluation may involve checking the accuracy and effectiveness of the technique. Furthermore, there is a need for regular monitoring of the performance of the techniques that have been implemented. Every enterprise evolves with time and so must the data mining system. Therefore, monitoring is necessary from time to time and this may lead to the refinement of tools and techniques that have been implemented. Details of implementation and evaluation should be documented in a report. Furthermore, instructions for monitoring should also be described perhaps in a separate report.

1.4.6 Step 6: Results Visualisation

Explaining the results of data mining to the decision makers is an important step of a data mining process. Most commercial data mining tools include data visualisation modules. These tools are often vital in communicating results to the managers, although a problem dealing with a number of dimensions must often be visualised using a two-dimensional computer screen or printout. Better data visualisation tools are being developed to display results that deal with more than two dimensions. The visualisation tools available should be tried and used if found effective for the given problem. A user's guide for visualisation should be prepared.

We now present another approach to implementing data mining.

1.5 THE DATA MINING PROCESS—THE CRISP-DM APPROACH

As noted earlier, the approach given above is similar to the software development approach that may be used for a data mining project. This approach has a number of steps that are not included in classical software development life cycle. These include Steps 2, 3 and perhaps Step 6.

A number of other, often similar, methodologies have been proposed. For example, SPSS recommends the 5As approach that consists of five steps—assess, access, analyse, act and automate. SAS on the other hand uses another five-step approach that consists of the steps—sample, explore, modify, model and assess. These two approaches do not appear to emphasise data cleaning and data preparation, although it is quite likely that these steps are included in the steps recommended.

In 1998, a consortium of vendors and users (including DaimlerChrysler, SPSS and NCR) have proposed yet another approach. This approach, claimed to be more practical, successful and widely adopted, is called CRISP-DM for Cross-Industry Standard Process for Data Mining. It consists of six steps that are: business understanding – data understanding – data preparation – modelling – evaluation – deployment. The steps are shown in Figure 1.3.

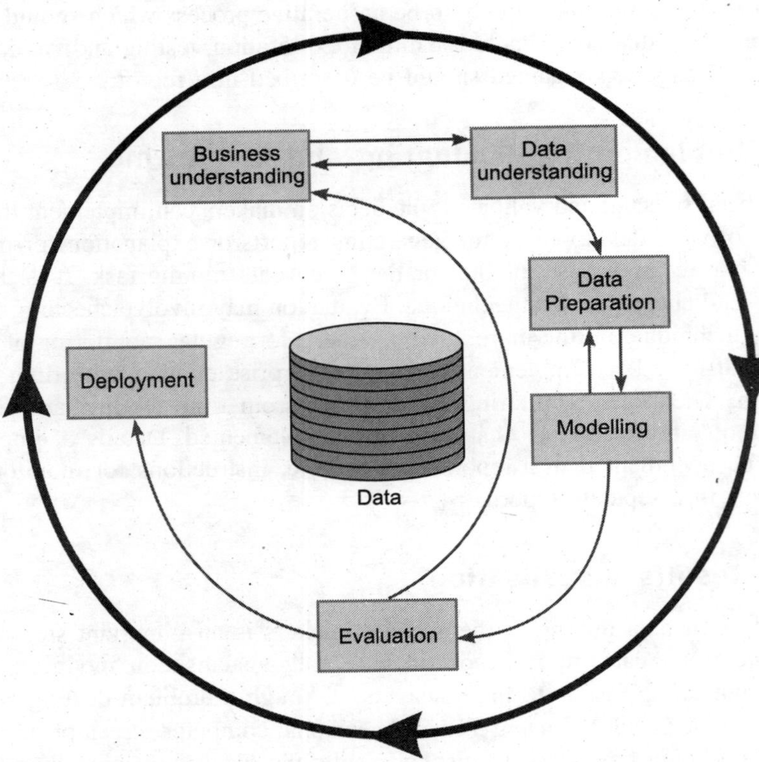

Figure 1.3 CRISP data mining process model.
Source: http://www.crisp-dm.org/Process/index.htm

Although, the CRISP-DM process was conceived in 1998, it has been developed and refined and in August 2000, a document describing it in detail was produced. This document by Chapman et al. is the basis of our description of CRISP-DM that follows. For further details the original document should be consulted.

We now discuss the six steps of the CRISP process.

1.5.1 Step 1: Business Understanding

To start a new data mining project, the senior management of the enterprise needs to understand the project from their business perspective. What are the aims of the project? What problems are likely to be solved by the project? It includes determining business objectives and assessing the current situation in the enterprise. The management can then define the project's objectives as well as requirements. Criteria for determining if the project has been a success should also be clearly specified. The management should also allocate a budget, perhaps only a preliminary budget, and define benefits expected from the project. A timeline should perhaps be specified. Following that a project team should be appointed. Initially, the project team should carry out the following tasks:

- Clearly describe the project goals including outcomes expected and prepare a report describing the business objectives.
- Assess the project situation and environment.
- List the assumptions being made and prepare a report listing all assumptions and contingencies.
- Explain the terminology that will be used and produce a report listing the terminology.
- Make a list of resources including data and human resources required.
- List project constraints, project risks and contingencies. These should be included in a report.
- What software will be required, would it be purchased or developed in-house? Prepare a report describing feasible options and recommendations.
- Produce a project plan. The plan should include data mining goals, data mining success criteria and details of tools and techniques to be used.

Once all these tasks have been completed, the data mining task may begin with data understanding followed by data preparation. We describe them now.

Before moving to the next step, it is worth noting that in Table 1.1, data was presented without any objectives. If a clear objective was defined, for example finding groupings of states, then a number of other questions are likely to arise. For example, what is the basis of the groupings that we want? What data is required to determine that type of groupings? We leave these questions as an exercise for the reader.

1.5.2 Step 2: Data Understanding

As noted earlier, to start the project, the project team needs to assess the project environment and the data requirements. What data needs to be collected? What data attributes are required? Data types are different for example, geographical data, quantitative data and gender data. Where is the data coming from? Does the enterprise have a number of computer systems that will need to be used to extract and integrate data? Does the enterprise have a data warehouse[5] that has all the data that is required?

The data attributes should not be related closely; they should be independent. If they are not independent then pre-processing of the data should ensure that they are. This data needs to be loaded and integrated in order to successfully complete the data collection. Since data may be collected from many different sources, the data is likely to be of poor quality requiring data pre-processing.

Data understanding is likely to include the following steps:

- Collect data and prepare an initial data collection report
- Describe the collected data and prepare a data description report
- Explore data and prepare a data exploration report
- Verify data quality and prepare a data quality report

[5]Data warehousing will be discussed in detail in Chapter 8.

Once again if we consider the data in Table 1.1, it might be necessary to document where the data came from. Such data is not conveniently available from one source and a number of sources had to use to collect the data in the table.

1.5.3 Step 3: Data Preparation

Once the data understanding phase has been completed, the data preparation phase can start. Data preparation is a substantial task and may consume as much as 80% of the project time if the data has been collected from a number of different sources. Data preparation is likely to include filtering data, aggregating some data and filling of missing values. It may also require identification of outliers. Duplicate records and redundant data may need to be identified and eliminated. The outcome of the data preparation phase is the final data set. Once data sources available are identified during the data understanding phase, the data need to be selected, cleaned, constructed and formatted into the desired form. It includes data pre-processing that we discuss in more detail in Chapter 2.

Data preparation is likely to include the following steps:

- Select data and prepare a report that presents a list of data and why it has been selected
- Clean data and prepare a data cleaning report
- Construct data and prepare a report that describes all the derived attributes
- Integrate data and prepare a data integration report
- Format data and prepare a report describing formatting and the final dataset

We should ask if a small data set like that in Table 1.1 requires some data preparation? Surprisingly even this data set required data preparation. Perhaps the most important data preparation needed was to scale all the attributes so that no attribute dominated the data set. As it is clear from the table we have already scaled the data.

1.5.4 Step 4: Modelling

A good understanding of the data is essential in identifying the data mining technique to be selected to analyse the prepared data set. The technique obviously will depend on the business objectives of the project and the type of data that has been collected. Next, the test scenario must be generated to validate the models' quality and validity. Running the modelling tool on the prepared data set may help in creating one or more models. Last but not least, models need to be assessed carefully involving stakeholders to make sure that created models meet the business objectives.

Modelling is likely to include the following steps:

- Select a modelling technique and prepare a report listing assumptions
- Generate test design and prepare a test design report
- Build model and select parameters and prepare a report listing parameters and model description
- Evaluate the model and prepare a report describing the evaluation

What models may be used for analysing the data in Table 1.1? It may be difficult to identify an appropriate model since we have not yet studied the techniques that are available to us.

1.5.5 Step 5: Evaluation

The role of the fifth step is to evaluate what has been done so far. Is the project likely to achieve the business objectives? Does the model have any deficiencies? Is the model likely to produce useful results? This involves evaluating the model and reviewing the first four steps of the model. Have all important business issues been carefully considered? It may be possible to use some test data to evaluate the proposed model.

Evaluation is likely to include the following steps:

- Review the process and prepare a report that summarises the results of the review
- Evaluate the results and prepare a report that thoroughly reviews the project and notes any deficiencies
- Determine the next steps and prepare a report that lists further actions and the reasons for each of these actions as well as how these actions may be implemented

Evaluation and deployment steps are perhaps not applicable for the data in Table 1.1 given that the example is so small.

1.5.6 Step 6: Deployment

Once the evaluation is accepted by the management, the last step is the deployment step. Assuming that deployment is successful, it should be possible to generate a report of the project. Implement changes in the processes of the organisation. Implement a repeatable data mining process. For successful deployment the customer must understand the actions to be carried out by the software.

Deployment is likely to include the following steps:

- Plan deployment and produce a report summarising the plan including how the plan is to be implemented.
- Plan monitoring and maintenance involving monitoring the deployment of the project and a plan to maintain it so it continues to perform as expected. A report describing the monitoring and maintenance strategy including how to implement it should be produced.
- Produce the final report. Once the deployment has been successful, the project team should complete a final report of the project. This final report may be a comprehensive report including all the reports produced earlier.
- Review project and document what went right and what went wrong and how the project could have been done better. A report documenting the experience of the team should be produced.

1.6 DATA MINING APPLICATIONS

Data mining is being used for a wide variety of applications. We group the applications in the following six groups. These are related groups, not disjoint groups.

1.6.1 Prediction and Description

It is clearly important for any enterprise to be able to predict some aspects of the business to assist in planning for the future. Even in a university, prediction or forecasting the number of students for the next year plays an important role in planning. Also, looking at Table 1.1, it would be very useful to be able to forecast the growth rate and perhaps change in the literacy rate of each state for the next 2–3 years or even longer. Such forecasting requires more historical data than what is available in a single table.

Describing some of the data can also be important. For example, BIMARU is one description of a number of states in Table 1.1.

Data mining may be used to answer questions like "would this customer buy a product?" or "is this customer likely to leave?" Usually prediction involves selecting some or all the attributes available in the database to predict variables of interest.

It can be useful to describe classes in the data. For example, considering data given in Table 1.1, it may be possible to label some states as small states or tiny states while others may be classified as large states or developed states. Once we label states by a class label, we may be able to summarise some of the characteristics of the states.

Data visualisation can be useful in describing some data. For example, we may wish to use a pie chart to show how much of the Indian population lives in the poorer states and how much of the population lives in developed states.

1.6.2 Relationship Marketing

For many enterprises, marketing is of considerable importance. In particular, telecommunications companies are keen to recruit new customers and retain the current customers. In fact a new business culture is developing and within the economics of customer relationships are changing in fundamental ways. Many modern businesses are focussed on customer relationships as the central business issue. These businesses are concerned with increasing customer value through analysis of the customer life cycle. A new term is being used in businesses called customer relationship management (CRM) that provides new opportunities for businesses to act on the concepts of relationship marketing.

Usually customers have a lifetime value, not just the value of a single sale. Customer relationship deals with building a long term relationship between a customer and an enterprise. This may include customer identification, customer value, and customer retention as well as customer development. Data mining can help in analysing customer profiles, discovering sales triggers, and in identifying critical issues that determine client loyalty and help in improving customer retention. This also includes analysing customer profiles and improving direct marketing plans. A number of data mining techniques may be used in relationship marketing. For example, it may be possible to use cluster analysis to identify customers suitable for cross-selling other products.

1.6.3 Customer Profiling

Once again it may be said that customer profiling can be useful for most enterprises. Even if we take the example of a university, customer profiling of its students might be useful. A car insurance company may carry out customer profiling and may decide it is useful to label different customer as A, B, C, etc. depending on the type of car they own, whether they have fully paid for it and their driving history.

Customer profiling is the process of using relevant and available information to describe the characteristics of a group of customers and to identify their discriminators from other customers and drivers for their purchasing decisions.

Profiling can help an enterprise identify its most valuable customers so that the enterprise may differentiate their needs and values. Customer profiling may also help in increasing the lifetime value of some customers. Profiling may also facilitate, for example, loan and credit card approvals as well as approval of insurance applications.

Customer profiles may include information on how customers spend money, where and what they tend to buy, who are the most profitable customers and where could the enterprise find more prospects similar to the most valuable customers.

1.6.4 Customer Segmentation

We may say that customer segmentation can also be useful in many situations. Going back to the example given in Table 1.1, a segment of interest may be the small north-eastern states (for example Assam, Meghalaya, Nagaland) where there is no tradition of dowry. We may group some states where the literacy is high or where the GDP per capita is high.

Customer segmentation is related to relationship marketing and customer profiling. Essentially, it is a process of finding sub-groups of similar people within a data set and can be useful in marketing.

There can be a number of types of segmentation. It may be demographic. It may be attitudinal. For example, it may be possible to learn whether some customers are happy or unhappy, perhaps by using a survey or by looking at return visits. Segmentation may also be behavioural, for example, by looking at customer's surfing the website.

It is a way to assess and view individuals based on their status and needs. Data mining can be used for customer segmentation, promoting the cross-selling of services, and in increasing customer retention. Data mining may also be used for branch segmentation and for evaluating performance of various banking channels, such as phone or online banking. Furthermore, data mining may be used to understand and predict customer behaviour and profitability, to develop new products and services, and to effectively market new offerings.

1.6.5 Outliers Identification and Detecting Fraud

There are many applications of data mining in identifying outliers including fraud or unusual cases. These might be as simple as identifying unusual expense claims by a staff member, identifying anomalies in expenditure patterns between similar units of an enterprise, perhaps during auditing, or identifying fraud. Data mining techniques are being used in a variety of fraud detection. For example:

- Credit card fraud
- Social welfare fraud
- Insurance fraud

- Medical fraud
- Tax fraud
- Customs fraud and smuggling
- Telecommunication fraud

1.6.6 Website Design and Promotion

If we look at some major websites, for example, india.gov.in or india.gov.in/topics/foreign-affairs, it is essential to study that why these websites are designed for, who are the visitors to these sites and what parts of the websites the visitors look at. It is only then that these very average websites may be improved. Surprisingly, most websites are not user-friendly since almost everyone believes that they can design a good website.

Web mining may be used to discover how users navigate a website and the results can help in improving the site design and making it more visible on the web. Data mining may also be used in cross-selling by suggesting to a Web customer items that he/she may be interested in by correlating properties about the customer, or items the person has ordered, with a database of items that other customers have ordered previously.

1.7 DATA MINING TECHNIQUES

Use of data mining for applications is based on a number of techniques. It is difficult to cover all of them in this textbook so we have included a number of important techniques including the following. We will use the data in Table 1.1 as the basis of some examples.

1.7.1 Association Rules Mining (ARM) or Market Basket Analysis

Association rules mining (discussed in Chapter 3) is a technique that analyses a set of transactions like those captured at a supermarket checkout in one of the malls, each transaction being a list of products or items purchased by one customer. The aim of association rule mining is to determine which items are purchased together frequently so that they may be grouped together on store shelves or the information may be used for cross-selling. Sometimes the term *lift* is used to measure the power of association between items that are purchased together. Lift essentially indicates how much more likely an item is to be purchased if the customer has bought the other item that has been identified as having an association with the first item compared to the likelihood of it being purchased without the other item being purchased. Obviously, lift must be above 1.0 for the association to be of interest.

Association rules mining has many applications other than market basket analysis, including applications in marketing, customer segmentation, medicine, electronic commerce, classification, clustering, Web mining, bioinformatics and finance. To illustrate the applications of ARM, let us consider the data in Table 1.1. We might be interested in finding if one of the attributes, for example the literacy rate, is associated with another attribute, for example the population growth rate. We cannot apply ARM to Table 1.1 because much of the data is numeric. Therefore, the data has to be transformed into categorical values before ARM may be used. We will describe the ARM technique in more detail in Chapter 3.

A simple algorithm called the *Apriori algorithm* may be used to find associations, but the algorithm becomes inefficient for applications where the data is large. Much research has been done in finding more efficient algorithms for determining association rules. The Apriori algorithm and a number of other algorithms are discussed in Chapter 3.

1.7.2 Supervised Classification

Supervised classification (discussed in Chapter 4) is an important data mining technique that has its origins in machine learning. The technique is appropriate to use if the data is known to have a small number of classes, the classes are already known and some training data with their classes known is available. The model built based on the training data may then be used to assign a new object to a predefined class. Supervised classification can be used in predicting the class to which an object or individual is likely to belong. This is useful, for example, in predicting whether an individual is likely to respond to a direct mail solicitation, a good candidate for a surgical procedure, a good risk for granting a loan or insurance.

Once again it is possible to apply supervised classification to Table 1.1 but the table needs to be transformed. We need some training data and for example, we can assert that there are only two classes; the poor states and non-poor states. We may further assert that Bihar is an example of a poor state and Gujarat is an example of a non-poor state. Furthermore, the table may require some further transformation. Supervised classification may then be carried out with the transformed data. We will show`how it may be done in Chapter 4.

One of the most widely used supervised classification techniques is the decision tree. The decision tree technique is widely used because it generates easily understandable rules for classifying data. Decision tree method and another method called Naïve Bayes are discussed in Chapter 4.

1.7.3 Cluster Analysis

Cluster analysis or clustering (discussed in Chapter 5) is similar to classification but, in contrast to supervised classification, cluster analysis is useful when the classes in the data are not already known and training data is not available. The aim of cluster analysis is to find groups that are similar within each group and very different from other groups in a collection of data. Cluster analysis breaks up a single collection of perhaps diverse data into a number of groups. Often these techniques require that the user specify how many groups are expected. Also, in some cases it is necessary to specifies starting points for the groups. Normally, every data point in the data set is allocated to one of the groups and only to one group.

Yet again we consider if cluster analysis is an appropriate technique for the data in Table 1.1 to find if any groups of similar states could be found. The table does not need to be transformed and no training data is required. We do however need some starting points or seeds. It is necessary to have three starting point if we believe there are three groups. The starting points may be Rajasthan, Kerala and Maharashtra. Cluster analysis may now be carried out. We will show how it may be done in Chapter 5.

One of the most widely used cluster analysis methods is called the *K-means algorithm*. It requires that the user specifies not only the number of clusters but also their starting seeds. The algorithm assigns each object in the given data to the closest seed that provides the initial clusters. The algorithm then iteratively reviews the clusters obtained and refines them. There are a number of other algorithms available including hierarchical methods. The results of cluster analysis often have to be interpreted by someone who is knowledgeable about the business. K-means and hierarchical methods are discussed in Chapter 5.

1.7.4 Web Data Mining

In the short time of not much more than 20 years, the Web revolution has had a profound impact on the way we search and find information at home and at work. From its beginning in the early 1990s, the Web has grown to billions of pages in 2013. It is estimated that more than two billion people from all over the world are accessing the Web[6]. Therefore, the Web has now become a huge widely distributed database that has information about news, shopping, financial institutions, education, and governments, etc. In addition, this information is very dynamic, including huge variety of content which may be textual or multimedia as well as hyperlinks. Given its rich structure, the Web provides a fertile ground for data mining applications.

Web mining, discussed in Chapter 6, is the application of data mining techniques to find interesting and potentially useful patterns from Web data. It is normally expected that either the hyperlink structure of the Web or the Web log data or both are available for the mining process. Web data mining is usually organised into three main parts. These three areas are Web usage mining, Web content mining and Web structure mining.

Web usage mining involves understanding user behaviour in interacting with the Web or with a website. It may find interesting structures using Web logs. This type of mining can be used to improve the quality of service of a website. Web content mining on the other hand involves discovering useful content or knowledge from the Web. Finally, Web structure mining involves discovering and modelling the link structure of the Web and extracting interesting patterns from the hyperlink structures.

These techniques are discussed in Chapter 6.

1.7.5 Search Engines

Search engines, discussed in Chapter 7, are huge databases of billions of Web pages as well as software packages for indexing and retrieving the pages that enable users to find information of interest to them. Normally the search engine databases of Web pages are built and updated automatically by Web crawlers. Increasingly the crawlers are becoming more intelligent and frequently visit dynamic pages like news sites. When one searches the Web using one of the search engines, one is not searching the entire Web. Instead one is only searching the database that has been compiled by the search engine. There are a number of challenging problems related to search engines that we

[6]Some Web statistics may be found at http://www.worldwidewebsize.com and at http://www.internetworldstats.com.

will discuss in Chapter 7 including how to assign a ranking to each Web page that is retrieved in response to a user query.

In a health study that was noted at the beginning of this chapter, Google researchers found that one way to improve early detection of influenza was to monitor health-seeking behaviour in the form of online Web search queries. Search queries are submitted by millions of users around the world each day. A method of analysing large numbers of Google search queries is a viable way to track influenza-like illness in a population. Because the relative frequency of certain queries is highly correlated with the percentage of physician visits in which a patient presents with influenza-like symptoms, the queries accurately estimate the current level of weekly influenza activity in each region of the world, with a reporting lag of about one day. This approach makes it possible to use search queries to detect influenza epidemics in areas with a large population of Web search users.

1.7.6 Data Warehousing and OLAP

Data warehousing and OLAP are discussed in Chapters 8 and 9 respectively. Data warehousing is a process by which an enterprise collects data from the whole enterprise to build a single version of the truth. This information is useful for decision makers and may also be used for data mining. A data warehouse can be of real help in data mining since data cleaning and other problems of collecting data would have already been overcome. OLAP tools are decision support tools that are often built on top of a data warehouse or another database (called multidimensional database). OLAP goes further than traditional query and report tools in that a decision maker already has a hypothesis which he/she is trying to test. Data mining is different from OLAP since in data mining a hypothesis is not being tested. Instead data mining is used to uncover novel patterns in the data.

1.8 PRACTICAL EXAMPLES OF DATA MINING

In a recent poll, Kdnuggests (http://www.kdnuggets.com/polls) found that data mining was used most widely in the following industries/fields: banking, direct marketing, fraud detection, scientific data, bioinformatics, insurance, medical/pharmaceutical, telecommunications, and E-commerce/Web.

We now briefly present a number of examples from some of these applications. The original papers describing some of these examples as well as a number of others are included in the bibliography at the end of this chapter. These original papers should be carefully studied to better understand the data mining applications and the data mining process.

1.8.1 Astronomy

An interesting data mining application area is astronomy. Astronomers produce huge amounts of data every night on the fluctuating intensity of around 20 million stars which are classified by their spectra and their surface temperature. Some 90% of stars are called *main sequence stars* including some stars that are very large, very hot and blue in colour. The main sequence stars are fuelled by nuclear fusion and are very stable, lasting billions of years. Smaller main sequence stars include the Sun (type G in Table 1.3). There are a number of classes including stars called yellow dwarf, red dwarf and white dwarf. We show the seven major classes in Table 1.3.

Table 1.3 Different types of stars

Star type	*Colour*	*Approximate temperature*	*Average brightness* (Sun = 1)	*Average radius* (Sun = 1)
O	Blue	> 25,000 K	> million	60
B	Blue	11,000 to 25,000 K	20,000	18
A	Blue	7,500 to 11,000 K	80	3.2
F	Blue to White	6,000 to 7,500 K	6	1.7
G	White to Yellow	5,000 to 6,000 K	1.2	1.1
K	Orange to Red	3,500 to 5,000 K	0.4	0.8
M	Red	< 3,500 K	0.04	0.3

Clearly the classes O and B stars are very bright but only few of them have been found. A star by the name "10 Lacertra" belonging to class O has been found and another called "Rigel" belonging to class B has been discovered. Stars by the names "Sirius" and "Canopus" belong to classes A and F respectively. Class G has many stars including the Sun and "Capella". The next two classes have many stars that are quite dim. Two stars belonging to these classes are "Arcturus" and "Antares".

Using the enormous amount of data that is being collected, astronomers want to classify stars and galaxies and find any new classes of objects that might be out there. Decision trees and cluster analysis techniques have been used for such data mining.

As an example, when a clustering program was used to group a large amount of astronomical data, four classes corresponding to stars, galaxies with bright central cores, galaxies without bright central cores and stars with visible "fuzz" around them were found. The clustering program found unexpected but meaningful results without any understanding of astronomical data.

1.8.2 Banking and Finance

Banking and finance is a rapidly changing competitive industry. The industry is using data mining for a variety of tasks including building customer profiles to better understand them, to identify fraud, to evaluate risks in insurance as well as personal and home loans, and to better forecast stock prices, interest rates, exchange rates and commodity prices. In the field of credit evaluation, data mining may be able to assist in establishing an automated decision support system which would allow credit card or loan providing companies to quickly and accurately assess risk and approve or reject an application.

The magazine "Network Magazine" India reports a case study about the Standard Chartered Bank (SCB). The bank established a group of 25 people in Bangalore to analyse the large amount of data from its 2.2 million customers and 1.3 million credit card holders. SCB discovered that a significant proportion of their business came from the upwardly mobile Indian women and this was likely to grow substantially. The bank successfully launched a specially designed women's international credit card with several features including discounts and zero interest rates on categories like jewellery, cosmetics, apparel, consumer durables, leather products, and mobile phones.

In Table 1.4, an example in which a number of attributes from a collection of artificial loan applications is presented. Each row is data about one customer assuming that for each customer the bank has some loan history as well as some personal information. Information is also available for a number of past customers.

Table 1.4 Sample data for past and current credit customers

ID	*Sex*	*Education*	*Work length*	*Marital status*	*Income*	*House*	*Dependents*	*Age*	*Risk*
100379	M	HS	H	M	L	O	1	30	G
102760	M	HS	S	D	U	O	2	29	G
100022	F	HS	S	D	L	N	2	60	B
133300	M	U	S	D	L	O	2	52	M
299000	M	U	S	M	M	O	3	30	B
345699	F	L	H	M	H	O	1	37	G
411745	M	L	H	M	H	N	1	55	G
276500	F	L	H	M	M	N	0	35	B
377762	M	HS	M	M	L	N	2	29	B
400012	M	U	M	S	L	O	1	59	?
423900	M	U	S	M	L	O	3	48	?
333000	F	HS	S	S	L	O	4	42	?
300012	M	L	H	S	M	N	2	41	?
200055	M	L	H	D	M	O	1	35	?
233227	M	HS	H	D	H	O	1	39	?
211100	F	HS	H	D	M	L	1	40	?

The attributes in the table are as follows. The first two columns are self-explanatory. The third column is also obvious although the value L has been used for people who did not finish high school. The next column deals with the number of years employed with only three values H, M and S for more than 20 years, between 10–20 years and below 10 years respectively. The next column is self-explanatory. The income column has several values; H, M, L and U; U being unemployed. The next column deals with house ownership followed by number of dependents and then age.

The final column gives the class of each customer in the data set. The first nine rows of the data set therefore is about past customers which may be considered as training data and the remaining rows are for new customers, for which the class is not known. These rows are called the test data.

Based on such information, the bank may be able to build a useful profile of a good credit risk customer and use the profile in assessing current and future loan applications. We will discuss the techniques that may be used in Chapter 4. It should be understood that results of such data mining are not definitive and care must be taken in using the results. Similar analysis is possible for mortgage lending and insurance underwriting (e.g. life insurance, car insurance, health insurance). It is possible to discover rules like "male drivers under 30 years, driving model xyz car that is more than 5 years old, are bad insurance risks".

Another application of data mining in banking and finance is to identify high-value customers, since not all customers are equally profitable. Often an 80–20 or similar rule may apply—that is 20% of the customers might be responsible for 80% of the profit or 30% of the customers might account for 70% of the profit.

Customer churn has been an area of considerable interest in banking, retail and telecommunications. There have been a large number of data mining studies that have investigated customer churn. One of these studies from Finland has investigated churn in consumer retail banking sector. It investigated customers who were at risk of leaving and whether those customers were worth retaining. A company will usually have a sense of how much is it really worth retaining a customer that is likely to leave therefore the scale of effort that would be appropriate for a retention campaign.

1.8.3 Business

In a study, the company SAS has used their customer data as a tool for discovering underlying patterns of software and support issues. They investigated two years of help desk calls (3,854 calls). Basic exploration and pre-processing of textual data was carried out. Mining textual information was able to deliver strategic insights to suggest improvements to the business process. The study was able to recommend a number of improvements that led to better user satisfaction, faster speed of responses to users' queries and happy renewing customers.

Another study looked at the problem of buying prominent advertising positions on search engines' sponsored link space. It is not just about how many clicks these links generate. More important is the revenue generated by the clicks and lifetime value associated with these customers. While calculating profitability of a few search terms may not sound that difficult, keeping track of profitability due to hundreds of search terms on a periodic basis is intractable. Once a system is built to compute 'Return on Investment (ROI)' of search terms on a periodic basis, the next step is to analyse their performance. Improving landing pages, optimising titling strategies and determining most cost effective positions for each term can further improve the overall ROI. By implementing simple decision tree modelling approach, it was possible to reduce cost to revenue ratio from 108% to 47%, whilst increasing clicks 34%.

In another study of online advertising, it was found that an advertiser that has many products to promote will typically find that even after segmentation of their audience using techniques such as decision trees across all leaf nodes one product will have a higher response rate than all other products. The consequence for an advertiser is that it will be optimal to show just one product all of the time to maximise response rates. However, from an advertiser perspective this solution can be suboptimal due to the fact that the remaining products must also be advertised at least at a minimal level. The objective of this study was to demonstrate how data mining techniques can be applied to decision trees to optimally override the default recommendations in order to optimally meet business objectives.

Yet another study considers the problem of estimating customer lifetime value, when a large number of features are present in the data. In order to measure lifetime value survival analysis models may be used to estimate customer tenure. In a paper the authors show how these ideas and methods can be adapted for estimation of customer's life cycles. In such a context, a number of data mining modelling challenges may arise. For example, a client that is lost can come back.

1.8.4 Crime Prevention

A number of case studies have been published about use of data mining techniques in analysing crime data. A highly disputed area in criminology is whether there are criminal offender types. Many criminologists argue against the possibility of separate criminal types while others strongly support their existence

In a study, juvenile offenders (N = 1572) from three U.S. state juvenile justice systems were assessed on a battery of crime risks and needs factors as well as official criminal histories. Data mining techniques were applied with the goal of identifying intrinsic patterns in this data set and to assess whether these replicate any of the main patterns previously proposed in the criminological literature.

The first major problem encountered in the study was that the data was noisy and often unreliable. This is not an unusual problem as discussed in some detail in Chapter 2. Second, the empirical clusters were not clear cut so that cases ranged from strongly classified to poorly classified boundary cases with only weak cluster affiliations. It was found that there were a large number of hybrid cases that belonged to two or more classes. To eliminate these cases a method that combines the results of Bagged K-means and the consistency method, a semi-supervised learning technique were used.

Seven clusters were found. Each of the clusters was found to relate fairly clearly to criminal types previously identified in various studies in criminology literature but had never been identified at the same time in one data set using clustering methods.

In another study, data mining techniques were used to link serious sexual crimes to other crimes that might have been committed by the same offenders. The data used related to more than 2000 offences (the number of offenders was much smaller, since most offenders committed multiple crimes) involving a variety of sexual crimes.

As in most case studies, the data was not complete and there were errors and discrepancies in the data supplied by the police. Some of the values were missing. Data was encoded and two sets of variables were selected for two different studies. In one of the studies, three clusters were identified. In the other study only one "super cluster" was found. The results of the study were verified and it was found that the members of each cluster did have strong similarities within them and they identified crime patterns that police officers thought made sense.

Another case study dealing with crime prevention follows this chapter.

1.8.5 Education

Several researchers have developed prediction models for student dropout rates since dropout rates are an important concern for educational institutions. A study carried out in Holland showed that rather simple classifiers gave useful results with accuracies between 75 and 80% that is better than other more sophisticated models. The study found that the strongest predictor of success was the grade for the Linear Algebra course, which was in general not been seen as the decisive course. Other strong predictors were grades for Calculus and Networks.

Work carried out in Spain is concerned with developing methods for exploring the unique types of data from educational context. This study deals with application of data mining in Moodle learning management systems and a case study tutorial with the Moodle system. Full process for mining e-learning data step by step is described as well as how to apply data mining techniques such as statistics, visualisation, classification, clustering, association rule mining, pattern mining and text mining to the data. Free data mining tools were used. The authors describe how different data mining techniques can be used in order to improve the course and students' learning.

Another educational data mining study found that data exploration focused on the number of attempted exercises combined with classification was able to identify students at risk. Clustering and cluster visualisation was able to identify a particular behaviour among failing students. A timely and appropriate warning to students at risk was able to help many students passing in the final exam.

1.8.6 Government

The Internal Revenue Service (IRS) in the USA has found that high income individuals are a primary contributor to the unrecovered taxes (or tax losses) to the government. This case study addresses the use of data mining techniques for the purpose of helping the IRS target high-income individuals engaging in abusive tax shelters. Kernel based analysis of known abuse allows targeting individual taxpayers while associative analysis allows targeting groups of taxpayers who appear to be participating in a tax shelter being promoted by a common financial advisor. This analysis task requires estimating risk, a weighted combination of both the likelihood of abuse and the potential revenue losses.

In a study reported by the USA Department of Agriculture (USDA) it was found that there were anomalies in some crop insurance policies perhaps because of collusion between either three parties (agent, adjuster and producer) or between two parties (agent and producer). The agent-producer was found to account for the greatest proportion of waste, fraud or abuse in the insurance program. A total of 24 million records were analysed.

1.8.7 Healthcare

Health care is perhaps an area in which much research is being carried out in applying data mining techniques to a variety of applications. It has been found, for example, that in drug testing, data mining may assist in isolating those patients where the drug is most effective or where the drug is having unintended side effects. Data mining has been used in determining factors influencing the survival rate of heart transplant patients when survival rate data were available for a significant number of patients over several years. It has been claimed that data mining may be able to identify factors that influence doctors' ability to recommend new drugs on the market. In Australia, the Health Insurance Commission has been able to identify doctors who tend to over-service their patients. In one data mining application, it was found that there were a small number of patients who tended to go doctor shopping, that is, they visited several different doctors during a month or a fortnight.

In a data mining case study in the USA, data from a number of veterans hospitals was analysed. The aim of the study was to be able to predict the length of hospital stay for patients suffering from spinal cord injuries. The study was undertaken because spinal injury patients often had extended hospital stays and the hospital system wanted to know if the length of stay could be reduced and the efficiency of the hospital improved.

The study required data validation and data cleaning. Data used in the study was manually checked to ensure accuracy and reliability. Errors in the data were discovered and in many cases missing values were found from paper records. Close to 5000 clean data records were thus extracted to be used for data mining. The data belonged to some 20 diagnostic categories of spinal cord injuries. The length of stay varied from one day to more than two years, with a mean of about two months. Much time was spent in visualising the data. After visualisation, it was decided to focus the study on patients who had stayed less than 40 days, since this duration included the vast majority of cases. Models were built which could correctly predict length of stay in up to 80% of the cases.

A number of data mining case studies deal with breast cancer which is a common cause of death among women in Western countries. In one study that is devoted to identifying high-risk patients in order to provide them with specialised treatment because access to experienced oncologists was not possible. The study was carried out in Sweden where 3699 breast cancer patients were admitted to south-east hospitals from 1986 to 1995. A decision tree was trained with all patients except for the 100 cases that were used for testing. Two domain experts were asked for their opinions about the probability of recurrence of a certain outcome for the 100 test patients. After comparing the predictions from a model built by data mining with predictions made by two domain experts, no significant differences were noted. Therefore if no experienced oncologist was available, predictive models created with data mining techniques can be used to support physicians in decision making with acceptable accuracy.

Another medical case study deals with cancer management, especially the management of Acute Lymphoblastic Leukemia or ALL, which is the most common type of cancer in Children in Egypt. The study concluded that the data mining technique decision trees, as a data mining technique was very useful especially in the domains where available data had many limitations like inconsistent and missing values. Also, decision tree results were simple to understand. Furthermore using better quality of data influences the whole process of knowledge discovery takes less time in cleaning and integration and assures better results from the mining process.

1.8.8 Manufacturing

Data mining tools have been used to identify factors that lead to critical manufacturing situations to warn the engineers of impending problems. It has been reported in a case study that data mining was able to predict and prevent the failure of critical manufacturing components in some manufacturing companies. Hewlett Packard has been reported to have used data mining to improve the quality of their scanners by identifying factors that impacted quality.

Data mining applications have also been reported in power stations, petrochemical plants and other types of manufacturing plants. For example, in a study involving a power station, the company wanted to reduce its operating costs. Data mining was used to identify variables like manifold pressure, steam flow to secondary turbines and the total steam flow as the major variables on which cost depended. The company was able to control these variables better to save about 5% on the cost of running the power station.

1.8.9 Telecommunications

As we have noted earlier, the telecommunications industry in many countries is in turmoil due to deregulation. Also, the telecommunications business is changing through consolidation in the market place and the convergence of new technologies, for example, video, voice, data. Furthermore, in some countries, on the one hand there is an infrastructure capacity explosion and the Internet is impacting the telecommunications business significantly. In this environment, the carriers are offering a variety of products including packaged landline, broadband and mobile phone services. They also have to deal with technologies like voice over IP.

The telecommunications industry is interested in answering a wide variety of questions with the help of data mining. For example:

- How does one retain customers and keep them loyal?
- Which customers are most likely to churn?

- What characteristics make a customer likely to be most profitable?
- What products and services yield the highest amount of profit?
- How does one recognize and predict when mobile phone fraud occurs?
- What characteristics indicate customers who will increase their line usage?

A widely discussed data mining application in the telecommunications industry is churn analysis. Essentially, given the highly competitive nature of the industry, there is extreme competition to retain customers and to poach other companies' customers. Data mining can provide information about customers who are most likely to remain loyal and those who are most likely to switch. The industry places high importance on retaining customers since retaining a good customer is much cheaper than recruiting a good new customer.

A telecommunications company has to deal with a large number of variables including cost of local calls, cost of international calls, mobile phone plans, installation and disconnection rates, customer satisfaction data, or data about customers who do not pay their bills or do not pay them on time. Furthermore, companies would like to improve their profitability by identifying customers who might wish to buy new products and to profile customers' use of telephone cards in an attempt to reduce fraud.

A variety of data mining tools including data warehousing, OLAP, classification, clustering and association rules are being used in the telecommunications sector.

1.8.10 Transportation

In a report published by NASA, experiments were carried out to automatically analyse textual incident reports from aviation incidents. These reports usually describe situations that were encountered during flight operations.

Wipro some years ago reported a study of frequent flyer data from an Indian airline. Before carrying out data mining, the data was selected and prepared. It was decided to use only the three most common sectors flown by each customer and the three most common sectors when points are redeemed by each customer. It was discovered that much of the data supplied by the airline was incomplete or inaccurate. Also, it was found that the customer data captured by the company could have been more complete. For example, the airline did not know customers' marital status or their income or their reasons for taking a journey.

In spite of this, there were some interesting results including some simple facts that most customers fly between metropolitan cities of India. It was found that customers flying Mumbai-Delhi also flew to other cities, for example Mumbai-Chennai, Mumbai-Kolkata and Mumbai-Bangalore. Most customers flying Bangalore-Hyderabad also travelled Delhi-Bangalore. Those who flew Guwahati to Bagdogra did not fly back to Guwahati but instead flew to Delhi.

These results provided the airline with a better understanding of its business and may have helped it to refine flight programming to better suit the customers.

1.9 THE FUTURE OF DATA MINING

Predicting the future is always risky but we will make some comments about future of data mining. Who could have predicted the emergence of the Web in the early 1990s?

Although the use of data mining in business is growing as data mining techniques move from research algorithms to business applications and as storage prices continue to decline and enterprise data continues to grow, data mining is still not being used widely. Thus there is considerable potential for data mining to continue to grow. The number of jobs in the area of data analytics has certainly been growing.

Since most time spent in data mining is actually spent in data extraction, data cleaning and data manipulation, it is expected that technologies like data warehousing will grow in importance. It has been found that as much as 40% of all collected data has errors in them. To deal with such large error rates, there is likely to be more emphasis in the future data cleaning. Data mining effectiveness would improve if these tasks could be carried out more efficiently.

Much of the innovation in the data mining field is coming from the academic community. Business users often find the techniques difficult to understand and integrate into business processes. The academic community is more interested in developing new techniques that perform better than those that are already known. To make data mining techniques more accessible to business, academics need to put more effort into understanding the kind of business problems that need to be solved, the kind of business processes that exist and explain to businesses which data mining techniques are suitable for which applications. They need to provide suitable training, without hype, to business people so that they develop familiarity with the techniques and build confidence to use them. To use data mining, the business user must be able to comprehend the techniques and understand how they may be applied to the problem that he/she is trying to solve. Such problems may be in marketing or credit scoring. In some cases, the business user already has a technique that has been used for years. The user will adopt a new technique only if he/she is convinced that the new technique will help the business to either save money or increase revenue.

As noted earlier, data mining techniques depend upon a lot of careful analysis of the business and a good understanding of the techniques and software available. Often a model needs to be built (e.g. for classification), tested and validated before it can be used. This needs considerable expertise and time. The team building a data mining application should have the business expertise as well as the data mining expertise.

Data mining techniques that are likely to become important in the future include techniques that better determine "interestingness" of a discovered pattern and are able to compare current data with an earlier set of data to determine if there is a change of pattern in the data. Other techniques that are likely to receive more attention in the future are text and Web-content mining, bio-informatics and multimedia data mining.

The issues related to information privacy and data mining will continue to attract serious concern in the community in future. In particular, privacy concerns related to use of data mining techniques by governments, in particular perhaps in fighting terrorism.

The area of visualisation has not yet received the attention in data mining that it deserves. The importance of visualisation is expected to grow and there should be more tools available with better visualisation capabilities in the future.

1.10 GUIDELINES FOR SUCCESSFUL DATA MINING

For a successful data mining application in an organisation, it is perhaps best to identify one particular area that needs to be explored. This may require a small project team with suitable expertise. The focus of this team should be in analysing only that particular area using perhaps one or two of the available techniques. The area may be to explain why the sales of a particular product have been going down or going up, or how to make more reliable demand forecasts for the next three years, or how to improve the response rate of customers to some promotional mail out, or how to detect opportunities for cross-selling or detect fraud. Only by solving an important problem can the team hope to persuade the senior managers of an organisation to support data mining initiatives.

It should be noted that every data mining project is different but the projects do have some common features. A very nice article describing these is by Lavrac, Motoda, Fawcett, Holte and Langley. First of all they discuss some basic requirements for a data mining project to be successful. These are:

- The data must be available
- The data must be relevant, adequate and clean
- There must be a well-defined problem
- The problem should not be solvable by means of ordinary query or OLAP tools
- The results must be actionable

Once the above basic prerequisites have been met, the following guidelines may be appropriate for a data mining project. A useful and much more detailed document is the CRISP-DM guide to which we have referred earlier.

1. Data mining projects should be carried out by small teams with a strong internal integration and a loose management style.
2. Before starting a major data mining project, it is recommended that a small pilot project be carried. This may involve a steep learning curve for the project team. This is of vital importance.
3. A clear problem owner should be identified who is responsible for the project. Preferably this is not a technical analyst or a consultant but someone with direct business responsibility, e.g. someone in a sales or marketing environment. This will benefit the external integration.
4. The positive return on investment should be realised within 6 to 12 months.
5. Since the roll-out of the results in a data mining application mostly involves larger groups of people and is technically less complex, it should be a separate and more strictly managed project.
6. The whole project should have the support of the top management of the company.

1.11 LIMITATIONS OF DATA MINING

Unless the data quality is high after pre-processing the data and an appropriate technique has been applied, it is possible that the results obtained from a data mining project are not relevant. The results may get contaminated if the data quality is not high. Also, using one of the large expensive data mining software without developing sufficient understanding of the data and the technique being used may produce misleading results that are not what the project was expected to have produced. It may be that the project team does not fully understand the different data mining techniques and has decided to choose the technique that is most popular or that recommended in the software documentation.

Furthermore, it should be understood that it is almost impossible to test if the results of a data mining project are the best that could be obtained. There is a no goodness-of-fit guarantee in data mining.

1.12 USING WEKA SOFTWARE IN CLASS

Waikato environment for knowledge analysis (WEKA) is a collection of open source software for data mining developed at the University of Waikato in New Zealand. It was developed in the mid-1990s and is now being used in teaching all over the world. We recommend instructors use Weka in their class to encourage students to experience some hands-on experience of carrying out at least some data mining tasks.

WEKA provides a collection of software. It allows data to be uploaded from files, URLs and databases. It provides a graphical interface for each of the following:

1. Data pre-processing—allows data to be uploaded and transformed
2. Classification and regression—allows data to be classified using supervised classification
3. Clustering—this is for unsupervised classification
4. Attribute selection
5. Visualisation—this provides the user to generate colour-coded scatter plots
6. Experimentation

It should be noted that a number of other open source software packages are also available. Rapid Miner is one that is widely used. It may be downloaded from rapid-i.com.

1.12.1 File Format for Using Weka

The data file used by Weka is called the Attribute-Relation File Format (or ARFF). This file has two sections; the first section is the *Header* information and the second is the *Data* information. A number of websites explain the format. One of the Web pages that explains the format is http://weka.wikispaces.com/ARFF+(stable+version).

1.13 DATA MINING SOFTWARE

There is considerable data mining software available in the market. Most major computing companies, for example IBM, Oracle and Microsoft, are providing data mining packages. Some data mining software has now also been included in most major database management systems.

Some data mining software can be expensive while other data mining software is available free. Therefore a user should spend some time selecting an appropriate tool for the task that he/she faces. We list a number of data mining software below but we do not claim the list to be a comprehensive list or a list of the best products on the market.

- Angoss Software—Angoss has data mining software called Knowledge SEEKER. It is a complete data mining package that includes facilities for classification, cluster analysis and prediction. It claims to provide a visual, easy-to-use interface.

- CART and MARS—software from Salford Systems includes CART Decision Trees, MARS predictive modelling, TreeNet classification and regression, data access, preparation, cleaning and reporting modules, RandomForests predictive modelling, clustering and anomaly detection.
- Clementine—from SPSS is a well-known and comprehensive package that provides association rules, classification, cluster analysis, factor analysis, forecasting, prediction and sequence discovery.
- DBMiner Technologies—DBMiner provides techniques for association rules, classification and cluster analysis. This software comes from Han and Kamber who are authors of the book Data Mining: Concepts and techniques.
- Enterprise Miner—SAS Institute has a comprehensive, integrated data mining package. Enterprise Miner provides a user-friendly icon-based GUI front-end using their process model called SEMMA (Sample, Explore, Modify, Model, Assess).
- GhostMiner—is a complete data mining suite, including data pre-processing, feature selection, k-nearest neighbours, neural nets, decision tree, SVM, PCA, clustering, and visualisation. GhostMiner was developed in Poland but is now a subsidiary of Fujitsu.
- Intelligent Miner—this is a comprehensive data mining package from IBM. Intelligent Miner uses DB2 but can access data from other databases. Its functionality includes association rules, classification, cluster analysis, prediction, sequential patterns and time series. It also includes Intelligent Miner for Text for text mining, including mining of email and Web pages. Intelligent miner provides support for processes from data preparation to mining and presentation.
- JDA Intellect—JDA Software Group has a comprehensive package called JDA Intellect that provides facilities for association rules, classification, cluster analysis and prediction. A GUI interface is provided. http://www.jda.com/Intellect.asp
- Mantas—Mantas software is a small company that was a spin-off from SRA International. The Mantas suite is now designed to focus on detecting and analysing suspicious behaviour in the financial market and assist companies comply with global regulations. http://www.mantas.com/
- MineSet—originally developed by SGI; now owned and further developed by Purple Insight. MineSet specialises in visualisation and provides a variety of visualisation tools including scatter visualiser, tree visualiser, statistics visualiser and map visualiser. http://www.purpleinsight.com/products/index.shtml
- MiningMart developed at University of Dortmund in Germany. The software focuses on data cleaning and provides a graphical tool for data pre-processing. It provides mining on relational databases; supports development, documentation, re-use and exchange of complete KDD processes. Free for non-commercial purposes. http://www-ai.cs.uni-dortmund.de/MMWEB/index.html
- Oracle—Oracle 10g has data mining facilities embedded in it. Users of Oracle therefore have access to techniques for association rules, classification and prediction. Oracle Data Miner is a graphical user interface for Oracle Data Mining. Oracle also has a product called Darwin which includes cluster analysis, prediction, classification and association rules. Darwin provides a GUI interface. http://www.oracle.com/technology/products/bi/odm/index.html

- WEKA 3—as noted earlier, it is a collection of machine learning algorithms for solving data mining problems. It is written in Java that runs on almost any platform. Witten and Frank who are authors of the book "Data Mining" have developed it. http://www.cs.waikato.ac.nz/ml/weka/

1.13.1 Software Evaluation and Selection

It should be noted at the outset that there is no software tool or suite of tools that could be considered the best data mining software. What a user looking for data mining software needs to do is to find the package or packages that are best suited to meet the needs of his/her enterprise. Many factors must be considered in evaluating the suitability of software. Some of the important factors are:

1. Product and vendor information
   - (a) Is the vendor reliable?
   - (b) What is the vendor's background? Industry expertise? How long has the vendor been in business?
   - (c) Does the software run on the platform that is to be used for the software? Are there satisfied customers already using the software?
   - (d) Was the software originally designed for this platform?
   - (e) Does the software use client-server architecture if that is the environment in which the software is to be used?
   - (f) How easy is it to upload information in the software? Is it easy to upload information from a relational database system?
2. Total cost of ownership
   - (a) How much will the product cost?
   - (b) Does it include the cost of maintenance?
   - (c) What kind of contract of sale is offered? Can the software be used by more than one user if necessary?
3. Performance
   - (a) How does the product perform compared to its competitors?
   - (b) If performance information is provided, is the information reliable?
   - (c) How does the software deal with large data sets? Is the performance linear or quadratic or exponential?
4. Functionality and modularity
   - (a) What techniques and algorithms does the software provide? Do they include the ones needed and likely to be needed in the near future?
   - (b) Do the techniques accept a variety of data, e.g. numeric, categorical, etc.?
   - (c) Is the software modular? Can the software be customised? Is customisation going to be expensive?
   - (d) Does the software provide tools for data cleaning, data filtering, data binning?
   - (e) Does the tool deal well with missing values?
   - (f) Does the software provide too many features compared to what is required?

5. Training and support
   (a) What documentation is provided? How current is the documentation?
   (b) Does the vendor provide training and help in installation?
   (c) Is computer based training for the software available?
   (d) Are there articles that have been written about the product by third parties?
   (e) Is technical support available in case problems arise? Is this support available via telephone or via email?
   (f) How far away is the nearest branch of the vendor?
   (g) Is the vendor large enough to provide adequate support?
   (h) Does the vendor have knowledgeable support staff?
6. Reporting facilities and visualisation
   (a) Are the results of data mining presented in a variety of ways?
   (b) Are good graphical and visualisation tools available to communicate results?
   (c) Are tools available to provide a summary of results?
   (d) Can reporting be customised to meet the user's needs?
7. Usability
   (a) Is the user interface intuitive given the machine platform?
   (b) Is the software easy to learn? Is simple documentation available?
   (c) Is the software flexible? Can it be easily adapted to a variety of problems?

Much information about each software may be obtained from the software vendors' website but one must be particularly careful in evaluating the information available there. We have discovered that many data mining software websites are uninformative about what techniques the software uses and about the software's performance.

Also, when one is attempting to compare a number of software packages, it is best to use a matrix by which all the different packages may be compared against all the important criteria. One can thus develop a 'score card' for each piece of software. Insist on receiving relevant technical information before evaluation. Once the evaluation is complete, it may be possible to ask the vendors on the short list to make a presentation of their product. In some cases that will not be possible. In any case, it is prudent to ask the vendors for a list of references. It may then be appropriate to contact the references and ask each of them a carefully prepared list of questions. This should provide some very useful information in making the final decision.

SUMMARY

In this chapter we have explained what data mining is and have presented a definition. The reasons for current interest in data mining were discussed and a number of areas of growth in data were described. The data mining process was discussed and the techniques discussed in this book are introduced. A number of application areas of data mining have been presented and several case studies from different applications areas have been briefly described. We have also presented a list of some data mining software available and a list of issues that should be considered when purchasing data mining software.

We have noted that for data mining to be effective, the user must carefully analyse the business and develop a good understanding of the data mining techniques and software available. Often a model needs to be built, tested and validated before it can be used. This needs considerable expertise and time. The team building a data mining application should have the business expertise as well as the data mining expertise.

REVIEW QUESTIONS

1. Briefly explain data mining and define it. (Sections 1.1, 1.2)
2. Discuss some of the reasons for growth in enterprise data. (Section 1.3)
3. Why is data mining being used more widely now? (Section 1.3)
4. List the steps of a data mining process. How is it different than the waterfall software engineering process? (Section 1.4)
5. Discuss the six steps of the CRISP-DM data mining process. (Section 1.5)
6. List some of the major applications of data mining. (Section 1.6)
7. What is the aim of Association Rule Mining? When can this technique be useful? (Section 1.7.1)
8. Explain an application of Supervised Classification. (Section 1.7.2)
9. Introduce briefly Cluster Analysis. (Section 1.7.3)
10. What is the aim of Web Data Mining? Explain how it might be useful for a website that you know. (Section 1.7.4)
11. Explain what Data Warehousing and OLAP aim to achieve that cannot be achieved by OLTP systems. (Section 1.7.6)
12. Briefly describe a number of case studies of successful use of data mining. (Section 1.8)
13. What is the future of data mining? (Section 1.9)
14. Explain the guidelines for successful data mining. Why are these guidelines helpful? (Section 1.10)
15. Explain briefly some limitations of data mining. (Section 1.11)
16. Explain how data mining software should be evaluated and selected for purchase. (Section 1.13)

EXERCISES

1. Explore one or two areas of data mining and show how the developments in these areas would not have been possible without growth in electronic data.
2. Study how much health data is collected in India. Would this collection help in health policy making? Would more careful data collection help? Discuss.
3. Discuss the advantages of data mining over other approaches of analysing data.

4. Can data mining in some areas assist in identifying corruption? Select one area and study the possibilities.
5. Describe the steps that are required in a typical data mining process and explain the importance of each step.
6. Briefly describe one data mining case study, listing objectives and results, in each of the following areas:
   (a) Astronomy
   (b) Marketing
   (c) Telecommunications
7. List the guidelines that have been recommended to ensure data mining is implemented successfully. Discuss the importance of each recommendation.
8. What objectives might be suitable for analysing the data in Table 1.1? Is the data suitable given the objectives?

MULTIPLE CHOICE QUESTIONS

1. Which of the following are the major concerns in designing OLTP systems?
   (a) Performance
   (b) Availability
   (c) Efficiency of data analysis
   (d) Efficiency of data aggregation
2. Which one of the following questions can be easily answered without using any data mining tools?
   (a) How many different types of customers are there?
   (b) What customers are the most profitable?
   (c) Which state in India did most students come from?
   (d) Which patient has a high risk of breast cancer?
3. Which one of the following may be considered a data mining task
   (a) Computing the total sales of each company branch
   (b) Predicting the outcome of a roulette wheel given its history
   (c) Predicting the future enrolments of a university given its history
   (d) None of the above
4. Which of the following a successful data mining technique is not expected to deliver?
   (a) Unknown patterns
   (b) Actionable patterns
   (c) Valid patterns
   (d) Confirm expected patterns
5. Which of the following areas have applications for data mining?
   (a) Telecommunications

(b) Education
(c) Health care
(d) Astronomy
(e) All of the above

6. Which one of the following is the most important step of the data mining process?
(a) Getting management support
(b) Data selection
(c) Visualisation
(d) Monitoring

7. Which of the following are features of data mining?
(a) It is an automatic process
(b) It is about discovering novel patterns
(c) It usually deals with large data sets
(d) All of the above

8. Which one of the following is not a step in the data mining process?
(a) Visualisation
(b) Report production
(c) Requirements analysis
(d) Testing and validation

9. Which one of the following is not a data mining technique?
(a) Association rule mining
(b) Clustering
(c) Multiple regression
(d) Supervised classification

10. Which one of the following is true?
(a) Association rule mining is same as market basket analysis
(b) Market basket analysis is same as computing correlation
(c) Clustering is same as classification
(d) Web data mining is same as page rank analysis

11. Which one of the following is true if the classical algorithm was being used?
(a) Association rules require numeric data
(b) Supervised classification requires categorical data
(c) Clustering requires categorical data
(d) All of the above are true

12. Which of the following is one of the guidelines for successful data mining?
(a) The enterprise must have a data warehouse
(b) There must be a well-defined problem
(c) There must be good visualisation tools available
(d) The enterprise must have OLAP experience

BIBLIOGRAPHY

During the last few years a number of good books on data mining have been published. Different books seem to have different focus. For example, the book by Han and Kamber is written from a database perspective while Hand, Mannila and Smyth are more theoretical and write more from the perspective of statistics. The books by Witten and Frank and Dhar and Stein deal with data mining issues from the perspective of machine learning. Both books by Berry and Linoff reflect a business perspective. The book edited by Fayyad et al. is a collection of papers and so is the book edited by Klösgen and Zytkow. The latter has a large number of papers that describe data mining software as well as others that describe data mining applications. The paper by Lavrac et al. is a very useful summary of what a person starting on a data mining project should know.

Recommended Reading for Students

We list a number of articles and tutorial slides that are easy to understand and may prove useful for students wishing to look at a different view of data mining.

Berry, M. and Linoff, G., *Mastering Data Mining*, John Wiley & Sons, 1999.

Bramer, M., *Principles of Data Mining*, Springer, 2013.

Dhar, V. and Stein, R., *Seven Methods for Transforming Corporate Data into Business Intelligence*, Prentice Hall, 1997.

Moore, A., Statistical Data Mining Tutorials, Tutorial Slides (Carnegie-Mellon University) http://www-2.cs.cmu.edu/~awm/tutorials/

SQL Server 2000 Resource Kit, Effective Strategies for Data Mining, Chapter 24, URL: http://www.microsoft.com/resources/documentation/sql/2000/all/reskit/en-us/default.mspx, September 2004.

Two Crows Corporation, *Introduction to Data Mining and Knowledge Discovery*, 3rd ed., 1999. http://www.twocrows.com/intro-dm.pdf

Recommended Reading for Lecturers

Chapman, P., Clinton, J., Kerber, R., Khabaza, T., Reinartz, T., Shearer, C., and Wirth, R., CRISP-DM 1.0 Step-by-Step Data Mining Guide, 2000. http://www.crisp-dm.org/crispwp-0800.pdf.

CRISP-DM, http://www.crisp-dm.org/ and at http://dms.irb.hr/tutorial/tut_main.php.

Fayyad, U.M., Piatetsky–Shapiro, G., Smyth, P., and Anduthurusamy, R. (Eds.), *Advances in Knowledge Discovery and Data Mining*, MIT Press, 625 pp., 1996.

Ghosh, J., Obradovic, Z., Dy, J., Zhou, Z., Kamath, C., and Parthasarathy, S. (Eds.), *Proceedings of the 2013 SIAM International Conference on Data Mining*, 804 pp., 2013.

Hall, M., Frank, E., Holmes, G., and Pfahringer, B., The WEKA Data Mining Software: An Update, SIGKDD Explorations, Volume 11, Issue 1, pp. 11–18, 2009.

Han, J., Kamber, M., and Pei, J., *Data Mining: Concepts and Techniques*, Morgan Kaufmann, 3rd ed., 703 pp., 2012. The Book website is http://www.cs.uiuc.edu/~hanj/bk2/.

Klösgen, W. and Zytkow, J.M. (Eds.), *Handbook of Data Mining and Knowledge Discovery*, Oxford University Press, 980 pp., 2002.

Kudyba, S., Big Data, *Mining, and Analytics: Components of Strategic Decision Making*, Auerbach Publications, 325 pp., 2014.

Lavrac, N., Motoda, H., Fawcett, T., Holte, R., Langley, P., and Adriaans, P., Lessons Learned From Data Mining Applications and Collaborative Problem Solving: Machine Learning, Vol. 57, No. 1–2, pp. 5–11, 2004.

North, M.A., Data Mining for the Masses, Global Text Project, 264 pp., 2012.

Russell, M.A., Mining the Social Web: Data Mining Facebook, Twitter, Linkedin, Google+, Github, and More, O'Reilly Media, 488 pp., 2013.

Tan, P.N., *Introduction to Data Mining*, Addison-Wesley, 792 pp., 2014.

Tan, P.N., Steinbach, M., and Kumar, V., *Introduction to Data Mining,* Pearson/Addison-Wesley, 769 pp., 2006.

Tsiptsis, K. and Chorianopoulos, A., *Data Mining Techniques in CRM: Inside Customer Segmentation*, Wiley, 2010.

Witten, I.H., Frank, E., and Hall, M.A., *Data Mining: Practical Machine Learning Tools and Techniques*, 3rd ed., Morgan Kaufmann, 2011. The book's website is www.mkp.com/datamining. The WEKA software is available from www.cs.waikato.ac.nz/weka.

Wu, X. and Kumar, V. (Eds.), *The Top Ten Algorithms in Data Mining*, Chapman & Hall/CRC, 2009.

Data Mining Web Resources

A List of Data Mining Books
http://www3.shore.net/~kht/books.htm#dbm

ACM Special Interest Group on Knowledge Discovery and Data Mining (SIGKDD)
http://www.acm.org/sigkdd/explorations/

Bibliography on Association Rules Mining
http://wwwai.wu-wien.ac.at/~hahsler/research/bib/association_rules/

Bibliography on Data Warehousing and OLAP
http://www.ondelette.com/OLAP/dwbib.html

Class Notes—Stanford Data Mining Course by Professor J.D. Ullman
http://www-db.stanford.edu/~ullman/mining/allnotes.pdf

Data Mining and Knowledge Discovery (Journal)
http://www.kluweronline.com/issn/1384-5810

Grossman, R., Kamath, C., and Kumar, V., 2001, Data Mining Scientific and Engineering Applications, More than 400 Slides used for Tutorial at SC2001
http://www-users.cs.umn.edu/~kumar/Presentation/sc2001.html

How much Data is there in the World?
http://www.lesk.com/mlesk/ksg97/ksg.html

IBM Intelligent Miner Redbooks
http://publib-b.boulder.ibm.com/cgi-bin/searchsite.cgi?query=intelligent+miner

IBM Quest Data Mining Site
http://www.almaden.ibm.com/software/quest/

Slides on Association Rule Mining.
datamining.anu.edu.au/student/dm_course2004/imstut.pdf

The Serendip Data Mining Project at Bell Labs
http://www.bell-labs.com/project/serendip/

For Data Mining Case Studies

Crime Case Study

Chen, H., Chung, W., Xu, J.J., Wan, G., Qin, Y., and Chan, M., Crime Data Mining: A general framework and some examples, *IEEE Computer*, pp. 50–56, 2004.

Wang, G., Chen, H., and Atabakhsh, H., Automatically detecting deceptive criminal identities, *Comm. ACM*, pp. 70–76, 2004.

Healthcare Case Study

Silver, M., Sakata, T., Su, H-C., Herman, C., Dolins, S.B., and O'Shea, M.J., Case Study: How to apply data mining techniques in a healthcare data warehouse, *J. Healthcare Information Management*, Vol. 15, No. 2, pp. 155–64, 2001.

Wisniewski, M.F., Kieszkowski, P., Zagorski, B.M., Trick, W.E., Sommers, M., and Weinstein, R.A., Development of a clinical data warehouse for hospital infection control, *J. Am. Med. Infor. Assoc.*, Vol. 10, Issue 5, pp. 454–62, 2003.

Inventory Control Case Study

Dhond, A., Gupta, A., and Vadhavkar, S., Data mining techniques for optimising inventories for electronic commerce, *Proc. Sixth ACM SIGKDD Int. Conf. on Knowledge Discovery and Data Mining*, pp. 480–486, 2000.

Loan Risk Assessment Case Study

Assessing Loan Risks: A Data Mining Case Study http://www.exclusiveore.com/casestudies/dm_at_usda_(itpro).pdf

Manufacturing Case Study

Gardner, M. and Bieker, J., Data mining solves tough semiconductor manufacturing problems, *Proc. Sixth ACM SIGKDD Int. Conf. on Knowledge Discovery and Data Mining*, pp. 376–383, 2000.

Medical and Engineering Case Study

Kusiak, A., Kernstine, K.H., Kern, J.A., McLaughlin, K.A., and Tseng, T.L., 2000, Data mining: medical and engineering case studies, *Proc. Industrial Engineering 2000 Conf.*, Cleveland, Ohio. http://www.icaen.uiowa.edu/~ankusiak/Res-in-Prog/IIE-0.pdf

Wipro's Frequent Flyer Program Case Study
http://www.bitpipe.com/data/detail?id=1024577555_848&type=RES&x=1106840343

CASE STUDY 1A

Data Mining Techniques for Optimizing Inventories for Electronic Commerce*

ABSTRACT

As part of their strategy for incorporating electronic commerce capabilities, many organizations are involved in the development of information systems that will establish effective linkages with their suppliers, customers, and other channel partners involved in transportation, distribution, warehousing and maintenance activities. These linkages have given birth to comprehensive data warehouses that integrate operational data with supplier, customer, channel partners and market information. Data mining techniques can now provide the technological leap needed to structure and prioritize information from these data warehouses to address specific end-user problems. Emerging data mining techniques permit the semi-automatic discovery of patterns, associations, changes, anomalies, rules, and statistically significant structures and events in data. Very significant business benefits have been attained through the integration of data mining techniques with current information systems aiding electronic commerce. This paper explains key data mining principles that can play a pivotal role in an electronic commerce environment. The paper also highlights two case studies in which neural network-based data mining techniques were used for inventory optimization. The results from the data mining prototype in a large medical distribution company provided the rationale for the strategy to reduce the total level of inventory by 50% (from a billion dollars to half a billion dollars) in the particular organization, while maintaining the same level of probability that a particular customer's demand will be satisfied. The second case study highlights the use of neural network-based data mining techniques for forecasting hot metal temperatures in a steel mill blast furnace.

Keywords: Inventory Optimization, Temporal Data Mining, Data Massaging.

1. INTRODUCTION

The past two decades have witnessed a dramatic increase in information being stored in electronic format. This surge will be further compounded by an ever-growing number of organizations embracing the paradigm of electronic commerce. The amount of information in the world is estimated to double every 20 months and the size and the numbers of databases are increasing at a still faster pace. The increase in the use of electronic data gathering devices, such as point-of-sale devices and remote sensing devices, is one factor for this explosive growth.

In electronic commerce environments, the rapidly escalating volume of data makes timely and accurate data analysis beyond the reach of the best human domain expert, even hordes of them working day and night. Instead, emerging data mining techniques offer far superior abilities to discover hidden knowledge, interesting patterns and new business rules hidden within huge repositories of

*Dhond, A., A. Gupta, and S. Vadhavkar, 2000, Data mining techniques for optimizing inventories for electronic commerce, *Proc. Sixth ACM SIGKDD Int. Conf. on Knowledge Discovery and Data Mining*, pp. 480–486.

adhond@mit.edu agupta@mit.edu vada@mit.edu

electronic databases. Currently regarded as the key element of the more elaborate process of Knowledge Discovery in Database (KDD), the data-mining paradigm integrates theoretical perspectives from the realms of statistics, machine learning and artificial intelligence. From the standpoint of technology implementation, it relies on advances in data modeling, data warehousing and information retrieval. However, the more important challenges lie in organizing business practices around the knowledge discovery activity. As organizations gear towards a web-enabled economy and increasingly rely on online information sources for a variety of decision support applications, one will witness a growing reliance on data mining techniques in the electronic commerce space.

Data mining involves the semi-automatic discovery of patterns, associations, changes, anomalies, rules, and statistically significant structures and events in data. In other words, data mining attempts to extract knowledge from data. Data mining differs from traditional statistics in several ways: formal statistical inference is assumption-driven in the sense that a hypothesis is formed and validated against the data. Data mining in contrast, is discovery driven in the sense that patterns and hypotheses are automatically extracted from large data sets. Further, the goal in data mining is to extract qualitative models, which can easily be translated into business patterns, logical rules or visual representations. Therefore, the results of the data mining process may be patterns, insights, rules, or predictive models that are frequently beyond the capabilities of the best human domain experts.

In the electronic commerce space, data mining techniques have the potential of providing companies with competitive advantages in optimizing their use of information. Potential applications include the following [16][17][18][19]:

- To manage customer relationships by predicting customer buying habits, calibrating customer loyalty and retention, analyzing customer segments, target marketing and promotion effectiveness, customer profitability, customer lifetime value, and customer acquisition effectiveness.
- To enable financial management through analytical fraud detection, claims reduction, detection of high cost to serve orders or customers, risk scoring, credit scoring, audit targeting and enforcement targeting.
- To position products by product affinity analysis that shows opportunities for cross selling, up selling and strategic product bundling.
- To develop efficient and optimized inventory management systems based on Web customer demand predictions.
- To implement more efficient supply chains with suppliers and contractors.

2. CASE STUDIES

2.1 Medicorp—Pharmaceutical Distribution Company

Large organizations, especially geographically dispersed organizations, are usually obliged to carry large inventories of products ready for delivery on customer demand. Inventory optimization pertains to the problem of how much quantity of each product should be kept in the inventory at each store and each warehouse. If too little inventory is carried relative to demand, unsatisfied customers could turn to competitors. On the other hand, a financial cost is incurred for carrying excessive inventory. In addition, some products have short expiration periods and shelf life and therefore, must be replaced periodically. Inventories take a lot of money to maintain. The best way to manage an inventory is through the development of better techniques for predicting customer demands and managing stock inventories accordingly. In this way, the size and the constitution of the inventory can be optimized with respect to changing demands.

With hundreds of chain stores and with revenues of several billion dollars per annum, "*Medicorp*" is a large retail distribution company. *Medicorp* revenues exceeded $15 billion from over 4100 stores in 25 states in the United States. *Medicorp* dispenses approximately 12% of all retail prescriptions in the

United States. In keeping with its market-leading position, *Medicorp* is forced to have a large standing inventory of products ready to deliver on customer demand. The problem is how much quantity of each drug should be kept in the inventory at each store and warehouse. Because of unfulfilled prescriptions, unsatisfied customers may switch company loyalties, relying on other pharmacy chains for their needs. On the other hand, *Medicorp* incurs a financial cost if it carries excessive inventories. In addition, pharmaceutical drugs have a short expiration date and must be renewed periodically.

Historically, *Medicorp* has maintained an inventory of approximately a billion dollars on a continuing basis, using traditional regression models to determine inventory levels for each drug item. The corporate policy of *Medicorp* is governed by two competing principles: minimize total inventory and achieve highest level of customer satisfaction. The former principle is not quantified in numerical terms. On the latter issue, *Medicorp* strives to achieve a 95% fulfillment level. That is, if a random customer walks into a random store on a random day for a random drug, the probability for the availability of the particular item must be 95%. The figure of 95% is based on the type of goods that *Medicorp* carries, and the service levels offered by competitors of *Medicorp* for the same items. *Medicorp* has a corporate wide data warehouse system that maintains data on what was sold, at what price, and to whom at each store.

After reviewing various options, and using conventional inventory optimization techniques, *Medicorp* adopted a "three-weeks of supply" approach. This approach involved the regression study of historical data to compute a seasonally-adjusted estimate of the forecasted demand for the next three week period. This estimated demand is the inventory level that *Medicorp* keeps, or strives to keep, on a continuing basis. Each store within the *Medicorp* chain orders replenishments on a weekly basis and receives the ordered items 2–3 days later from a regional data warehouse. Historically, this model has yielded the 95% target for customer satisfaction.

To find the best solution to the inventory problem, we analyzed data maintained within the transactional data warehouse at *Medicorp*. The *Medicorp* data warehouse is of the order of several gigabytes in size. In the modeling phase, we extracted a portion of the recent data fields, which was deemed to provide adequate raw data for a preliminary analysis:

- Date field—Indicates the date of the drug transaction
- NDC number—Uniquely identifies a drug (equivalent to a drug name)
- Customer number—Uniquely identifies a customer (useful in tracking repeat customers)
- Quantity number—Identifies the amount of the drug purchased
- Sex field—Identifies the sex of the customer
- Days of Supply—Identifies how long that particular drug purchased will last
- Cost Unit Price—Establishes the per unit cost to *Medicorp* of the particular drug
- Sold Unit Price—Identifies per unit cost to the customer of the particular drug

Before adopting neural network based data mining techniques, preliminary data analysis was utilized to help search for seasonal trends, correlation between field variables and significance of variables, etc. Our preliminary data provided evidence for the following patterns:

- Most sales of drug items showed minimal correlation to seasonal changes.
- Women are more careful about consuming medication than men, indicating that women customers were more likely to complete the prescription fully than men.
- Drug sales are heaviest on Thursdays and Fridays, indicating that inventory replenishment would be best ordered on Monday.
- Drug sales (in terms of quantity of drug sold) show differing degrees of variability.
- *Maintenance type drugs* (for chronic ailments) show low degrees of sales variability.
- *Acute type drugs* (for temporary ailments) show high degrees of sales variability.

There is no general theory that specifies the type of neural network, number of layers, number of nodes (at various layers), or learning algorithm for a given problem. As such, data mining analysts must experiment with a large number of neural networks before converging upon the appropriate one for the problem in hand. In order to evaluate the relative performance of each neural network, we used statistical techniques to measure the error values in predictions. Most major neural network architectures and major learning algorithms were tested using sample data patterns from *Medicorp*. Multi Layer Perceptron (MLP) models and Time Delay Neural Network (TDNN) models yielded promising results and were studied in greater detail.

Modeling short time-interval predictions is difficult, as it requires a greater number of forecast points, shows greater sales demand variability, and exhibits lesser dependence on previous sales history. Using MLP architectures and sales data for one class of products, we initially attempted to forecast sales demand on a daily basis. The results were unsatisfactory: the networks produced predictions with very low correlation (generally below 20%) and very high absolute error values (generally above 80%). Hence, modeling for larger time intervals was attempted next.

As expected, forecasting for a week proved more accurate than for a day and forecasting for one month proved more accurate than for a week. Indeed, when predicting aggregate annual sales demand, we obtained average error values of only 2%. Keeping a weekly prediction interval provided the best compromise between the accuracy of prediction and the usefulness of the predicted information for *Medicorp*. The weekly forecasts are useful for designing inventory management systems for individual *Medicorp* stores, while the yearly forecasts are useful for determining the performance of a particular item in a market and the overall financial performance of the organization.

The neural network was trained with historic sales data using two methods: the standard method and the rolling method. The difference between these two methods is best explained with an example. Assume that weekly sales data (in units sold) were 10, 20, 30, 40, 50, 60, 70, 80, 90, 100, etc. In the standard method, we would present the data: "10, 20, 30" and ask the network to predict the fourth value: "40". Then, we would present the network with "40, 50, 60" and ask it to predict the next value: "70". We would continue this process until all training data were exhausted. On the other hand, using the rolling method, we would present historic data as "10, 20, 30" and ask the network to predict the fourth value: "40"; then, we would present the network with "20, 30, 40" and ask it to predict the fifth value: "50". We would continue using the rolling method until all the training data were exhausted.

The rolling method has an advantage over the standard method in that it produces a greater quantity of training examples from the same data sample, but at the expense of training data quality. The rolling method can "confuse" the neural network because of the close similarity between training samples. Using the previous example for instance, the rolling method would produce "10, 20, 30"; "20, 30, 40"; "30, 40, 50". Each of these training samples differs from another data set by a single number only. This minuscule difference may reduce the neural network's ability to understand the underlying pattern in the data.

At *Medicorp*, some items sell infrequently. In fact, some of the specialized drugs may sell only twice or thrice a year at a particular store. This lack of sales data is a major problem in training neural networks. To solve it, we used other methods for transformation of data, reuse, and aggregation of data. The one we found most effective involved changing future data sets with some known fraction of past data sets. If $X[i]'$ represents the ith changed data set, $X[i]$ represents the ith initial data set, $X[i-1]$ represents the initial $(i-1)$th initial data set and μ is some numerical factor, then the new time series can be computed as $X[i]' = X[i] + \mu * X[i-1]$, $X[0]' = X[0]$. The modified time series thus has data elements that retain a fraction of the information of past elements. By modifying the actual time series with the proposed scheme, the memory of non-zero sales items is retained for a longer period of time, making it easier to train the neural networks with the modified time series.

As mentioned before, the policies at *Medicorp* are governed by two competing principles: minimize drug inventories and enhance customer satisfaction via high availability of items in stock. As such, we calibrated the different inventory models using two parameters: "undershoot" and "days of supply". The number of "undershoots" denotes the number of times a customer would be turned away if a particular inventory model were used over the "test" period. The "days-of-supply" statistic is the number of days the particular item in the inventory is expected to last. By using the latter parameter, one reduces the complexity and allows for equitable comparisons across different categories of items. For example, items in the inventory are measured in different ways: by weight or by volume or by number. If one talked in terms of raw amount, one would need to take into account different units of measure. However, the "days-of-supply" parameter allows all items to be specified in terms of one unit: days. The level of popularity of the item gets factored into the "days-of-supply" parameter. While maintaining a 95% probability of customer, the MLP model reduces "days-of-supply" for items in the inventory by 66%. On the average, the neural network "undershoots" only three times (keeping the 95% customer satisfaction policy of *Medicorp*).

Our models suggested that, as compared to the "three-weeks of supply" thumb rule, the level of inventory needs to be "reduced" for popular items and "increased" for less popular or unpopular items. This inference appears counter-intuitive at first glance. However, since fast moving items are already carried in large amounts, and since they can be replenished at weekly intervals, one can reduce the inventory level without adversely impacting the likelihood of availability when needed. This is the factor that permits significant reduction in the size of the total inventory, and has been highlighted by a number of observers in the popular press.

To summarize the effort, we developed the neural network based data mining model for reducing the inventory at *Medicorp* from over a billion dollars worth of drugs to about one-half billion dollars (reduction by 50%) while maintaining the original customer satisfaction level (95% availability level).

2.2 Steelcorp—Iron and Steel Company

The blast furnace is the heart of any steel mill. Inside the blast furnace, the oxygen from the iron oxides is removed to yield nearly pure liquid iron. This liquid iron, or pig iron, is the raw material used in the steel plants. As with any product, the quality of this pig iron can vary. The most important determinants of the quality are (1) the amount and composition of any impurities, and (2) the temperature of the hot metal when it is tapped from the blast furnace [8]. The quality of the pig iron produced is important in determining how costly it will be to produce steel from the pig iron, as well as constraining what final types of steel into which the pig iron can be made. Therefore, it is crucial that hot metal temperature be maintained within an optimal range of values [9]. A blast furnace is very difficult to model due to the complex flow conditions with mass and heat transfer inside. For many years, blast furnace operators have been aware of the fact that there are no universally accepted methods for accurately controlling blast furnace operation and predicting the outcome. The Hot Metal Temperature and Silicon Content are important indicators of the internal state of a blast furnace as well as of the quality of the pig iron being produced. The production of pig iron involves complicated heat and mass transfers and introduces complex relationships between the various chemicals used.

This case study presents preliminary results from the use of Artificial Neural Networks (ANNs) as a means of modeling these complex inter-variable relationships. The research is based on three months of operational data collected from the blast furnace of *"Steelcorp"*. *Steelcorp* is one of Asia's largest manufacturers of iron and steel and has multiple blast furnaces operating in tandem at multiple locations. Most of the blast furnaces are state-of-the-art and automatically collect and store data at periodic intervals on a number of input and output parameters for future analysis.

There have been many attempts by researchers to use AI techniques in order to predict different state variables of the blast furnace based on measured conditions within the furnace. However, modeling the relationships between various variables in the blast furnace has been quite difficult using standard statistical techniques· [5]. The main reason is that non-linearities exist between the different parameters used in pig iron (hot metal) production. Production of hot metal in a blast furnace is the result of complex chemical reactions that scientists have not been able to model explicitly. Therefore, many have turned to neural networks in order to predict various blast furnace parameters. For example, Bulsari and Saxen [5] used feed-forward neural networks when trying to classify the state of a blast furnace based on the measurement of blast furnace temperatures. Bulsari et al. [9] used multi-layered feed-forward artificial neural networks to predict the silicon content of hot metal from a blast furnace. Several different artificial neural network models were tried by Singh et al. [7] in order to predict the silicon content of hot metal using: coke rate, hot blast temperature, slag rate, top pressure, slag basicity and the logarithm of blast kinetic energy.

The raw data from the blast furnace was not consistent/enough for direct use during modeling. Reasons for this ranged from problems inherent to the data, such as missing or very anomalous values, to more subtle flaws such as not taking into account the effect of time lags in the production process. Several steps were involved in preprocessing the raw data into a dataset that would be suitable for training an artificial neural network.

Extremely abnormal data values were adjusted to make the data more consistent. Values that were more than two standard deviations from the mean were modified so that they would be two standard deviations away from the mean. In some cases a minimum value for a variable was specified. If two standard deviations below the mean is smaller than the minimum then the data was adjusted to the minimum value. This process removed any outliers from the dataset. A major problem with the original data was inaccurate values of HMT for many of the data points. HMT can be measured only approximately once every hour while the other data points were taken every five minutes. Linear interpolation between measurements of HMT was used to approximate values for the missing data points.

The raw data from the blast furnace contained a total of 9100 data points taken every five minutes. This five minute level data may see some inputs changing rapidly from one value to another, but since the temperature changes slowly over a longer period of time these short-term changes do not have a noticeable effect on the output. Domain knowledge from *Steelcorp* indicated that an effective unit for considering the data would be in blocks of one hour. Therefore, groups of twelve data points were averaged to create one data point, which represented a one-hour block. While hourly averaging of the data improved the predictive ability of the network, it had a side effect of greatly reducing the number of data points available for training the networks. The hourly averaging reduced the number of data points to approximately 760. A moving window technique was used to deter this problem. The moving window takes the first twelve data points and averages them, but in the next step it shifts over by a five-minute interval and averages the new data point with the previous eleven data points. The window continues to slide one data point at a time, until the end of the set is reached. This technique allowed the use of almost the same number of data points as in the original data set.

The initial data contained 35 input parameters. Analysis of the data revealed that some of the input variables were redundant and others were not useful in predicting HMT or Silicon content. In order to discover which variables were the most important, a sensitivity analysis was performed on all of the 35 input variables. The way this was done was to calculate the correlation coefficient between each input variable and the corresponding output variable (HMT). The reasoning is that the higher the correlation between a particular input and HMT, the more 'important' that particular input variable must be in determining HMT. Therefore, such a variable should be included in the dataset. Using correlation relationships and information from the blast furnace experts at *Steelcorp*, the number of input variables was narrowed down from 35 to 11. These 11 variables were: total coke, carbon oxide, hydrogen, steam, group 1 heat flux, group 2 heat flux, actual coke injection, % oxygen enrichment, ore/coke ratio, hot blast temperature (degrees C), charge time for 10 semi charges, and the previous measured hot metal temperature (HMT).

Two distinct types of data sets were created in order to model future silicon content. The first type of data set consisted of 38 of the 39 input/output columns of the five minute interval HMT data (the only column omitted was the time column). These variables were used as the inputs in order to predict the lone output variable, Si%, which is a column that was extracted from hot metal chemistry data.

Since Si% was measured at a less frequent rate than the HMT input variables, the addition of the silicon column as the output column resulted in having large, contiguous regions of the output variable that had the same, constant value. Therefore, linear interpolation and hourly averaging were performed. In addition, the usual practices of implementing the best lags for each input column, filling of missing values with previous values, and normalization of each column were also implemented. The second type of silicon data set was processed in the same manner as above, but, includes additional variables as inputs. Specifically, the additional inputs used were taken from the Coke and Sinter data sets, and include the following: Coke Ash, Coke V.M., C.S.R., C.R.I., RDI, CaO, SiO_2, MgO, Al_2O_3, FeO and Fe.

To present some of the key results from the modeling exercise, prediction results from modeling HMT 2 and 4 hours into the future are shown below (Figures 1 and 2). Figure 1 shows the graph of predicted Hot Metal Temperature, two hours ahead of time, against the observed value. The network with the lowest mean squared error (MSE) had 19 hidden nodes. A noticeable lag is present which indicates that the most important variable (as far as the model is concerned) for predicting future HMT is the previous known HMT.

Similar analysis was performed for modeling silicon content. Preliminary results from the modeling are shown in Figures 3 and 4. From Figures 1–4 and comparing the absolute error values from the analyses, our results indicate that the addition of coke and sinter as inputs did not provide any clear advantage in terms of predicting silicon content. One interesting point to notice is that, unlike in the HMT case, there is no deterioration in the quality of silicon predictions as the prediction horizon increases. In addition, the predictions do not seem to "lag" the actual values. This is a problem that we had with HMT estimation. This means that the networks are not focusing on just the previous silicon value when predicting into the future.

The research group is currently looking at other artificial intelligence techniques such as genetic algorithms and pattern matching to control the conditions in the blast furnace. A prediction can indicate the future condition of the blast furnace based on the current conditions. This is extremely useful when the blast furnace operator can alter the current conditions in order to keep the future conditions within a desirable range. In order to perform the task, the relationships between the variables being controlled and the variables affecting them must be known. But some characteristics of the problem make it difficult: (1) each variable being controlled is affected by a large number of variables, (2) the relationships between the variables being controlled and the variables affecting them are non-linear, and (3) these non-linear relationships change over time. The first step towards

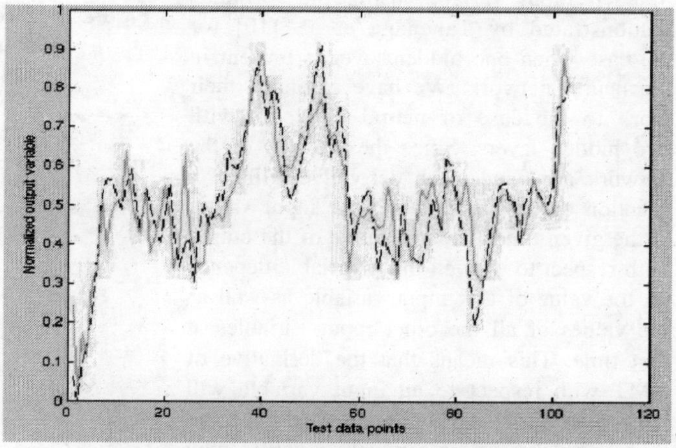

Figure 1: HMT 2 Hours: Solid—Predicted, Dashed—Actual.

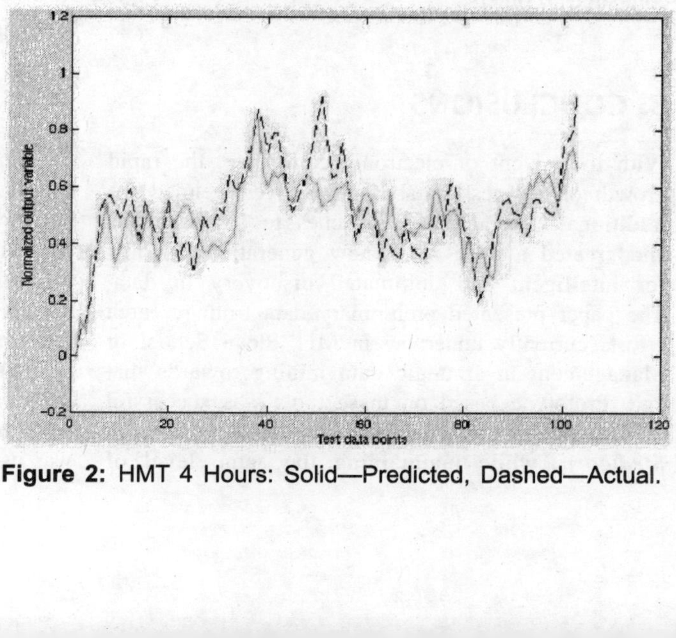

Figure 2: HMT 4 Hours: Solid—Predicted, Dashed—Actual.

controlling the conditions in a blast furnace involves finding out which input variables are most influential in producing an output. Our analysis uses HMT as the output variable.

Since we have been able to train networks that can predict HMT with a relatively high degree of accuracy, we now will find what kind of importance the neural network itself assigns each input variable when predicting HMT. The neural network will provide us with some insight into which variables we should pay special attention to when trying to predict and control HMT. We calculate the derivative of the output (HMT) with respect to each input variable using the formulas demonstrated by Takenaga et al. [10] for the case when one hidden layer is present in the neural network. We have extended their work to the case of neural networks with two hidden layers. Since the weights of the network are fixed, each derivative will be a function of the weights and the input values at the given time. The derivative of the output with respect to a given input variable depends on the value of that input variable as well as the values of all the other input variables at that time. This means that the derivative of HMT with respect to an input variable will vary over time. This approach is expected to give us insights into which variables may be more influential in predicting HMT when compared to others.

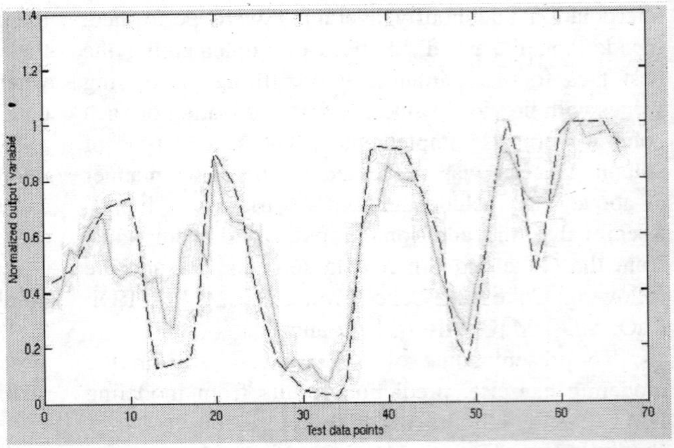

Figure 3: Silicon Content 2 Hour Network with coke and sinter as inputs: Solid—Predicted, Dashed—Actual.

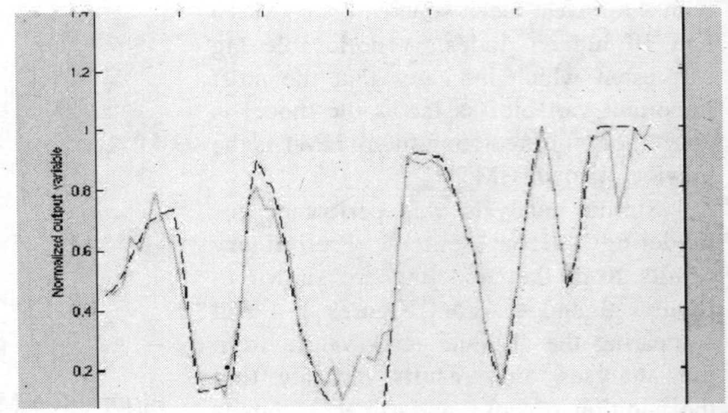

Figure 4: Silicon Content 4 Hour Network with coke and sinter as inputs: Solid—Predicted, Dashed—Actual.

3. CONCLUSIONS

With the advent of electronic commerce, the rapid growth of business databases has overwhelmed the traditional, interactive approaches to data analysis and created a need for a new generation of tools for intelligent and automated discovery in data. The paper presented preliminary data from research efforts currently underway in MIT Sloan School of Management in strategic data mining towards that end. Prototype based on these tools was successful in reducing the total level of inventory by 50% in *Medicorp*, while maintaining the same level of probability that a particular customer's demand will be satisfied.

The paper also highlighted many interesting challenges within the context of providing neural network based data mining tools for Inventory control. In neural network based data mining, the most difficult problems were encountered at the data preparation stage. The problem of too few and relatively irregular timing of data points was addressed in multiple ways. Linearization was used to overcome the erratic frequency with which the input variables were measured. The concept of "moving windows" was used to boost the number of data points reduced by the use of linearization. Both methods are good at resolving the problems they are intended for, but distort the way the input parameters are represented in the modeling stage. This is a side effect which one has to cope with, in situations involving missing and/or infrequent data.

In the modeling stage, different neural network algorithms were experimented with, along with different input-hidden-output node configurations, different randomizing algorithms and different learning rates. The variations on the number of nodes and the different algorithms did not produce very different results, indicating that these factors are not important. Even though in general, the Time-Delay family of neural networks are more powerful networks in time series analysis because of their ability to capture time-dependencies in the data set, in this case, they did not outperform simple Feed-Forward neural networks. For both the case studies, time-dependencies of the data set were explicitly defined and compensated in the modeling stage.

4. CHECKLIST FOR POTENTIAL BENEFICIARIES

Based on our experience with many data mining projects, we have the following suggestions to offer for using data mining techniques for electronic commerce related applications:

Have a clearly articulated business problem and then determine whether data mining is the proper solution technology. It might be tempting to use data mining to solve every business problem related to databases—but some problems are unsuited to data mining. A question such as "What were my sales from Web customers in Massachusetts last month?" can be best answered with a database query or on-line analytical processing tool. Data mining is about answering questions such as: "What are the characteristics of my most profitable Web customers from Massachusetts?" "How do I optimize my inventory for the next month?" In the electronic commerce space, data mining can be used effectively to increase market share by knowing who your most valuable customers are, defining their features and then using that profile to either retain them or target new, similar customers.

Have business division(s) intimately involved in the endeavor from the beginning. Data mining is gradually evolving from a technology-driven concept to a business solution-driven concept. Earlier, information technology consumers were eager to employ data mining technologies without much regard to its incumbent business processes and organizational disciplines. Now business divisions, rather than technology divisions, are spearheading the data mining efforts in major corporations.

Understand and deliver the fundamentals. At the heart of any data mining effort, there must be a business process. No amount of technology firepower can take its place. The fundamentals of the business must be incorporated seamlessly in the data mining effort. For example, it may be important to keep in mind that Web customers are different from non-Web customers; therefore, any data mining results derived from analyzing an entire customer base may not be applicable to a Web-customer base. In fact, data mining tools can be used to model the differences in the two types of customer bases thereby creating a more effective experience for the customer.

Have your technology folks involved too. Software vendors are responding to the technology-to-business migration by growing emphasis on one-button data mining products. Vendors can repackage data mining tools, enhancing their graphical user interface and automating some of their more esoteric aspects. However, it still falls on the analyst to acquire, clean, and feed data to the software; make dynamic selection of appropriate algorithms; validate and assimilate the results of the data mining runs; and generate business rules from the patterns in the data. Most of the operational complexity, time consumption and potential benefits of data mining lie in performing these steps and performing them well.

ACKNOWLEDGMENTS

The authors would like to thank various members of the Data Mining research group at the Sloan School of Management for their help in building training data for the ANNs and testing various ANN models. Proactive support from the top manage-ment of *Medicorp* and *Steelcorp* throughout the research is greatly appreciated.

REFERENCES

[1] Knoblock, C., Ed., "Neural networks in real-world applications," in *IEEE Expert*, August 1996, pp. 4–10.

[2] Bhat, N. and McAvoy, T.J., "Use of Neural Nets for Dynamic Modeling and Control of Chemical Process Systems," in *Computers in Chemical Engineering*, Vol. 14, No. 4/5, pp. 573–583.

[3] Rumelhart D. and McClelland J., *Parallel Distributed Processing: Exploration in the Microstructure of Cognition*, Vol. 1, MIT Press 1986.

[4] Pal S.K. and Mitra S., "Multilayer perceptron, fuzzy sets and classification", in *IEEE Transactions on Neural Networks,* Vol. 3, No. 5, September 1992.

[5] Bulsari, A. and Saxen, H., "Classification of blast furnace probe temperatures using neural networks," in *Steel Research*, Vol. 66, 1995.

[6] Biswas A.K., *Principles of Blast Furnace Ironmaking*, SBA Publications, 1984.

[7] Singh, H. and Sridhar, Nallamali and Deo, Brahma, "Artificial neural nets for prediction of silicon content of blast furnace hot metal," in *Steel Research*, Vol. 67 (1996). No. 12.

[8] Osamu, L. and Ushijima, Yuichi and Toshiro, Sawada, "Application of AI techniques to blast furnace operations," in *Iron and Steel Engineer*, October 1992.

[9] Bulsari, A. and Saxen, Henrik and Saxen Bjorn, "Timeseries prediction of silicon in pig iron using neural networks," in *International Conference on Engineering Applications of Neural Networks* (EANN '92).

[10] Takenaga, H. et al., "Input Layer Optimization of Neural Networks by Sensitivity Analysis and Its Application to Recognition of Names," in *Electrical Engineering in Japan*, Vol. 111, No. 4, 1991.

[11] Elvers, B., Ed., *Ullman's Encyclopedia of Industrial Chemistry*, John Wiley and Sons, New York, 1996.

[12] Smith, Murray, *Neural Networks for Statistical Modeling*, Van Nostrand Reinhold, New York, 1993.

[13] Chauvin, Y., "Generalization Performance of Overtrained Back-Propagation Networks," in *Neural Networks, Lecture Notes in Computer Science*, pp. 46–55, Springer-Verlag, New York, 1990.

[14] Bhattacharjee, D., Dash S.K., Das, A.K., "Application of Artificial Intelligence in Tata Steel," *Tata Search*, 1999.

[15] Weigend, A.S. and Gershenfeld, N.A., "Results of the time series prediction competition at the Santa Fe Institute," in *IEEE International Conference on Neural Networks*, pp. 1786–1793. IEEE Press, Piscataway, NJ, 1993.

[16] Reyes, Carlos, Ganguly, A., Lemus, G. and Gupta, A., "A hybrid model based on dynamic programming, neural networks, and surrogate value for inventory optimization applications", in *Journal of the Operational Research Society,* Vol. 49, 1998, pp. 1–10.

[17] Bansal, K., Gupta, A., Vadhavkar, S., "Neural Networks Based Forecasting Techniques for Inventory Control Applications," in *Data Mining and Knowledge Discovery*, Vol. 2, 1998.

[18] Gupta, A., Vadhavkar, S. and Au, S., "Data Mining for Electronic Commerce," in *Electronic Commerce Advisor*, Vol. 4, Number 2, September/October 1999, pp. 24–30.

[19] Bansal, K., Vadhavkar, S. and Gupta, A., "Neural Networks Based Data Mining Applications for Medical Inventory Problems", in *International Journal of Agile Manufacturing*, Vol. 1, Issue 2, 1998, pp. 187–200, Urvashi Press, India.

CASE STUDY 1A SUMMARY

This case study was published in the ACM SIGKDD conference in year 2000 and has been reproduced here with the permission of the Association of Computing Machinery, New York, USA.

Dhond, A., Gupta, A., and Vadhavkar, S., 2000, Data Mining Techniques For Optimising Inventories for Electronic Commerce, *Proc Sixth ACM SIGKDD Int. Conf. On Knowledge Discovery and Data Mining*, pp. 480–486.

The case study reports results of using data mining in inventory control of a US pharmaceutical company Medicorp which is the largest retail distribution company with 4100 stores in 25 US states.

The company maintained an inventory worth almost one billion dollars to ensure that any drug required by a customer had a 95% chance of being available from any outlet of the company. To achieve this goal, the company had a rule of thumb to maintain "three weeks of supply" of every drug. The study involved collecting relevant data and then carrying out some preliminary studies. Models were developed for predicting demand for various drugs. The models were not very accurate for daily predictions but more accurate for weekly forecasts and even better for monthly forecasts. The weekly forecasting model was chosen, since that better suited the company's need. The study concluded that the company needed to change its rule of thumb of maintaining three weeks supply of drugs and recommended that the three weeks should be reduced for popular drugs and needed to be extended for less popular items, since large selling items can be easily replenished on a weekly basis. The company was reported to have reduced its inventory by half, resulting in considerable savings.

CASE STUDY 1A EXERCISES

1. Describe clearly the aims of Case Study 1A.
2. What were the major conclusions of Case Study 1A? How did this help the company Medicorp?
3. Case Study 1A also discusses the operations of Steel Corp. Provide a clear summary of the problem that was studied at Steelcorp and the results obtained.

CASE STUDY 1B

Crime Data Mining: A General Framework and Some Examples*

By increasing efficiency and reducing errors, crime data mining techniques can facilitate police work and enable investigators to allocate their time to other valuable tasks.

Concern about national security has increased significantly since the terrorist attacks on 11 September 2001. The CIA, FBI, and other federal agencies are actively collecting domestic and foreign intelligence to prevent future attacks. These efforts have in turn motivated local authorities to more closely monitor criminal activities in their own jurisdictions.

A major challenge facing all law-enforcement and intelligence-gathering organizations is accurately and efficiently analyzing the growing volumes of crime data. For example, complex conspiracies are often difficult to unravel because information on suspects can be geographically diffuse and span long periods of time. Detecting cybercrime can likewise be difficult because busy network traffic and frequent online transactions generate large amounts of data, only a small portion of which relates to illegal activities.

Data mining is a powerful tool that enables criminal investigators who may lack extensive training as data analysts to explore large databases quickly and efficiently.[1] Computers can process thousands of instructions in seconds, saving precious time. In addition, installing and running software often costs less than hiring and training personnel. Computers are also less prone to errors than human investigators, especially those who work long hours.

We present a general framework for crime data mining that draws on experience gained with the Coplink project (http://ai.bpa.arizona.edu/coplink), which researchers at the University of Arizona have been conducting in collaboration with the Tucson and Phoenix police departments since 1997.

1. CRIME TYPES AND SECURITY CONCERNS

A criminal act can encompass a wide range of activities, from civil infractions such as illegal parking to internationally organized mass murder such as the 9/11 attacks. Law-enforcement agencies across the US compile crime statistics using well-established standards such as the FBI's Uniform Crime Reporting System and its successor, the National Incident-Based Reporting System (www. fbi.gov/hq/cjisd/ucr.htm), as well as other criteria defined by jurisdictional needs and requirements.

Table 1 lists eight crime categories on which local and federal authorities maintain data, ordered by their increasing degree of harm to the general public. We devised these categories, which include numerous offenses classified by different law-enforcement agencies in various ways, in consultation with a local detective with more than 30 years of experience.

Some types of crime, such as traffic violations and arson, primarily concern police at the city, county, and state levels. Other crime types are investigated by local law-enforcement units as well as by national

*Chen, H., W. Chung, J.J. Xu, G. Wang, Y. Qin, and M. Chau, 2004, Crime data mining: a general framework and some examples, *IEEE Computer,* Vol. 37, No. 4, pp. 50–56.

Table 1: Crime types at different law-enforcement levels

Crime type	*Local law enforcement*	*National and international security*
Traffic violations	Speeding, reckless driving, causing property damage or personal injury in a collision, driving under the influence of drugs or alcohol, hit-and-run, "road rage"	—
Sex crime	Sexual abuse, rape, sexual assault, child molestation, child pornography, prostitution	Trafficking in women and children for sexual exploitation, including prostitution and pornography
Theft	Robbery, burglary, larceny, motor vehicle theft	Theft of national secrets or weapon information, illicit trafficking in stolen art and vehicles
Fraud	Money laundering, counterfeiting, insurance fraud, corruption and bribery, misappropriation of assets	Transnational money laundering, fraud, and corruption; trafficking in stolen software, music, movies, and other intellectual property
Arson	Intentionally setting fires to damage property, such as a warehouse or apartment building	—
Gang/drug offenses	Possessing, distributing, and selling illegal drugs	Transnational drug trafficking, organized racketeering and extortion, people smuggling
Violent crime	Murder, aggravated assault, armed robbery, forcible rape, hate crime	Terrorism, air and maritime piracy, bombings
Cybercrime	Internet fraud, such as credit card and advance fee fraud, fraudulent Web sites, and illegal online gambling and trading; network intrusion and hacking; virus spreading; cyberpiracy and cyberterrorism; distributing child pornography; identity theft	

and international agencies. For example, a city police department's sex crimes unit may track local pedophiles and prostitutes, while the FBI and the International Criminal Police Organization focus on transnational trafficking in children and women for sexual exploitation.

Many crimes, such as the theft of nuclear weapons data, can have profound implications for both national and global security. Transnational fraud and trafficking in stolen property or contraband can severely impact trade, business, and government revenue. Local gangs as well as foreign-based drug cartels and criminal organizations exact a large financial cost as well as threaten public health and safety. Although most types of violent crime—such as murder, robbery, forcible rape, and aggravated assault—are local police matters, terrorism is a global problem that relies on cooperation at all levels of government. The Internet's pervasiveness likewise makes identity theft, network intrusion, cyberpiracy, and other illicit computer-mediated activities a challenge for many law-enforcement bodies.[2]

2. CRIME DATA MINING TECHNIQUES

Traditional data mining techniques such as association analysis, classification and prediction, cluster analysis, and outlier analysis identify patterns in structured data.[3] Newer techniques identify patterns from both structured and unstructured data. As with other forms of data mining, crime data mining raises privacy concerns.[4] Nevertheless, researchers have developed various automated data mining techniques for both local law enforcement and national security applications. *Entity extraction* identifies particular patterns from data such as text, images, or audio materials. It has been used to automatically identify persons, addresses, vehicles, and personal characteristics from police narrative reports.[5] In computer forensics, the extraction of software metrics[6]—which includes the data structure, program flow, organization and quantity of comments, and use of variable names—can facilitate further investigation by, for example, grouping similar programs written by hackers and tracing their behavior. Entity extraction provides basic information for crime analysis, but its performance depends greatly on the availability of extensive amounts of clean input data.

Clustering techniques group data items into classes with similar characteristics to maximize or minimize intraclass similarity—for example, to identify suspects who conduct crimes in similar ways or distinguish among groups belonging to different gangs. These techniques do not have a set of predefined classes for assigning items. Some researchers use the statistics-based *concept space* algorithm to automatically associate different objects such as persons, organizations, and vehicles in crime records.[7] Using link analysis techniques to identify similar transactions, the Financial Crimes Enforcement Network AI System[8] exploits Bank Secrecy Act data to support the detection and analysis of money laundering and other financial crimes. Clustering crime incidents can automate a major part of crime analysis but is limited by the high computational intensity typically required.

Association rule mining discovers frequently occurring item sets in a database and presents the patterns as rules. This technique has been applied in network intrusion detection to derive association rules from users' interaction history. Investigators also can apply this technique to network intruders' profiles to help detect potential future network attacks.[9]

Similar to association rule mining, *sequential pattern mining* finds frequently occurring sequences of items over a set of transactions that occurred at different times. In network intrusion detection, this approach can identify intrusion patterns among time-stamped data. Showing hidden patterns benefits crime analysis, but to obtain meaningful results requires rich and highly structured data.

Deviation detection uses specific measures to study data that differs markedly from the rest of the data. Also called *outlier detection,* investigators can apply this technique to fraud detection, network intrusion detection, and other crime analyses. However, such activities can sometimes appear to be normal, making it difficult to identify outliers.

Classification and common properties among different crime entities and organizes them into predefined classes. This technique has been used to identify the source of e-mail spamming based on the sender's linguistic patterns and structural features.[10] Often used to predict crime trends, classification can reduce the time required to identify crime entities. However, the technique requires a predefined classification scheme. Classification also requires reasonably complete training and testing data because a high degree of missing data would limit prediction accuracy.

String comparator techniques compare the textual fields in pairs of database records and compute the similarity between the records. These techniques can detect deceptive information—such as name, address, and Social Security number—in criminal records.[11] Investigators can use string comparators to analyze textual data, but the techniques often require intensive computation.

Social network analysis describes the roles of and interactions among nodes in a conceptual network. Investigators can use this technique to construct a network that illustrates criminals' roles, the flow of tangible and intangible goods and information, and associations among these entities. Further analysis can reveal critical roles and subgroups and vulnerabilities inside the network. This approach enables visualization of criminal networks, but investigators still might not be able to discover the network's true leaders if they keep a low profile.

3. CRIME DATA MINING FRAMEWORK

Many efforts have used automated techniques to analyze different types of crimes, but without a unifying framework describing how to apply them. In particular, understanding the relationship between analysis capability and crime type characteristics can help investigators more effectively use those techniques to identify trends and patterns, address problem areas, and even predict crimes.

Based on the Tucson Police Department's crime classification database, which contains approximately 1.3 million suspect and criminal records ranging from 1970 to the present, and on the existing literature, we have developed the general framework for crime data mining shown in Figure 1.

The framework shows relationships between data mining techniques applied in criminal and intelligence analysis and the crime types listed in Table 1. The vertical axis arranges the techniques in increasing order of analysis capability. We identified four major categories of crime data mining techniques: entity extraction, association, prediction, and pattern visualization. Each category represents a set of techniques for use in certain types of crime analysis.

For example, investigators can use neural network techniques in crime entity extraction and prediction. Clustering techniques are effective in crime association and prediction. Social network analysis can facilitate crime association and pattern visualization. Investigators can apply various techniques independently or jointly to tackle particular crime analysis problems.

Guided by our detective consultant, we have arranged the eight crime types in increasing order of public harm on the horizontal axis. The shaded regions represent research using various analytical techniques on certain crime types. Although they can apply any technique to any crime type, when highly organized criminal enterprises involve many people and have a pervasive societal impact, investigators must apply a spectrum of techniques to discover associations, identify patterns, and make predictions.

We believe that our framework has general applicability to crime and intelligence analysis because it encompasses all major crime types as well as both traditional and new intelligence-specific data mining techniques.

4. COPLINK CASE STUDY

To illustrate our crime data mining framework, we describe three examples of its use in the Coplink project: named-entity extraction, deceptive-identity detection, and criminal-network analysis.

4.1 Named-entity Extraction

Most criminal justice databases capture only structured data that first in predefined fields. Our

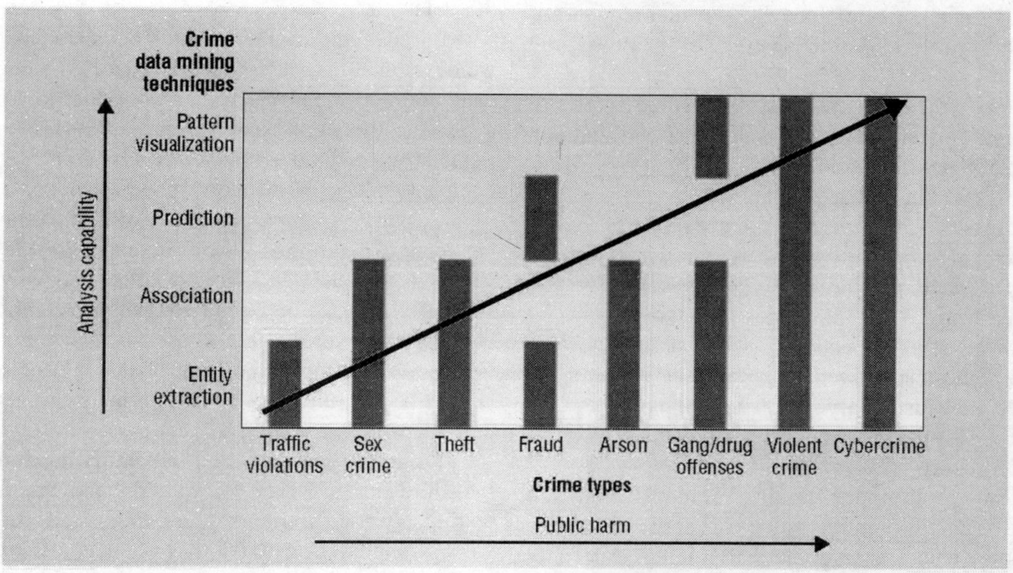

Figure 1: Crime data mining framework. The framework identifies relationships between techniques applied in criminal and intelligence analysis at the local, national, and international levels.

first data mining task involved extracting named entities from police narrative reports, which are difficult to analyze using automated techniques. We randomly selected 36 narcotics-related reports from the Phoenix Police Department that were relatively *noisy*—all were written in uppercase letters and contained many typos, spelling errors, and grammatical mistakes.

We adopted a modified version of the AI Entity Extractor system, which uses a three-step process to identify the names of persons, locations, and organizations in a document. First, it identifies noun phrases according to linguistic rules. Second, the system calculates a set of feature scores for each phrase based on pattern matching and lexical lookup. Third, it uses a feedforward/backpropagation neural network to predict the most likely entity type for each phrase.

The AI Entity Extractor has been compared to systems reported at the Sixth Message Understanding Conference (MUC-6) and achieved above-average performance. To adopt the system for crime analysis applications, we modified it to identify five entity types: person names, addresses, vehicles, narcotic names, and physical characteristics.[5]

Working from the selected reports, our detective consultant manually identified all entities that belong to the five categories of interest. We then conducted threefold cross-validation testing to evaluate the system.

The modified extractor performed well in identifying person names (74.1 percent) and narcotic drugs (85.4 percent) from the test data set, but not as well for addresses (59.6 percent) and personal properties (46.8 percent). Recalls for the same categories were 73.4, 77.9, 51.4, and 47.8 percent, respectively. Vehicle name results were not analyzed because only four references to vehicles occurred in the 36 reports.

> ***Crime Investigators must apply a spectrum of techniques to discover associations, identify patterns, and make predictions.***

These preliminary results demonstrated the feasibility and potential value of applying entity extraction techniques to crime data mining, especially considering that the narrative reports were much noisier than the news articles used in the MUC-6 evaluations. Although we tested only 36 reports in our study, we plan to use training and testing data typical of other practical data mining applications to more thoroughly evaluate the system. We also are exploring interactive ways to integrate human knowledge into the extractor's learning component.

Using advanced analysis techniques to further extract information from narrative documents, such as the roles of entities and the relationships among them, is an important future research direction. Often, entities provide the unit of analysis in other crime data mining applications.

4.2 Deceptive-identity Detection

Suspects often give false names, birth dates, or addresses to police officers and thus have multiple database entries, making it difficult for officers to determine a suspect's true identity and relate past incidents involving that person. Our second data mining task involved automatically detecting deceptive criminal identities from the Tucson Police Department's database, which contains information such as name, gender, address, ID number, and physical description. Our detective consultant manually identified 120 deceptive criminal records involving 44 suspects from the database.

Based on the criminal identity deception taxonomy we developed in a case study, we selected name, birth date, address, and Social Security number to represent a criminal's identity and ignored other less reliable fields. Our method employed string comparators to compare values in the corresponding fields of each record pair.[11] Comparators measure the similarity between two strings. We normalized the similarity values between 0 and 1, and calculated an overall similarity measure between two records as a Euclidean vector norm over the four chosen fields. A Euclidean vector norm is the square root of the sum of squared similarity measures and is also normalized between 0 and 1.

We employed a holdout validation method using two-thirds of the data for training and the rest for testing. In the training stage, we tried threshold values ranging from 0.00 to 1.00 that differentiated between deceptive and not-deceptive records. We first determined the optimal threshold to be reached when the association decisions best matched our expert's judgments, 0.48, then used this value to assess our algorithm's predicted association accuracy in the testing stage.

In the training stage, the algorithm achieved its highest accuracy, 97.4 percent, with a low 2.6 percent false-negative rate and 2.6 percent false-positive rate. In the testing stage, the algorithm achieved an accuracy of 94.0 percent in linking deceptive records that pointed to the same suspect.

The results again demonstrated that crime data mining is feasible and promising. Testing errors that occurred in the false-negative category, in which unrelated suspects were recognized as being related, might be caused by the overall threshold value obtained from the training stage. Thus, an adaptive threshold might be more desirable for developing an automated process in future research.

With this technique, law-enforcement officers can retrieve existing identity records relating to a suspect in their databases that traditional exact-match techniques often fail to locate. They also can use this technique as a preprocessing tool to combine identity records representing the same person for other crime data mining applications, thereby improving subsequent data analysis.

4.3 Criminal-network Analysis

Criminals often develop networks in which they form groups or teams to carry out various illegal activities. Our third data mining task consisted of identifying subgroups and key members in such networks and then studying interaction patterns to develop effective strategies for disrupting the networks. Our data came from 272 Tucson Police Department incident summaries involving 164 crimes committed from 1985 through May 2002.

We used a concept-space approach to extract criminal relations from the incident summaries and create a likely network of suspects. Co-occurrence weight measured the relational strength between two criminals by computing how frequently they were identified in the same incident.[7] We used hierarchical clustering to partition the network into subgroups and the block-modeling approach to identify interaction patterns between these subgroups.[12] We also calculated centrality measures—degree, betweenness, and closeness—to detect key members in each group, such as leaders and gatekeepers.

As Figure 2a shows, data mining uncovered 16 target gang members from the resulting network. In Figure 2b, the circles represent subgroups the system found, and they bear the labels of their leaders' names. A circle's size is proportional to the number of members in that subgroup. The thickness of straight lines connecting circles indicates the strength of relationships between subgroups.

We conducted a two-hour field study with three Tucson Police Department domain experts who evaluated the analysis's validity by comparing the results against their knowledge of gang organization. They confirmed that the system-found subgroups correctly represented the real groups' organization. For example, the biggest group consisted of gang members involved in many murders and assaults. The second largest group specialized in drug distribution and sales. Interaction patterns between subgroups found in the network were valid as well.

According to the experts, members from the two biggest groups associated frequently, and their leaders were good friends. In most cases, the analysis also correctly identified central members who played important roles. For example, the leader of the second largest subgroup made considerable money from selling and distributing drugs.

All three experts believed that this system could greatly increase crime analysts' work productivity by efficiently extracting criminal association information from data and using that information to generate and visualize criminal networks. More importantly, it would help discover knowledge about criminal organizations that requires many hours to uncover manually. In addition, the system would help novice investigators understand the structure and operations of criminal enterprises relatively quickly. Finally, it could suggest investigative leads that would otherwise be overlooked and help prevent crimes by disrupting criminal networks effectively.

Studying criminal networks requires additional data mining capabilities: entity extraction and co-occurrence analysis to identify criminal entities and associations, clustering and block modeling for discovering subgroups and interaction patterns, and visualization for presenting analysis results. One drawback of our current approach is that it generates mostly static networks. Given that criminal networks are dynamic, future research will focus on the evolution and prediction of criminal networks.

Human investigators with years of experience can often analyze crime trends precisely, but as the incidence and complexity of crime increases, human errors occur, analysis time increases, and criminals have more time to destroy evidence and escape arrest. By increasing efficiency and reducing errors, crime data mining techniques can facilitate police work and enable investigators to allocate their time to other valuable tasks.

Much work remains in this emerging field. For example, investigators can use crime entity-extraction techniques to analyze the behavioral patterns of serial offenders. Crime association and clustering techniques can reveal the identities of cyber-criminals who use the Internet to spread illegal messages or malicious code. Investigators can use machine-learning algorithms—such as ID3, neural networks, Support Vector Machines, and genetic algorithms—to predict crimes by analyzing factors such as time, location, vehicle, address, physical characteristics, and property. They also can use these tools to develop more intuitive techniques for crime pattern and network visualization.

We are continuing our research in crime data mining using Coplink data as our tested. We intend to supplement this work with information from the US Secret Service and the US Citizenship and Immigration Services, public infrastructure data, terrorists' and extremists' Web sites, television news archives, and disease and biological agent statistics. Currently, we are creating a multilingual cybercrime database with the help of experts from the Tucson and Phoenix police departments and the Taiwan Criminal Investigation

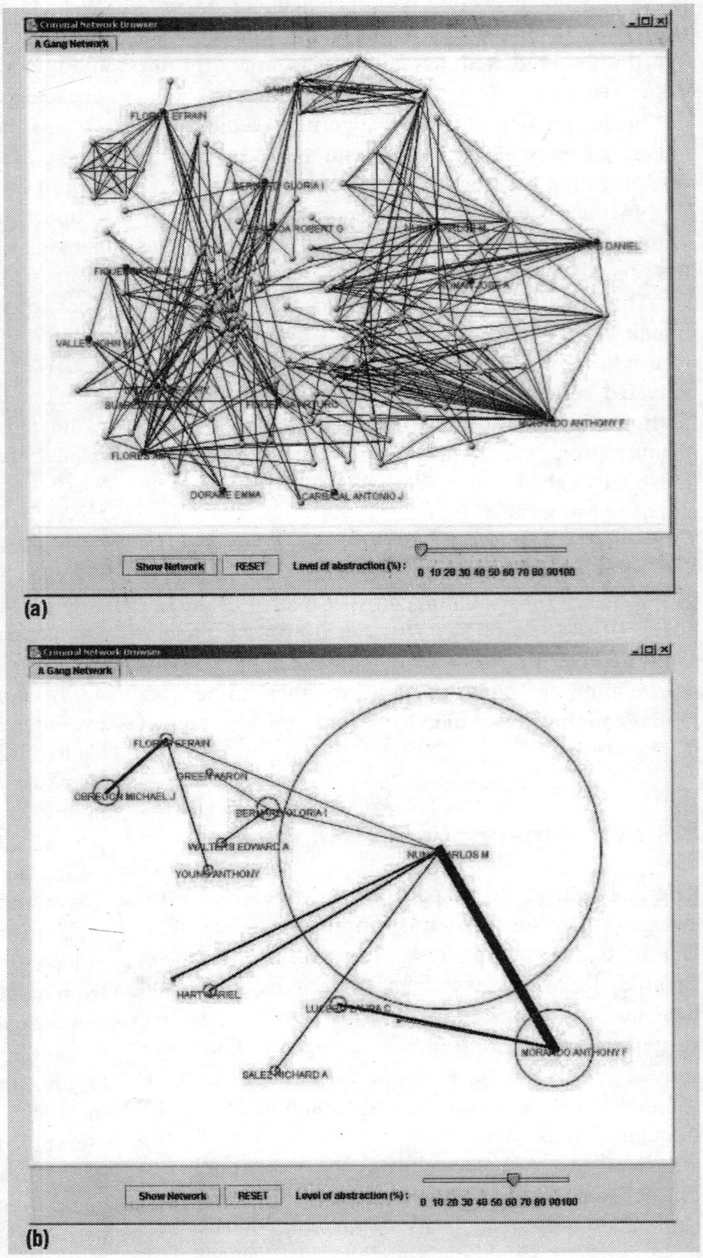

Figure 2: Criminal-network analysis. (a) Data mining uncovered 16 target gang members from a network of 164 criminals in the Tucson Police Department database. (b) The circles represent subgroups and are tagged with their leaders' names. Each circle's size is proportional to the number of members in the subgroup.

Bureau, our research partner. This effort will monitor suspicious Internet newsgroups, chat rooms, peer-to-peer network messages, and Web sites in the US and Taiwan and download messages for further analysis.

ACKNOWLEDGMENT

The Coplink project was funded by the National Institute of Justice and the National Science Foundation.

REFERENCES

[1] U.M. Fayyad and R. Uthurusamy, "Evolving Data Mining into Solutions for Insights," *Comm. ACM*, Aug. 2002, pp. 28–31.

[2] W. Chang et al., "An International Perspective on Fighting Cybercrime," *Proc. 1st NSF/NIJ Symp. Intelligence and Security Informatics*, LNCS 2665, Springer-Verlag, 2003, pp. 379–384.

[3] J. Han and M. Kamber, *Data Mining: Concepts and Techniques*, Morgan Kaufmann, 2001.

[4] H. Kargupta, K. Liu, and J. Ryan, "Privacy-Sensitive Distributed Data Mining from Multi-Party Data,"*Proc. 1st NSF/NIJ Symp. Intelligence and Security Informatics*, LNCS 2665, Springer-Verlag, 2003, pp. 336–342.

[5] M. Chau, J.J. Xu, and H. Chen, "Extracting Meaningful Entities from Police Narrative Reports, *Proc. Nat'l Conf. Digital Government Research*, Digital Government Research Center, 2002, pp. 271–275.

[6] A. Gray, P. Sallis, and S. MacDonell, "Software Forensics: Extending Authorship Analysis Techniques to Computer Programs," *Proc. 3rd Biannual Conf. Int'l Assoc. Forensic Linguistics*, Int'l Assoc. Forensic Linguistics, 1997, pp. 1–8.

[7] R.V. Hauck et al., "Using Coplink to Analyze Criminal-Justice Data," *Computer*, Mar. 2002, pp. 30–37.

[8] T. Senator et al., "The FinCEN Artificial Intelligence System: Identifying Potential Money Laundering from Reports of Large Cash Transactions," *AI Magazine,* Vol. 16, no. 4, 1995, pp. 21–39.

[9] W. Lee, S.J. Stolfo, and W. Mok, "A Data Mining Framework for Building Intrusion Detection Models," *Proc. 1999 IEEE Symp. Security and Privacy*, IEEE CS Press, 1999, pp. 120–132.

[10] O. de Vel et al., "Mining E-Mail Content for Author Identication Forensics," *SIGMOD Record*, Vol. 30, no. 4, 2001, pp. 55–64.

[11] G. Wang, H. Chen, and H. Atabakhsh, "Automatically Detecting Deceptive Criminal Identities," *Comm. ACM*, Mar. 2004, pp. 70–76.

[12] S. Wasserman and K. Faust, *Social Network Analysis: Methods and Applications*, Cambridge Univ. Press, 1994.

Hsinchun Chen is the McClelland Professor of Management Information Systems at the University of Arizona's Eller College of Business and Administration. His research interests include medical informatics, homeland security, semantic retrieval, search algorithms, knowledge management, and Web computing. Chen received a PhD in information systems from New York University. Contact him at hchen@eller.arizona.edu.

Wingyan Chung is a doctoral candidate in the Department of Management Information Systems at the University of Arizona, where he is a research associate in the Artificial Intelligence Lab. His research interests include knowledge management, knowledge discovery on the Web, text mining, security informatics, and human-computer interaction. Chung received an MS in information and technol-ogy management from the Chinese University of Hong Kong. He is a member of the IEEE Computer Society, the ACM, and the Association for Information Systems. Contact him at wchung@eller.arizona.edu.

Jennifer Jie Xu is a doctoral candidate in the Department of Management Information

Systems at the University of Arizona, where she is a member of the Artificial Intelligence Lab. Her research interests include knowledge management, social network analysis, computer-mediated communication, and information visualization. Xu received an MS in computer science from the University of Mississippi. She is a member of the IEEE Computer Society. Contact her at jxu@eller.arizona.edu.

Gang Wang is a doctoral student in the Department of Management Information Systems at the University of Arizona. His research interests include deception detection, data mining, Web mining, and knowledge discovery. Wang received an MS in industrial engineering from Louisiana State University. Contact him at gang@eller.arizona.edu.

Yi Qin was a member of the Artificial Intelligence Lab at the University of Arizona. Her research interests include medical informatics and cyber-crime analysis. Qin received an MS in management information systems from the University of Arizona. Contact her at yiqin@eller.arizona.edu.

Michael Chau is a research assistant professor in the School of Business at the University of Hong Kong and was formerly a research associate at the University of Arizona's Artificial Intelligence Lab. His research interests include text mining, Web mining, digital libraries, knowledge management, and intelligent agents. Chau received a PhD in management information systems from the University of Arizona. He is a member of the IEEE Computer Society, the ACM, the Association for Information Systems, and the American Society for Information Science and Technology. Contact him at mchau@business.hku.hk.

CASE STUDY 1B SUMMARY

This case study was published in the magazine IEEE Computer in April 2004 and has been reproduced here with the permission of the IEEE.

Chen, H., Chung, W., Xu, J.L., Wang, G., Qin, Y. and Chan, M., Crime Data Mining: A General Frame Work and Some Examples, *IEEE Computer*, April 2004, pp. 50–56.

In this case study, crime data was grouped into eight categories comprising traffic violation, sex crime, theft, fraud, arson, gang/drug offences, violent crimes and cybercrime. Some of the major crimes are included in the category violent crime, which includes murder, assault, armed robbery, sexual and hate crimes. The study focussed on three aspects of crime: extracting named entities from narrative reports, detecting deceptive criminal identities and identifying criminal groups and key members of the groups.

CASE STUDY 1B EXERCISES

1. Describe clearly the aims of Case Study 1B.
2. Briefly describe the approach taken in Case Study 1B. What were the major conclusions of the case study?

CHAPTER

2 Data Understanding and Data Preparation

LEARNING OBJECTIVES

After completing this chapter, you will be able to:

- Better understand the steps of the Cross Industry Standard Process (CRISP) used in data mining
- Explain the various steps of data pre-processing and data cleaning
- Understand the problems of missing data and the techniques of identifying outliers
- Explain the different types of data
- Understand and explain the different methods of computing distance between the two multidimensional points
- Appreciate how some statistical properties of the data can describe data
- Understand some techniques for displaying data graphically
- Find other suitable literature on topics covered in this chapter

2.1 INTRODUCTION

In Section 1.8 we presented a number of data mining case studies in brief. Although details of the case studies were not presented, it was clear that many of the case studies had to deal with significant issues of data quality. It was necessary for these projects to invest a lot of resources in data collection and data cleaning.

Improving the quality of data in databases for use in data mining is a challenging task. The presence of incorrect and inconsistent data can significantly impact the result of any data mining analysis and therefore the potential benefits of using data mining may not be achieved. Given that the size of data is often large, it is not possible to identify errors and correct them manually. One therefore must find automatic or semi-automatic procedures to identify errors and correct them. We discuss some procedures in this chapter.

We have discussed the data mining process in Section 1.4 (Chapter 1). The CRISP data mining process was described in some detail. The process consists of the following six phases:

1. Business understanding
2. Data understanding
3. Data preparation
4. Modelling
5. Evaluation
6. Deployment

We also presented a set of guidelines for successful data mining in Section 1.10. The guidelines included a number of basic requirements including:

1. The data must be available
2. The data must be relevant, adequate and clean
3. There must be a well-defined problem

Both the CRISP process and the guidelines highlight the importance of having clearly defined business objectives and ensuring that the data mining project has access to clean relevant data. In this chapter we discuss the issue of data pre-processing before presenting a number of data mining techniques starting from the next chapter.

CHAPTER OVERVIEW

This chapter covers various aspects of data collection and data preparation. Section 2.2 provides an introduction and lists a number of steps that are required in pre-processing data. The Extraction, Transformation and Loading (ETL) process is discussed in Sections 2.2.1, 2.2.2 and 2.2.3. Section 2.3 deals with outliers and Section 2.4 presents techniques for mining outliers. Section 2.5 deals with missing data and how to manage it in a dataset. Section 2.6 describes different types of data and the following section describes various distance metrics. Section 2.8 presents a number of basic statistical measurements of data. Section 2.9 discusses some data visualisation techniques including box plots, histograms and scatter plots. A brief discussion of multidimensional data visualisation is given in Section 2.10.

2.2 DATA COLLECTION AND PRE-PROCESSING

As noted earlier, data collection and pre-processing is time consuming. Even looking at Table 1.1, data collection for such a small dataset was not easy since such data is not available in one place. To build the table, it was necessary to consult a number of sources including several Wikipedia pages and some United Nations reports. In spite of this the different columns of the table perhaps are not about the same year and therefore the table is not 100% accurate. Also, some data items are missing. Once the data was collected it was necessary to do some pre-processing to ensure that the magnitude of the different columns was similar. Clearly, for a larger dataset the task is much more challenging.

We now present a simple definition of data cleaning.

> **Data Cleaning**
> It is a process used to determine inaccurate, incomplete or unreasonable data items of a dataset and then improving the data quality through corrections of the detected errors and omissions.

As noted earlier, most enterprises currently store their operational data in relational OLTP databases. The data in OLTP systems is usually current and historical data is not stored in them unless customer services require such data to be accessible by customer support staff. Most data therefore is transient and changes as information is updated. Some databases like banking databases usually need to store all historical data should a customer enquire about a transaction of some weeks (or even months) ago. Even information about closed accounts may need to be stored for some time for online access.

Data from OLTP databases is usually not sufficient to carry out most data mining operations. Usually data required for data mining needs to be extracted from a number of databases, integrated, and perhaps cleansed and transformed. This process is called ETL (extraction, transformation and loading). As discussed in this chapter, errors have to be detected and removed. Missing data values may have to be dealt with in that estimates may have to be used.

When datasets are large, it is inevitable that there will be errors in the data because data collection techniques are never perfect. Data collection involves humans and machines and both can be prone to errors. A variety of errors including noise, missing data, duplicate data and input errors may result. The errors may also include some data values that are too large or too small (these are often called *outliers*) or missing values. To carry out reliable data mining we must ensure that the results of data mining are not influenced by such errors.

It has been estimated that the level of errors in data is usually between 1% and 10%. Even the FBI database in 2013 was found to have wrong spelling of one of the Boston bombers' name. Therefore anomalies are sufficiently common that a data mining technique should not be used without pre-processing data.

Although there is need to pre-process data even when all the data comes from one source, the need for pre-processing increases significantly when the data comes from multiple sources. Integrating data from multiple sources can also lead to redundant data because the same data may be represented in different ways in different data sources. The aim of data cleaning therefore should not only be to identify and correct data errors and inconsistencies in each source before data integration but also to identify and remove data errors that may result from integrating data. Software tools are available that could be used.

Data pre-processing involves the following steps[1]:

- **Data understanding:** As noted when discussing CRISP-DM in Chapter 1, it is difficult to start data pre-processing without a good understanding of the data and the types of errors that may be present in the data. This may require considerable manual effort on the part of the data mining team. Careful study of the metadata for each data source may be required. This would also assist in learning about the data properties and perhaps also in making judgments about the data quality. Furthermore studying the schema of each data source would also enable

[1]This discussion is based on the paper by Rahm and Do.

the data mining project team developing some understanding of the integrity constraints that have been specified on the data. All this knowledge can assist in data cleaning including in making estimates of any missing values.

- **Mapping rules:** When the data has been obtained by integrating a number of data sources, it is usually necessary to devise mapping rules to transform data that uses different conventions. Data pre-processing software may help in supporting this step. It may be useful to talk to the managers of the source databases to fully understand their data.
- **Verification:** Before carrying out any data mining project, the data obtained after the above two steps (or a smaller sample from it) should be tested and evaluated to ensure that the two steps were indeed effective. A single step of verification may not be sufficient in some cases because some errors are not immediately visible.
- **Transformation:** The transformation phase of the procedure can now be carried out. Considerable metadata is required before ETL software is used for transformation. The metadata that has been collected should be saved so that it can be used the next time it is required. Information about transformation also needs to be documented and saved.
- **Backflow:** Once the errors in the source systems data are identified in the above process, the errors may be reported back to staff members who manage the source systems. These staff should replace the dirty data with clean data.

We now discuss the ETL process that includes most of the five steps above. Backflow is not part of the ETL and therefore must be handled separately.

2.2.1 Extraction, Transformation and Loading (ETL)

As noted earlier, building an integrated dataset requires data collecting, data cleaning and data integration.

Data errors at least partly arise because of unmotivated data entry staff. Since data entry positions are often poorly paid and the work of such staff is rarely recognised, staff tend to have low morale which leads to error rates higher than would be expected. Much can be done in improving data entry staff morale and thus reducing error rates.

ETL requires skills in management, business analysis and technology and the process tends to be somewhat different for every data mining project. It should not be assumed that an off-the-shelf ETL system can magically solve all data problems. It is best to use a flexible ETL approach combining perhaps an off-the-shelf tool with some in-house developed software to perform the tasks that are required. It is essential that the ETL process be adequately documented so that at a later stage another staff member(s) can understand what exactly was done. It should be noted that the source systems and the dataset may evolve with time as enterprise needs change.

Successful implementation of an ETL system involves resolving many issues including the following:

What are the source systems?

These systems may include relational database systems (e.g. Oracle, SQL Server, MySQL), legacy systems, flat files as well as other systems.

To what extent are the source systems and the target system interoperable?

The more different the sources and the target, the more complex the ETL process is likely to be.

What ETL technology will be used?

One approach might be to use an in-house custom-built solution. Some tools may be available to help in building such a solution. Another approach is to acquire a generic ETL package that will either meet the needs of the enterprise or can be modified to meet these needs. As noted earlier, a large variety of tools are available in the market. We list some at the end of the chapter.

How will the quality and integrity of the data be monitored?

During the ETL process much effort is required to ensure data quality. As noted earlier, data cleaning will often be required to deal with issues like missing values, date formats, code values, primary key and referential integrity.

How will a log of the dataset be maintained?

Once the dataset is being used, a dispute may arise about the origin of some data. It is therefore necessary to be able to log which information came from and when.

How will recovery take place?

Although database systems normally have a well-defined recovery procedure, the dataset may also need to be recovered if it fails.

How will the transformation be carried out?

Transformation could be done within each of the source OLTP systems but that implies that additional load will be placed on the source systems. It may therefore be useful to have a staging area that is a temporary database separate from the source systems so that the data can be copied across to it and then transformed and copied to another area. If anything is going to go wrong, it is likely to happen to the staging database without creating any major problems.

How will data be copied from non-relational legacy systems that may still be operational?

It is necessary to work out a sensible methodology of copying data from such systems and transforming it to eventually load it across to the staging area.

2.2.2 ETL Functions

As the name implies, the ETL process consists of data extraction from source systems, data transformation which includes data cleaning, and loading data in a separate staging area. One may look at ETL as the plumbing which gets the data from the source systems to the staging area.

Let us first consider an example of ETL. Suppose we have extracted Tables 2.1, 2.2 and 2.3 from three source systems and the three records belong to the same supplier. We have the task of cleaning and integrating them.

Table 2.1 Supplier record extracted from the first source system

Supplier ID	*345627*
Business name	Krishna Software Inc
Address	65 Gandhi Road
City	Secunderabad
State	Andhra
PIN	500003
Telephone	040-7766027
Fax	040-7766022
Email	info@krishna.co.in
Owner	Sumitra Singh
Last updated	7/12/2005

Table 2.2 Supplier record extracted from the second source system

Supplier ID	
Business name	Krishna Software Inc
Address	P.O. Box 123
City	Hyderabad
State	Andhra Pradesh
PIN	500001
Telephone	7766027
Fax	
Email	
Owner	Dr S.S. Singh
Last updated	12/7/1999

Table 2.3 Supplier record extracted from the third source system

Supplier ID	*345627*
Business name	Krishna Inc
Address	201, 2nd Floor, 65 Gandhi Road
City	New Delhi
State	AP
PIN	50001
Telephone	776027
Fax	
Email	
Owner	Dr Sumitra
Last updated	7/17/2002

There are many errors and missing values in the records extracted from the three different source systems. We leave it as an exercise for the reader to list all the errors in them.

We now present what the record could look like after it has gone through an ETL process:

Table 2.4 is the best information we are able to derive from the three tables. It is still likely to have some errors in it but they cannot be corrected without additional information.

Table 2.4 Supplier record after ETL

Supplier ID	*345627*
Business Name	Krishna Software Inc
Address	201, 2nd Floor, 65 Gandhi Road
City	Secunderabad
State	Andhra Pradesh
PIN	500003
Postal address	P.O. Box 123
City	Hyderabad
State	Andhra Pradesh
PIN	500001
Telephone	040-7766027
Fax	040-7766022
Email	info@krishna.co.in
Owner	Dr Sumitra Singh
Last updated	7/12/2005

2.2.3 Sources of Errors in the Data

Building an integrated database from a number of source systems may involve dealing with some or all of the following data errors. Some of these errors may be single-source errors while others may be multiple-source errors:

Instance identity errors

As noted above, the same individual may be represented slightly differently in different source systems. For example, my name is represented as Gopal Gupta in some systems and as GK Gupta in others. Given that the name is unusual for data entry staff in Western countries, it is sometime misspelled as Gopal Gopta or Gopal Gupka or some other way. The name may also be represented as Professor GK Gupta, Dr GK Gupta or Mr GK Gupta. There is thus a high possibility of mismatching between the different systems that needs to be identified and corrected. In fact it has been claimed that there are more than 200 different ways to spell Mohammed and more than 300 different variants of the name Moammar Gaddafi, the former leader of Libya. Checking for homonyms (different items with the same identifier) and synonyms (same item with more than one identifier) is therefore necessary. It has been reported that achieving high consistency (i.e., close to 100%) in names and addresses requires huge amount of resources.

Data errors

Many different types of data errors other than identity errors are possible. For example:

- Data may have some missing attribute values

- Coding of some values in one database may not match with coding in other databases (i.e., different codes with the same meaning or same code for different meanings)
- Meanings of some code values may not be known
- There may be duplicate records
- There may be wrong aggregations
- There may be inconsistent use of nulls, spaces and empty values
- Some attribute values may be inconsistent (i.e., outside their domain)
- Some data may be wrong because of input errors
- There may be inappropriate use of address lines
- There may be non-unique identifiers

The ETL process needs to ensure that all these types of errors are resolved using a sound methodology.

Record linkage problem

Record linkage relates to the problem of linking information from different databases that relates to the same customer or client. The problem can arise if a unique identifier is not available in all databases that are being linked. Perhaps records from a database are being linked to records from a legacy system or to information from a spreadsheet. Record linkage can involve a large number of record comparisons to ensure linkages that have a high level of accuracy.

Semantic integration problem

Data integration is the problem of combining the data residing at different sources and building a unified view of the data. Such a unified view is structured according to a so-called global schema. Therefore this step also deals with integration of information found in heterogeneous OLTP and legacy sources. As noted above, some of the sources may be relational, some may not be. Some may be even in text documents. Some data may be character strings while others may be integers.

Data integrity problem

The database source schema is usually expressed in the relational model. Integrity constraints of the source system should also be available during data integration. Data integrity deals with issues like referential integrity, null values, domain of values, etc.

Overcoming all these problems is often tedious work. Many errors can be difficult to identify. In some cases one may be forced to ask the question how accurate the data ought to be since improving the accuracy is always going to require more and more resources and fixing all problems may be unrealistic. Many techniques for correcting errors have been developed. For example, if a variable has numerical values then using the mean and standard deviation of the variable, the values may be checked. The outliers can then be identified and checked for validity.

Telephone numbers in most countries have a given format and can be checked against that format. Similarly, postcodes have a fixed number of digits and/or letters in every country and values may be checked for legality. It may be possible to correct invalid values using other information that may be available. Many different formats for dates are used and it is should be possible to identify errors since it is relatively easier to check for invalid dates. Some dates may be entered in American format while others in British format. Some dates may be using 2005 and others 05.

Checking for duplicates is also not easy. The data can be sorted and duplicates removed although for large files sorting can be expensive. In some cases duplicate records are not identical. In these cases check for primary key may be required. If more than one record has the same primary key then it is likely to be because of duplicates.

Data entry errors

When data is being entered by humans, errors are not uncommon. Data errors at least partly arise because of unmotivated data entry staff. Since data entry positions are often poorly paid and the work of such staff is rarely recognised, staff tend to have low morale which leads to error rates higher than would be expected. Fatigue can also be an issue. Much can be done in improving data entry staff morale, perhaps by providing regular breaks, and thus reducing error rates.

Data entry errors may also be reduced if high quality data entry software is used. The software should require that any data integrity specifications are enforced. Any data that violates any of the integrity constraints should not be allowed to be entered.

Measurement errors

Data is often captured by instruments since there is an increasing tendency to use sensor technology, for example capturing car speeds or temperatures or share indexes. Errors can creep in either because of an instrument malfunctioning, poor calibration or poor design of the software used in the instrument.

Filtering errors

As noted earlier, data collection may involve a number of steps including filtering, smoothing and summarisation, perhaps to reduce the volume of data. Each of these steps has the potential to produce errors.

Data often cannot be cleaned without human involvement. Sometime substantial human involvement may be necessary. It may be necessary to use data visualisation software. In some cases exploratory data mining may help since that can help in understanding properties of the data and the data sources.

2.2.4 Selecting an ETL Tool

Selection of an appropriate ETL tool is an important decision. The ETL tool is required to provide coordinated access to multiple data sources so that relevant data may be extracted from them. An ETL tool would normally include tools for data cleaning, reorganisation, transformation, aggregation, calculation, and automatic loading of data into the target database.

An ETL tool should provide an easy user interface that allows data cleaning and data transformation rules to be specified using a point-and-click approach. When all mappings and transformations have been specified, the ETL tool should automatically generate the data extract/transformation/load programs, which may run in batch mode.

It should be noted that it is often difficult to switch from one ETL tool to another since there are no standards regarding data definitions and transformation rules.

2.3 OUTLIERS

Essentially an outlier is a data point (or an observation) that appears to deviate markedly from other data points in the dataset. We present a definition given by Hawkins in his book, 1980.

> **Outlier**
> An outlier is an observation which deviates so much from the other observations as to arouse suspicions that it was generated by a different mechanism.

Looking at it another way, an outlier is far from the centre of the distribution, perhaps several standard deviations away. For example, in normal distribution, 99.7% of values occur within three standard deviations. If a data point is say four or more standard deviations away then it could be considered an outlier although it should be noted that outliers are not only far away from the centre of the distribution but also far away from other values in the dataset. Therefore if a number of data values are far from the centre of the distribution then they perhaps should not be labelled outliers.

In Figures 2.1 and 2.2, we show two different scatter diagrams for two similar datasets. Given the scatter diagrams, it is clear that it is not easy to identify outliers precisely. In fact different data mining software appear to include different criteria for identifying outliers. In essence all criteria involve determining what the nominal (or values that are not outliers) data values are and what data values are outside the set of nominal values. In the two figures, identify any points that you consider as outliers and explain the reasons for selecting them.

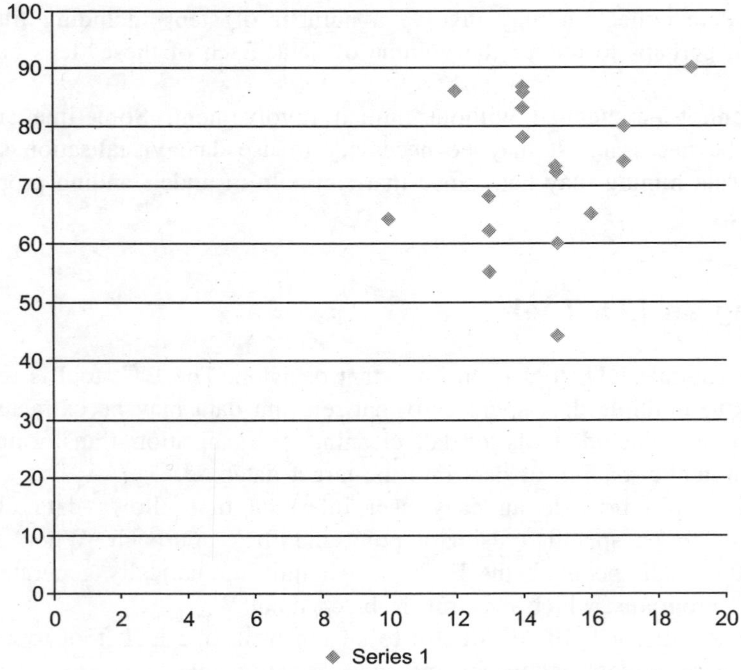

Figure 2.1 Scatter diagram of a dataset.

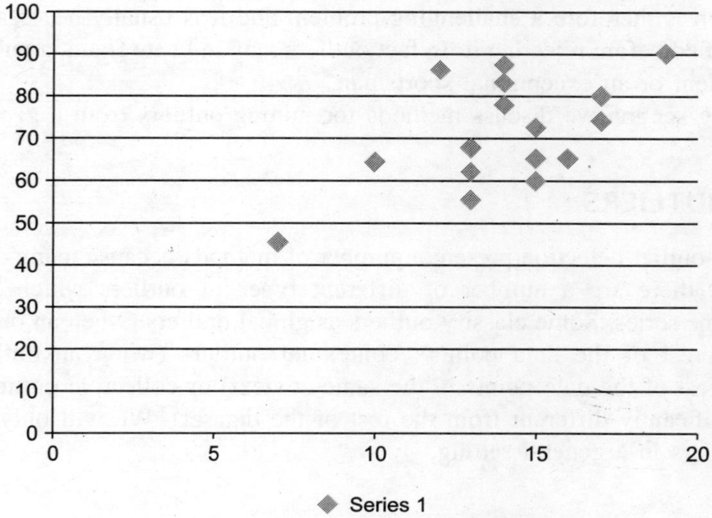

Figure 2.2 Scatter diagram of another dataset.

It is often thought that outliers should be quickly identified and eliminated but outliers can contain useful information. For example in some of the following situations outliers may contain useful information.

- In a dataset about number of visas or passports issued by different offices or branches in a country, an outlier may show that too many visas or passports were issued by one agency or a branch. Although this data point could well be an outlier, it is also possible that there were genuine reasons for the unexpected large number of visas or passports,
- In a dataset of expenditure incurred by each branch or each division of a company, many overseas trips funded by one overseas branch of a multinational company may be considered an outlier once again; it is also possible that there were genuine reasons for the unexpected number of overseas trips.
- In a dataset of investment properties, one of the investment buildings is not earning any rental income. Although this data point may be an outlier it is also possible that the property with unusually low rental income is in a area that is not popular or the building is in need of some repairs.
- In a dataset about a chain of hotels owned by a company, a hotel losing money while others in the same city are doing well may be considered an outlier but it is also possible that there were some genuine reasons for the unexpected low income from the hotel.
- In a dataset of an Indian telephone company that shows number of calls made and cost of the calls from each of millions of phones, a telephone account is suddenly making a lot more international calls than it usually does. Although this data point may be an outlier, it is also possible that the owner of the handset is travelling overseas for holidays or business.
- In a computer system that has software that monitors behaviours of its users, a user's behavior may be found to be very different than what is normally expected. This user may be flagged and the system manager informed. Such an approach is sometimes used in what is called *anomaly detection*.

Outlier detection is therefore a challenging problem and it is usually necessary to look at every outlier that is identified before rejecting it. In fact outliers may indicate fraud, a public health problem, an outstanding student or an exceptional sportsman.

In the following section we discuss methods for mining outliers from a given dataset.

2.4 MINING OUTLIERS

Research papers on outlier detection present a number of methods because many different approaches are possible. Also, there are a number of different types of outliers which may be univariate, multivariate or a time series. Some classify outliers as global outliers (when an outlier is significantly different from the rest of the data points), contextual outliers (when an outlier is significantly different from the rest of the data points in the same context) or collective outliers (when a number of outliers are significantly different from the rest of the dataset). We will only look at techniques for identifying outliers in a general setting.

2.4.1 Mining Univariate Outliers

The simplest case of outliers is when the data is univariate. It is a single dimension variable. Often this can be one of the most useful cases since each attribute in a dataset can also be analyzed separately. It has been found that many errors, for example, mistyping, may be discovered using univariate analysis.

This variable for example may be speed of vehicles that are travelling on a road (perhaps a road camera sensor is recording the speed of every vehicle). What are the nominal values for this dataset and what are the outliers? Assuming that it is a major road in India, the average speed might be say 75 km/h. If we were to plot a scatter graph of all the speeds say between 5 pm and 6 pm then speed value below 20 km/h and above 80 km/h might be outliers. However if many drivers are driving at high speeds then we cannot classify speeds above 80 km/h as outliers.

In most situations we assume that the data values are independent random observations. In the case of almost similar values, we can calculate the mean and standard deviation to determine the nominal values. In the case of uniform or normal distribution, the standard deviation will need to be estimated and then outliers identified based on that estimate, perhaps using the distance to be greater than three standard deviations. It should be noted that with outliers as part of the data the estimates of the average and the standard deviation must be assumed to be somewhat corrupted. *Robust statistics* may be used to overcome this problem but further discussion of robust statistics is beyond the scope of this book.

Let us now consider how univariate outliers may be detected. Let the mean of a univariate dataset be μ and the standard deviation μ then we could accept all values within three standard deviations or between $(\mu - 3\sigma, \mu + 3\sigma)$. All values outside this interval may then be considered outliers.

The above method assumes that the univariate variable is normally distributed. In most cases, even if the variable is not normally distributed, the above method will lead to acceptable results. Other approaches may however be used if it is clear that the data is not normally distributed. A histogram may be used to get some idea about the distribution of the data.

2.4.2 Multivariate Outliers

The situation is much more complex in the case of multivariate data. A multivariate dataset is a set of vectors, each data point being a vector.

Although univariate outliers can provide useful information when we consider one attribute of a multivariate data at a time; it is sometime necessary to consider a number of attributes together. For example, in Table 1.1, we may consider each column separately but some combination of columns (for example, population and population growth rate or literacy and population growth rate) may provide more useful information.

Let us consider a bivariate case first and assume both variables are independent of each other. In this case, it is possible to find the mean value of the pair (x, y) and a single standard deviation to define the dispersion around the mean. Now that the centre of the data and an estimate of the dispersion have been calculated, it is possible to determine how far each point is from the centre estimate. A benefit of considering bivariate distribution is that the data, after appropriate pre-processing, may be examined visually, for example with scatter plots. Outliers may then be identified visually.

It is possible to extend this definition of mean value and standard deviation to more than two dimensions but it becomes quite complex if the number of points is large.

A detailed discussion of algorithms for mining outliers from large datasets is given in the paper by Ramaswamy, Rastogi and Shim (it is listed in the bibliography at the end of the chapter).

2.4.3 Distance-based Outliers

In the discussion of outliers above we have assumed that the variables were distributed according to a normal distribution. In many cases this assumption is not true and then a non-parametric model-free approach needs to be used. Such an approach essentially involves computing the pair wise distances and defining outliers those points that are far from the centre of the data and furthest from the nearest points.

This approach makes no assumptions about the probability distribution of the data points.

2.4.4 Other Techniques

There are a number of other methods for detecting outliers. We should remember that most data is multidimensional although most theoretical models assume univariate data with an underlying one simple normal distribution. Most methods are based on the assumption that outliers are rare observations.

As noted earlier, there are many methods for detecting outliers. Some methods are based on classification methods including supervised classification and unsupervised classification; techniques that are discussed in Chapters 4 and 5. Supervised classification requires training data which is not normally available and therefore unsupervised classification is often more appropriate.

Some outlier detection methods use statistical tests while others may use distance based approach. Outliers in some cases may also be identified by examination of unique rules, consecutive rules, and null rules. A unique rule says that each value of the given attribute must be different from all other values for that attribute. A consecutive rule says that there can be no missing values between the lowest and highest values for the attribute and that all values must also be unique (e.g., as in check numbers). A null rule specifies the use of blanks, question marks, special characters, or other strings that may indicate the null condition (e.g., where a value for a given attribute is not available) and how such values should be handled. For a detailed description of such methods other books can be consulted.

Finally, a common outlier detection method is based on displaying data using good data visualisation software. The display is likely to show one or more data values that are not like the remaining values. These may be the outliers. It is of course not always possible to display the data and pick the outliers because the data may be large and multidimensional and some values may be non-numeric.

2.5 MISSING DATA

As noted earlier, in a large dataset it is inevitable that some data values are missing. There can be a number of reasons for missing values including:

- The particular data has no value associated with it.
- The field was not applicable, the event did not happen, or the data was not available.
- It could be that the person who entered the data did not know the right value, or did not care if a field was filled in.
- The value is to be provided by a later step of the process.

For example, an employee may not have a date of birth because he/she comes from an area where birth records were not maintained properly. May be he/she was a refugee as a child and had no papers when he/she came. It is for such a reason that it has been found that in an employee database, values for one or two employees' age is often missing. Another example is when data is automatically collected from sensors. For example, a number of sensors may be reading pollution in the environment. If the power goes off even momentarily some data values may not be recorded.

In some cases missing data values may not have a significant impact on the data mining process, it depends on what fraction of the data values are missing and what type of data values are missing, but handling missing data values correctly is an important part of data pre-processing. In a dataset, missing values might be represented in many ways: as nulls, as the value N/A or some other code, or as an artificial value such as 9999. However, for purposes of data mining, only nulls are considered missing values.

However, there are many data mining scenarios in which missing values provide important information. The meaning of a missing value depends largely on the context. For example, a missing value for the date in a list of invoices has a meaning substantially different from the lack of a date in column that indicates an employee hire date. Generally, some approaches treat missing values as informative and adjusts the probabilities to incorporate the missing values into its calculations. By doing so, you can ensure that models are balanced and do not weight existing missing values too heavily.

We discuss two different mechanisms for managing and calculating missing values. The first method controls the handling of nulls at the level of the mining structure. The second method differs in implementation, but generally defines how missing values are processed and counted in models that permit null values.

One approach of dealing with missing data suggests a number of ways missing data may be handled in data mining. These are:

- **Ignore the tuple:** This is usually done when the class label is missing (that is, assuming the mining task involves classification). This method is not very effective, unless the tuple contains several attributes with missing values. It is especially poor when the percentage of missing values per attribute varies considerably.
- **Fill in the missing value manually:** In general, this approach is time consuming and may not be feasible given a large dataset with many missing values.
- **Use the attribute mean to fill in the missing value:** For example, suppose that the average income of customers is Rupees Five Lakhs. Use this value to replace the missing value for income.
- **Use the most probable value to fill in the missing value:** This may be determined with regression, inference-based tools using a Bayesian formalism, or decision tree induction. For example, using the other customer attributes in the dataset, it may be possible to replace the missing value.
- **Use the attribute mean for all samples belonging to the same class as the given tuple:** For example, if classifying customers according to credit risk, replace the missing value with the average income value for customers in the same credit-risk category as that of the given tuple.

As noted in the last chapter, most enterprises have a number of databases; large data is often obtained by combining data from a number of sources. These data sources may not have been designed for integration. It has been found that combining data from a number of sources usually leads to data that has a variety of missing data errors.

2.6 TYPES OF DATA

Datasets come in a number of different forms and may include data that may be quantitative, binary, nominal or ordinal. When collecting data, it is important to decide on the type of data to be used for each variable.

2.6.1 Quantitative (or Numerical) Data

Real data or continuous data is quite common. It is obtained when a quantity is being measured, e.g. weight, marks, height, price, salary, and count. It may be integers or floating point numbers. It may be a sequence of numbers. Continuous data has a number of attractive properties. It has order, scale, and distance. This type of data is therefore easiest to use and interpret. Numerical data may have constraints, for example, the daily rate cannot be below the minimum wage and height may not be above a predefined maximum height. Bank balance normally is positive although negative balance may be allowed in exceptional circumstances. Quantitative data also normally have a clear meaning of zero. It may be necessary to identify outliers if any. There are a number of methods for computing similarity between quantitative data. These methods are discussed later in the chapter.

2.6.2 Binary Data

Binary data is also quite common, for example gender, marital status, permanent employee or not. As we have noted earlier, computing similarity or distance between categorical variables is not as simple as for quantitative data but a number of methods have been proposed. A simple method involves counting how many attribute values of the two objects are different amongst the n attributes and using this as an indication of distance.

2.6.3 Qualitative Nominal Data or Categorical Data

Nominal or categorical data is similar to binary data which may take more than two values but have no natural order, e.g. religion, foods, account type (savings, cheque, or fixed term), credit card type (Visa, MasterCard, Amex) and colours. Such data does not have a natural concept of order, scale or distance between them. Also, with textual values it may be necessary to ensure that the values are spelled correctly. In finding distance, an approach similar to that suggested for computing distance for binary data may be used.

Sometime there may be temptation to transform nominal data to numerical data (for example by a series of integers) since the technique that is to be used does not handle nominal data well. This can introduce an order in the original data which can introduce a variety of problems. Such transformation is therefore not recommended. Therefore it is important to retain the lack of order. Perhaps it is best to represent such data as strings.

2.6.4 Qualitative Ordinal (or Ranked) Data

Ordinal data is similar to nominal data except that the data has an order associated with it, for example, grades A, B, C, D, sizes S, M, L, and XL. We can now say that A > B and S < L. The problem of measuring distance between ordinal variables is different than for nominal variables since the order of the values is important. One method of computing distance involves transferring the values to numeric values according to their rank. For example grades A, B, C, D could be transformed to 4.0, 3.0, 2.0 and 1.0 and then one of the methods for the quantitative data may be used. This approach however cannot be recommended since it assumes that distance between the grade A and B is same as between B and C and half of the distance between A and C.

Another problem may arise when dealing with ordinal data. When the data has a large number of values for example age or number of times a person has visited a website, it is sometime suggested that the number of values to be stored may be reduced by *binning*. For example, all ages under 18 may be labelled as A, 19–40 as B, 41–65 as C and over 65 as D. Usually this should not be done since binning reduces the granularity of data and A, B, C and D do not convey the meaning of age.

2.6.5 Identifiers, Names and Addresses

These are usually special cases of categorical data but they may have to be dealt with separately since they usually have special structure. An identifier is usually unique. It may be a number, a series of alphabets or a mixture. For example, in India a PAN is something like ABCDE1234F. Aadhaar has its own identifier and so do a passport and a driver's licence. The structure of each of them is clearly defined. Internet IP addresses are unique, for example, 172.16.254.19.

Addresses may be free text and pre-processing may be necessary to remove redundancy and ambiguity. For example, 123 Shastri Nagar, Defence Colony, New Delhi may be considered to have some redundancy. In Australia, my address may include the last line of address Monash University,

Clayton, Victoria 3800, Australia. There is some redundancy there since Clayton is not required in the address.

Names in India can be complex since the structure of names varies from region to region. In Tamil Nadu, most people have initials and the name; there is no concept of a family name. Initials are usually the person's father's name, mother's name, and the village name but some people have only one initial and other have two initials. It is possible for people to have even four initials. In North India, the names are usually like western names that include a first name, a second name and a family name.

Other types of data are also possible. For example, data may include text strings or a sequence of Web pages visited. Data may also be *date* or *time* but date and time are often not useful in data mining but they could be converted to difference between two values or difference between a value and a fixed reference value. For example, it may be more useful to use a person's age rather than the person's date of birth.

Some techniques, for examples, classical cluster analysis methods do not accept categorical data.

2.7 COMPUTING DISTANCE

A number of data mining techniques require that distance between two sets of data be computed. There are a number of methods for computing distance in a multidimensional environment that we now discuss. There is no distance metric that one can say is the best in all applications.

First we note that distance is a well understood concept that has a number of simple properties.

- Distance is always positive.
- Distance from point x to itself is always zero.
- Distance from point x to point y cannot be greater than the sum of the distance from x to some intermediate point z and distance from z to y.
- Distance from x to y is always the same as from y to x.

Before the data is subjected to analysis, it is best to ensure that only the most descriptive and discriminatory attributes are used in the input. Furthermore the unit of measurement of data can significantly influence the result of analysis. Assuming we want to place similar importance on each of the attributes, it is best that the magnitudes of the attributes are similar. One approach might be to transform all attribute values to the standard distribution, that is, to have a mean of zero and standard deviation of 1. We discuss scaling and weighting attributes later.

The distance measures discussed below assume that equal importance is being given to each attribute. It is possible to assign weights to some of the attributes indicating their importance. The distance measure will then use these weights in computing the total distance.

We note that a multidimensional point is usually represented as a vector. Let the distance between two points **x** and **y** (both vectors) be $D(\mathbf{x}, \mathbf{y})$. We now define a number of distance measures.

2.7.1 Euclidean Distance

Euclidean distance (called the L_2 norm in Mathematics) of the two vectors is magnitude of the difference vector is most commonly used to compute distances and has an intuitive appeal. It is the sum of the square of each element in the difference vector (**x** – **y**), where **x** and **y** are two vectors whose distance needs to be computed. Since squares of the elements are being summed, the largest valued attribute may dominate the distance. It is therefore essential that the attributes are properly scaled.

$$D(\mathbf{x}, \mathbf{y}) = \sqrt{\sum_i (x_i - y_i)^2}$$

The summation in the formula is over all the elements in the difference vector (**x** – **y**).

It is possible to use this distance measure without the square root if one wanted to place lower weight on differences that are large.

A Euclidean distance measure is more appropriate when the data is not standardised but as noted above the distance measure can be greatly affected by the scale of the data. That is why we have noted earlier that data should be scaled so that each column has similar magnitude.

2.7.2 Manhattan Distance

Another commonly used distance metric is the Manhattan distance (called the L_1 norm in Mathematics) of the difference vector (**x** – **y**). In most cases, the results obtained by the Manhattan distance are similar to those obtained by using the Euclidean distance. Once again the largest valued attribute can dominate the distance, although not as much as in the Euclidean distance.

$$D(x, y) = \sum_i |x_i - y_i|$$

2.7.3 Tchebychev Distance

This distance metric is based on the maximum attribute difference. In mathematics, it is called the L_∞ norm of the difference vector.

$$D(x, y) = \text{Max } |x_i - y_i|$$

2.7.4 Categorical Data Distance

This distance measure may be used if the attributes have categorical values with only a small number of values (e.g. binary values). Let N be the total number of categorical attributes.

$$D(x, y) = (\text{number of } x_i \neq y_i)/N$$

Although other distance measures are available, the above four are the most common.

2.7.5 Distances and Similarity

In some data mining techniques it is necessary to define either a similarity measure between two points (both vectors) or a distance measure which may be considered a measure of dissimilarity. We have presented a number of measures of distance above. Often a measure of similarity called the cosine of the angle between the vectors may also be used. The cosine similarity between two vectors calculates the cosine of the angle between the vectors. Therefore the cosine similarity is a measure of the orientation and not a measure of the magnitude. It therefore shows how related the two vectors are.

2.8 DATA SUMMARISING USING BASIC STATISTICAL MEASUREMENTS

We assume that the dataset is multidimensional. For example, it may be a table that has a number of columns (or attributes). To get an overall picture of such multidimensional data that has been collected, it is often useful to compute some basic statistical properties of the data. Computing these values gives us an idea of what the data is like.

2.8.1 Central Tendency of Data—Mean

Mean is well known as representing a typical value of the data elements that is why the mean is also called the *expected value*. The mean is the weighted average of all the values of an attribute in the data. Weights are sometime used to indicate the value of its likelihood of occurrence.

Since the data is only a sample of the whole population, the mean is calculated by summing all the values of the attribute and dividing the sum by the number of data points. Let the attribute be X_i. We may then write the mean as:

$$\text{Mean}(X) = \frac{\Sigma X_i}{N}$$

Since this mean is the mean of the values of attribute X of the sample data that we have, the mean may vary somewhat depending on the sample. There is considerable literature about the mean of a sample and its relationship with the actual mean of the whole population. We do not discuss such details here except noting that more values provide a better estimate of the mean.

2.8.2 Median

The sample median of an attribute is another very useful measurement that estimates the centre (or middle) of the values of the attribute. The median is a value which divides the given values of an attribute into two equal parts. An important property of the median is its stability since the median does not move much unless almost half the data is changed.

2.8.3 Mode

Another metric of data that can be useful is mode. It is the most likely value of an attribute in the dataset. It is particularly useful for categorical attributes since then mean and median for such data have little meaning. Mode is not as widely used as the mean or the median.

2.8.4 Dispersion of Data—Variance and Standard Deviation

These two measurements are related and they play important role in describing the dispersion of the data around the mean. The variance is computed by multiplying the first value minor the mean of the first value multiplied by the first value minus the mean of the second value. These products are then added and divided by $N - 1$ where N is the number of elements. Standard deviation is the square root of the variance. A small variance (and therefore a small standard deviation) indicates that most of the data values are close to the mean while a large variance suggests a much larger dispersion.

2.8.5 Covariance and Correlation

Just like variance and standard deviation, covariance and correlation are two similar measures for determining how much two attributes in a table are similar. We find that in most datasets not all attributes are independent since there are often relationships between attributes. Two statistical measurements that measure relationships are covariance and correlation. We describe them now.

Two attributes that change together have a positive covariance between them. If the two attributes are independent of each other then the covariance will be small.

Let two attributes of a dataset be X and Y. The individual values are X_i and Y_i and let the means of the values be μ_x and μ_y respectively. The covariance of the two attributes $C(X, Y)$ is given by

$$C(x, y) = \frac{\Sigma(X_i - \mu_x)(Y_i - \mu_y)}{N - 1}$$

This expression clearly depends on the means of the two attributes but is not affected by the standard deviations. Correlation coefficient is a normalised by the two standard deviation values giving us a measurement that is always between –1 and 1. A correlation coefficient of 1 means both attributes are almost the same while –1 means that the attributes are the opposites, meaning if X doubles in value then Y halves and so on. The correlation of the two attributes Cor(X, Y) often written as $r(X, Y)$ is given by

$$\text{Cor}(X, Y) = r(X, Y) = \frac{C(X, Y)}{\sigma_x \sigma_y}$$

$C(X, Y)$ is the covariance computed earlier and $\sigma_x \sigma_y$ is the product of the two standard deviations.

All these statistical measures may be computed using a speadsheet like MS Excel.

2.8.6 Quantiles

The quantiles are values which divide the distribution such that there is a given proportion of an observation below the quantile. For example, the median is a quantile. The median is the central value of the distribution, such that half the points are less than or equal to it and half are greater than or equal to it. We can estimate any quantiles easily from the cumulative frequency distribution.

2.8.7 Range of Values

Range of value is the difference between the maximum and minimum values of an attribute.

2.8.8 An Example

We present an example of multidimensional data in a tabular form (Table 2.5). It has been created using some cricket batsmen data. The table has a number of attributes. To get an overall picture of such multidimensional data, we compute the basic statistical properties of the data that has been described above.

Table 2.5 Example dataset

M	*I*	*R*	*A*	*S*	*C*
442	431	17598	45.12	86.26	46
444	432	13428	32.43	91.22	28
351	342	13072	42.85	80.84	29
378	350	11739	39.52	74.24	10
311	300	11363	41.02	73.70	22
303	289	10838	45.72	72.72	17
339	313	10765	39.43	71.17	12
299	289	10405	40.48	79.51	19
282	267	9624	42.39	75.15	15
287	279	9619	35.89	96.94	16

The statistical properties are given in the Table 2.6. They are explained after this table.

Table 2.6 Some statistical properties

	M	*I*	*R*	*A*	*S*	*C*
Mean	344	329	11845	40	80	21
Median	325	306	11100	41	77	18
Variance	3635	3584	5721550	16	76	113
SD	60	60	2392	4	9	11
Correlation (column a and a+1)	0.99	0.89	0.21	−0.55	0.42	
Correlation (column a and a+2)	0.86	−0.20	0.26	0.23		
Correlation (column a and a+3)	−0.21	0.38	0.90			
Correlation (column a and a+4)	0.31	0.72				
Correlation (column a and a+5)	0.65					

Mean

The first row of Table 2.5 gives the mean of each column. The average of the first column is about 344, of the second 329, of the third 11845 followed by 40, 80 and 21.

Median

The second row presents the median of each column. The median value is the value that has half values above and half below. These values are often not very different than the mean values which indicate that there are no large outliers in these values. Comparing values in the first row with those in the second, we find that the corresponding values do not differ so much.

Variance and Standard Deviation

The third row in the table (Table 2.5) indicates for each column how much those values are spread out around the mean. The largest variance is in the third column. This column was derived from the number of runs scored by a player during his batting career. The values go down from a high of 17598 to a low of 9619 and therefore the variance is high

The standard deviation (SD) is the square root of variance.

Correlations

The correlations show interesting relationships between the column values. The fifth row presents correlations between two adjacent columns. Not surprisingly the first two columns derived from the number of matches and number innings are very strongly correlated (0.99). One of these two almost identical columns could therefore be eliminated before any analysis is carried out. Some other large correlations are between the number of matches and runs (0.86) and runs and number of 100s (0.9). All large correlations should be removed by either deleting one of the two columns that are correlated or by transforming the data.

The following rows show correlation between a column and the column two away, a column and a column three away and so on. The last row gives just one value, correlation between the first column and the last.

2.9 DISPLAYING DATA GRAPHICALLY

Although statistical values provide useful information about a dataset, graphical representation of data can also be useful. We present a number of graphical representations in the following section.

2.9.1 Box Plots

Box plots are useful visual presentations to provide a summary and a comparison of one or more datasets. It is sometime called a five-number summary of the data. Before defining the five numbers we assume that each dataset is ordered. That is we are able to arrange data in the dataset from the smallest to the largest. It is assumed that the data is single-dimensional. More dimensions may be displayed using a box plot for each dimension.

The five numbers in a box plot are:

1. The maximum value (end of the fourth quartile Q_4)
2. The minimum value (beginning of the first quartile Q_1)
3. The median (sometime labelled, the end of the second quartile Q_2)
4. The upper quartile (sometime labelled the end of the third quartile Q_3)
5. The lower quartile

The ends of a box plot are maximum and minimum values; these are sometime called whiskers. Therefore the length of a box plot shows the variation of values. The median of the data in a box plot is marked within the box. If the data is evenly distributed then the median should be near the middle. If some values are a lot more common than the remaining ones then the median will be nearer the more common values. The box essentially shows the range of middle half of the data values. The top quarter of the values (Q_4) are above the box and the bottom quarter (Q_1) is below the box.

More specifically, details of a box plot are explained in Figure 2.3 and the characteristics needed have been explained above.

Figure 2.4 shows how box plots can assist in comparing data from different sources.

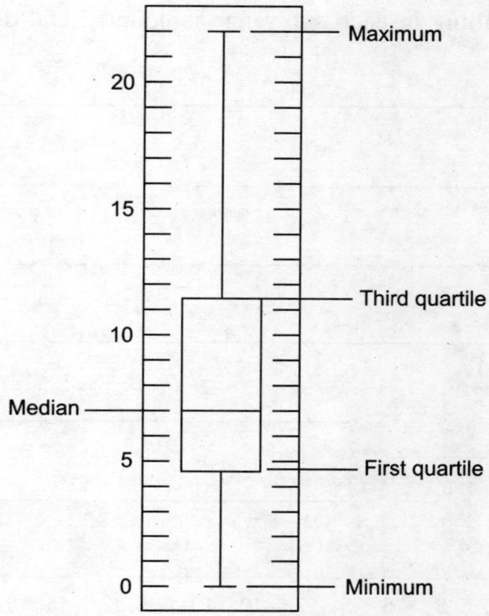

Figure 2.3 Basic components of a box plot.

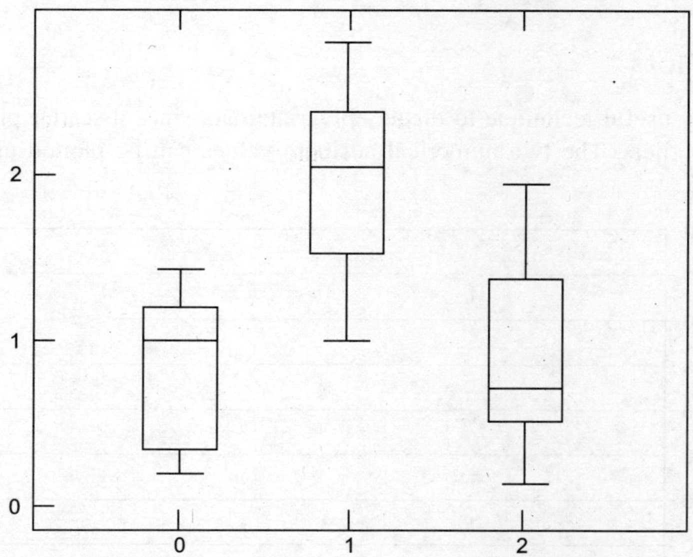

Figure 2.4 Comparing data by comparing their box plots.

2.9.2 Histograms

Histograms are an old and well-known way of displaying data. A histogram is best used for displaying numeric data. The range of values is divided into a number of sub-ranges (sometime called buckets) and number of data values falling in each sub range is counted and displayed. A typical histogram is shown in Figure 2.5.

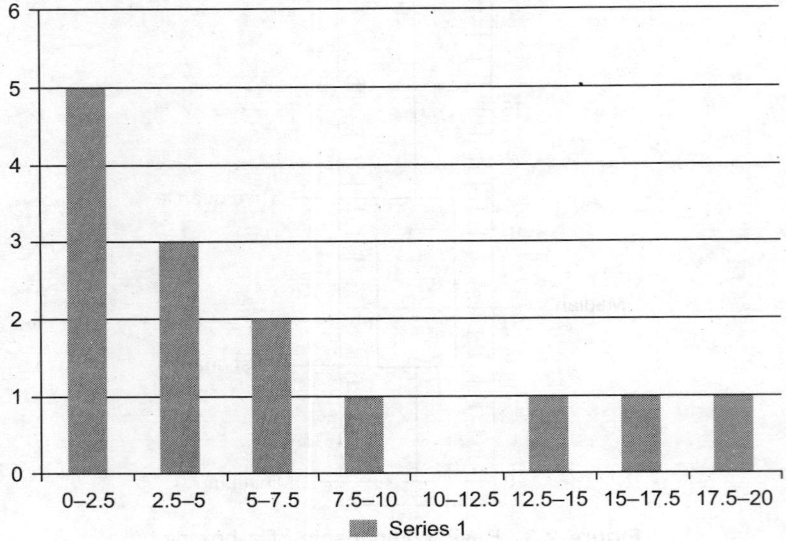

Figure 2.5 An example of a histogram.

2.9.3 Scatter Plots

A scatter plot is very useful technique to display bivariate data since a scatter plot can show clusters of data as well as outliers. The two numerical attribute values can be plotted using the two axes as shown in Figure 2.6.

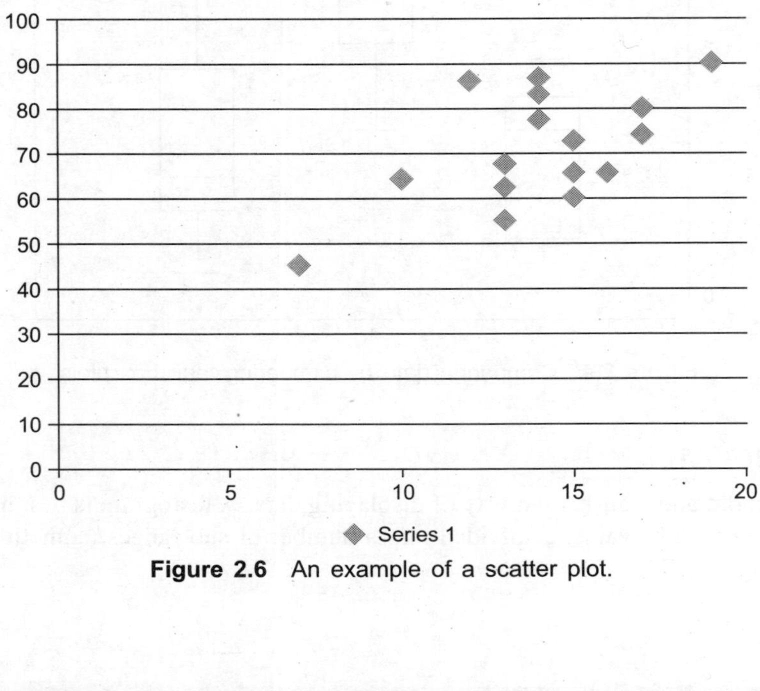

Figure 2.6 An example of a scatter plot.

2.10 MULTIDIMENSIONAL DATA VISUALISATION

Data visualisation is different than graphical representation of data because data visualisation is used to communicate data effectively to users or managers. As computer become more powerful, data visualisation is being in a variety of applications, for example, in computer games.

The field of data visualisation is complex but we present some basic concepts here. We assume that the data we wish to visualize is multidimensional. The simplest data visualisation involves using colour of pixels to display a value of a dimension, for example dark red may mean a large value and light red may display lower values. An example is shown below that shows rainfall variation in India. Since data is normally multidimensional, it may be necessary to have a number of displays; each displaying a different dimension.

Although pixel-based approach is simple, it provides the user only limited understanding of the multidimensional data. It is difficult to identify cluster of data that have high values or low values of all the variables. In some ways, scatter plots convey better information if the data is only two-dimensional or three-dimensional.

Other widely used visualisation techniques include Chernoff faces which essentially display multidimensional data using cartoon-type human faces.

There are a number of ways of visualisations in Weka. It is possible to select an area of the graph to zoom in on. It is also possible to save the visualisation data out to an ARFF file which can be loaded back for further manipulation.

Further details of visualisation are beyond the scope of this book.

SUMMARY

In this chapter, we have explained the importance of data collection, data understanding and data preparation. The process of data extraction from a variety of courses, data transformation and data loading (ETL) was discussed in some detail using an example. Reasons for data errors were discussed. The issue of outliers was explained and methods of identifying presented. Missing data problems were considered and different methods for overcoming missing data were presented. Different types of data were explained followed by different distance metrics. Summarising data using a number of statistical measures was presented. Finally a number of ways of displaying data graphically were presented.

REVIEW QUESTIONS

1. Review briefly the CRISP-DM process and the data mining guidelines from the last chapter. (Section 2.1)
2. Discuss data collection and data pre-processing. (Section 2.2)
3. Describe the extraction, transformation and loading (ETL) process. (Sections 2.2.1 and 2.2.2)
4. Discuss what an outlier is. (Section 2.3)
5. Explain methods for mining outliers. (Section 2.4)
6. Discuss the problems of missing data. (Section 2.5)
7. Explain different types of data. (Section 2.6)

8. List a number of measures of computing distance between two vectors. (Section 2.7)
9. Describe the basic statistical measurements of data. (Section 2.8)
10. Discuss the basic methods for displaying data graphically. (Sections 2.9 and 2.10)

EXERCISES

1. Suppose you are required to collect data similar to that in Table 1.1. Using the web, find out all the sources that are required to collect such data. What data pre-processing you might require before you can use the data for data mining.
2. Consider the table below which gives crime statistics about crime against women. The data has been obtained from one of the reports titled "Crime Statistics in India" published by National Crimes Bureau, Ministry of Home Affairs, 2012.

	Approximate population	*Number of rapes*	*Number of kidnappings and abductions*	*Number of dowry deaths*	*Cruelty by husband and relatives*
Andhra Pradesh	847	1442	1612	599	13376
Arunachal Pradesh	14	42	60	0	18
Assam	312	1700	3192	121	5246
Bihar	1038	93	3050	1413	2607
Chhattisgarh	255	1053	365	104	834
Goa	15	29	17	1	18
Gujarat	604	439	1442	30	6052
Haryana	254	733	733	255	2740
Himachal Pradesh	69	168	191	4	239
Jammu & Kashmir	129	277	1023	11	286
Jharkhand	330	784	660	282	659
Karnataka	611	636	715	267	3712
Kerala	334	1132	221	15	5377
Madhya Pradesh	726	3406	1088	811	3732
Maharashtra	1124	1701	1252	339	7136
Manipur	27	53	116	1	39
Meghalaya	30	130	37	1	21
Mizoram	11	77	0	0	9
Nagaland	20	23	3	0	1
Odisha	420	1112	1008	465	2320
Punjab	277	479	517	143	1136
Rajasthan	686	1800	2713	514	12218
Sikkim	6	16	10	0	4
Tamil Nadu	721	677	1743	152	1812
Tripura	37	205	116	30	702
Uttar Pradesh	1996	20422	7525	2322	7121
Uttrakhand	101	129	283	83	307
West Bengal	913	2363	3711	510	19772
Delhi	168	572	2085	142	1575

You are required to do the following:

(a) Compute mean value of each column.

(b) Compute correlations between each column and the other columns. How many correlations are required?

(c) Scale each column so that each of them is a similar size. Explain how the scaling was done and why.

(d) Now carry out the correlations again. Are there different than those obtained in (b) above? Why?

(e) List some data mining that you might like to carry out on the data in the table.

3. What data formats do Association Rule Mining, Supervised Classification and Clustering require before you can use the technique? Present a dataset that can be used for all three techniques.

4. Select two case studies in which the authors discovered significant problems of data collection and/or data pre-processing. Get the original case study papers and outline the problems. This should be no more than 1000 words. Do not cut and paste. Instead use your own description of the issues.

MULTIPLE CHOICE QUESTIONS

1. Which one of the following is not a step in CRISP-DM?
   (a) Outlier detection
   (b) Data understanding
   (c) Evaluation
   (d) Modelling
2. Which one of the following is a step in data pre-processing?
   (a) Data understanding
   (b) Mapping rules
   (c) Verification
   (d) Transformation
   (e) All of the above
3. Which one of the following is not included in ETL?
   (a) Extraction
   (b) Transformation
   (c) Loading
   (d) Finding the source systems
4. Which of the following issues is not resolved by ETL?
   (a) Data extraction
   (b) Data transformation

(c) Loading data in a separate staging area
(d) All of the above are resolved

5. Which one of the following is not resolved during data cleaning?
   (a) Instance identity problem
   (b) Different types of data problems
   (c) Record linkage problem
   (d) Referential integrity problem
6. Data cleaning must involve the following
   (a) Outliers
   (b) Missing data
   (c) Duplicate data
   (d) All of the above
7. Which one of the following is not a reason for missing data?
   (a) A particular data has no value
   (b) The data field is not applicable
   (c) The event did not happen
   (d) The data was not available
   (e) All of the above are reasons
8. Which one of the following may be used to handle missing data?
   (a) Ignore the tuple
   (b) Use the most probably value
   (c) Use the attribute mean
   (d) Replace the value manually
   (e) All of the above
9. Which one of the following is not a data type?
   (a) Numerical data
   (b) Binary data
   (c) Floating point data
   (d) Ordinal data
10. Which one of the following is not a technique for computing distance between two points?
   (a) Chebyshev distance
   (b) Polynomial distance
   (c) Euclidean distance
   (d) Manhattan distance

11. Which one of the following is a good metric to measure spread of a dataset?
    (a) Mean
    (b) Median
    (c) Correlation
    (d) Variance
12. Which one of the following is a good display technique for multidimensional data?
    (a) Box plots
    (b) Histograms
    (c) Scatter plots
    (d) None of the above

BIBLIOGRAPHY

Recommended Reading for both Students and Lecturers

Aggarwal, C., *Outlier Analysis*, Springer, 450 pp., 2013.

Brown, J.L. and Kros, J.F., The Impact of Missing Data on Data Mining, In J. Wang (Ed.), *Data Mining: Opportunities and Challenges, Idea Group*, S. Chakrabarti et al., Data Mining—Know it all, Chapters 2 and 3, pp. 37–112, Morgan Kauffman, 2009.

Chapman, P., Clinton, J., Kerber, R., Khabaza, T., Reinartz, T., Shearer, C., and Wirth, R., CRISP-DM 1.0: Step-by-Step Data Mining Guide, 2000.

Dasu, T. and Johnson, T., *Exploratory Data Mining and Data Cleaning*, Wiley 2003

Hawkins, D., *Identification of Outliers*, Chapman & Hall, 1980.

Hellerstein, J.M., Quantitative Data Cleaning for Large Databases, White Paper, United Nations Economic Commission for Europe, February, 2008. http://db.cs.berkeley.edu/jmh/papers/cleaning-unece.pdf

Hernandez, M.A. and Stolfo, S.J., Real-World Data is Dirty: Data Cleansing and the Merge/Purge Problem, *Data Mining and Knowledge Discovery*, 2, pp. 9–37, 1998.

Hodge, V.J. and Austin, J., A Survey of Outlier Detection Methodologies, *Artificial Intelligence Review*, Vol. 22, pp. 85–126, 2014.

Kim, W., Choi, B.J., Hong E.K., Kim S.K., and Lee, D., A Taxonomy of Dirty Data, *Data Mining and Knowledge Discovery*, 7(1), pp. 81–99, 2003.

Knorr, E.M. and Ng, R.T., Algorithms for Mining Distance Based Outliers In Large Datasets, *Pro. 24th VLDB Conference*, pp. 392–403, 1998.

Maletic, J.I. and Marcus, A., Data Cleaning: A Prelude to Knowledge Discovery, In *Data Mining and Knowledge Handbook*, Maimon, O. and Rokach, L. (Eds.), Springer, pp. 21–36, 2005.

Osborne, J.W., *Best Practices in Data Cleaning: A Complete Guide to Everything You Need to Do before and after Collecting Your Data*, 2012.

Pearson, R.K., Mining Imperfect Data: Dealing with Contamination and Incomplete Records, *SIAM*, 2005

Pyle, D., *Data Preparation for Data Mining*, Morgan Kaufmann, 1999.

Rahm, E. and Do, H.H., Data Cleaning: Problems and Current Approaches, *IEEE Data Engineering Bulletin*, Vol. 23, 2000.

Ramaswamy, S., Rastogi R., and Shim, K., Efficient Algorithms for Mining Outliers from Large Datasets, *Proceedings of the SIGMOD Conference*, pp. 427–438, ACM, 2000.

CHAPTER

3 Association Rules Mining

LEARNING OBJECTIVES

After completing this chapter, you will be able to:

- Understand what association rules mining is and learn a naïve algorithm
- Learn the basic terminology and the Apriori algorithm
- Describe examples of using the Apriori algorithm
- Understand the efficiency of the Apriori algorithm and how it may be improved
- Describe briefly a number of more efficient algorithms
- Understand where to find more information about the ARM methods

3.1 INTRODUCTION

In all retail outlets the amount of electronic data stored has grown enormously in recent years due to barcoding of all goods sold. As an extreme example, Wal-Mart, with more than 4000 branches, collects about 20 million point-of-sale transactions each day. Given this mountain of data, it is good business sense to try to analyse it to find useful information.

A conceptually simple yet interesting example is that of analysing a large database of supermarket transactions with the aim of finding association rules. This is called *Association Rules Mining* (ARM) or *Market Basket Analysis.* It involves searching for interesting customer habits by looking at associations. The classical example is the one where a store was reported to have discovered that people buying nappies tended also to buy beer. It is not quite clear if this is really true but it makes an interesting example!

Association rules mining has many applications other than market basket analysis, including applications in marketing, customer segmentation, medicine, electronic commerce, classification, clustering, Web mining, bioinformatics and finance.

CHAPTER OVERVIEW

The next section presents some of the basic concepts and terminology used in ARM. A simple example is presented. Section 3.3 describes the task and presents a naïve algorithm as well as an improved naïve algorithm. Section 3.4 presents the classical Apriori algorithm. A stepwise algorithm is presented and a small as well as a larger example using these steps is given. The concepts of closed and maximal itemsets are described using an example. Section 3.5 deals with improving the efficiency of the Apriori algorithm. Other algorithms are presented in Sections 3.6, 3.7 and 3.8. Section 3.9 describes an algorithm called FP-Growth. A stepwise description and an example are presented. Performance of the algorithms is discussed in Section 3.10.

3.2 BASICS

Let us first describe the association rule mining task informally and define some of the terminology by using an example of a small shop. To keep the example simple we assume that the shop sells only a small variety of products:

- Bread
- Cheese
- Coffee
- Juice
- Milk
- Tea
- Biscuits
- Newspaper
- Sugar

We assume that the shopkeeper has an electronic register that keeps records of what each customer purchases. Such records of ten customers are given in Table 3.1. Each row in the table gives the set of items one customer bought.

Table 3.1 Transaction for a simple example

Transaction ID	*Items*
10	Bread, Cheese, Newspaper
20	Bread, Cheese, Juice
30	Bread, Milk
40	Cheese, Juice, Milk, Coffee
50	Sugar, Tea, Coffee, Biscuits, Newspaper
60	Sugar, Tea, Coffee, Biscuits, Milk, Juice, Newspaper
70	Bread, Cheese
80	Bread, Cheese, Juice, Coffee
90	Bread, Milk
100	Sugar, Tea, Coffee, Bread, Milk, Juice, Newspaper

The shopkeeper wants to find which products (call them *items*) are sold together frequently. If for example, sugar and tea are two items that are sold together frequently then he/she might consider having a sale on one of them in the hope that it will not only increase the sale of that item but also increase the sale of the other. We will not find a solution to this example just now. Similar examples are used later in the chapter when we illustrate a number of methods for solving it.

3.2.1 Terminology

We now define some terminology. We assume that the number of items the shop stocks is n (for example, $n = 9$ for this shop) and these items are represented by the vector $I(i_1, i_2, \ldots, i_n\}$. We assume that there are N transactions ($N = 10$ for the shop data in Table 3.1). We denote them by the vector (or *tuple*) $T\{t_1, t_2, \ldots, t_N\}$ each with a unique tuple identifier (*TID*) and each specifying a subset of items (possibly a small subset) from the itemset I purchased by one customer. Let each transaction of m items be $(i_1, i_2, \ldots, i_m\}$ with $m < n$. Typically transactions differ in the number of items. We now wish to find association relationships given a large number of transactions such that items that tend to occur together are identified. It should be noted that association rules mining does not take into account the quantities of items bought.

Association rules are often written as $X \rightarrow Y$ meaning that whenever X appears Y also tends to appear. X and Y may be single items or sets of items (in which the same item does not appear in both). X is often referred to as the rule's *antecedent* and Y as the *consequent*.

$X \rightarrow Y$ is a probabilistic relationship found empirically. It indicates only that X and Y have been found together frequently in the given data and does not show causal relationship implying that buying of X by a customer causes him/her to buy Y.

As noted above, we assume that we have a set of transactions, each transaction being a list of items. Suppose items (or itemsets) X and Y appear together in only 10% of the transactions but whenever X appears there is a 80% chance that Y also appears. The 10% presence of X and Y together is called the *support* (or *prevalence*) of the rule and the 80% chance is called the *confidence* (or *predictability*) of the rule. Essentially the support and confidence are measures of interestingness of the rule. A high level of support indicates that the rule is frequent enough for the business to be interested in it and a high level of confidence shows that the rule is true often enough to justify a decision based on it.

Let us define support and confidence more formally. As noted earlier, the total number of transactions is N. Support of X is the number of times it appears in the database divided by N and support for X and Y together is the number of times they appear together divided by N. Therefore, using $P(X)$ to mean probability of X in the database, we have:

$$\text{Support } (X) = \frac{\text{Number of times } X \text{ appears}}{N} = P(X)$$

$$\text{Support } (XY) = \frac{\text{Number of times } X \text{ and } Y \text{ appear together)}}{N} = P(X \cup Y)$$

Confidence for $X \rightarrow Y$ is defined as the ratio of the support for X and Y together to the support for X. Therefore if X appears much more frequently than X and Y appear together, the confidence will be low. It does not depend on how frequently Y appears.

$$\text{Confidence of } (X \rightarrow Y) = \frac{\text{Support } (XY)}{\text{Support } (X)} = \frac{P(X \cup Y)}{P(X)} = P(Y|X)$$

$P(Y \mid X)$ is the probability of Y once X has taken place, also called the conditional probability of Y.

Sometime the term lift is used to measure the power of association between items that are purchased together. Lift essentially indicates how much more likely an item *Y* is to be purchased if the customer has bought the item *X* that has been identified as having an association with the first item *Y* compared to the likelihood of *Y* being purchased without the other item being purchased. Obviously lift must be above 1.0 for the association to be of interest.

Lift may be defined as

$$\frac{P(Y|X)}{P(Y)}$$

It should be noted that considerable care is needed in interpreting association rules. For example, if the consequent is very popular, like Coca-Cola which is a very frequently bought item in most Australian supermarkets, then the confidence of the rule is likely to be high irrespective of whether the two items are associated. We will discuss such issues later in the chapter.

3.3 THE TASK AND A NAÏVE ALGORITHM

We are now able to define our task more precisely. Given a large set of transactions, we seek a procedure to discover all association rules which have at least *p*% support with at least *q*% confidence such that all rules satisfying these constraints are found and the rules are found efficiently. In addition, we would prefer only to find rules that are actionable, but this aspect of the task is beyond the scope of this book.

Example 3.1—A Naïve Algorithm

Let us consider a naïve brute force algorithm to do the task. Consider the following example which is even simpler than what we considered earlier in Table 3.1. We now have only four items for sale (Bread, Cheese, Juice and Milk) and we have only the four transactions given in Table 3.2, each transaction showing the purchases of one customer. We are interested in finding association rules with a minimum support of 50% and minimum confidence of 75%. It is worth noting that these numbers need to be high because there are so few transactions. For large set of transactions, the support and confidence are likely to be much smaller.

Table 3.2 Transactions for Example 3.1

Transaction ID	*Items*
100	Bread, Cheese
200	Bread, Cheese, Juice
300	Bread, Milk
400	Cheese, Juice, Milk

The basis of our naïve algorithm is as follows. If we can list all the combinations of the items that we have in stock and find which one of these combinations are frequent then we can find the association rules that have the confidence from these frequent combinations.

The four items and all combinations of the four items and their frequencies of occurrence in the transaction "database" in Table 3.2 are given in Table 3.3.

Table 3.3 List of all itemsets and their frequencies

Itemsets	*Frequency*
Bread	3
Cheese	3
Juice	2
Milk	2
(Bread, Cheese)	2
(Bread, Juice)	1
(Bread, Milk)	1
(Cheese, Juice)	2
(Cheese, Milk)	1
(Juice, Milk)	1
(Bread, Cheese, Juice)	1
(Bread, Cheese, Milk)	0
(Bread, Juice, Milk)	0
(Cheese, Juice, Milk)	1
(Bread, Cheese, Juice, Milk)	0

Given the required minimum support of 50%, we must find the itemsets that occur in at least two transactions. Such itemsets are called *frequent*. The above list of frequencies shows that all four items (Bread, Cheese, Juice and Milk) are frequent. The frequency goes down as we look at 2-itemsets (only two out of a possible six are frequent), 3-itemsets (none are frequent) and 4-itemsets (again, none frequent).

The frequent itemsets are given in Table 3.4.

Table 3.4 The set of all frequent item sets

Itemsets	*Frequency*
Bread	3
Cheese	3
Juice	2
Milk	2
(Bread, Cheese)	2
(Cheese, Juice)	2

We can now proceed to determine if the two 2-itemsets (Bread, Cheese) and (Cheese, Juice) lead to association rules with required confidence of 75%. Every 2-itemset (A, B) can lead to two rules $A \rightarrow B$ and $B \rightarrow A$ if both satisfy the required confidence. As defined earlier, confidence of $A \rightarrow B$ is given by the support for A and B together divided by support for A.

We therefore have four possible rules and their confidence as follows:

Bread → Cheese with confidence of 2/3 = 67%

Cheese → Bread with confidence of 2/3 = 67%

Cheese → Juice with confidence of 2/3 = 67%

Juice → Cheese with confidence of 100%

Therefore only the last rule Juice → Cheese has confidence above the minimum 75% required and qualifies. Rules that have more than user-specified minimum confidence are called *confident*.

This is not an interesting example since there were only four items in Table 3.2. We had to use a small number of items because Table 3.3 grows quickly with the number of items. There are 15 different combinations in Table 3.3 and if we include a null combination (a combination with no items) as well we obtain 16 or 2^4 combinations. You will understand that if the example had six items it would have produced 64 combinations and if the number of items was 10 then we would have a table with 1024 combinations.

This simple algorithm works well with four items but if the number of items is say 100, the number of combinations is much larger, in billions. The number of combinations becomes about a million with 20 items since the number of combinations is 2^n with n items. The naïve algorithm can be improved to deal more effectively with larger datasets. We discuss one improvement.

3.3.1 Improved Naïve Algorithm

Rather than counting all possible item combinations we can look at each transaction and count only the combinations that actually occur (that is, we don't count itemsets with zero frequency). For example let us look at the combinations in each transaction in Table 3.2.

Table 3.5 All possible combinations with non-zero frequencies

Transaction ID	*Items*	*Combinations*
100	Bread, Cheese	{Bread, Cheese}
200	Bread, Cheese, Juice	{Bread, Cheese}, {Bread, Juice}, {Cheese, Juice}, {Bread, Cheese, Juice}
300	Bread, Milk	{Bread, Milk}
400	Cheese, Juice, Milk	{Cheese, Juice}, {Cheese, Milk}, {Juice, Milk}, {Cheese, Juice, Milk}

We therefore only need to look at the following combinations and their frequencies given in Table 3.6.

Table 3.6 Frequencies of all itemsets with non-zero frequencies

Itemsets	*Frequency*
Bread	3
Cheese	3
Juice	2
Milk	2
(Bread, Cheese)	2
(Bread, Juice)	1
(Bread, Milk)	1
(Cheese, Juice)	2
(Juice, Milk)	1
(Bread, Cheese, Juice)	1
(Cheese, Juice, Milk)	1

We can now proceed as before.

This works better since the list of item combinations is significantly reduced (from 15 to 11) and this reduction is likely to be much larger for bigger problems. Regardless of the extent of the reduction, this list will also become very large for say 1000 items since it includes all the non-zero itemsets that exist in the transactions database whether they have minimum support or not. Therefore the naïve algorithm or any improvement of it is not suitable for large problems. We discuss a number of algorithms for more efficiently solving the association rule problem starting with the classical Apriori algorithm.

3.4 THE APRIORI ALGORITHM

The basic algorithm for finding association rules was first proposed in 1993. In 1994, an improved algorithm was proposed. Our discussion is based on the 1994 algorithm called the *Apriori algorithm*. This algorithm may be considered to consist of two parts. In the first part, those itemsets that exceed the minimum support requirement are found. As noted earlier, such itemsets are called frequent itemsets. In the second part, association rules that meet the minimum confidence requirement are found from the frequent itemsets. The second part is relatively straightforward so much of the focus of the research in this field has been to improve the first part.

3.4.1 First Part—Frequent Itemsets

The first part of the algorithm itself may be divided into two steps (Steps 2 and 3). The first step essentially finds itemsets that are likely to be frequent or candidates for frequent itemsets. The second step finds a subset of these candidate itemsets that are actually frequent.

The algorithm works as follows for a given set of transactions (it is assumed that we require minimum support of $p\%$):

Step 1: Scan all transactions and find all frequent items that have support above p%. Let these frequent items be L_1.

Step 2: Build potential sets of k items from L_{k-1} by using pairs of item sets in L_{k-1} such that each pair has the first $k - 2$ items common. Now the $k - 2$ common items and the one remaining item from each of the two itemsets are combined to form a k itemset. The set of such potentially frequent k itemsets is the candidate set C_k. (For $k = 2$, build potential frequent pairs by using the frequent item set L_1 so that every item in L_1 appears with every other item in L_1. The set so generated is the candidate set C_2.) This step is called a priori-gen.

Step 3: Scan all transactions and find all k-itemsets in C_k that are frequent. The frequent set so obtained is L_k. (For $k = 2$, C_2 is the set of candidate pairs. The frequent pairs are L_2.)

Terminate when no further frequent itemsets are found otherwise continue with Step 2.

The main notation for association rule mining that is used in the Apriori algorithm is the following:

- A k-itemset is a set of k items.
- The set C_k is a set of candidate k-itemsets that are potentially frequent.
- The set L_k is a subset of C_k and is the set of k-itemsets that are frequent.

It is now worthwhile to discuss the algorithmic aspects of the Apriori algorithm. Some of the issues that need to be considered are:

1. **Computing L_1:** We scan the disk-resident database only once to obtain L_1. An item vector of length n with count for each item stored in the main memory may be used. Once the scan of the database is finished and counts for each item found, the items that meet the support criterion can be identified and L_1 determined.
2. **A priori-gen function:** This is Step 2 of the Apriori algorithm. It takes an argument L_{k-1} and returns a set of all candidate k-itemsets. In computing C_3 from L_2, we organise L_2 so that the itemsets are sorted in their lexicographic order. Observe that if an itemset in C_3 is (a, b, c) then L_2 must have items (a, b) and (a, c) since all subsets of C_3 must be frequent. Therefore to find C_3 we only need to look at pairs in L_2 that have the same first item. Once we find two such matching pairs in L_2, they are combined to form a candidate itemset in C_3. Similarly when forming C_i from L_{i-1}, we sort the itemsets in L_{i-1} and look for a pair of itemsets in L_{i-1} that have the same first $i - 2$ items. If we find such a pair, we can combine them to produce a candidate itemset for C_i.
3. **Pruning:** Once a candidate set C_i has been produced, we can prune some of the candidate itemsets by checking that all subsets of every itemset in the set are frequent. For example, if we have derived $\{a, b, c\}$ from $\{a, b\}$ and $\{a, c\}$, then we check that $\{b, c\}$ is also in L_2. If it is not $\{a, b, c\}$ may be removed from C_3. The task of such pruning becomes harder as the number of items in the itemsets grows, but the number of large itemsets tends to be small.
4. **A priori subset function:** To improve the efficiency of searching, the candidate itemsets C_k are stored in a hash tree. The leaves of the hash tree store itemsets while the internal nodes provide a roadmap to reach the leaves. Each leaf node is reached by traversing the tree whose root is at depth 1. Each internal node of depth d points to all the related nodes at depth d + 1 and the branch to be taken is determined by applying a hash function on the dth item. All nodes are initially created as leaf nodes and when the number of itemsets in a leaf node exceeds a specified threshold, the leaf node is converted to an internal node. We do not discuss the data structure any further.
5. **Transactions storage:** We assume the data is too large to be stored in the main memory. Should it be stored as a set of transactions, each transaction being a sequence of item numbers? Alternatively should each transaction be stored as a Boolean vector of length n (n being the number of items in the store) with 1's showing for the items purchased? We discuss this issue later in this section.
6. **Computing L_2 (and more generally L_k):** Assuming C_2 is available, in the main memory, each candidate pair needs to be tested to find if the pair is frequent. Given that C_2 is likely to be large, this testing must be done efficiently. In one scan, each transaction can be checked for the candidate pairs.

3.4.2 Second Part—Finding the Rules

To find the association rules from the frequent itemsets, we take a large frequent itemset, say p, and find each non-empty subset a. The rule $a \rightarrow (p - a)$ is possible if it satisfies the confidence. Confidence of this rule is given by support (p)/support (a).

It should be noted that when considering rules like $a \rightarrow (p - a)$, it is possible to make the rule generation process more efficient as follows. We only want rules that have the minimum confidence required. Since confidence is given by support (p)/support (a), it is clear that if for some a, the rule $a \rightarrow (p - a)$ does not have the minimum confidence then all rules like $b \rightarrow (p - b)$ where b is a subset of a will also not have the confidence since support (b) cannot be smaller than support (a). It, therefore, makes sense to generate all subsets a in a recursive fashion and once we find a subset a for which the rule $a \rightarrow (p - a)$ does not have minimum confidence then no smaller subsets need to be checked. As an example if $ABC \rightarrow D$ does not have the minimum confidence then $AB \rightarrow CD$ or $A \rightarrow BCD$ also will not have the confidence.

Another way to improve rule generation is to consider rules like $(p - a) \rightarrow a$. If this rule has the minimum confidence then all rules $(p - b) \rightarrow b$ will also have minimum confidence if b is a subset of a since $(p - b)$ has more items than $(p - a)$ given that b is smaller than a and so cannot have support higher than that of $(p - a)$. As an example, if $A \rightarrow BCD$ has the minimum confidence then all rules like $AB \rightarrow CD$, $AC \rightarrow BD$ and $ABC \rightarrow D$ will also have the minimum confidence. Once again this can be used in improving the efficiency of rule generation.

In both improvements noted above, the total number of items and therefore support(p) stays the same.

3.4.3 Implementation Issue—Transaction Storage

Let us now deal with the representation of the transactions. To illustrate the different options, let the number of items be six. Let them be {A, B, C, D, E, F}. Let there be only eight transactions with transaction IDs {10, 20, 30, 40, 50, 60, 70, 80}. This set of eight transactions with six items can be represented in at least three different ways as follows.

The first representation (Table 3.7) is the most obvious horizontal one. Each row in the table provides the transaction ID and the items that were purchased.

Table 3.7 A simple representation of transactions as an item list

Transaction ID	*Items*
10	*A, B, D*
20	*D, E, F*
30	*A, F*
40	*B, C, D*
50	*E, F*
60	*D, E, F*
70	*C, D, F*
80	*A, C, D, F*

In the second horizontal representation (Table 3.8), rather than listing the items that were purchased we may list all the items and indicate purchases by putting a 1 against the item that occurs in a transaction and 0 against the rest. Each row is still a transaction, but the items purchased are represented by a binary string.

Table 3.8 Representing transactions as a binary item list

TID	*A*	*B*	*C*	*D*	*E*	*F*
10	1	1	0	1	0	0
20	0	0	0	1	1	1
30	1	0	0	0	0	1
40	0	1	1	1	0	0
50	0	0	0	0	1	1
60	0	0	0	1	1	1
70	0	0	1	1	0	1
80	1	0	1	1	0	1

In the third representation (Table 3.9), call it the vertical representation, the transaction list is turned around. Rather than using each row to represent a transaction of the items purchased, each row now represents an item and indicates transactions in which the item appears. The columns now represent the transactions. This representation is also called a *TID-list* since for each item it provides a list of TIDs.

Table 3.9 Representing transactions as binary columns

Items	10	20	30	40	50	60	70	80
A	1	0	1	0	0	0	0	1
B	1	0	0	1	0	0	0	0
C	0	0	0	1	0	0	1	1
D	1	1	0	1	0	1	1	1
E	0	1	0	0	1	1	0	0
F	0	1	1	0	1	1	1	1

How the data is represented can have an impact on the efficiency of an algorithm. A vertical representation can facilitate counting of items by counting the number of 1's in each row and for example the number of 2-itemsets can be counted by finding the intersection of the two TID lists, but the representation is not storage efficient if there is a very large number of transactions involved. Also, if an algorithm needs data in the vertical representation then there would be a cost in transforming data from the horizontal representation to the vertical one.

We now present two examples of using the Apriori algorithm, one very simple and another more complex.

Example 3.2—A Simple Apriori Example

Let us first consider an example of only five transactions and six items. The example is similar to Example 3.1 in Table 3.2 at the beginning of this chapter but we have added two more items and another transaction. We still want to find association rules with 50% support and 75% confidence. The transactions are given in the Table 3.10.

Table 3.10 Transactions for Example 3.2

Transaction ID	*Items*
100	Bread, Cheese, Eggs, Juice
200	Bread, Cheese, Juice
300	Bread, Milk, Yogurt
400	Bread, Juice, Milk
500	Cheese, Juice, Milk

We first find L_1. Since we have only a small number of items, we can see that Bread appears 4 times, Cheese 3 times, Juice 4 times, Milk 3 times and Eggs and Yogurt only once. We require 50% support and therefore each frequent item must appear in at least three transactions. Therefore L_1 is given by items in Table 3.11.

Table 3.11 Frequent items L_1 for Example 3.2

Item	*Frequency*
Bread	4
Cheese	3
Juice	4
Milk	3

The candidate 2-itemsets or C_2 therefore has six pairs. These pairs and their frequencies are given in Table 3.12.

Table 3.12 Candidate item pairs C_2 for Example 3.2

Item Pairs	*Frequency*
(Bread, Cheese)	2
(Bread, Juice)	3
(Bread, Milk)	2
(Cheese, Juice)	3
(Cheese, Milk)	1
(Juice, Milk)	2

We therefore have only two frequent item pairs that are {Bread, Juice} and {Cheese, Juice}. This is L_2. From these two frequent 2-itemsets, we do not obtain a candidate 3-itemset since we do not have two 2-itemsets that have the same first item.

The two frequent 2-itemsets above lead to the following possible rules:

Bread $\rightarrow$ Juice
Juice $\rightarrow$ Bread
Cheese $\rightarrow$ Juice
Juice $\rightarrow$ Cheese

The confidence of these rules is obtained by dividing the support for both items in the rule by the support for the item on the left hand side of the rule. The confidence of the four rules therefore is

3/4 = 75%, 3/4 = 75%, 3/3 = 100%, and 3/4 = 75% respectively. Since all of them have a minimum 75% confidence, they all qualify.

Example 3.3—A Larger Apriori Example

Consider a bakery having 16 items for sale as listed in Table 3.13. Now consider the 25 transactions given in Table 3.14. As usual, each row in the table represents one transaction, that is, the items bought by one customer.

In this example, we want to find association rules that satisfy the requirement of 25% support and 70% confidence.

Table 3.13 The list of bakery items for Example 3.3

Item number	*Item name*
1	Biscuits
2	Bread
3	Cereal
4	Cheese
5	Chocolate
6	Coffee
7	Donuts
8	Eggs
9	Juice
10	Milk
11	Newspaper
12	Pastry
13	Rolls
14	Sugar
15	Tea
16	Yogurt

3.4.4 Transaction Storage

In Table 3.14 shows 25 transactions, we list the names of items for interest but it would be more storage efficient to use item numbers.

3.4.5 Computing L_1

To find the frequent set L_1 we count the number of times each of the 16 items has been sold. Since we wish to scan the transaction database only once, we first set up a list of items and we look at one transaction at a time and update the count of every item that appears in that transaction. We obtain the list given in Table 3.15.

Table 3.14 Transaction data for Example 3.3

TID	*Items*
1	Biscuits, Bread, Cheese, Coffee, Yogurt
2	Bread, Cereal, Cheese, Coffee
3	Cheese, Chocolate, Donuts, Juice, Milk
4	Bread, Cheese, Coffee, Cereal, Juice
5	Bread, Cereal, Chocolate, Donuts, Juice
6	Milk, Tea
7	Biscuits, Bread, Cheese, Coffee, Milk
8	Eggs, Milk, Tea
9	Bread, Cereal, Cheese, Chocolate, Coffee
10	Bread, Cereal, Chocolate, Donuts, Juice
11	Bread, Cheese, Juice
12	Bread, Cheese, Coffee, Donuts, Juice
13	Biscuits, Bread, Cereal
14	Cereal, Cheese, Chocolate, Donuts, Juice
15	Chocolate, Coffee
16	Donuts
17	Donuts, Eggs, Juice
18	Biscuits, Bread, Cheese, Coffee
19	Bread, Cereal, Chocolate, Donuts, Juice
20	Cheese, Chocolate, Donuts, Juice
21	Milk, Tea, Yogurt
22	Bread, Cereal, Cheese, Coffee
23	Chocolate, Donuts, Juice, Milk, Newspaper
24	Newspaper, Pastry, Rolls
25	Rolls, Sugar, Tea

Table 3.15 Frequency count for all items

Item no	*Item name*	*Frequency*
1	Biscuits	4
2	Bread	13
3	Cereal	10
4	Cheese	11
5	Chocolate	9
6	Coffee	9
7	Donuts	10
8	Eggs	2
9	Juice	11
10	Milk	6
11	Newspaper	2
12	Pastry	1
13	Rolls	2
14	Sugar	1
15	Tea	4
16	Yogurt	2

The items that have the necessary support (25% support in 25 transactions) must occur in at least seven transactions. The frequent 1-itemset or L_1 is now given in Table 3.16.

Table 3.16 The frequent 1-itemset or L_1

Item	*Frequency*
Bread	13
Cereal	10
Cheese	11
Chocolate	9
Coffee	9
Donuts	10
Juice	11

3.4.6 Computing C_2

Given L_1, we now form candidate pairs or C_2. The seven items in the list above form 21 pairs, or $(d)(d–1)/2$ pairs for d frequent items, shown in Table 3.17. The number of pairs in this list is a quadratic function of the number of frequent items and grows rapidly with the number of frequent items. It may also be written as L_1 X L_1 where X is a special concatenation operation. These 21 pairs are the only ones worth investigating since they are the only ones that could be frequent:

Table 3.17 The 21 candidate 2-itemsets or C_2

{Bread, Cereal}
{Bread, Cheese}
{Bread, Chocolate}
{Bread, Coffee}
{Bread, Donuts}
{Bread, Juice}
{Cereal, Cheese}
{Cereal, Chocolate}
{Cereal, Coffee}
{Cereal, Donuts}
{Cereal, Juice}
{Cheese, Chocolate}
{Cheese, Coffee}
{Cheese, Donuts}
{Cheese, Juice}
{Chocolate, Coffee}
{Chocolate, Donuts}
{Chocolate, Juice}
{Coffee, Donuts}
{Coffee, Juice}
{Donuts, Juice}

3.4.7 Computing L_2

This step is the most resource intensive step. We scan the transaction database once and look at each transaction and find out which of the candidate pairs occur in that transaction. This then requires scanning the list C_2 for every pair of items that appears in the transaction that is being scanned.

Table 3.18 presents the number of times each candidate 2-itemset appears in the example transaction database in Table 3.14.

Table 3.18 Frequency count of candidate 2-itemsets

Candidate 2-itemsets	*Frequency*
{Bread, Cereal}	9
{Bread, Cheese}	8
{Bread, Chocolate}	4
{Bread, Coffee}	8
{Bread, Donuts}	4
{Bread, Juice}	6
{Cereal, Cheese}	5
{Cereal, Chocolate}	4
{Cereal, Coffee}	5
{Cereal, Donuts}	4
{Cereal, Juice}	6
{Cheese, Chocolate}	4
{Cheese, Coffee}	9
{Cheese, Donuts}	3
{Cheese, Juice}	4
{Chocolate, Coffee}	1
{Chocolate, Donuts}	7
{Chocolate, Juice}	7
{Coffee, Donuts}	1
{Coffee, Juice}	2
{Donuts, Juice}	9

From this list we can find the frequent 2-itemsets or the set L_2. It is given in Table 3.19. Usually L_2 is smaller than L_1 but in this example they both have seven itemsets and each member of L_1 appears as a subset of some member of L_2 . This is unlikely to be true when number of items is large.

Table 3.19 The frequent 2-itemsets or L_2

Frequent 2-itemset	*Frequency*
{Bread, Cereal}	9
{Bread, Cheese}	8
{Bread, Coffee}	8
{Cheese, Coffee}	9
{Chocolate, Donuts}	7
{Chocolate, Juice}	7
{Donuts, Juice}	9

3.4.8 Computing C_3

To find the candidate 3-itemsets or C_3, we combine appropriate frequent 2-itemsets from L_2 (these must have the same first item) and obtain four such itemsets. Now we again scan the transaction database to find frequencies. These are given in Table 3.20.

Table 3.20 Candidate 3-itemsets or C_3 and their frequencies

Candidate 3-itemset	*Frequency*
{Bread, Cereal, Cheese}	4
{Bread, Cereal, Coffee}	4
{Bread, Cheese, Coffee}	8
{Chocolate, Donuts, Juice)	7

3.4.9 Computing L_3

Now Table 3.21 presents the frequent 3-itemset or L_3. Note that only one member of L_2 is not a subset of any itemset in L_3. That 2-itemset is {Bread, Cereal}.

Table 3.21 The frequent 3-itemsets or L_3

Frequent 3-itemset	*Frequency*
{Bread, Cheese, Coffee}	8
{Chocolate, Donuts, Juice)	7

This is the end of frequent itemset generation since there cannot be any candidate 4-itemsets.

3.4.10 Finding the Rules

To derive association rules, we find the rules and their confidence and proceed as follows. We know that:

$$\text{Confidence } (A \to B) = P(B \mid A) = P(A \cup B)/P(A)$$

The rules obtained from frequent 3-itemsets would always include some rules that we could obtain from L_2 embedded in them but some additional rules will be obtainable from itemsets in L_2 which are not subsets of itemsets in L_3, for example, {Bread, Cereal}. We now use a single letter for each item for brevity. Thus we write {Bread, Cheese, Coffee} as $\{B, C, D\}$ and obtain a rule $B \to CD$ which may be written as $B \to C$ and $B \to D$.

A 3-itemset, for example BCD, will always result in six possible rules, three possible association rules with one item on the left side and three rules with one item on the right side. That is:

$$\begin{aligned} B &\to CD \\ C &\to BD \\ D &\to BC \\ CD &\to B \\ BD &\to C \\ BC &\to D \end{aligned}$$

The support for all these rules is 8. We need to compute (Table 3.22) the frequencies of the left hand side itemsets to compute confidence.

Table 3.22 Confidence of association rules from {Bread, Cheese, Coffee}

Rule	*Support of BCD*	*Frequency of LHS*	*Confidence*
$B \rightarrow CD$	8	13	0.61
$C \rightarrow BD$	8	11	0.72
$D \rightarrow BC$	8	9	0.89
$CD \rightarrow B$	8	9	0.89
$BD \rightarrow C$	8	8	1.0
$BC \rightarrow D$	8	8	1.0

Confidence of all these rules, except the first one, is higher than 70% and so five association rules qualify. Similarly, looking at the other 3-itemset {Chocolate, Donuts, Juice} and writing it as $\{N, M, P\}$ we find values as given in Table 3.23.

Table 3.23 Confidence of association rules from {Chocolate, Donuts, Juice}

Rule	*Support*	*Frequency of LHS*	*Confidence*
$N \rightarrow MP$	7	9	0.78
$M \rightarrow NP$	7	10	0.70
$P \rightarrow NM$	7	11	0.64
$MP \rightarrow N$	7	9	0.78
$NP \rightarrow M$	7	7	1.0
$NM \rightarrow P$	7	7	1.0

Again, the confidence of all these rules, except the third, is higher than 70%, and so five of them also qualify.

As noted earlier, the rules obtained from L_3 do not always include all the rules that could be derived from L_2 if there are frequent 2-itemsets that are not subsets of frequent 3-itemsets. For each member of L_3 there should be three 2-itemsets in L_2 although these might overlap. We therefore need to check L_2.

The only rules that may be derived from L_2 that have not been derived already are Bread → Cereal and Cereal → Bread and they both have the confidence required.

The full list of all the rules is now given in Table 3.24.

Table 3.24 All association rules for Example 3.3

Cheese → Bread
Cheese → Coffee
Coffee → Bread
Coffee → Cheese
Cheese, Coffee → Bread
Bread, Coffee → Cheese
Bread, Cheese → Coffee
Chocolate → Donuts
Chocolate → Juice
Donuts → Chocolate
Donuts → Juice
Donuts, Juice → Chocolate
Chocolate, Juice → Donuts
Chocolate, Donuts → Juice
Bread → Cereal
Cereal → Bread

Note that we have replaced rules like Cheese → (Bread, Coffee) by two rules Cheese → Bread and Cheese → Coffee in Table 3.24. That concludes this example.

3.4.11 Comments about the Apriori Algorithm and Further Terminology

1. In the three examples that we have used so far in this chapter, we have required support of 25%, 30% and 60%. These support values are very high if the number of items and/or number of transactions is large. For example, 25% support in a supermarket transaction database of a day would mean searching for items that have been purchased by one in four customers! Not many items would probably qualify. Practical applications therefore deal with much smaller support, sometimes even down to 1% or lower.
2. *A* and *B* are related events, they are not independent so we cannot use probability theory for independent events. The interestingness of a rule $A \rightarrow B$ can in fact be related to $P(A \cup B) - P(A)\, P(B)$.
3. **Closed and maximal itemsets:** A frequent *closed* itemset is a frequent itemset *X* such that there exists no superset of *X* with the same support count as *X*. A frequent itemset *Y* is *maximal* if it is not a proper subset of any other frequent itemset. Therefore a maximal itemset is a closed itemset but a closed itemset is not necessarily a maximal itemset. In Example 3.3, we found $\{B, D\}$ and $\{B, C, D\}$ had the same support of 8 while $\{C, D\}$ had a support of 9. $\{C, D\}$ is therefore a closed itemset but not maximal. On the other hand {Bread, Cereal} was frequent but no superset of the two items is frequent. This pair therefore is maximal as well as closed.
4. **Frequent maximal itemsets:** The frequent maximal itemsets uniquely determine all frequent itemsets. Therefore the aim of any association rule algorithm is to find all maximal frequent itemsets.

Example 3.4—Closed and Maximal Itemsets

We consider an example to further demonstrate the concepts of closed frequent itemsets and maximal frequent itemsets.

Consider the transaction database in Table 3.25 with minimum support required to be 40%.

Table 3.25 A transaction database to illustrate closed and maximal itemsets

100	Bread, Cheese, Juice
200	Bread, Cheese, Juice, Milk
300	Cheese, Juice, Egg
400	Bread, Juice, Milk, Egg
500	Milk, Egg

All the frequent itemsets from transaction database in Table 3.25 are given in Table 3.26.

Table 3.26 Frequent itemsets for database in Table 3.25

Itemset	*Support*	*Closed?*	*Maximal?*	*Both?*
{Bread}	3	No	No	No
{Cheese}	3	No	No	No
{Juice}	4	Yes	No	No
{Milk}	3	Yes	No	No
{Egg}	3	Yes	No	No
{Bread, Cheese}	2	No	No	No
{Bread, Juice}	3	Yes	No	No
{Bread, Milk}	2	No	No	No
{Cheese, Juice}	3	Yes	No	No
{Juice, Milk}	2	No	No	No
{Juice, Egg}	2	Yes	Yes	Yes
{Milk, Egg}	2	Yes	Yes	Yes
{Bread, Cheese, Juice}	2	Yes	Yes	Yes
{Bread, Juice, Milk}	2	Yes	Yes	Yes

There are 14 frequent itemsets and the closed and maximal itemsets amongst them have been identified in the table. The number of closed itemsets is 9 and the number of maximal frequent itemsets is 4.

It should be noted that closed and maximal frequent itemsets are often orders of magnitude fewer than all frequent itemsets and yet all frequent itemsets and the association rules can be generated from them. Therefore an algorithm mining only the maximal frequent itemsets is likely to be efficient. The reader is encouraged to look at the maximal frequent itemsets and check whether all possible rules from this database can be derived from them.

The relationship between frequent itemsets, closed frequent itemsets and maximal frequent itemsets may be shown as in Figure 3.1.

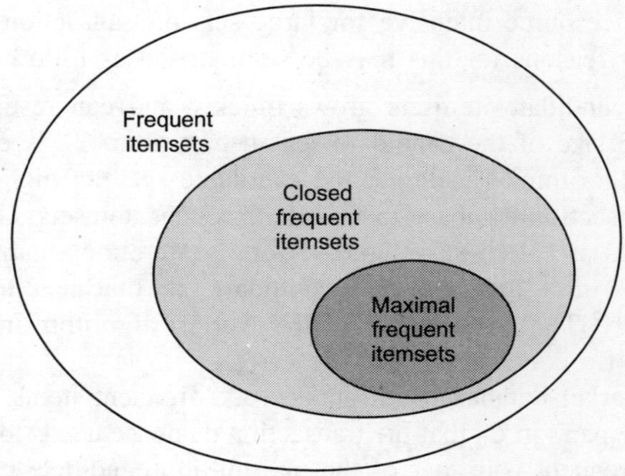

Figure 3.1 Frequent, closed and maximal itemsets.

We consider the Apriori algorithm again since it finds potentially frequent itemsets and then scans the database to find frequent itemsets. It is useful to look at the following lattice structure (Figure 3.2):

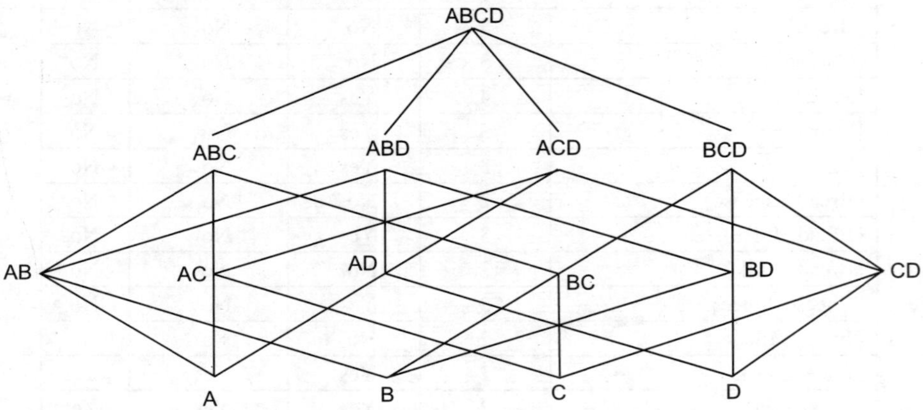

Figure 3.2 Lattice showing subsets of itemset *ABCD*.

The lattice structure shows the basic concept in association rule mining that an itemset can be frequent only if all the subsets of the itemset are frequent. For the four-itemset *ABCD* to be frequent, itemsets *ABC*, *ABD*, *ACD* and *BCD* must be frequent which in turn require that *AB*, *AC*, *AD*, *BC*, *BD* and *CD* be frequent which finally require *A*, *B*, *C* and *D* to be frequent.

Looking at the lattice we can say that the Apriori algorithm works bottom up one level at a time. It first computes frequent 1-itemsets, the candidate 2-itemsets, then frequent 2-itemsets, etc. The number of scans of the transaction database is thus equal to the maximum number of items in a candidate itemset. Thus if *ABCD* is the final candidate itemset then that would require a final scan of the transaction database whether *ABCD* is found to be frequent or not.

3.5 IMPROVING THE EFFICIENCY OF THE APRIORI ALGORITHM

.The Apriori algorithm is resource intensive for large sets of transactions that have a large set of frequent items. The major reasons for this may be summarised as follows:

1. The number of candidate itemsets grows quickly and can result in huge candidate sets. For example, the size of the candidate set, in particular C_2, is crucial to the performance of the Apriori algorithm. The larger the candidate set, the higher the processing cost for scanning the transaction database to find the frequent itemsets. Given that the early sets of candidate itemsets are often very large, the initial iterations dominate the cost. In the later stages of the algorithm, the number of candidate sets that need to be checked usually goes down dramatically. The performance of the Apriori algorithm in the later stages therefore is not so much of a concern.

   In a supermarket database with about 1000 frequent items, there will be almost one million candidate pairs in C_2 that the transaction database needs to be scanned for. Generally the number of frequent pairs out of the one million candidate pairs will be much smaller and the number of three-itemsets will be even smaller.

2. The Apriori algorithm requires many scans of the database. If n is the length of the longest itemset then $(n + 1)$ scans are required.
3. Many trivial rules (e.g. buying milk with Tic Tac) are derived and it can often be difficult to extract the most interesting rules from all the rules derived. For example, one may wish to remove all the rules involving very frequently sold items. Progress is being made in developing techniques in which constraints may be specified so that, for example, rules with the most frequent items may be pruned.
4. Some rules can be inexplicable and very fine grained, for example toothbrush was the most frequently sold item on Thursday mornings.
5. Redundant rules are generated. For example if $A \rightarrow B$ is a rule then any rule $AC \rightarrow B$ is redundant. A number of approaches have been suggested to avoid generating redundant rules.
6. The Apriori algorithm assumes sparsity since the number of items in each transaction is small compared with the total number of items. The algorithm works better with sparsity. Some applications produce dense data (i.e. many items in each transaction) which may also have many frequently occurring items. A priori is likely to be inefficient for such applications.

A number of techniques for improving the performance of the Apriori algorithm have been suggested. They can be classified in four categories:

- Reduce the number of candidate itemsets. For example, use pruning to reduce the number of candidate 3-itemsets and, if necessary, larger itemsets.
- Reduce the number of transactions. This may involve scanning the transaction data after L_1 has been computed and deleting all the transactions that do not have at least two frequent items. More transaction reduction may be done if frequent 2-itemset L_2 is small.
- Reduce the number of comparisons. There may be no need to compare every candidate against every transaction if we use an appropriate data structure.
- Generate candidate sets efficiently. For example, it may be possible to compute C_k and from it compute C'_{k+1} rather than wait for L_k to be available. One could then search for both k-itemsets and $(k + 1)$-itemsets in one pass.

We now discuss a number of algorithms that use one or more of the above approaches to improve the Apriori algorithm. The last method, the Frequent Pattern Growth, does not generate candidate itemsets and is not based on Apriori algorithm.

- Apriori-TID
- Direct Hashing and Pruning (DHP)
- Dynamic Itemset Counting (DIC)
- Frequent Pattern Growth

3.6 APRIORI-TID

Apriori-TID uses the a priori's candidate generating function to determine candidate itemsets before the beginning of a pass but it does not use the database for counting support after the first pass.

Rather it builds another, hopefully smaller, database by encoding of the candidate itemsets used in the previous pass denoted by T_k. In the first pass, T_1 corresponds to the database. In the following steps, each member of T_k corresponding to a transaction t such that it contains at least one candidate k-itemset, that is T_k is given by $\{t.TID,\ c \in C_k | c \text{ contained in } t\}$. If a transaction does not contain any candidate k-itemset, then T_k will not have an entry for that transaction. The size of T_k is therefore expected to be smaller, in particular as k grows, than the number of transactions in the original transaction database. Also, for large k values, each entry in T_k is likely to be smaller than the corresponding transaction, as few candidates would be expected to be contained in each transaction. However, for small values of k, each entry may be larger than the corresponding transaction as we show in the example below.

The a priori-TID algorithm is outlined below:

1. The entire transaction database is scanned to obtain T_1 in terms of itemsets (i.e. each entry of T_1 contains all items in the transaction along with the corresponding TID).
2. Frequent 1-itemset L_1 is calculated with the help of T_1.
3. C_2 is obtained by applying the a priori-gen function discussed under the Apriori algorithm.
4. The support for the candidates in C_2 is then calculated by using T_1.
5. Entries in T_2 are then calculated.
6. L_2 is then generated from C_2 by the usual means and then C_3 can be generated from L_2.
7. T_3 is then generated with the help of T_2 and C_3. This process is repeated until the set of candidate k-itemsets is an empty set.

Example 3.5—Apriori-TID

We consider the transactions in Example 3.2 again. As a first step, T_1 is generated by scanning the database. It is assumed throughout the algorithm that the itemsets in each transaction are sorted in lexicographical order. T_1 is essentially the same as the whole database, the only difference being that each of the itemsets in a transaction is represented as a set of one item.

As in Example 3.2, we will use minimum support of 50% and minimum confidence of 75%.

Step 1: We first scan the entire database and obtain T_1 by treating each item as a 1-itemset. This is given in Table 3.27.

Table 3.27 The transaction database T_1

Transaction ID	*Items*
100	{Bread} {Cheese} {Eggs} {Juice}
200	{Bread} {Cheese} {Juice}
300	{Bread} {Milk} {Yogurt}
400	{Bread} {Juice} {Milk}
500	{Cheese} {Juice} {Milk}

Steps 2 and 3: The next step is to generate L_1. This is generated with the help of T_1. C_2 is calculated as previously in the Apriori algorithm. See Table 3.28.

Table 3.28 The sets L_1 and C_2

L_1		C_2
Itemset	*Support*	*Itemset*
{Bread}	4	$\{B, C\}$
{Cheese}	3	$\{B, J\}$
{Juice}	4	$\{B, M\}$
{Milk}	3	$\{C, J\}$
		$\{C, M\}$
		$\{J, M\}$

In Table 3.28, we have used single letters B(Bread), C(Cheese), J(Juice) and M(Milk) for C_2.

Step 4: The support for itemsets in C_2 is now calculated with the help of T_1, instead of scanning the actual database as in the Apriori algorithm and the result is shown in Table 3.29.

Table 3.29 Frequency of itemsets in C_2

Itemset	*Frequency*
$\{B, C\}$	2
$\{B, J\}$	3
$\{B, M\}$	2
$\{C, J\}$	3
$\{C, M\}$	1
$\{J, M\}$	2

Step 5: We now find T_2 by using C_2 and T_1 as shown in Table 3.30.

Table 3.30 Transaction database T_2

TID	*Set-of-itemsets*
100	$\{\{B, C\}, \{B, J\}, \{C, J\}\}$
200	$\{\{B, C\}, \{B, J\}, \{C, J\}\}$
300	$\{\{B, M\}\}$
400	$\{\{B, J\}, \{B, M\}, \{J, M\}\}$
500	$\{\{C, J\}, \{C, M\}, \{J, M\}\}$

$\{B, J\}$ and $\{C, J\}$ are the frequent pairs and they make up L_2. C_3 may now be generated but we find that C_3 is empty. If it was not empty we would have used it to find T_3 with the help of the transaction set T_2. That would have results in a smaller T_3 and it might have resulted in the removal of a transaction or two (e.g. TID 300) from T_2. This is the end of this simple example.

The generation of association rules from the derived frequent set can be done in the usual way.

The main advantage of the a priori-TID algorithm is that the size of T_k is usually smaller than the transactions database. Furthermore, each entry in T_k may be smaller, in some cases significantly smaller, than the entry in the corresponding transaction for larger k values. Since the support for each candidate k-itemset is counted with the help of the corresponding T_k, the algorithm is often faster than the basic Apriori algorithm.

It should be noted that both a priori and a priori-TID use the same candidate generation algorithm, and therefore they count the same itemsets. Experiments have shown that the Apriori algorithm runs more efficiently during the earlier phases of the algorithm because for small values of k, each entry in T_k may be larger than the corresponding entry in the transaction database. However, in the later phases, a priori-TID becomes more efficient than the Apriori algorithm because the number of candidate itemsets reduces in the later stages of the algorithm while a priori still examines every transaction in the database. When T_k can fit in memory, then the process becomes even more efficient, because the cost of writing data to the disk is not incurred.

3.7 DIRECT HASHING AND PRUNING (DHP)

This algorithm proposes overcoming some of the weaknesses of the Apriori algorithm by reducing the number of candidate k-itemsets, in particular the 2-itemsets, since that is the key to improving performance. Also, as noted earlier, as k increases, not only is there a smaller number of frequent k-itemsets but there are fewer transactions containing these itemsets. Thus it should not be necessary to scan the whole transaction database as k becomes larger than 2.

The direct hashing and pruning (DHP) algorithm claims to be efficient in generation of frequent itemsets and effective in trimming the transaction database by discarding items from the transactions or removing whole transactions that do not need to be scanned. The algorithm uses a hash-based technique to reduce the number of candidate itemsets generated in the first pass (that is, a significantly smaller C_2 is constructed), it is claimed that the number of itemsets in C_2 generated using DHP can be orders of magnitude smaller, so that the scan required to determine L_2 is more efficient.

The algorithm may be divided into the following three parts. The Part 1 finds all frequent 1-itemsets and all candidate 2-itemsets. The second part is the more general part including hashing and the third part is without the hashing. Both the second and the third part include pruning. Part 2 is used for early iterations and Part 3 for later iterations.

Part 1—Essentially the algorithm goes through each transaction counting all 1-itemsets. At the same time all possible 2-itemsets in the current transaction are hashed to a hash table. The algorithm uses the hash table in the next pass to reduce the number of candidate itemsets. Each bucket in the hash table has a count, which is increased by one each time an itemset is hashed to that bucket. Collisions can occur when different itemsets are hashed to the same bucket. A bit vector is associated with the hash table to provide a flag for each bucket. If the bucket count is equal or above the minimum support count, the corresponding flag in the bit vector is set to 1, otherwise it is set to 0.

Part 2—This part has two phases. In the first phase, C_k is generated. In the Apriori algorithm C_k is generated by L_{k-1} X L_{k-1} but the DHP algorithm uses the hash table to reduce the number of candidate itemsets in C_k. An item is included in C_k only if the corresponding bit in the hash table bit vector has been set, that is the number of items hashed to the location is greater than the support. Although having the corresponding bit vector bit se does not guarantee that the itemset is frequent due to collisions but the hash table filtering does reduce C_k significantly. Each itemset that passes the hash filtering is a member of C_k and is stored in a hash tree, which is used to count the support for each itemset in the second phase of Part 2.

In the second phase, the hash table for the next step is generated. Both in the support counting and when the hash table is generated, pruning of the database is carried out. Only itemsets that are important to future steps are kept in the database. An k-itemset is not considered useful in a frequent $k + 1$ itemset unless it appears at least k times in a transaction. The pruning not only trims each transaction by removing unwanted itemsets but also removes transactions that have no itemsets that could be frequent.

Part 3—The third part of the algorithm continues until there are no more candidate itemsets. Instead of using a hash table to find frequent itemsets, the transaction database is now scanned to find the support count for each itemset. The database is likely to be now significantly smaller because of the pruning. When the support count is established the algorithm determines the frequent itemsets as before by checking against the minimum support. The algorithm then generates candidate itemsets like the Apriori algorithm does.

Example 3.6—DHP Algorithm

We now use an example to illustrate the DHP algorithm. The transaction database is the same as we used in Example 3.2. We want to find association rules that satisfy 50% support and 75% confidence. Table 3.31 presents the transaction database and Table 3.32 presents possible 2-itemsets for each transaction.

Table 3.31 Transaction database for Example 3.6

Transaction ID	*Items*
100	Bread, Cheese, Eggs, Juice
200	Bread, Cheese, Juice
300	Bread, Milk, Yogurt
400	Bread, Juice, Milk
500	Cheese, Juice, Milk

We will use letters B(Bread), C(Cheese), E(Egg), J(Juice), M(Milk) and Y(Yogurt) in Tables 3.32 to 3.35.

Table 3.32 Possible 2-itemsets

100	(B, C) (B, E) (B, J) (C, E) (C, J) (E, J)
200	(B, C) (B, J) (C, J)
300	(B, M) (B, Y) (M, Y)
400	(B, J) (B, M) (J, M)
500	(C, J) (C, M) (J, M)

The possible 2-itemsets in Table 3.32 are now hashed to a hash table. The last column shown in Table 3.33 is not required in the hash table but we have included it for explaining the technique.

Assuming a hash table of size 8 and using a very simple hash function described below leads to the hash Table 3.33.

Table 3.33 Hash table for 2-itemsets

Bit vector	*Bucket number*	*Count*	*Pairs*	C_2
1	0	3	(*C*, *J*) (*B*, *Y*) (*M*, *Y*)	(*C*, *J*)
0	1	1	(*C*, *M*)	
0	2	1	(*E*, *J*)	
0	3	0		
0	4	2	(*B*, *C*)	
1	5	3	(*B*, *E*) (*J*, *M*)	(*J*, *M*)
1	6	3	(*B*, *J*)	(*B*, *J*)
1	7	3	(*C*, *E*) (*B*, *M*)	(*B*, *M*)

The simple hash function is obtained as follows:

- For each pair, a numeric value is obtained by first representing *B* by 1, *C* by 2, *E* by 3, *J* by 4, *M* by 5 and *Y* by 6 and then representing each pair by a two digit number, for example (*B*, *E*) by 13 and (*C*, *M*) by 26.
- The two digits are then coded as modulo 8 number (dividing by 8 and using the remainder). This is the bucket address.

For a support of 50%, the frequent items are *B*, *C*, *J* and *M*. This is L_1 which leads to C_2 of (*B*, *C*), (*B*, *J*), (*B*, *M*), (*C*, *J*), (*C*, *M*) and (*J*, *M*). These candidate pairs are then hashed to the hash table and pairs that hash to locations where the bit vector bit is not set are removed. Table 3.33 shows that (*B*, *C*) and (*C*, *M*) can be removed from C_2. We are therefore left with the four candidate item pairs or the reduced C_2 given in the last column of the hash table in Table 3.33. We now look at the transaction database and modify it to include only these candidate pairs (Table 3.34):

Table 3.34 Transaction database with candidate 2-itemsets

100	(*B*, *J*) (*C*, *J*)
200	(*B*, *J*) (*C*, *J*)
300	(*B*, *M*)
400	(*B*, *J*) (*B*, *M*)
500	(*C*, *J*) (*J*, *M*)

It is now necessary to count support for each pair and while doing it further trim the database by removing items and deleting transactions that will not appear in frequent 3-itemsets. The frequent pairs are (*B*, *J*) and (*C*, *J*). The candidate 3-itemsets must have two pairs with the first item being the same. Only transaction 400 qualifies since it has candidate pairs (*B*, *J*) and (*B*, *M*). Others can therefore be deleted and the transaction database now looks like Table 3.35.

Table 3.35 Reduced transaction database

400	(*B*, *J*, *M*)

In this simple example we can now conclude that (*B*, *J*, *M*) is the only potential frequent 3-itemset but it cannot qualify since transaction 400 does not have the pair (*J*, *M*) and the pairs (*J*, *M*) and (*B*, *M*) are not frequent pairs. That concludes this example.

The DHP algorithm usually performs better than the Apriori algorithm during the initial stages, especially during L_2 generation. Added to this improvement is also the feature that trims and prunes the transaction set progressively, thereby improving the overall efficiency of the algorithm. The startup phase of DHP does consume some extra resources when the hash table is constructed but this is outweighed by the advantages gained during the later phases when both the number of candidate itemsets and the transaction set are reduced.

Efficiency

As one of the major aims of the algorithm is to reduce the size of C_2, it is essential that the hash table is large enough so that collisions are low. If the hash table is small and collisions are high, more than one itemset will hash to most buckets resulting in loss of effectiveness of the hash table in reducing the number of candidate itemsets in C_2. This is what happened in the example above in which we had collisions in three of the eight buckets. If the minimum support count is low, it is even more important that all collisions be avoided. Also, it is best to ensure that the hash table resides in the main memory. If the hash table does not fit in the main memory, additional disk I/O costs will apply which may again reduce the efficiency.

The algorithm is most efficient when the number of itemsets for L_2 is a lot smaller than C_2 generated by a priori. Reduction in database size will also then have an impact on the efficiency of the algorithm. Because of this efficient pruning of the database, the algorithm can achieve a significantly shorter execution time than the Apriori algorithm.

3.8 DYNAMIC ITEMSET COUNTING (DIC)

As noted earlier, the Apriori algorithm must do as many scans of the transaction database as the number of items in the last candidate itemset that was checked for its support. The Dynamic Itemset Counting (DIC) algorithm reduces the number of scans required by not just doing one scan for the frequent 1-itemset and another for the frequent 2-itemset but combining the counting for a number of itemsets as soon it appears that it might be necessary to count it.

The basic algorithm is as follows:

1. Divide the transaction database into a number of say q partitions.
2. Start counting 1-itemsets in the first partition of the transaction database.
3. At the beginning of the second partition, continue counting the 1-itemsets but also start counting 2-itemsets using the frequent 1-itemsets from the first partition.
4. At the beginning of the third partition, continue counting the 1-itemsets and 2-itemsets but also start counting 3-itemsets using results from the first two partitions.
5. Continue like this until the whole database has been scanned once. We now have the final set of frequent 1-itemsets.
6. Go back to the beginning of the transaction database and continue counting 2-itemsets and 3-itemsets, etc.
7. At the end of the first partition in the second scan of the database, we have scanned the whole database for 2-itemsets and thus have the final set of frequent 2-itemsets.
8. Continue the process in a similar way until there are no frequent k-itemsets are found.

DIC algorithm works well when the data is relatively homogeneous throughout the file since it starts the 2-itemset count before having a final 1-itemset count. If the data distribution is not homogeneous, the algorithm may not identify an itemset to be large until most of the database has been scanned. In such cases it may be possible to randomise the transaction data although this is not always possible. Essentially DIC attempts to finish the itemset counting in two scans of the database while a priori would often take three or more scans.

3.9 MINING FREQUENT PATTERNS WITHOUT CANDIDATE GENERATION (FP-GROWTH)

This algorithm uses an approach that is different than that used by methods based on Apriori algorithm. The major difference between frequent pattern-growth (FP-growth) and the other algorithms is that FP-growth does not generate the candidates, it only tests. In contrast the Apriori algorithm generates the candidate itemsets and then tests.

The motivation for the FP-tree method is as follows:

- Only frequent items are needed to find the association rules so it is best to find the frequent items and ignore the others.
- If the frequent items can be stored in a compact structure then the original transaction database does not need to be used repeatedly.
- If multiple transactions share a set of frequent items, it may be possible to merge the shared sets with the number of occurrences registered as count.

To be able to do this, the algorithm involves generating a frequent pattern tree (FP-tree).

Generating a FP-tree

The algorithm works as follows:

1. Scan the transaction database once, as in the Apriori algorithm, to find all frequent items and their support.
2. Sort the frequent items in descending order of their support.
3. Initially, start creating the FP-tree with a root "null".
4. Get the first transaction from the transaction database. Remove all non-frequent items and list the remaining items according to the order in the sorted frequent items.
5. Use the transaction to construct the first branch of the tree with each node corresponding to a frequent item and showing that items frequency, which is 1 for the first transaction.
6. Get the next transaction from the transaction database. Remove all non-frequent items and list the remaining items according to the order in the sorted frequent items.
7. Insert the transaction in the tree using any common prefix that may appear. Increase the item counts.
8. Continue with Step 6 until all transactions in the database are processed.

We show building of a FP-tree using an example.

Example 3.7—FP-Tree

We again use the transaction database in Example 3.2 as shown in Table 2.36. The minimum support required is again 50% and confidence is 75%.

Table 3.36 Transaction database for Example 3.7

Transaction ID	*Items*
100	Bread, Cheese, Eggs, Juice
200	Bread, Cheese, Juice
300	Bread, Milk, Yogurt
400	Bread, Juice, Milk
500	Cheese, Juice, Milk

The frequent items sorted by their frequency as shown in Table 3.37.

Table 3.37 Frequent items for database in Table 3.36.

Item	*Frequnecy*
Bread	4
Juice	4
Cheese	3
Milk	3

Now we remove the items that are not frequent from the transactions and order the items according to their frequency as above (Table 3.38).

Table 3.38 Database after removing non-frequent items and reordering

Transaction ID	*Items*
100	Bread, Juice, Cheese
200	Bread, Juice, Cheese
300	Bread, Milk
400	Bread, Juice, Milk
500	Juice, Cheese, Milk

In a large transaction database, Table 3.37 will be much smaller than Table 3.36.

We start building the FP-tree now. We use symbols *B*, *J*, *C*, *M* for the items.

The item-header table on the left-hand side of the tree is to help in tree traversal, as we will see later. Each item in this list points to its first occurrence in the FP-tree. Nodes with the same item name in the tree are linked via dotted node-links.

The FP-tree is compact and often orders of magnitude smaller than the transaction database. Once the FP-tree is constructed, the transaction database is not required.

An FP-tree consists of nodes. A node contains three fields: an item name, a count, and a node link as illustrated in Figure 3.3. The count tells the number of occurrences the path (constructed from the root node to this node) has in the transaction database. The node link is a link to the next node in the FP-tree containing the same item name or a null pointer if this node is the last one with this name. The FP-tree also consists of a header table with an entry for each itemset and a link to the first item in the tree with the same name. This linking is done to make traversal of the tree more efficient.

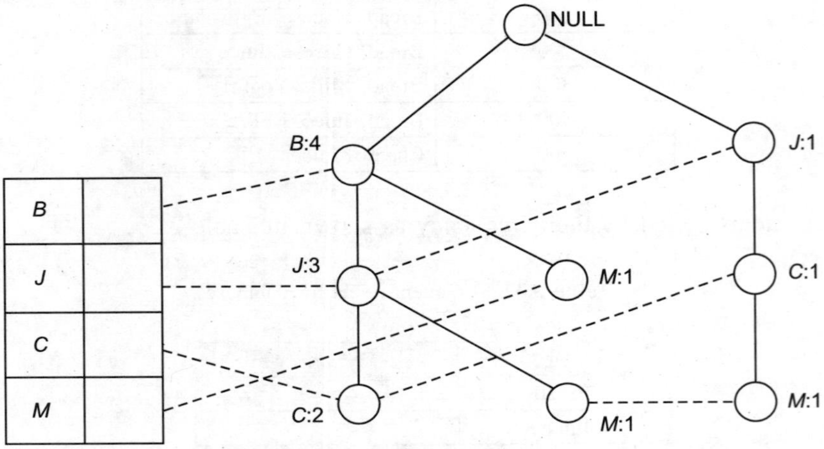

Figure 3.3 FP-tree for Example 3.7.

The tree is built by making a root node labelled null. A node is made for each frequent item in the first transaction and the count is set to 1. The nodes near the root in the tree are more frequent than those further down the tree. The algorithm goes through all sorted transactions, which includes second scan of the database. If the path already exists in the tree, a counter is increased; otherwise a new node is inserted into the tree with a count of 1. Each identical path is only stored in the FP-tree once, which often makes the size of an FP-tree smaller than the corresponding transactional database. The height of an FP-tree is always equal to the maximum number of itemsets in a transaction excluding the root node.

Mining the FP-tree for frequent items

To find the frequent itemsets we should note that for any frequent item a, all the frequent itemsets containing a can be obtained by following a's node-links, starting from a's head in the FP-tree header.

The mining on the FP-tree structure is done using an algorithm called the frequent pattern growth (FP-growth). This algorithm starts with the least frequent item, that is the last item in the header table. Then it finds all the paths from the root to this item and adjusts the count according to this item's support count.

We first look at using the FP-tree in Figure 3.3 built in the example earlier to find frequent itemsets. We start with item M and find the following patterns:

$BM(1)$
$BJM(1)$
$JCM(1)$

No frequent itemset is discovered from these since no itemset appears three times. Next we look at *C* and find the following:

BJC(2)

JC(1)

These two patterns give us a frequent itemset *JC*(3). Looking at *J*, the next frequent item in the table, we obtain:

BJ(3)

J(1)

Again we obtain a frequent itemset, *BJ*(3). There is no need to follow links from item *B* and there are no other frequent itemsets.

The process above may be represented by the following "conditional" trees for *M*, *C* and *J* in Figures 3.4, 3.5 and 3.6.

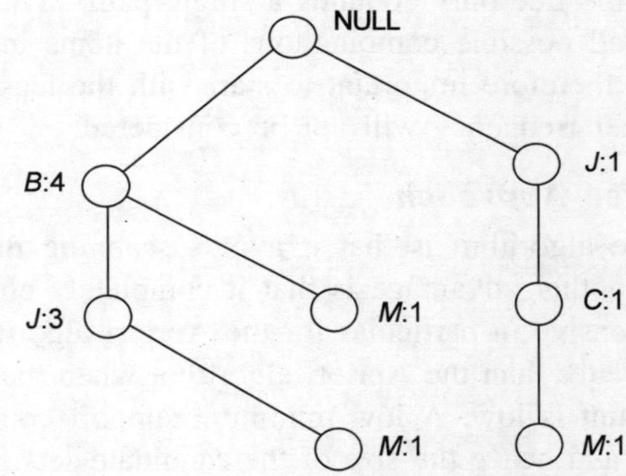

Figure 3.4 Conditional tree for *M*.

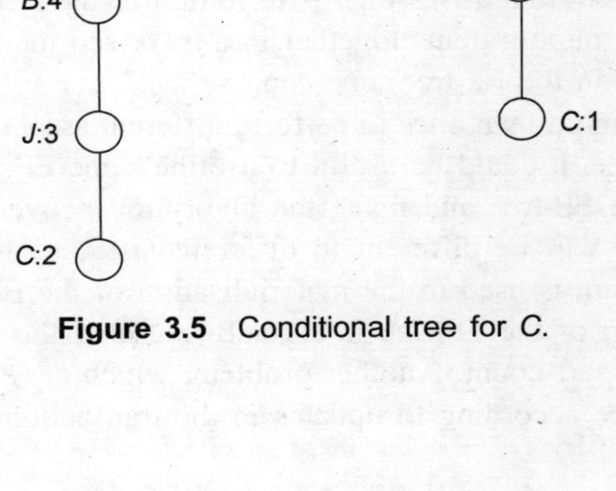

Figure 3.5 Conditional tree for *C*.

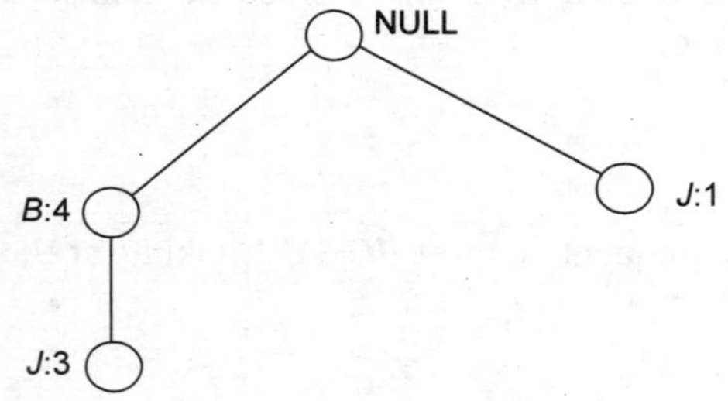

Figure 3.6 Conditional tree for *J*.

We now describe this procedure in algorithmic form. The algorithm finds the conditional pattern base for each item. The conditional pattern base of an item consists of all patterns leading to the specific item. Then the conditional frequent pattern tree is constructed from the conditional pattern base where only the frequent items are included. This conditional FP-tree also contains a header table. Then the algorithm is called again with this new conditional FP-tree. This recursion is ended when the tree is empty or if the tree only contains a single path. When the tree only contains one path, the algorithm will find all possible combinations of the items in the itemset that support the minimum support count. It is therefore important to start with the least frequent item the first time otherwise the items with higher frequency will not be considered.

Advantages of the FP–tree Approach

One advantage of the FP-tree algorithm is that it avoids scanning the database more than twice to find the support counts. Another advantage is that it completely eliminates the costly candidate generation, which can be expensive in particular for the Apriori algorithm for the candidate set C_2. The FP-growth algorithm is better than the Apriori algorithm when the transaction database is huge and the minimum support count is low. A low minimum support count means that a lot of items will satisfy the support count and hence the size of the candidate sets for a priori will be large. FP-growth uses a more efficient structure to mine patterns when the database grows.

Further improvements

In spite of these advantages there are possibilities to make the algorithm even more efficient and scalable. This algorithm works best if the FP-tree fits in main memory. However, in large databases this will not always be possible. There are two solutions proposed to overcome this problem. The first divides the database and then constructs a FP-tree for each of the databases. The second constructs a FP-tree on disk. One problem that arises then is to minimize the I/O cost. Removing all the node-links from the FP-tree and grouping items together in a traversed manner can reduce this cost. Also to get faster access to items in the FP-tree, one can use a B^+-tree to index the FP-tree.

If the same data is used more than once to perform different association rule mining perhaps with different minimum confidence, it could be useful to use the same FP-tree results. This will save the initial cost of generating the FP-tree and make the algorithm in overall more efficient. Sometimes the minimum support count will be different in different tasks, so to overcome this problem, the lowest minimum support count is used in the materialisation of the FP-tree. When a higher support count is wanted only the top of the FP-tree is used. Because of the organisation of the FP-tree, it is easy to have different support count. Another problem, which arises with a materialisation of the tree is how to update the tree according to updates in the transactional database.

3.10 PERFORMANCE EVALUATION OF ALGORITHMS

Performance evaluation of a number of implementations of different association mining algorithms has been carried out. In one study that compared a number of methods including a priori, CHARM (an algorithm for enumerating all closed itemsets) and FP-growth methods using real world data as well as artificial data, it was concluded that:

(a) The FP-growth method was usually better than the best implementation of the Apriori algorithm.
(b) CHARM was also usually better than a priori. In some cases, CHARM was better than FP-growth method.
(c) Apriori was generally better than other algorithms if the support required was high since high support leads to a smaller number of frequent items which suits the Apriori algorithm.
(d) At very low support, the number of frequent items became large and none of the algorithms was able to handle large frequent sets gracefully.

Another more comprehensive annual evaluation of software that implements association rule mining algorithms was started in 2003. The first Frequent Itemset Mining Implementations (FIMI) workshop was held in 2003 and the second was held in November 2004. These evaluations have provided many new and surprising insights into association rule mining. In the 2003 performance evaluation of programs, it was found that two algorithms were perhaps the best. These were:

(a) An efficient implementation of the FP-tree algorithm
(b) An algorithm that combined a number of algorithms using multiple heuristics

The performance evaluation also included algorithms for closed itemset mining as well as for maximal itemset mining. The performance evaluation in 2004 found an implementation of an algorithm that involves a novel tree traversal as the most efficient algorithm for finding frequent, frequent closed and maximal frequent itemsets.

SUMMARY

We have introduced the association rules mining problem and have presented the classical Apriori algorithm. Association rule mining is an interesting problem with many applications. The algorithm used is conceptually simple and the resulting rules are clear and understandable. The algorithms work on data of variable length.

The process of mining association rules can be made more efficient than the Apriori algorithm. Some of the proposed algorithms make changes to the existing Apriori algorithm like a priori-TID and DHP, while others present completely new solutions like FP-growth. In performance evaluation of many algorithms it is becoming clear that tree-based algorithms perform the best although how efficient an algorithm is also depends on the nature and size of the data in the database and the minimum support count required. More research is being carried out on further improving all these algorithms.

It should be noted that lowering the support threshold results in many more frequent itemsets and often increases the number of candidate itemsets and maximum length of frequent itemsets resulting in cost increases. Also, in case of denser datasets (i.e. those with many items in each transaction) the maximum length of frequent itemsets is often higher and therefore the cost of finding the association rules is higher.

One of the major problems in association rules mining is the large number of rules discovered. To overcome this a variety of algorithms that use constraints have been proposed. For example, it has been proposed that constraints be specified for each rule to provide a minimum improvement than the confidence of any of its proper subset-rules. In such algorithms one specifies not only minimum support and minimum confidence but also minimum improvement. Other proposed algorithms involve specifying the maximum number of rules to be found. A new term, succinctness, has been coined to label only those itemsets which satisfy the constraints.

Software for Association Rule Mining

Packages like Clementine and IBM Intelligent Miner include comprehensive association rule mining software. We present some software designed for association rules.

- A priori, FP-growth, Eclat and DIC implementations by Bart Goethals. The algorithms generate all frequent itemsets for a given minimal support threshold and for a given minimal confidence threshold. (Free)
  http://www.adrem.ua.ac.be/~goethals/software/index.html
- ARMiner is a client-server data mining application specialised in finding association rules. ARMiner has been written in Java and it is distributed under the GNU General Public License. ARMiner has been developed at UMass/Boston as a Software Engineering project in Spring 2000.
  http://www.cs.umb.edu/~laur/ARMiner/
- ARtool has also been developed at UMass/Boston. It a collection of algorithms and tools for the mining of association rules in binary databases. Distributed under the GNU General Public License.
  http://www.cs.umb.edu/~laur/ARtool/
- Magnum Opus (marketed by Rulequest Research) employs k-most-interesting rule discovery techniques. Developed by Geoff Webb of Monash University. Claims to discard spurious rules.
  http://www.rulequest.com/index.html
- FIMI, Frequent Itemset Mining Implementations repository is the result of the workshops on Frequent Itemset Mining Implementations, FIMI'03 and FIMI'04 which took place at IEEE ICDM'03, and IEEE ICDM'04 respectively.
  http://fimi.cs.helsinki.fi/

REVIEW QUESTIONS

1. What is the aim of association rule mining? Why is this aim important in some applications? (Section 3.1)
2. Define the concepts of support and confidence. Define these concepts using probabilities. Why do we need those concepts? (Section 3.2)
3. Define lift. What is the relation between support, confidence and lift of an association rule $X \rightarrow Y$? (Section 3.2)

4. In our examples, we have used support and confidence figures such that minimum confidence required is always higher than the minimum support required. Is this necessary? What does it mean if the minimum confidence required is lower than the minimum support required? (Section 3.2)
5. Explain the Naïve algorithm for finding association rules. (Section 3.3)
6. Prove that all nonempty subsets of a frequent itemset must also be frequent. (Section 3.4)
7. What is the weakness of the Naïve algorithm? (Section 3.4)
8. Show how the Apriori algorithm works on an example dataset. (Section 3.4)
9. What is the basis of the Apriori algorithm? Describe the algorithm briefly. Which step of the algorithm can become a bottleneck? (Section 3.4)
10. What are closed and maximal itemsets? What is their relevance to association rule mining? (Section 3.4)
11. List some ways of improving the Apriori algorithm. What is pruning? (Section 3.5)
12. What does a priori-TID do? Is it an improvement of the a priori Method? (Section 3.6)
13. The Direct Hashing and Pruning (DHP) algorithm is quite a different approach to ARM. Analyse the effectiveness of DHP. (Section 3.7)
14. What is Dynamic Itemset Counting (DIC)? Explain the algorithm. (Section 3.8)
15. Show using an example how FP-tree algorithm solves the ARM problem. (Section 3.9)
16. Which methods have been evaluated? Which ones were found to be efficient? (Section 3.10)

EXERCISES

1. Define support and confidence for an association rule.
2. The Apriori algorithm makes use of prior knowledge of subset support properties.
   (a) Prove that all nonempty subsets of a frequent itemset must also be frequent.
   (b) Prove that the support of any nonempty subset s' of itemset s must be as great as the support for s.
3. The Apriori algorithm makes use of prior knowledge of subset support properties:
   (a) Prove that all nonempty subsets of a frequent itemset must also be frequent.
   (b) Prove that the support of any nonempty subset of itemset must be as great as the support for the itemset.
   (c) If a database D of transactions is divided into n nonoverlapping partitions, prove that any itemset that is frequent in D must be frequent in at least one partition of D.
   (d) Prove that if an association rule $A \rightarrow B$ holds then the rule $B \rightarrow A$ may or may not hold.

(e) Consider the following four transactions:

T100	*K, A, D, B*
T200	*D, A, C, E, B*
T300	*C, A, B, E*
T400	*B, A, D*

Assuming minimum support of 60% and minimum confidence of 80%, find all frequent items and list all association rules using the Apriori algorithm.

4. Consider the following transactions for association rules analysis:

TransactionID	*Date*	*Items*
100	10/1/2000	Bread, Milk, Juice, Cheese
200	12/1/2000	Bread, Milk, Cheese
300	20/2/2000	Bread, Milk
400	25/2/2000	Bread, Cheese, Juice

(a) Use the Apriori algorithm for finding frequently itemsets with minimum support of 90% and minimum confidence of 90%.

(b) Repeat the algorithm for minimum support of 40% and minimum confidence of 90%.

5. Use the Apriori algorithm for finding frequently itemsets, given the following data from a transactional database. Minimum Support = 30%. Minimum Confidence = 70%

Transaction Database (D)

Transaction ID	*Items*
T1	Pencil, Eraser, Sharpener
T2	Eraser, Sharpener, Ruler
T3	Eraser
T4	Pencil, Eraser

6. How many operations it will take if there were a million transactions in a database that was being analysed for association rules?

7. Suppose that frequent itemsets and association rules are saved for a large transaction database. Discuss how to efficiently mine the (global) association rules under the same minimum support and confidence threshold, if a set of new transactions is added to the database.

8. Show that if the rule $ABC \rightarrow D$ does not have the minimum confidence required then rules like $AB \rightarrow CD$, $A \rightarrow BCD$ and $C \rightarrow ABD$ will also not have the minimum confidence.

9. Show that if the rule $A \rightarrow BCD$ has the minimum confidence required then rules like $AB \rightarrow CD$ and $ABC \rightarrow D$ will also have the minimum confidence.

10. What does the lattice structure of itemsets show?

11. Discuss frequent itemsets, closed frequent itemsets and maximal frequent itemsets. Which one is the most common and which one is least common? How are these concepts useful in solving the association rules problem?

12. Explain the association rule mining problem. Consider an example with the following set of transactions. There are 10 items.

TID	*Items bought*
001	*B, M, T, Y*
002	*B, M*
003	*A, T, S, P*
004	*A, B, C, D*
005	*A, B*
006	*T, Y, E, M*
007	*A, B, M*
008	*B, C, D, T, P*
009	*D, T, S*
010	*A, B, M*

13. Assume that we wish to find association rules with at least 30% support and 60% confidence. Find the frequent itemsets and then the association rules.
14. Consider the data in the last example and answer the following:
    (a) How many 3-itemsets are possible?
    (b) How many 4-itemsets are possible?
    (c) What is the maximum size of frequent itemsets possible in this dataset?
15. How can the efficiency of a priori method for association rules be improved?
16. Explain how the hashing method will work. Estimate how much work will be needed to compute association rules compared to a priori. Make suitable assumptions.
17. Explain how transaction reduction might work. Estimate how much saving can be made using this method. Make suitable assumptions.

MULTIPLE CHOICE QUESTIONS

1. Which one of the following is true?
   (a) Support and confidence are the same
   (b) Frequent itemset and a candidate itemset are the same
   (c) Apriori algorithm may be used for supervised classification
   (d) Association rule mining should not be used for medical applications
2. Which one of the following $X \rightarrow Y$ rule is the least interesting from a business point of view?
   (a) Support(X, Y) = 80% and Confidence $(X \rightarrow Y)$ = 75%
   (b) Support(X, Y) = 10% and Confidence $(X \rightarrow Y)$ = 80%
   (c) Support(X, Y) = 1% and Confidence $(X \rightarrow Y)$ = 90%
   (d) Support(X, Y) = 50% and Confidence $(X \rightarrow Y)$ = 50%
3. Let the support of three items X, Y and Z together be 20%. Which one of the following must be true about support for the two pairs X and Y and Y and Z?
   (a) Support(X, Y) = 20%

(b) Support(Y, Z) = 20%
(c) Support (X, Y) ≥ 20%
(d) Support (X, Y) < 20%

4. Let the support of the three itemsets (p, q, r), (p, r, t) and (p, q, s) be above the minimum support required. Now in attempting to find frequent 4-itemsets which of the following itemsets must be looked at?
   (a) (p, q, r, s)
   (b) (p, s, q, t)
   (c) (p, q, s, t)
   (d) (p, q, r, t)
5. Which one of the following makes the brute force approach to finding association rules not viable?
   (a) Too many items
   (b) Too many transactions
   (c) Too many itemset combinations
   (d) Too many rules
6. Which one of the following is not true about association rule mining?
   (a) Support of X is equal to the number of times X occurs in the transactions
   (b) An item is frequent if it meets the minimum support specified
   (c) An association rule is confident if its confidence is above the user specified minimum confidence
   (d) A candidate set of itemsets is potentially frequent set of itemsets
7. Three frequent pairs (p, q), (r, s) and (t, u) have been found in association rule mining. What is the maximum number of rules that may be derived from these three pairs?
   (a) 3
   (b) 4
   (c) 6
   (d) 8
8. Three frequent pairs (p, q), (r, s) and (t, u) have been found in association rule mining. What is the minimum number of rules that may be derived from these three pairs?
   (a) 0
   (b) 1
   (c) 3
   (d) 6
9. Given the association rules $A \rightarrow CD$ and $PQ \rightarrow R$ which one of the following is **not** true?
   (a) $A \rightarrow C$
   (b) $A \rightarrow D$
   (c) $P \rightarrow R$
   (d) $Q \rightarrow R$
   (e) $Q \rightarrow PR$

10. A very large dataset of transactions has been stored on a disk. A quarter of the dataset at a time can be brought into the main memory and analysed to find frequent itemsets. To find frequent itemsets for the full dataset, which one of the following is correct?
    (a) A frequent itemset need not be frequent in any of the four quarters of the dataset to be frequent in the whole dataset.
    (b) A frequent itemset in only one quarter of the dataset can be frequent in the whole dataset.
    (c) A frequent itemset must exist in at least two quarters of the dataset to be frequent in the whole dataset.
    (d) A frequent itemset must exist in all four quarters of the dataset to be frequent in the whole dataset.

PROJECT 1—USING ARM FOR TABLE 1.1

Consider Table 1.1. Suppose we want to consider if any two attributes values occur together. May be high literacy rate is almost always found with high GDP per capita. How do we use ARM in analyzing the data in Table 1.1?

- First explain how the data in Table 1.1 needs to be transformed for using ARM? (Hint: ARM does not deal with numerical values. Therefore all attributes in the table must be converted to non-numeric values.)
- Now write down some objectives for analyzing the data in the table using ARM.
- Use ARM software from Weka and analyse the data.
- Discuss the results.
- Which association rules obtained by applying ARM to Table 1A are the most significant and why?

PROJECT 2—DESIGNING A SHOPPING MALL

An interesting case study is to look at a shopping mall. So many shopping malls are opening in India that is why we consider how the enterprises that establish shopping malls decide what shops will go where. Looking at a number of shopping malls we find that some of the stores included in the malls are as given in the list below.

A	Formal apparel	J	Sports	S	Bedroom
B	Men's casual wear	K	Food & Beverage	T	Dining
C	Luggage	L	Restaurant	U	Living room
D	Women's casual wear	M	Ethnic formal	V	Electronics
E	Women's accessories	N	Gifts and celebration	W	Audio systems
F	Women apparel	O	Fashion accessories	X	Electricals and home appliances
G	Kids wear	P	Bathroom	Y	Kitchen
H	Furnishings	Q	Music and movies	Z	Mobile phones
I	Books and stationary	R	Toys		

- Explain how Association Rule Mining could be used in this shopping mall design. What data do you require?
- Assume that in an attempt to generate some data on which the company could base the design, the company issues shopping loyalty cards to shoppers that they must scan at every shop they go to. To encourage scanning, the company announces that a few prizes will be offered to some of the shoppers who do the scanning.
- Now to generate some data for this project, hand out a list of these store names to all the students in your class and ask them to tick the stores they are likely to visit when they go to the shopping mall. Also, ask them to mark on a separate sheet the stores that their mother or sister is likely to visit. It may help if codes are assigned to all the 26 stores above. You will need at least 100 transaction records, more would help. Use association rule software from the web or use Weka from New Zealand to run this software using your data. Analyze the results and write a report.

PROJECT 3—DISTRIBUTED ARM

Suppose that a large store has a transaction database that is distributed among four locations. Transactions in each component database have the same format, namely T_j: $\{i_1, \ldots, i_m\}$, where T_j is a transaction identifier, and i_k $(1 \leq k \leq m)$ is the identifier of an item purchased in the transaction. Propose an efficient algorithm to mine global association rules. Present your algorithm in the form of an outline. Your algorithm should not require shipping all the data to one site and should not cause excessive network communication overheads.

BIBLIOGRAPHY

Association rule mining has been an area of very active research for last several years. A comprehensive bibliography is available at
http://wwwai.wu-wien.ac.at/~hahsler/research/bib/association_rules/.

Another very good list is
http://www.comp.nus.edu.sg/~ssung/research/association_rule.htm.

Our aim here is to present only a small number of important references.

Recommended Reading for Students

We have selected some survey/tutorial type papers that are easy to read.

Association Rules Mining: A Recent Overview, Gests International Transactions on Computer Science and Engineering, V 32, 1, pp. 71–82, 2006.

Goethals, B., Survey on Frequent Pattern Mining, 2003.
www.cs.helsinki.fi/u/goethals/publications/survey.pdf

Hipp, J., Guntzer, U., and Nakaeizadeh, G., Algorithms for Association Rule Mining—A General Survey and Comparison, *ACM SIGKDD Explorations*, **2**(1), pp. 58–64, June 2000.
http://suraj.lums.edu.pk/~cs536a03/handouts/association_mining_survey.pdf

Slides on Association Rule Mining.
datamining.anu.edu.au/student/dm_course2004/imstut.pdf

Zhao, Q. and Bhowmick, S.S., Association Rule Mining: A Survey, Technical Report, Nanyang Technological University, Singapore, 2003.
http://www.cais.ntu.edu.sg/~qkzhao/pdf/ars.pdf

Recommended Reading for Lecturers

The classical papers on the topic are the papers by Agrawal, Imielinski, and Swami in 1993 and by Agarwal and Srikant in 1994. As noted, this is an area of considerable research. One of the reasons for such activity perhaps is because the problem looks so simple and everyone at first sight thinks that they can do better than an algorithm like *a priori*.

The paper by Brin, Motwani, Ullman, and Tsur presents the DIC algorithm. The hashing algorithm DHP is presented by Park, Chen, and Yu and the FP-growth algorithm is given in Han, Pei, and Yin. Performance evaluation of association rules algorithms is discussed by Zheng, Kohavi, and Mason and by Goethals and Zaki.

Agrawal, R., Imielinski, T., and Swami, A., Mining Association Rules between Sets of Items in Large Databases, *Proc. Int. Conf. on Management of Data* (*SIGMOD ’93*), Washington, D.C., pp. 207–216, 1993.

Agrawal, R. and Srikant, R., Fast Algorithms for Mining Association Rules, in *VLDB ’94*, Santiago, Chile, pp. 487–499, 1994.

Agrawal, R., Mannila, H., Srikant, R, Toivonen, H., and Verkamo, A.I., Fast Discovery of Association Rules, in Fayyad, U.M., Piatetsky-Shapiro, G., Smyth, P., and Uthurusamy, R., (Eds.), *Advances in Knowledge Discovery and Data Mining*, MIT Press, pp. 307–328, 2006.

Bayardo, R.J. and Agrawal, R., Mining the Most Interesting Rules, *Proc. Int. Conf. Knowledge Discovery and Data Mining* (*KDD '99*), San Diego, CA, pp. 145–154, 1999.

Bayardo, R., Goethals, B., and Zaki, M.J. (Eds.), FIMI '04: *Proceedings of the IEEE ICDM Workshop on Frequent Itemset Mining Implementations*, CEUR Workshop Proceedings, 2004. http://sunsite.informatik.rwth-aachen.de/publications/ceur-ws//Vol-126/

Brin, S., Motwani, R., Ullman, J.D., and Tsur, S., Dynamic Itemset Counting and Implication Rules for Market Basket Data, *Proc. Int. Conf. on Management of Data* (*SIGMOD '97*), Tucson, Arizona, pp. 255–264, 1997.

Brin, S., Motwani, R., and Silverstein, C., Beyond Market Basket: Generalizing Association Rules to Correlations, *Proc. Int. Conf. on Management of Data* (*SIGMOD '97*), Tucson, Arizona, pp. 265–276, 1997.

Goethals, B. and Zaki, M.J., FIMI '03: Workshop on Frequent Itemset Mining Implementations, 2003. http://fimi.cs.helsinki.fi/

Han, J., Pei, J., and Yin, Y., Mining Frequent Patterns without Candidate Generation: A Frequent Pattern Approach, *Data Mining and Knowledge Discovery*, Vol. 8, No. 1, pp. 53–87, 2004.

Park, J.S., Chen, M.S., and Yu, P.S., An Effective Hash-Based Algorithm for Mining Association Rules, *Proc. Int. Conf. on Management of Data* (*SIGMOD '95*), San Jose, CA, pp. 175–186, 1995.

Srikant, R. and Agrawal, R., Mining Generalized Association Rules, *VLDB '95*, Zurich, Switzerland, pp. 407–419, 1995.

Srikant, R. and Agrawal, R., Mining Quantitative Association Rules in Large Relational Tables, *Proc. Int. Conf. on Management of Data* (*SIGMOD '96*), Montreal, Canada, pp. 1–12, 1996.

Srikant, R. and Agrawal, R., Mining Sequential Patterns: Generalizations and Performance, *Proc. Int. Conf. Extending Database Technology* (*EDBT '96*), Avignon, France, pp. 3–17, 1996.

Uno, T., Kiyomi, M., and Arimura, H., LCM Ver. 2: Efficient Mining Algorithms for Frequent/Closed/Maximal Itemsets, *Proceedings of the IEEE ICDM Workshop on Frequent Itemset Mining Implementations*, Bayardo, R., Goethals, B., and Zaki, M.J. (Eds.), CEUR Workshop Proceedings, 2004.
http://sunsite.informatik.rwth-aachen.de/publications/ceur-ws//vol-126/

Zaki, M.J., Parthasarathy, S., Ogihara, M., and Li, W., New Algorithms for Fast Discovery of Association Rules, In Heckerman, D. Mannila, H., Pregibon, D., and Uthurusamy, R. (Eds.), *Proc. Int. Conf. on Knowledge Discovery and Data Mining* (*KDD '97*), Newport Beach, CA, pp. 283–296, 1997.

Zaki, M.J., Mining Non-Redundant Association Rules, *Data Mining and Knowledge Discovery*, Vol. 9, No. 3, pp. 223–248, 2004.

Zheng, Z., Kohavi, R., and Mason, L., Real World Performance of Association Rule Algorithms, *Proc. Int. Conf. on Knowledge Discovery and Data Mining* (*KDD '01*), 2001.
http://ai.stanford.edu/users/ronnyk/realworldassoclongpaper.pdf

RAKESH AGRAWAL—INVENTOR OF ASSOCIATION RULES MINING

Rakesh Agrawal has developed a number of fundamental data mining concepts and technologies and has made contributions to key concepts in data privacy, including Privacy-Preserving Data Mining. Rakesh is the recipient of the ACM-SIGKDD First Innovation Award, ACM-SIGMOD Edgar F. Codd Innovations Award, ACM-SIGMOD Test of Time Award and the VLDB 10-Yr Most Influential Paper Award. He is a Member of the National Academy of Engineering, a Fellow of ACM, and a Fellow of IEEE.

Dr Agarwal is presently a Microsoft Technical Fellow. Before joining Microsoft, he was an IBM Fellow and led the Quest group at the IBM Almaden Research Center. Earlier, he was with the Bell Laboratories, Murray Hill from 1983 to 1989. He also worked for 3 years at the Bharat Heavy Electricals Ltd.

Dr Agrawal received the M.S. and Ph.D. degrees in Computer Science from the University of Wisconsin-Madison. He is a graduate of the University of Roorkee (now IIT-Roorkee).

CASE STUDY 3

Mining Customer Value: From Association Rules to Direct Marketing*

Reproduced with permission
from Springer Science

ABSTRACT

Direct marketing is a modern business activity with an aim to maximize the profit generated from marketing to a selected group of customers. A key to direct marketing is to select a subset of customers so as to maximize the profit return while minimizing the cost. Achieving this goal is difficult due to the extremely imbalanced data and the inverse correlation between the probability that a customer responds and the dollar amount generated by a response. We present a solution to this problem based on a creative use of association rules. Association rule mining searches for *all* rules above an interestingness threshold, as opposed to *some* rules in a heuristic-based search. Promising association rules are then selected based on the observed value of the customers they summarize. Selected association rules are used to build a model for predicting the value of a future customer. On the challenging KDD-CUP-98 dataset, this approach generates 41% more profit than the KDD-CUP winner and 35% more profit than the best result published thereafter, with 57.7% recall on responders and 78.0% recall on non-responders. The average profit per mail is 3.3 times that of the KDD-CUP winner.

Keywords: association rule, classification, direct marketing, regression

1. INTRODUCTION

Direct marketing makes it possible to offer goods or services or transmit messages to a specific, targeted segment of the population by mail, telephone, email or other direct means.[1] Direct marketing is one of the most effective and measurable methods of marketing available. For example, retail industries need to identify buyers of certain products; banks and insurance companies need to promote loan insurance products to customers; and fundraising organizations need to identify potential donors. Direct marketing campaigns are only as successful as the mailing list used. A good mailing list will target only the consumers that are potential or valuable customers. Typically, direct marketing models select addresses by predicting future response behavior. In management and marketing science, Stochastic models are used to describe the response behavior of customers, including binary choice models (Bult and Wansbeek, 1995), latent class models (Desarbo and Ramaswamy, 1994), neural networks (Levin and Zahavi, 1996; Potharst et al., 2002) and Markov chains (Bitran and Mondschein, 1996).

In this paper, we propose a data mining method for determining the mailing list. Available is a *historical* data base containing information about previous mailing campaigns, including whether a customer responded and the dollar amount collected if responded. The task is to build a model to predict *current* customers who are likely to respond. The goal is to maximize the sum of net profit, Σ(*dollar amount − mailing cost*), over the contacted customers. We choose the KDD-CUP-98 dataset (KDD98, 1998a) as the case study. This dataset was collected from

---

* Wang, K., S. Zhou, Q. Yang, and J.M.Y. Yeung, 2005, Mining customer value: from association rules to direct marketing, *Data Mining and Knowledge Discovery,* Vol. 11, pp. 57–79.
wangk@cs.sfu.ca szhoua@cs.sfu.ca qyang@cs.ust.hk yeung@ cs.sfu.ca

the result of the 1997 Paralyzed Veterans of America fundraising mailing campaign (more details in Section 2) and only 5% of records are responders. Thus, simply classifying all customers into non-responders would give 95% accuracy, but this does not generate profit.

A principled method is ranking customers by the estimated probability to respond and selecting some top portion of the ranked list (Ling and Li, 1998; Masand and Shapiro, 1996). For example, if the top 5% of the ranked list contains 30% of all responders, the lift model gives the lift of 30/5 = 6 (Ling and Li, 1998; Masand and Shapiro, 1996). A significant drawback of this approach is that the actual customer value, e.g., the donation amount in the example of fundraising, is ignored in the ranking, or it requires a uniform customer value for all customers. As pointed out in KDD98 (1998b) for the KDD-CUP-98 task, there is an inverse correlation between the likelihood to buy (or donate) and the dollar amount to spend (or donate). This inverse correlation reflects the general trend that the more dollar amount is involved, the more cautious the buyer (or donor) is in making a purchase (or donation) decision. As a result, a probability based ranking tends to rank down, rather than rank up, valuable customers.

The realization that a cost-sensitive treatment is required in applications like direct marketing has led to a substantial amount of research. Domingos (1999) proposed the MetaCost framework for adapting accuracy-based classification to cost-sensitive learning by incorporating a *cost matrix* $C(i, j)$ for misclassifying true class j into class i. Zadrozny and Elkan (2001) examined the more general case where the *benefit* $B(i, j, x)$ depends not only on the classes involved but also on the individual customers x. For a given customer x, the "optimal prediction" is the class i that leads to the minimum expected cost

$$\Sigma_j P(j|x)C(i, j)$$

or the maximum expected benefit

$$\Sigma_j P(j|x)B(i, j, x).$$

Both methods require to estimate the conditional class probability $P(j|x)$. In this phase, since only the frequency information about x, not the customer value of x, is examined, valuable customers, who tend to be infrequent because of the "inverse correlation", are likely to be ignored. The customer value is factored only at the end via the factor $B(i, j, x)$. In this paper, we propose a novel approach to address the above issues. First, we exploit association rules (Agrawal et al., 1993; Agrawal and Srikant, 1994) of the form $X \rightarrow$ *respond* to extract features for responders, where X is a set of items that is correlated with the "respond" class. Unlike traditional rule induction (Michalski, 1969; Quinlan, 1983; Clark and Niblett, 1989) that examines *one variable at a time*, association rules evaluate *a combination of variables* (i.e., X) *at a time*, therefore, better represent correlated features. We select a small subset of association rules to identify potential customers in the current campaign. We address two key issues, namely, push the customer value in selecting association rules, and maximize profitability over the customers (instead of historical ones). On the challenging KDD-CUP-98 task, which has 5% responders and 95% non-responders, this method generated 41% more profit than the winner of the competition and 35% more profit than the best known result after the competition, and the average profit per mail is 3.3 times that of the winner. This method identifies correctly 57.7% of responders and 78% of non-responders, thus, also provides a competitive solution to the cost-sensitive classification.

The motivation of association rules in the market basket analysis has led to several attempts to extend and apply such rules in business environments. Savasere et al. (1998) considers negative association rules that tell what items a customer will not likely buy given that he/she buys a certain set of other items. Tan et al. (2000) considers indirect association rules where the association of two items is conditional on the presence of some set of other items. Such associations are purely count or occurrence based and have no direct relationships with the "inverse correlation" considered here that addresses profit. We focus on *using* association rules based on customer value, whereas these works focus on *finding* association rules based on count information. This distinction is substantial because association rules themselves do not tell how to maximize an objective function, especially in the presence of the "inverse correlation". Our work differs from the product recommendation in Wang et al. (2002) and item selection in Brijs et al. (1999) and Wang and Su (2002) in that we identify valuable customers instead of items or products.

The rest of this paper is organized as follows. In Section 2, we examine the challenges in the KDD-CUP-98 dataset and outline our approach. In Section 3, we present the detailed algorithm. We evaluate our method using the KDD-CUP-98 task in Section 4. Finally, we conclude the paper.

2. CHALLENGES AND OUR PROPOSALS

The KDD-CUP-98 dataset (KDD98, 1998a) contains 191,779 records about individuals contacted in the 1997 mailing campaign. Each record is described by 479 nontarget variables and two target variables indicating the "respond"/"not respond" classes and the actual donation in dollars. About 5% of records are "respond" records and the rest are "not respond" records. The dataset has been pre-split into 50% for learning and 50% for validation. The validation set is reserved for evaluation and is held out from the learning phase. The competition task is to build a prediction model of the donation amount using the learning set. The participants are contested on Σ(*actual donation* – $0.68) over the validation records with predicted donation greater than the mailing cost $0.68.

We chose this fundraising task because it shares several key requirements with direct marketing. Both activities are only as successful as the mailing list used, and require identifying a subset of "valuable" individuals to maximize some objective function (e.g., sales, customer services, donation amount). The fundraising dataset contains offerings and responses in previous campaigns, similar to those kept in a typical direct marketing campaign. The target variable "actual donation" corresponds to the sales value on a contacted customer, and $0.68 corresponds to the cost associated with contacting a customer. In fact, this problem is more general than the direct marketing considered in Ling and Li (1998) in that it allows to model a different profitability for different customers, just as a different sale could yield a different sales profit due to the difference in products, quantity and promotion. However, this generalization raises some new issues as explained below.

2.1 The Challenges

This real life dataset presents two challenges.

Challenge 1. Quoted from KDD98 (1998b), "there is often an inverse correlation between the likelihood to respond and the dollar amount of the gift". This inverse correlation could exist in the offerings to the same customer or different customers. For the same customer, a standard handling is avoiding multiple offerings with a certain time period. For different customers, it means that there are many "small customers" making small purchases and few "big customers" making big purchases. We focus on this type of inverse correlation. A pure probability based ranking tends to favor "small customers" because of higher likelihood to respond, and ignore "big customers". Previous researches addressed this issue in two steps: obtain the probability estimation from a standard classification model such as decision tree (Ling and Li, 1998; Masand and Shapiro, 1996), bagging (Domingos, 1999) and smoothing (Zadrozny and Elkan, 2001), and re-rank the probability based ranking by taking into account the customer value (Masand and Shapiro, 1996; Zadrozny and Elkan, 2001). The disadvantage of this approach is that the customer value is ignored in the first step.

Challenge 2. The high dimensionality and the scare target population present a significant challenge for extracting the features of the "respond" class. The dataset is very high in dimensionality, i.e., 481 variables, and very scare in the "respond" class population, only 5% of the dataset. Since any subset of variables can be a feature for distinguishing the "respond" class from "not respond" class, searching for such features is similar to searching for a needle from a haystack. The "one attribute at a time" gain criterion (Quinlan, 1993) does not search for correlated variables as features. Though, the independence assumption of the Naive Bayesian classifier is quite robust to classification, which only depends on the maximum class probability (Domingos and

Pazzani, 1996), it suffers from distortion if used for probability estimation where non-maximum class probabilities are also used for ranking customers. Our study on the KDD-CUP-98 dataset shows that taking into account this correlation yields a significantly higher profit.

2.2 The Proposed Approach

We address these challenges in two steps.

In the first step, we propose the notion of *focused association rules* to focus on the features that are typical of the "respond" class and not typical of the "not respond" class. A focused association rule has the form $X \rightarrow respond$, where X is a set of items for non-target variables, such that X occurs *frequently* in the "respond" class and each item in X occurs *infrequently* in the "not respond" class. A formal definition will be given in Section 3.1. A focused association rule makes use of only items that have higher frequency and correlation in the "respond" class. The search space is determined by "respond" records and items that occur infrequently in the "not respond". This prunes all "not respond" records (to deal with the scarcity of the target class) and all items that occur frequently in the "not respond" class (to deal with the high dimensionality).

In the second step, we convert focused association rules into a model for predicting the donation amount for a given customer. This involves determining how to cover customers using rules, pruning over-fitting rules that do not generalize to the whole population, and estimating the donation amount for rules, therefore, for customers. In the presence of Challenge 1, innovative solutions are needed because statistically insignificant rules could generate a significate profit. Our approach is to push the customer value into the model building/pruning so that the estimated profit over the whole population is maximized.

In the rest of the paper, the following terms are interchangeable: customer and record, responder and "respond" record, non-responder and "not_respond" record.

3. ALGORITHM

Historical records are stored in a relational table of m nontarget variables $A_1, \ldots, A_m$ and two target variables *Class* and *V*. *Class* takes one of the "respond"/"not respond" classes as the value. V represents a continuous donation amount. Given a set of records of this format, our task is to build a model for predicting the donation profit over current customers represented by the validation set in the KDD-CUP-98 dataset. Precisely, we want to maximize $\Sigma(V - \$0.68)$ over the current customers who are predicted to have a donation greater than the mailing cost \$0.68. An implicit assumption is that current customers follow the same class and donation distribution as that of historical records. Since the donation amount V for a current customer is not known until the customer responds, the algorithm is evaluated using a holdout subset from the historical data, i.e., the validation set.

Algorithm 1 outlines the algorithm for building the model. There are three main steps: *Rule Generating*, *Model Building*, and *Model Pruning*. The Rule Generating step finds a set of good rules that capture features of responders. The Model Building step combines such rules into a prediction model for donation amount. The Model Pruning step prunes over-fitting rules that do not generalize to the whole population. We discuss these steps in detail.

Algorithm 1 The overall algorithm

Input: The learning set, minimum support and maximum support
Output: A model for predicting the donation amount
1: Rule Generating;
2: Model Building;
3: Model Pruning;

3.1 Step 1: Rule Generating

We discretize continuous non-target variables using the utility at http://www.sgi.com/tech/mlc before generating rules. After discretization, each value a_{ij} is either a categorical value or an interval. We are interested in "respond" rules of the form

$$A_{i1} = a_{i1}, \ldots, A_{ik} = a_{ik} \rightarrow \textit{respond}$$

that are potentially useful for discriminating responders from non-responders. The generality of a rule is defined by the percentage of the records that contain all the equalities on the left-hand side of the rule, called *support*. Despite many efficient algorithms for mining association rules (see (Agrawal et al., 1993, 1996; Agrawal and Srikant, 1994), for example), we encountered a significant difficulty in this step: to find respond rules, we have to set the minimum support well below 5%, i.e., the percentage of "respond" records in the dataset; however, with 481 variables and 95% records in the "not respond" class, the number of "not respond" rules satisfying the minimum support is so large that finding "respond" rules is similar to searching a needle from a haystack. Sampling techniques cannot reduce the "width" of records that is the real curse behind the long running time. This situation of extremely high dimensionality and extremely low target proportion also occurs in computational biology (Rigoutsos and Floratos, 1998), network intrusion detection and fraud detection (Joshi et al., 2001). We consider a simple but efficient solution to this problem by focusing on items that *occur frequently in "respond" records but occur infrequently in "not_respond" records*. Let D_r be the set of "respond" records and let D_n be the set of "not_respond" records.

Definition 3.1 (Focused association rules). The *support* of item $A_i = a_i$ in D_r or D_n is the percentage of the records in D_r or D_n that contain $A_i = a_i$. The *support* of a rule in D_r or D_n is the percentage of the records in D_r or D_n that contain all the items in the rule. Given a minimum support for D_r and a maximum support for D_n, an item $A_i = a_i$ is *focused* if its support in D_n is not more than the maximum support and its support in D_r is not less than the minimum support. A "respond" rule is a *focused association rule* (*FAR*) if it contains only focused items and its support in D_r is not less than the minimum support.

In words, a FAR occurs frequently in D_r (as per the minimum support) but none of its items occurs frequently in D_n (as per the maximum support). Notice that FARs exclude the "respond" rules that as a whole do not occur frequently in D_n but some of its items does. This "incompleteness" trades for the data reduction achieved by pruning all non-focused items. For the KDD-CUP-98 dataset, this prunes all "not_respond" records, which accounts for 95% of the dataset, and all items that occur frequently in D_n, which accounts for 40%–60% of all items. In fact, for our purpose, the completeness of rules is not a concern, but finding some rules that can influence the final profit is. Our experiments show that the notion of FARs works exactly towards this goal.

Algorithm 2 finds FARs for given minimum support in D_r and maximum support in D_n. First, it computes the support in D_n for the items in D_r (line 1–11) and removes those items from D_r for which this support exceeds the maximum support (line 12–15). Then, it applies any association rule mining algorithm such as Agrawal et al. (1993) to the updated D_r to find "respond" rules above the minimum support (line 16–17). This association rule mining is expensive, but is applied to only "respond" records and only items whose support in D_n is not more than

---

Algorithm 2 Rule Generating

Input: D_r, D_n, the minimum support for D_r and the maximum support for D_n
Output: FARs
1: /* compute the support in D_n for items in D_r */
2: **for all** tuple t in D_r **do**
3:     **for all** item in t **do**
4:         create a counter for the item if not yet created;
5:     **end for;**
6: **end for;**
7: **for all** tuple t in D_n **do**
8:     **for** all item in t **do**
9:         increment the counter for the item if found;
10:     **end for;**
11: **end for;**
12: /* remove the items from D_r whose support in D_n exceeds the maximum support */
13: **for all** tuple t in D_r **do**
14:     remove the items from t whose support in D_n exceeds the maximum support;
15: **end for;**
16: /* find frequent "respond" rules in D_r */
17: find "respond" rules above the minimum support in D_r such as in Agrawal et al. (1993);

---

the maximum support. After finding the FARs, we add to the rule set the (only) "not_respond" rule of the form

$$\emptyset \rightarrow \textit{not respond}.$$

This rule, called the *default rule,* is used only if a customer matches no FAR.

Example 3.1. Consider the database in Table 1(a). There are 10 records (tuples), 5 in D_r and 5 in D_n. Each record has 3 attributes *A, B, C* and donation *V*. Suppose that both minimum support for D_r and maximum support for D_n are 40%. The lower table in Table 1(b) shows the support count for each item in D_r. The items exceeding the maximum support in D_n (i.e., occur in more than 2 records in D_n) are marked with "*". The upper table of Table 1(b) shows D_r with such items removed. Table 2 shows the FARs found from D_r, plus the default rule.

In the rest of the paper, a "rule" refers to either a FAR or the default rule, *Supp(r)* denotes the support of rule *r* in $D_r \cup D_n$, i.e., the percentage of all records containing both sides of the rule, *lhs*(*r*)

Table 1: (a) Before applying maximum support. (b) After applying maximum support

D_r					D_n				
TID	A	B	C	V	TID	A	B	C	V
(a)									
p_1	a_1	b_1	c_3	\$30.68	n_1	a_1	b_1	c_1	\$0.00
p_2	a_1	b_2	c_3	\$50.68	n_2	a_2	b_1	c_3	\$0.00
p_3	a_1	b_2	c_1	\$40.68	n_3	a_2	b_2	c_1	\$0.00
p_4	a_2	b_2	c_2	\$20.68	n_4	a_2	b_1	c_3	\$0.00
p_5	a_2	b_1	c_3	\$20.68	n_5	a_3	b_2	c_1	\$0.00

D_r					Count of items		
TID	A	B	C	V	Item	Count in D_n	Count D_r
(b)							
p_1	a_1	/	c_3	\$30.68	a_1	1	3
p_2	a_1	b_2	c_3	\$50.68	a_1^*	3	2
p_3	a_1	b_2	/	\$40.68	b_1^*	3	2
p_4	/	b_2	c_2	\$20.68	b_2	2	3
p_5	/	/	c_3	\$20.68	c_1^*	3	1
					c_2	0	1
					c_3	2	3

Table 2: The FARs generated with minimum support and maximum support of 40%

RID	Rules	Support in *D*
r_1	$\emptyset \rightarrow$ *not_respond*	5/5 = 100%
r_2	$A = a_1 \rightarrow$ *respond*	3/5 = 60%
r_3	$B = b_2 \rightarrow$ *respond*	3/5 = 60%
r_4	$C = c_3 \rightarrow$ *respond*	3/5 = 60%
r_5	$A = a_1,\ B = b_2 \rightarrow$ *respond*	2/5 = 40%
r_6	$A = a_1,\ C = c_3 \rightarrow$ *respond*	2/5 = 40%

denotes the set of items on the left-hand side of rule *r*, |*lhs*(*r*)| denotes the number of items in *lhs*(*r*). We say that a rule *r matches* a record *t*, or vice versa, if *t* contains all the items in *lhs*(*r*). We say that a rule *r* is *more general than* a rule *r′* if $lhs(r) \subseteq lhs(r')$.

3.2 Step 2: Model Building

Given a customer, we need to choose one rule to predict the donation amount on the customer. To maximize the profit generated, we prefer the rule that matches the customer and has the largest observed profit on the learning set. The observed profit of a rule *r* is the average profit generated on the learning records that match the rule. Let *profit*(*r, t*) denote the profit generated by the prediction of *r* on a learning record *t*. The observed profit of *r* is defined as:

$$O\_avg(r) = \Sigma_t profit(r, t)/M,$$

where *t* is a learning record that matches *r* and *M* is the number of such records. A large *O_avg*(*r*) means that the customers (in the learning set) matched by *r* make a large donation on average.

Table 3 gives two models for defining *profit*(*r, t*). The *Reward/Penalty* model rewards each dollar saved or earned and penalizes each dollar wasted or not earned. The *Profit* model simply measures the net profit generated. Let us explain each case in Table 3.

- Case 1: a responder *t* is predicted as a responder. Both models reward this decision by the net profit earned, i.e., *V* – 0.68.
- Case 2: a responder *t* is predicted as a non-responder. The Reward/Penalty model

Table 3: Two models of profit (r, t) (V is the donation amount in r)

	Rule r	Record t	Reward/Penalty model	Profit model
Case 1	"respond" rule	"respond" record	$V - 0.68$ (earned)	$V - 0.68$
Case 2	default rule	"respond" record	$-(V - 0.68)$ (not earned)	0
Case 3	"respond" rule	"not_respond" record	-0.68 (wasted)	-0.68
Case 4	default rule	"not_respond" record	0.68 (saved)	0

penalizes this decision by the loss of the supposedly earned dollars, i.e., $-(V - 0.68)$ and the Profit model does it by the zero profit generated.

- Case 3: a non-responder t is predicted as a responder. Both models penalize this decision by the mailing cost wasted, i.e., -0.68.
- Case 4: a non-responder t is predicted as a non-responder. The Reward/Penalty model rewards this decision by the mailing cost saved, i.e., 0.68, and the Profit model does it by the zero profit generated (i.e., no mailing cost wasted).

The difference between the two models is that, for each non-responder prediction (i.e., Case 2 and 4), there is zero profit generated in the Profit model, but there is the mailing cost saved (if the prediction is correct) or the customer value lost (if the prediction is wrong) in the Reward/Penalty model.

To maximize the profit on a current customer, we prefer the matching rule of the largest possible *O_avg*. The effect is predicting the profit using the most portable customer group that matches a current customer. We formalize this preference below.

Definition 3.2 (Covering rules). For any two rules r and r', r is *ranked higher than* r'

- (Average profit) if $O\_avg(r) > O\_avg(r')$, or
- (Generality) if $O\_avg(r) = O\_avg(r')$, but $Supp(r) > Supp(r')$, or
- (Simplicity) if $Supp(r) = Supp(r')$, but $|lhs(r)| < |lhs(r')|$, or
- (Totality of order) if $|lhs(r)| = |lhs(r')|$, but r is generated before r',

in that order. Given a record t, *a* rule r is the *covering rule* of t, or r *covers* t, *if* r matches t and has the highest possible rank.

Table 4: Coverage and rank of rules

RID	Records matched	Records covered	*O_avg*	Ranking
r_5	p_2, p_3	p_2, p_3	\$45.00	1st
r_6	p_1, p_2	p_1	\$40.00	2nd
r_2	p_1, p_2, p_3, n_1	n_1	\$29.83	3rd
r_3	p_2, p_3, p_4, n_3, n_5	p_4, n_3, n_5	\$21.73	4th
r_4	p_1, p_2, p_5, n_2, n_4	p_5, n_2, n_4	\$19.73	5th
r_1	$p_1 - p_5, n_1 - n_5$	Ø	\$0.00	6th

Given a current customer, we use the covering rule of the customer to estimate the profit. We will discuss the profit estimation shortly. Though possibly matched by more than one rule, each record is covered by exactly one rule (i.e., the covering rule). To find the covering rule of a given record, we store rules of size k in a hash tree of depth k (Agrawal et al., 1993). Associated with each rule is the quadruple <*O_avg, Supp, |lhs|, generation_time*> that determines the rank of the rule. Given a record t, we find the covering rule of t by finding all matching rules using the hash trees of depth smaller than the size of t. The covering rule of t is the matching rule of the highest possible rank.

A rule is useless if it matches a record, some rule of a higher rank also matches the record. Therefore, a useless rule has no chance to cover any record and can be removed without affecting prediction. Precisely, a rule is *useless* if some other rule is more general and ranked higher.

Example 3.2. Continue with Example 3.1. Rules are ranked by *O_avg* in Table 4, where the Profit model for $profit(r, t)$ is used. For example, r_2 matches 4 records p_1, p_2, p_3, and n_1. $O\_avg(r_2) = \Sigma_t\, profit(r_2, t)/4 = (\$30 + \$50 + \$40 - \$0.68)/4 = \$29.83$. *O_avg* for other rules is similarly computed. p_2 is matched by all 6 rules and is covered by r_5, the matching rule of highest rank. Similarly, the covering rules of other records can be determined.

3.3 Step 3: Model Pruning

The above rule ranking favors specific rules that match a small number of customers of a high profit. In the classic classification problem, such rules are pruned due to statistical insignificance. In the presence of inverse correlation between the likelihood to respond and the dollar amount generated by a response, extra care should be taken because valuable customers do not show up very often and pruning their rules could lead to the loss of significant profit. To address this issue, we propose pruning rules *on the basis of increasing the estimated profit over the whole population.* Below, we describe this new pruning method.

First, we explain how to estimate the profit of a rule r over the whole population; then, we give a method for pruning rules based on this estimation. The profit of r (over the whole population) can be estimated in two steps. First, we estimate the "hits" of r over the whole population. Second, we compute the profit of the estimated hits using the observations in the learning set. We borrow the *pessimistic estimation* (Clopper and Pearson, 1934; Quinlan, 1993) for estimating the "hits" of r.

Definition 3.3 Let *Cover*(r) denote the set of learning records covered by r. Let M denote the number of records in *Cover*(r), E of which do not match the class in r.

E/M is the observed error rate of r on the learning sample. To estimate the error rate of r over the whole population, we regard these E errors as observing E events in M trials, assuming that such events follow the binomial distribution. Given a confidence level CF, the probability that the real error rate of r in the whole population exceeds the upper limit $U_{CF}(M, E)$ is no more than $CF/2$. The exact computation of $U_{CF}(M, E)$ is less important and can be found in the C4.5 code (Quinlan, 1993), and a theoretical account can be found in Clopper and Pearson (1934). The idea is that a smaller sample size M is penalized by a larger upper limit $U_{CF}(M, E)$ to guarantee the specified confidence level CF. The default value of CF in C4.5 is 25%. If we use r to classify M customers randomly chosen from the whole population, we have $1 - CF/2$ confidence that the number of "hits" is at least $M \times (1 - U_{CF}(M, E))$, and the number of "misses" is at most $M \times U_{CF}(M, E)$

Consider a "respond" rule r. The average profit per hit in *Cover*(r) *is*

$$avg_h(r) = \Sigma_t(V - 0.68)/(M - E)$$

for the "respond" records t in *Cover*(r), **where V is the** donation amount in t. The average profit per miss in *Cover*(r) is the cost of mailing to a non-responder, i.e., 0.68. We extend these averages to the above estimated hits and misses.

Definition 3.4 (Estimated profit). Assume that r covers M learning records, E incorrectly. The *estimated profit* of r is

$$Estimate(r) = \begin{cases} M \times (1 - U_{CF}(M,E)) \times avg_h(r) \\ -M \times U_{CF}(M,E) \times 0.68 & \text{If } r \text{ is a "respond" rule} \\ 0 & \text{If } r \text{ is the default rule} \end{cases}$$

The *estimated average profit* of r, denoted *E_avg*(r), is *Estimated*(r)/M. The *estimated profit* of a model is Σ_r*Estimated*(r) over all rules r (for $|D_r| + |D_n|$ customers randomly chosen from the whole population).

Notice the difference between *O_avg*(r) and *E_avg*(r). *O_avg*(r) *is* the average profit *observed* for the learning records that are *matched* by r. The matching rule of largest *O_avg*(r) is the covering rule of a given record. *E_avg*(r) is the average profit *estimated* for the records in the whole population that are *covered* by r. We use *E_avg*(r) to estimate the profit generated by each prediction of r over the whole population. *E_avg*(r) depends on *O_avg*(r) to define the notion of covering rules.

Now we return to the main topic of pruning overfitting rules to maximize Σ_r*Estimated*(r) over unpruned rules r. If a specific rule is pruned, we choose the general rule of highest rank to cover the records that were covered by the pruned rule. This specific/general rule relationship is defined by the covering tree below.

Definition 3.5 (Covering tree). In the *covering tree,* a rule r' is the *parent* of a rule r if r' is more general than r and has the highest possible rank. If a rule r is pruned, the parent of r replaces r as the covering rule of the records previously covered by r.

A child rule always has a higher rank than its parent; otherwise, the parent rule will cover all records matched by the child rule and the child rule is useless, which contradicts the fact that all useless rules have been removed. The most general default rule is the root of the covering tree. As we walk down the tree, rules are increasingly more specific and ranked higher.

Algorithm 3 shows the algorithm for pruning rules in a bottom-up order of the covering tree. It first builds the covering tree (line 1). This can be done as follows. Assume that rules of size k are stored in a hash tree of depth k. We examine rules of larger size before examining rules of smaller size. For each rule r of size k, we find all general rules by searching the hash trees of depth smaller than k. If the general rule of highest possible rank has a lower rank than r, we make it the parent rule of r; otherwise, we discard r because it is useless. In this step, we also compute M and E for every rule r in the covering tree. For this, we scan every record t in $D_r \cup D_n$, find the covering rule r of t using the hash trees, and increment M for r. If t and r does not match in class, we also increment E for r.

Algorithm 3 Model Pruning

Input: A set of rules
Output: The pruned covering tree
1: build the covering tree;
2: **for all** node r in the bottom-up order
3: compute *Estimated*(r);
4: **if** r is a non-leaf node and *E_tree*(r) ≤ *E_leaf*(r) **then**
5: prune the subtree at r;
6: **end if;**
7: **end for;**
8: return the unpruned rules;

After building the covering tree, the algorithm examines the nodes in the bottom-up order. At a leaf node r, it computes *Estimated*(r). At a non-leaf node r, it computes the estimated profit for the subtree at r, denoted by *E_tree*(r), and the estimated profit of r after pruning the subtree, denoted by *E_leaf*(r). *E_tree*(r) is Σ*Estimated*(u) over all nodes u within the subtree at r. *E_leaf*(r) is the same as *Estimated*(r), except that r now covers all the learning records covered by the subtree at r. If *E_tree*(r) ≤ *E_leaf*(r), it prunes the subtree at r by making r a new leaf node in the covering tree and removing the rules in the subtree from the hash trees. If *E_tree*(r) > *E_leaf*(r), it does nothing at r. The nodes outside the subtree at r are not considered because their estimated profit remains unchanged. Essentially, the bottom-up pruning has t he effect of cutting off some lower portion of the covering tree to maximize Σ_r *Estimated*(r) over remaining rules r.

Example 3.3. Let us build the covering tree for Example 3.2. Consider rule r_5 for example. r_1, r_2 and r_3 are more general than r_5, but r_2 has the highest rank among them. So, r_2 is the parent of r_5. In this way, we build the covering tree on the left of figure 1.

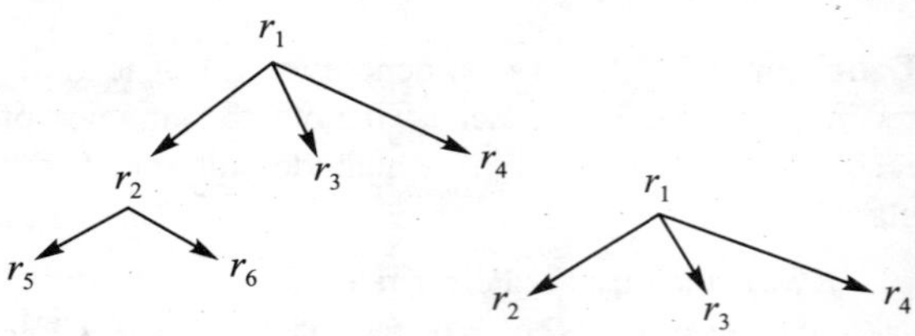

Figure 1: Left: the covering tree before pruning. Right: the covering tree after pruning.

Table 5 shows *Estimated*(r) before and after the pruning at r. For example, r_5 covers correctly p_2 and p_3, so $M = 2$ and $E = 0$. The estimated number

Table 5: *Estimated*(r) before and after pruning

	Before pruning at the rule	After pruning at the rule
RID	*Cover*(r)(M, E), *Estimated*(r)	*Cover*(r) (M, E), *Estimated*(r)
r_5	p_2, p_3(2, 0), \$44.32	
r_6	p_1(1, 0), \$6.99	
r_2	n_1(1, 1), –\$0.68	p_1, p_2, p_3, n_1(4, 1), \$70.50
r_3	p_4, n_3, n_5(3, 2), \$2.10	
r_4	p_5, n_2, n_4(3, 2), \$2.10	
r_1	∅(0, 0), \$0.00	∅(0, 0), \$0.00 (pruning not performed)

of misses is $2 \times U_{CF}(2, 0) = 2 \times 0.50 = 1.00$, and the estimated number of hits is $2 \times (1 - U_{CF}(2, 0)) = 2 \times 0.50 = 1.00$. $avg_h(r_5) = [(50.68 - 0.68) + (40.68 - 0.68)]/(2 - 0) = \$45.00$. >From Definition 3.4, $Estimated(r_5) = 1.00 \times avg_h(r_5) - 1.00 \times 0.68 = \$44.32$.

After examining nodes r_5 and r_6, the bottom-up pruning examines the node r_2. $E\_tree(r_2) = Estimated(r_2) + Estimated(r_5) + Estimated(r_6) = -0.68 + 44.32 + 6.99 = \$50.63$. Pruning the subtree at r_2 makes r_2 cover p_1, p_2, p_3 and n_1, and $M = 4$ and $E = 1$. In this case, the estimated number of misses is $4 \times U_{CF}(4, 1) = 4 \times 0.55 = 2.20$, the estimated number of hits is $4 \times (1 - U_{CF}(4, 1)) = 4 \times 0.45 = 1.80$, and $avg_h(r_2) = [(50.68 - 0.68) + (40.68 - 0.68) + (30.68 - 0.68)]/(4 - 1) = \$40.00$. Following Definition 3.4,

$E\_leaf(r_2) = Estimated(r_5) = 1.80 \times 40.00 - 0.68 \times 2.20 = \$70.50$.

Since $E\_tree(r_2) \leq E\_leaf(r_2)$, the subtree at r_2 is pruned. After examining nodes r_2, r_3, r_4, the bottom-up pruning examines the root r_1. We have

$$E\_tree(r_1) = \sum_{i=1}^{4} Estimated(r_i)$$

$$= 0.00 + 70.50 + 2.10 + 2.10 = \$74.70$$

If the subtree at r_1 is pruned, r_1 would cover all records in $D_r \cup D_n$. Since r_1 is a "not_respond" rule, $Estimated(r_1) = 0$ (Definition 3.4), and $E\_leaf(r_1) = 0$. We have $E\_tree(r_1) > E\_leaf(r_1)$. So, no pruning is done at r_1. The final pruned covering tree is shown on the right of figure 1.

We can prove the following optimality of the above bottom-up pruning. A *cut* of a tree contains exactly one node on each root-to-leaf path in the tree. A cut generates a tree by making the nodes in the cut as the leaf nodes.

Theorem 3.1. *The pruned covering tree has the maximum Σ_r Estimated(r) among all pruned covering trees generated by a cut of the given covering tree.*

Proof: It essentially follows from the fact that the pruning decision at a sibling node is independent of the decisions at other sibling nodes. This implies that, if the pruning at a sibling node increases estimated profit, so does it in any "optimal cut" because it does not affect the pruning at other sibling nodes. Therefore, the pruning should be done in any "optimal cut". ❑

The cost of Model Pruning consists of building the covering tree and pruning the tree. Pruning the covering tree takes only one scan of the nodes in the tree. The cost of building the covering tree involves finding all general rules for each rule and finding the covering rule for every learning record. These costs are comparable to the cost of counting the support of candidates for item sets in the Apriori algorithm (Agrawal and Srikant, 1994).

3.4 Choosing Threshold Values

A remaining issue is how to choose the minimum support (for D_r) and the maximum support (for D_n). Our method is less sensitive to specific rules because of its own pruning step, i.e., Step 3. For this reason, a smaller minimum support is preferred to avoid losing portable rules. The choice of maximum support is dictated by how much resource we can afford for mining "respond" rules. The rule of thumb is that, for a smaller minimum support, the Rule Generating step becomes more time/space-consuming, and a smaller maximum support should be used to exclude more items.

We suggest the following procedure for choosing the minimum support and maximum support as follows. We split the learning set into *building set* and *testing set*, and run Algorithm 1 on the building set. Some initial minimum support, usually 1%, and initial maximum support, which is usually the percentage of "respond" records in the learning set, are used. After building the model, we compute the *sum of actual profit,* as defined in Section 4, on the testing set. If the current run results in an increase in the sum of actual profit, we rerun the algorithm with a reduced minimum support and, if necessary, a reduced maximum support to allow efficient rule generating. This procedure is repeated several times until the sum of actual profit cannot be increased "significantly". The model built in the last run is returned. We shall experimentally study this procedure in Section 4. The testing set serves to tune parameters in our method, therefore, should not be confused with the validation set.

3.5 Making Prediction

The prediction model is given by the set of unpruned rules returned in the last run. To make prediction on a customer *t,* we use the hash trees to find the covering rule *r* of *t*. The decision on the customer is "contact the customer" if and only if *r* is a "respond" rule and the predicted profit *E_avg*(*r*) (Definition 3.4) is positive.

4. VALIDATION

In this section, we validate the proposed method using the standard split of the KDD98-learning-set (95,412 records) and KDD98-validation-set (96,367 records) used by the KDD competition (KDD98, 1998a). The KDD98-learning-set is used for learning a model. In our method, we split the KDD98-learning-set randomly into 70% for the building set (66,788 records, 3,390 "respond" records) and 30% for the testing set (28,624 records, 1,453 "respond" records), as described in Section 3.4. The testing set is used for tuning the minimum and maximum support in our method, not for evaluation purpose. The evaluation is performed using the standard KDD98-validation-set, which is held out from the learning phase of all algorithms. The competition criterion is the *sum of actual profit* on the KDD98-validation-set, defined as $\Sigma_t(V - 0.68)$ for all validation records *t* predicted to have a positive profit, where *V* is the donation amount in *t*. We report our results based on the Profit model in Table 3. No significant difference is found on the Reward/Penalty model.

We compare our method with three categories of published results. The first includes the top five results from the KDD-CUP-98 competition. As pointed out by KDD98 (1998b), these contestants used state-of-the-art techniques such as *2-stage, multiple strategies, combined boosting and bagging.* The second category includes the results produced by the Meta-Cost technique (Domingos, 1999). The third category includes the results produced by the direct cost-sensitive decision-making (Zadrozny and Elkan, 2001). The results from the latter two categories are taken from Zadrozny and Elkan (2001), which implemented Meta-Cost and direct cost-sensitive decision-making using advanced techniques for probability estimation and donation estimation, including *multiple linear regression, C4.5, naive Bayes, smoothing, curtailment, binning, averaging,* and *Heckman* procedure. Interested readers are referred to Zadrozny and Elkan (2001) for more details.

The evaluation results in Sections 4.1-4.4 are based on the KDD98-validation-set, which has 96,367 records and 4,873 "respond" records. Figures 2 and 3 show the distribution of donation amount for "respond" records. There is a clear inverse correlation between the probability that a customer responds and the dollar amount generated by a response.

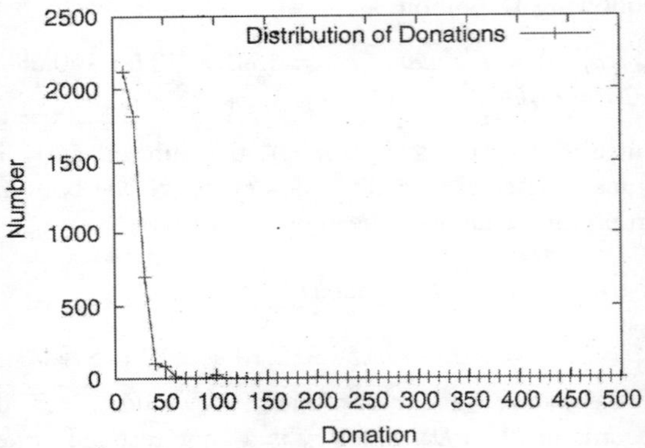

Figure 2: The distribution of donation.

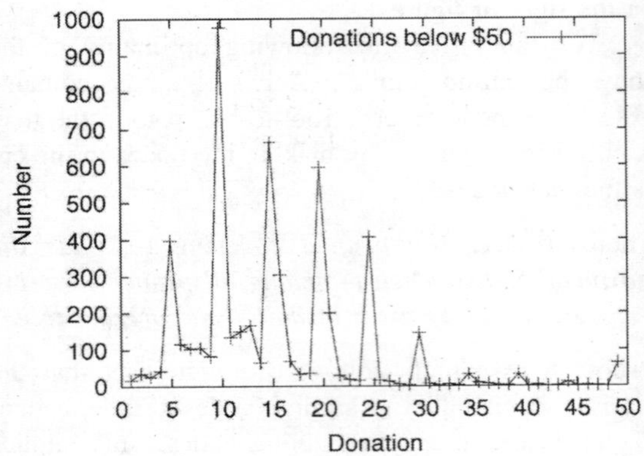

Figure 3: The distribution of donation below $50.

4.1 Sum of Actual Profit

The summary of comparison is shown in Table 6, based on the KDD98-validation-set. The first row (in boldface) is our result. Next come the three categories of published results: the top five contestants of the KDD-CUP-98 as reported in KDD98 (1998b), five algorithms of MetaCost and five algorithms of direct cost-sensitive decision making as reported in Zadrozny and Elkan (2001).

Our method generated the sum of actual profit of $20,693. This is 41% more than the KDD-CUP-98 winner ($14,712.24), 47% more than the best profit of MetaCost ($14,113), and 35% more than the best profit of direct cost-sensitive decision making ($15,329). According to the analysis in (Zadrozny and Elkan, 2001), a minimum difference of $1,090 is required to be statistically significant. Our performance gain far exceeds this requirement. Our average profit per mail is $0.88. This is 3.38 times that of the KDD-CUP-98 winner, and 8 times that of the Mail to Everyone Solution. Compared to the KDD-CUP winner, we generated 41% more profit by predicting less than an half number of contacts. Zadrozny and Elkan (2001) did not report the number of mailed, so we cannot compute their average profit. These higher total profit and average profit suggest that the proposed method is highly successful in focusing on valuable customers. This success is credited to the novel feature extraction based on the global search of association rule mining, and the profit estimation that pushes the customer value as the first class information.

4.2 Profit Lift

We extend the concept of "lift" in the literature (Ling and Li, 1998; Masand and Shapiro, 1996) to evaluate the "profit lift" of our result. In the *cumulative lift curve* (Ling and Li, 1998; Masand and Shapiro, 1996), validation records are ranked by the estimated probability of belonging to the "respond" class, and each point (x, y) on the curve represents that the top x percent of the ranked list contains y percent of all actual responders. In

Table 6: Comparison with published results

Category	Algorithm	Sum of actual profit	# Mailed	Average profit
	Our Algorithm	$20,693	23,437	$0.88
KDD-CUP-98 Results *in* (KDD98, 1998b)	GainSmarts (The winner)	$14,712.24	56,330	$0.26
	SAS/Enterprise Miner (#2)	$14,662.43	55,838	$0.26
	Quadstone/Decision house (#3)	$13,954.47	57,836	$0.24
	ARIAI/CARRL (#4)	$13,824.77	55,650	$0.25
	Amdocs/KDD Suite (#5)	$13,794.24	51,906	$0.27
MetaCost *in* (Domingos, 1999) and (Zadrozny and Elkan, 2001)	Smoothed C4.5 (sm)	$12,835		
	C4.5 with curtailment (cur)	$11,283		
	Binned naive Bayes (binb)	$14,113		
	Average (sm, cur)	$13,284		
	Average (sm, cur, binb)	$13,515		
Direct Cost-Sensitive *in* (Zadrozny and Elkan, 2001)	Smoothed C4.5 (sm)	$14,321		
	C4.5 with curtailment (cur)	$14,161		
	Binned naive Bayes (binb)	$15,094		
	Average (sm, cur)	$14,879		
	Average (sm, cur, binb)	$15,329		
	Maximum possible profit	$72,776	4,873	$14.93
	Mail to Everyone	$10,548	96,367	$0.11

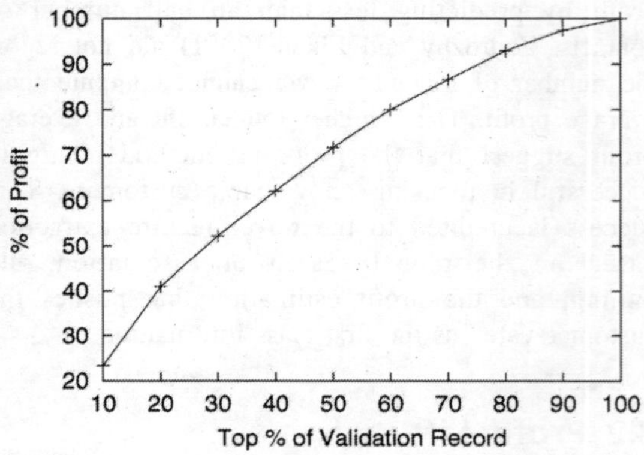

Figure 4: The accumulative profit lift curve.

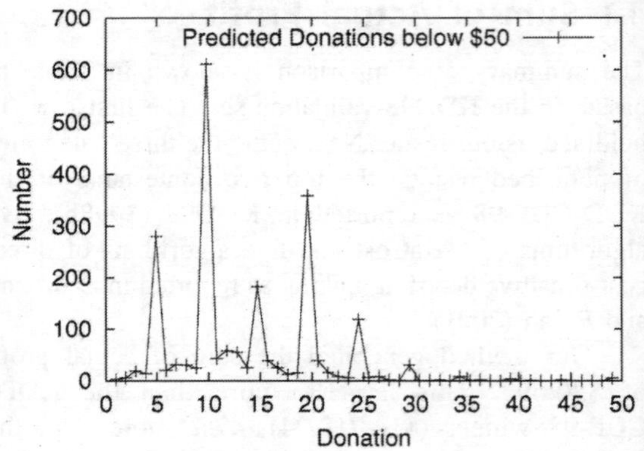

Figure 5: The predicted responders below $50.

the *cumulative profit lift curve*, each point (*x*, *y*) represents that the top *x* percent of the ranked list generates *y* percent of the total profit. Thus, the cumulative lift curve is a special case of the cumulative profit lift curve when every responder generates the same profit. Figure 4 shows the cumulative profit lift curve of our result. For example, the top 20% of the ranked list generates 42% of the total actual profit, giving the profit lift of 2.1. The bend toward the upper-left corner suggests that our method ranks valuable customers toward the top of the list.

4.3 Classification

Table 7 shows the confusion matrix for the KDD98-validation-set. 2,813 of the 4,873 responders are predicted as responders (i.e., contacted), and 71,389 of the 91,494 non-responders are predicted as non-responders (i.e., not contacted), giving the "hit rate" of 57.7% on responders and 78.0% on non-responders. In other words, the hit rate for responders is more than 10 times the percentage of responders in the data (i.e., 5%). This strongly suggests that our method has achieved the goal of identifying valuable customers. This is further confirmed by the striking similarity between the number of identified responders in figure 5 and the number of actual responders in figure 3.

Table 7: The confusion matrix

	Not contacted	Contacted
Non-responder	71,389	20,105
Responder	2,060	2,813

4.4 The Top 10 Rules

Figure 6 shows the 10 "respond" rules in terms of the profit generated on the KDD98-validation-set. The top portion describes the involved variables, copied from the data source. Each rule is listed in the following format:

Rule#: *Profit Supp Conf* $A_{i1} = a_{i1}, \ldots, A_{ik} = a_{ik}$

where *Profit* is the total profit generated on validation records by the rule, *Supp* and *Conf* are the support (in number of records) and confidence of the rule. A_{i1} is a nontarget variable and a_{i1} is either a single value or a range of the form [*a, b*]. We have omitted the right-hand side *respond* from all rules.

Examining these rules reveals some interesting points. First, neither the most general rule 8 (with the largest support) nor the most confident rule 9 is the most portable rule, i.e., rule 1. Second, the support of rules is very small. Recall that the learning set, $D_n \cup D_r$, has 66,788 records, 3,390 of which are "respond" records, D_r. The smallest support of 7 here corresponds to 0.01% of $D_n \cup D_r$

Variables	Meanings
AGE904	Average Age of Population
CHIL2	Percent Children Age 7 - 13
DMA	DMA Code
EIC16	Percent Employed in Public Administration
EIC4	Percent Employed in Manufacturing
ETH1	Percent White
ETH13	Percent Mexican
ETHC4	Percent Black < Age 15
HC6	Percent Owner Occupied Structures Built Since 1970
HHD1	Percent Households w/ Related Children
HU3	Percent Occupied Housing Units
HUPA1	Percent Housing Units w/ 2 thru 9 Units at the Address
HVP5	Percent Home Value >= $50,000
NUMCHLD	NUMBER OF CHILDREN
POP903	Number of Households
RAMNT_22	Dollar amount of the gift for 95XK
RFA_11	Donorís RFA status as of 96X1 promotion date
RFA_14	Donorís RFA status as of 95NK promotion date
RFA_23	Donorís RFA status as of 94FS promotion date
RHP2	Average Number of Rooms per Housing Unit
TPE11	Mean Travel Time to Work in minutes
WEALTH2	Wealth Rating

Rule	Profit	Supp	Conf	Rule
1	$81.11	13	0.11	ETHC4=[2.5,4.5], ETH1=[22.84,29.76], HC6=[60.91,68.53]
2	$61.73	8	0.17	RFA_14=f1d, ETH1=[29.76,36.69]
3	$47.07	12	0.12	HHD1=[24.33,28.91], EIC4=[33.72,37.36]
4	$40.82	16	0.12	RFA_23=s2g, ETH13=[27.34,31.23]
5	$35.17	11	0.16	EIC16=[11.25,13.12], CHIL2=[33,35.33], HC6=[45.69,53.30]
6	$28.71	7	0.16	RHP2=[36.72,40.45], AGE904=[42.2,44.9]
7	$24.32	10	0.14	HVP5=[56.07,63.23], ETH13=[31.23,35.61], RAMNT_22=[7.90,10.36]
8	$19.32	31	0.08	NUMCHLD=[2.5,3.25], HU3=[66.27,70.36]
9	$17.59	8	0.25	RFA_11=f1g, DMA=[743,766.8], POP903=[4088.208,4391.917], WEALTH2=[6.428571,7.714286]
10	$9.46	9	0.23	HUPA1=[41.81+,], TPE11=[27,64,31.58]

Figure 6: The top 10 "respond" rules found.

and 0.2% of D_r. With 481 variables, mining the whole learning set with the minimum support of 0.01% is infeasible according to our experience. However, by mining FARs from D_r only, we can set the minimum support to 0.2%, in which case the mining task is feasible. Third, these rules are explicit in terms of customer demographic information, thus, are potentially useful for devising campaign strategies.

4.5 Choosing Threshold Values

Now we report how the maximum support/minimum support were selected in our algorithm. At first, we included all items by setting maximum support at 100%. The rule generating (i.e., association rule mining) took a significantly long time for any minimum support small enough to produce sufficient "respond" rules; or to finish the rule generating within a reasonable amount of time, we had to use a high minimum support that generated very few "respond" rules, therefore, very low profit. Therefore, we have to exclude unpromising items using a lower maximum support. Our algorithm iteratively adjusted the maximum support and minimum support based on the feedback on the testing set. The last column in Table 8 shows the sum of actual profit on the testing set for several settings of maximum support/minimum support. Recall that the testing set is a 30% random sample of the KDD98-learning-set.

Table 8: Choosing maximum support/minimum support

Max sup.	Min sup.	#Rules	#Rules Aft. Prune	Time (second)	#Mailed	Sum of Act. Prof.
5% (40% remain)	3%	956	714	825	5470	$3757
	2%	31850	1117	1019	6270	$4566
	1.5%	46348	1363	2227	8559	$4690
3% (25% remain)	3%	1819	973	716	6785	$5722
	0.8%	2510	1064	754	6898	$5640
	0.5%	6530	1303	913	7796	$6733
	0.3%	16446	1522	1067	7812	$6760
	0.2%	**47665**	**1863**	**2178**	**8739**	**$7382**
	0.15%	71626	2317	2841	8383	$7103
1% (8% remain)	0.1%	4451	793	1001	5802	$4757
	0.05%	13871	1173	975	6017	$5128

In general, reducing maximum support/minimum support increases the sum of actual profit. Reducing the minimum support increases the number of rules, and reducing the maximum support allows more efficient mining. After reaching 3% for maximum support and 0.2% for minimum support, i.e., the row in boldface, further reducing these thresholds will decrease the sum of actual profit, due to the excessive over-fitting of specific rules. Therefore, our algorithm chooses 3 and 0.2% for maximum support and minimum support.

This study reveals the effectiveness of maximum support in reducing the number of items. The first column of Table 8 gives the remaining file size in percentage after applying the maximum support. A large portion of items was removed by using maximum support, which is extremely important for scaling up the association rule mining. A question is whether such dimension reduction will reduce the profitability of the final model. To answer this question, figure 7 compares the models built at varied maximum support of 15, 10 and 5%, with minimum support fixed at 3%. A smaller maximum support sharply reduces the number of rules, but not the sum of actual profit (on the testing set). In fact, many rules pruned by the maximum support are ranked lower than some general rules. Such rules are never used according to our ranking of rules.

Table 8 also shows the number of rules before and after the model pruning in Step 3 (i.e., columns 3 and 4). The pruning effect is dramatic, especially when the initial model is large.

For example, at the maximum support of 3% and the minimum support of 0.2%, the model has 47,665

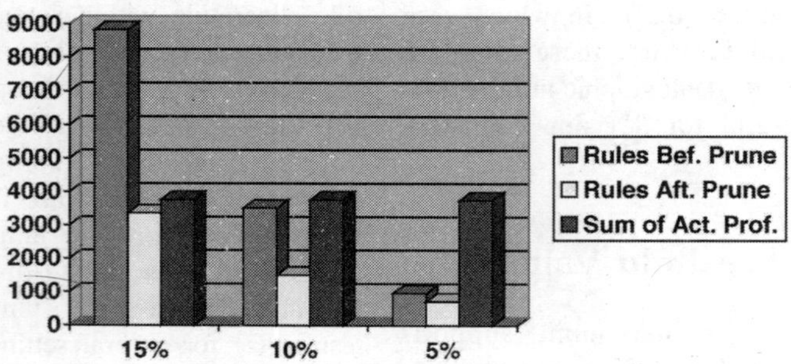

Figure 7: The effectiveness of maximum support.

rules before the pruning and only 1,863 rules after the pruning.

5. CONCLUSION

Direct marketing becomes increasingly important in retail, banking, insurance and fundraising industries. In a recent KDnuggets poll on the question "where do you plan to use data mining in 2002", direct marketing/fundraising received the second highest vote among 15 application areas (KDnuggets, 2001). A challenge to the prediction problem in direct marketing is the inverse correlation between the likelihood to buy and the dollar amount to spend, which implies that the class probability based ranking will rank valuable customers low rather than high! Previous approaches are "after the fact" in that they re-rank the probability based ranking using the customer value in the second step. Another challenge is the extremely high dimensionality and extremely low proportion of the target class. In such cases, finding rules to distinguish the target class from non-target classes is similar to finding a needle from a haystack.

In this paper, we directly estimate the profit generated on a customer without estimating the class probability. This methodology opens up new possibilities for profit estimation. In particular, we use association rules to summarize customer groups and to build a model for profit prediction. The advantage of the association rule approach is its stability of finding correlated features that may never be found in a local search. Evaluation on the well known, large, and challenging KDD-CUP-98 task demonstrates the benefits of this approach.

ACKNOWLEDGMENT

Research was supported in part by research grants from the Natural Science and Engineering Research Council of Canada. Qiang Yang's work was supported by the research grant 611261 from NSERC.

Note

1. http://www.commerce-database.com/directmarketing.htm

REFERENCES

Agrawal, R., Imilienski, T., and Swami, A. 1993. Mining association rules between sets of items in large datasets. In *Proceedings of the 1993 ACM SIGMOD International Conference on Management of Data* (*SIGMOD'93*), Washington, D.C., USA, pp. 207–216.

Agrawal, R., Mannila, H., Srikant, R., Toivonen, H., and Verkamo, A. 1996. Fast discovery of association rules. In *Advances in Knowledge Discovery and Data Mining*. AAAI/MIT Press, pp. 307–328.

Agrawal, R. and Srikant, R. 1994. Fast algorithm for mining association rules. In *Proceedings of the 20th International Conference on Very Large Data Bases* (*VLDB'94*), Santiago de Chile, Chile, pp. 487–499.

Bitran, G. and Mondschein, S. 1996. Mailing decisions in the catalog sales industry. *Management Science*, 42:1364–1381.

Brijs, T., Swinnen, G., Vanhoof, K., and Wets, G. 1999. Using association rules for product assortment decisions: a case study. In *Proceedings of the Fifth ACM SIGKDD International Conference on Knowledge Discovery and Data Mining* (*SIGKDD'99*), San Diego, CA, USA.

Bult, J.R. and Wansbeek, T. 1995. Optimal selection for direct mail. *Marketing Science*, 14:378–394.

Clark, P. and Niblett, T. 1989. The CN2 induction algorithm. *Machine Learning Journal*, 3(4): 261–283.

Clopper, C. and Pearson, E. 1934. The use of confidence or fiducial limits illustrated in the case of the binomial (http://www.jstor.org/journals/bio.html). *Biometrika*, 26(4):404–413.

Desarbo, W. and Ramaswamy, V. 1994. CRISP: Customer response based iterative segmentation procedures for response modeling in direct marketing. *Journal of Direct Marketing*, 8:7–20.

Domingos, P. and Pazzani, M. 1996. Beyond independence: Conditions for the optimality of the simple Bayesian classifier. In *Proceedings of the Thirteenth International Conference on Machine Learning* (*ICML'96*), Bari, Italy, pp. 105–112.

Domingos, P. 1999. MetaCost: A general method for making classifiers cost sensitive. In *Proceedings of the Fifth ACM SIGKDD International Conference on Knowledge Discovery and Data Mining* (*SIGKDD'99*), SanDiego, CA, USA, pp. 155–164.

Joshi, M., Agarwal, R., and Kumar, V. 2001. Mining needles in a haystack: Classifying rare classes via two-phase rule induction. In *Proceedings of the 2001 ACM SIGMOD International Conference on Management of Data* (*SIGMOD'01*), Santa Barbara, California, USA, pp. 91–102.

KDD98. 1998a. The KDD-CUP-98 dataset. http://kdd.ics.uci.edu/databases/kddcup98/kddcup98.html.

KDD98. 1998b. The KDD-CUP-98 result. http://www.kdnuggets.com/meetings/kdd98/kdd-cup-98.html.

KDnuggets. 2001. KDnuggets poll results: Data mining applications in 2002. http://www.kdnuggets.com/news/2001/n25.

Levin, N. and Zahavi, J. 1996. Segmentation analysis with managerial judgement. *Journal of Direct Marketing*, 10:28–37.

Ling, C. and Li, C. 1998. Data mining for direct marketing: Problems and solutions. In *The Fourth International Conference on Knowledge Discovery and Data Mining* (*KDD'98*), New York, New York, USA, pp. 73–79.

Masand, B. and Shapiro, G.P. 1996. A comparison of approaches for maximizing business payoff of prediction models. In *Proceedings of the Second International Conference on Knowledge Discovery and Data Mining* (*KDD'96*), Portland, Oregon, USA, pp. 195–201.

Michalski, R.S. 1969. On the quasi-minimal solution of the general covering problem. In *Proceedings of the Fifth International Symposium on Information Processing* (*FCIP 69*) (*Switching Circuits*), Vol. A3, Bled, Yugoslavia, pp. 125–128.

Potharst, R., Kaymak, U., and Pijls, W. 2002. Neural networks for target selection in direct marketing. *Neural Networks in Business: Techniques and Applications*, 89–110.

Quinlan, J. 1993. C4.5: *Programs for Machine Learning*. San Mateo, CA, USA: Morgan Kaufmann.

Quinlan, R.J. 1983. Learning efficient classification procedures and their application to chess endgames. *Machine Learning: An Artificial Intelligence Approach,* 1:463–482.

Rigoutsos, I. and Floratos, A. 1998. Combinatorial pattern discovery in biological sequences. *Bioinformatics*, 14(2):55–67.

Savasere, A., Omiecinski, E., and Navathe, S. 1998. Mining for strong negative associations in a large database of customer transactions. In *Proceedings of the Fourteenth International Conference on Data Engineering* (*ICDE'98*), Orlando, Florida, USA, pp. 494–502.

Tan, P.N., Kumar, V., and Srivastav, J. 2000. Indirect association: Mining higher order dependencies in data. In *The Fourth European Conference on Principles and Practice of Knowledge Discovery in Databases* (*PKDD'00*), Lyon, France, pp. 632–637.

Wang, K. and Su, M.Y. 2002. Item selection by hub-authority profit ranking. In *Proceedings of the Eighth ACM SIGKDD International Conference on Knowledge Discovery and Data Mining* (*SIGKDD'02*), Edmonton, Alberta, Canada, pp. 652–657.

Wang, K., Zhou, S., and Han, J. 2002. Profit mining: From patterns to actions. In *Proceedings of the Eighth International Conference on Extending Database Technology* (*EDBT'02*), Prague, Czech Republic, pp. 70–87.

Zadrozny, B. and Elkan, C. 2001. Learning and making decisions when costs and probabilities are both unknown. In *Proceedings of the seventh ACM SIGKDD International Conference on Knowledge Discovery and Data Mining* (*SIGKDD'01*), San Francisco, CA, USA, pp. 204–213.

CASE STUDY 3 SUMMARY

This case study was published in the journal Data Mining and Knowledge Discovery:
Wang, K., Zhou, S., Yang, Q., and Yeung, J.M.Y., Mining Customer Value: Association Rules to Direct Marketing, *Data Mining and Knowledge Discovery*, Vol: 11, pp. 57–79, 2005.

Data mining in the field of direct marketing often involves selecting those customers that are likely to be most profitable. Most direct marketing companies have large databases of potential customers and a lot of information about them including their history of purchases but the direct marketing response rates are often low, even as low as 5% is some cases. It therefore makes sense to select those customers that are more likely to respond and not contact customers that are unlikely to respond. This case study analyses direct marketing data from a fundraising campaign in which each record had 481 variables. The response rate was only 5%. Association rule mining is used to improve the response rate.

CASE STUDY 3 EXERCISES

1. Describe the most important features of the data used in this case study.
2. What are the major steps in the overall algorithm used to improve the response rate? Discuss each step and explain its importance.
3. What is a focused item? What is a focused association rule?
4. Why is validation required in this case study?
5. Consider the information given in Figure 6 and discuss the role of support and confidence in discovering the most profitable rules. Explain why the rule with the highest support or the rule with the highest confidence are both not the most profitable.

CHAPTER

4 Classification

LEARNING OBJECTIVES

After completing this chapter, you will be able to:

- Explain the concept of classification
- Describe the decision tree method
- Give an example using the decision tree method
- Describe the Naïve Bayes method
- Give an example using the Naïve Bayes method
- Discuss accuracy of classification methods and how accuracy may be improved
- Find further information about classification techniques

4.1 INTRODUCTION

Classification, as a means of estimating associations, is a classical problem extensively studied by statisticians and machine learning researchers. The word classification is difficult to define precisely. We present one definition.

Classification
Classification is the separation or ordering of objects (or things) into classes.

If the classes are created without looking at the data (non-empirically), the classification is called *a priori classification*. If however the classes are created empirically (by looking at the data), the classification is called *posteriori classification*. In most literature on classification it is assumed that the classes have been deemed a priori and classification then consists of training the system so that when a new object is presented to the trained system it is able to assign the object to one of the existing classes. This approach is also called *supervised learning*. Some techniques are available for posteriori or unsupervised classification in which the classes are determined based on the given data. These are discussed in Chapter 5 on *cluster analysis*.

Data mining has generated renewed interest in classification. Since the datasets in data mining are often large, new classification techniques have been developed to deal with millions of objects having perhaps dozens or even hundreds of attributes.

A classification process in which classes have been pre-defined needs a method that will train the classification system to allocate objects to the classes. The training is based on a training sample, a set of sample data where for each sample the class is already known. We assume each object to have a number of attributes, one of which tells us which class the object belongs to. This attribute is known for the training data but for data other than the training data (we call this other data the *test data*) we assume that the value of the class attribute is unknown and is to be determined by the classification method. This attribute may be considered as the output of all other attributes and is often referred to as the *output attribute* or the *dependent attribute*. The attributes other than the output attribute are called the *input attributes* or the *independent attributes*. In supervised learning schemes, it is assumed that we have sufficient training data to build an accurate model during the training phase. The model that we build from the training data is never 100% accurate and classification based on the model will always lead to errors in some cases. In spite of such errors, classification can be useful for prediction and better understanding of the data.

The attributes may be of different types as discussed in Chapter 2. Attributes whose domain is numerical are called *numerical attributes* while attributes whose domain is not numerical are called *categorical attributes*. Categorical attributes may be ordered (e.g. a student's grade) or may be unordered (e.g. gender). Usually, the dependent attribute is assumed to be categorical if it is a classification problem and then the value of the attribute is the class label. If the problem is not a classification problem, the dependent attribute may be numerical. Usually such problems are called *regression problems.* Obviously, the two problems are closely related and one type of problem may sometimes be converted to another type if necessary by simple transformation of variables from either categorical to continuous (by converting categories to numerical values which may not be always possible) or from continuous to categorical (by bracketing numerical values and assigning categories, e.g. High, Medium and Low for salaries). Binning of continuous data into categories is quite simple although the selection of ranges can have a significant impact on the results.

Classification has many applications, for example prediction of customer behaviour (e.g. predicting direct mail responses or identifying telecom customers that might switch companies) and identifying fraud. In many applications, for example in assessing credit card applicants, a credit card company may already have sample data based on past applicants and knowledge about the applicants that were good credit risks and those that were not. A classification method may use the sample to derive a set of rules for allocating new applications to either of the two classes.

CHAPTER OVERVIEW

This chapter deals with supervised learning that requires training data to build a classification model. This data has been preclassified. We first discuss the classification technique based on the decision tree method. A simple example is presented before a step-wise algorithm for building a decision tree is presented in Section 4.3. One of the steps in this algorithm requires a *split algorithm.* Two split algorithms are presented. Section 4.4 presents the first split algorithm based on information theory. Section 4.5 describes the other split algorithm; based on the *Gini Index*. Section 4.6 deals with the problems of overfitting and pruning the decision tree followed by deriving rules from a decision tree in Section 4.7. Another classification method, the Naïve Bayes method, is described in Section 4.9. In the classification techniques discussed in this chapter, testing and validation play an important role. Classifying the test data and comparing the results with the known results can then determine the accuracy. The number of cases classified correctly provides us with an estimate of the accuracy of the model. Although accuracy is a very useful metric, it does not provide sufficient information about the utility of the model. For example, efficiency may be paramount in some applications. These issues are discussed in Sections 4.10 and 4.11. Our aim is to find the most accurate models that are easy to understand and which are efficient when dealing with large datasets. Section 4.12 presents a number of evaluation criteria.

4.2 DECISION TREE

A decision tree is a popular classification method that results in a flow-chart like tree structure where each node denotes a test on an attribute value and each branch represents an outcome of the test. The tree leaves represent the classes.

Let us imagine that we wish to classify a group of (mostly Australian) animals. We have some training data of 16 animals that has already been classified. It is given in Table 4.1. We want to build a model based on this already classified data.

It should be noted that this is a very simple example and the data has only three classes, namely, Bird, Mammal and Marsupial. If we had a larger set of animals, we are likely to have more classes and may need more attributes than the three we use in Table 4.1. Furthermore, note that all attributes are binary.

Table 4.1 Training data for a classification problem

Name	*Eggs*	*Pouch*	*Flies*	*Class*
Cockatoo	Yes	No	Yes	Bird
Dugong	No	No	No	Mammal
Eagle	Yes	No	Yes	Bird
Echidna	Yes	Yes	No	Marsupial
Emu	Yes	No	No	Bird
Flying Fox	No	No	Yes	Mammal
Kangaroo	No	Yes	No	Marsupial
Koala	No	Yes	No	Marsupial
Kookaburra	Yes	No	Yes	Bird
Owl	Yes	No	Yes	Bird
Penguin	Yes	No	No	Bird
Platypus	Yes	No	No	Mammal
Possum	No	Yes	No	Marsupial
Wallaby	No	Yes	No	Marsupial
Whale	No	No	No	Mammal
Dolphin	No	No	No	Mammal

Decision tree is a model that is both predictive and descriptive. A decision tree is a tree that displays relationships found in the training data. The tree consists of zero or more internal nodes and one or more leaf nodes with each internal node being a decision node having two or more child nodes. Using the training data, the decision tree method generates a tree that consists of nodes that are rules, very similar to those used in "20 questions"[1] to determine the class of an object after the training is completed. Each node of the tree represents a choice between a number of alternatives (in "20 questions" the choices are binary) and each leaf node represents a classification or a decision. The training process that generates the tree is called *induction*. The decision tree technique is popular since the rules generated are easy to describe and understand, the technique is fast unless the data is very large. Also, there is a variety of software available. Furthermore, the decision tree approach does not make any assumptions about the underlying probability distributions of the attributes' values.

Just like in the game of "20 questions", we must select questions that help discriminate well. There is little point in asking a question like "Is the person Mahatma Gandhi?" because if the answer is no then we have not learned a lot. A better question might be "Is the person a man?" We will later discuss techniques for deciding which question at each stage is the best.

As an example of a decision tree, we show a possible result in Figure 4.1 of classifying the data in Table 4.1:

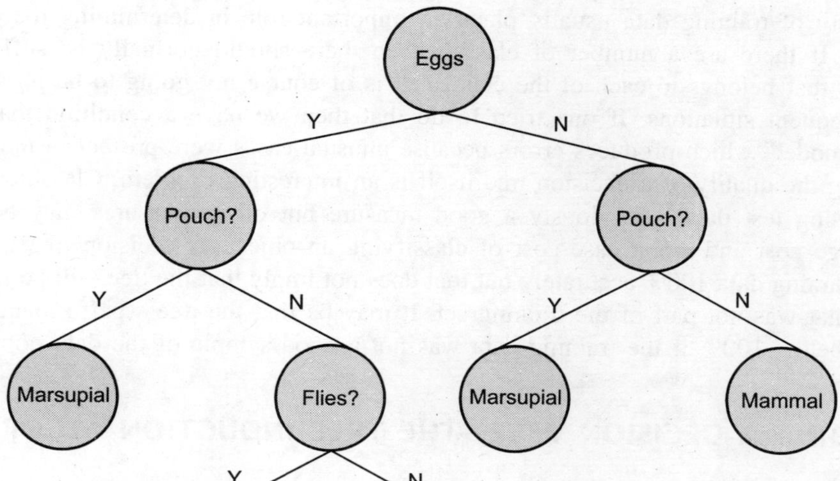

Figure 4.1 A decision tree for data in Table 4.1.

Note that each node of the tree is a decision while the leaves are the classes.

[1] 20 questions is a simple game in which one person selects an object that others need to guess by asking simple questions like "Is it a living thing?" and getting a reply yes or no. The game continues until the object is guessed correctly or 20 questions have been asked.

We should note that given a dataset, the decision tree obtained is not unique. In the above example, we used the first attribute first by asking the question "does the animal lay eggs?" followed by the question "does the animal have a pouch?" which is followed by the third question. We could have instead started with a question based on either the second or third attribute followed by the remaining two questions. In all there are six different sequences of questions that we could ask because the first question could be any of the three possible questions and the next question could be either of the two remaining ones. Obviously if there were 10 attributes then the number of different sequences of questions would be 1024 if all attributes are binary. Given such a large number of sequences we must have an automatic way of selecting the next question to ask.

It should be noted that there needs to be a balance between the number of training samples and the number of independent attributes. Generally, the number of training samples required is likely to be relatively small if the number of independent attributes is small and the number of training samples required is likely to be large when the number of attributes is large. It is not unusual to have hundreds of objects in the training sample if the number of attributes is 10 or more although the examples in this chapter must consider only a small number of attributes and a small training set.

Normally, the complexity of a decision tree increases as the number of attributes increases, although in some situations it has been found that only a small number of attributes can determine the class to which an object belongs and the rest of the attributes have little or no impact.

The quality of training data usually plays an important role in determining the quality of the decision tree. If there are a number of classes, then there should normally be sufficient training data available that belongs to each of the classes. It is of course not going to be possible to model the most infrequent situations. If one tried to do that then we have a condition that is called an "overtrained model" which produces errors because unusual cases were present in the training data.

Measuring the quality of a decision tree itself is an interesting problem. Classification accuracy determined using test data is obviously a good measure but other measures may be used. These include average cost and worst case cost of classifying an object. A decision tree may be able to classify the training data 100% accurately but that does not imply that the tree will be just as accurate on test data that was not part of the training set. It may be that the tree's performance on test data will be well below 100% if the training data was not a good sample of the data population.

4.3 BUILDING A DECISION TREE—THE TREE INDUCTION ALGORITHM

As noted earlier, a decision tree consists of internal nodes where decisions need to be made and leaf nodes, each of which is given a class label.

The decision tree algorithm is given below. It is a relatively simple top-down greedy algorithm. The aim of the algorithm is to build a tree that has leaves that are as homogeneous as possible. The major step of the algorithm is to continue to divide leaves that are not homogeneous into leaves that are as homogeneous as possible until no further division is possible.

1. Let the set of training data be S. If some of the attributes are continuous-valued, they should be discretised. For example, age values may be binned into the following categories (under 18), (18–40), (41–65) and (over 65) and transformed into *A*, *B*, *C* and *D* or more descriptive labels may be chosen. Once that is done, put all of S in a single tree node.
2. If all instances in S are in the same class, then stop.

3. Split the next node by selecting an attribute A from amongst the independent attributes that best divides or splits the objects in the node into subsets and create a decision tree node.
4. Split the node according to the values of A.
5. Stop if either of the following conditions is met otherwise continue with Step 3:
   (a) If this partition divides the data into subsets that belong to a single class and no other node needs splitting.
   (b) If there are no remaining attributes on which the sample may be further divided.

In the decision tree algorithm decisions are made locally and the algorithm at no stage tries to find a globally optimum tree.

The major step in the decision tree building algorithm is Step 3, where an attribute that best splits the data needs to be selected. We assume that only one attribute is to be used for the split, although methods that use a combination of attributes have been proposed in the literature. Therefore the split rules in our algorithm are based on simple tests, for example "salary = high", while algorithms that use more than one split attribute may use split rules such as "salary = high and age = A".

To find a split attribute, all the attributes that have not yet been used need to be somehow given goodness value that shows the discrimination power of the attribute. The attributes then may be ranked according to that value and the highest ranked attribute selected.

The discriminatory power of each attribute may be evaluated in a number of different ways. We will only discuss the following two most commonly used evaluation rules:

- Rules based on information theory
- Rules based on Gini index

It has been shown that the split attributes selected and the quality of decision trees obtained by using these approaches do not differ significantly.

We have assumed that the algorithm will stop gracefully in Step 5, but knowing when to stop can be a nontrivial issue. The quality of the tree will depend on stopping at a point when the decision tree provides good accuracy and is of the "right" size. Often once the tree building is complete (that is, no further improvement is possible given the training data), *pruning* may be required to reduce the tree size and improve its performance. We will discuss this in Section 4.6.

4.4 SPLIT ALGORITHM BASED ON INFORMATION THEORY

One of the techniques for selecting an attribute to split a node is based on the concept of information theory or entropy. The concept is quite simple, although often difficult to understand for many. It is based on Claude Shannon's idea that if you have uncertainty then you have information and if there is no uncertainty there is no information. For example, if a coin has a head on both sides, then the result of tossing it does not produce any information but if a coin is normal with a head and a tail then the result of the toss provides information.

Essentially information is defined as $-p_i \log p_i$ where p_i is the probability of some event. Since the probability p_i is always less than 1, $\log p_i$ is always negative and $-p_i \log p_i$ is always positive. For those who cannot remember their high school mathematics, we note that log of 1 is always zero whatever the base, the log of any number greater than 1 is always positive and the log of any number smaller than 1 is always negative. Also,

$$\log_2\left(\frac{1}{2}\right) = -1$$

$$\log_2\left(\frac{1}{2^n}\right) = -n$$

Information of any event that is likely to have several possible outcomes is given by

$$I = \sum_i (-p_i \log p_i)$$

Consider an event that can have one of two possible values. Let the probabilities of the two values be p_1 and p_2. Obviously if p_1 is 1 and p_2 is zero then there is no information in the outcome and $I = 0$. If $p_1 = 0.5$ and $p_2 = 0.5$ then the information is

$$I = -0.5 \log (0.5) - 0.5 \log (0.5)$$

This comes out to 1.0 (using log base 2) and is the maximum information that you can have for an event with two possible outcomes. This is also called entropy and is in effect a measure of the minimum number of bits required to encode the information.

If we consider the case of a die (singular of dice) with six possible outcomes with equal probability, then the information is given by:

$$I = 6(-(1/6) \log (1/6)) = 2.585$$

Therefore three bits are required to represent the outcome of rolling a dice. Of course if the die was loaded so that there was a 50% or a 75% chance of getting a 6 then the information content of rolling the die would be lower as given below. Note that we assume that the probability of getting any of 1 to 5 is equal (that is, equal to 10% for the 50% case and 5% for the 75% case).

$$(50\%)\ I = 5(-(0.1) \log (0.1)) - 0.5 \log (0.5) = 2.16$$

$$(75\%)\ I = 5(-(0.05) \log (0.05)) - 0.75 \log (0.75) = 1.39$$

Therefore we will need three bits to represent the outcome of throwing a die that has 50% probability of throwing a six but only two bits when the probability is 75%.[2]

The idea of selecting a split attribute is to select an attribute that reduces the uncertainty by the largest amount. So the attribute ought to distribute the objects such that each attribute value results in objects that have as little uncertainty as possible. Ideally, each attribute value should provide us with objects that belong to only one class and therefore have zero information.

Information gain

We will use the term *information gain*. It is a measure of how good an attribute is for predicting the class of each of the training data. We will select the attribute with the highest information gain as the next split attribute. In Table 4.1 we can look at each attribute and it is possible to work out which attribute is the best to use based on the uncertainty.

[2]The reader may be wondering how two bits will represent the outcomes of throwing a die that could produce any of the six numbers. When probability of getting a 6 is 75%, four die throws should result on the average in three 6's and one other number. A code may therefore be developed in which each six is represented by just one bit (say a 1) allowing five bits to represent a number 1 to 5. Try to work out a code for this situation!

Perhaps the term information gain is somewhat confusing because what we really mean is that information gain is a measure of reduction in uncertainty once the value of an attribute is known. If the uncertainty is reduced by a large amount, knowing the value of the attribute has provided a lot of information and thus we have a large information gain.

Assume there are two classes, P and N and let the set of training data S (with a total number of objects s) contain p elements of class P and n elements of class N. The amount of information is defined as

$$I = -(n/s)\log(n/s) - (p/s)\log(p/s)$$

Obviously if $p = n$, I is equal to 1 and if $p = s$ then $I = 0$. Therefore, if there was an attribute for which almost all the objects had the same value (for example, gender when most people are male), using the attribute would lead to no information gain (that is, not reduce uncertainty) because for gender = female there will be almost no objects while gender = male would have almost all the objects even before we knew the gender. If on the other hand an attribute divided the training sample such that gender = female resulted in objects that all belong to Class A and gender = male all belong to Class B, then uncertainty has been reduced to zero and we have a large information gain. We define information gain for sample S using attribute A as follows:

$$\text{Gain}(S, A) = I - \sum_{i \in \text{values}(A)} \left(\frac{t_i}{s}\right) I_i$$

I is the information before the split and $\sum_{i \in \text{values}(A)} \left(\frac{t_i}{s}\right) I_i$ is the sum of information after the split where I_i is the information of node i and t_i is the number of objects in node i. Thus the total information after the split $\sum_{i \in \text{values}(A)} \left(\frac{t_i}{s}\right) I_i$ which is the sum of the information of each node.

Once we have computed the information gain for every remaining attribute, the attribute with the highest information gain is selected.

Example 4.1—Using the Information Measure

We consider an artificial example of building a decision tree classification model to classify bank loan applications by assigning applications to one of three risk classes (Table 4.2).

Table 4.2 Training data for Example 4.1

Owns Home?	*Married*	*Gender*	*Employed*	*Credit rating*	*Risk class*
Yes	Yes	Male	Yes	*A*	*B*
No	No	Female	Yes	*A*	*A*
Yes	Yes	Female	Yes	*B*	*C*
Yes	No	Male	No	*B*	*B*
No	Yes	Female	Yes	*B*	*C*
No	No	Female	Yes	*B*	*A*
No	No	Male	No	*B*	*B*
Yes	No	Female	Yes	*A*	*A*
No	Yes	Female	Yes	*A*	*C*
Yes	Yes	Female	Yes	*A*	*C*

There are 10 (s = 10) samples and three classes. The frequencies of these classes are:

$A = 3$
$B = 3$
$C = 4$

Information in the data due to uncertainty of outcome regarding the risk class each person belongs to is given by:

$$I = -(3/10) \log (3/10) - (03/10) \log (3/10) - 4/10 \log (4/10) = 1.57$$

Let us now consider using each attribute in turn as a candidate to split the sample.

1. **Attribute "Owns Home"**

   Value = Yes. There are five applicants who own their home. They are in classes
   $$A = 1, B = 2, C = 2.$$
   Value = No. There are five applicants who do not own their home. They are in classes
   $$A = 2, B = 1, C = 2.$$
   Given the above values, it does not appear as if this attribute will reduce the uncertainty by much. Let us compute the information gain by using this attribute. We divide persons into those who own their home and those who do not. Computing information for each of these two subtrees.
   $$I(\text{Yes}) = I(y) = -(1/5) \log (1/5) - (2/5) \log (2/5) - (2/5) \log (2/5) = 1.52$$
   $$I(\text{No}) = I(n) = -(2/5) \log (2/5) - (1/5) \log (1/5) - (2/5) \log (2/5) = 1.52$$
   Total information of the two subtrees = $0.5\ I(y) + 0.5\ I(n) = 1.52$

2. **Attribute "Married"**

   There are five applicants that are married and five that are not.

   Value = Yes has $A = 0$, $B = 1$, $C = 4$, total 5

   Value = No has $A = 3$, $B = 2$, $C = 0$, total 5

   Looking at the values above, it appears that this attribute will reduce the uncertainty by more than the last attribute. Computing the information gain by using this attribute we obtain the following:
   $$I(y) = -(1/5) \log (1/5) - (4/5) \log (4/5) = 0.722$$
   $$I(n) = -(3/5) \log (3/5) - (2/5) \log (2/5) = 0.971$$
   Information of the subtrees = $0.5I(y) + 0.5I(n) = 0.846$

3. **Attribute "Gender"**

   There are three applicants that are male and seven are female.

   Value = Male has $A = 0$, $B = 3$, $C = 0$, total 3

   Value = Female has $A = 3$, $B = 0$, $C = 4$, total 7

The values above show that the uncertainty is reduced even more by using this attribute since for Value = Male we have only one class. Let us compute the information gain by using this attribute.

$$I(\text{Male}) = 0$$

$$I(\text{Female}) = -(3/7) \log (3/7) - (4/7) \log (4/7) = 0.985$$

Total information of the subtrees = $0.3I(\text{Male}) + 0.7\,I(\text{Female}) = 0.69$

4. **Attribute "Employed"**

   There are eight applicants that are employed and two that are not.

   Value = Yes has $A = 3$, $B = 1$, $C = 4$, total 8

   Value = No has A = 0, $B = 2$, $C = 0$, total 2

   The values above show that this attribute will reduce uncertainty but most attribute values are Yes while the No value leads to only one class. Computing the information gain by using this attribute we obtain the following:

   $$I(y) = -(3/8) \log (3/8) - (1/8) \log (1/8) - (4/8) \log (4/8) = 1.41$$

   $$I(n) = 0$$

   Total information of the subtrees = $0.8I(y) + 0.2I(n) = 1.12$

5. **Attribute "Credit Rating"**

   There are five objects that have credit rating A and five that have B.

   Value = A has $A = 2$, $B = 1$, $C = 2$, total 5

   Value = B has $A = 1$, $B = 2$, $C = 2$, total 5

   Looking at the values above, we can see that this is like the first attribute that does not reduce uncertainty by much. The information gain for this attribute is the same as for the first attribute.

   $$I(A) = -(2/5) \log (2/5) - (1/5) \log (1/5) - (2/5) \log (2/5) = 1.52$$

   $$I(B) = -(1/5) \log (1/5) - (2/5) \log (2/5) - (2/5) \log (2/5) = 1.52$$

   Total information of the subtrees = $0.5I(A) + 0.5I(B) = 1.52$

The values for information gain can now be computed in Table 4.3.

Table 4.3 Information gain for the five attributes

Potential split attribute	*Information before split*	*Information after split*	*Information gain*
Owns home	1.57	1.52	0.05
Married	1.57	0.85	0.72
Gender	1.57	0.69	0.88
Employed	1.57	1.12	0.45
Credit rating	1.57	1.52	0.05

Hence the largest information gain is provided by the attribute "Gender" and that is the attribute that is used for the split.

Now we can reduce the data by removing the attribute Gender and removing the Class *B* since all Class *B* have Gender = Male. See Table 4.4.

Table 4.4 Data after removing attribute "Gender" and Class B

Owns home?	*Married*	*Employed*	*Credit rating*	*Risk class*
No	No	Yes	*A*	*A*
Yes	Yes	Yes	*B*	*C*
No	Yes	Yes	*B*	*C*
No	No	Yes	*B*	*A*
Yes	No	Yes	*A*	*A*
No	Yes	Yes	*A*	*C*
Yes	Yes	Yes	*A*	*C*

The information in this data of two classes due to uncertainty of outcome regarding the class each person belongs to is given by:

$$I = -(3/7)\log(3/7) - (4/7)\log(4/7) = 1.33$$

Let us now consider each attribute in turn as a candidate to split the sample.

1. **Attribute "Owns Home"**

   Value = Yes. There are three applicants who own their home, who are in classes

   $$A = 1 \text{ and } C = 2$$

   Value = No. There are four applicants who do not own their home, who are in classes

   $$A = 2 \text{ and } C = 2$$

   Given the above values, it does not appear as if this attribute will reduce the uncertainty by much. Computing information for each of these two subtrees:

   $$I(\text{Yes}) = I(y) = -(1/3)\log(1/3) - (2/3)\log(2/3) = 0.92$$

   $$I(\text{No}) = I(n) = -(2/4)\log(2/4) - (2/4)\log(2/4) = 1.00$$

   Total information of the two subtrees = $(3/7)I(y) + (4/7)I(n) = 0.96$

2. **Attribute "Married"**

   There are four applicants that are married and three that are not.

   Value = Yes has $A = 0$, $C = 4$, total 4

   Value = No has $A = 3$, $C = 0$, total 3

   Looking at the values above, it appears that this attribute will reduce the uncertainty by a lot more than the last attribute since for each value the persons belong to only one class and therefore information is zero.

   $$I(y) = -(4/4)\log(4/4) = 0.0$$

   $$I(n) = -(3/3)\log(3/3) = 0.0$$

   Information of the subtrees = 0.0

There is no need to consider other attributes now, since no other attribute can be better. The split attribute therefore is "Married" and we now obtain the following decision tree in Figure 4.2 which concludes this very simple example. It should be noted that a number of attributes that were available in the data were not required in classifying it.

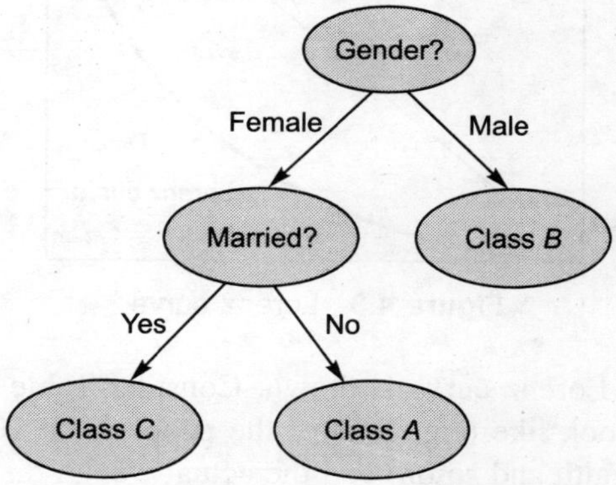

Figure 4.2 Decision tree for Example 4.1.

The decision tree may be written as a set of rules like "if Gender = Male then Class *B*". We discuss rule generation in Section 4.7.

Note: The attribute comparison based on information gain is not necessarily always fair. The approach tends to favour attributes that have a large number of values. For example, if there was an attribute that had a large number of values such that each value resulted in only one element of the dataset then that attribute will be selected although it might not be the optimum split attribute in that it leads to a very wide tree with depth one. Such a tree may be even quite inaccurate for unseen data.

4.5 SPLIT ALGORITHM BASED ON THE GINI INDEX

We have considered the information theory approach of splitting a node. This approach is used in the well-known software package C4.5. Another commonly used split approach is called the Gini index which is used in the widely used packages CART and IBM Intelligent Miner.

An Italian economist, Corrado Gini (1884–1965) proposed the Gini index as a measure of resource inequality in a population. The index varies from 0 to 1, zero means no inequality (similar to saying no uncertainty and hence $I = 0$) and 1 means maximum possible inequality (in other words, maximum uncertainty). The index is based on the Lorenz curve, which plots cumulative family income against the number of families from poorest to richest.

Figure 4.3 shows the Lorenz curve which is the basis of the Gini index. The index is the ratio of the area between the Lorenz curve and the 45-degree line to the area under the 45-degree line. The smaller the ratio, the less is the area between the two curves and the more evenly distributed is the wealth. When wealth is evenly distributed, asking any person about his/her wealth provides no information at all since every person has the same wealth while in a situation where wealth is very unevenly distributed finding out how much wealth a person has provides information because of the uncertainty of wealth distribution.

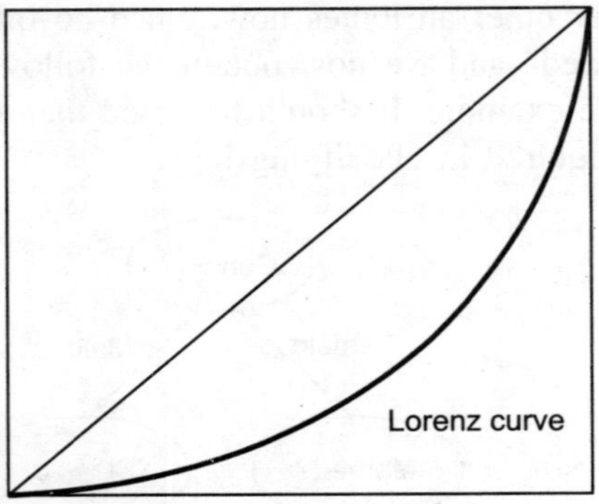

Figure 4.3 Lorenz curve.

We now explain how the Lorenz curve is drawn. Consider Table 4.5 that gives what the equal distribution of wealth would look like (e.g. 10% of the people own 10% of the wealth and 20% of the people own 20% of the wealth and so on) and the actual wealth distribution figures for Australia. Note that wealth is measured in many different ways and the data in the table below is based on the total household wealth as the indicator. Surprisingly the poor half of the Australian population has very little wealth (only 6%) since most of them do not own a home (and if they do they have large mortgages) and they often have credit card debts and other debts. This is in contrast to 45% of the nation's wealth being held by the wealthiest 10% of the population.[3]

Table 4.5 Wealth distribution in Australia

Fraction of population	*Fraction of wealth if equal distribution (cumulative)*	*Actual fraction of wealth in Australia (cumulative)*
0.1	0.1	0.00
0.2	0.2	0.00
0.3	0.3	0.00
0.4	0.4	0.02
0.5	0.5	0.06
0.6	0.6	0.14
0.7	0.7	0.23
0.8	0.8	0.36
0.9	0.9	0.55
1.0	1.0	1.00

We may compute areas below the two curves using the Trapezoidal Rule. The area under the 45-degree line is the area of the triangle, which is 0.5. The area under the Lorenz curve for Australia may be computed and comes to approximately 0.19. The ratio of the area between the 45-degree line and the Lorenz curve to the area below the 45-degree line is (0.5 – 0.19)/0.5 which is 0.62. A more accurate value (0.35) is given in Table 4.6.

[3] The wealth distribution is even worse in the USA where the wealthiest 10% of the population has 71% of the wealth and top 1% has 33%. Bottom 60% of the population in the USA has only 4.3% of the wealth! This wealth distribution has been reported to be getting worse in recent years.

Table 4.6 Income distribution Gini index in a number of countries

Country	Gini index
Brazil	0.59
Mexico	0.55
Malaysia	0.49
Russia	0.46
China	0.45
USA	0.41
UK	0.36
Australia	0.35
Indonesia	0.34
India	0.32
Sweden, Japan	0.25

Source: http://hdr.undp.org/reports/global/2004/pdf/hdr04_HDI.pdf

We now, in Table 4.6, using figures from the United Nations Human Development Report 2004, show that there is wide variation in family income distribution in the countries of the world. Note that the income distribution and wealth distribution are not the same. The wealth distribution is usually worse than income distribution. Again, note that a Gini index of zero means equal distribution of income and value 1 is for most unequal distribution. Therefore income distribution is best in Sweden and Japan and worst in Brazil. Not surprisingly, income distribution in USA is even worse than in countries like Indonesia and India which are sometimes used as examples of uneven income distribution.

Gini index may also be calculated for the whole world since the population and GNP per capita of each country in the world is known. If we assume that Gini index within each country is zero (i.e. income within each country is evenly distributed, far from reality as seen above), the Gini index for the world for 2003 was 0.67. However if we consider Gini index within each country to be 0.40 the Gini index for the world goes up to about 0.77. Perhaps not surprisingly, it shows that income within the world is very unevenly distributed and wealth is even more unevenly distributed. If countries like China, India and Brazil continue to grow at the current fast pace the world Gini index could well reduce significantly in the next 20–30 years.

The Gini index has been used in a wide variety of applications in addition to measuring wealth distribution. For example, the Queensland Government has analysed crime data using the Gini index to find how different types of crimes are distributed in the state. The results obtained are given in Table 4.7.

Table 4.7 Crime distribution in Queensland Gini index

Crime type	*Gini index*
Prostitution offences	0.65
Liquor offences	0.52
Armed robbery	0.38
Kidnapping	0.33
Motor vehicle theft	0.30
Fraud	0.26
Drug offences	0.22
Unlawful entry shops	0.21
Stealing from homes	0.17

It is clear that crimes like stealing from homes are fairly evenly distributed in the state since the Gini index for such crimes is small, while crimes like prostitution offences are, perhaps not surprisingly, not evenly distributed since such crimes are more frequent in larger cities than in smaller cities and towns.

If a dataset S contains examples from n classes, the Gini index, $G(S)$, is defined as

$$G(S) = 1 - \sum p_i^2$$

where p_i is the relative frequency of class i in S. If a dataset S with s elements is split into two subsets S_1 and S_2 with number of elements n_1 and n_2 respectively, the Gini index of the split data contains examples from n classes, and is defined as

$$G(S) = (n_1/s)G(S_1) + (n_2/s)G(S_2)$$

Computing the Gini index for the outcome of tossing a true coin:

$$G = 1 - (0.5)^2 - (0.5)^2 = 0.5$$

0.5 is the maximum value for an event with two possible values.

Consider a loaded coin with 70% chance of a head and another coin with heads on both sides.

$$G = 1 - (0.7)^2 - (0.3)^2 = 0.42$$

$$G = 1 - (1.0)^2 = 0$$

Clearly, there is no uncertainty about the coin with two heads and so the index is zero. With heads having a probability of 70%, the uncertainty is lower than with a coin with equal probabilities and therefore the index is again lower.

The Gini index for a die with six possible outcomes with equal probability is:

$$G = 1 - 6(1/6)^2 = 5/6 = 0.833$$

If a loaded die had much more chance of getting a 6, say 50% (and therefore only a 10% chance of getting each number other than a 6) or even 75% (and therefore only a 5% chance of getting other than a 6), the Index is given by:

$$50\%: \quad G = 1 - 5(0.1)^2 - (0.5)^2 = 0.70$$

$$75\%: \quad G = 1 - 5(0.05)^2 - (0.75)^2 = 0.425$$

Clearly, the index is largest with the largest uncertainty.

It is perhaps interesting to compare values obtained for the Gini index with those information gain obtained in Section 4.4. Figures in Table 4.8 show that there is no relationship between the two measures and the trends are similar.

Table 4.8 Information and Gini index for a number of events

Event	*Information*	*Gini index*
Toss of a true coin	1.0	0.5
Toss of a biased coin (70% heads)	0.881	0.42
Throw of a true die	2.585	0.83
Throw of a biased die (50% chance of a 6)	2.16	0.7
Throw of a biased die (75% chance of a 6)	1.39	0.425

It should be noted that the maximum value the Gini index can have is 1. There is no such maximum value for information.

Example 4.2—Using the Gini Index

We use the same example (Table 4.2) as we have used before to illustrate the Gini index.

Owns home?	*Married*	*Gender*	*Employed*	*Credit rating*	*Risk class*
Yes	Yes	Male	Yes	*A*	*B*
No	No	Female	Yes	*A*	*A*
Yes	Yes	Female	Yes	*B*	*C*
Yes	No	Male	No	*B*	*B*
No	Yes	Female	Yes	*B*	*C*
No	No	Female	Yes	*B*	*A*
No	No	Male	No	*B*	*B*
Yes	No	Female	Yes	*A*	*A*
No	Yes	Female	Yes	*A*	*C*
Yes	Yes	Female	Yes	*A*	*C*

There are 10 ($s = 10$) samples and three classes. The frequencies of these classes are:

$A = 3$

$B = 3$

$C = 4$

The Gini index for the distribution of applicants in the three classes is:

$$G = 1 - (3/10)^2 - (3/10)^2 - (4/10)^2 = 0.66$$

Now consider using each of the attributes to split the sample.

1. **Attribute "Owns Home"**

   Value = Yes. There are five applicants who own their home, who are in classes

   $$A = 1, B = 2, C = 2$$

   Value = No. There are five applicants who do not own their home, who are in classes

   $$A = 2, B = 1, C = 2.$$

   Using this attribute will divide objects into those who own their home and those who do not. Computing the Gini index for each of these two subtrees:

   $$G(y) = 1 - (1/5)^2 - (2/5)^2 - (2/5)^2 = 0.64$$

   $$G(n) = G(y) = 0.64$$

   Total value of Gini index = $G = 0.5G(y) + 0.5G(n) = 0.64$

2. **Attribute "Married"**

   There are five applicants that are married and five that are not.

   Value = Yes has $A = 0, B = 1, C = 4$, total 5

   Value = No has $A = 3, B = 2, C = 0$, total 5

$$G(y) = 1 - (1/5)^2 - (4/5)^2 = 0.32$$
$$G(n) = 1 - (3/5)^2 - (2/5)^2 = 0.48$$

Total value of Gini index = $G = 0.5G(y) + 0.5G(n) = 0.40$

3. **Attribute "Gender"**

   There are three applicants that are male and seven are female.

   Value = Male has $A = 0$, $B = 3$, $C = 0$, total 3

   Value = Female has $A = 3$, $B = 0$, $C = 4$, total 7

   $$G(\text{Male}) = 1 - 1 = 0$$
   $$G(\text{Female}) = 1 - (3/7)^2 - (4/7)^2 = 0.511$$

   Total value of Gini index = $G = 0.3G(\text{Male}) + 0.7G(\text{Female}) = 0.358$

4. **Attribute "Employed"**

   There are eight applicants that are employed and two that are not.

   Value = Yes has $A = 3$, $B = 1$, $C = 4$, total 8

   Value = No has $A = 0$, $B = 2$, $C = 0$, total 2

   $$G(y) = 1 - (3/8)^2 - (1/8)^2 - (4/8)^2 = 0.594$$
   $$G(n) = 0$$

   Total value of Gini index = $G = 0.8G(y) + 0.2G(n) = 0.475$

5. **Attribute "Credit Rating"**

   There are five applicants that have credit rating *A* and five that have *B*.

   Value = *A* has $A = 2$, $B = 1$, $C = 2$, total 5

   Value = *B* has $A = 1$, $B = 2$, $C = 2$, total 5

   $$G(A) = 1 - 2(2/5)^2 - (1/5)^2 = 0.64$$
   $$G(B) = G(A)$$

   Total value of Gini index = $G = 0.5G(A) + 0.5G(B) = 0.64$

So the values for the Gini index are as given in Table 4.9.

Table 4.9 Gini index gain for the attributes

Attribute	*Gini Index before split*	*Gini index after split*	*Gain*
Owns home	0.66	0.64	0.02
Married	0.66	0.40	0.26
Gender	0.66	0.358	0.302
Employed	0.66	0.475	0.185
Credit rating	0.66	0.64	0.02

The attribute with the largest reduction in the Gini index is selected as the split attribute. So the split attribute is Gender.

We can now take "Gender" out of consideration and take the three instances where the Gender value was Male also out of consideration since they have already been classified. The same approach is used with the remaining data until the algorithm terminates. The tree obtained for this example is exactly the same as using information gain.

4.6 OVERFITTING AND PRUNING

The decision tree building algorithm given earlier continues until either all leaf nodes are single class nodes or no more attributes are available for splitting a node that has objects of more than one class. When the objects being classified have a large number of attributes and a tree of maximum possible depth is built, the tree quality may not be high since the tree is built to deal correctly with the training set. In fact, in order to do so, it may become quite complex, with long and very uneven paths. Some branches of the tree may reflect anomalies due to noise or outliers in the training samples. Such decision trees are a result of overfitting the training data and may result in poor accuracy for unseen samples.

According to the Occam's razor principle (due to the medieval philosopher William of Occam) it is best to posit that the world is inherently simple and to choose the simplest model from similar models since the simplest model is more likely to be a better model. We can therefore "shave off" nodes and branches of a decision tree, essentially replacing a whole subtree by a leaf node, if it can be established that the expected error rate in the subtree is greater than in the single leaf. This makes the classifier simpler. A simpler model has less chance of introducing inconsistencies, ambiguities and redundancies.

Pruning is a technique to make an overfitted decision tree simpler and more general.

There are a number of techniques for pruning a decision tree by removing some splits and subtrees created by them. One approach involves removing branches from a "fully grown" tree to obtain a sequence of progressively pruned trees. The accuracy of these trees is then computed and a pruned tree that is accurate enough and simple enough is selected. It is advisable to use a set of data different from the training data to decide which is the "best pruned tree".

Another approach is called pre-pruning in which tree construction is halted early. Essentially a node is not split if this would result in the goodness measure of the tree falling below a threshold. It is however quite difficult to choose an appropriate threshold.

4.7 DECISION TREE RULES

The decision tree method is a popular and relatively simple supervised classification method that involves each node of the tree specifying a test of some attribute and each branch from the node corresponding to one of the values of the attribute. Each path from the root to a leaf of the decision tree therefore consists of attribute tests, finally reaching a leaf that describes the class. The popularity of decision trees is partly due to the ease of understanding the rules that the nodes specify. One could even use the rules specified by a decision tree to retrieve data from a relational database satisfying the rules using SQL.

There are a number of advantages in converting a decision tree to rules. Decision rules make it easier to make pruning decisions since it is easier to see the context of each rule. Also, converting to rules removes the distinction between attribute tests that occur near the root of the tree and those that occur near the leaves. As noted earlier, rules are easier to read than a decision tree and they are easier for people to understand.

IF-THEN rules may be derived based on the various paths from the root to the leaf nodes. Although the simple approach will lead to as many rules as the leaf nodes, rules can often be combined to produce a smaller set of rules. For example:

If Gender = "Male" then class = *B*

If Gender = "Female" and Married = "Yes" then class = *C*, else class = *A*

Once all the rules have been generated, it may be possible to simplify the rules. Rules with only one antecedent (for example, if Gender = "Male" then class = *B*) cannot be further simplified, so we only consider those with two or more antecedents. It may be possible to eliminate unnecessary rule antecedents that have no effect on the conclusion reached by the rule. Some rules may be unnecessary and these may be removed. In some cases a number of rules that lead to the same class may be combined.

As noted earlier, the quality of the decision tree and that of the rules depends on the quality of the training sample. If the training sample is not a good representation of the population, then one should be careful in reading too much into the rules derived.

4.8 DECISION TREE SUMMARY

Information measure and the Gini index are both concave measures. That is, the total value of the measure is never less than the total value of the branch nodes after a split. Information gain is therefore always non-negative. Information measure and Gini index often produce the same decision trees and it has been shown that they differ in only about 2% of cases.

We have noted earlier that information split measure prefers split attributes that have many values and lead to shallow trees. It has been found that the Gini index has difficulty when there are a relatively large number of classes.

It should be noted that a small entropy or small Gini index does not guarantee a small classification error.

Decision tree approach is widely used since it is efficient, can deal with both continuous and categorical variables (although we have not discussed continuous variables) and generates understandable rules. The split variables used in building decision trees provide a clear indication of which attributes are most important for classification. The decision tree approach is perhaps best if each attribute takes only a small number of possible values (e.g. very unlikely, unlikely, likely, very likely). The decision tree approach is able to deal with missing values in the training data and can also tolerate some errors in the data.

On the other hand, decision trees are less appropriate for tasks where the goal is to predict the value of a continuous variable such as share price or interest rate. Furthermore, decision trees can lead to large errors if the number of training examples per class is small. This can happen when the tree has a number of classes and many attributes and the depth of the tree grows so that towards the bottom of the tree the number of training samples is small. This leads to overfitting the training data.

For larger problems, with lots of training data and many attributes, finding split attribute at each node can become expensive. Also, since the decision tree algorithm usually only deals with one split attribute at a time, the result leads to rectangular classification boxes which is not always suitable.

In some situations, a decision tree will not be 100% accurate even on the test data. Usually the leaf node is given a class label based on the label of the majority of instances in the leaf. In some cases, there may not be a majority class available. In such situations either the leaf should be labelled "unknown" or it should be given a label that is most common amongst the instances available to the leaf.

4.9 NAÏVE BAYES METHOD

The Naïve Bayes method is based on the work of Thomas Bayes (1702–1761). Bayes was a British minister and his theory was published only after his death. It is a mystery what Bayes wanted to do with such calculations.

Bayesian classification is quite different from the decision tree approach. In Bayesian classification we have a hypothesis that given data belongs to a particular class. We then calculate the probability for the hypothesis to be true. This is among the most practical approaches for certain types of problems. The approach requires only one scan of the whole data. Also, if at some stage there are additional training data then each training example can incrementally increase/decrease the probability that a hypothesis is correct.

Before we define the Bayes' theorem, we will define some notation. The expression $P(A)$ refers to the probability that event A will occur. $P(A|B)$ stands for the probability that event A will happen, given that event B has already happened. In other words $P(A|B)$ is the conditional probability of A based on the condition that B has already happened. For example, A and B may be probabilities of passing a course A and passing another course B respectively. $P(A|B)$ then is the probability of passing A when we know that B has been passed.

Now here is Bayes' theorem:

$$P(A|B) = P(B|A)P(A)/P(B)$$

One might wonder where this theorem came from. Actually it is rather easy to derive since we know the following:

$$P(A|B) = P(A \text{ \& } B)/P(B)$$

and

$$P(B|A) = P(A \text{ \& } B)/P(A)$$

Dividing the first equation by the second gives us Bayes' theorem.

Continuing with A and B being courses, we can compute the conditional probabilities if we knew what the probability of passing both courses was, that is $P(A \text{ \& } B)$, and what the probabilities of passing A and B separately were. If an event has already happened then we divide the joint probability $P(A \text{ \& } B)$ with the probability of what has just happened and obtain the conditional probability.

If we consider to be an object to be classified then Bayes' theorem may be read as giving the probability of it belonging to one of the classes C_1, C_2, C_3, etc by calculating $P(C_i|X)$. Once these probabilities have been computed for all the classes, we simply assign X to the class that has the highest conditional probability.

Let us now consider how probabilities $P(C_i|X)$ may be calculated. We have

$$P(C_i|X) = [P(X|C_i)P(C_i)]/P(X)$$

- $P(C_i|X)$ is the probability of the object X belonging to Class C_i.
- $P(X|C_i)$ is the probability of obtaining attribute values X if we know that it belongs to Class C_i.
- $P(C_i)$ is the probability of any object belonging to Class C_i without any other information.
- $P(X)$ is the probability of obtaining attribute values X whatever class the object belongs to.

Given the attribute values X, what probabilities in the formula can we compute? The probabilities we need to compute are $P(X|C_i)$, $P(C_i)$ and $P(X)$. Actually the denominator $P(X)$ is independent of C_i and is not required to be known since we are interested only in comparing probabilities $P(C_i|X)$. Therefore we only need to compute $P(X|C_i)$ and $P(C_i)$ for each class. Computing $P(C_i)$ is rather easy since we count the number of instances of each class in the training data and divide each by the total number of instances. This may not be the most accurate estimation of $P(C_i)$ but we have very little information, the training sample, and we have no other information to obtain a better estimate. This estimate will be reasonable if the training sample was large and was randomly chosen.

To compute $P(X|C_i)$ we use a Naïve approach (that is why it is called the Naïve Bayes model) by assuming that all attributes of are independent which is often not true.

Using the independence of attributes assumption and based on the training data, we compute an estimate of the probability of obtaining the data X that we have by estimating the probability of each of the attribute values by counting the frequency of those values for class C_i.

We then determine the class allocation of X by computing $[P(X|C_i)P(C_i)]$ for each of the classes and allocating X to the class with the largest value.

The beauty of the Bayesian approach is that the probability of the dependent attribute can be estimated by computing estimates of the probabilities of the independent attributes.

We should also note that it is possible to use this approach even if values of all the independent attributes were not known since we can still estimate the probabilities of the attribute values that we know. This is a significant advantage of the Bayesian approach.

Example 4.3—Naïve Bayes Method

Once again we go back to the example in Table 4.2 that we have used before.

Owns home?	*Married*	*Gender*	*Employed*	*Credit rating*	*Risk class*
Yes	Yes	Male	Yes	*A*	*B*
No	No	Female	Yes	*A*	*A*
Yes	Yes	Female	Yes	*B*	*C*
Yes	No	Male	No	*B*	*B*
No	Yes	Female	Yes	*B*	*C*
No	No	Female	Yes	*B*	*A*
No	No	Male	No	*B*	*B*
Yes	No	Female	Yes	*A*	*A*
No	Yes	Female	Yes	*A*	*C*
Yes	Yes	Female	Yes	*A*	*C*

There are 10 (s = 10) samples and three classes:

Credit risk class A = 3
Credit risk class B = 3
Credit risk class C = 4

The prior probabilities are obtained by dividing these frequencies by the total number in the training data (that is, 10)

$$P(A) = 0.3, \quad P(B) = 0.3, \quad \text{and } P(C) = 0.4$$

If the data that is presented to us is {yes, no, female, yes, A} for the five attributes, we can compute the posterior probability for each class as noted earlier. For example:

$P(X|C_i)$ = P({yes, no, female, yes, A}|C_i) = P(Owns Home = yes|C_i) × P(Married = no|C_i) × P(Gender = female|C_i) × P(Employed = yes|C_i) × P(Credit Rating = A|C_i).

Using expressions like that given above, we are able to compute the three posterior probabilities for the three classes, namely that the person with attribute values X has credit risk Class A or Class B or Class C. We compute $P(X|C_i)P(C_i)$ for each of the three classes given P(A) = 0.3, $P(B)$ = 0.3 and P(C) = 0.4 and these values are the basis for comparing the three classes.

To compute $P(X|C_i)$ = P({yes, no, female, yes, A}|C_i) for each of the classes, we need the following probabilities for each:

P(Owns home = yes|C_i)
P(Married = no|C_i)
P(Gender = female|C_i)
P(Employed = yes|C_i)
P(Credit rating = A|C_i)

These probabilities are given in Table 4.10. We order the data by risk class to make it convenient.

Table 4.10 Probability of events in the Naïve–Bayes method

Owns home	*Married*	*Gender*	*Employed*	*Credit rating*	*Class*
No	No	Female	Yes	A	A
No	No	Female	Yes	B	A
Yes	No	Female	Yes	A	A
1/3	1	1	1	2/3	Probability of having {yes, no, Female, yes, A} attribute values given risk class A
Yes	Yes	Male	Yes	A	B
Yes	No	Male	No	B	B
No	No	Male	No	B	B
2/3	2/3	0	1/3	1/3	Probability of having {yes, no, Female, yes, A} attribute values given risk class B
Yes	Yes	Female	Yes	B	C
No	Yes	Female	Yes	B	C
No	Yes	Female	Yes	A	C
Yes	Yes	Female	Yes	A	C
0.5	0	1	1.0	0.5	Probability of having {yes, no, Female, yes, A} attribute values given risk class C

Given the estimates of the probabilities in the table above we can compute the posterior probabilities:

$$P(X|A) = 2/9$$

$$P(X|B) = 0$$

$$P(X|C) = 0$$

Therefore the values of $P(X|C_i)P(C_i)$ are zero for Classes B and C and $0.3 \times 2/9 = 0.0666$. Therefore X is assigned to Class A. It is unfortunate that in this example two of the probabilities came out to be zero. This is most unlikely in practice.

Bayes' theorem assumes that all attributes are independent and that the training sample is a good sample to estimate probabilities. These assumptions are not always true in practice, as attributes are often correlated but in spite of this the Naïve Bayes method performs reasonably well. Other techniques have been designed to overcome this limitation. One approach is to use Bayesian networks that combine Bayesian reasoning with causal relationships between attributes.

4.10 ESTIMATING PREDICTIVE ACCURACY OF CLASSIFICATION METHODS

The accuracy of a classification method is the ability of the method to correctly determine the class of a randomly selected data instance. It may be expressed as the probability of correctly classifying unseen data. Estimating the accuracy of a supervised classification method can be difficult if only the training data is available and all of that data has been used in building the model. In such situations, overoptimistic predictions are often made regarding the accuracy of the model. The accuracy estimation problem is much easier when much more data is available than is required for training the model.

Often when a great deal of past data is available, only a part of this data is used for training and the rest, which does not include the training set, can be used for testing the method. As noted earlier, the training set should normally be obtained by random sampling since just using the last n cases or using just the data from head office can lead to bias in the training data which should be avoided. Different sets of training data would often lead to somewhat different models and therefore testing is very important in determining how accurate each model is. When several models are built, the most accurate may then be selected.

We would obviously like to obtain an accuracy estimate (for example, a mean value and variance) that has low bias and low variance. Accuracy may be measured using a number of metrics. These include sensitivity, specificity, precision and accuracy. The methods for estimating errors include holdout, random sub-sampling, K-fold cross-validation and leave-one-out. Some of the methods may be used when the data available is limited.

We will define some terminology before discussing the error estimation methods.

Let us assume that the test data has a total of T objects. When testing a method we find that C of the T objects are correctly classified. Error rate then may be defined as:

$$\text{Error rate} = C/T$$

This error rate is only an estimate of the true error rate and it is expected to be a good estimate if the number of test data T is large and representative of the population. A method of estimating the error rate is considered biased if it either tends to underestimate the error or tends to overestimate it. That is why we prefer unbiased methods.

A "confusion matrix" is sometime used to represent the result of testing in more detail as shown in Table 4.11. The advantage of using this matrix is that it not only tells us how many got misclassified but also what misclassifications occurred. For example in Table 4.11 we can see that 1 out of 10 objects that belonged to Class 3 got misclassified to *Class* 1.

Table 4.11 A confusion matrix for three classes

Predicted class	*True class*		
	1	2	3
1	8	1	1
2	2	9	2
3	0	0	7

Using Table 4.11 we can define the terms "false positive" (FP) and "false negative" (FN). False positive cases are those that did not belong to a class but were allocated to it. For example, there were 2 false positives for Class 1 and 4 for Class 2. Class 3 had no false positives. False negative on the other hand are cases that belong to a class but were not allocated to it. For example, there were 2 false negatives for Class 1, 1 for Class 2 and 3 for Class 3. Therefore there were a total of 6 false positives and 6 false negatives for the example in Table 4.11.

We now define sensitivity and specificity.

$$\text{Sensitivity} = TP/(TP + FN)$$

$$\text{Specificity} = TN/(TN + FP)$$

where *TP* (total positives) is the total correctly classified objects and *TN* (total negatives) is the total number of objects that did get classified to a class they did not belong to. Let us explain this further.

Consider Class 1 in Table 4.11. There are 10 objects that belong to this class and 20 do not. Only 8 are classified correctly. Out of the 20 that did not belong to Class 1, 2 objects are classified wrongly to belong to it. So we have $TP = 8$, $TN = 18$, $FN = 2$, $FP = 2$. For Class 2, $TP = 9$, $TN = 16$, $FN = 1$, $FP = 4$ and for Class 3, $TP = 7$, $TN = 20$, $FN = 3$ and $FP = 0$. Now we can compute:

$$\text{Sensitivity} = TP/(TP + FN) = 24/30 = 80\%$$

$$\text{Specificity} = TN/(TN + FP) = 54/60 = 90\%$$

Sometime terms like "false acceptance rate" (FAR) and "false rejection rate" (FRR) or Type 1 and Type 2 errors are also used.

Now we discuss a number of methods for estimating accuracy of a method.

4.10.1 Holdout Method

The Holdout Method (sometimes called the Test Sample method) requires a training set and a test set. The sets are mutually exclusive. It may be that only one dataset is available which has been divided into two subsets (perhaps 2/3 and 1/3), the training subset and the test or holdout subset. Once the classification method produces the model using the training set, the test set can be used to estimate the accuracy. Interesting questions arise in this estimation since a larger training set would produce a better classifier, while a larger test set would produce a better estimate of the accuracy. A balance must be achieved. Since none of the test data is used in training, the estimate is not biased, but a good estimate is obtained only if the test set and the training set are large enough and representative of the whole population.

4.10.2 Random Sub-sampling Method

Random sub-sampling is very much like the holdout method except that it does not rely on a single test set. Essentially the holdout estimation is repeated several times and the accuracy estimate is obtained by computing the mean of the several trials. Random sub-sampling is likely to produce better error estimates than the holdout method.

4.10.3 *K*-fold Cross-validation Method

In *k*-fold cross-validation, the available data is randomly divided into *k* disjoint subsets of approximately equal size. One of the subsets is then used as the test set and the remaining $k - 1$ sets are used for building the classifier. The test set is then used to estimate the accuracy. This is done repeatedly *k* times so that each subset is used as a test subset once. The accuracy estimate is then the mean of the estimates for each of the classifiers. Cross-validation has been tested extensively and has been found to generally work well when sufficient data is available. A value of 10 for *k* has been found to be adequate and accurate.

4.10.4 Leave-one-out Method

Leave-one-out is a simpler version of *k*-fold cross-validation. In this method, one of the training samples is taken out and the model is generated using the remaining training data. Once the model is built, the one remaining sample is used for testing and the result is coded as 1 or 0 depending if it was classified correctly or not. The average of such results provides an estimate of the accuracy. The leave-one-out method is useful when the dataset is small. For large training datasets, leave-one-out can become expensive since many iterations are required. Leave-one-out is unbiased but has high variance and is therefore not particularly reliable.

4.10.5 Bootstrap Method

In this method, given a dataset of size *n*, a Bootstrap Sample is randomly selected uniformly with replacement (that is, a sample may be selected more than once) by sampling *n* times and used to build a model. It can be shown that only 63.2% of these samples are unique. The error in building the model is estimating by using the remaining 36.8% of objects that are not in the bootstrap sample. The final error is then computed as 0.632 times the training error plus 0.368 times the testing error.

The figures 0.632 and 0.368 are based on the assumption that if there were n samples available initially from which n samples with replacement were randomly selected for training data then the expected percentage of unique samples in the training data would be 0.632 or 63.2% and the number of remaining unique objects used in the test data is 0.368 or 36.8% of the initial sample. This is repeated and the average of error estimates is obtained. The bootstrap method is unbiased and in contrast to leave-one-out has low variance but many iterations are needed for good error estimates if the sample is small, say 25 or less.

k-fold cross-validation, leave-one-out and bootstrap techniques are used in many decision tree packages including *CART* and *Clementine*.

4.11 IMPROVING ACCURACY OF CLASSIFICATION METHODS

Bootstrapping, *Bagging* and *Boosting* are techniques for improving the accuracy of classification results. They have been shown to be very successful for certain models, for example, decision trees. All three involve combining several classification results from the same training data that has been perturbed in some way. The aim of building several decision trees by using training data that has been perturbed is to find out how these decision trees differ from those that have been obtained earlier.

The bootstrapping method is described earlier. It can be shown that all the samples selected are somewhat different from each other since, on the average, only 63.2% of the objects in them are unique. The bootstrap samples are then used for building decision trees which are then combined to form a single decision tree.

Bagging (the name is derived from **B**ootstrap and **Agg**regat**ing**) combines classification results from multiple models or results of using the same method on several different sets of training data. Bagging may also be used to improve the stability and accuracy of a complex classification model with limited training data by using sub-samples obtained by resampling, with replacement, for generating models. With small samples to start, the sub-samples can lead to very different decision trees. To derive a single decision tree from these trees, simple voting is used to combine all the decision trees built by sub-samples. Thus the final tree is the one that is most often found in the sub-sample trees.

Bagging essentially involves simple voting (with no weights) so the final model is the one that is predicted by the majority of the trees. The different decision trees obtained during bagging should not be so different if the training data is good and large enough. If the trees obtained are very different, it only indicates instability, perhaps due to the training data being too small or not being random. In such a situation, bagging will often provide a better result than using the training data only once to build a decision tree.

In contrast to simple voting used in bagging, weighted voting can also be used. A technique called *boosting* involves applying weights to different instances of training data depending on the quality of the previous result. Often the idea is to give more weight to those instances that are not being correctly classified and less weight to those that are frequently classified correctly. One approach is that different weights can be applied to data in different classes. For example, the weights could be inversely proportional to the accuracy of prediction in each class. Thus classes that are not being classified with a high level of accuracy will get a higher weight and the data from these classes will be selected more frequently in resampling. When the classifier is used again, the result can improve the performances of classes that were doing poorly in the last result. This is followed by another iteration of computing weights and so on until some stopping criterion is met.

There is a lot of literature available on bootstrapping, bagging and boosting. This brief introduction only provides a glimpse into these techniques but some of the points made in the literature regarding the benefits of these methods are:

- These techniques can provide a level of accuracy that usually cannot be obtained by a large single-tree model.
- Creating a single decision tree from a collection of trees in bagging and boosting is not difficult.
- These methods can often help in avoiding the problem of overfitting since a number of trees based on random samples are used.
- Boosting appears to be on the average better than bagging although it is not always so. On some problems bagging does better than boosting.

On the other hand, it should be noted that it is more difficult to visualise a large set of decision trees as compared to a single tree. Also, generally bagging and boosting produce a final classifier that is much more difficult to understand. Nevertheless, bagging and boosting generally do improve accuracy and are being used in several decision tree software packages.

4.12 OTHER EVALUATION CRITERIA FOR CLASSIFICATION METHODS

In the last section we discussed estimating predictive accuracy of classification methods and some techniques for improving the accuracy. Other criteria for evaluation of classification methods, like those for all data mining techniques, are:

1. Speed
2. Robustness
3. Scalability
4. Interpretability
5. Goodness of the model
6. Flexibility
7. Time complexity

We now discuss these criteria briefly.

4.12.1 Speed

Speed involves not just the time or computation cost of constructing a model (e.g. a decision tree), it also includes time required to learn to use the model. Obviously a user wishes to minimise both times although it has to be understood that any significant data mining project will take time to plan and prepare the data. If the problem to be solved is large, careful study of the methods available may need to be carried out so that an efficient method may be chosen.

4.12.2 Robustness

In Chapter 2, we discussed the problems associated with preprocessing data. Data errors are common, in particular when data is being collected from a number of sources and errors may remain even after data cleaning. It is therefore desirable that a method be able to produce good results in spite of some errors and missing values.

4.12.3 Scalability

As noted earlier, many data mining methods were originally designed for small datasets. Many have been modified to deal with large problems. Given that large datasets are becoming common, it is desirable that a method continue to work efficiently for large disk-resident databases.

4.12.4 Interpretability

An important task of a data mining professional is to ensure that results of data mining are explained to the decision makers. It is therefore desirable that the end-user be able to understand and gain insight from the results produced by the method.

4.12.5 Goodness of the Model

For a model to be effective, it needs to fit the problem that is being solved. For example, in a decision tree classification, it is desirable to find a decision tree of the "right" size and compactness with high accuracy.

4.13 CLASSIFICATION SOFTWARE

4.13.1 C4.5

There are a number of software packages available for classification. One of the most well-known is **C4.5**; J. Ross Quinlan initially developed it.

To use **C4.5**, the dataset must have a number of instances of objects or things that are described by a number of attributes. Some of these objects must form the training data. The remaining objects are the test data that we wish to classify. It is assumed that each object belongs to only one class.

Let us consider an example where each object is an Indian states, each described by a number of attributes that denote some social attributes.

C4.5 is based on using the decision trees approach. As already discussed the approach uses a series of questions that are so arranged that the first question discriminates between the objects the most while the lowest level question provides the least discrimination.

It should be noted that

1. **C4.5** allows binary questions as well as questions that have more than two possible answers. Since the algorithm is based on decision trees, a node may lead either to just two branches or more than two branches. Obviously a node with only one branch does not make much sense.

2. As noted above and in this chapter earlier, the highest-level questions are chosen to be the most discriminatory. For example, the question to be chosen first is the one that divides 10 objects into two groups of five each than a question that divides 10 objects into two groups of 8 and 2 objects.
3. The growth of a decision tree terminates when the number of growth in all nodes are either single objects or the objects cannot be discriminated any further.
4. Each terminating leaf is a class and a label is assigned to it.

C4.5 tree pruning

Sometime decision tree obtained by classification of a given dataset may be overfitting the data. For example, if the classification of the states data in Table 1.1 results in each state appearing in its own class then we may believe that the classification algorithm has gone too far. In such instances, it may be desirable to prune the tree and thus obtain a classification that makes more sense. A similar overfitting may be assumed if we have 500 largest cities in India being classified and we obtain more than 300 classes.

There are a number of different tree pruning algorithms that may be used.

4.13.2 CART

CART is yet another well-known classification software. **CART** stands for *Classification and Regression Trees*. Breiman, Friedman, Olshen and Stone first presented the approach in a research paper in 1984. The paper has been cited a large number of times.

CART is also based on decision trees, just as **C4.5**. The **CART** decision tree is a binary tree. The raw data in a dataset is first divided into two descendants. Each of these descendants is then divided in two descendants each. The process continues until there is no need to divide the nodes.

All packages listed in Chapter 1 include modules on classification. Decision tree is one of the major techniques in these packages. Some include the Naïve-Bayes method as well as other classification methods. The list of software given here is for classification only. It should be noted that different software using the same technique (e.g. decision tree) may not produce the same results since there are subtle differences in the techniques used.

This is not a comprehensive list but it includes some of the most widely used classification software. A more comprehensive classification software list is available at kdnuggets site (http://www.kdnuggets.com/software/classification.html).

- **C4.5**, version 8 of the "classic" decision-tree tool, developed by J.R. Quinlan (free, restricted distribution) http://www.rulequest.com/Personal/
- **C5.0/See5** from Rulequest Research, is designed to deal with large datasets. It constructs classifiers in the form of decision trees or a set of if-then-else rules. Software uses boosting to reduce errors on unseen data. C5.0 is included in Clementine. Links to a large number of publications of case studies of its use are available at http://www.rulequest.com/see5-pubs.html.
- **CART 5.0** and TreeNet from Salford Systems are well-known decision-tree software packages. TreeNet provides boosting. CART is the decision tree software. The packages incorporate facilities for data pre-processing and predictive modelling including bagging and arcing. http://www.salford-systems.com/

- **DTREG**, from a company with the same name, generates classification trees, when the classes are categorical, and regression decision trees, when the classes are numerical intervals, and finds optimal tree size. In both cases, attribute values may be discrete or numerical. Software modules TreeBoost and Decision Tree Forest generate an ensemble of decision trees. In TreeBoost, each tree is generated based on input from a previous tree while Decision Tree Forest generates an ensemble independently of each other. The ensemble is then combined. http://www.dtreg.com/
- **SMILES**, provides new splitting criteria, non-greedy search, new partitions, extraction of several and different solutions. It has a quite effective handling of (misclassification and test) costs. SMILES also uses boosting and cost-sensitive learning. http://www.dsic.upv.es/~flip/smiles/

SUMMARY

In this chapter we have discussed supervised classification, which is an extensively studied problem in statistics and machine learning. Classification is probably the most widely used data mining technique.

We have described the decision tree approach of classification using information measure and Gini index for splitting attributes. In the decision tree approach, decisions are made locally by considering one attribute at a time thus considering the most important attribute first. We have discussed decision tree pruning and testing. Another classification method, the Naïve-Bayes method, has been described.

Finally, we have discussed a number of methods for estimating the predictive accuracy of classification and have discussed bootstrapping, bagging and boosting for improving the accuracy of classification methods.

REVIEW QUESTIONS

1. What is supervised classification? In what situations can this technique be useful? (Section 4.1)
2. What is a training sample? What is used for? (Section 4.1)
3. What is the idea behind decision trees? How does it explain structure for a given set of data? (Section 4.2)
4. What types of attributes does the decision tree approach work for? (Section 4.2)
5. Explain the decision tree induction algorithm. (Section 4.3)
6. Describe the building algorithm for decision tree using information theory. Explain how information of an event is calculated. (Section 4.4)
7. What is the split algorithm based on information theory? (Section 4.4)
8. Describe the split algorithm based on the Gini index and explain what the Lorenz curve is. (Section 4.5)
9. Describe the concept of Occam's Rajor, overfitting and pruning a decision tree. (Section 4.6)

10. Present an example decision tree and derive the rules from the tree. (Section 4.7)
11. What is Bayes Theorem and show how it is used as the basis of Naïve-Bayes method? Describe the Naïve-Bayes method. (Section 4.9)
12. How can the predictive accuracy of classification methods be estimated including holdout method and K-fold cross-validation method? (Section 4.10)
13. Explain how bootstrapping, bagging and boosting improve accuracy of classifications. (Section 4.11)
14. Discuss the importance of the evaluation criteria for classification methods. (Section 4.12)

EXERCISES

1. Briefly outline the major steps of decision tree classification.
2. Why is tree pruning useful in decision tree induction? What is the drawback of using a separate set of samples to evaluate pruning?
3. Given a decision tree, you have the option of
   (a) converting the decision tree to rules and then pruning the resulting rules, or
   (b) pruning the decision tree and then converting the pruned tree to rules.
   What advantage does (a) have over (b)?
4. Why is Naïve Bayesian classification called "Naïve"? Briefly outline the major ideas of Naïve Bayesian classification.
5. Study the table given below and construct a decision tree based on the Greedy algorithm using Information Gain.

RID	*Age*	*Income*	*Student*	*Credit_rating*	*Class: Buys_computer*
1	<=30	High	No	Fair	No
2	<=30	High	No	Excellent	No
3	31–40	High	No	Fair	Yes
4	>40	Medium	No	Fair	Yes
5	>40	Low	Yes	Fair	Yes
6	>40	Low	Yes	Excellent	No
7	31–40	Low	Yes	Excellent	Yes
8	<=30	Medium	No	Fair	No
9	<=30	Low	Yes	Fair	Yes
10	>40	Medium	Yes	Fair	Yes
11	<=30	Medium	Yes	Excellent	Yes
12	31–40	Medium	No	Excellent	Yes
13	31–40	High	Yes	Fair	Yes
14	>40	Medium	No	Excellent	No

6. What kind of data is the decision tree method most suitable for? Briefly outline the major steps of the algorithm to construct a decision tree. Explain each step.

7. Assume we have 10 training samples. There are four classes A, B, C and D. Compute the information in the samples for the five training datasets given below (each row is a dataset and each has 10 objects) when the number of samples in each class are:

Class	*A*	*B*	*C*	*D*
Dataset 1	1	1	1	7
Dataset 2	2	2	2	4
Dataset 3	3	3	3	1
Dataset 4	1	2	3	4
Dataset 5	0	0	1	9

Use the log values from the following table:

p	$\log(p)$	$-p\log(p)$
0.1	–3.32	0.332
0.2	–2.32	0.464
0.3	–1.74	0.521
0.4	–1.32	0.529
0.5	–1.00	0.500
0.6	–0.74	0.442
0.7	–0.51	0.360
0.8	–0.32	0.258
0.9	–0.15	0.137

8. Consider the classification problem that has been used in this chapter. The association rule algorithm may also be used to find classification rules from data like that. Clearly present a step-by-step algorithm explaining how such an algorithm might work.
9. Explain the meaning of each of the following four probabilities (X is an object to be classified and C_i are the classes) and show how they are used in the Bayes Theorem.
   (a) $P(C_i|X)$
   (b) $P(X|C_i)$
   (c) $P(C_i)$
   (d) $P(X)$
10. What is overfitting of a decision tree? What problems can overfitting lead to?
11. List five criteria for evaluating classification methods. Discuss them briefly.
12. Describe three methods of estimating accuracy of a classification method.
13. Explain the terms bootstrapping, bagging and boosting for improving accuracy of a classification method.
14. What is the difference between bootstrapping, bagging and boosting?
15. Briefly outline the major steps in building a decision tree. Why is tree pruning useful in building decision trees?

16. How are attributes selected for a split in a decision tree?
17. Try the following technique. Split the original training data into a small training set and a large test set. If the decision tree formed from the training set classifies test objects incorrectly, add some of the incorrectly classified objects to the training set and re-calculate the tree. Test Quinlan's assertion (1986, p. 88) that accurate decision trees are usually found more quickly by this iterative method than by forming a tree directly from the entire training dataset.
18. What is Bayes Theorem? How can it be used in classification? Write a program to implement this technique and test it using some test dataset from one of the data mining websites. How do the results compare with those of the decision tree method?

MULTIPLE CHOICE QUESTIONS

1. Which one of the following is true?
   (a) Classification is separation of objects into classes
   (b) Supervised classification is posterior classification
   (c) Cluster analysis is a priori classification
   (d) No training data is needed in supervised classification
2. Which one of the following is true?
   (a) Output attribute is also called independent attribute
   (b) Input attributes are also called dependent attributes
   (c) An input attribute must always be a numerical attribute
   (d) An output attribute must always be a categorical attribute
3. Which one of the following is true?
   (a) The decision tree algorithm finds a globally optimum tree
   (b) The aim of the split algorithm is to find the most discriminating attribute
   (c) The discriminating power of each attribute is based on the number of different values an attribute has
   (d) Stopping the decision tree algorithm is very simple
4. Which two of the following are true?
   (a) Information gain is based on the idea of increase in uncertainty
   (b) Gini index value of zero shows very uneven wealth distribution
   (c) Pre-pruning involves stopping decision tree construction early
   (d) IF-THEN rules may be derived from a decision tree
5. Which of the following are methods for supervised classification?
   (a) Decision tree
   (b) K-Means
   (c) Hierarchical
   (d) Naïve Bayes

6. Which one of the following is true?
   (a) Decision tree is not predictive
   (b) Decision tree is not descriptive
   (c) Quality of training data is important for decision trees
   (d) Measuring the quality of a decision tree is relatively easy
7. Which one of the following is true?
   (a) Decision tree algorithm requires a split algorithm
   (b) A split algorithm may be based on computing Euclidean distances
   (c) A split algorithm may be based on Bayes theorem
   (d) All of the above are true
8. Which one of the following is true?
   (a) Decision tree can be useful in decision making
   (b) Decision tree is similar to OLAP
   (c) Decision tree is similar to cluster analysis
   (d) None of the above is true
9. Which of the following are the main reasons for the popularity of the decision tree approach?
   (a) It is efficient
   (b) It can deal with both continuous and categorical variables
   (c) It generates understandable rules
   (d) All of the above
10. Which of the following probabilities are used in the Naïve Bayes Method?
   (a) $P(C_i|X)$
   (c) $P(C_i)$
   (b) $P(X|C_i)$
   (d) $P(X)$
   (e) All are used

PROJECTS

Project 1: Consider the data in Table 1.1. First of all covert all the numerical attributes into categorical attributes. Initially use only binary values. Now select six of the states so and classify two of them each from the six as H, I, and L. H stands for a state that is doing well, I stands for one that is middle of the road and L stands for a state that is relatively poor. These six states now become the training data. You may select nine states as training data if that is what you believe will produce better results. Now build a decision tree and classify the remaining states.

Discuss the results and suggest how a better classification could have been obtained.

Project 2: Consider the data about some Australian animals in the table below. Label each animal as bird or mammal or marsupial. Now build a decision tree using the data. Note that C stands for carnivorous, O for omnivorous and H for herbivorous.

Name	*Eggs*	*Pouch*	*Flies*	*Feathers*	*Eats*	*Nocturnal*	*Habitat*
Bandicoot	No	Yes	No	No	C	Yes	Bushes
Cassowary	Yes	No	No	Yes	O	No	Ground
Cockatoo	Yes	No	Yes	Yes	C	No	Trees
Crocodile	Yes	No	No	No	C	No?	Water
Dingo	No	No	No	No	C	No	Ground
Dugong	No	No	No	No	H	No	Water
Echidna	Yes	Yes	No	No	C	No	Ground
Emu	Yes	No	No	Yes	C	No	Ground
Kangaroo	No	Yes	No	No	H	Yes	Grass
Koala	No	Yes	No	No	H	Yes	Trees
Kookaburra	Yes	N	Yes	Yes	C	No	Trees
Penguin	Yes	No	No	Yes	C	No	Burrows
Platypus	Yes	No	No	No	C	No	Streams
Possum	No	Yes	No	No	H	Yes	Trees
Wombat	No	Yes	No	No	H	Yes	Burrows

BIBLIOGRAPHY

Recommended Reading for Students

A number of survey/tutorial papers are included in the list below if you need a different view of classification or if you require more information on the topics discussed.

Majoros, W., Naïve Bayes Model for Classification: A Tutorial,
http://www.geocities.com/researchtriangle/forum/1203/naïvebayes.html

Moore, A., Tutorial Slides on Decision Trees, Carnegie-Mellon University.
http://www-2.cs.cmu.edu/~awm/tutorials/dtree.html

A Tutorial on Decision Trees
http://dms.irb.hr/tutorial/tut_dtrees.php

Decision Tree Learning, An Interactive Tutorial.
http://www.decisiontrees.net/index.html

Overview of Decision Trees
http://www2.cs.uregina.ca/~dbd/cs831/notes/ml/dtrees/4_dtrees1.html (A good overview. Includes a step-by-step example to show workings of decision tree construction.)

Recommended Reading for Lecturers

Some of the most highly cited papers are included here. Papers on decision trees by Ross Quinlan have been highly cited, for example Quinlan (1986) and Quinlan (1987). Other highly cited papers include those by Breiman (1996), and by Freund and Schapire (1996).

Ankerst, M., Ester, M., and Kriegel, H.P., Towards an effective cooperation of the user and the computer for classification, *Proc. Int. Conf. Knowledge Discovery and Data Mining (KDD '00)*, Boston, MA, pp. 179–188, 2000.

Bauer, E. and Kohavi, R., An empirical comparison of voting classification algorithms: Bagging, boosting, and variants, *Machine Learning*, Vol. 36, No. 1–2, pp. 105–139, 1999.

Breiman, L., Bagging predictors, *Machine Learning*, Vol. 24, No. 2, pp. 123–140, 1996.

Breiman, L., Friedman, J., Olshen, R., and Stone, C., *Classification and Regression Trees*, Wadsworth, California, USA, 1984.

Freund, Y. and Schapire, R.E., Experiments with a new boosting algorithm, *International Conference on Machine Learning*, pp. 148–156, 1996.

Freund, Y. and Schapire, R.E., A decision-theoretic generalization of online learning and an application to boosting, *Journal of Computer and System Sciences*, Vol. 55, No. 1, pp. 119–139, 1997.

Gehrke, J., Ramakrishnan, R., and Ganti, V., Rain Forest—A framework for fast decision tree construction of large datasets, *Data Mining and Knowledge Discovery*, Vol. 4, No. 2/3, pp. 127–162, 2000.

Gehrke, J., Ganti, V., Ramakrishnan, R., and Loh, W.Y., BOAT– optimistic decision tree construction, *Proc. Int. Conf. Management of Data (SIGMOD '99)*, Philadelphia, PA, pp. 169–180, 1999.

Kohavi, R., A study of cross-validation and bootstrap for accuracy estimation and model selection, *Int. Joint Conference on Artificial Intelligence* (*IJCAI*), 1995.

Li, W., Han, J., and Pei, J., CMAR: Accurate and efficient classification based on multiple class-association rules, *Proc. 2001 Int. Conf. on Data Mining (ICDM '01)*, San Jose, CA, pp. 369–376, 2001.

Mitchell, T., Decision tree learning, *Machine Learning*, McGraw-Hill, pp. 52–78, 1997.

Murthy, S.K., Automatic construction of decision trees from data: A multi-disciplinary survey, *Data Mining and Knowledge Discovery*, Vol. 2, No. 4, pp. 345–389, 1998.

Patil, D.V. and Bichkar, R.S., Issues in Optimization of Decision Tree Learning: A Survey, *International Journal of Applied Information Systems* (*IJAIS*), *Foundation of Computer Science*, Vol. 3, No. 5, 2012

Quinlan, J.R., Induction of decision trees, *Machine Learning*, Vol. 1, pp. 81–106, 1986.

Quinlan, J.R., Simplifying decision trees, *International Journal of Man-Machine Studies*, Vol. 27, pp. 221–234, 1987.

ROSS QUINLAN—LEADING RESEARCHER IN DECISION TREES

Ross Quinlan is a computer scientist who has made significant contributions in the field of data mining and decision theory. He is well-known for his development of decision tree algorithms, including development of the C4.5 and ID3 algorithms.

Ross completed BSc degree in Physics and Computing from the University of Sydney and his computer science PhD at the University of Washington.

CASE STUDY 4A

KDD for Insurance Risk Assessment: A Case Study*

This case study is a technical report from the Australian CSIRO Division of Information Technology. It is reproduced here with the permission of Dr Graham Williams.

ABSTRACT

Insurance is a business of risks. Identifying and understanding areas of risk is an important task performed by an insurer. An assessment of risk is used to set the appropriate premium for insurance policies. This paper describes a KDD exercise which uses decision tree techniques to identify significant areas of risk within an insurance portfolio. The real world dataset used contains information about policies and insurance claims on those policies. Decision trees can be constructed to identify and describe areas of high risk which are then evaluated, as a separate exercise, in terms of claim frequency and claim costs. The paper stresses the idea of interactive post-processing, or evaluation, of the patterns that are illuminated by traditional data mining tools.

Keywords: Knowledge discovery in databases, KDD Process, data mining, insurance risk analysis.

1. INTRODUCTION

Assessing the performance of an insurance portfolio requires both overall and within-portfolio analyses. The overall analysis demonstrates whether the portfolio in the past was profitable or not, whereas a detailed within-portfolio analysis reveals which particular areas within the portfolio made significant profits and losses (Coutts 1984). The latter information is particularly important for a company to know in order to maintain both its competitiveness in the market and its profitability. Without knowing where the areas of significant risk are in its portfolio an insurer will be unable to sustain operation, even though the overall portfolio may perform well temporarily. A portfolio should balance its exposure to risk.

The overall analysis of an insurance portfolio can be performed using straightforward statistical techniques, based on the total premiums earned and the total of the claims paid. More sophisticated approaches are required for within-portfolio analysis (Brockman and Wright 1992, Coutts 1984).

A common approach to within-portfolio analysis is to partition the risk of the whole portfolio into small areas of risk. These are identified by a set of risk rating factors usually represented by a contingency table. Only a few variables are usually considered at a time (the claim frequency, the claim cost, and the exposure, for example) for each cell of the contingency table.

When a portfolio is partitioned a model can be fitted to each cell relating the level of the risk rating factors to the claim frequency and claim cost. Historical data is used to estimate parameters of the model. The model can then be used to predict the expected claim frequencies and claim costs for different risk rating factor levels.

With such an approach, the risk rating factors must be categorical. A continuous factor has to be categorised into a small number of levels. A trade-off

*Williams, G.J. and Z. Huang, CSIRO Division of Information Technology, GPO Box 664, Canberra 2601, Australia. Email: Graham.Williams@br.dit,csiro.au.

The authors acknowledge the support provided by the Cooperative Research Centre for Advanced Computational Systems (AC-Sys) established under the Australian Government's Cooperative Research Centres Program.

is needed in the detail of the analysis and fit of the model. Also, the interaction between factors is often ignored because of the difficulty with handling them. With many variables and with categorical variables with many values, the number of possible interactions is very large.

Alternative approaches to the task of insurance risk analysis have primarily been explored within the statistical/actuarial domains. Siebes (1994), however, considered the problem of insurance risk analysis in the context of data mining by employing probability theory. Insurance claims on policies in any one year were viewed in terms of Bernoulli experiments. This work led to the idea of developing equal probability, homogeneous descriptions of classes of the insurance portfolio.

In this paper we consider some initial exploratory work in using an iterative and interactive approach to insurance risk analysis within the KDD context. The approach is motivated by the desire to involve expert intuition as an integral aspect of the process, supported by formal analyses. The approach is also driven by the view of KDD as an iterative process involving a number of stages, one of which is the traditional Data Mining stage (Fayyad, Piatetsky-Shapiro and Smyth 1996, Williams and Huang 1996b).

While the primary focus of this paper is on the data mining and evaluation (post data mining) stages, the pre data mining stages are also highlighted. Section 2 describes the concept of an insurance portfolio database which serves as the starting point of the KDD exercise. Section 3 summarises the process through which the data supplied by our collaborators was transformed into a Working Dataset for the data mining stage. Section 4 describes the data mining tool used for this exploratory analysis and Section 5 demonstrates the types of results and post data mining evaluations performed. NRMA Insurance Limited, one of Australia's largest general insurers, were the collaborators for the project and supplied the database and domain expertise.

2. INSURANCE PORTFOLIO DATABASES

A portfolio database in an insurance company contains a set of insurance policies purchased by customers. A policy insures up to a specified value a particular entity (motor vehicle, household contents, buildings) from loss. When damage or loss occurs to the insured entity a claim is made against the policy for compensation. A policy is valid for a certain time period and is usually renewed upon payment of the premium. The period during which a policy is active is referred to as the period of exposure (as in the insurer's exposure to risk) and is usually measured in days. At any particular time the exposures associated with active policies in the portfolio database will differ depending upon their dates of validity.

A key factor to the success of an insurance portfolio is balancing the trade-off between the setting of competitive premiums and covering the risk associated with the exposure. The insurance market is very competitive and setting premiums too high leads to a loss of market share. Yet setting premiums too low leads to loss of profit. Premiums are generally based on a small number of key factors (such as age of driver, type of vehicle, and address of owner) identified by various analyses and intuitions. Because of the size of many insurance portfolios, analysis is often restricted to straightforward techniques.

The performance of a portfolio is usually assessed in the context of the previous year's data. The analyses performed on the data are used by the underwriter to envisage the near future performance of the portfolio and to adjust the policy rating structure to reflect changes in the market and in the behaviour of the insured. Essentially the analyses are used each year to tune the rules which set premiums for the coming year.

There are two extremes in setting premiums: all policies attract the same premium; or each individual policy has an individual premium determined for it based on all of the details of the policy. Neither extreme is particularly useful nor practical. The former would likely penalise those who are less likely to lodge claims in favour of those who are more likely to do so, and would probably drive them to the competitors! The latter would generally be impractical because of the complexity of the rules that would be required. However, the goal of good insurance premium setting is likely to lean towards the latter than to the former. An insurer would prefer to fine tune their premium setting more so than is often currently performed, identifying more factors that affect the risk and taking more information into account in setting premiums.

With the focus on dealing with very large databases, Data Mining (and KDD in general) provides an environment in which to perform such extended analyses of insurance portfolio databases. The ACSys Data Mining Environment (Williams and Huang 1996a)—consisting of a collection of integrated tools together with a variety of commercial and research data mining systems based on high performance parallel computers—provides the framework in which these analyses are performed.

3. PREPROCESSING

As observed elsewhere (Brachman and Anand 1996, Williams and Huang 1996b), while data mining is a key stage of the whole KDD process, the other stages of the process often require considerable (and often considerably more) effort. Starting from the data extracted from the source database maintained by NRMA Insurance Limited (consisting of many millions of policies), a number of transformations had to be performed before a suitable Working Dataset was built. This involved many iterations, some of which were performed after the initial data mining runs were performed. (The initial runs indicated different directions to take, different data to obtain, and different transformations to be performed.)

The Source Dataset was extracted from the NRMA's motor vehicle insurance portfolio database. An initial trial dataset of some 125,000 records, covering a time period of only 6 months (1 July 1994 to 31 December 1994), was used prior to working with the full dataset. Each record contained 93 fields of data. Figure 1 summarises the preprocessing performed.

The first task was to remove from the database those fields/attributes/variables which were irrelevant to the task at hand. This process was complicated by the fact that some "obviously" irrelevant attributes (e.g., office at which application for insurance was lodged) could contain surprising information. On the other hand, leaving irrelevant attributes in the data set can lead to aberrant results.

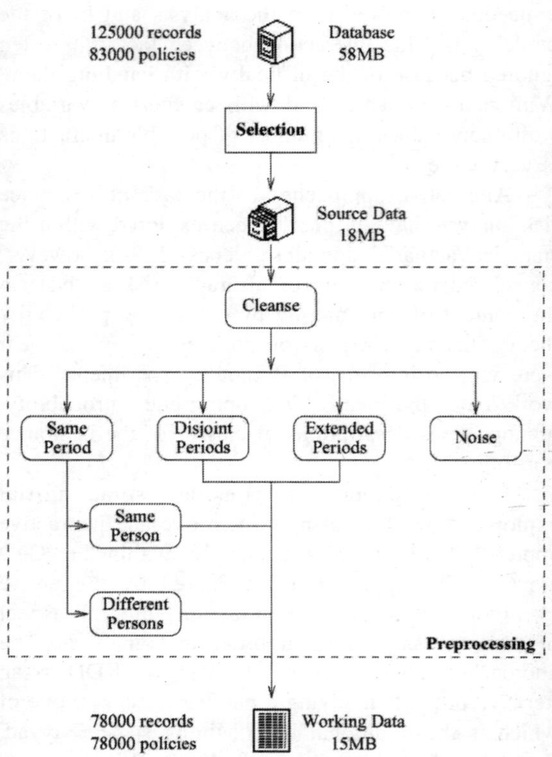

Figure 1: Preprocessing.

A panel of KDD experts (from Machine Learning, Statistics, and Databases) and domain experts (from the NRMA) considered each attribute in turn, removing only those that were seen as clearly irrelevant by all.

The second task, labelled "Cleansing" in Figure 1, involved performing various transformations on the data (e.g., birth dates transformed into ages). Various computed fields were also added to the data at this stage. One, for example, calculated the period of exposure associated with the policy in the context of the period of interest (last six months of 1994).

The third task involved collapsing the transaction-oriented data that was supplied into a policy-oriented dataset which is required for the types of analyses intended to be performed. The original database was oriented towards managing the insurance portfolio—it was not designed with Data Mining in mind. A transaction in the original database records some change made to, or incident associated with, a policy. Hence, in the 125,000 records, there were only about 83,000 policies. Some policies had multiple owners (hence multiple records) while others had a variety of changes, such as renewals, cancellations, etc. Other policies appeared more than once when there was more than a single claim made on the policy in the period of interest.

A careful study of the dataset had to be made to understand all of its nuances. This finally resulted in the definition of a set of rules to merge the multi-record policies into single policy records. These rules were implemented as a variety of operations and were tuned iteratively as the data and problems became better understood.

An intermediate dataset was created with some 78,000 individual policies, each described by 43 attributes, some of which were generated in the merging process to record, for example, the number of owners of each individual policy and the total amount of all claims made against a policy. Policies that were cancelled or met other criteria (e.g., contained critical but missing data) were also removed from the dataset.

The intermediate dataset was intended to be used for multiple data mining objectives (e.g., fraud detection). Consequently, some of its attributes were still irrelevant to the risk analysis and thus further processing was performed to build the final risk analysis Working Dataset. This dataset contained some 75,000 unique policies, each being represented by 23 attributes, including exposure and total claims cost.

An initial observation that has some impact upon the type of analysis performed was that of the 75,000 policies, only about 4,000 of them actually had claims against them. While not particularly surprising, such a low relative occurrence (about 5%) of an important aspect of the data does require attention (e.g., appropriate use of prior probabilities), but is beyond the immediate scope of this paper.

A second observation of relevance to the data mining is that different policies have different exposures, even though the majority have exposure for the whole period. This indicates that the exposure should be used to weight the examples in some way. This important aspect of the data is also left for future exposition.

4. DECISION TREES

The ACSys Data Mining Environment uses StarTree, for example, which is an implementation of the classification and regression tree software CART (Breiman, Friedman, Olshen and Stone 1984). This parallel implementation by Thinking Machines Corporation is part of the Darwin toolkit (Thinking Machines Corporation 1995). CART is similar in many ways to the traditional machine learning decision tree induction algorithm C4.5 (Quinlan 1993).

StarTree consists of three operations: *grow tree*; *evaluate tree*; and *apply tree*. The *grow tree* stage actually implements the usual divide-and-conquer strategy in a parallel architecture for building a full decision tree based on a training set. The *evaluate tree* stage evaluates the generated tree in the context of a test dataset. It is here that pruning is performed and a variety of test datasets can be used to explore the performance of the tree in the context of pruning. The *apply tree* stage simply applies any resulting trees to new unseen data. StarTree provides a variety of output options, including a $\LaTeX$ formatted decision tree or a collection of rules.

5. RISK ANALYSIS

5.1 Methodology

The claim cost attribute in the final database was selected as the target attribute (or dependent variable) and the remainder (excluding exposure) as the independent variables. All policies were classified into two classes: those with claims and those with no claims—the claim cost was effectively reclassified as 1 or 0. The dataset was processed with *grow tree* to produce a complete decision tree.

Using StarTree a rule base can be built from a generated decision tree. A rule base consists of a set of rules, each corresponding to a different path through the tree representing a conjunction of the conditions associated with the nodes of the tree. An example rule might be:

If age ≤ 20
and sex = Male
and insured amount ≥ 5000
and insured amount < 10000
Then insurance claimed = 1, cost = 0, (0, 15)

This rule indicates that under the given conditions an insurance policy is claimed against (with a misclassification cost of 0). There are 15 examples from which this rule was generated.

The primary rule base generated by StarTree is now extended within the ACSys Data Mining Environment with new information that is derived from other sources, including the Source Dataset and original database. Significant areas of risk were explored by viewing those leaf nodes containing claims. The frequency of claims at any leaf together with the total of the claim costs at the leaf nodes provide important information. However, since claims cost had been factored out of the training set used by StarTree to build the decision tree, this information was incorporated as an extra step following on from the data mining. The rules are thus extended with information that records the total exposure and the total claim cost for each rule. Other information such as the total of the premiums associated with the "area of risk" could also have been determined.

The generation of this extra information is an important step in the KDD task which, as we emphasise above, is more than just the application of Data Mining tools. This post processing of the learned rules is an important part in the final stage of the KDD process—the evaluation of discovered patterns.

The additional information can be used to determine whether the information embodied as a rule is useful as knowledge. Such an exploration of the rules discovered turns data mining, in a sense, back onto itself. This is particularly the case where we are dealing with very large datasets with many attributes from which very large trees (and hence very many rules) are generated without pruning (and hence over fitting). The generated rules themselves need to be data mined (in the context of this evaluation stage).

5.2 Initial Results

Some initial results from the analysis of the NRMA Insurance Limited sample database are presented here.

Due to the commercial nature of the data the actual variables will be referred to as `F01`, `F02`, `...`, `F23`.

For illustration, three decision trees were generated using different selection measures for the partitions—we will refer to the three trees as the entropy, gini, and error trees. (Refer to Mingers (1989) for a discussion of selection measures.) An idea of the size and organisation of the trees produced from the sample data is gained from the statistics of the various trees grown (Table 1).

Table 1: Using alternative decrease functions

Tree name:	Entropy	Gini	Error
Decrease Function	entropy	gini	error
Number of Nodes	10215	10887	8197
Depth	43	38	39
Total leaves	5062	5391	3331
Positive leaves (Pl)	1967	2188	1192
Negative leaves (Nl)	3095	3203	2139
Policies by Pl	3815	3795	1682
Policies by Nl	71993	72013	74126

It is clear from Table 1 that very large trees are generated given the large number of attributes (and possible values) and the large number of examples. (Refer to Catlett (1991) for a discussion of using decision tree induction on large datasets.) The row in the table giving the total number of leaves corresponds also to the number of rules generated from the tree. Similarly the positive leaves and the negative leaves. The Entropy tree, for example, generates 1967 rules for claims.

Although 21 independent variables were used in the input data, only 19 were selected by the Entropy and Gini trees and 20 by the Error tree. Table 2 lists the selected variables and the frequencies with which the variables appear in each tree. Thus, the variable `F01` appears 111 times in the Error tree. Such information can be of use in gaining some insights into which variables appear to be important. (The

Table 2: Attribute frequencies

Variable	Entropy	Gini	Error
F02	0	0	0
F01	0	0	111
F14	465	840	60
F21	668	711	52
F19	1756	1367	119
F22	2223	2177	85
F18	2258	2034	374
F12	2667	2589	289
F16	3013	2461	82
F07	3051	2947	1407
F15	3543	3122	189
F13	4629	4928	224
F20	4843	5175	19
F17	6164	6197	1023
F04	6773	6743	4041
F10	6799	6431	3975
F06	8760	9122	10195
F08	10771	11772	20842
F09	11362	10200	7895
F03	12073	12349	11464
F11	12329	12989	1480

Table 3: Claims associated with each risk area

Claims	Number of Rules		
	Entropy	Gini	Error
1	1090	1493	941
2	494	404	150
3	192	135	48
4	82	51	27
5	38	31	7
6	15	16	7
7	18	17	3
8	9	7	3
9	5	6	2
10	5	5	1
11	4	5	1
12	2	4	
13	4	5	
14	4		2
15	2	1	
16	2	1	
17		2	
18		1	
22	1	2	
24		1	
36		1	

location of the variable within the tree and the type of the variable—categorical versus continuous—are other important indicators.) Table 3 records the number of claims associated with the rules generated from each of the three trees, aggregated by the number of claims. There are 1090 rules from the Entropy tree, for example, which have just a single claim. On the other hand, there are 36 claims associated with one of the rules from the Gini tree. Those rules associated with a higher number of claims would tend to indicate areas of high risk.

Table 4 summarises the rules from each tree with more than 14 claims against them or with a high average claim cost with respect to the exposure. For each such rule the tables record the number of claims, the total amount of exposure, and the sum of the claim costs. Each row represents a single rule. In the Gini sub-table, for example, there are 36 claims associated with a single rule. These claims cover 442 days of exposure and have a total claim cost of $159,472. Such information can again be used to target areas described by the rules for further explorations.

Armed with such "post data mining" analyses areas of significant insurance risk can be identified and further investigated. Such investigations could be expected to lead to a better understanding of insurance risk and to a finer tuning of insurance premium setting.

Table 4: High claim risk areas

Gini		
Claims	Exposure	Cost
11	221	139673
15	1868	74367
16	2513	54750
17	2635	33152
17	2637	52721
22	2305	70558
22	3839	86988
24	3399	98918
36	442	159472

Entropy		
Claims	Exposure	Cost
15	1745	43308
15	197	55921
16	2198	50213
16	2471	52201
22	265	85678

Error		
Claims	Exposure	Cost
10	349	27827
14	2183	49883
14	2023	49889

6. SUMMARY

In this paper we have followed the KDD process and highlighted a novel approach to its application to the domain of insurance risk assessment. A particular focus has been on the interaction between the data mining stage and the evaluation stage of the KDD process. StarTree was used to analyse the large insurance dataset, generally building very large decision trees (and hence large rule sets). The rules were used only as an aid in the "discovery" of interesting areas of the data. By understanding such hot spots, better insights into policy premium setting can be gained.

ACKNOWLEDGEMENTS

This work has been performed within the Divisions of Information Technology (DIT) and Mathematics and Statistics (DMS) of the Australian Governments' Commonwealth Scientific and Industrial Research Organisation (CSIRO). The KDD team also includes Peter Milne of DIT and Murray Cameron, Glenn Stone, Petra Kuhnert, and David Chan of DMS. Industry collaborators from NRMA Insurance Limited include Keith Forster, Philip Woods, and Hong Ooi. Thanks to all for their comments on this paper.

REFERENCES

Brachman, R.J. and Anand, T.: 1996, The process of knowledge discovery in databases: A human-centered approach, in Fayyad, Piatetsky-Shapiro, Smyth and Uthurusamy (1996), chapter 2.

Breiman, L., Friedman, J.H., Olshen, R.A. and Stone, C.J.: 1984, *Classification and regression trees*, Wadsworth, Belmont, CA.

Brockman, M.J. and Wright, T.S.: 1992, Statistical motor rating: Making effective use of your data, *Journal of Institute of Actuaries* 119, 457–543.

Catlett, J.: 1991, *Megainduction: Machine learning over very large databases*, PhD thesis, Basser Department of Computer Science, University of Sydney.

Coutts, S.M.: 1984, Motor insurance rating: An actuarial approach, *Journal of Institute of Actuaries* 111, 87–148.

Fayyad, U.M., Piatetsky-Shapiro, G. and Smyth, P.: 1996, From data mining to knowledge discovery: An overview, in Fayyad, Piatetsky-Shapiro, Smyth and Uthurusamy (1996), chapter 1.

Fayyad, U.M., Piatetsky-Shapiro, G., Smyth, P. and Uthurusamy, R. (eds): 1996, *Advances in Knowledge Discovery and Data Mining*, AAAI Press.

Mingers, J.: 1989, An empirical comparison of selection measures for decision-tree induction, *Machine Learning* 3(4), 319–342.

Quinlan, J.R.: 1993, *C4.5: Programs for machine learning*, Morgan Kaufmann.

Siebes, A.: 1994, Homogeneous discoveries contain no surprises: Inferring risk porfiles from large databases, *Technical Report CS-R9430*, CWI.

Thinking Machines Corporation: 1995, The Darwin solution: A family of prediction and classifica- tion tools for large databases, *Technical report*, Thinking Machines Corporation, available from http://www.think.com/.

Williams, G.J. and Huang, Z.: 1996a, The ACSys data mining environment, *Technical Report TR-DM-96001*, CSIRO Division of Information Technology.

Williams, G.J. and Huang, Z.: 1996b, Modelling the KDD process: A four stage process and four element model, *Technical Report TR-DM-96013*, CSIRO Division of Information Technology, available from Graham. Williams@dit.csiro.au.

CASE STUDY 4A SUMMARY

Williams G.J. and Huang, Z., KDD for Insurance Risk Assessment: A Case Study, CSIRO Division of Information Technology, GPO Box 664, Canberra 2601, March 1996.

This case study uses the decision tree approach for assessing insurance risk for NRMA Insurance Limited, one of Australia's largest general insurers. The case study describes preprocessing of data and then use of decision tree. Large decision trees, some with thousand of nodes, were generated.

CASE STUDY 4A EXERCISES

1. Explain the preprocessing that was required in Case Study 4A to transform data from NRMA for classification.
2. Case Study 4A generated very large decision trees. Can you explain the reasons for this? How could the size of the trees be reduced?

CASE STUDY 4B

A Data Mining Approach for Retailing Bank Customer Attrition Analysis*

This case study was published in the journal *Applied Intelligence* Vol. 22, pp. 47–60. It is reproduced here with permission from Springer Science and Business Media

ABSTRACT

Deregulation within the financial service industries and the widespread acceptance of new technologies is increasing competition in the finance marketplace. Central to the business strategy of every financial service company is the ability to retain existing customers and reach new prospective customers. Data mining is adopted to play an important role in these efforts. In this paper, we present a data mining approach for analyzing retailing bank customer attrition. We discuss the challenging issues such as highly skewed data, time series data unrolling, leaker field detection etc, and the procedure of a data mining project for the attrition analysis for retailing bank customers. We use lift as a proper measure for attrition analysis and compare the lift of data mining models of decision tree, boosted naïve Bayesian network, selective Bayesian network, neural network and the ensemble of classifiers of the above methods. Some interesting findings are reported. Our research work demonstrates the effectiveness and efficiency of data mining in attrition analysis for retailing bank.

Keywords: data mining, classification method, attrition analysis

1. INTRODUCTION

Deregulation within the financial service industries and the widespread acceptance of new technologies is increasing competition in the finance marketplace. Central to the business strategy of every financial service company is the ability to retain existing customers and reach new prospective customers. Data mining is adopted to play an important role in these efforts. Data mining is an *iterative* process that combines business knowledge, machine learning methods and tools and large amounts of accurate and relevant information to enable the discovery of non-intuitive insights hidden in the organization's corporate data. This information can refine existing processes, uncover trends and help formulate policies regarding the company's relation to its customers and employees [1]. In the financial area, data mining has been applied successfully in determining:

- Who are the likely attriters in the next two months?
- Who are likely to be your profitable customers?
- What is your profitable customers' economic behavior?
- What products are different segments likely to buy?
- What value propositions service different groups?
- What attributes characterize your different segments and how does each play in the person's profile?

In this paper, our focus is on applying data mining techniques to help retailing banks for the attrition analysis. The goal of attrition analysis is to identify

*Hu, Xiaohua, College of Information Science, Drexel University, Philadelphia, PA, USA 19104.
xiaohua_hu@acm.org; thu@cis.drexel.edu

a group of customers who have a high probability to attrite, and then the company can conduct marketing campaigns to change the behavior in the desired direction (change their behavior, reduce the attrition rate). In data mining based direct marketing campaigns, it is well understood that targeting every customer is unprofitable and ineffective.

With limited marketing budget and staff, data mining models are used to rank the customers and only a certain percentage of customers are contacted via mail, phone etc. If the data mining model is good enough and target criteria are well defined, the company can contact a much smaller group of people with a high concentration of potential attriters [1–5]. The process of data mining for bank attrition analysis can be described in the following steps:

1. Problem definition: formulation of business problems in the area of customer retention.
2. Data review and initial selection
3. Problem formulation in terms of existing data
4. Data gathering, cataloging and formatting
5. Data Processing: (a) Data cleansing, data unfolding and time-sensitive variable definition, target variable definition, (b) Statistical analysis, (c) Sensitivity analysis, (d) Leaker detection, (e) Feature selection
6. Data modeling via classification models: Decision Trees, Neural Networks, Boosted Bayesian Networks, Selective Bayesian Network, an ensemble of classifiers
7. Result review and analysis: use the data mining model to predict the likely attriters among the current customers
8. Result Deployment: target the likely attriters (called rollout)

The paper represents a data mining approach for a retailing bank attrition analysis. The purpose is the identification of rules, trends, patterns and groups that can serve as potential indicators of attrition and identify the potential attriters in advance so the bank can take proactive actions to reduce the attrition rate. The paper is organized as follows: we first define the problem and formulation of business problems in the area of customer retention in Section 2. In Section 3, we discuss data selection, data review and initial, then data gathering, cataloging and formatting, data unfolding and time-sensitive variable definition. Then we discuss sensitivity analysis, leaker detection and feature selection. Next we describe data modeling via decision trees, neural networks, Bayesian networks, selective Bayesian network and an ensemble of classifiers with the above four methods in Section 4. In Section 5, we discuss the major findings, and fields test results. Finally we conclude with our next step in Section 6.

2. BUSINESS PROBLEM

2.1 Brief Explanation of the Problem

Our client is one of the top 10 retailing banks in the world. It offers many types of financial retail products to various customers. The product we discussed in this paper belongs to a certain type of loan service. Over 750,000 customers currently use this service with \$1.5 billion outstanding, the product has had significant losses. Revenue is constantly challenged by a high attrition rate: every month, the call centers receive over 4500 calls from customers wishing to close their accounts. This, in addition to approximately 1,200 write-ins, "slow" attriters (no balance shown over 12 consecutive months) and pirated accounts constitutes a serious challenge to the profitability of the product, which totals about 5,700/ month mostly due to rate, credit line, and fees. In addition to that, many customers will use the product as long as the introductory or "teaser" rate is in effect and lapse thereafter. There are customer management program costs and acquisition costs for each account: mailing costs \$1/customer, telemarketing costs \$5/customer. Cost of incentives (i.e. lowering rates to retain customers) needs to be considered and is dependent upon the offer. Our client didn't have a proactive or reactive retention effort. In most cases, it's come down to price reduction although there is a feeling that this need not be the only or most effective policy. However, the situation described above has motivated the business and technology executives of our client to review the possibility of setting a knowledge based retention effort through a combination of effective segmentation, customer profiling, data mining and credit scoring that can retain more customers, while maximizing revenue. The result of this initiative was the launching of the project described in this paper.

2.2 Problem Definition

The section presents the steps to understand and define the problem in terms of data available, time periods, and target fields. In this exercise, as in all data mining projects, the longest and most laborious part of the process is the selection, preparation and organization of the data [1, 6, 7].

There are different types of attriters in the product line:

- Slow attriters: Customers who slowly pay down their outstanding balance until they become inactive. Attrition here is understood comprehensively, where voluntary attrition can show more than one behavior.
- Fast attriters: Customers who quickly pay down their balance and either lapse it or close it via phone call or write-in.
- Cross selling: Identify customers who are likely to purchase alternative products offered to existing loan customers such as life insurance and the like. The increase in relationships is believed to serve as a deterrent to attrition.
- High risk: Customers who are likely to become high risk.
- Pirating: Identify customers likely to transfer their relationship to competing products and away from our client.

These patterns are not unidimensional: a customer can display a subset of these behaviors over the life of the loan. At the same time, he/she can be influenced to change the behavior through the effective use of policies and incentives. Given this, the customer can be thought of as operating within a state diagram such as the one depicted in Figure 1.

As the figure shows, a customer, through his actions, can migrate between activity and attrition where each state is defined in terms of a grouping of attributes. Based on this diagram, we decided to concentrate on two attrition problems, namely:

1 Utilizing data on accounts that remained continuously open in the last 4 months, predict, with 60 days advance notice, the likelihood that a particular customer will opt

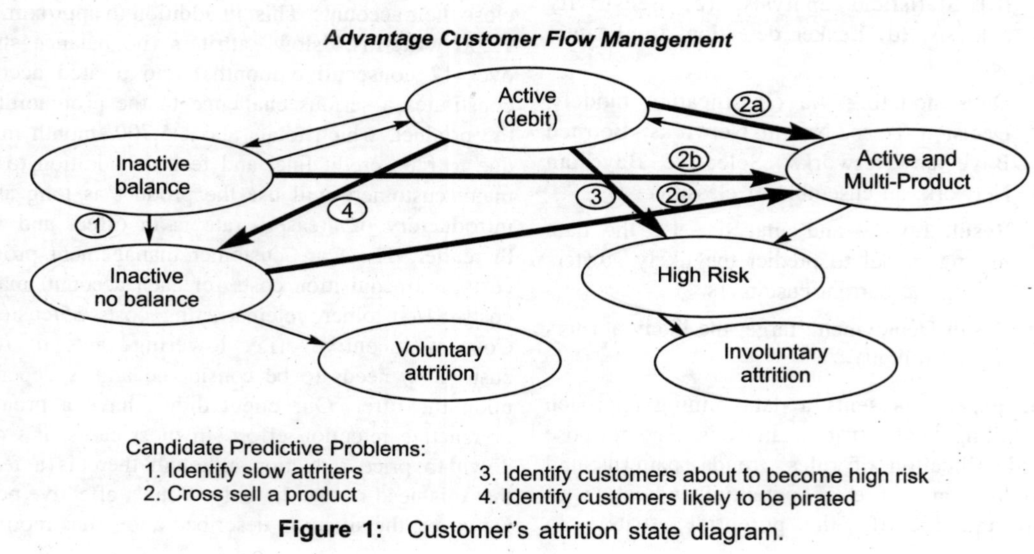

Figure 1: Customer's attrition state diagram.

to voluntarily close his/her account either by phone or write-in.

2 Utilizing data on accounts that remained continuously open in the last 4 months, predict, with 60 days advance notice, the likelihood that a particular customer will have his account transferred to a competing institution. The account may or may not remain open.

The focus of the modeling process, and subsequent campaigns, will revolve around the resolution of the two classes of business problems related to improving customer retention and activation for the product line as identified by the business:

Problem Class #1: Retention of Existing Customers

The problem requires the stratification of customer segments by leveraging the current segmentation model in order to:

- Develop models that predict the customers who are likely to attrite within 30 to 60 days on an ongoing basis.
- Identify the characteristics of the most profitable/desirable customer segments in order to develop policies to ensure their continued support, to grow the group, and to acquire more customers with similar characteristics.

Problem Class #2: Customer Activation Policies

Identify customer groups whose characteristics lend them to migrating from unprofitable/dormant to profitable. Once identified, the characteristics can enable the development of risk, maintenance and opportunity policies tailored to a successful migration.

3. DATA SELECTION

Like all data mining exercises, the identification of relevant data in the right quantity and over a significant period of time is critical for the development of meaningful models [1, 8, 9]. Given this and working with the domain experts, we proceeded to identify the necessary data sources available and those readily accessible for initial review. Table 1 summarizes the data sources identified and their expected functions.

Table 1: Description of identified (Potential) data sources for related data

Data source	Description & relevance to attrition modeling
DDS warehouse	Credit Card Data Warehouse containing about 200 product specific fields. Originating at various points (Write-ins, external database, scores, etc.), the data is compacted according to a set of operational rules that reduce size for non-changing fields. The Warehouse contains 6 months of data and is rotated on a monthly basis. In some cases, additional attributes allow for data to cover up to 18 months. For the current exercise, the period includes 4 month history information. The Credit Card Data warehouse is the primary source of data for retention modeling problems.
Third party data	A set of account related demographic and credit bureau information. The data is available from an external provider, Dynamark, Inc. The data is linked to DDS Warehouse data to provide additional predictive data
Segmentation files	Set of account related segmentation values based on our client's segmentation scheme, which combines Risk, Profitability and External potential. The segment data combine with DDS data extract to overlay with results of models.
Payment database	Database that stores all checks processed. The database can categorize source of checks. This data set allows the finding of date, balance and originator of checks and is used to identify pirated accounts

3.1 Data Preprocessing Goals

The data preprocessing state consists of the series of activities necessary to create a compacted file that:

- Reflects data changes over time.
- Recognizes and removes statistically insignificant fields
- Defines and introduces the "target" field
- Allows for second stage preprocessing and statistical analysis.

This was accomplished through three steps, detailed in the sections below:

- Time series "unrolling"
- Target value definition
- First stage statistical analysis

3.1.1 Data Period Identification

Given the data availability and its time periodicity, we decided to start the data selection by extracting a subset of records of accounts whose status was "Open" i.e. currently appearing as bonafide users for the period of **12/2001–3/2002**. In addition, and for comparison purposes, we also requested data on accounts whose status is either "Closed" or "Charged Off" on a date not prior to 11/2001. This will allow us to review the characteristics of attriters and enable the creation of a voluntary attriter. Based on this consideration, 45,814 random records were selected, each representing one account of which 42,547 are open and the remainder, or 3267 have been closed since December, 2001. The records obtained are stored in a temporary table to be used to join with all relevant tables that will produce, for every account, the status of the account FOR EACH MONTH for the past 4 months. This means that we are able to reproduce ALL THE FIELDS for each month starting in December 2001 and not only those for March, 2002.

3.1.2 Time Series "Unrolling"

The data extracted from the data source had one row per account for each month. In our application, historical customers records are used to group customers into two classes—those who are attriters and those who are not. In order to save space, every month a query checks every field against the previous month. If there is no change, no rows are added and the value of Effective Start Date (EFF_START_DT) remains as that during which a change was last recorded (which is the same as "a new row was inserted"). If any attribute changes, a whole new row is added with the corresponding EFF_START_DT updated. Therefore, it is very likely that some of the accounts will have less than the corresponding number of months in cases where no activity is recorded. For example, if an account has had no activity since December 2001, the last row will be the one for that month and it is up to the user to extrapolate it all the way to the current month. Understanding this when arranging the files is critical to developing the attrition model.

Since data records in the data file is one row per account for each month, we need to use the last 4-month historical information to build a predictive model. To reflect the data changes over time and maintain the seasonal behavior of the data, it is necessary to combine the 4 individual monthly data files into one data file, in which each account has one row with all the last 4 months financial information. The data format used is required for the implicit data to be made explicit and the time periods to be itemized into individual fields. To accomplish this, we classify the variables into static variables and time sensitive variables [1]. The values of static variables do not change over time. Examples of this are: Account Number, Mother's Maiden name, Address, and the like. The values of time sensitive variables change from month to month and it is essential to retain all these different values for the last 4 months in order to find some seasonal/temporal behavior related to the account activity. The time sensitive variables were assigned a time prefix (T0 means the last month, T1 one month back from the last month, T2 two months back from last month and T3 three months back from the last month). So, for example, the variable *CURRENT_BALANCE* for the

Table 2: Naming convention for time sensitive DDS data for the 4 months period.

Period	Nomenclature
Last month (March 2002)	T0_CURRENT_BALANCE
One month back (Feb 2002)	T1_CURRENT_BALANCE
Two months back (Jan 2002)	T2_CURRENT_BALANCE
Three months back (Dec 2001)	T3_CURRENT_BALANCE

period of December 2001 to March 2002 is redefined in Table 2.

Given this, the next task consisted of generating the additional fields on the "clean" formatted files and adding them to the resulting file. After the time-series data unrolling (Table 3), the fields in the data set increased from 250 to around 870.

3.1.3 Target Value Definition

Like many real data mining applications, normally there is no data mining target field defined directly in the data warehouse. It is part of the data mining procedure to define the proper target field based on the business objective for the data mining analysis. With the help of the business domain experts, we define the target value in terms of existing data and, with these, define the value of the target variable, i.e., the variable that determines the voluntary attriters, hereby (Table 4) defined as **VA_ACCTS (1: attriter, 0: non-attriter)**. It is defined in terms of:

1. Status code (*CRD_ST_CD*)
2. Status change date (*CRD_STATUS_CHANGE_DATE*)
3. Closed reason code (*CRD_CLS_REA_CD*)

The formula for definition is:

CRD_ST_CD = C (Closed) &&

CRD_STATUS_CHANGE_DATE Between Dec-1-2001 and March-31-2002 &&

CRD_CLS_REA_CD (reason code) in

[0 1 23 25 26 28 29 30 35 36 40 41 42 80 81 82 83 84 97 98 31 32 33 34]

The reason codes for a voluntary attriter (customer requested) are: "0 1 23 25 26 28 29 30 35 36 40 41 42", the reason codes for a voluntary attriter (customer requested) related to pricing issues are: "31 32 33 34". According to this definition, the average attrition rate for the section of the data received is 2.2% of all customers for a 4-month period.

3.1.4 First Stage Statistical Analysis

Of the 870 fields in the time-series data set, a significant portion of them is constants, null fields. Filtering them out in the early stage can dramatically reduce the data mining time and improve the model accuracy. The statistical analysis, the first in a series, is done in order to obtain an initial understanding of the data quality: number of unknown fields, relative frequency, early indicators, averages and target data distribution. As an initial field discrimination step, the fields where a single value appeared in more than 99.95% of all records or null was deemed statistically insigni-ficant and removed from the set of attributes. These fields are removed from both the data and meta-data files to ensure their removal from the modelling process, thus reducing the computing time required. This process reduced the fields from 870 to 655.

3.2 Data Premodeling

The data premodeling stage is the next critical step in the generation of the files used for modeling. This stage consists of three main steps, namely:

(1) field sensitivity analysis to filter fields with low correlation to target the field and detect data "*leakers*",

(2) field reduction to create a compacted file with highly relevant fields,

(3) file set generation of all balanced and unbalanced sets required for training, testing and iterative verification of results and model refinement.

3.2.1 Field Sensitivity Analysis and Field Reduction

The field sensitivity analysis is used to determine each attribute's "contribution" to the modeling process. We use a rough set based field selection algorithm [4]. Our algorithm generates a merit value for each field, consider the interaction/correlation among the fields and identify a minimum subset of fields from the entire field. On the other hand, if a field whose merit value is too high, it is considered to be a potential *leaker* [10]. Leakers are fields that "leak" information on the target. For example, a field with a value representing account closure could leak information on attrition, and would confound modeling efforts. While some leakers are readily explained, many times they are included in

Table 3: Data file after time-series unrolling

Account#	Name	. . .	T0_Current_balance	T1_Current_balance	T2_Current_balance	T3_Current_balance	. . .	. . .
1	Jim	. . .	1234.7	2345.6	1489.87	234.9	. . .	. . .
2	Tom	. . .	0.0	0.0	769.09	0	. . .	. . .
. . .	. . .	. . .	. . .	. . .	. . .	. . .	. . .	. . .
15000	Ana	. . .	200.0	215.0	250.0	278.0	. . .	. . .
. . .	. . .	. . .	. . .	. . .	. . .	. . .	. . .	. . .
45814	Mike	. . .	780.0	1200.90	300	100.0	. . .	. . .

Table 4: Data after target defined

Account#	Name	. . .	T0_Current_balance	T1_Current_balance	T2_Current_balance	T3_Current_balance	. . .	VA_ACCTS
1	Jim	. . .	1234.7	2345.6	1489.87	234.9	. . .	0
2	Tom	. . .	0.0	0.0	769.09	0	. . .	1
. . .	. . .	. . .	. . .	. . .	. . .	. . .	. . .	. . .
15000	Ana	. . .	200.0	215.0	250.0	278.0	. . .	0
. . .	. . .	. . .	. . .	. . .	. . .	. . .	. . .	. . .
45814	Mike	. . .	780.0	1200.90	300	100.0	. . .	0

business rules whose relation to the target is not apparent. In this case, the best way to determine if a field is indeed a leaker is to discuss the findings with those familiar with the data schema and the business problem. Some of the leaker fields we identified from the data sets are *bankruptcy score, risk level, bankruptcy reason code, number of times the person used the cards, number of sales, the closed reason code* etc. In many circumstances, field names and values are not always representative of their function, and need clarification. One the other hand, fields that are suspected but turn out *not* to be leakers constitute potential predictors in the model. In some cases, the values for a field are constant (i.e., have a standard deviation of zero) and thus the merit value is zero. These fields should be removed in order to improve data mining processing speed and to generate better models. After the leaker field analysis, we applied our novel feature selection algorithm [4] on the data set to identify a minimum subset of features related to the target field. For example, through this effort, the initial set of 655 attributes in the data set was reduced to 242 after processing.

3.2.2 Files Set Generation

Our sample file comprises of 45814 records, the average monthly attrition rate is 0.55%, and the accumulated attrition rate of the last 4 months is around 2.2%. In order to build a good model from this highly skewed data set, we need to build a more balanced representation of attriters and non-attriters in the training data set. The reason is that in the original data file, we have high non-attriters percentage (97.8%) vs. a very low attriter rate (2.2%); a learning model can achieve high accuracy by always predicting every customer to be a non-attriter. Obviously, such a high accurate model is useless for attrition analysis [10, 11]. We created a random sample file where we include about 938 attriters and then we add enough non-attriters into it to make it a dataset with 50–50 percentage of each class category (attriters vs. non-attriters), then file was divided into *balanced, train* and *test* files as well as *raw* (i.e., unbalanced) *test* and *held aside* files for verification purposes. The *balanced train file* consisted of 50% of the records containing target values, i.e., for whom VA_ACCTs = 1. The *balanced test, raw test*, and *raw held aside files* consisted of approximately 1/6 of the targets each. As defined earlier in Section 3.1.3, targets in the raw files represent 2.2% of the total number of records for the files being reviewed. These files were handed over to the data mining component for further statistical analysis, data mining and clustering work.

4. DATA MINING MODEL DEVELOPMENT PROCESS

4.1 Evaluation Criterion: Lift

As pointed in [4, 5, 11, 12], prediction accuracy, which was used to evaluate the mining algorithms, is not a suitable evaluation criterion for the data mining applications such as attrition analysis. The main reasons are:

1. Classification errors (false negative, false positive) are treated equally, but in attrition analysis, false positive and false negative have different impact and different consequences, they should be dealt with differently,
2. Accuracy is used to measure the performance of the learning algorithm on the whole dataset, The goal of the attrition analysis is not to predict the behavior of every customer, but find a good subset of customers where the percentage of attriters is high. For attrition analysis, the dataset is highly skewed and noisy, it is very difficult to build a model with good accuracy.

In attrition analysis, our goal is to use history information to build an effective data mining model and then use the data mining model to predict the most likely attriters and then take proactive action to prevent the customer attrition. So it is required that learning algorithms need to classify with a confidence measurement, such as a probability estimation factor or certainty factor (also called scores in attrition analysis). The scores will allow us to rank customers for promotion or targeting marketing. Lift instead of the predictive accuracy is used as an evaluation criterion. As pointed out in [9], if the data mining model is good enough, we should find a high concentration of attriters at the top of the list and this higher proportion of attriters can be measured in terms of "lift" to see how much better than random the model-based targeting is. Generally, lift can be calculated by looking at the cumulative targets captured up to $p\%$ as a percentage of all targets and dividing by $p\%$[9]. For example, the top 10% of the sorted list may contain 35% of likely attriters, then the model has a lift of 35/10 = 3.5. A lift reflects the redistribution of responders in the testing set after the testing examples are ranked. After the learning algorithm ranks all testing examples from most likely responders to least likely responders, we divide the ranked list into some deciles (the top 10% is finer partitioned in our test experiments: we measure the lift in each percentage), and see how the original responders distributed in these deciles. Lift measures the increased accuracy for a target subset based on a model-scored ranked list. Using past information collected over several months on usage of the financial service, our task is to build a model for predicting the customer class in the next two months and apply it to the whole customers. The prediction model is used to rank the customers based on their likelihood of attrition. As shown in section, the attrition rate for our clients is low (2.2%) and it is difficult or impossible to predict with high accuracy for all customers, and usually it is not necessary to predict all the customers because in practice, for attrition analysis, it is a good practice to contact a small percentage of customers and hope this small percentage of customers contains a higher concentrated percentage of attriters than random sample.

4.2 Data Mining Models Based on Different Algorithms

We are interested in models that maximize lift. A good model in our analysis should concentrate the likely attriters near the top in the sorted list based on the attrition scores generated by the model. We need to use learning algorithms that can produce scores in order to rank the testing examples. Algorithms such as Naïve Bayesian, decision tree, neural network satisfy our requirement. We performed several data mining analyses using four different data mining algorithms and an ensemble of classifiers of the above 4 algorithms [4]. These are:

1. Boosted Naïve Bayesian (BNB)
2. Neural Network (NeuralWare Predict: a commercial neural network from NeuralWare Inc)
3. Decision Tree (C4.5 with some modifications for scoring and ranking [10])
4. Selective Naïve Bayesian (SNB).
5. An ensemble of classifiers of the above four methods

4.2.1 Boosted Naïve Bayesian Networks (BNB)

The BNB data mining method combines boosting and naive Bayesian learning [6, 13–15]. Boosting is a general method of improving the predictive accuracy of any two-class learning algorithm, which works in successive stages. In the first stage, all the training examples are weighted equally and the two-class learning algorithm is used to acquire a classifier. In the second stage, the examples that are misclassified by this first classifier are upweighted, and a second classifier is learned that focuses on these examples. In the third stage, the examples misclassified by the second classifier are upweighted, and a third classifier is learned. The boosting process can be repeated for as many stages as desired. Applied with naive Bayesian learning, generally five to twenty stages are beneficial. The results described here use just five stages.

Like other software, our BNB software identifies which attributes are most predictive of an example being a target. Unlike most other software, BNB reports which values (or numerical ranges) of an attribute are most predictive. For example, BNB automatically identifies that the value 2 of the attribute T1_CRD_ACCOUNT_FORMAT is an important predictor. According to the supplied documentation, this value 2 signifies "account which has been active but is currently not active." Also unlike other software, BNB evaluates the statistical significance of the predictors that it reports. The significance of a predictor depends on both its lift (i.e. predictive benefit) and on its coverage (i.e. number of examples to which it applies). BNB does not report predictors that may be spurious, because they have low coverage or low lift. The lift chart of BNB is shown in Figure 2.

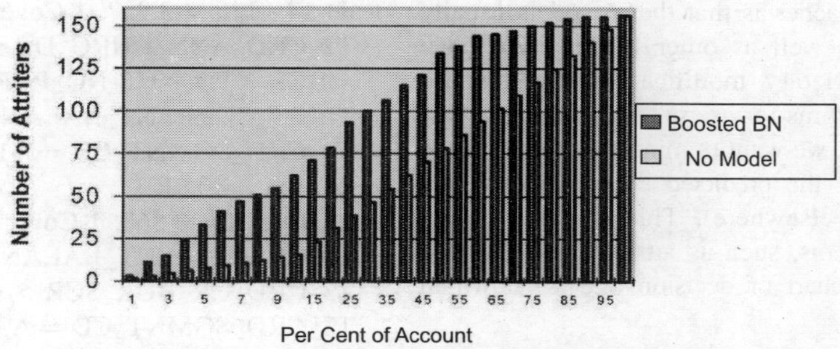

Figure 2: Boosted Naive Bayesian model lift chart.

Results

		Hits			Hits
PCT	Cases	Boosted BN	% hits	Lift	no model
1	70	3	4.3	1.9	1.5
2	141	11	7.8	3.5	3.1
3	212	15	7.1	3.2	4.7
4	283	24	8.5	3.9	6.2
5	354	33	9.3	4.2	7.8
6	425	41	9.6	4.4	9.3
7	496	47	9.5	4.3	10.9
8	567	51	9.0	4.1	12.5
9	638	55	8.6	3.9	14.0
10	709	62	8.7	4.0	15.6
15	1063	71	6.7	3.0	23.4
20	1418	78	5.5	2.5	31.2
25	1772	93	5.2	2.4	39.0
30	2127	100	4.7	2.1	46.8
35	2481	106	4.3	1.9	54.6
40	2836	115	4.1	1.8	62.4
45	3190	121	3.8	1.7	70.2
50	3545	134	3.8	1.7	78.0
55	3900	138	3.5	1.6	85.8
60	4254	144	3.4	1.5	93.6
65	4609	145	3.1	1.4	101.4
70	4963	147	3.0	1.3	109.2
75	5318	150	2.8	1.3	117.0
80	5672	152	2.7	1.2	124.8
85	6027	154	2.6	1.2	132.6
90	6381	155	2.4	1.1	140.4
95	6736	155	2.3	1.0	148.2
100	7091	156	2.2	1.0	156.0

Variables of Interest

There are 14 most significant positive predictors of the target class picked up by BNB. The top 4 attributes are listed as below in order. Each predictor is a certain value (or numerical range) of a certain attribute. A value of "z" means zero in the original dataset. "counts" is the number of targets versus non-targets with this value of the attribute. "zscore" is the measure of statistical significance.

- Attribute 84 T0_CURRENT_BALANCE {Current Balance carried in hundreds of cents} between –1840.52 and 1277.62: counts 209/86, odds 2.43418, zscore 7.17529
- Attribute 119 T1_CRD_ACCOUNT_FORMAT {Record Format of the Account. Values are: 1 = Never-Active Account, 2 = Account which has been active but is not currently active, 3 = Currently Active Account, 4 = Delinquent Account} between 1.9 and 2.2 : counts 281/154, odds 1.82764, zscore 6.10613
- Attribute 56 T0_NON_CF_LS_MIN_PY_DUE value z {This figure corresponds to the minimum payment due on the last statement. It is used in conjunction with accrued arrears and the number of cycles delinquent to permit automatic delinquency adjustment.} counts 353/214, odds 1.65221, zscore 5.8568
- Attribute 40_T0_NON_CF_LS_OS_BAL {The actual ending balance as it appeared on the cardholder's last statement. This field is not affected by adjustments.} between –1840.52 and 1277.62: counts 189/98, odds 1.93171, zscore 5.38532

4.2.2 Decision Trees

Decision tree methods build a collection of rules for use as a predictive model [10, 16, 17]. The advantage of this approach is that the rules are easy to understand, and they are frequently useful for discovering underlying business processes. The disadvantage of decision tree approaches is that these models usually do not perform as well as other models. We have developed a proprietary modification for standard decision tree algorithms for use in "lift" problems [10] where, for example, we want to minimize performance in the top 25% of the predicted data (and care less about performance elsewhere). This is the situation for common problems, such as attrition and targeted mailings. The lift chart of decision tree is shown in Figure 3.

Results

PCT	Cases	Hits decision tree	% hits	Lift	Hits no model
1	70	6	8.6	3.9	1.5
4	283	25	8.8	4.0	6.2
8	567	47	8.3	3.8	12.5
9	638	56	8.8	4.0	14.0
10	709	60	8.5	3.8	15.6
20	1418	95	6.7	3.0	31.2
25	1772	101	5.7	2.6	39.0

Some of the rules are:

Rule 8: (Lift = 5.347, 1-Cover = 0.029)
T0_CF HD_ACT_MNTHS ≤ 2
T3_CRD_SGMNT_CD = A1
-> class 1 [0.889]

Rule 12: (Lift = 4.102, 1-Cover = 0.162)
T0_ CF_CURRENT_BALANCE ≤ 407.06
T2_CF_DATE_LAST_STATEMENT ≤ 1998.055
T3_CRD_SGMNT_CD = A2
-> class 1 [0.859]

Rule 14: (Lift = 3.927, 1-Cover = 0.318)
T2_CRD_ANN_CHRG_DT ≤ 1998.164
T0_CF_YTD_NET_NO_PURCHASE ≤ 0
T0_CF_CURRENT_BALANCE ≤ 407.06
T3_CRD_SGMNT_CD = A1
-> class 1 [0.812]

Rule 9: (Lift = 3.868, 1-Cover = 0.385)
T0_CF_CURRENT_BALANCE ≤ 407.06
T3_CRD_CR_BUR_SCR > 606
T3_CRD_SGMNT_CD = A3
T3_CRD_BKRPCY_REA_CD 3 > 9260
-> class 1 [0.889]

4.2.3 Neural Networks

Neural networks are a well-established approach for modeling data [7, 14, 18]. The advantage of this approach is that neural network models tend to be among the most predictive models. The disadvantage of neural network models is that it can be harder to understand their output. For our work we have used a commercial package (NeuralWare Predict) that:

- Selects appropriate input transfer functions for fields
- Selects subsets of the variables to model the data, and
- Builds "constructive" neural network models.

The lift chart of neural network is shown in Figure 4.

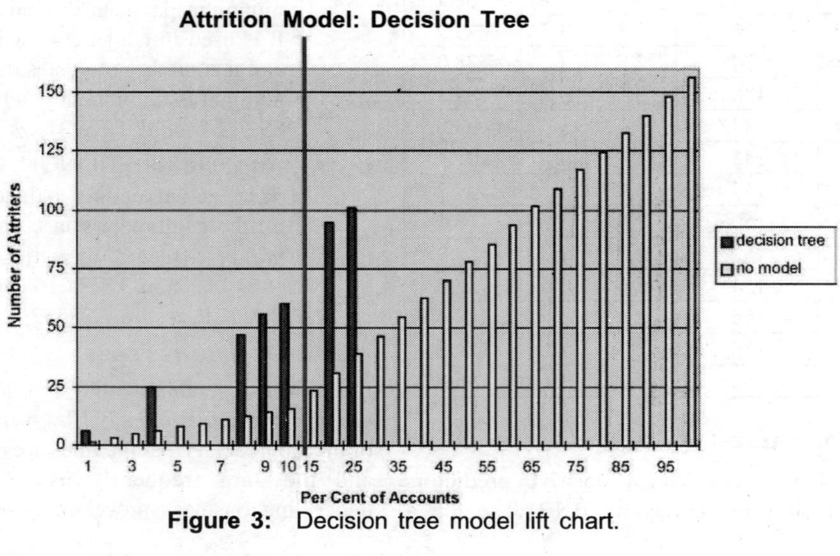

Figure 3: Decision tree model lift chart.

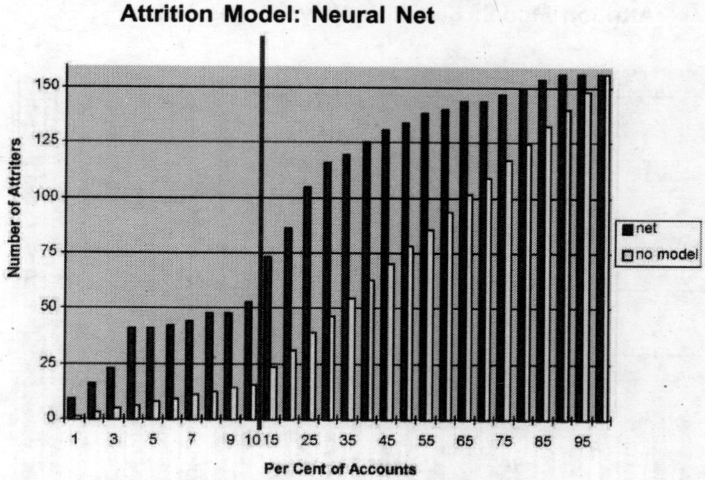

Figure 4: Neural net model lift chart.

Results

PCT	Cases	Hits Neural Net	% hits	Lift	Hits no model
1	70	9	12.9	5.8	1.5
2	141	16	11.3	5.2	3.1
3	212	23	10.8	4.9	4.7
4	283	41	14.5	6.6	6.2
5	354	41	11.6	5.3	7.8
6	425	42	9.9	4.5	9.3
7	496	44	8.9	4.0	10.9
8	567	48	8.5	3.8	12.5
9	638	48	7.5	3.4	14.0
10	709	53	7.5	3.4	15.6
15	1063	73	6.9	3.1	23.4
20	1418	86	6.1	2.8	31.2
25	1772	105	5.9	2.7	39.0
30	2127	116	5.5	2.5	46.8
35	2481	120	4.8	2.2	54.6
40	2836	125	4.4	2.0	62.4
45	3190	131	4.1	1.9	70.2
50	3545	134	3.8	1.7	78.0
55	3900	138	3.5	1.6	85.8
60	4254	140	3.3	1.5	93.6
65	4609	144	3.1	1.4	101.4
70	4963	144	2.9	1.3	109.2
75	5318	147	2.8	1.3	117.0
80	5672	150	2.6	1.2	124.8
85	6027	154	2.6	1.2	132.6
90	6381	156	2.4	1.1	140.4
95	6736	156	2.3	1.1	148.2
100	7091	156	2.2	1.0	156.0

4.2.4 Selective Naïve Bayesian Networks

The naive Bayesian classifier is a probabilistic, predictive model that assumes that all attributes are conditionally independent of each other given the target variable [19] i.e. within each class, the attributes are unrelated. The naive Bayesian classifier is simple, inherently robust with respect to noise, and scales well to domains that involve many irrelevant features. Moreover, despite its simplicity and the strong assumption that attributes are independent within each class, it has been shown to give remarkably high accuracies in many natural domains. The selective naive Bayesian classifier that we used is an extension to the naive Bayesian classifier designed to perform better in domains with highly correlated (redundant) features. The intuition is that, if highly correlated features are not selected, the classifier should perform better given its feature independence assumptions. Attributes are selected by starting with an empty set of attributes, and then incrementally adding that single attribute (from the set of unselected attributes) the attribute that most improves the accuracy of the resultant classifier on the test set. Attributes are selected until the addition of any other attribute results in a fall in accuracy of the classifier. The lift chart of the selective Bayesian networks is shown in Figure 5.

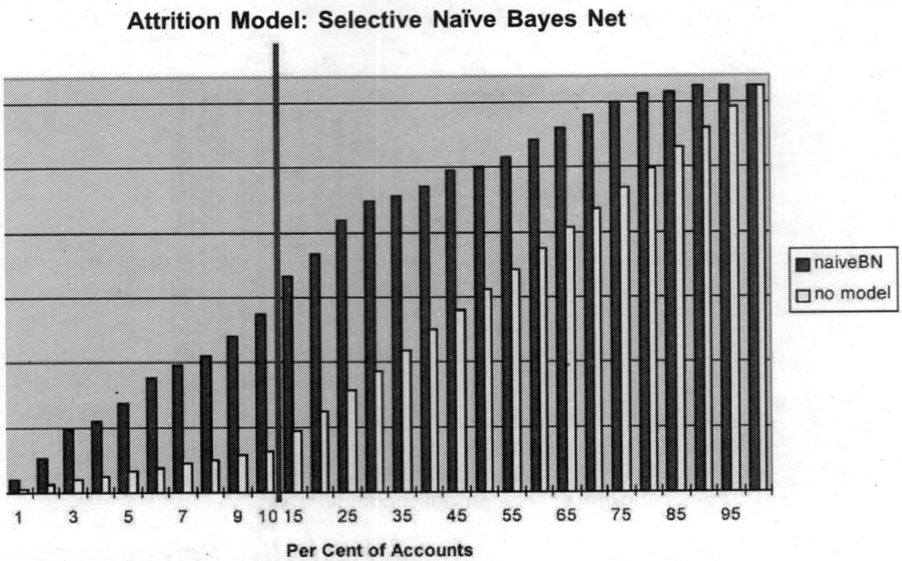

Figure 5: Selective Naïve Bayesian network model lift chart.

Results

PCT	Cases	Hits Selective BN	% hits	Lift	Hits no model
1	70	5	7.1	3.2	1.5
2	141	13	9.2	4.2	3.1
3	212	24	11.3	5.1	4.7
4	283	27	9.5	4.3	6.2
5	354	34	9.6	4.4	7.8
6	425	44	10.4	4.7	9.3
7	496	49	9.9	4.5	10.9
8	567	53	9.3	4.2	12.5
9	638	60	9.4	4.3	14.0
10	709	69	9.7	4.4	15.6
15	1063	83	7.8	3.5	23.4
20	1418	92	6.5	2.9	31.2
25	1772	105	5.9	2.7	39.0
30	2127	112	5.3	2.4	46.8
35	2481	114	4.6	2.1	54.6
40	2836	118	4.2	1.9	62.4
45	3190	124	3.9	1.8	70.2
50	3545	125	3.5	1.6	78.0
55	3900	129	3.3	1.5	85.8
60	4254	136	3.2	1.5	93.6
65	4609	140	3.0	1.4	101.4
70	4963	145	2.9	1.3	109.2
75	5318	150	2.8	1.3	117.0
80	5672	153	2.7	1.2	124.8
85	6027	154	2.6	1.2	132.6
90	6381	156	2.4	1.1	140.4
95	6736	156	2.3	1.1	148.2
100	7091	156	2.2	1.0	156.0

4.2.5 A Hybrid Approach: An Ensemble of Classifiers

An ensemble of classifiers is to generate a set of classifiers instead of one classifier for the classification of new objects, hoping that the combination of answers of multiple classifiers result in better accuracy [4, 15, 20, 21]. Ensemble of classifiers has been proved to be a very effective way to improve classification accuracy because uncorrelated errors made by the individual classifier can be removed by voting. A classifier, which utilizes a single minimal set of classification rules to classify future examples, may lead to mistakes. An ensemble of classifiers is a set of classifiers whose individual decisions are combined in some way to classify new examples. Many methods for constructing ensembles of classifiers have been developed, some are general and some are specific to particular algorithms [4, 8]. We adopted a hybrid approach: we first built 4 classifiers using Boosted Naïve Bayesian (BNB), NeuralWare predict, Decision Tree, Selective Naïve Bayesian (SNB), then we ensembled a classifier from the 4 classifiers based on the majority vote of them [4]. The ensembled classifier does have a better lift measure than any of the 4 individual classifiers.

Results

PCT	Cases	Hits ensemble of classifier	% hits	Lift	Hits no model
1	70	7	10.0	4.7	1.5
2	141	16	11.3	5.2	3.1
3	212	23	10.8	4.9	4.7
4	283	42	14.8	6.8	6.2
5	354	42	11.9	6.8	7.8
6	425	43	10.1	5.4	9.3
7	496	48	9.7	4.4	10.9
8	567	52	9.3	4.2	12.5
9	638	61	9.6	4.4	14.0
10	709	63	8.9	4.0	15.6
15	1063	81	7.7	3.5	23.4
20	1418	96	6.5	3.0	31.2
25	1772	104	5.9	2.6	39.0
30	2127	121	5.7	2.6	46.8
35	2481	131	5.3	2.4	54.6
40	2836	144	5.1	2.3	62.4
45	3190	153	4.8	2.1	70.2
50	3545	154	4.4	2.0	78.0
55	3900	155	4.0	1.8	85.8
60	4254	156	3.6	1.7	93.6
65	4609	156	3.3	1.5	101.4
70	4963	156	3.1	1.4	109.2
75	5318	156	2.9	1.3	117.0
80	5672	156	2.7	1.2	124.8
85	6027	156	2.5	1.1	132.6
90	6381	156	2.4	1.1	140.4
95	6736	156	2.3	1.0	148.2
100	7091	156	2.2	1.0	156.0

5. DATA MINING FINDINGS

The initial studies unveiled a number of relationships between variables as well as threshold values that justify further discussion and analysis. Following is a summary of the more salient points and their possible meaning:

The table below shows that several specific values (or ranges of numerical values) of several attributes are useful predictors of retention and/or attrition. These explanations increase our confidence that these values of these attributes will continue to be predictors in the future.

Field Test

To test the effectiveness of the data mining models, our client conducted a field test on their customers. The test wanted to show two points:

1. The top percentage of the customer attrition list does contain concentrated attriters,
2. The data mining based marketing approach is effective for retention purposes.

They ran the model generated from the ensemble of classifiers approach on the current customers and then sorted the customers based on the attrition scores. They decided to contact the top 4% of the existing customers (around 750,000) from the list, which was around 30,000 customers. They divided the customers into 2 groups randomly, each with 15,000 customers and took different proactive actions to each group: for group1, the marketing department contacted each customer and offered some incentive packages to encourage the customers to stay with the company, for group 2, there is no contact. After two months later, they examined the list and found out, for group 1, the attrition rate is very low (0.12%), for group two, the attrition rate is very high, almost 5.6%, while the accumulated average attrition rate for two months is 1.1%, thus achieved a lift of 5.0 (consistent with the list of 4.6 in the test dataset). The lower attrition rate among group 1 did indicate, if the proactive action is in time and proper, it does have an impact on the customers' behavior, the high attrition rate among group 2 demonstrates that our data mining model is accurate and the top 4% captured a high concentrated proportion of attriters.

Variables	Results & implications
Most recent Current Balance *(CURRENT_BALANCE)*	The most recent current balance showed a strong predictive value when the amount fell below approximately \$1000.00. A small but significant segment was of those with negative balances, i.e., of customers who overpay. Review of accounts whose previous balance falls below the threshold may be candidates for proactive action. Such candidates can also be "Possibilities" subjects during inbound calls. It can also be an indicator of "Balance Attriters" in the case of negative balances.
Current Balance with constant values *(CURRENT_BALANCE=12*	The accounts with values of \$12.00 and \$15.00 dlls. Showed prominently among the results for attrition.
NON CF_CURRENT_BALANCE=15)	If these are interest charges or related to annual charges, it could hint at policies for retention/exiting/ win back of customers.
Segment *(CRD_SGMNT_CD)*	The association of a group to a specific segment (as defined in the DDS Data Warehouse) was a significant value for segments A1–A4. With a larger sample group, we intend to allocate groups to segments (as defined by the Marketing group) in order to run more focused models.
Annual charge date *(CRD_ANN_CHRG_DT)*	The billing period within the first trimester of the year is predictive of impending attrition for customers with reduced balance *(CURRENT_BALANCE*<407). The results point an attrition pattern for lagging users of "zero balance" users who take the charge as a disincentive to maintain the product.
Number of payments *(NO_PY)*	Accounts with a number of payments made over the same billing period or payments made to cover low balances over a continuous period *(YTD_NET_PURCHASE_AMT* ≤ 62.0) can be predictive of attrition. A request for Payoff could indicate, for some accounts, a likelihood of closing (due to a recent annual charge or competitor's bid) which could be averted.
Incentive Interest *(INCENT_PRI_ANN MRCH_R)*	Incentive pricing appeared to be somewhat predictive at the value of 4.9%. This result may warrant a more in-depth study of segment-based review of "rate chaser" population.

6. CONCLUSION

In this paper, we present a data mining approach for retailing bank customer attrition analysis. We discuss the challenging issues such as highly skewed data, time series data unrolling, leaker field detection etc., and procedure of a data mining task for the attrition analyses for retailing bank. We discuss the use of lift as a proper measure for attrition analysis and compare the lift of data mining models of decision tree, boosted naïve Bayesian network, selective Bayesian network, neural network and the ensemble of class of the above methods. Our initial findings show some interesting results. The field test conducted by our clients proved that the data mining prediction model for attrition is very accurate and the target-oriented campaign is very effective. Based on above results and new source files available on segmentation; we plan to review the voluntary attrition trends on a segment-by-segment basis. A thorough clustering study is also planned for the data to review the natural grouping of the data and how it lines up with the segmentation in terms of incidence, variables and number of groups.

REFERENCES

1. A.M. Hughes, The *Complete Database Marketer: Second-generation Strategies and Techniques for Tapping the Power of Your Customer Database*, McGraw-Hill, 1996.
2. B. Baesens, M. Egmont-Petersen, R. Castelo, and J. Vanthienen, "Learning Bayesian network classifiers for credit scoring using Markov chain Monte Carlo search," *Tech report*, Utrecht University, Institute of Information and Computer Science, Netherlands.
3. S. Bhattacharya, "Direct marketing response models using genetic algorithms," in *Proc. of the 4th International Conference on Knowledge Discovery and Data Mining*, 1998, pp. 144–148.
4. X. Hu, "Using rough sets theory and database operations to construct a good ensemble of classifiers for data mining application," in *Proc. of the 2001 IEEE International Conf. on Data Mining*, 2001, pp. 233–240.
5. F. Provost and T. Fawcett, "Analysis and visualization of classifiers performance: Comparison under imprecise class and cost distribution," in *Proc. of the 3rd International Conference on Knowledge Discovery and Data Mining*, pp. 43–48.
6. M. Berry and G. Linoff, *Mastering Data Mining: The Art and Science of Customer Relationship Management*, John Wiley & Sons, 1998.
7. T. Masters, *Neural, Novel & Hybrid Algorithms for Time Series Predictions*, John Wiley & Sons Inc., 1995.
8. N. Indurkhya and M. Sholom, "Solving regression problems with rule-based ensemble classifiers," in *Proc. of the ACM SIGKDD*, 2001, pp. 287–292.
9. G. Piatetsky-Shapiro and B. Masand, "Estimating campaign benefits and modeling lift," in *Proc. of the 5th SIGKDD International Conference on Knowledge Discovery and Data Mining*, pp. 185–193.
10. X. Hu, "Comparison of classification methods for customer attrition analysis" in *Proc. of the Third International Conference on Rough Sets and Current Trends in Computing*, Springer, 2002, pp. 487–492.
11. C. Ling and C.Li, "Data mining for direct marketing: Problems and solutions," in *Proc. of the 4th International Conference on Knowledge Discovery & Data Mining*, 1998, pp. 73–79.
12. B. Masand and G. Piatetsky-Shapiro, "A comparison of approaches for maximizing business payoff of prediction models," in *Proc. of the 2nd International Conference on Knowledge Discovery and Data Mining*, 1996, pp. 195–201.
13. C. Elkan, "*Boosting* and naïve bayesian learning," *Technical Report* No. CS97–557, University of California, San Diego, Sept. 1997.
14. M. Klenin, "A simple neural network predictor for volatile time series data

nonlinear financial forecasting," in *Proc. of the 4th International Conference on Neural Networks in the Capital Market*, 1996, pp. 134–140.

15. R.E. Schapire, Y. Freund, P. Bartlett, and W.S. Lee, "Boosting the margin: A new explanation for the effectiveness of voting methods," *The Annals of Statistics,* to appear.
16. J.R. Quinlan, "Induction of decision tree," *Machine Learning*, vol. 1, no. 1, pp. 81–96.
17. J.R. Quinlan, "Bagging, boosting, and C4.5." in *Proceedings of the Thirteenth National Conference on Artificial Intelligence*, 1996, pp. 725–730.
18. G. Grudnitski and A. Quang, "Important factors in neural networks' forecasts of gold futures prices," in *Proc. of the 4th International Conference on Neural Networks in the Capital Market*, 1996, pp. 163–176.
19. Friedman, J., D. Geiger, and M. Goldszmidt, "Bayesian network classifiers," *Machine Learning,* vol. 29, pp. 131–163, 1997.
20. R.E. Schapire, "The boosting approach to machine learning: An overview," MSRI Workshop on Nonlinear Estimation and Classification, 2002.
21. R.E. Schapire, M. Rochery, M. Rahim, and N. Gupta, "Incorporating prior knowledge into boosting," in *Proc. of the Nineteenth International Conference on Machine Learning*, 2002.
22. Hu, X., and N. Cercone, "Data mining via discretization, generalization and rough set feature selection," *Knowledge and Information System: An International Journal,* vol. 1, pp. 33–60, 1999.

CASE STUDY 4B SUMMARY

Hu, X., A Data Mining Approach for Retailing Bank Customer Attrition Analysis, Applied Intelligence, 22, 47–60, 2005

This is a case study of using a number of classification techniques to analyse a large retailing bank's 750,000 customers of a loss-making loan product and identify those that have high probability to attrite.

938 attriters and an equal number of non-attriters were selected randomly and combined to make the training dataset. Monthly data for four months was combined into one record with 870 fields, which were reduced to 242 fields after filtering and sensitivity analysis.

Four algorithms, Boosted Naïve Bayesian, Neural Network, Decision Tree and Selective Naïve Bayesian as well as a hybrid algorithm combining the four were used to rank customers from those most likely to attrition to those least likely. The decision tree algorithm was modified to do so. The effectiveness of each algorithm was evaluated by calculating "lift" defined as the ratio of attritioners found in the top p% of the result to the number expected in a random sample.

Finally the results were tested in a field trial in which top 4% of around 750,000 customers ranked by the hybrid method were chosen and divided into two groups of 15,000 customers each. Each customer in one of the groups was contacted by the bank and offered an incentive package while no contact was made with the other group. The attrition rate of the two groups at the end of two months was 0.12% and 5.6% respectively. Although the 0.12% result appears attractive, it may not be a good basis for action by the bank since over 94% of the 15,000 customers who were contacted were not expected to attrition and the incentives were wasted on them.

Further work that will isolate the attritioners better rather than identifying a large number of customers that have a relatively large percentage of attritioners but more than 90% of non-attritioners is worth investigating.

CASE STUDY 4B EXERCISES

1. Explain the preprocessing that was required in Case Study 4B to transform the bank data for classification.
2. Do you think classification was the best data mining technique for the problem in Case Study 4B? Could association rule mining have been used? If yes, explain how you would use association rule mining and why this might be a suitable technique.
3. Explain the results obtained in Case Study 4B. Are the results actionable? Briefly explain your answer.

CHAPTER

5 Cluster Analysis

LEARNING OBJECTIVES

After completing this chapter, you will be able to:

- Explain what cluster analysis is
- Describe some desirable features of a cluster analysis method
- Discuss the types of cluster analysis techniques available
- Describe the K-Means Method, a partitioning technique
- Describe two hierarchical techniques—the Agglomerative method and the Divisive method
- Find other learning resources about cluster analysis

5.1 INTRODUCTION

We like to organise observations or objects or things (e.g. plants, animals, chemicals) into meaningful groups so that we are able to make comments about the groups rather than individual objects. Such groupings are often rather convenient since we can talk about a small number of groups rather than a large number of objects although certain details are necessarily lost because objects in each group are not identical. A classical example of a grouping is the chemical periodic table where chemical elements are grouped into rows and columns such that elements adjacent to each other within a group have similar physical properties. Elements in each of the groups are similar and dissimilar to elements in other groups. Class formation is often based on a small number of common characteristics.

Fauna and flora have also been grouped. The groupings at the top level are *Animalia, Fungi, Monera, Plantae, Protista and Viruses*. Every one of these groups is then divided into further groupings which are in turn divided further. Another interesting example, noted earlier in

Chapter 1, comes from Astronomy where the aim is to group the stars. Yet another example is the grouping of topics in a library.

Classification and cluster analysis (or clustering) are important techniques that partition objects that have many attributes (multidimensional data) into meaningful disjoint subgroups so that objects in each group are more similar to each other in the values of their attributes than they are to objects in other groups.

There is a major difference between cluster analysis and classification. In supervised classification, the classes are predefined, the user already knows what classes there are, and some training data that is already labelled by their class membership is available to train or build a model. The classification problem then is to build a model that would be able to label or classify newly encountered data. The example from the last chapter is given in Table 5.1.

Table 5.1 An example of classification training data

Owns home?	*Married*	*Gender*	*Employed*	*Credit rating*	*Risk class*
Yes	Yes	Male	Yes	*A*	*B*
No	No	Female	Yes	*A*	*A*
Yes	Yes	Female	Yes	*B*	*C*
Yes	No	Male	No	*B*	*B*
No	Yes	Female	Yes	*B*	*C*
No	No	Female	Yes	*B*	*A*
No	No	Male	No	*B*	*B*
Yes	No	Female	Yes	*A*	*A*
No	Yes	Female	Yes	*A*	*C*
Yes	Yes	Female	Yes	*A*	*C*

The financial risk classes for this training data have been specified and this data is used in building a model (e.g. a decision tree).

In cluster analysis, one does not know what classes or clusters exist and the problem to be solved is to group the given data into meaningful clusters. We illustrate a cluster analysis problem by using the same example without the last column which specified the class, as shown in Table 5.2.

Table 5.2 An example without training data

Owns home?	*Married*	*Gender*	*Employed*	*Credit rating*
Yes	Yes	Male	Yes	*A*
No	No	Female	Yes	*A*
Yes	Yes	Female	Yes	*B*
Yes	No	Male	No	*B*
No	Yes	Female	Yes	*B*
No	No	Female	Yes	*B*
No	No	Male	No	*B*
Yes	No	Female	Yes	*A*
No	Yes	Female	Yes	*A*
Yes	Yes	Female	Yes	*A*

We now have no prior information about the classes. We have the attribute values but we do not know if there are a (small) number of groups that might be interesting. Cluster analysis is useful for such analysis although we will see that normally the data in cluster analysis is not categorical. A more typical cluster analysis example may include numerical attributes like:

1. Age
2. Salary
3. Length of residence at current address
4. Length of employment with current employer
5. Loan amount sought

and so on. We first present a definition of cluster analysis.

> **Cluster Analysis**
> Cluster analysis is the task of grouping a set of objects in such a way that objects in the same group are more similar, based on some measure, to each other than to those in other groups. No preclassified training data is assumed to be available.

The aim of cluster analysis is often exploratory, to find if data naturally falls into meaningful groups with small within-group variations and large between-group variation. Often we may not have a hypothesis that we are trying to test. The aim is to find any interesting grouping of the data. It is possible to define cluster analysis as an optimisation problem in which a given function consisting of within cluster (intra-cluster) similarity and between clusters (inter-cluster) dissimilarity needs to be optimised. This function can be difficult to define and the optimisation of any such function is a challenging task. Clustering methods therefore only try to find an approximate or local optimum solution.

We assume that each object belongs to only one cluster and overlapping of clusters is not allowed. There are methods that consider overlapping clusters but we will not explore them in this book.

Just like applications of supervised classification, cluster analysis has applications in many different areas such as in marketing. In a university one may wish to find clusters of students. In medicine, one may be interested in finding clusters of patients or clusters of diseases. In business, for example in banking and finance, one may want to identify clusters of customers. In real estate, one may wish to find clusters of properties. Practical applications of cluster analysis have also been found in character recognition, Web analysis and classification of documents, classification of astronomical data and classification of objects found in an archaeological study.

Work on clustering has been carried out in statistics for many years. Most of the algorithms developed are based on some concept of similarity or distance so that groups of objects that are similar or near to each other and dissimilar or far away from other objects may be put together in a cluster. The technique may appear simple but it can be rather challenging because to find objects that are similar amongst a large collection of objects requires comparing each object with every other object which may be prohibitively expensive for large sets. Also, the cost of computing distances between a group of objects grows as the number of attributes grows. Finally, it is easier to compute distances between objects with numeric attributes but computing distances between categorical attributes is more difficult.

The classical clustering algorithms developed in statistics assumed small data sets but with the advent of computing, bar codes and the Web, users wish to apply cluster analysis to large datasets.

Old methods have therefore been modified to manage large datasets and new methods are being developed.

CHAPTER OVERVIEW

In this chapter the major issues in cluster analysis are discussed. In the next section, we look at the desired features of cluster analysis. The next section, Section 5.3, briefly describes a number of cluster analysis methods followed by a description of partitioned methods in Section 5.4. This includes a discussion of the widely used K-Means method. An example is included. The issue of scaling and weighting is explained in Section 5.4.2 and the problem of choosing starting values is discussed in Section 5.4.3. The Expectation Maximization Method is discussed in Section 5.4.4. Hierarchical Methods then discussed in Section 5.5. This section also includes a discussion of distance between clusters. Agglomerative Method is then presented in Section 5.5.7. An example is included followed by discussion of Divisive Hierarchical Method. Section 5.6 presents a brief discussion of the Density-based Methods. Section 5.7 considers how very large datasets may be clustered efficiently. Section 5.8 presents a discussion of quality and validity of cluster analysis methods. The chapter concludes with a summary of cluster analysis software.

5.2 DESIRED FEATURES OF CLUSTER ANALYSIS

Given that there are a large number of cluster analysis methods on offer, we make a list of desired features that an ideal cluster analysis method should have. The list is given below:

1. **(For large datasets) Scalability:** As noted earlier, data mining problems can be large and therefore it is desirable that a cluster analysis method be able to deal with small as well as large problems gracefully. Ideally, the performance should be linear with the size of the data. The method should also scale well to datasets in which the number of attributes is large.
2. **(For large datasets) Only one scan of the dataset:** For large problems, the data must be stored on the disk and the cost of I/O from the disk can then become significant in solving the problem. It is therefore desirable that a cluster analysis method not require more than one scan of disk-resident data.
3. **(For large datasets) Ability to stop and resume:** When the dataset is very large, cluster analysis may require considerable processor time to complete the task. In such cases, it is desirable that the task be able to be stopped and then resumed when convenient.
4. **Minimal input parameters:** The cluster analysis method should not expect too much guidance from the user. A data mining analyst may be working with a dataset about which his/her knowledge is limited. It is therefore desirable that the user not be expected to have domain knowledge of the data and not be expected to possess insight into clusters that might exist in the data.
5. **Robustness:** Most data obtained from a variety of sources has errors. It is therefore desirable that a cluster analysis method be able to deal with noise, outliers and missing values gracefully.

6. **Ability to discover different cluster shapes:** Clusters come in different shapes and not all clusters are spherical. It is therefore desirable that a cluster analysis method be able to discover cluster shapes other than spherical. Some applications require that various shapes be considered.
7. **Different data types:** Many problems have a mixture of data types, e.g. numerical, categorical and even textual. It is therefore desirable that a cluster analysis method be able to deal with not only numerical data but also boolean and categorical data.
8. **Result independent of data input order:** Although this is a simple requirement, not all methods satisfy it. It is therefore desirable that a cluster analysis method not be sensitive to data input order. Whatever the order, the result of cluster analysis of the same data should be the same.

Very few cluster analysis methods have all these features.

5.3 TYPES OF CLUSTER ANALYSIS METHODS

Cluster analysis methods may be divided into the following categories:

5.3.1 Partitional Methods

Partitional methods obtain a single level partition of objects. These methods usually are based on greedy heuristics that are used iteratively to obtain a local optimum solution. Given n objects, these methods make $k \leq n$ clusters of data and use an iterative relocation method. It is assumed that each cluster has at least one object and each object belongs to only one cluster. Objects may be relocated between clusters as the clusters are refined. Often these methods require that the number of clusters be specified apriori and this number usually does not change during the processing.

5.3.2 Hierarchical Methods

Hierarchical methods obtain a nested partition of the objects resulting in a tree of clusters. These methods either start with one cluster and then split into smaller and smaller clusters (called divisive or top down) or start with each object in an individual cluster and then try to merge similar clusters into larger and larger clusters (called agglomerative or bottom up). In this approach, in contrast to partitioning, tentative clusters may be merged or split based on some criteria.

5.3.3 Density-based Bethods

In this class of methods, typically for each data point in a cluster, at least a minimum number of points must exist within a given radius. Density-based methods can deal with arbitrary shape clusters since the major requirement of such methods is that each cluster be a dense region of points surrounded by regions of low density.

5.3.4 Grid-based Methods

In this class of methods, the object space rather than the data is divided into a grid. Grid partitioning is based on characteristics of the data and such methods can deal with non-numeric data more easily. Grid-based methods are not affected by data ordering.

5.3.5 Model-based methods

A model is assumed, perhaps based on a probability distribution. Essentially the algorithm tries to build clusters with a high level of similarity within them and a low level of similarity between them. Similarity measurement is based on the mean values and the algorithm tries to minimise the squared-error function.

A simple taxonomy of cluster analysis methods is presented in Figure 5.1.

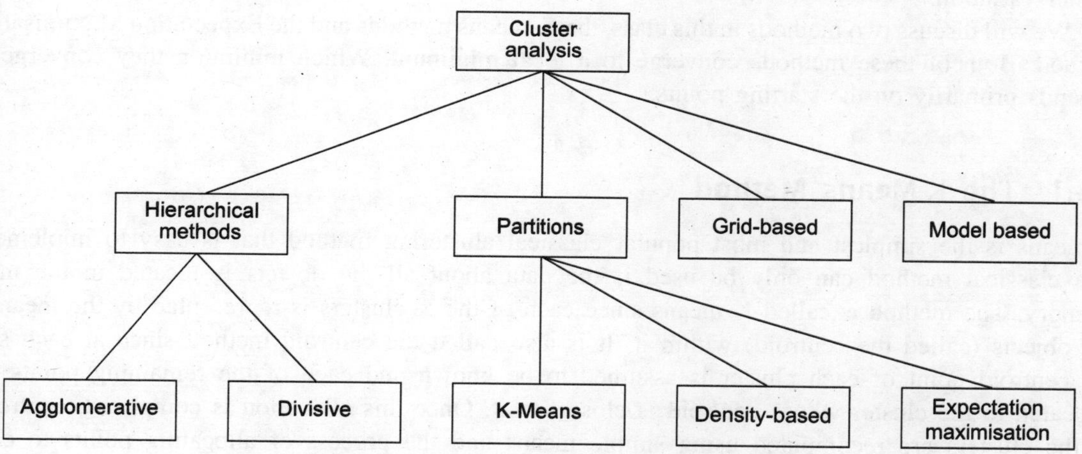

Figure 5.1 Taxonomy of cluster analysis method.

Cluster analysis has been an area of research for several decades and there are too many different methods for all to be covered even briefly in this chapter. Many new methods are still being developed. We discuss only the partitional and hierarchical methods in the sections that follow. First, in the next section, the partitional methods are discussed. In section 5.5, the hierarchical methods are discussed.

5.4 PARTITIONAL METHODS

Partitional methods are popular since they tend to be computationally efficient and are more easily adapted for very large datasets. The hierarchical methods tend to be computationally more expensive.

As noted earlier, the algorithms in this section are iterative refinement methods (sometimes called hill-climbing or greedy methods) and they converge to a local minimum rather than the global minimum. These methods not only require specifying the number of clusters a priori, they also require the user to normally specify the starting states (or seeds) of the clusters. This may be difficult for a user since the user may not have such knowledge and there is no simple reliable method for finding initial conditions for the clusters. We do however discuss some possible methods for obtaining initial conditions when the user is not able to provide them.

Often, as noted earlier, the user may have to resort to an iterative approach in which he/she has to run the method many times specifying different starting seeds and different numbers of clusters, then selecting the best solution.

The aim of partitional methods is to reduce the variance within each cluster as much as possible and have large variance between the clusters. Since the partitional methods do not normally explicitly control the inter-cluster variance, heuristics (e.g. choosing seeds as far apart as possible) may be used for ensuring large inter-cluster variance. One may therefore consider the aim to be minimising a ratio like a/b where a is some measure of within cluster variance and b is some measure of between cluster variation.

We will discuss two methods in this class, the K-means methods and the Expectation Maximisation method. Both of these methods converge to a local minimum. Which minimum they converge to depends primarily on the starting points.

5.4.1 The K-Means Method

K-means is the simplest and most popular classical clustering method that is easy to implement. The classical method can only be used if the data about all the objects is located in the main memory. The method is called K-means since each of the K clusters is represented by the mean of the objects (called the centroid) within it. It is also called the centroid method since at each step the centroid point of each cluster is assumed to be known and each of the remaining points are allocated to the cluster whose centroid is closest to it. Once this allocation is completed, centroids of the clusters are recomputed using simple means and the process of allocating points to each cluster is repeated until there is no change in the clusters (or some other stopping criterion, e.g. no significant reduction in the squared error, is met). The method may also be looked at as a search problem where the aim is essentially to find the optimum clusters given the number of clusters and seeds specified by the user. Obviously we cannot use a brute-force or exhaustive search method to find the optimum so we consider solutions that may not be optimal but may be computed efficiently.

The K-means method uses the Euclidean distance measure, which appears to work well with compact clusters. If instead of the Euclidean distance, the Manhattan distance is used the method is called the K-median method. The K-median method can be less sensitive to outliers.

The K-means method may be described as follows:

1. Select the number of clusters. Let this number be k.
2. Pick k seeds as centroids of the k clusters. The seeds may be picked randomly unless the user has some insight into the data.
3. Compute the Euclidean distance of each object in the dataset from each of the centroids.

4. Allocate each object to the cluster it is nearest to based on the distances computed in the previous step.
5. Compute the centroids of the clusters by computing the means of the attribute values of the objects in each cluster.
6. Check if the stopping criterion has been met (e.g. the cluster membership is unchanged). If yes, go to step 7. If not, go to step 3.
7. [Optional] One may decide to stop at this stage or to split a cluster or combine two clusters heuristically until a stopping criterion is met.

The method is scalable and efficient (the time complexity is of O(n)) and is guaranteed to find a local minimum. We first discuss an example and then discuss heuristics that can generally improve the chances of the method finding a global minimum.

Example 5.1

Consider the data about students given in Table 5.3. The only attributes are age and three marks.

Table 5.3 Data for Example 5.1

Student	*Age*	*Mark*1	*Mark*2	*Mark*3
S_1	18	73	75	57
S_2	18	79	85	75
S_3	23	70	70	52
S_4	20	55	55	55
S_5	22	85	86	87
S_6	19	91	90	89
S_7	20	70	65	60
S_8	21	53	56	59
S_9	19	82	82	60
S_{10}	47	75	76	77

Steps 1 and 2: Let the three seeds be the first three students as shown in Table 5.4.

Table 5.4 The three seeds for Example 5.1

Student	*Age*	*Mark*1	*Mark*2	*Mark*3
S_1	18	73	75	57
S_2	18	79	85	75
S_3	23	70	70	52

Steps 3 and 4: Now compute the distances using the four attributes and using the sum of absolute differences for simplicity (i.e. using the K-median method). The distance values for all the objects are given below. Columns 6, 7 and 8 give the three distances from the three seeds respectively. Based on these distances each student is allocated to the nearest cluster. The result is as shown in Table 5.5.

Table 5.5 First iteration—allocating each object to the nearest cluster

					Distances from clusters			
C_1	*18.0*	*73.0*	*75.0*	*57.0*	*From C_1*	*From C_2*	*From C_3*	*Allocation to the nearest cluster*
C_2	*18.0*	*79.0*	*85.0*	*75.0*				
C_3	*23.0*	*70.0*	*70.0*	*52.0*				
S_1	18.0	73.0	75.0	57.0	0.0	34.0	18.0	C_1
S_2	18.0	79.0	85.0	75.0	34.0	0.0	52.0	C_2
S_3	23.0	70.0	70.0	52.0	18.0	52.0	0.0	C_3
S_4	20.0	55.0	55.0	55.0	42.0	76.0	36.0	C_3
S_5	22.0	85.0	86.0	87.0	57.0	23.0	67.0	C_2
S_6	19.0	91.0	90.0	89.0	66.0	32.0	82.0	C_2
S_7	20.0	70.0	65.0	60.0	18.0	46.0	16.0	C_3
S_8	21.0	53.0	56.0	59.0	44.0	74.0	40.0	C_3
S_9	19.0	82.0	82.0	60.0	20.0	22.0	36.0	C_1
S_{10}	47.0	75.0	76.0	77.0	52.0	44.0	60.0	C_2

The first iteration leads to two students in the first cluster and four each in the second and third clusters.

Step 5: The new cluster means of clusters found in Table 5.6 are given below and are compared with the original seeds:

Table 5.6 Comparing new centroids and the seeds

	Age	*Mark* 1	*Mark* 2	*Mark* 3
C_1	18.5	77.5	78.5	58.5
C_2	26.5	82.5	84.3	82.0
C_3	21	61.5	61.5	56.5
Seed1	18	73	75	57
Seed2	18	79	85	75
Seed3	23	70	70	52

It is interesting to note that the mean marks for C_3 are significantly lower than for C_1 and C_2.

Steps 3 and 4: Use the new cluster means to recompute the distance of each object to each of the means, again allocating each object to the nearest cluster. Table 5.7 shows the second iteration result.

Table 5.7 Second iteration—allocating each object to the nearest cluster

					Distances from clusters			
C_1	*18.5*	*77.5*	*78.5*	*58.5*	*From C_1*	*From C_2*	*From C_3*	*Allocation to the nearest cluster*
C_2	*26.5*	*82.5*	*84.3*	*82.0*				
C_3	*21.0*	*62.0*	*61.5*	*56.5*				
S_1	18.0	73.0	75.0	57.0	10.0	52.3	28.0	C_1
S_2	18.0	79.0	85.0	75.0	25.0	19.8	62.0	C_2
S_3	23.0	70.0	70.0	52.0	27.0	60.3	23.0	C_3
S_4	20.0	55.0	55.0	55.0	51.0	90.3	16.0	C_3
S_5	22.0	85.0	86.0	87.0	47.0	13.8	79.0	C_2
S_6	19.0	91.0	90.0	89.0	56.0	28.8	92.0	C_2
S_7	20.0	70.0	65.0	60.0	24.0	60.3	16.0	C_3
S_8	21.0	53.0	56.0	59.0	50.0	86.3	17.0	C_3
S_9	19.0	82.0	82.0	60.0	10.0	32.3	46.0	C_1
S_{10}	47.0	75.0	76.0	77.0	52.0	41.3	74.0	C_2

The number of students in cluster 1 is again 2 and the other two clusters still have four students each. A more careful look shows that the clusters have not changed at all. Therefore the method has converged rather quickly for this very simple dataset.

The cluster membership is as follows:

Cluster 1: S_1, S_9

Cluster 2: S_2, S_5, S_6, S_{10}

Cluster 3: S_3, S_4, S_7, S_8

It should be noted that the above method was K-median rather than K-means because we wanted to use a simple distance measure that a reader could check without using a computer or a calculator. Interestingly, when K-means is used the result is exactly the same and the method again converges quickly.

Another point worth noting is about the within cluster variance and the between cluster variance. In Table 5.8 we present the average Euclidean distance of objects in each cluster to the cluster centroids. Therefore average distance within C_1 of objects within it from its centroid is 5.9 while average distance between objects in C_2 and the centroid of C_1 is 26.5 and between objects in C_3 and the centroid of C_1 is 23.3. These numbers do show that the clustering method has done well in minimising within cluster variance and maximising between cluster variance although these numbers do not show if there is another result that is better. We do get different results if we start with different seeds. For example, when we started with the last three objects as the seeds we obtained C_1 with 4 students, C_2 with 5 students and C_3 with only one student. The one object in C_3 was the starting seed for C_3. Therefore we chose as one of the seeds an object that was an outlier and it therefore appeared as a cluster of one object in the final result.

Table 5.8 Within cluster and between clusters distances

Cluster	C_1	C_2	C_3
C_1	5.9	26.5	23.3
C_2	29.5	14.3	42.6
C_3	23.9	41.0	10.7

5.4.2 Scaling and Weighting

In Example 5.1 using K-means, the clusters were determined primarily based on the three attributes Mark 1, Mark 2 and Mark 3. The attribute Age did not have much influence on determining which cluster an object belonged to since the values of this attribute were smaller than other attributes and the variation within the attribute was small except for the object S_{10} which was an outlier.

For clustering to be effective all attributes should be converted to a similar scale unless we want to give more weight to some attributes that are relatively large in scale. There are a number of ways to transform the attributes. As noted earlier, one possibility is to transform them all to a normalised score or to a range (0, 1). Such transformations are called scaling. Some other approaches to scaling are:

1. Divide each attribute by the mean value of that attribute. This reduces mean of each attribute to 1. It does not control the variation, some values may still be large, others small.
2. Divide each attribute by the difference between the largest value and the smallest value. This reduces the mean of attributes that have large range of values and increases mean of attributes that have small range of values but does not reduce each attribute's mean to the same value. The scaling reduces the difference between the largest value and the smallest value to 1 and therefore does control the variation.
3. Covert the attribute values to "standardised scores" by subtracting the mean of the attribute from each attribute value and dividing it by the standard deviation. Now the mean of the each attribute will be zero and standard deviation one. This not only scales the magnitude of each attribute to a similar range but also scales the standard deviation.

Scaling removes the bias due to different scales of the attributes and then gives equal importance to all attributes. In some cases, one or two attributes may be much more important than the rest and then it may be desirable to give more weight to these attributes. The purpose of giving weights to some attributes essentially is to introduce bias in the clustering process by purposely giving higher weights to some important attributes.

5.4.3 Starting Values for the K-Means Method

Often the user has little basis for specifying the number of clusters and starting seeds. This problem may be overcome by using an iterative approach. For example, one may first select three clusters and choose three starting seeds randomly. Once the final clusters have been obtained, the process may be repeated with a different set of seeds. Attempts should be made to select seeds that are as far away from each other as possible. Also, during the iterative process if two clusters are found to be close together, it may be desirable to merge them. Also, a large cluster may be split in two if the variance within the cluster is above some threshold value.

Another approach involves finding the centroid of the whole dataset and then perturbing this centroid value to find seeds. Yet another approach recommends using a hierarchical method like the agglomerative method on the data first since that method does not require starting values and then using the results of that method as the basis for specifying the number of clusters and starting seeds.

Yet another approach is based on using a number of small samples of the given data and using random seeds for each sample. The result of cluster analysis of these samples can then help in finding seeds for the whole data.

Summary of the K-means method

K-means is an iterative-improvement greedy method. A number of iterations are normally needed for convergence and therefore the dataset is processed a number of times. If the data is very large and cannot be accommodated in the main memory the process may become inefficient.

Although the K-means method is most widely known and used, there are a number of issues related to the method that should be understood:

1. The K-means method needs to compute Euclidean distances and means of the attribute values of objects within a cluster. The classical algorithm therefore is only suitable for continuous data. K-means variations that deal with categorical data are available but not widely used.
2. The K-means method implicitly assumes spherical probability distributions.
3. The results of the K-means method depend strongly on the initial guesses of the seeds.
4. The K-means method can be sensitive to outliers. If an outlier is picked as a starting seed, it may end up in a cluster of its own. Also, if an outlier moves from one cluster to another during iterations, it can have a major impact on the clusters because the means of the two clusters are likely to change significantly.
5. Although some local optimum solutions discovered by the K-means method are satisfactory, often the local optimum is not as good as the global optimum.
6. The K-means method does not consider the size of the clusters. Some clusters may be large and some very small.
7. The K-means method does not deal with overlapping clusters.

Versions of the K-means method have been suggested. A simple version involves recomputing the cluster mean after each object reallocation. This appears to work somewhat better.

5.4.4 Expectation Maximisation Method

The K-means method does not explicitly assume any probability distribution for the attribute values. It only assumes that the dataset consists of groups of objects that are similar and the groups can be discovered because the user has provided cluster seeds.

In contrast to the K-means method, the Expectation Maximisation (EM) method is based on the assumption that the objects in the dataset have attributes whose values are distributed according to some (unknown) linear combination (or mixture) of simple probability distributions. While the K-means method involves assigning objects to clusters to minimise within-group variation, the EM method assigns objects to different clusters with certain probabilities in an attempt to maximise expectation (or likelihood) of assignment.

The simplest situation is when there are only two distributions. For every individual we may assume that it comes from distribution 1 with probability p and therefore from distribution 2 with probability $1-p$. Such mixture models appear to be widely used because they provide more parameters and therefore more flexibility in modelling.

The EM method consists of a two-step iterative algorithm. The first step, called the estimation step or the E-step, involves estimating the probability distributions of the clusters given the data. The second step, called the maximisation step or the M-step, involves finding the model parameters that maximise the likelihood of the solution.

The EM method assumes that all attributes are independent random variables. In a simple case of just two clusters with objects having only a single attribute, we may assume that the attribute values vary according to a normal distribution. The EM method requires that we now estimate the following:

1. The mean and standard deviation of the normal distribution for cluster 1
2. The mean and standard deviation of the normal distribution for cluster 2
3. The probability p of a sample belonging to cluster 1 and therefore probability $1-p$ of belonging to cluster 2

The EM method then works as follows:

1. Guess the initial values of the five parameters given above.
2. Use the two normal distributions (given the two guesses of means and two guesses of standard deviations) and compute the probability of each object belonging to each of the two clusters.
3. Compute the likelihood of data coming from these two clusters by multiplying the sum of probabilities of each object.
4. Re-estimate the five parameters and go to step 2 until a stopping criterion has been met.

The EM method is based on a statistical model that, when appropriate, shows optimal results. The method assumes that all attributes are independent and normally distributed. Further details of the EM method are beyond the scope of this book.

5.5 HIERARCHICAL METHODS

Hierarchical methods produce a nested series of clusters as opposed to the partitional methods which produce only a flat set of clusters. Essentially the hierarchical methods attempt to capture the structure of the data by constructing a tree of clusters. This approach allows clusters to be found at different levels of granularity.

As noted earlier, two types of hierarchical approaches are possible. In one approach, called the Agglomerative approach for merging groups (or bottom up approach), each object at the start is a cluster by itself and nearby clusters are repeatedly merged resulting in larger and larger clusters until some stopping criterion (often a given number of clusters) is met or all the objects are merged into a single large cluster which is the highest level of the hierarchy. In the second approach, called the Divisive approach (or the top down approach), all the objects are put in a single cluster to start. The method then repeatedly performs splitting of clusters resulting in smaller and smaller clusters until a stopping criterion is reached or each cluster has only one object in it.

5.5.1 Distance between Clusters

The hierarchical clustering methods require distances between clusters to be computed. These distance metrics are often called linkage metrics. There are a number of them proposed in the literature. We discuss some of the most widely used distance metrics below.

Computing distances between large clusters can be expensive. Suppose one cluster has 50 objects and another has 100, then computing most of the distance metrics listed below would require computing distances between each object in the first cluster with every object in the second. Therefore 5,000 distances would need to be computed just to compute a distance between two clusters. This can be expensive if each object has many attributes.

We discuss the following methods for computing distances between clusters:

1. Single-link algorithm
2. Complete-link algorithm
3. Centroid algorithm
4. Average-link algorithm
5. Ward's minimum-variance algorithm

5.5.2 Single-link

The single-link (or nearest neighbour) algorithm is perhaps the simplest algorithm for computing distance between two clusters. The algorithm determines the distance between two clusters as the minimum of the distances between all pairs of points (a, x) where a is from the first cluster and x is from the second. The algorithm therefore requires that all pair-wise distances be computed and the smallest distance (or shortest link) found. The algorithm can form chains and can form elongated clusters.

Figure 5.2 shows two clusters *A* and *B* and the single-link distance between them.

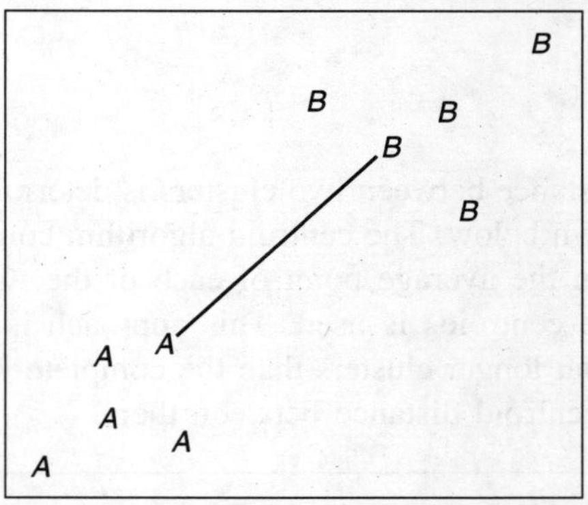

Figure 5.2 Single-link distance between two clusters.

5.5.3 Complete-link

The complete-link algorithm is also called the farthest neighbour algorithm. In this algorithm, the distance between two clusters is defined as the maximum of the pair-wise distances (a, x). Therefore if there are m elements in one cluster and n in the other, all mn pair-wise distances therefore must be computed and the largest chosen. Complete link is strongly biased towards compact clusters. Figure 5.3 shows two clusters *A* and *B* and the complete-link distance between them. Complete-link can be distorted by moderate outliers in one or both of the clusters.

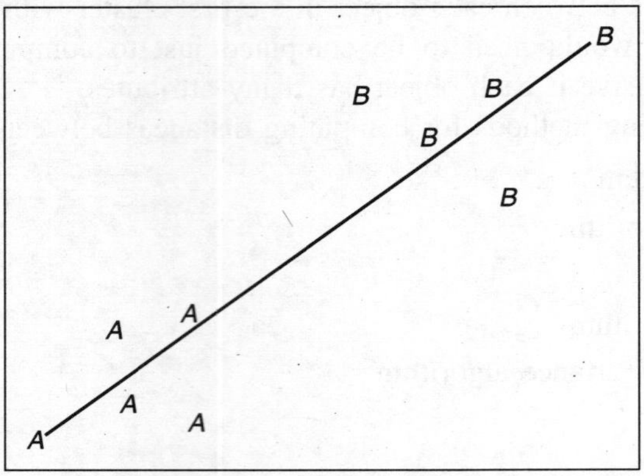

Figure 5.3 Complete-link distance between two clusters.

Both single-link and complete-link measures have their difficulties. In the single-link algorithm, each cluster may have an outlier and the two outliers may be nearby and so the distance between the two clusters would be computed to be small. Single-link can form a chain of objects as clusters are combined since there is no constraint on the distance between objects that are far away from each other. On the other hand, the two outliers may be very far away although the clusters are nearby and the complete-link algorithm will compute the distance as large. The complete-link algorithm generally works well but if a cluster is naturally of a shape say like a banana then perhaps complete-link is not appropriate.

5.5.4 Centroid

In the centroid algorithm the distance between two clusters is determined as the distance between the centroids of the clusters as shown below. The centroid algorithm computes the distance between two clusters as the distance between the average point of each of the two clusters. Usually the squared Euclidean distance between the centroids is used. This approach is easy and generally works well and is more tolerant of somewhat longer clusters than the complete-link algorithm. Figure 5.4 shows two clusters *A* and *B* and the centroid distance between them.

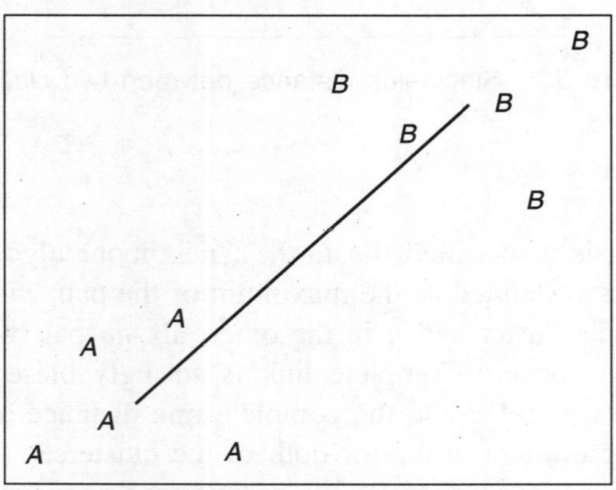

Figure 5.4 The centroid distance between two clusters.

5.5.5 Average-link

The average-link algorithm on the other hand computes the distance between two clusters as the average of all pair-wise distances between an object from one cluster and another from the other cluster. Therefore if there are *m* elements in one cluster and *n* in the other, there are *mn* distances to be computed, added and divided by *mn*. This approach also generally works well. It tends to join clusters with small variances although it is more tolerant of somewhat longer clusters than the complete-link algorithm. Figure 5.5 shows two clusters *A* and *B* and the average-link distance between them.

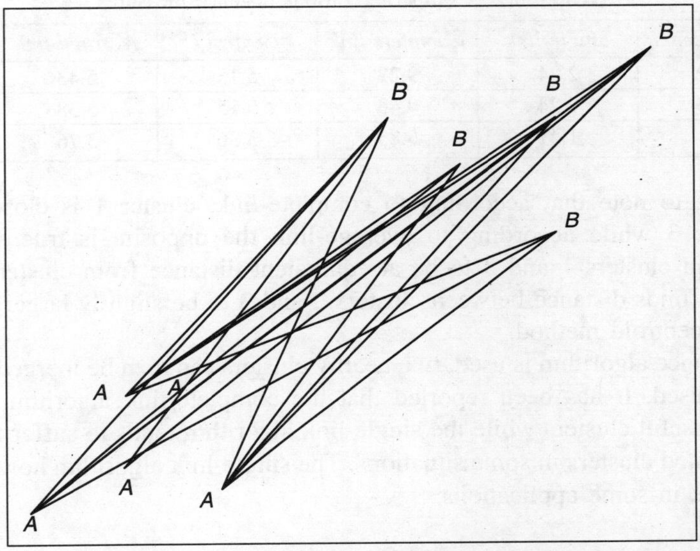

Figure 5.5 The average-link distance between two clusters.

5.5.6 Ward's Minimum-variance Method

Ward's minimum-variance distance measure on the other hand is different. The method generally works well and results in creating small tight clusters. Ward's distance is the difference between the total within the cluster sum of squares for the two clusters separately and within the cluster sum of squares resulting from merging the two clusters.

An expression for Ward's distance may be derived. It may be expressed as follows:

$$D_W(A, B) = \frac{N_A N_B D_C(A, B)}{(N_A + N_B)}$$

where $D_W(A, B)$ is the Ward's minimum-variance distance between clusters *A* and *B* with N_A and N_B objects in them respectively. $D_C(A, B)$ is the centroid distance between the two clusters computed as squared Euclidean distance between the centroids. It has been observed that Ward's method tends to join clusters with a small number of objects and is biased towards producing clusters with roughly the same number of objects. The distance measure can be sensitive to outliers.

Example 5.2

Consider the following three clusters, each with four members:

Cluster 1: {(1,5) (2,4) (3,3) (2,1)}
Cluster 2: {(5,4) (6,6) (7,5) (8,8)}
Cluster 3: {(4,1) (3,0) (5,1) (6,2)}

The distances between these clusters using different distance metrics are given in Table 5.9.

Table 5.9 Comparing various distance measures

Distance between	*Single-link*	*Complete-link*	*Centroid*	*Average-link*	*Ward's*
Clusters 1 & 2	2.24	9.22	5.15	5.43	53.0
Clusters 2 & 3	2.24	9.43	5.15	5.38	53.1
Clusters 3 & 1	1.41	5.83	3.36	3.76	22.6

It is interesting to note that according to complete-link, cluster 1 is closer to cluster 2 than cluster 2 to cluster 3 while according to average-link the opposite is true. Single-link and the centroid method find clusters 1 and 3 to be at equivalent distance from cluster 2 although a more accurate calculation finds distance between clusters 2 and 3 to be slightly larger than between 1 and 2 according to the centroid method.

Whichever distance algorithm is used, two nearby clusters can then be merged if an agglomerative approach is being used. It has been reported that the complete-link algorithm generally produces compact and more useful clusters while the single-link algorithm tends to suffer from chaining effect and produces elongated clusters in some situations. The single-link algorithm however has been found to be more effective in some applications.

5.5.7 Agglomerative Method

Some applications naturally have a hierarchical structure. For example, the world's fauna and flora have a hierarchical structure. The agglomerative clustering method tries to discover such structure given a dataset.

The basic idea of the agglomerative method is to start out with n clusters for n data points, that is, each cluster consisting of a single data point. Using a measure of distance, at each step of the method, the method merges two nearest clusters, thus reducing the number of clusters and building successively larger clusters. The process continues until the required number of clusters has been obtained or all the data points are in one cluster. The agglomerative method leads to hierarchical clusters in which at each step we build larger and larger clusters that include increasingly dissimilar objects.

The agglomerative method is basically a bottom-up approach which involves the following steps. An implementation however may include some variation of these steps.

1. Allocate each point to a cluster of its own. Thus we start with n clusters for n objects.
2. Create a distance matrix by computing distances between all pairs of clusters either using, for example, the single-link metric or the complete-link metric. Some other metric may also be used. Sort these distances in ascending order.

3. Find the two clusters that have the smallest distance between them.
4. Remove the pair of objects and merge them.
5. If there is only one cluster left then stop.
6. Compute all distances from the new cluster and update the distance matrix after the merger and go to step 3.

Example 5.3

We now use agglomerative clustering for clustering the data in Example 5.1. This data is reproduced in Table 5.10. We will use the centroid method for computing the distances between clusters.

Table 5.10 Data for Example 5.3

Student	*Age*	*Mark*1	*Mark*2	*Mark*3
S_1	18	73	75	57
S_2	18	79	85	75
S_3	23	70	70	52
S_4	20	55	55	55
S_5	22	85	86	87
S_6	19	91	90	89
S_7	20	70	65	60
S_8	21	53	56	59
S_9	19	82	82	60
S_{10}	47	75	76	77

Steps 1 and 2: Allocate each point to a cluster and compute the distance matrix using the centroid method. The distance matrix is symmetric, so we only show half of it in Table 5.11. The last column would be for S_{10} but the diagonal element is zero.

Table 5.11 Distance matrix for data in Example 5.3

	S_1	S_2	S_3	S_4	S_5	S_6	S_7	S_8	S_9
S_1	0								
S_2	34	0							
S_3	18	52	0						
S_4	42	76	36	0					
S_5	57	23	67	95	0				
S_6	66	32	82	106	15	0			
S_7	18	46	16	30	65	76	0		
S_8	44	74	40	8	91	104	28	0	
S_9	20	22	36	60	37	46	30	115	0
S_{10}	52	44	60	90	55	70	60	98	99

The above matrix gives distance of each object with every other object.

Steps 3 and 4: The smallest distance is 8 between object S_4 and object S_8. They are combined and removed and we put the combined cluster (C_1) where object S_4 was.

Table 5.12 shows is the new distance matrix. All distances except those with cluster C_1 remain unchanged.

Table 5.12 Distance matrix after merging S_4 and S_8 into cluster C_1

	S_1	S_2	S_3	C_1	S_5	S_6	S_7	S_9
S_1	0							
S_2	34	0						
S_3	18	52	0					
C_1	41	75	38	0				
S_5	57	23	67	93	0			
S_6	66	32	82	105	15	0		
S_7	18	46	16	29	65	76	0	
S_9	20	22	36	59	37	46	30	0
S_{10}	52	44	60	88	55	70	60	58

Steps 5 and 6: The smallest distance now is 15 between objects S_5 and S_6. They are combined in a cluster and S_5 and S_6 are removed.

Steps 3, 4, 5 and 6: Table 5.13 is the updated distance matrix.

Table 5.13 Distance matrix after merging S_5 and S_6 into cluster C_2

	S_1	S_2	S_3	C_1	C_2	S_7	S_9
S_1	0						
S_2	34	0					
S_3	18	52	0				
C_1	41	75	38	0			
C_2	61.5	27.5	74.5	97.5	0		
S_7	18	46	16	29	69.5	0	
S_9	20	22	36	59	41.5	30	0
S_{10}	52	44	60	88	62.5	60	58

We find the shortest distance again.

S_3 and S_7 are at a distance 16 apart. We merge them and put C_3 where S_3 was. Although we do not show any further distance matrices, the next step would show that C_3 and S_1 have the smallest distance. They are then merged and the process continues.

The result of using the agglomerative method could be something like that shown in Figure 5.6. The cluster numbers show an example sequence of cluster mergings. The first one being merging of objects S_4 and S_8 followed by merging of S_5 and S_6 and so on.

As noted earlier, it is possible to use any measure of distance between cluster centroids.

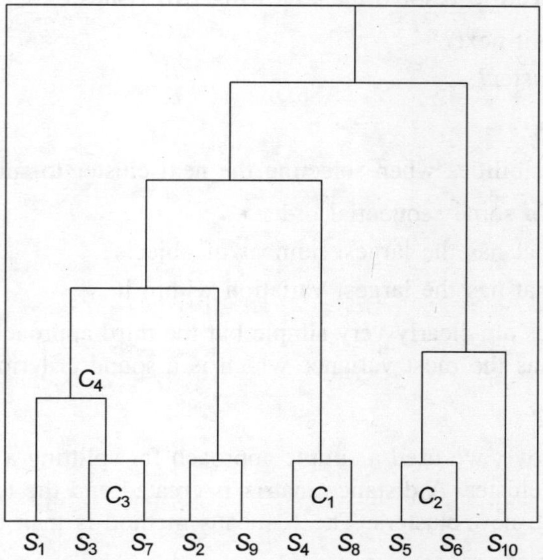

Figure 5.6 A possible result of using the agglomerative method.

5.5.8 Divisive Hierarchical Method

The divisive method is the opposite of the agglomerative method in that the method starts with the whole dataset as one cluster and then proceeds to recursively divide the cluster into two sub-clusters and continues until each cluster has only one object or some other stopping criterion has been reached. There are two types of divisive methods:

Monothetic: It splits a cluster using only one attribute at a time. An attribute that has the most variation could be selected.

Polythetic: It splits a cluster using all of the attributes together. Two clusters far apart could be built based on distance between objects.

A typical polythetic divisive method works like the following:

1. Decide on a method of measuring the distance between two objects. Also decide a threshold distance.
2. Create a distance matrix by computing distances between all pairs of objects within the cluster. Sort these distances in ascending order.
3. Find the two objects that have the largest distance between them. They are the most dissimilar.
4. If the distance between the two objects is smaller than the pre-specified threshold and there is no other cluster that needs to be divided then stop, otherwise continue.
5. Use the pair of objects as seeds of a K-means method to create two new clusters.
6. If there is only one object in each cluster then stop otherwise continue with step 2.

In the above method, we need to resolve the following two issues:

- Which cluster to split next?
- How to split the cluster?

Which cluster to split?

There are a number of possibilities when selecting the next cluster to split:

1. Split the clusters in some sequential order
2. Split the cluster that has the largest number of objects
3. Split the cluster that has the largest variation within it

The first two approaches are clearly very simple but the third approach is better since it is based on splitting a cluster that has the most variance which is a sound criterion.

How to split a cluster?

In the method presented above, we used a simple approach for splitting a cluster based on distances between the objects in the cluster. A distance matrix is created and the two most dissimilar objects are selected as seeds of two new clusters. The K-means method is then used to split the cluster.

Example 5.4

Consider once again the distance matrix in Table 5.14 that gives distances between each pair of objects in the single starting cluster.

Table 5.14 Distance matrix for objects in Example 5.4

	S_1	S_2	S_3	S_4	S_5	S_6	S_7	S_8	S_9
S_1	0								
S_2	34	0							
S_3	18	52	0						
S_4	42	76	36	0					
S_5	57	23	67	95	0				
S_6	66	32	82	106	15	0			
S_7	18	46	16	30	65	76	0		
S_8	44	74	40	8	91	104	28	0	
S_9	20	22	36	60	37	46	30	115	0
S_{10}	52	44	60	90	55	70	60	98	99

The largest distance is 115 between the objects is between S_8 and S_9 (Table 4.15). They become the seeds of two new clusters. K-means is used to split the group in two clusters.

The two clusters may be derived based on distances in the distance matrix in Table 5.14.

Table 5.15 Distances from the seeds of the two clusters

	S_1	S_2	S_3	S_4	S_5	S_6	S_7	S_8	S_9	S_{10}
S_8	44	74	40	8	91	104	28	0	115	98
S_9	20	22	36	60	37	46	30	115	0	99

Cluster C_1 includes S_4, S_7, S_8, S_{10}

Cluster C_2 includes S_1, S_2, S_3, S_5, S_6, S_9

Since none of the stopping criteria has been met, we decide to split the larger cluster next and then repeat the process.

We find the largest distance in C_2 first. The distance matrix given in Table 5.16 may be built using distances given in the distance matrix in Table 5.14.

Table 5.16 Distance matrix for objects in cluster C_2

	S_1	S_2	S_3	S_5	S_6
S_1	0				
S_2	34	0			
S_3	18	52	0		
S_5	57	23	67	0	
S_6	66	32	82	15	0
S_9	20	22	36	37	46

The largest distance in C_2 is 82 between S_3 and S_6. C_2 can therefore be split with S_3 and S_6 as seeds.

The distance matrix of cluster 1 is given in Table 5.17. The largest distance is 98 between S_8 and S_{10}. C_1 can be split with S_8 and S_{10} as seeds.

The method continues like this until one of the stopping criteria is met.

Table 5.17 Distance matrix for objects in cluster C_1

	S_4	S_7	S_8
S_4	0		
S_7	30	0	
S_8	8	28	0
S_{10}	90	60	98

It should be noted that the splitting criterion does not take into account the shape of the cluster and essentially assumes that each cluster is spherical. It has been suggested that the next cluster to be split should be selected based on scatter and centroid distance.

5.5.9 Summary of Hierarchical Methods

Agglomerative clustering finds distance between all clusters (starting from each object being in a cluster of its own) and merges the closest clusters until there is just one cluster or some other stopping criterion is met. Since the method requires distances between each object, a distance matrix $n \times n$ must be stored making it difficult for very large datasets. The size of the matrix can be reduced by omitting some entries. For example, large distances are of little interest in the agglomerative method while the opposite is true for the divisive method. It should be noted that in the agglomerative method, any distance metric may be used. It need not be based on Euclidean distance.

Advantages of the hierarchical approach

1. The hierarchical approach can provide more insight into the data by showing a hierarchy of clusters than a flat cluster structure created by a partitioning method like the K-means method.
2. Hierarchical methods are conceptually simpler and can be implemented easily.
3. In some applications only proximity data is available and then the hierarchical approach may be better.
4. Hierarchical methods can provide clusters at different levels of granularity.

Disadvantages of the hierarchical approach

1. The hierarchical methods do not include a mechanism by which objects that have been incorrectly put in a cluster may be reassigned to another cluster.
2. The time complexity of hierarchical methods can be shown to be $O(n^3)$.
3. The distance matrix requires $O(n^2)$ space and becomes very large for a large number of objects.
4. Different distance metrics and scaling of data can significantly change the results.

Hierarchical methods are quite different from partition-based clustering. In hierarchical methods there is no need to specify the number of clusters and the cluster seeds. The agglomerative approach essentially starts with each object in an individual cluster and then merges clusters to build larger and larger clusters. The divisive approach is the opposite of that. There is no metric to judge the quality of the results.

Different distance functions can lead to different shapes of hierarchical clusters, but hierarchical clusters provide a useful display of cluster relationships.

5.6 DENSITY-BASED METHODS

The density-based methods are based on the assumption that clusters are high density collections of data of arbitrary shape that are separated by a large space of low density data (which is assumed to be noise). Therefore the basis for density-based methods is that for each data point in a cluster, at least a minimum number of points must exist within a given distance. Data that is not within such high-density clusters is regarded as outliers or noise.

Another way of looking at density-based clustering is that the clusters are dense regions of probability density in the datasets. We assume that generally the data is very sparsely distributed in the n-dimensional space but there are regions where the density is much higher and we wish to find these regions.

DBSCAN (density based spatial clustering of applications with noise) is one example of a density-based method for clustering. The method was designed for spatial databases but can be used in other applications. It requires two input parameters: the size of the neighbourhood (R) and the minimum points in the neighbourhood (N). Essentially these two parameters determine the density within the clusters the user is willing to accept since it specifies how many points must be in a region. The number of points determines not only the density of acceptable clusters, it also determines which objects will be labelled outliers or noise. Objects are declared to be outliers if there are few other objects in their neighbourhood. The size parameter R determines the size of the clusters found. If R is big enough, there would be one big cluster and no outliers. If R is small, there will be small dense clusters and there might be many outliers.

We now define a number of concepts that are required in the DBSCAN method:

1. ***Neighbourhood:*** The neighbourhood of an object y is defined as all the objects that are within the radius R from y.
2. ***Core object:*** An object y is called a core object if there are N objects within its neighbourhood.
3. ***Proximity:*** Two objects are defined to be in proximity to each other if they belong to the same cluster. Object x_1 is in proximity to object x_2 if two conditions are satisfied:
   (a) the objects are close enough to each other, i.e. within a distance of R, and
   (b) x_2 is a core object as defined above.
4. ***Connectivity:*** Objects x_1 and x_n are connected if there is a path or chain of objects $x_1, x_2, \ldots, x_n$ from x_1 to x_n such that each x_{i+1} is in proximity to object x_i.

We now outline the basic algorithm for density-based clustering:

1. Select values of R and N.
2. Arbitrarily select an object p.
3. Retrieve all objects that are connected to p given R and N.
4. If p is a core object, a cluster is formed.
5. If p is a border object, no objects are in its proximity. Choose another object. Go to step 3.
6. Continue the process until all of the objects have been processed.

Essentially the above algorithm forms clusters by connecting neighbouring core objects and those non-core objects that are boundaries of clustering. The remaining non-core objects are labelled outliers. If one is trying to cluster data with significant level of noise, the density specified must be significantly higher than the expected density of the noise. By doing so, density-based methods can extract clusters in spite of high level of noise.

The performance of DBSCAN has been found to be sensitive to the parameters R and N and some time the user has no sound basis to chose good values of these parameters. If R and N are not chosen carefully, an algorithm like DBSCAN may result in either a large number of very small clusters or a few very large clusters.

5.7 DEALING WITH LARGE DATABASES

As noted earlier, most clustering methods implicitly assume that all data is accessible in the main memory. Often the size of the database is not considered but an method requiring multiple scans of data that is disk-resident could be quite inefficient for large problems.

As noted earlier, old methods have been modified to deal with large datasets and some new methods have been devised for cluster analysis of large datasets. We briefly introduce some such methods although full details of the methods are beyond the scope of the book.

One possible approach to deal with large datasets that could be used with any type of clustering method is to draw as large a sample from the large dataset as could be accommodated in the main memory. The sample is then clustered. Each remaining object is then assigned to the nearest cluster obtained from the sample. This process could be repeated several times and the clusters that lead to the smallest within clusters variance could be chosen.

5.7.1 K-means Method for Large Databases

We discuss one modification of the K-means methods for data that is too large to fit in the main memory. The modified method is based on the assumption that centroids or starting seeds have been specified and these seeds are reasonable in that the actual cluster is likely to have attribute values normally distributed around the seeds. The method first picks the number of clusters and their seed centroids and then attempts to classify each object to belong to one of the following three groups:

(a) Those that are certain to belong to a cluster. These objects together are called the *discard* set. Some information about these objects is computed and saved. This includes the number of objects n, a vector sum of all attribute values of the n objects (a vector S) and a vector sum of squares of all attribute values of the n objects (a vector Q). These values are sufficient to recompute the centroid of the new cluster and its variance.

(b) Those that are sufficiently close to each other to be replaced by their summary. The objects are however sufficiently far away from each cluster's centroid that they cannot yet be put in the discard set of objects. These objects together are called the *compression* set.

(c) The remaining objects that are too difficult to assign to either of the two groups above. These objects are called the *retained* set and are stored as individual objects. They cannot be replaced by a summary.

An iterative procedure is used based on the statistics computed for the discard set to allocate some of the objects in the compression set and the retained set to the discard set. The statistics of the discard set are recomputed and the remaining members of the compression set and retained set are then looked at again until there are no more members in the two sets.

5.7.2 Hierarchical Method for Large Databases—Concept of Fractionation

Dealing with large datasets is difficult using hierarchical methods since the methods require a $N \times N$ distance matrix to be computed for N objects. If N is large, say 100,000, the matrix has 10^{10} elements making it impractical to use a classical hierarchical method.

A modification of classical hierarchical methods that deals with large datasets was proposed in 1992. It is based on the idea of splitting the data into manageable subsets called "fractions" and then applying a hierarchical method to each fraction. The concept is called fractionation. The basic algorithm used in the method is as follows, assuming that M is the largest number of objects that the hierarchical method may be applied to. The size M may be determined perhaps based on the size of the main memory. Now the algorithm:

1. Split the large dataset into fractions of size M.
2. The hierarchical clustering technique being used is applied to each fraction. Let the number of clusters so obtained from all the fractions be C.

3. For each of the C clusters, compute the mean of the attribute values of the objects in it. Let this mean vector be m_i, $i = 1, \ldots, C$. These cluster means are called meta-observations. The meta-observations now become the data values that represent the fractions.
4. If the C meta-observations are too large (greater than M), go to step 1 otherwise apply the same hierarchical clustering technique to the meta-observations obtained in step 3.
5. Allocate each object of the original dataset to the cluster with the nearest mean obtained in step 4.

The cost of this algorithm is linear in terms of the size of the dataset. The accuracy of the results is related to the accuracy of the clustering algorithm used. The effectiveness of this approach has not yet been fully investigated.

5.8 QUALITY AND VALIDITY OF CLUSTER ANALYSIS METHODS

An interesting issue in cluster analysis is how to evaluate the results. Evaluation is particularly difficult since all clustering methods will produce clusters even if there are no meaningful clusters in the data. In cluster analysis there is no test data available as there often is in classification. Also, even if the process has been successful and clusters have been found, two different methods may produce different clusters. How to judge which clusters are better? Often it is left to the user to judge which of the two results are better by judging which results make more sense in terms of similar objects being together and dissimilar objects being in different clusters.

Different methods are biased towards different types of clusters. For example, minimising the maximum distance between the points in a cluster is trying to favour a spherical shape.

The results of K-means may in the first instance be evaluated by examining each attribute's mean for each cluster in an attempt to assess how far each cluster is from the other. Another approach is based on computing within cluster variation (I) and between clusters variation (E). These variations may be computed as follows:

Let the number of clusters be k and let the clusters be C_i, $i = 1, \ldots, k$. Let the total number of objects be N and let the number of objects in cluster C_i be M_i so that

$$M_1 + M_2 + \cdots + M_k = N$$

The within-cluster variation between the objects in a cluster C_i is defined as the average squared distance of each object from the centroid of the cluster. That is, if μ_i is the centroid of the cluster C_i then the mean of the cluster is given by

$$\mu_i = \frac{\sum_j x_j}{M_i}$$

and the internal cluster variation is given by:

$$I_i = \frac{\sum_j (x_j - \mu_i)^2}{M_i}$$

We may then write an expression for I, the average within-cluster variation as follows:

$$I = \left(\frac{1}{k}\right)(I_1 + I_2 + \cdots + I_k) = \frac{\sum I_i}{k}$$

The between cluster distances E may now be computed given the centroids of the clusters. It is the average sum of squares of pairwise distances between the centroids of the k clusters. We may write E as:

$$E = \left(\frac{1}{k^2}\sum_i \sum_j (\mu_i - \mu_j)^2\right)$$

Note that there are k^2 distances between k clusters because we include the distance of every cluster from each of the k clusters including distance from itself (which obviously is zero).

To choose the best result of cluster analysis, one possible approach might be choosing the result that has the largest E/I from the results available.

If I is small, it means that we have tight clusters. Similarly if E is small (relative to say I) it means that the clusters are not well separated and thus the result of clustering may not be so good. A large E is desirable since it shows good separation between the clusters.

There are no satisfactory methods for determining the number of clusters in a given set of data. A visualisation tool may assist the user in estimating how many clusters are likely. Another approach may be to use a method like K-means and use the method with several different numbers of clusters and different seeds and then compare the results.

As noted earlier, evaluating the quality of clustering methods or results of a cluster analysis is a challenging task. Quality of a method involves a number of criteria:

1. Efficiency of the method
2. Ability of the method to deal with noisy and missing data
3. Ability of the method to deal with large problems
4. Ability of the method to deal with a variety of attribute types and magnitudes

These are of course related to the desirable features of cluster analysis methods that we listed in Section 5.2.

Just like bagging and boosting is used in classification, the techniques may also be used in cluster analysis. For example, it is possible to obtain samples of size n from the data of size n using replacement and carry out clustering. Once several clustering results have been obtained, they can be combined, hopefully providing better results than just one clustering of the given data. Experiments using these techniques suggest that they can lead to improved quality and robustness of results.

In an interesting paper, Kleinberg notes that although there is a bewildering array of clustering methods, they are based on diverse underlying principles and they often lead to qualitatively different results. He notes that there has been little work done in independent reasoning about clustering without considering any of the methods. He suggests that clustering ought to obey at least three properties. These are scale-invariance, richness and consistency. We discuss these properties briefly.

Scale-invariance does not need to be discussed further since we have already seen in the examples we have considered that clustering results using the same method can change if the scale of one or more of the attributes is changed. Richness refers to the possibility of achieving any or all possible partitions depending on the attribute values and the method. Consistency requires that if we shrink distances between points inside a cluster and expand distances inside another cluster, the results are still the same.

No clustering method satisfies all three, scale-invariance, richness and consistency.

5.9 CLUSTER ANALYSIS SOFTWARE

Most general data mining software packages listed at the end of Chapter 1 include cluster analysis software. For example, packages like Intelligent Miner from IBM or Clementine from SPSS. In this section we only include some software that is primarily for cluster analysis. A more comprehensive list of cluster analysis software is available at http://www.kdnuggets.com/software/clustering.html.

- ClustanGraphics7 from Clustan offers a variety of clustering methods including K-means, density-based and hierarchical cluster analysis. The software provides facilities to display results of clustering including dendograms and scatterplots. http://www.clustan.com/index.html
- CViz Cluster Visualization from IBM is a visualisation tool designed for analysing high-dimensional data in large, complex datasets. It displays the most important factors relating clusters of records. http://www.alphaworks.ibm.com/tech/cviz
- AutoClass, an unsupervised Bayesian classification system, based on SNOB mentioned below, is available from NASA. (Free). http://ic.arc.nasa.gov/ic/projects/bayes-group/autoclass/
- Cluster 3.0, open source software originally developed by Michael Eisen at Stanford. It uses the K-means method, which includes multiple trials to find the best clustering solution. This is crucial for the K-means method to be reliable. http://bonsai.ims.u-tokyo.ac.jp/~mdehoon/software/cluster/software.htm
- CLUTO provides a set of clustering methods including partitional, agglomerative, and graph-partitioning based on a variety of similarity/distance metrics. http://www-users.cs.umn.edu/~karypis/cluto/ (Free).
- SNOB is based on MML (Minimum Message Length). SNOB (and also AutoClass above) does not require the number of classes or the starting seeds to be specified. From Monash University in Australia. http://www.csse.monash.edu.au/~dld/Snob.html (Free).

SUMMARY

Cluster analysis is a collection of methods that assist the user in putting different objects from a collection of objects into different groups. In some ways one could say that cluster analysis is best used as an exploratory data analysis exercise when the user has no hypothesis to test. Cluster analysis therefore can be used to uncover hidden structure which may assist further exploration.

We have discussed a number of clustering methods. In the K-means method it was required that the user specify the number of clusters and starting seeds for each cluster. This may be difficult to do without some insight into the data that the user may not have. One possible approach then might be to combine a partitioning method like K-means with a hierarchical method like the agglomerative method. The agglomerative method can then be used to better understand the data and help in estimating the number of clusters and the starting seeds. The strength of cluster analysis is that it works well with numeric data. Techniques are available that work well with categorical and textual data as well. Cluster analysis is easy to use.

We have noted that the performance of cluster analysis methods can be dependent on the choice of the distance metric. It can be difficult to devise a suitable distance metric for data that contains a mixture of variable types. It can also be difficult to determine a proper weighting scheme for disparate variable types. Furthermore, since cluster analysis is exploratory, results of cluster analysis sometime can be difficult to interpret. On the other hand quite unexpected results may be obtained. For example, at NASA two subgroups of stars were distinguished, where previously no difference was suspected.

REVIEW QUESTIONS

1. Explain the aims of cluster analysis. (Section 5.1)
2. What is clustering? How is it different than supervised classification? In what situations clustering can be useful? (Section 5.1)
3. List and explain desired features of cluster analysis. (Section 5.2)
4. Explain the different types of cluster analysis methods and discuss their features. (Section 5.3)
5. What are the features of the partitional methods? (Section 5.4)
6. Describe the K-means algorithm and discuss its strengths and weaknesses. How does the distance metric affect the result of clustering. (Section 5.4.1)
7. Describe the role of scaling and weighting in K-means algorithm. (Section 5.4.2)
8. How are the starting values in the K-means method selected? (Section 5.4.3)
9. What is the expected maximisation method? (Section 5.4.4)
10. Describe the features of Hierarchical clustering methods? In what situations are these methods useful? (Section 5.5)
11. What is the role of distance between clusters in Hierarchical methods? (Section 5.5.1)
12. Describe single-link, complete-link, centroid and Ward's algorithm. Which one is used most frequently? (Sections 5.5.2, 5.5.3, 5.5.4 and 5.5.6)
13. What is the Agglomerative method and in what situations this method is suitable? (Section 5.5.7)
14. What is the Divisive Hierarchical method and in what situations this method is suitable? (Section 5.5.8)
15. How should a cluster be split in Hierarchical methods? (Section 5.5.8)
16. What are density-based methods? (Section 5.6)
17. How should clustering be carried out for very large datasets? (Section 5.7)
18. Explain how the quality of a clustering algorithm may be determined (Section 5.8)

EXERCISES

1. Given two objects represented by the attribute values (1, 6, 2, 5, 3) and (3, 5, 2, 6, 6)
   (a) Compute the Euclidean distance between the two objects
   (a) Compute the Manhattan distance between the two objects.
2. List four desirable features of a cluster analysis method. Which of them are important for large datasets? Discuss.
3. Suppose that the data mining task is to cluster the following eight points [with (x, y) representing location] into three clusters.

   $A_1(4, 6)$, $A_2(2, 5)$, $A_3(9, 3)$, $A_4(6, 9)$, $A_5(7, 5)$, $A_6(5, 7)$, $A_7(2, 2)$, $A_8(6, 6)$

   Suppose initially we assign A_1, A_2 and A_3 as the seeds of three clusters that we wish to find. Use the K-means method to show:
   (a) The three cluster centroids after the first iteration using the Manhattan distance
   (b) The final three clusters
   (c) Repeat the exercise using the Euclidean distance.
4. Using the data in the last exercise, use the first two points as starting seeds of two clusters. Using K-means, obtain the clusters and compare the result with the result of Exercise 2.
5. What kind of shapes would the different distance metrics deliver? Devise a new distance measure that could lead to sausage type clusters.
6. The following six objects, each with two attributes, are to be clustered:

   $A_1(4, 6)$, $A_2(2, 5)$, $A_3(9, 3)$, $A_4(6, 9)$, $A_5(7, 5)$, $A_6(5, 7)$

   (a) Show the distance matrix for the six objects using Manhattan distance
   (b) Using the divisive method, determine the two objects that should form the basis for splitting the above dataset
   (c) Now split the dataset using the two objects identified in part (b) using the K-means method.
7. Consider the data in Exercise 6. Find the distance matrix between the objects using Manhattan distance and use the agglomerative method to build hierarchical clusters.

MULTIPLE CHOICE QUESTIONS

1. Which one of the following makes the clustering problem difficult to solve?
   (a) Too much data
   (b) Too many attributes
   (c) Not all attributes are numeric
   (d) The number of clusters is not given
2. Which one of the following is true?
   (a) In cluster analysis, the number of clusters is predefined
   (b) The aim of cluster analysis is often exploratory

(c) Overlapping of clusters is normally allowed
(d) All of the above

3. Which one of the following is not a desired feature of cluster analysis?
   (a) Scalability for large datasets
   (b) Minimum input parameters
   (c) No more than three scans of large datasets
   (d) Independent of data input order
4. A distance metric used in cluster analysis must have the following properties?
   (a) Always positive
   (b) Distance from x to x is zero
   (c) Distance from x to y is same as y to x
   (d) All of the above
5. In cluster analysis, which one of the following is not a distance metric?
   (a) Euclidean distance
   (b) Manhattan distance
   (c) Chebyshev distance
   (d) Maximum data value distance
6. Which one of the following is true about clustering?
   (a) K-means is the only clustering method available
   (b) Most clustering algorithms require that the number of clusters be specified
   (c) Changing distance metric does not change the results of clustering
   (d) Training data must be available
7. Which one of the following is correct?
   (a) The centroid of each cluster in K-means usually changes at each iteration
   (b) The number of clusters in K-means usually changes at each iteration
   (c) The number of objects in each cluster usually changes at each iteration
   (d) The total number of objects in the clusters in K-means may change at each iteration
8. Which one of the following is correct?
   (a) K-means algorithm is guaranteed to always terminate
   (b) K-means algorithm is guaranteed to always find the best set of clusters
   (c) K-means algorithm always uses Euclidean distance metric
   (d) All of the above
9. Which one of the following is not a metric used in computing distance between clusters?
   (a) Single-link
   (b) Double-link
   (c) Complete-link
   (d) Ward's minimum variance
10. Which one of the following is correct about the Divisive hierarchical clustering methods?
   (a) The Divisive method is opposite of the Agglomerative method
   (b) The Divisive method starts with the whole dataset as a single cluster

(c) The clusters are divided using either monothetic or polythetic method
(d) All of the above

11. Which two of the following are not correct?
    (a) Agglomerative hierarchical clustering always starts with each object being a cluster of its own
    (b) Agglomerative hierarchical clustering always ends with all objects being in one cluster
    (c) Agglomerative hierarchical clustering never requires computing of distances
    (d) Agglomerative hierarchical clustering at each step merges the closest pair of clusters
12. Which one of the following is correct?
    (a) Agglomerative hierarchical clustering always involves $n - 1$ mergers for a problem with n objects
    (b) Agglomerative hierarchical clustering always involves $n - 1$ levels of merging assuming lowest level as level 1
    (c) Agglomerative hierarchical clustering requires K-means algorithm at each step
    (d) Agglomerative hierarchical clustering requires that the last cluster includes all the objects

PROJECTS

Four datasets are given below. Choose one of them as a class project. The students should:

- Consider the data set chosen carefully and suggest what data mining technique could be used to find structure of the data.
- Would it help if the chosen dataset was modified by scaling and/or deleting some data?
- Use software from the Web to run an appropriate Weka program and analyze the results.

Dataset 1

Consider the following data about nutrients for a number of regional foods in Assam. This data is based on a paper "Nutrient Composition of Some Regional Recipes of Assam, India" published in Ethno-Med, Volume 3, No. 2, 2009, pp. 111–117. Many more foods are listed in that paper if a bigger dataset is required for analysis.

Food	*Water*	*Protein*	*Fat*	*Minerals*	*Fibre*	*Carbohydrate*	*Energy*
Mandhania Chutney	89.6	1.7	0.6	1.2	0.6	6.3	37.4
Kalmou Sak Bhaji	64.8	1.2	11.8	3.0	5.4	13.8	166.2
Aloo Bilahi Pitika	82.8	3.3	0.8	1.7	0.3	10.9	64.8
Bhat Kerala Bhaji	65.8	0.9	9.8	2.8	12.6	8.1	124.2
Rou Masar Tenga	81.9	2.0	2.7	1.7	0.2	11.5	78.3
Boriola Mas Bhoja	29.3	27.0	26.7	8.8	—	8.2	381.0
Bhoja Murgi	44.1	26.9	16.3	1.9	0.6	10.2	295.1
Pura Aloo Pitika	70.5	3.0	1.3	2.1	0.3	22.8	114.9

Dataset 2

The following dataset is about the G20 countries. The table actually has only 19 countries since the 20th country is the European Union. The fourth column provides the GDP in terms of the "Purchase Power Parity" or PPP. The fifth column is the United Nations "Human Development Index" or HDI.

Would scaling the data help in applying a clustering technique? What scaling do you recommend? Explain the reasons for your choice.

G20 Member name	*Trade* (Million USD)	*Nominal GDP* (Million USD)	*PPP GDP* (Million USD)	*HDI*	*Population* (Millions)
Argentina	152,690	474,954	743,121	0.811	40,117
Australia	522,000	1,541,797	970,764	0.938	22,328
Brazil	494,800	2,395,968	2,355,586	0.73	201,032
Canada	962,600	1,819,081	1,488,311	0.911	34,088
China	3,801,000	8,227,037	12,406,870	0.699	1,339,724
France	1,226,400	2,608,699	2,254,067	0.893	65,447
Germany	2,768,000	3,400,579	3,197,069	0.92	81,757
India	809,400	1,824,832	4,684,372	0.554	1,210,193
Indonesia	384,100	878,196	1,216,738	0.629	237,556
Italy	953,000	2,014,079	1,832,916	0.881	60,325
Japan	1,649,800	5,963,969	4,627,891	0.912	127,390
Mexico	756,800	1,177,116	1,758,896	0.775	112,211
Russia	900,600	2,021,960	2,513,299	0.788	143,400
Saudi Arabia	518,300	727,307	906,806	0.782	27,123
South Africa	208,000	384,315	582,391	0.629	53,000
South Korea	1,068,700	1,155,872	1,613,921	0.909	50,004
Turkey	370,800	794,468	1,123,380	0.722	72,561
United Kingdom	1,127,000	2,440,505	2,336,295	0.875	62,041
United States	3,969,000	15,684,750	15,684,750	0.937	316,173

Dataset 3

All shopping malls have food malls which might include dishes like those given below. Use clustering to find structure in this data. You may use Weka software.

Food item	*Calories*	*Carbohydrates*	*Protein*	*Total fat*
Aloo-Baigan	103	32	1	5
Aloo Curry	105	15	1	5
Bhindi (Okra)	161	12	4	11
Cabbage	131	7	2	5
Chole	74	3	4	4
Besan Khadi	100	15	3	5
Mutter Paneer	147	11	9	8
Pumpkin	67	7	2	4
Kofta Curry	147	13	3	9

Food item	*Calories*	*Carbohydrates*	*Protein*	*Total fat*
Chana Dahl	99	13	5	3
Moong Dahl	211	31	13	4
Sambhar	5	3	15	2
Boiled Rice	111	25	2	0.2
Milk (buffalo)	117	5	4	7
Milk (Cow)	67	4	3	4
Khoa	421	21	20	26
Cheese	348	6	24	25

Dataset 4

Consider the following data about animals. Classify it using the agglomerative method. Please note that the data was collected from a variety of sources and may have some inaccuracies.

Discuss problems caused by such large variation in the scale of different attributes in the last example. Show how you might overcome it.

Animal name	*Average weight* (kg)	*Average gestation period* (days)	*Milk protein* (%)	*Milk fat* (%)
Buffalo	500	280	5.9	7.9
Camel	400	405	3.5	3.4
Cat	10	60	10.1	6.3
Cow	400	270	3.9	4.9
Deer	75	200	10.4	19.7
Dog	25	60	9.3	9.5
Elephant	4000	625	3.6	17.6
Fox	50	54	6.6	5.9
Goat	75	150	3.6	3.9
Guinea-pig	2	21	7.4	7.2
Hippopotamus	1500	237	0.6	4.5
Horse	400	330	2.6	1
Human	80	270	1.1	4.5
Monkey	40	165	2.2	2.7
Orangutan	50	180	1.4	3.5
Pig	60	110	7.1	5.1
Rabbit	2	30	12.3	13.1
Rat	2	20	9.2	12.6
Sheep	80	145	5.6	6.4
Whale	20000	425	11.1	21.2
Zebra	120	365	3	4.8

BIBLIOGRAPHY

Recommended Reading for Students

A number of tutorial papers and lecture slides have been included below. Of course there is much more material available on the Web but these in my view are some of the better ones.

Berkhin, P., Survey of Clustering Data Mining Techniques, 56 pages.
http://www.ee.ucr.edu/~barth/ee242/clustering_survey.pdf

Fung, G., A Comprehensive Overview of Basic Clustering Methods, 20 pages, 2001.
http://www.cs.wisc.edu/~gfung/clustering.pdf

Mercer, D.P., Clustering Large Datasets, 48 pages, 2003.
http://www.stats.ox.ac.uk/~mercer/documents/transfer.pdf

Moore, A., K-means and Hierarchical Clustering Tutorial Slides, Carnegie-Mellon University.
http://www-2.cs.cmu.edu/~awm/tutorials/kmeans.html

A Tutorial on Clustering Methods,
http://www.elet.polimi.it/upload/matteucc/clustering/tutorial_html/

Cluster Analysis,
http://www.statsoft.com/textbook/stcluan.html.

Recommended Reading for Lecturers

The book by Hartigan is the classical book on cluster analysis. Another good book is by Jain and Dubes. The survey paper by Jain, Murthy and Flynn is highly cited. The 1992 paper by Cutting et al., proposed the concept of fractionation. The 1996 paper by Ester et al. introduced the DBSCAN method.

A good bibliography on clustering is available at
http://www.ece.northwestern.edu/~harsha/clustering/clus.html

Another site for a number of clustering papers is
http://www.cs.utexas.edu/users/dml/

Aggarwal, C.C. and Reddy, C.K., *Data Clustering: Algorithms and Applications*, CRC Press, Taylor and Francis Group, 617 pp., 2014.

Bradley, P.S., Fayyad, U.M., and Reina, C.A., Scaling Clustering Algorithms to Large Databases, *Proc. Int. Conf. Knowledge Discovery and Data Mining (KDD'98)*, New York, pp. 9–15, 1998.

Chawla, S. and Gionis, A., K-means: A Unified Approach to Clustering and Outlier Detection, *Proceedings of the 2013 SIAM International Conference on Data Mining*, 2013.

Cutting, D.R., Karger, D.R., Pedersen, J.O., and Tukey, J.W., 1992, Scatter/Gather: A Cluster-based Approach to Browsing Large Document Collections, *Proc. Int. Conf. on Research and Development in Information Retrieval (SIGIR'92)*, Copenhagen, Denmark, Belkin, N., Ingwersen P., and Pejtersen A. (Eds.), ACM Press, pp. 318–329, 1992.

Ester, M., Kriegel, H., Sander, J., and Xu, X., A Density-based Algorithm for Discovering Clusters in Large Spatial Databases with Noise, *Proc. Int. Conf. Knowledge Discovery and Data Mining (KDD'96)*, Portland, Oregon, Simoudis, E., Han, J., and Fayyad U. (Eds.), AAAI Press, pp. 226–231, 1996.

Fayyad, U.M., Reina, C.A., and Bradley, P.S., Initialization of Iterative Refinement Clustering Algorithms, *Proc. Int. Conf. Knowledge Discovery and Data Mining (KDD'98)*, New York, Agrawal, R., Stolorz, P., and Piatetsky-Shapiro, G. (Eds.), AAAI Press, pp. 194–198, 1998.

Ganti, V., Ramakrishnan, R., Gehrke, J., Powell, A., and French, J., Clustering Large Datasets in Arbitrary Metric Spaces, *ICDE*, Sydney, Australia, pp. 502–511, 1999.

Ghosh, J., Scalable Clustering Methods for Data Mining, *Handbook of Data Mining*, Erlbaum, L. and Ye, N. (Eds.), pp. 247–277, 2003.

Hartigan, J., *Cluster Algorithms*, John Wiley & Sons, New York, 351 pp., 1975.

Iqbal, F., Binsalleeh, H., Fung, B.C.M., and Debbabi, M., A Unified Data Mining Solution for Authorship Analysis in Anonymous Textual Communications, Information Sciences, Vol. 231, pp. 98–112, 2013.

Jain, A.K., Data Clustering: 50 Years Beyond K-means, *Pattern Recognition Letters*, Vol. 31, No. 8, pp. 651–666, 2010.

Jain, A.K. and Dubes, R., *Algorithms for Clustering Data*, Prentice Hall, New Jersey, 320 pp., 1988.

Jain, A.K., Murty, M.N., and Flynn, P.J., Data Clustering: A Review, *ACM Computing Surveys*, Vol. 31, No. 3, pp. 263–323, 1999.

Karypis, G., Han, E.H., and Kumar, V., Chameleon: A Hierarchical Clustering Algorithm Using Dynamic Modelling, *Computer*, Vol. 32, No. 8, pp. 68–75, 1999.

Kaufman, L. and Rousseeuw, P.J., *Finding Groups in Data: An Introduction to Cluster Analysis*, John Wiley & Sons, 1990.

Kleinberg, J., An Impossibility Theorem for Clustering, *NIPS 15*, pp. 446–453, 2002.

Meila, M. and Heckerman, D., Experimental Comparison of Several Clustering and Initialization Methods, *Proceedings of the Fourteenth Conference on Uncertainty in Artificial Intelligence* (*UAI1998*), 1998.

Wang, H., Wang, W., Yang, J., and Yu, P.S., Clustering by Pattern Similarity in Large Datasets, *Proc. Int. Conf. on Management of Data (SIGMOD'02)*, Madison, Wisconsin, pp. 394–405, 2002.

Zhang, T., Ramakrishnan, R., and Livny, M., BIRCH: An Efficient Data Clustering Method for Very Large Databases, *Proc. Int. Conf. on Management of Data (SIGMOD'96)*, Montreal, Canada, pp. 103–114, 1996.

CASE STUDY 5

Efficient Clustering of Very Large Document Collections*

ABSTRACT

An invaluable portion of scientific data occurs naturally in text form. Given a large unlabeled document collection, it is often helpful to organize this collection into clusters of related documents. By using a vector space model, text data can be treated as high-dimensional but sparse numerical data vectors. It is a contemporary challenge to efficiently preprocess and cluster very large document collections. In this paper we present a time and memory efficient technique for the entire clustering process, including the creation of the vector space model. This efficiency is obtained by (i) a memory-efficient multi-threaded preprocessing scheme, and (ii) a fast clustering algorithm that fully exploits the sparsity of the data set. We show that this entire process takes time that is linear in the size of the document collection. Detailed experimental results are presented—a highlight of our results is that we are able to effectively cluster a collection of 113,716 NSF award abstracts in 23 minutes (including disk I/O costs) on a single workstation with modest memory consumption.

Keywords: clustering, large document collections, hash tables, spherical k-means, vector space model

1. INTRODUCTION

Large collections of documents are becoming increasingly common. The public internet currently has more than 1.5 billion web pages, while private intranets also contain an abundance of text data. A vast amount of important scientific data appears as technical abstracts and papers. Given such large document collections it is important to organize them into structured ontologies. This organization facilitates navigation and search, and at the same time provides a framework for continual maintenance as document repositories grow in size.

Manual construction of structured ontologies is one possible solution and has been adopted to organize the internet (`www.yahoo.com`) and to structure library content. However, this process has the obvious disadvantage of being too labor intensive, and is viable only in large corporations. Thus it is desirable to seek automatic methods for organizing unlabeled document collections. Given a collection of unlabeled data points, *clustering* refers to the problem of automatically assigning class labels to the data and has been widely studied in statistical pattern recognition and machine learning [DH73, Mit97].

A starting point for applying clustering algorithms to unstructured text data is to create a *vector space model,* alternatively known as a *bag-of-words model* [SM83]. The basic idea is (a) to extract unique content-bearing words from the set of documents treating these words as *features* and (b) to then represent each document as a vector of certain weighted word frequencies in this feature space. Observe that we may regard the vector space model of a text data set as a *word-by-document matrix* whose rows are words and columns are document vectors. Typically, a large

*Dhillon, I.S., J. Fan, and Y. Guan, 2001, Efficient clustering of very large document collections, in *Data Mining for scientific and engineering applications,* Kamath, C., P. Kegelmeyer, and R.L. Grossman (Eds.), Kluwer Academic, pp. 357–381.

number of words exist in even a moderately sized set of documents where a few thousand words or more are common. Thus for large document collections, both the row and column dimensions of the matrix are quite large. However, as we will discuss later in greater detail, this matrix is typically very sparse with almost 99% of the matrix entries being zero.

Using the vector space model various classical clustering algorithms such as the k-means algorithm and its variants, hierarchical agglomerative clustering, and graph-theoretic methods have been explored in the text mining literature; for detailed reviews, see [Ras92, Wil88]. Recently, there has been a flurry of activity in this area, see [BGG+98, CKPT92, SS97, ZE98]. A substantial amount of this work has concentrated on clustering web search results where the document collections to be clustered are not very large.

In this paper, our main concern is in obtaining a highly efficient process for clustering very large document collections. Our main motivation is that we want to cluster collections in excess of more than 100,000 documents in a reasonable amount of time on a single processor. Thus our main emphasis is on high speed and scalability with modest main memory consumption. The clustering process involves reading the text documents from disk, and preprocessing them to form the vector space model before using a particular clustering algorithm. It turns out that main memory consumption and disk I/O costs in this process can be prohibitive. In order to alleviate these problems, we employ a memory efficient multi-threaded approach to reading and preprocessing the document. For creating the vector space model, we use efficient and scalable data structures such as local and global hash tables. Finally, we use the highly efficient and effective ispherical k-means algorithm that fully exploits the sparsity of the data [DM01]. The above steps lead to a highly efficient clustering process—as a result we are able to preprocess and cluster a collection of 113,716 NSF award abstracts documents in 23 minutes on a Sun workstation with modest memory consumption.

This paper is organized as follows. In Section 2 we highlight the challenges in obtaining an efficient and effective process for clustering large document collections. Section 3 describes our multi-threaded algorithm for creating the vector space model. In Section 4 we present the spherical k-means algorithm which is ideally suited for clustering high-dimensional sparse text data. Section 5 presents speed and memory consumption results on some document collections, in particular we examine the results on a collection of 113,716 NSF award abstracts. Finally, Section 6 concludes with a short summary and discussion of future work.

A quick word about notation. Lower-case bold letters such as $\mathbf{x}$, $\mathbf{c}$ will denote vectors while $\|\mathbf{x}\|$ will denote the 2-norm of the corresponding vector. Thus when we say that $\|\mathbf{x}\| = 1$ we mean that $\mathbf{x}^T\mathbf{x} = 1$.

2. CHALLENGES

As mentioned above, the preprocessing phase leads to the creation of the vector space model. Given a large document collection, the following steps are involved in this phase: (a) read all input documents from disk, (b) parse into word tokens using efficient regular expression pattern matching, (c) lookup words rapidly in hash tables to track the number of occurrences of each word, and finally, (d) output the vector space model.

Efficient parsing using regular expression pattern matching is a well-studied problem. Existing software tools such as FLEX provide a quick and easy way to construct the required parser [Pax96]. Also, efficient hash table indexing and access is provided in public-domain software [MS96]. Thus effective solutions to steps (b) and (c) above are easy to obtain.

However I/O costs in steps (a) and (d) can be substantial, especially if the documents need to be accessed from a Network File System(NFS) [Cal99]. In such a case, the time taken by these steps can be quite large and often unpredictable depending on other traffic on the NFS. Our approach to solve this problem is to use multiple threads [NBF96] so that input documents can be read in a parallel fashion.

Another challenge is main memory consumption. After all the documents have been read and processed there is a final phase which involves a sweep and modification of the entire vector space model. One simple approach to facilitate this phase is to retain the partially formed vector space model in main memory while the rest of the documents are being processed. We implemented such an approach and on our test collection of 113,716 documents, this required nearly 500 MBytes of main memory. Extrapolating this memory requirement to 1 million documents, we can see that this main-memory based implementation will require several gigabytes of memory. This cost is unacceptable since our goal is to preprocess and cluster a million documents on current workstations consuming less than 256 MBytes of main memory. In Section 3 we introduce such a memory efficient algorithm that allows us to preprocess a large number of documents without sacrificing much speed.

In our test collection of 113,716 documents there are a total of more than 150,000 unique words. After a pruning step, we retain 26,000 unique words in the vector space model. Thus, the document vectors are very *high-dimensional.* However, typically, most documents contain only a small subset of the total number of words. Hence, the document vectors are very *sparse*—a sparsity of 99% is common. The major challenge is to find a clustering algorithm that can yield good effective solutions for very high-dimensional data and at the same time, exploit the sparsity of the vector space model. Since we are interested in clustering very large document collections we seek algorithms that consume time and memory that is linear in the size of the document collection.

3. EFFICIENT PREPROCESSING

In this section, we describe our preprocessing algorithm for creating the vector space model. Before we describe the details we give a high level description of the task at hand.

3.1 Vector Space Model

The basic idea is to represent each document as a vector of certain weighted word frequencies. In order to do so, the following parsing and extraction steps are needed.

1. Ignoring case, extract all unique words from the entire set of documents.
2. Eliminate non-content-bearing "stopwords" such as "a", "and", "the", etc. For sample lists of stopwords, see [FBY92, Chapter 7].
3. For each document, count the number of occurrences of each word.
4. Using heuristic or information-theoretic criteria, eliminate non-content-bearing "high-frequency" and "low-frequency" words [SM83].
5. After the above elimination, suppose w unique words remain. Assign a unique identifier between 1 and w to each remaining word, and a unique identifier between 1 and d to each document.

The above steps outline a simple preprocessing scheme. In addition, one may extract word phrases such as "New York," and one may reduce each word to its "root" or "stem", thus eliminating plurals, tenses, prefixes, and suffixes [FBY92, Chapter 8].

The above preprocessing yields the number of occurrences of word j in document i, say, f_{ji}, and the number of documents which contain the word j, say, d_j. Using these counts, we can represent the ith document as a w-dimensional vector $\mathbf{x}_i$ as follows. For $1, \leq j \leq w$, set the jth component of $\mathbf{x}_i$, to be the product of three terms

$$x_{ji} = t_{ji} \cdot g_j \cdot s_i$$

where t_{ji} is the *term weighting component* and depends only on f_{ji}, while g_j is the *global weighting component* and depends on d_j, and s_i is the *normalization component* for x_i. Intuitively, t_{ji} captures the relative importance of a word in a document, while g_j captures the overall importance of a word in the entire set of documents. The objective of such weighting schemes is to enhance discrimination between various document vectors for better retrieval effectiveness [SB88].

There are many schemes for selecting the term, global, and normalization components, see [Ko197] for various possibilities. In this paper we use the popular tfn scheme known as *normalized term frequency-inverse document frequency.* This scheme uses $t_{ji} = f_{ji}$, $g_j = \log(d/d_j)$ and $s_i = \Sigma_{j=1}^{w}(t_{ji}(t_{ji}g_j)^2)^{-1/2}$. Note that this normalization implies that $\|\mathbf{x}_i\| = 1$, i.e., each document vector lies on the surface of the unit sphere in R^w. Intuitively, the effect of normalization is to retain only the *proportion* of words occurring in a document. This ensures that documents dealing with the same subject matter (that is, using similar words), but differing in length lead to similar document vectors.

3.2 Preprocessing Algorithm

The input to the preprocessing step is a data directory that contains all the documents to be processed. The documents may also be contained within subdirectories of the input directory. The output is the vector space model described in the above section. which can be represented as a highly sparse word-by-document matrix. We store this sparse matrix by using the Compressed Column Storage(CCS) format [DGL89]. In this format, we record the value of each non-zero element, along with its row and column index. The column indices represent the input documents, the row indices represent ids of distinct words present in the document collection, and the non-zero entries in the matrix represent the frequencies of words in documents.

Figure 1.1 gives an outline of the preprocessing algorithm. The algorithm first initializes a global hash table. To resolve whether a word has been encountered previously, a local and a global hash table are used. Both these hash tables use words as keys and store the corresponding row indices and frequencies as values. As the names suggest, the global hash table keeps track of words and their occurrences in the entire document collection while the local hash table does so for just one document. After initializing the global hash table, the algorithm recursively walks through the input directory to obtain the list of documents to be processed. The preprocessing algorithm then creates several threads of computation. The purpose of each thread is to process a set of documents independently and output its results into temporary files. Details of this processing are given in Figure 1.2 which we discuss in the next paragraph. After all the threads have finished, the global hash table is examined, and words that are too common or too rare are removed from the global hash table. Unique word ids are assigned to the words that still remain in the global hash table. The temporary files are then reloaded, the word ids are resolved and then the final vocabulary and word-by-document matrix are output.

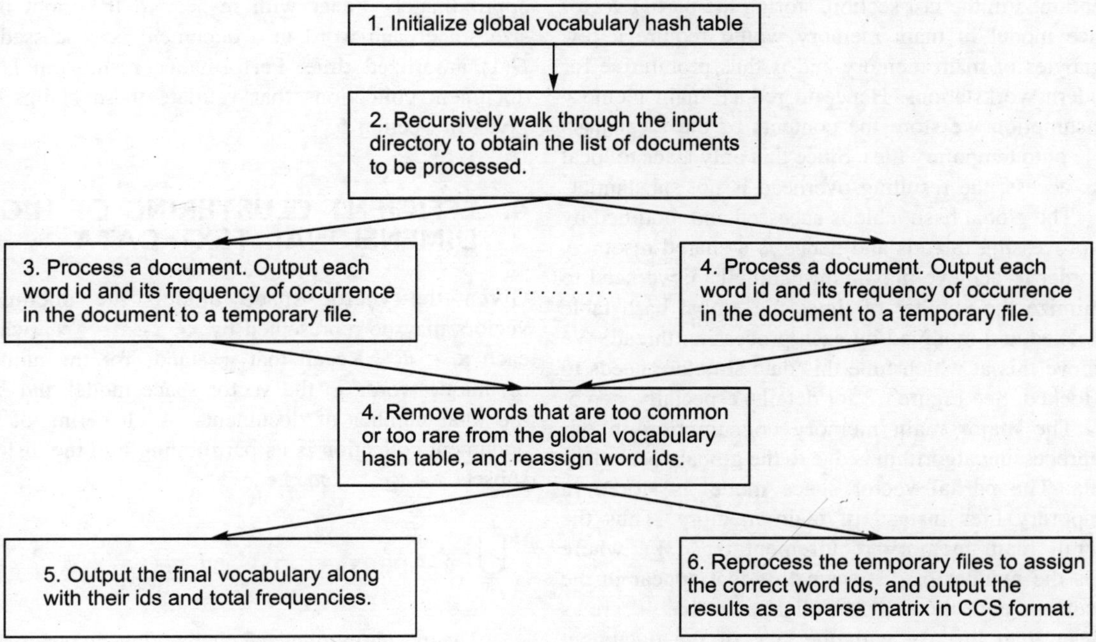

Figure 1.1: Outline of the preprocessing algorithm.

1. Initialize the local hash table (this hash table uses words as keys, and stores row indices and frequencies as values).
2. Get a token from the document, and convert the token to lower-case.
3. Discard the token if it is too long or too short or is a non-content "stopword" such as "a", "and", "the", etc.
4. If the word already exists in the local hash table, increment the frequency of that entry, otherwise insert the word into the local hash table with row index –1 and frequency 1.
5. After the whole document has been processed, set the row indices in the local hash table to the corresponding ones in the global hash table. If a word in the local hash table does not exist in the global hash table, assign a new row index to the word and add to the global hash table (note that this requires locking the global hash table to prevent simultaneous modification by another thread).
6. Output the contents of the local hash table (row indices and frequencies) to a temporary file, and discard the local hash table.

Figure 1.2: Details of the processing of a document by each thread (step 3 of Figure 1.1).

Figure 1.2 describes the various steps performed by each preprocessing thread. Two decisions warrant further explanation—the use of temporary files for storing the partial vector space model and the way in which the local and global hash tables are accessed. As mentioned in the last section, storing the partial vector space model in main memory would require a few gigabytes of main memory and is thus prohibitive for modern workstations. Hence to reduce main memory consumption we store the contents of the local hash table onto temporary files. Since this only leads to local disk access, the resulting overhead is not substantial.

The global hash table is accessed and modified by all processing threads and hence is a shared resource. In order to achieve maximum parallelism, we need to minimize the number of times the global hash table is locked and modified by each processing thread. We achieve this at which time this data structure needs to be locked. See Figure 1.2 for details, especially step 5.

The major main memory consumption in our preprocessing algorithm is due to the global vocabulary table. The partial vector space model is stored in temporary files instead of main memory. Thus the overall main memory requirement is $O(W)$, where W is the number of distinct words that appear in the document collection. It is well known that W grows slower than linearly with the size of the document collection—*Heaps' Law* states that the number of unique words in a text of size d grows as $O(d^{\beta})$, where β is a positive number less than one [Hea78]. Thus the main memory consumption grows slower than linearly with the size of the document collection. The computation time for the preprocessing step is approximately linear with respect to the input data size since each word in a document is processed in $O(1)$ amortized time. Performance results on large document collections that validate these claims are given in Section 5.

4. EFFICIENT CLUSTERING OF HIGH-DIMENSIONAL TEXT DATA

Given the vector space model, the document vectors may be represented by $\mathbf{x}_1, \mathbf{x}_2, \ldots, \mathbf{x}_d$, where each $\mathbf{x}_i \in R^w$. Recall that w stands for the number of unique words in the vector space model and d is the total number of documents. A clustering of the document collection is its partitioning into the disjoint subsets $\pi_1, \pi_2, \ldots, \pi_k$, i.e.,

$$\bigcup_{j=1}^{k} \pi_j = \{\mathbf{x}_1, \mathbf{x}_1, \ldots, \mathbf{x}_d\} \text{ and } \pi_j \cap \pi_l = \phi, \; j \neq l.$$

The most important and challenging characteristics of the vector space models that arise from text data are high dimensionality and sparsity. Typically, w is in the thousands and a sparsity of 99% is common. For purposes of efficiency, it is important that the clustering algorithm exploit the sparsity of the data while giving meaningful results at the same time. The spherical k-means algorithm satisfies both these properties and hence is our algorithm of choice. We now briefly formalize this algorithm highlighting its salient features. More details may be found in [DM01].

Any text clustering algorithm needs an objective notion of similarity between documents. A widely used measure of similarity is the cosine of the angle between two document vectors (FBY92, SM83]. Cosine similarlity is easy to interpret and simple to compute for sparse vectors and has been used in other information retrieval applications, such as query retrieval. Based on cosine similarity, we can define the "goodness" or "coherence" of cluster π_j as

$$\sum_{\mathbf{x}_i \in \pi_j} \mathbf{x}_i^T \mathbf{c}_j, \tag{4.1}$$

where each $\mathbf{x}_i$ is assumed to be normalized such that $\|\mathbf{x}_i\| = 1$ and $\mathbf{c}_j$ is the normalized centroid of cluster π_j,

$$\mathbf{c}_j = \frac{\sum_{\mathbf{x}_i \in \pi_j} \mathbf{x}_i}{\| \sum_{\mathbf{x}_i \in \pi_j} \mathbf{x}_i \|}.$$

By the Cauchy-Schwarz inequality,

$$\sum_{\mathbf{x}_i \in \pi_j} \mathbf{x}_i^T \mathbf{z} \le \sum_{\mathbf{x}_i \in \pi_j} \mathbf{x}_i^T \mathbf{c}_j, \qquad \forall \mathbf{z} \in R^w$$

and thus the normalized centroid is the vector that is closest in cosine similarity (in an average sense) to all the document vectors in the cluster π_j. As a result, we also call the vector $\mathbf{c}_j$'s as *concept vectors.*

Aggregating (4.1) over all clusters, we can measure the goodness of any given partitioning $\{\pi_j\}_{j=1}^k$ using the following *objective junction:*

$$Q(\{\pi_j\}_{j=1}^k) = \sum_{j=1}^{k} \sum_{\mathbf{x}_i \in \pi_j} \mathbf{x}_i^T \mathbf{c}_j. \tag{4.2}$$

Intuitively, the objective function measures the combined coherence of all the k clusters. Having posed the objective function, we now present an algorithm that attempts to maximize its value.

4.1 Spherical k-means Algorithm

It is well known that finding the partitioning that maximizes (4.2) is NP-Complete [KPR98, Theorem 3.1]; also, see [GJW82]. Thus we seek a heuristic algorithm that can quickly find a good local maximum. For this purpose, we use a variant of the classical k-means algorithm [DH73] that uses the cosine similarity measure. Since both the document and concept vectors lie on the surface of a high-dimensional sphere, we call this variant the *spherical k-means* algorithm. This algorithm proceeds as follows.

1. Initialize clustering. Start with some initial partitioning of the document vectors, namely $\{p_j^{(0)}\}_{j=1}^k$. Let $\{\mathbf{c}_j^{(0)}\}_{j=1}^k$ be the concept vectors of the associated partitioning. Set the iteration count t to 0.
2. Re-assign document vectors. For each document vector $\mathbf{x}_i$, $1 \le i \le d$, do the following:
   - **a.** Compute $\mathbf{x}_i^T \mathbf{c}_l^{(t)}$ for all $l = 1, 2, \ldots, k$.
   - **b.** From among all $\mathbf{x}_i^T \mathbf{c}_i^{(t)}$ computed above, find $j = \arg\max_l \mathbf{x}_i^T \mathbf{c}_l^{(t)}$ (break ties arbitrarily if $\mathbf{x}_i$ has largest cosine similarity with more than one concept vector).

   This induces the new partitioning

   $$\pi_j^{(t+1)} = (\mathbf{x}_i : j = \arg\max_l \mathbf{x}_i^T \mathbf{c}_l^{(t)}\}, \quad 1 \le j \le k.$$
3. Update concept vectors. Compute the concept vectors corresponding to the new partitioning:

   $$s_j = \sum_{\mathbf{x}_i \in \pi_j} \mathbf{x}_i, \quad \mathbf{c}_j^{(t+1)} = \frac{s_j}{\| s_j \|}, \quad 1 \le j \le k.$$
4. Check the stopping criterion. If the stopping criterion is satisfied, then exit. Otherwise increase t by 1 and go to step 2 above.

In our implementation, the stopping criterion is:

$$| Q(\{\pi_j^{(t)}\}_{j=1}^k) - Q(\{\pi_j^{(t+1)}\}_{j=1}^k) | \le 10^{-3} \cdot | Q(\{\pi_j^{(t)}\}_{j=1}^k) |.$$

It can be shown that the above algorithm yields a gradient-ascent scheme. In particular, we can show that the objective function value in (4.2) does not decrease from one iteration to the next, i.e.,

$$Q(\{\pi_j^{(t)}\}_{j=1}^k) \le Q(\{\pi_j^{(t+1)}\}_{j=1}^k).$$

Like any other gradient-ascent scheme, the spherical k-means algorithm is prone to local maxima. A careful selection of initial partitions $(\{\pi_j^{(0)}\}_{j=1}^k$ is important. One can either (a) randomly assign each document to one of the k clusters, (b) first compute the concept vector for the entire document collection and randomly perturb this vector to get k starting concept vectors or (c) try several initial clusterings and select the best in terms of the largest objective function. We use strategy (b) in our implementation.

We now examine the time and memory complexity of the above algorithm. We assume that the number of non-zero entries in the sparse matrix is nz, and that the above algorithm iterates τ times before stopping. Using our initialization strategy, step 1 of the algorithm costs $O(nz + k \cdot w)$ operations. For each iteration, step 2a costs $O(nz \cdot k)$ operations while 2b costs $O(k \cdot d)$ comparisons. Step 3 updates the concept vectors and costs $O(nz + k \cdot w)$ operations. Thus the total time complexity for τ iterations is

$$O((nz \cdot k + k \cdot d + k \cdot w) \cdot \tau).$$

Typically $nz \gg \max(d, w)$, hence it is clear that step $2a$ is the most computationally expensive step in the algorithm and the overall complexity of the algorithm is $O(nz \cdot k \cdot \tau)$.

The main memory consumed by the algorithm is for storing the document vectors and for old and new copies of the concept vectors. Storing the document vectors in the CCS sparse matrix form requires $4(2nz + d + 4)$ bytes while the concept vectors require $8kw$ bytes; hence the memory consumption is modest.

4.2 Similarity Estimation

The computational bottleneck in the spherical k-means algorithm is the dot product computation between all the document vectors and concept vectors (see step 2a). During the course of the algorithm it turns out that the first few iterations lead to a lot of movement of documents between clusters. However, just after a few iterations the clusters become more stable, see the solid line in the left plot of Figure 1.3. Consequently, the overall objective function value also settles down after 4.5 iterations as seen in the right plot of Figure 1.3.

When the clusters become stable, there are potential savings if we can somehow avoid computing unnecessary dot products between document vectors and 'far away' concept vectors.

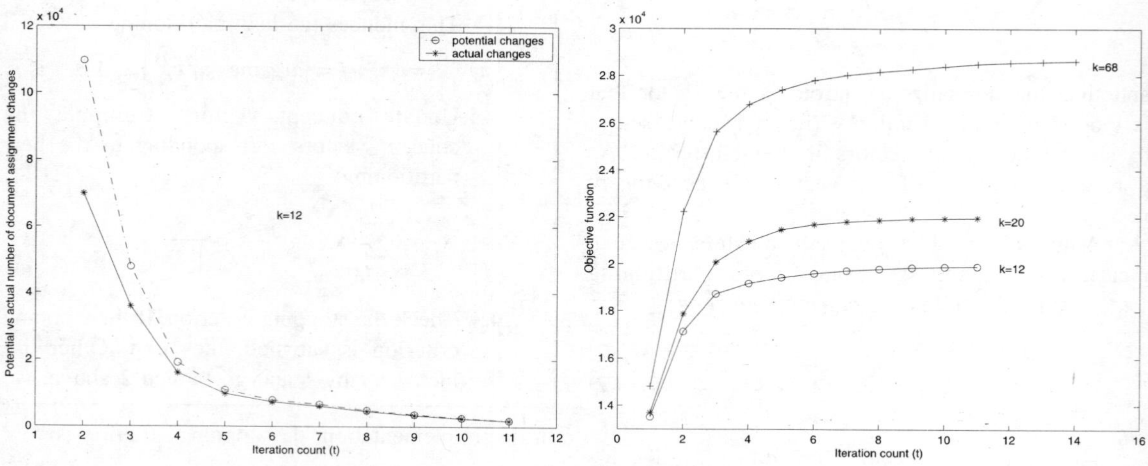

Figure 1.3: Clusters stabilize after just a few iterations.

We now introduce a technique for estimating cosine similarties which allows us to avoid such dot product computations.

Suppose $\mathbf{c}_l^{(t)}$ is the concept vector of cluster l at iteration t and x is a document vector. Then,

$$|\mathbf{x}^T\mathbf{c}_l^{(t)} - \mathbf{x}^T\mathbf{c}_l^{(t+1)}| \leq \|\mathbf{x}\|\,\|\mathbf{c}_l^{(t)} - \mathbf{c}_l^{(t+1)}\|$$
$$= \|\mathbf{c}_l^{(t)} - \mathbf{c}_l^{(t+1)}\|$$
$$\Rightarrow \mathbf{x}^T\,\mathbf{c}_l^{(t)} - \|\mathbf{c}_l^{(t)} - \mathbf{c}_l^{(t+1)}\| \leq \mathbf{x}^T\mathbf{c}_l^{(t+1)}$$
$$\leq \mathbf{x}^T\mathbf{c}_l^{(t)} + \|\mathbf{c}_l^{(t)} - \mathbf{c}_l^{(t+1)}\| \qquad (4.3)$$

The right side of inequality (4.3) gives a similarity upper bound which can be used profitably in the $(t + 1)$-st iteration to avoid computing $\mathbf{x}^T\mathbf{c}_l^{(t+1)}$. The idea is to store in memory the quantities $\|\mathbf{c}_l^{(t)} - \mathbf{c}_l^{(t+1)}\|$ and upper bounds for $\mathbf{x}^T\mathbf{c}_l^{(t)}$. Suppose $\mathbf{x}$ belongs to the cluster j at the t-th iteration. Then, at iteration $t + 1$, we can update in $O(1)$ time the similarity upper bound for $\mathbf{x}^T\mathbf{c}_l^{(t+1)}$, $i \varpi j$. If this similarity upper bound I is smaller than $\mathbf{x}^T\mathbf{c}_l^{(t+1)}$ (which is computed exactly) there is no need to explicitly compute $\mathbf{x}^T\mathbf{c}_l^{(t+1)}$, otherwise the exact value needs to be computed. As the clusters become more and more stable, this similarity estimation can dramatically cut down on computation (see Figure 1.4).

In our implementation, we store the similarity upper bounds in the $d \times k$ matrix U. We obtain the new algorithm by replacing step 2 of the spherical k-means algorithm by the following step (here we assume that similarity estimation is started after t_{min} iterations).

2. Re-assign document vectors. For each document vector X_i, $1 \leq i \leq d$, do the following:
   - **a.** If $t \leq t_{min}$, do step 2a as in Section 4.1. else if $t = t_{min}$, set $U(i, l) = \mathbf{x}_i^T\mathbf{c}_l^{(t)}$ for all $l = 1, 2, \ldots, k$.
     else if $t > t_{min}$, do the following steps for all $l = 1, 2, \ldots, k$,
     - **a1.** Set $U(i, l) = U(i, l) + \|\mathbf{c}_l^{(t)} - \mathbf{c}_l^{(t-1)}\|$.
     - **a2.** Compute $\mathbf{x}_i^T\mathbf{c}_j^{(t)}$ where x_i belongs to cluster j at iteration $t - 1$.
       If $U(i, l) > \mathbf{x}_i^T\mathbf{c}_j^{(t)}$, compute $\mathbf{x}_i^T\mathbf{c}_l^{(t)}$ and set $U(i, l) = \mathbf{x}_i^T\mathbf{c}_l^{(t)}$.
   - **b.** From among all $\mathbf{x}_i^T\mathbf{c}_l^{(t)}$ computed above, find $j = \arg\max_l \mathbf{x}_i^T\mathbf{c}_l^{(t)}$.

Figure 1.4 shows the considerable savings in the number of dot product computations as the

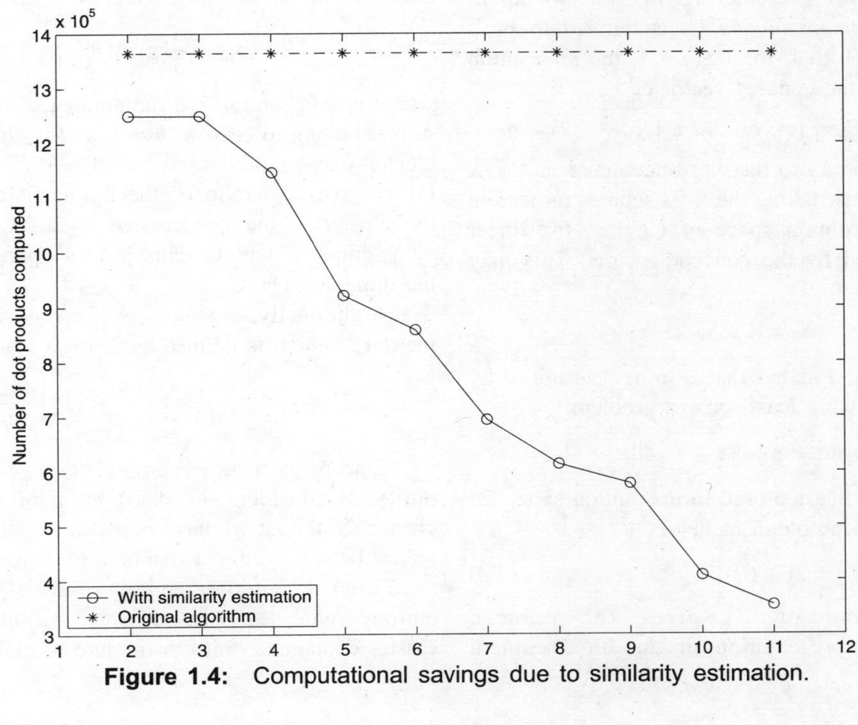

Figure 1.4: Computational savings due to similarity estimation.

iteration count increases in a typical run of the algorithm. To obtain these savings, an extra storage requirement of $4dk$ bytes is required to store the matrix U. Additionally, an extra $O(dk)$ operations to update the matrix U are required (see step a1 above).

However, these extra costs are small compared to the resulting savings in computation time, see Section 5.1.2 for an example.

4.3 Clustering for Dimensionality Reduction

We now highlight another use of our clustering algorithm. Using the vector space model, each document may be represented as a high-dimensional vector of words. Clearly the occurrence of one word in a document is not independent of other words. Thus there is a great deal of redundancy in this collection of vectors. Dimensionality reduction is a technique that tries to represent each document as a vector with fewer dimensions that are more independent. It turns out that the above clustering algorithm also yields a fast and effective technique for dimensionality reduction.

Let $\{\mathbf{c}_j\}^k_{j=1}$ denote the concept vectors corresponding to a clustering of the document vectors. The *concept matrix* C_k is defined to be a $d \times k$ matrix such that, for $1 \leq j \leq k$, the jth column of the matrix is the concept vector $\mathbf{c}_j$, i.e.,

$$C_k = [\mathbf{c}_1, \mathbf{c}_2, \ldots, \mathbf{c}_k].$$

An approximation X_k to the word-document matrix X may be obtained by taking the least squares projection of X onto the column space of C_k, i.e., the linear subspace spanned by the concept vectors. This may be expressed as

$$X_k = C_k Z^*_k,$$

where Z^*_k is a $k \times d$ matrix that is to be determined by solving the following least-squares problem:

$$Z^*_k = \arg_Z \min \|X - C_k Z\|^2_F.$$

It is well known that a closed form solution exists for this least-squares problem, namely,

$$Z^*_k = (C_k{}^T C_k)^{-1} C_k{}^T X. \quad (4.4)$$

The ith column of Z^*_k gives the reduced k-dimensional representation of the ith document vector. Typically the original dimensionalty w is in the thousands while k is much smaller. In previous work, we have shown that empirically, the quality of the reduced dimensional representation given by (4.4) is comparable to the "best" possible, namely the k-truncated SVD, see [DM01] for details. Thus our clustering process followed by dimensionality reduction can be used in various applications, such as query retrieval, text classification, etc.

5. EXPERIMENTAL RESULTS

In this section, we give experimental results for the entire clustering process—this includes time and memory consumed by the preprocessing phase as well as by the clustering algorithm. In addition, we need to evaluate the goodness of the clustering produced. Evaluating clustering results is a tricky business. However, in situations where documents are already categorized (labelled), we can compare the clusters with the "true" class labels. For this comparison we use the measures of purity and entropy as defined below, see also [SGM00].

Suppose we are given c categories (true class labels) while the clustering algorithm produces k clusters. Cluster π_l's *purity* can be defined as

$$P(\pi_l) = \frac{1}{n_l} \max_h (n_l^{(h)}),$$

where $n_l = |\pi_l|$ and $n_l^{(h)}$ is the number of documents in π_l that belong to class h, $h = 1, \ldots, c$. Note that each cluster may contain samples from different classes. Purity gives the ratio of the dominant class size in the cluster to the cluster size itself. A high purity value implies that the cluster is a "pure" subset of the dominant class.

Additionally, we also use *entropy* as a quality measure, which is defined as follows:

$$H(\pi_l) = -\frac{1}{\log c} \sum_{h=1}^{c} \frac{n_l^{(h)}}{n_l} \log\left(\frac{h_l^{(h)}}{n_l}\right)$$

Entropy is a more comprehensive measure than purity. It considers the distribution of classes in a cluster. Note that we have normalized entropy to take values between 0 and 1. An entropy value of 0 means the cluster is comprised entirely of one class, while an entropy value near 1 is bad since it implies that the cluster contains a uniform mixture of classes.

We now examine these quality measures on a sample collection. We formed a collection of 3893 documents by merging the popular MEDLINE, CISI, and CRANFIELD sets. MEDLINE consists of 1033 abstracts from medical journals, CISI consists of 1460 abstracts from information retrieval papers, while CRANFIELD consists of 1400 abstracts from aeronautical systems papers (ftp://ftp.cs.cornell.edu/pub/smart). We preprocessed this collection by proceeding as in Section 3. After removing common stopwords, the collection contained 22149 unique words from which we eliminated 17839 low-frequency words appearing in less than 8 documents (roughly 0.2% of the documents), and 7 high-frequency words appearing in more than 585 documents (roughly 15% of the documents). We were finally left with 4303 words using which we created 3893 document vectors using the `tfn` scheme. Each document vector has dimension 4303, however, on an average, each document vector is about 99% sparse.

For this contrived collection, we used our clustering algorithm to form 3 clusters. The following table shows the "confusion matrix" for this clustering, from which we can see that the clusters can be easily identified with the three classes—'MEDLINE', 'CISI' and 'CRANFIELD'.

	MEDLINE	CRANFIELD	CISI
patients (1023)	1020	2	1
boundary (1388)	1	**1383**	4
library (1481)	12	14	**1455**

In the above table the rows denote clusters. Note that we have denoted the clusters by the most frequently occurring word in the cluster from among the words in the vector space model 'patients', 'boundary' and 'library'. The above table says that the cluster 'patients' has 1023 documents of which 1020 belong to the 'MEDLINE' class, the 'boundary' cluster has 1388 documents while the 'library' cluster has 1481 documents. Notice that the confusion matrix is almost diagonal which shows that the clustering algorithm nearly recovered the three classes. This fact is also reflected by the high purity and low entropy values of the three clusters shown below.

Cluster#	Purity	Entropy
0	.996094	.0252647
1	.996398	.0233619
2	.982444	.0914646

5.1 Case Study on a Large Scientific Collection

To show the efficiency and effectiveness of our algorithms, we now present results on a large real-life collection of NSF award abstracts. We obtained the NSF data set by downloading abstracts of grants awarded by the National Science Foundation between Jan 1958 and August 1999 from `www.nsf.gov`. For our experiments we extracted titles and abstracts (ignoring fields such as 'Type', 'NSF Org', 'Date', etc.) of awards made in the 8 NSF organizations: Directorate for Biological Sciences (BIO), Directorate for Computer and Information Science and Engineering (CISE), Directorate for Education and Human Resources (EHR), Directorate for Engineering (ENG), Directorate for Geosciences (GEO), Directorate for Mathematical and Physical Sciences (MPS), Office of Polar Programs (OPP) and Directorate for Social, Behavioral, and Economic Sciences (SBE). This results in a total of 113716 abstracts. The number of documents per NSF organization is as follows:

Class label	ENG	CSE	MPS	BIO	GEO	EHR	SBE	OPP
# documents	19366	8275	23037	16768	15667	14112	13725	2767

The most populous class is MPS with over 23000 awards, with ENG being second. On the other hand, OPP contains the fewest (2767) number of documents. Both the mean and median class size is about 142000.

We preprocessed this NSF collection by proceeding as in Section 3. After removing common stopwords, the collection contained 153527 unique words from which we eliminated 127103 low-frequency and high-frequency words. We were finally left with 26424 words using which we created 113716 document vectors using the `tfn` scheme. Each document vector has dimension

26424, however, on an average, each document vector contains only about 72 nonzero components and thus is more than 99% sparse.

In terms of the words contained in these documents, Table 1.1 shows the top ten most common words in the NSF data set. Note that we refer to the most frequently occurring word as having rank 1, the second most frequent word as having rank 2, and so on. As is common in most document collections the majority of the words occur in very few documents. Figure 1.5 shows the distribution of all the word frequencies versus their rank on a log-log scale. This distribution approximately fits the so-called *Zipf's law* [Zip49].

Table 1.1: Top 10 most common words in the NSF data set

Rank	Word	Frequency
1	abstract	154467
2	research	152134
3	title	143257
4	project	73720
5	study	51178
6	data	43703
7	system	40314
8	university	39491
9	program	39203
10	science	38530

As mentioned above, there are a total of 153527 unique words in the NSF collection. In general, the number of unique words W grows slower than linearly with the number of documents, i.e., $W = O(d^{\beta})$ where $0 < \beta < 1$. This behaviour known as *Heap's law* [Hea78] is seen in Figure 1.6.

5.1.1 Preprocessing Results

We now show the results of our clustering process on this large NSFcollection. The preprocessing phase takes time that grows linearly with the size of the data set, while the main memory consumed also grows linearly with the number of unique words. Experiments on subsets of the NSF collection validate these claims, see Figures 1.7 and 1.8. Figure 1.7 shows

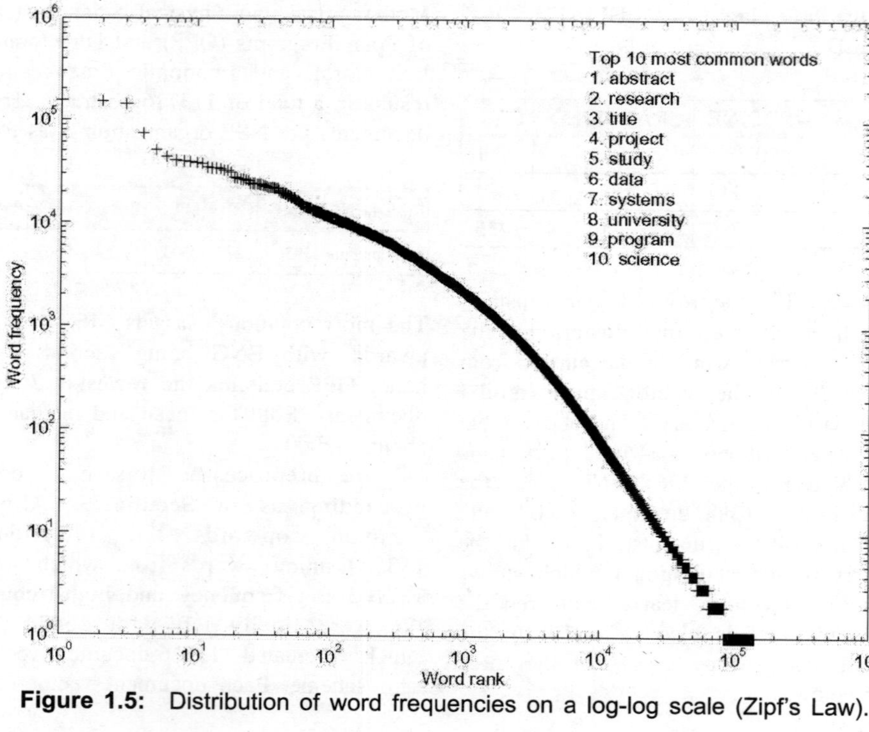

Figure 1.5: Distribution of word frequencies on a log-log scale (Zipf's Law).

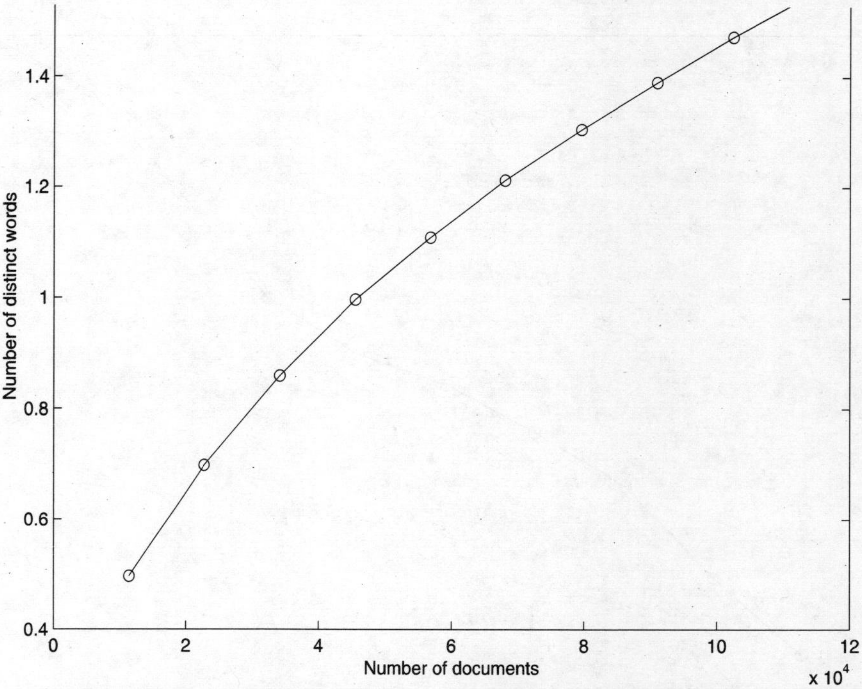

Figure 1.6: Vocabulary size vs. number of documents (Heap's Law).

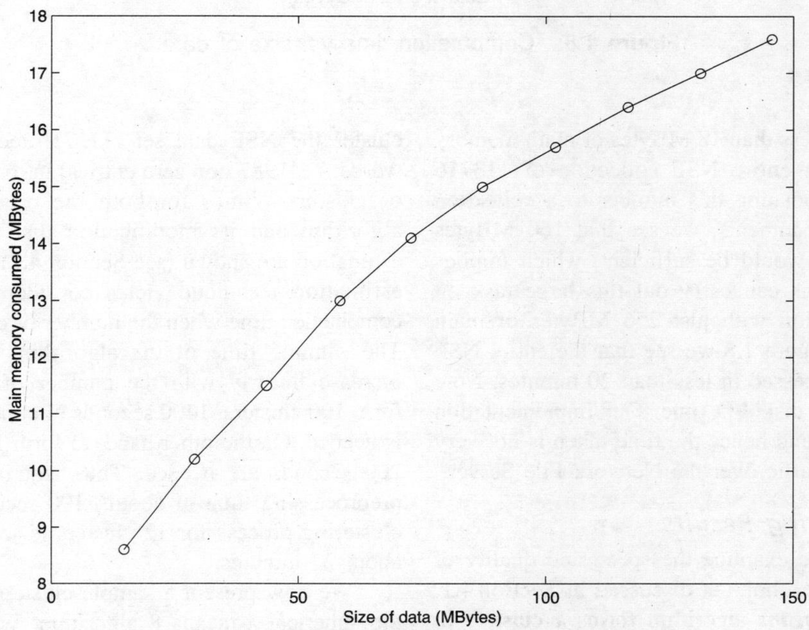

Figure 1.7: Main memory consumed vs. size of data.

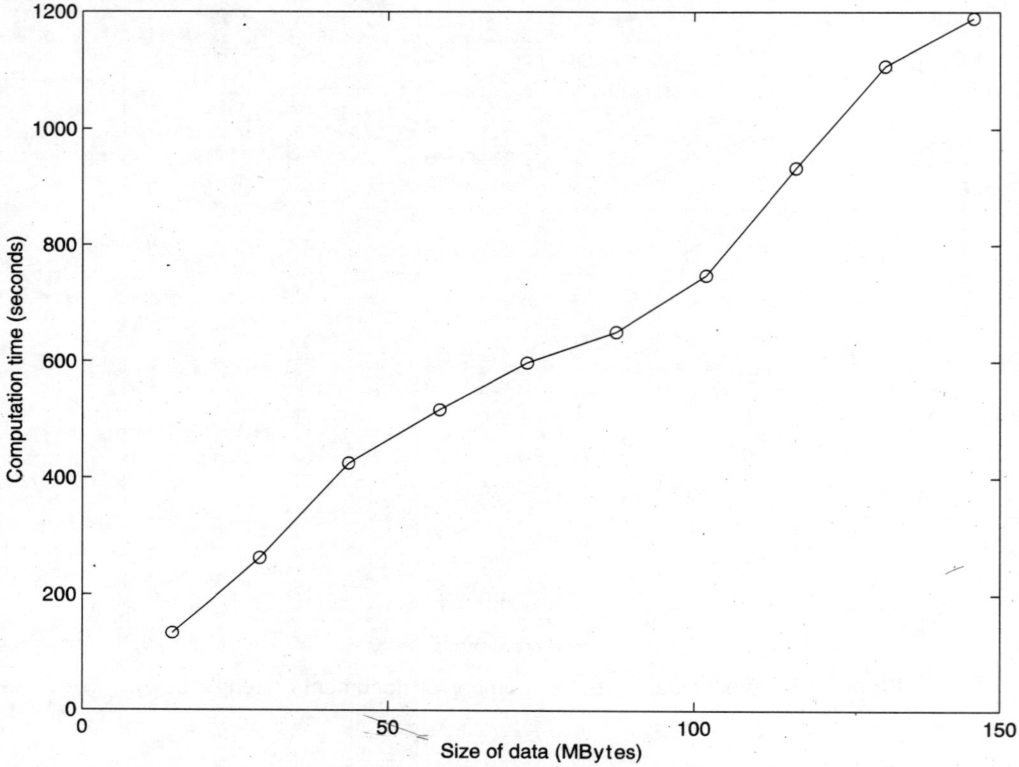

Figure 1.8: Computation time vs. size of data.

that we consume less than 18 MBytes of main memory to preprocess the entire NSF collection of 113716 documents. Extrapolating this number to a collection of one million documents, we see that 160 MBytes of main memory would be sufficient, which implies that our algorithms can carry out this large task on a single workstation with just 256 MBytes of main memory. From Figure 1.8 we see that the entire NSF data set is preprocessed in less than 20 minutes. Note that this includes disk I/O time. Our implementation is multi-threaded and hence the time taken is not very sensitive to the traffic over the Network File Server.

5.1.2 Clustering Results

In this section, we examine the speed and quality of the clustering algorithm. As discussed in Section 4.1, the spherical *k-means* algorithm forms *k* clusters in $O(nz \cdot k)$ time. Figure 1.9 gives the time taken to cluster the NSF data set (113716 documents, 26424 words, 8141987 non-zero entries) into a varied number of clusters. Times for both the original clustering algorithm and its modification that uses similarity estimation are shown (see Section 4.2). The similarity estimation technique yields considerable savings in computation time when the number of clusters is large. The running time of the algorithm is also seen to increase linearly with the number of clusters *k*. To form 100 clusters, 1400 seconds of computational time is needed. On the other hand, to form 12 clusters only 200 seconds are needed. Thus, combined with 4the preprocessing time of about 1190 seconds, the entire clustering process for 12 clusters is seen to take only about 23 minutes.

We now present a sample clustering obtained by the spherical *k*-means 8 algorithm. We clustered the entire set of 113716 documents into 12 clusters. In the

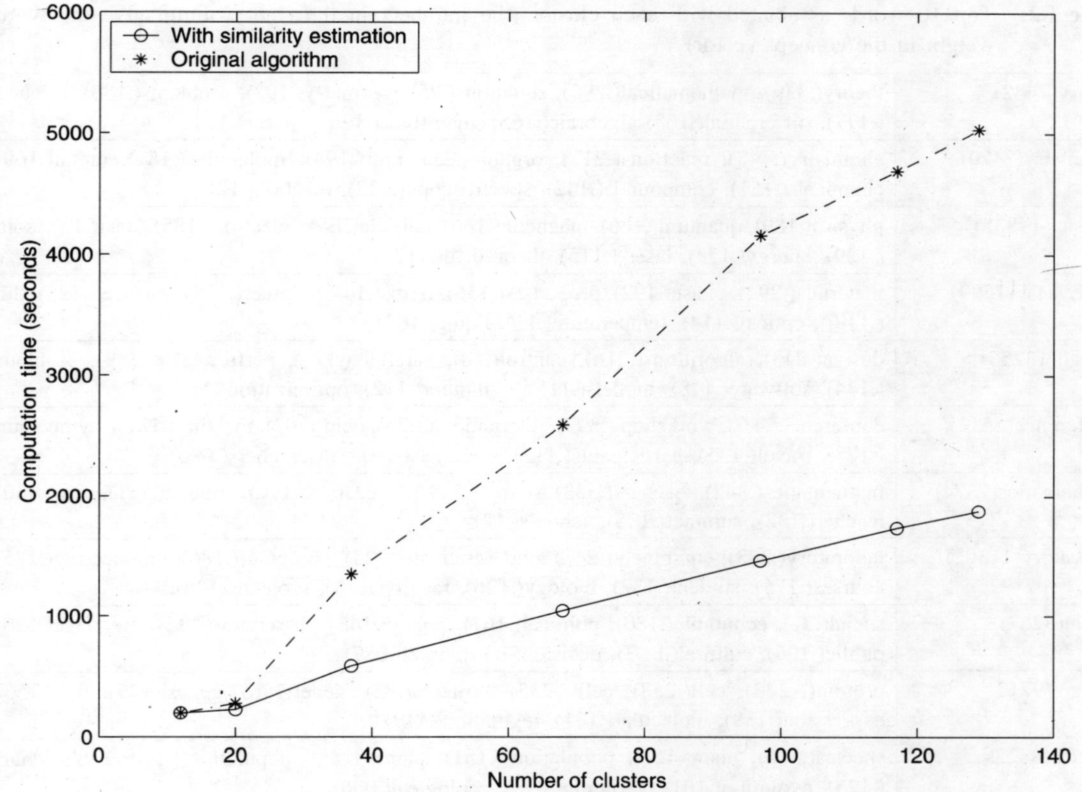

Figure 1.9: Time required to cluster the NSF collection.

following table, we have listed the 10 dominant words and their weights in each of the concept vectors that correspond to the 12 clusters. Note that we have denoted each of the 12 clusters by the dominant word, e.g., 'theory', 'chemistry', 'physics', etc. By examining the top 10 words it is easy to see the 'concept' contained in each cluster. For example, the 'conference' cluster containing 6652 documents appears to be about NSF awards that support conferences, meetings, workshops and symposiums for international scientists and researchers.

We now see the extent to which our clustering algorithm is able to recover the 8 NSF classes: BIO, CSE, EHR, ENG, GEO, MPS, OPP and SBE. The following gives the confusion matrix between the 12 clusters and 8 classes.

Note that the largest number in each row of the above table is boldfaced. We have ordered the clusters and classes so that the confusion matrix has large numbers near the diagonal. The fact that the numbers near the diagonal are larger than those away from the diagonals implies that many of the clusters can be identified with NSF organizations. For example, the 'theory' and 'chemistry' clusters can be identified with MPS, the 'social' cluster with SBE, the 'protein' and 'species' clusters with BIO and the 'ocean' cluster can be identified with GEO. Interestingly, some of the clusters indicate the multidisciplinary nature of some NSF organizations. The 'conference' cluster is seen to have many awards from MPS, ENG, SBE and BIO but no particular organization is dominant. Also, organizations such as MPS are seen to have subcategories 'mathematical theory', 'chemistry reactions' and 'quantum physics'.

The numbers in the confusion matrix also indicate the inter-relationships between various NSF

Table 1.2: Top 10 words associated with each cluster (the numbers in the right column give the word's weight in the concept vector)

theory(7442)	theory(.339), mathematical(.295), equations(.25), geometry(.192), problems(.186), sciences (.177), differential(.168) algebraic(.165), manifolds(.126), spaces(.114)
chemistry(7420)	chemistry(.448), reactions(.217), organic(.21), nmr(.194), molecules(.182), metal(.169), chemical (.151), compounds(.142), spectroscopy(.122), reaction(.12)
physics (9835)	physics(.189), quantum(.166), magnetic(.166), particle(.144), electron(.135), stars(.13), solar (.129), energy(.123), laser (.115), theoretical(.112)
materia1s(11589)	materials(.292), phase(.192), properties(.156), fi1ms(.14), polymer(.135), surface (.125), thin (.11.6), optical(.114), temperature(.11), liquid(.107)
design(13255)	design(.243), algorithms(.216), control(.18), parallel (.175), performance(.149), problems (.144), software(.118), models(.115), computer(.112), optimization(.1)
conference(6652)	conference(.4 7), workshop (.399), international(.23), held(.207), meeting(.181), symposium (.178), travel(.135), participants(.112), scientists(.107), researchers(.096)
mathematics(7374)	mathematics(.342), teachers(.333), school(.259), education(.177), college(.151), year(.150), teacher(.132), summer(.125), schools(.12)
laboratory(11302)	laboratory(.303), equipment(.241), undergraduate(.225), computer(.186), engineering(.185), courses(.175), student(.132), biology(.126), faculty(.124), projects(.124)
social(8267)	social(.27), economic(.180), political(.167), policy(.143), dissertation(.13), language(.126), public(.104), cultural(.1 03), decision(.1), market(.087)
protein(9212)	protein(. 273), cell(.258), cells(.235), proteins(.22), gene(.196), genes(.179), dna(.153), expression(.138), molecular(.131), regulation(.119)
species(8822)	species(.326), plant(.167), populations(.151), plants(.133), population(.125), evolutionary (.125), evolution(.101), variation(.098), ecological(.096)
ocean(12546)	ocean(.232), ice(.194), climate(.153), mantle(.147), sea(.134), water(.118), seismic(.1 06), circulation(.097), pacific(.096), isotopic(.092)

Table 1.3: Confusion matrix between the 8 "true" classes and 12 clusters for the entire NSF collection

	MPS	ENG	CSE	EHR	SBE	OPP	BIO	GEO
theory(7442)	**6502**	196	240	92	336	0	43	33
chemistry(7420)	**4747**	572	8	991	363	24	377	338
physics(9835)	**4901**	1649	31	146	849	147	176	1936
materials(11589)	3257	**7094**	33	171	541	12	89	392
design(13255)	952	4754	**5850**	357	840	5	349	148
conference(6652)	1149	**1767**	544	383	1176	146	947	540
mathematics(7374)	410	208	772	**5658**	143	21	65	97
laboratory(11302)	767	1344	541	**5658**	209	410	1036	1337
social(8267)	84	438	221	317	**6686**	126	326	69
protein(9212)	164	784	20	162	383	25	7578	96
species(8822)	61	153	7	121	1690	252	**5602**	936
ocean(12546)	43	406	8	56	509	1599	180	**9745**

organizations. For example, the 'materials' cluster indicates closeness between MPS and ENG while the 'design' cluster shows the closeness between ENG and CSE.

The quality measures of purity and entropy for this clustering are given in the following table.

Despite the above quality measures, it is sometimes best to have an informal way of examining a clustering. For this purpose, we have created a sequence of web pages to browse through the clusters, and the documents and keywords contained in them. The clustering presented above is available at: `http://www.cs.utexas.edu/users/dml/demos/nsfbrowser/`.

Table 1.4: Purity and entropy results for the computed clusters of the entire NSF collection

Cluster	Purity	Entropy
theory	.87369	.275307
chemistry	.639757	.585657
physics	.498322	.670075
materials	.612132	.499253
design	.441343	.643922
conference	.265634	.911829
mathematics	.76729	.429274
laboratory	.500619	.766223
social	.808758	.397713
protein	.822623	.347316
species	.635003	.535591
ocean	.776742	.389061

6. CONCLUSIONS AND FUTURE WORK

In this paper, we have presented a time and memory efficient scheme for clustering very large document collections. We employ a multithreaded approach to reading and preprocessing the documents to mitigate disk I/O costs, and use the effective spherical *k*-means algorithm to cluster the documents. Our experimental results show that we are able to preprocess and cluster 113,716 NSF award abstracts in 23 minutes on a Sun workstation with modest memory consumption. We have also demonstrated that the quality of the clustering is good. Based on the experiments we have done in this paper, we predict that we can use our scheme to cluster a million documents into 12 clusters in less than 4 hours on a Sun workstation.

In future work, we will continue our focus on improving the efficiency and scalability of our scheme. The dot product computation between all the document vectors and concept vectors is the computational bottleneck in the spherical *k*-means algorithm. To cut down on this computation, techniques like "truncation" which project each document vector onto a small subspace of the total word space will be investigated, see [SS97]. Meanwhile, more sophisticated handling of I/O threads will be studied in order to cut down the I/O cost which is the bottleneck for preprocessing. Parallelizing the whole process can be one of the approaches. Hierarchical clustering will also be studied in future work to discover the inherent hierarchical structure and the 'correct' number of clusters in the data set.

REFERENCES

[BGG+98] D. Boley, M. Gini, R. Gross, E.-H. Han, K. Hastings, G. Karypis, V. Kumar, B. Mobasher, and J. Moore. Document categorization and query generation on the World Wide-Web using WebACE. *AI Review,* 1998.

[Cal99] Brent Callaghan. *NFS Illustrated.* Addison-Wesley, 1999.

[CKPT92] D.R. Cutting, D.R. Karger, J.O. Pedersen, and J.W. Tukey. Scatter/gather: A cluster-based approach to browsing large document collections. In *ACM SIGIR,* 1992.

[DGL89] I. Duff, R. Grimes, and J. Lewis. Sparse matrix test problems. *ACM Trans Math Soft,* pages 1–14, 1989.

[DH73] R.O. Duda and P.E. Hart. *Pattern Classification and Scene Analysis.* Wiley, 1973.

[DM01] I.S. Dhillon and D.S. Modha. Concept decompositions for n large sparse text data using clustering. *Machine Learning,* 42(1):143–175, January 2001. Also appears as IBM Research Report RJ 10147, July 1999.

[FBY92] W.B. Frakes and R. Baeza-Yates. *Information Retrieval: Data Structures and Algorithms.* Prentice Hall, Englewood Cliffs, New Jersey, 1992.

[GJW82] M.R. Garey, D.S. Johnson, and H.S. Witsenhausen. The complexity of the generalized Lloyd-Max problem. *IEEE Trans. Inform. Theory,* 28(2):255–256, 1982.

[Hea78] J. Heaps. *Information Retrieval-Computational and Theoretical Aspects.* Academic Press, 1978.

[Kol97] T.G. Kolda. *Limited-Memory Matrix Methods with Applications.* PhD thesis, The Applied Mathematics Program, University of Maryland, College Park, Maryland, 1997.

[KPR98] Jon Kleinberg, C. H. Papadimitriou, and P. Raghavan. A microeconomic view of data mining. *Data Mining and Knowledge Discovery,* 2(4):311–324, December 1998.

[Mit97] Tom M. Mitchell. *Machine Learning.* McGraw-Hill, 1997.

[MS96] D. Musser and A. Saini. *STL Tutorial and Reference Guide.* Addison-Wesley, 1996.

[NBF96] Bradford Nichols, Bick Buttlar, and Jackie Proulx Farrell. *Pthreads Programming.* O'Reilly & Associates, Inc., 981 Chestnut Street, Newton, MA 02164, USA, 1996.

[Pax96] Vern Paxson. Flex user manual, November 1996.

[Ras92] E. Rasmussen. Clustering algorithms. In William B. Frakes and Ricardo Baeza-Yates, editors, *Information Retrieval: Data Structures and Algorithms,* pages 419–442. Prentice Hall, Englewood Cliffs, New Jersey, 1992.

[SB88] G. Salton and C. Buckley. Term-weighting approaches in automatic text retrieval. *Information Processing & Management,* 4(5):513–523, 1988.

[SGM00] A. Strehl, J. Ghosh, and R. Mooney. Impact of similarity measures on web-page clustering. In *Proceedings of the AAAI2000 Workshop on Artificial Intelligence for Web Search,* pages 58-64, Austin, Texas) July 2000. AAAI/ MIT Press.

[SM83] G. Salton and M.J. McGill. *Introduction to Modern Retrieval.* McGraw-Hill Book Company, 1983.

[SS97] H. Schütze and C. Silverstein. Projections for efficient document clustering. In *ACM SIGIR,* 1997.

[Wil88] P. Willet. Recent trends in hierarchic document clustering: a critical review. *Information Processing* and *Management,* 24(5):577–597, 1988.

[ZE98] O. Zamir and O. Etzioni. Web document clustering: A feasibility demonstration. In *ACM SIGIR,* 1998.

[Zip49] G.K. Zipf. *Human Behavior and the Principle of Least Effort.* Addison Wesley, Reading, MA, 1949.

CASE STUDY 5 SUMMARY

This case study comes from a book titled Data Mining for Scientific and Engineering Applications published in 2001. I am particularly grateful for Springer-Verlag to give permission for including this very good article in the book.

Dhillon, I.S., Fan, J., and Guan, Y., Efficient Clustering of Very Large Document Collections, in *Data Mining for Scientific and Engineering Applications*, Kamath, C., Kegelmeyer, P., and Grossman R.L. (Eds.), pp. 357–381, Kluwer, 2001.

The case study deals with clustering of a very large collection, more than 100,000, of documents efficiently. A preprocessing algorithm is presented to extract the required information followed by use of the K-means algorithm to cluster 113,736 documents.

CASE STUDY 5 EXERCISES

1. Explain what preprocessing was carried out and why it was necessary.
2. How was the K-means method used? Was it different from what is described in the chapter?
3. How was the efficiency of the K-means method improved to deal with large numbers of documents?
4. Comment on the results obtained in the case study. How can you judge if the results were good or not?

CHAPTER

6 Web Data Mining

LEARNING OBJECTIVES

After completing this chapter, you will be able to:

- Learn what Web data mining is about
- Understand relevant Web terminology
- Describe the main topics of Web content mining
- Understand Web structure mining
- Learn Web usage mining
- Find additional resources about Web data mining

6.1 INTRODUCTION

In a short time, since 1995, the Web revolution has had a profound impact on the way we search and find information at home and at work. The Web has also become an enormously important tool for communicating ideas, conducting business and entertainment. The exponential growth in the Web has been unbelievable. From the beginning in the early 1990s the Web has grown to more than ten billion pages indexed by Google in 2013[1] with millions of people from all over the world (some estimates suggest over 500 million or about 10% of the world's population) accessing them every day. In the USA, the use of the Web continues to grow and in 2013 about three-quarters of people went online and spent an average of 12.5 hours per week online. The Web has become the number

[1]Our estimate is based on the number of pages indexed by Google in 2013. In practice it is only a lower bound since no search index is able to index the entire Web (estimated to be more than one Trillion pages) and a union of Web pages indexed by all major search engines is larger than what Google indexes.

one source for information for Internet users although the credibility of Web information appears to have declined somewhat recently according to a 2013 survey.

Millions of Web pages are added every day (estimates vary between one and seven million pages a day) and millions of others are modified or deleted. Web pages are written in a variety of languages and they provide information in a variety of mediums including text, animation, images, photos, sound, music and video as well as a variety of scripts and symbols. The information is very diverse in content as well in topics ranging from Australian animals to symptoms of depression to rare books published in India hundreds of years ago. One of the most important features of the Web is the hyperlink by which one Web page provides links to other pages allowing a user to traverse the Web following links of interest to him or her. The links are set up by the author.

Growth in the Web and its use is also illustrated by the growth in Internet traffic. Analysis of data from a number of sources clearly shows that Internet traffic has been almost doubling every year since 1997. Although there is some indication that the rate of growth may have declined slightly, the traffic is still growing vigorously.

Pitkow (1998) presents a variety of interesting information about the Web although the information is several years old now and the Web has changed and grown enormously in the interim. He notes that page popularity follows Zipf's Law (the 20/80 rule), that is, some 20% of the sites are responsible for about 80% of requests on the Web. He also notes that small images dominate the Web traffic. This may be changing with better bandwidth becoming available to users. The life span of a Web page is estimated to be 50 days although some more recent investigations suggest that page life span is even shorter.

The Web is an open medium. There is no one monitoring what is published and there is no mechanism to control the quality or appropriateness of the content. The Web has hate sites, love sites, pornography and anti-pornography sites, sites on hobbies, sports, politics, religion, medicine, cults, academic disciplines, music, movies, scams and everything else under the sun. The quality of these sites varies from awful to superb with most sites somewhere in between. The Web does not have a catalogue like libraries do but it has search engines, directories, portals and indexes to help users browse a wide variety of information.

The openness has meant that the Web has grown exponentially which is its strength as well as its weakness. The strength is that one can find information on just about anything however esoteric the topic even if the quality of information varies. The weakness of an open Web is that there is the problem of abundance of information. For example searching for the phrase "data mining" on Google in March 2014 found more than 7.2 million pages. How does one plough through such a large collection of documents to find those that are the most useful? How reliable is the ranking provided by the search engines that retrieve such large numbers of documents? It is the aim of Web mining to help with problems like this.

Early attempts to assist users find what they were looking for resulted in the creation of directories like Yahoo! Some directories charged fees to place a website in a prominent position in the directory. Others tried to control the quality of links in the directory by human evaluation of sites. Some of this has come to an end due to the huge continued growth of the Web and the resulting high cost of maintaining such sites and the shortage of venture capital after the dotcom bust of 2000.

There is no agreed definition of Web mining but we present one simple definition.

Web Mining

Web Mining is the application of data mining techniques to find interesting and potentially useful knowledge from Web data. It is normally expected that either the hyperlink structure of the Web or the Web log data or both have been used in the mining process.

OVERVIEW

The next section, Section 6.2, explains briefly the three major categories of Web Mining. These are Web Content Mining, Web Structure Mining and Web Usage Mining. Section 6.3 defines some of the Web terminology as well as graph terminology. Some characteristics of the Web are also presented. Section 6.4 discusses locality and hierarchy in the Web. It briefly explains how most website are organised. The next section, Section 6.5, focuses on Web Content Mining. A number of techniques used for Web Content Mining are described including clustering and finding similar pages using fingerprinting. Section 6.6 deals with Web Usage Mining followed by Web Structure Mining in Section 6.7. This includes a description of the HITS algorithm for finding *hubs* and *authorities*. An example of the algorithm is presented. Finally Section 6.8 describes some Web mining software.

6.2 WEB MINING

Web mining is usually divided into the following three categories. We first briefly introduce the three topics. Detailed descriptions are then presented in the sections that follow.

6.2.1 Web Content Mining

Web content mining deals with discovering useful information or knowledge from the Web. It goes well beyond using keywords in a search engine. In contrast to Web usage mining and Web structure mining, Web content mining focuses on the content of the Web pages rather than the links. As noted earlier, Web content is a very rich information resource consisting of many types of information, for example unstructured free text, image, audio, video, animation and metadata as well as hyperlinks. A variety of techniques are therefore needed to retrieve content of interest. The content of web pages includes no machine readable semantic information. Search engines, *subject directories*, *intelligent agents, cluster analysis* and *portals* are employed to find what a user might be looking for. It has been suggested that users should be able to pose more sophisticated queries than just specifying the keywords.

6.2.2 Web Structure Mining

Web structure mining deals with discovering and modelling the link structure of the Web. Research has been carried out to model the Web based on the topology of the hyperlinks. This can help in discovering similarity between sites or in discovering important sites for a particular topic or discipline or in discovering Web communities.

6.2.3 Web Usage Mining

Web usage mining primarily deals with understanding user behaviour in interacting with the Web or with a website. One of the aims is to obtain information that may assist website reorganisation or assist site adaptation to better suit the user. The mined data often includes data logs of users' interactions with the Web. The logs include the Web server logs, proxy server logs and browser logs. The logs include information about the referring pages, user identification, time a user spends at a site and the sequence of pages visited. Information is also collected via cookie files. While Web structure mining shows that page *A* has a link to page *B*, Web usage mining shows who or how many people took that link, which site they came from and where they went when they left page B.

The three categories above are not independent since Web structure mining is closely related to Web content mining and both are related to Web usage mining.

We need to first describe some basic Web terminology and present some background about graphs before we discuss Web mining. We also present some results of investigations about the size and complexity of the Web.

6.3 WEB TERMINOLOGY AND CHARACTERISTICS

The Web is seen as having a two-tier architecture. The first tier is a Web server that serves the information to the client machine and the second tier is the client that displays that information to the user. This architecture is supported by three Web standards, namely HTML (Hyper-Text Markup Language) for defining the Web document content, URLs (Uniform Resource Locators) for naming and identifying remote information resources in the global Web world, and HTTP (Hyper-Text Transfer Protocol) for managing the transfer of information from the server to the client. We do not discuss these standards here.

We now define some of the Web terminology based on the work of World Wide Web Consortium (W3C).

The *World Wide Web (WWW)* is the set of all the nodes which are interconnected by hypertext links.

A *link* expresses one or more (explicit or implicit) relationships between two or more resources. Links may also be established within a document by using *anchors*.

A *Web page* is a collection of information, consisting of one or more Web resources, intended to be rendered simultaneously, and identified by a single URL. A *website* is a collection of interlinked Web pages, including a homepage, residing at the same network location.

In addition to simple text, HTML allows embedding of images, sounds and video streams.

A client *browser* is the primary user interface to the Web. It is a program which allows a person to view the contents of Web pages, and for navigating from one page to another. A Web browser allows launching of applications such as a Postscript reader, an Acrobat reader, a QuickTime player or an email client.

A *uniform resource locator (URL)* is an identifier for an abstract or physical resource, for example a server and a file path or index. URLs are location dependent and each URL contains four distinct parts, namely, the protocol types (usually http), the name of the Web server, the directory path and the file name. If a file name is not specified, index.html is assumed.

A *Web server* serves Web pages using http to client machines so that a browser can display them.

A *client* is the role adopted by an application when it is retrieving a Web resource.

A *proxy* is an intermediary which acts as both a server and a client for the purpose of retrieving resources on behalf of other clients. Clients using a proxy know the proxy is present and that it is an intermediary.

A *domain name server* is a distributed database of name to address mappings. When a DNS server looks up a computer name, it either finds it in its list, or asks another DNS server which knows more names.

A *cookie* is the data sent by a Web server to a Web client, to be stored locally by the client and sent back to the server on subsequent requests.

Obtaining information from the Web using a search engine is called information "*pull*" while information sent to users is called information "*push*". For example, users may register with a site and then information is sent ("pushed") to such users without them requesting it.

6.3.1 Graph Terminology

We define a *directed graph* as a set of *nodes* (that correspond to pages on the Web) denoted by, *V* and *edges* (which correspond to links on the Web) denoted by, *E*. Thus a graph is where all edges are directed, just like a link that points from one page to another, and may be considered as an ordered pair of nodes, the nodes that they link.

An undirected graph may also be represented by nodes and edges (*V*, *E*) but the edges have no direction specified. Therefore an undirected graph is not like the pages and links on the Web unless we assume the possibility of traversal in both directions. The back button on the browsers does provide the possibility of back traversal once a link has been traversed in one direction, but in general both way traversal of links is not possible on the Web.

A graph may be searched either by a *breadth first* search or by a *depth first* search. The breadth first search is based on first searching all the nodes that can be reached from the node where the search is starting and once these nodes have been searched, searching the nodes at the next level that can be reached from those nodes and so on. The depth first search is based on first searching any unvisited descendants of a given node first, then visiting the node and then any brother nodes. Essentially the search algorithm involves going down before going across to a brother node.

The diameter of the graph is defined as the maximum of the minimum distances between all possible ordered node pairs (*u*, *v*), that is, it is the maximum number of links that one would need to follow starting from any page *u* to reach any page *v* assuming that the best path has been followed.

Broder et al. (2000) carried out an investigation of the structure of the Web based on an analysis of about 200 million pages and 1.5 billion links. They first analysed the number of in-links (links pointing to a page) and the number of out-links (links pointing from a page) and found that most pages have only a few links pointing to them and only a few links being pointed by them. They found that both in-degrees and out-degrees follow power laws.

The results are very similar to what happens in academia. The number of publications of scholarly papers is important and is often used to evaluate an academic's research performance, but more recently people have started looking at not only how many papers a person has published but how many other people have referred to (or cited) the papers he/she has published (assuming that these people have not only read the papers but found them important). This generally works well although it may be possible that a group of researchers, perhaps working at the same institution, may make a pact that they will try to cite each other's papers as much as possible (one assumes that this does not happen frequently). As an example of the citation approach, in the decision tree field the most highly cited papers are by Ross Quinlan from Sydney. More than 1000 other researchers have cited his papers and he is therefore the foremost authority on decision trees. Very few papers in computing have been cited more than 1000 times or even 100 times, just like very few websites are very popular. We can use a similar approach to rank websites.

There is much interesting literature on citation analysis that is useful for analysing Web pages. For example, there is a law called Lotka's Inverse-Square Law that states that the number of authors publishing n papers is about $1/n^2$ of those publishing only one paper and the proportion of all authors that make a single contribution is about 60%. This asserts that most academics publish just one paper and the number of academics publishing multiple papers goes down so quickly that less than 1% publish 10 or more papers. Similarly there are many Web pages that are linked only to one other page (many not even linked to any) and the percentage of pages that have multiple links pointing to them declines rapidly.

As noted above, the number of *in-links* and the number of *out-links* follow a *power law*. The fraction of Web pages with i in-links was found to be proportional to $1/i^{2.1}$ and the fraction of Web pages with i out-links was found to be proportional to $1/i^{2.72}$. Thus there are only about 10% of pages that have three links pointing to them and there are only about 5% of pages with four links pointing to them. Therefore, relatively, only a small number of pages are popular in terms of in-links. A similar law applies to out-links, with only a small percentage of pages pointing to say five other pages. This phenomenon could be viewed as a "rich get richer" concept. The more links a page has, the more likely it is to get new links. However it appears that it is not quite true in some situations, in particular for smaller connectivities among Web pages of the same type.

It is interesting to note that the above conclusions apply not only to the Web as a whole but also to a significantly smaller subset of the Web, for example a thematic subset related to a particular sport or to a particular discipline or even to a particular company (e.g. IBM). The Web therefore displays self-similarity and is more like a fractal where various components have the same structure as the Web as a whole.

Broder et al. (2000) also investigated the structure of the Web and found that 90% of pages analysed, form a single undirected graph. If we could follow both forward and backward links then the Web is a very well connected graph, but considering the Web as a directed graph shows that most pairs of pages are not connected or are connected by a rather long chain of links.

It was found that the Web is not a ball of highly connected nodes. It displayed interesting structural properties (the structure appearing more like a 'bow-tie') and the Web could be conveniently divided into the following five components:

1. The strongly connected core (SCC)—This part of the Web was found to consist of about 30% of the Web, which is still very large given more than four billion pages on the Web in 2004. This core may be considered the heart of the Web and its main property is that pages in the core can reach each other following directed edges (i.e. hyperlinks).
2. The IN group—This part of the Web was found to consist of about 20% of the Web. The main property of the IN group is that pages in the group can reach the SCC but cannot be reached from it.

3. The OUT group—This part of the Web was found to consist of about 20% of the Web. The main property of the OUT group is that pages in this group can be reached from the SCC but cannot reach the SCC.
4. Tendrils—This part of the Web was found to consist of about 20% of the Web. The main property of pages in this group is that the pages cannot be reached by the SCC and cannot reach the SCC. It does not imply that these pages have no linkages to pages outside the group since they could well have linkages from the IN group and to the OUT group.
5. The disconnected group—This part of the Web was found to be less than 10% of the Web and is essentially disconnected from the rest of the Web world. These pages could include for example personal pages at many sites that link to no other page and have no links to them.

6.3.2 Size of the Web

Before discussing the size of the Web, we discuss the concept of *deep Web* and the *shallow Web*. The deep Web includes information stored in searchable databases often inaccessible to search engines. This information can often only be accessed by using each website's interface. Some of this information may be available only to subscribers. The shallow Web (or indexable Web) is the information on the Web that the search engines can access without accessing the Web databases.

Often large amounts of information, including large documents (e.g. technical reports, theses), are stored in the databases. It has been estimated[2] that the deep Web is about 500 times the size of the shallow Web. In some ways the nature of the information in the deep Web and shallow Web is somewhat different. In any case, search engines that access the deep Web as well as the shallow Web are being developed.

It has been found that the (shallow) Web is a rather large directed graph with a diameter of over 500. The diameter of the central core is about 30. The probability that a path exists from a randomly chosen source page to a randomly chosen destination page has been estimated to be only about 24% and when a directed path exists, its average length is about 16. It has been suggested that most pairs of pages on the Web are separated by less than 20 links. Some call it the "small world" phenomenon. Others have found that in many cases it is not even possible to get from any one page to another page while in other cases it cannot be done in the small number of clicks that the "small world" concept would have one believe.

We have noted above that the Web consisted of more than four billion pages in mid-2004. Assuming that each Web page is on the average 15K in size, the Web in 2004 was more than 60 Terabytes. The Web continues to grow rapidly, doubling in less than two years, and so, as noted earlier, it is estimated to be over 80 Terabytes at the end of 2004. If the growth of the Web continues (there are some suggestions that the growth is moderating) it will be approaching a Petabyte in size in the next 5–10 years. Also, if we include the size of the deep Web in estimating the size of the Web then the Web is already much larger than one Petabyte.

The Web pages are very dynamic, changing almost daily. One study found that 23% of pages

[2] Based on an article "Invisible Web Gets Deeper" by Danny Sullivan, 2 August 2000. http://searchenginewatch.com/sereport/article.php/2162871

changed daily while in the *dotcom domain* 40% changed daily, somewhat difficult to believe. It was found that in 10 days, half of the URLs were not valid, that is, the pages were removed or moved to another URL and could not be found. On the other hand, some people claim that perhaps as many as seven million new Web pages are added to the Web every day. Perhaps Web pages are being used for other purposes as well, e.g. communicating information to small number of individuals via the Web rather than via email. For example, my last travel itinerary was sent to me as an URL. In many cases such use of the Web makes good sense, for example it is better to put even short announcements in an enterprise on the Web rather than sending them by email since emails sit in many mailboxes wasting disk storage and putting information on the Web can be more effective as well as help in maintaining a record of communications. If such uses grow, which appears likely, then a very large number of such Web pages with a short life span and low connectivity to other pages are likely to be generated each day. The large numbers of websites that disappear every day do create enormous problems on the Web. Links from even well known sites do not always work. Not all results of a search engine search are guaranteed to work. URLs cited in scholarly publications also cannot be relied upon to be still available. A study of papers presented at the World Wide Web (WWW) conferences found that links cited in them had a decay rate that grew with the age of the papers. Abandoned sites therefore are much more than just an annoyance.

To overcome these problems, it may become necessary to categorise Web pages. The following categorisation is one possibility:

1. A Web page that is guaranteed not to change ever
2. A Web page that will not delete any content, may add content/links but the page will not disappear
3. A Web page that may change content/links but the page will not disappear
4. A Web page without any guarantee

The Web is increasingly becoming multi-lingual. In 2000, about 80% of all Web pages were in English and more than 90% of e-commerce websites were in English. There are now more non-English sites appearing on the Web.

6.3.3 Web Metrics

As we have seen in this section, there have been a number of studies that have tried to measure the Web, for example, its size and its structure. There are a number of other properties about the Web that are useful to measure. We discuss some of them briefly.

Some of the measures are based on distances between the nodes of the Web graph. It is possible to define how well connected a node is by using the concept of centrality of a node. *Centrality* may be *out-centrality* which is based on distances measured from the node using its out-links while *in-centrality* is based on distances measured from other nodes that are connected to the node using the in-links. Based on these metrics, it is possible to define the concept of compactness that varies from 0 to 1, 0 for a completely disconnected Web graph and 1 for a fully connected Web graph.

Perhaps the most important measurements about Web pages are about a page's relevance and its quality. Relevance is usually related to a user query since it concerns the user finding pages that are relevant to his/her query and may be defined in a number of ways. A simple approach involves relevance to be measured by the number of query terms that appear in the page. Another approach is based on in-links from relevant pages. In this approach relevance of a page may be defined as the sum of the number of query terms in the pages that refer to the page. Relevance may also use the concept of co-citation. In co-citation, if both pages *a* and *b*, point to a page *c*, then it is assumed that *a* and *b* have a common interest. Similarly if *a* points to both *b* and *c* then we may assume that *b* and *c* also share a common interest.

Quality is often independent of the user query and is not determined by page content since there is no automatic means of evaluating the quality of the content. Quality is primarily determined by the link structure. There are several notions of link structure that are used in determining quality. For example if page *a* points to page *b* then it is assumed that page *a* is endorsing page *b* and we can have some confidence in the quality of page *b*. Similar to the concept of citations index as used in scholarly publications, hyperlinks may be used to determine the impact or quality of a Web page. The concept of page rank discussed in the next chapter is also based on the idea of citation index.

6.4 LOCALITY AND HIERARCHY IN THE WEB

It is well known that most social structures tend to organise themselves as hierarchies. The Web is no different and shows a strong hierarchical structure. A website of any enterprise usually has the homepage as the root of the tree like in any hierarchical structure and as we go down the tree we find more and more detailed information about some aspects of the enterprise. For example, if one looks at a typical university website the homepage will provide some basic information about the institution and then provide links for example to:

Prospective students
Staff
Research
Information for current students
Information for current staff

The prospective students node will have a number of links for example to:

Courses offered
Admission requirements
Information for international students
Information for graduate students
Scholarships available
Semester dates

Similar structures would be expected for other nodes at this level of the tree.

In addition to the hierarchical nature of websites, it has been shown that Web structure has a strong locality feature to the extent that almost two thirds of all links are to sites within the enterprise domain. The one third links to sites outside the enterprise domain tend to have a higher percentage of broken links. The distance between local links tends to be quite small (distance may be measured by the number of URL directories that must be removed and added). About half of the local links have been found to be within the directory of the Web page (these links are often bidirectional) and a quarter of the local links refer to pages higher up or lower down the tree hierarchy.

Furthermore, websites are increasingly fetching information from a database to ensure that the information is accurate and timely. A recent study found that almost 40% of all URLs fetched information from a database.

It is possible to classify Web pages into several types:

- ***Homepage or the Head page:*** These pages representing an entry point for an enterprise website (and therefore often the most frequently visited) or a section within the enterprise or an individual's Web page.
- ***Index page:*** These pages that assist the user to navigate through the enterprise's website. A homepage in some cases may also act as an index page.
- ***Reference page:*** These pages that provide some basic information that is used by a number of other pages. For example, each page in a website may have a link to a page that provides the enterprise's privacy policy.
- ***Content page:*** These pages that only provide content and have little role in assisting a user's navigation. Often these pages are larger in size, have few out-links, and are well down the tree in a website. They are often the leaf nodes of a tree.

The above classification might suggest that large enterprises would have large, broad and deep trees. It appears not to be so. The directory trees of most enterprises have been found to be broad and shallow. Because of this, more than 80% of all URLs have been found to be leaf nodes in websites' trees. Perhaps such structures in which the homepage is also an index page are preferred because it has been found that pages close to the homepage tend to have higher hit rates compared to those that are further away. Also, it has been found that pages that have higher numbers of out-links have higher hit rates.

A website structure and content is best based on careful analysis of what the most common questions from the users are. The content should be organised in categories in such a way that traversing the site is simple and logical. Current topics can help and so can latest news to keep the visitor involved in the site.

Careful Web user data mining can help. Such mining can answer questions like: Is the user taking the action that the company wishes him/her to take? If not, why not? What should be done to change the content to help the users take the action the company wants them to take?

A number of simple principles have been developed to help design the structure and content of a website. For example, three basic principles are:

1. ***Relevant linkage principle:*** It is assumed that links from a page point to other relevant resources. This is similar to the assumption that is made for citations in scholarly publications, where it is assumed that a publication cites only relevant publications. Links are often assumed to reflect the judgement of the page creator. By providing a link to another page it is assumed that the creator is making a recommendation for the other relevant page.
2. ***Topical unity principle:*** It is assumed that Web pages that are co-cited (i.e. linked from the same pages) are related. Many Web mining algorithms make use of this relevance assumption as a measure of mutual relevance between Web pages.
3. ***Lexical affinity principle:*** It is assumed that the text and the links within a page are relevant to each other. Once again, it is assumed that the text on a page has been chosen carefully by the creator to be related to a theme.

Unfortunately not all pages follow these basic intuitive principles, resulting in difficulties for Web users and Web mining researchers.

Recently some researchers have suggested that it may be better to look at blocks of information on a page rather than the coarser page level since a single page often contains different sections, and hyperlinks in different sections of the page may point to pages that have different topics.

6.5 WEB CONTENT MINING

This area of Web content mining deals with discovering useful information from the Web. Normally when we need to search for content on the Web, we use one of the search engines like *Google* or a subject directory like *Yahoo!* Some search engines find pages based on location and frequency of keywords on the page although some now use the concept of page rank. We will look at the workings of search engines in detail in the next chapter.

If we consider the type of queries that are posed to the search engines we find that if the query is very specific we face the scarcity problem. For example searching for the phrase "when not to use data mining", no page was found on Google in November 2004. If the query is for a broad topic, we face the abundance problem. For example, as noted earlier, a query posed on Google for "data mining" resulted in some 2.6 million pages. How many of these pages are important? How does one work out which are the most important? Because of these problems, the keyword search using a search engine is called *suggestive* of the documents' relevance. The user is then left with the task of finding relevant documents.

Brin (1998) presents an interesting example of finding content on the Web. When one is searching the Web for something of interest, often the relevant material is spread amongst many servers and hosts all over the world. The example shows how the relevant information from a wide variety of sources presented in a wide variety of formats may be integrated for the user. The example involves extracting a relation of books in the form of (author, title) from the Web starting with a very small sample list.

The problem may be defined in more general terms. We wish to build a relation R that has a number of attributes. The information about tuples of R is found on Web pages but is unstructured. The aim is to extract the information and structure it with low error rate.

The algorithm proposed is called Dual Iterative Pattern Relation Extraction (DIPRE). It works as follows:

1. ***Sample:*** Start with a sample S provided by the user.
2. ***Occurrences:*** Find occurrences of tuples starting with those in S. Once tuples are found the context of every occurrence is saved. Let these be O.

$$O \leftarrow S$$

3. ***Patterns:*** Generate patterns based on the set of occurrences O. This requires generating patterns with similar contexts.

$$P \leftarrow O$$

4. ***Match patterns:*** The Web is now searched for the patterns.
5. Stop if enough matches found, else go to step 2.

Step 3 is the difficult part. In this example the pattern is defined as a tuple like (order, URL prefix, prefix, middle, suffix). It may then match strings like (author, middle, title) or (title, middle, author) where middle is some text appearing between the two items. In step 2 it is assumed that the occurrence consists of title and author with a variety of other information.

Web pages are usually semi-structured (e.g. HTML documents). Some Web pages, for example database generated HTML pages, are more structured. Often, however, Web pages consist of unstructured free text data which makes it more difficult to extract information from them.

Unstructured documents may be represented as a bag of words based on the statistics about single words in isolation, ignoring the sequence of words. The bag of words may then be used for classifying or clustering the Web pages. The semi-structured Web pages may be represented based on the HTML structures inside the documents. Some may also use the hyperlink structure. A different approach, called the database approach, involves inferring the structure of a website and transforming the website content into a database. Each of these approaches also needs to deal with the difficult problem of online multimedia resources.

As noted earlier, the Web pages are published without any external control on them. Unlike journal and most conference papers which are refereed, anyone can create a Web page on any topic and put it there for all the world to see. The situation is in fact even worse because in many situations businesses may create pages just to improve their presence on the Web. In the next chapter, we discuss the Google PageRank algorithm that attempts to measure the relative importance of Web pages.

Some of the sophisticated searching tools being developed are based on the work of the artificial intelligence community. These are called *intelligent Web agents*, they have been developed to meet the need for finding relevant content on the Web. Some Web agents replace the work of search engines in finding relevant information given some keywords or topic that the user is searching for. A good example of such agents is *ShopBot* that finds information about a product that the user is searching for. Other Web agents are designed to retrieve and filter information based on link information. Yet others are designed to help an individual by learning user preferences and discovering information based on those preferences. A more detailed discussion of these technologies is outside the scope of this book.

6.5.1 Web Document Clustering

Web document clustering is another approach to finding relevant documents on a topic or about query keywords. As discussed earlier, the popular search engines often return a huge, unmanageable list of documents which contain the keywords that the user specified. Finding the most useful documents from such a large list is usually tedious, often impossible. The user could apply clustering to a set of documents returned by a search engine in response to a query with the aim of finding semantically meaningful clusters, rather than a list of ranked documents, that are easier to interpret. It is not necessary to insist that a document can only belong to one cluster since in some cases it is justified to have the document belong to two or more clusters. Web clustering may be based on content alone, may be based on both content and links or may be exclusively based on links. We consider some different approaches.

Cluster analysis techniques have been discussed in the last chapter. In particular we discussed the K-means method and the agglomerative method. These methods can be used for Web document cluster analysis as well but these methods assume that each document has a fixed set of attributes that appear in all documents. Similarity between documents can then be computed based on these values. One could possibly have a set of words and their frequencies in each document and then use those values for clustering them. Such techniques have generally been found to be inadequate.

We will briefly discuss one approach that takes a different approach and is designed specifically for Web document cluster analysis. It is called Suffix Tree Clustering (STC) and it uses a *phrase-based clustering* approach rather than using single word frequency approach.

In STC, the key requirements of a Web document clustering algorithm include the following:

1. ***Relevance:*** This is the most obvious requirement. We want clusters that are relevant to the user query and cluster similar documents together.
2. ***Browsable summaries:*** The cluster must be easy to understand. The user should be quickly able to browse the description of a cluster and work out whether the cluster is relevant to the query.
3. ***Snippet tolerance:*** The clustering method should not require whole documents and should be able to produce relevant clusters based only on the information that the search engine returns.
4. ***Performance:*** The clustering method should be able to process the results of the search engine quickly and provide the resulting clusters to the user.

We briefly describe the STC algorithm which consists of document cleaning, identifying base clusters and combining base clusters.

STC does not carry out clustering after the full documents have been processed since it would be too time consuming. STC only requires the snippets of text that are returned by the search engine and removes unwanted text that might get in the way of identifying common phrases (e.g. prefixes, suffixes, sentence boundaries, non-word tokens, punctuation marks, etc).

The *second step* of the algorithm uses the cleaned snippets to mark sentence boundaries and then build a suffix tree to efficiently identify a set of documents that share common phrases.

Once a suffix tree has been constructed, a number of base clusters can be derived from it by reading the tree from the root to each leaf which gives a phrase. If such a phrase belongs to more than two snippets then the phrase is considered a base cluster. Each base cluster is given a score based on the number of words in the phrase and the number of snippets that have that phrase.

Many base clusters will be overlapping, since documents often share more than just one phrase. It is therefore necessary to consolidate the clusters. A similarity index for every pair of base clusters is created based on the documents that are in each cluster. If the base clusters are similar they are combined.

In experimentation, the STC algorithm resulted in clusters such that each document belonged to 2.1 clusters on the average. About 70% of the documents were placed in more than one cluster. It has been shown that STC is quite efficient in clustering Web documents.

The STC algorithm is just one approach of clustering Web documents retrieved by a search engine. It is an area of active research and many other techniques have been proposed. Some techniques use incoming links to the retrieved documents, based on the assumption that the incoming links contain more accurate information about a page than the page itself, as providing accurate keywords that describe a document. Another approach takes the list of titles and snippets of documents retrieved and calculate various properties of the phrases found. Clustering is then based on these properties. We will not discuss these methods further.

6.5.2 Finding Similar Web Pages

There is a proliferation of similar or identical documents on the Web. It has been found that almost 30% of all Web pages are very similar to other pages and about 22% (much of the 30%) are virtually identical to other pages. There are many reasons for identical pages. For example:

1. A local copy may have been made to enable faster access to the material
2. FAQs on important topics are duplicated since such pages may be used frequently locally
3. Online documentation of popular software like Unix or LATEX is may be duplicated for local use
4. There are mirror sites that copy highly accessed sites to reduce traffic (e.g. to reduce international traffic from India or Australia)

In some cases, documents are not exactly identical because different formatting might be used at different sites. There may be some customisation or use of templates at different sites. A large document may be split into smaller documents or a composite document may be joined together to build a single document.

In some cases documents that are found useful and are not copyrighted are duplicated because users do not trust the original site continuing to exist, given that a large fraction of URLs disappear regularly.

Copying a single Web page is often called *replication* while copying an entire website is called *mirroring*.

Similarity between Web pages usually means content-based similarity. It is also possible to consider link-based similarity and usage-based similarity. Link-based similarity is related to the concept of co-citation and is primarily used for discovering a core set of Web pages on a topic. Usage-based similarity is useful in grouping pages or users into meaningful groups. Our discussion is focused on content-based similarity which is based on comparing the textual content of the Web pages. The Web pages also have non-text content but we will not consider it.

We define two concepts:

1. ***Resemblance:*** Resemblance of two documents is defined to be a number between 0 and 1 with 1 indicating that the two documents are virtually identical and any value close to 1 indicating that the documents are very similar.
2. ***Containment:*** Containment of one document in another is also defined as a number between 0 and 1 with 1 indicating that the first document is completely contained in the second.

There are a number of ways similarity of documents can be assessed. One brute force approach is to compare two documents using software like the tool *diff* available in the Unix operating system which essentially compares the two documents as files. Other string comparison algorithms may be used to find how many characters need to be deleted, changed or added to transform one document into the other, but these approaches are very expensive if one wishes to compare millions of documents.

There are other issues that must be considered in document matching. Firstly, if we are looking to compare millions of documents then the storage requirement of the method should not be large. Secondly, documents may be in HTML, PDF, Postscript, FrameMaker, TeX, PageMaker or MS Word. They may need to be converted to text for comparison. The conversion can introduce some errors. Finally, the method should be robust, that is, it should not be possible to circumvent the matching process with modest changes to a document.

6.5.3 Fingerprinting

An approach for comparing a large number of documents is based on the idea of fingerprinting documents.

A document may be divided in all possible substrings of length. These substrings are called *shingles*. Based on the shingles we can define resemblance $R(X, Y)$ and containment $C(X, Y)$ between two documents X and Y as follows. We assume $S(X)$ and $S(Y)$ to be a set of shingles for documents X and Y respectively.

$$R(X, Y) = \{S(X) \cap S(Y)\}/\{S(X) \cup S(Y)\}$$

and

$$C(X, Y) = \{S(X) \cap S(Y)\}/\{S(X)\}$$

An algorithm like the following may now be used to find similar documents:

1. Collect all the documents that one wishes to compare
2. Choose a suitable shingle width and compute the shingles for each document
3. Compare the shingles for each pair of documents
4. Identify those documents that are similar

Unfortunately the algorithm is very inefficient for a large collection of documents. The Web is very large and this algorithm requires enormous storage to store the shingles and very long processing time to finish pairwise comparison for say even 100 million documents. This approach is sometimes called *full fingerprinting*.

One might think that perhaps the number of shingles could be reduced if the given documents were just chopped in strings that are L words wide. This unfortunately is unlikely to work since one additional word added to the beginning of one of the documents will result in mismatch between all substrings.

Example 6.1

Consider a simple example in which we wish to find if the two "documents" with the following content are similar:

Document 1 "the Web continues to grow at a fast rate"

Document 2 "the Web is growing at a fast rate"

The first step involves making a set of shingles from the content of each document. We obtain the following if we assume the shingle length to be three words.

Table 6.1 Shingles of length 3 in both documents in Example 6.1

Shingles in Document 1	*Shingles in Document 2*
the Web continues	the Web is
Web continues to	Web is growing
continues to grow	is growing at
to grow at	growing at a
grow at a	at a fast
at a fast	a fast rate
a fast rate	

Comparing the two sets of shingles we find that only two of them are identical. Thus, for this simple example, the documents are not very similar.

For millions of documents that are large compared to those in this simple example the comparison is very expensive. To improve the efficiency of the shingles algorithm, one simple approach could be that only a small number of shingles are selected from the set of all the shingles used for comparison. In the example above, we use three shingles that are the shortest in the number of letters including spaces.

Table 6.2 Number of letters in the shingles in Example 6.1

Shingles in Document 1	*Number of letters*	*Shingles in Document* 2	*Number of letters*
the Web continues	17	the Web is	10
Web continues to	16	Web is growing	14
continues to grow	17	is growing at	13
to grow at	10	growing at a	12
grow at a	9	at a fast	9
at a fast	9	a fast rate	11
a fast rate	11		

For comparison we select the three shortest shingles. For the first document, these are "to grow at", "grow at a" and "at a fast". For the second document the shortest shingles are "the Web is", "at a fast" and "a fast rate". There is only one match out of the three shingles, providing a resemblance ratio of 0.33.

False positives with the original document would be obtained for documents like "the Australian economy is growing at a fast rate". *False negatives* would be obtained for strings like "the Web is growing at quite a rapid rate".

It has been found that small length shingles cause many false positives while larger shingles result in more false negatives.

A better approach would involve randomly selecting shingles of various lengths, not just the shortest, by perhaps choosing shingles on some other basis. One possibility would be to choose them based on their hashed addresses and selecting those with the lowest hash addresses.

It should be noted that this is a rather trivial example that does not fully illustrate the method. If the document was 1000 times longer and we were using say 100 shingles, the performance of the algorithm would be much better.

There are many issues in comparing documents using fingerprinting that we have ignored in our discussion. For example:

1. How long should the shingle be for good performance?
2. Should shingle length be in number of words or number of characters?
3. How much storage would we need to store shingles?
4. Should upper case and lower case letters be treated differently?
5. Should spaces between words be removed?
6. Should punctuation marks be ignored?
7. Should end of line marker be ignored?
8. Should end of paragraph be ignored?

9. Should stop words like "to", "a" and "the" be removed?
10. Should stemming be carried out to transform "growing" into "grow"?

This is just one approach to finding similar pages. There are several modifications of the approach presented here as well as other approaches. In one recent approach it has been suggested that not only the content be compared but expression also be compared.

6.6 WEB USAGE MINING

The primary objective in Web usage mining is to be able to understand and/or be able to predict user behaviour in interacting with the Web or with a website in order to improve the quality of service. Other aims of Web usage mining are to obtain information and discover usage patterns that may assist website design or redesign, perhaps to assist navigation through the site. The mined data normally includes Web data repositories which may include data logs of users' interactions with the Web, Web server logs, proxy server logs, browser logs, and so on. The information collected in the Web server logs usually includes information about the access, referrer and agent. Access information includes the server's interaction with the user, the referrer information is about the referrer page and the agent information is about the browser used. Some of the routine information may be obtained by using tools that are available free or at a low cost. Using such tools it is generally possible to find at least the following information:

1. Number of hits—the number of times each page in the website has been viewed
2. Number of visitors—the number of users who came to the site
3. Visitor referring website—the website URL of the site the user came from
4. Visitor referral website—the website URL of the site where the user went when they left the website
5. Entry point—which website page the user entered from
6. Visitor time and duration—the time and day of visit and how long the visitor browsed the site
7. Path analysis—a list of the path of pages that the user took
8. Visitor IP address—this helps in finding which part of the world the user came from
9. Browser type
10. Platform
11. Cookies (record of having visited a site)

In addition, one can find which pages are the most popular, which search engines are referring visitors to the website, what keywords are being used in the search to find the site, how the visits vary by the hour, by the day and by the month.

Even this simple information about a website and pages within it can assist an enterprise to achieve the following:

1. Shorten the paths to high visit pages
2. Eliminate or combine low visit pages
3. Redesign some pages including the homepage to help user navigation

4. Redesign some pages so the search engines can find them
5. Help evaluate effectiveness of an advertising campaign

Web usage mining may also involve collecting much more information than what has been listed. For example, it may be desirable to collect information on:

1. ***Path traversed:*** What paths do the customers traverse? What are the most commonly traversed paths through a website? These patterns need to be interpreted, analysed, visualised and acted upon.
2. ***Conversion rates:*** What are the look-to-click, click-to-basket and basket-to-buy rates for each product? Are there significant differences in these rates for different products?
3. ***Impact of advertising:*** Which banners are pulling in the most traffic? What is their conversion rate?
4. ***Impact of promotions:*** Which promotions generate the most sales? Is there a particular level in the site where promotions are most effective?
5. ***Website design:*** Which links do the customer click most frequently? What links do customers buy from most frequently? Are their some features of these links that can be identified?
6. ***Customer segmentation:*** What are the features of customers who abandon trolley without buying? Where do the most profitable customers come from?
7. ***Enterprise search:*** Which customers use enterprise search? Are they more likely to purchase? What do they search for? How frequently does the search engine return a failed result? How frequently does the search engine return too many results?

These are some questions that an e-commerce site would like to explore. Many more questions are possible.

The data obtained from a Web server log which records users' requests to websites is not always an accurate reflection of the users. Web usage mining also needs to deal with issues like caching and proxy servers. Not all page requests are recorded in the server log because pages are often cached and served from the cache when the user requests them again. Caching occurs at several levels. The browser itself has a cache; the size of the cache varies and may be several Gigabytes, to keep copies of recently visited pages which may be retained only for a short time or for days depending on user preferences. Of course, any significant enterprise maintains a large (hundreds of Gigabytes) proxy server to reduce internet traffic and thus reduce cost and to improve performance, since proxy hit rates of up to 50% are possible in large well-designed proxies. In addition, there might be another level of an even bigger proxy server for the region or the country. The proxy server would intercept any requests for Web pages from any user in the enterprise and serve them from the proxy if a copy that has not expired is resident in the proxy. Other requests are generally forwarded to the Web server indicated in the URL with the requester identification intact. The use of caches and proxies therefore reduces the number of hits that the Web server log records. Also, the user navigation that is recorded by the log would often not be fully accurate as some back–button clicks would not be recorded since the proxy might be able to serve such pages. In spite of these issues, most Web usage mining is about mining Web server logs.

People who analyse user behaviour would prefer a tight coupling between user identity and user actions. Although such coupling sounds desirable since it should result in improving the quality of service, such an approach has serious personal privacy implications for the user. Does the user really want some tool to be monitoring every action on his/her machine that could be viewed by the employer or by another family member at home or by some third party? Nevertheless, a number of suggestions have been made including some that suggest browser modification and designing remote agents running on the client computer.

In some cases, one may be interested in the behaviour of users not just in one session but over several sessions. Returning visitors may be recognised by using *cookies*. As noted earlier, a cookie is issued by the Web server and stored on the client computer. The cookie is then presented to the Web server on return visits.

Log data analysis has been investigated using the following techniques:

- Using association rules
- Using composite association rules
- Using cluster analysis

Some researchers have suggested that association rule methodology may also be used in discovering affinity between pages on a site. Others have used methods for discovering sequential patterns from the logs. We discuss some of these techniques later in the section.

Log data may be converted into transactions like those used in market basket analysis with each node visited being treated like an item that is bought, but problems arise since in Web traversing it is not uncommon for a user to return to a node while in market basket there is no equivalent structure possible. Also, in usage analysis we would want to know the sequence of nodes visited by a user, which is not possible using association rules analysis.

To make the task simpler, some researchers discard backward movements in the data. Patterns may then be extracted using algorithms similar to those used for association rules mining. For example, if a support level of 30% and confidence level of 75% was to be specified for a site log data analysis, we would be able to find all those pages that are visited frequently together and be able to discover rules like whenever a user visits page *A* then he/she also visits page *B* with 75% confidence or more. This kind of association is useful since it may be that pages *A* and *B* can be restructured so that the information that the user is seeking from page *B* could even be made available on page *A* itself.

It should be noted that in association rules mining, patterns do not play any role. We are only interested in finding which items appear with which other items frequently. In fact, if pages *A* and *B* appear together in an association rule, it is difficult to tell if *A* was traversed first or *B* was. In Web usage mining, patterns are important and cannot be ignored.

In addition to mining Web log data, it is useful to analyse the click-stream data perhaps by using association rules or sequential mining. Once again such mining can assist in restructuring a site so that better service may be provided to the site visitor.

6.7 WEB STRUCTURE MINING

The aim of Web structure mining is to discover the link structure or the model that is assumed to underlie the Web. The model may be based on the topology of the hyperlinks. This can help in discovering similarity between sites or in discovering authority sites for a particular topic or discipline or in discovering overview or survey sites that point to many authority sites (such sites are called *hubs*). Link structure is only one kind of information that may be used in analysing structure of the Web.

As noted earlier, the links on Web pages provide a useful source of information that may be harnessed in Web searches. Kleinberg (1999) has developed a connectivity analysis algorithm called Hyperlink-Induced Topic Search (HITS) based on the assumption that links represent human judgement. His algorithm also assumes that for any query topic, there are a set of "authoritative" or "authority" sites that are relevant and popular focusing on the topic and there are "hub" sites that contain useful links to relevant sites on the topic including links to many related authorities.

6.7.1 The HITS Algorithm

The HITS algorithm is based on the idea that if the creator of page *p* provides a link to *q* then *p* confers some authority on page *q*. One must however realise that not all links confer authority, since some may be paid advertisements and others may be for navigational purposes, for example links to the homepage in a large website.

In searching, often a very large number of items are retrieved. One way to order these items may be by the number of in-links but it has been found that this approach does not always work.

We present some definitions before describing the HITS algorithm. As noted earlier, a graph may be defined as a set of vertices and edges (*V*, *E*). The vertices correspond to the pages and the edges correspond to the links. A directed edge (*p*, *q*) indicates a link from page *p* to page *q*.

The HITS algorithm has two major steps:

1. ***Sampling step:*** To collect a set of relevant Web pages given a topic
2. ***Iterative step:*** To find hubs and authorities using the information collected during sampling

In trying to use HITS, for example for a query "Web mining", the algorithm involves carrying out the sampling step by querying a search engine and then using the most highly ranked Web pages retrieved for determining the authorities and hubs. As noted earlier, posing a query to a search engine often results in abundance. For example "Java programming" might retrieve millions of pages and finding authority pages from these millions of pages is likely to be very expensive. Also, in some cases, the search engine may not retrieve all relevant pages for the query. The query for Java for example may not retrieve pages for object-oriented programming, some of which may also be relevant.

Therefore the pages retrieved by the search engine are a good starting point but relying solely on the retrieved pages does not guarantee an efficient and effective method for determining authorities and hub pages. The HITS method uses the following algorithm.

6.7.2 Step 1—Sampling Step

The first step involves finding a subset of nodes or a subgraph *S*, which is rich in relevant authoritative pages. To obtain such a subgraph, the algorithm starts with a root set of, say, 200 pages selected from the result of searching for the query in a traditional search engine. Let the root set be *R*. Starting from the root set *R*, we wish to obtain a set *S* that has the following properties:

1. S is relatively small
2. S is rich in relevant pages given the query
3. S contains most (or many) of the strongest authorities

The root set R usually satisfies conditions 1 and 2, that is, by 100 or 200 most highly ranked pages retrieved by a search engine. These pages may or may not satisfy condition 3 but pages in R must contain links to other authorities if there are any. In some cases, this may not be true. For example, searching for "Melbourne real estate" may return real estate agents' websites which are unlikely to refer to any other real estate website in Melbourne. HITS does not deal with such situations.

HITS algorithm expands the root set R into a base set S by using the following algorithm:

1. Let $S = R$
2. For each page in S, do steps 3 to 5
3. Let T be the set of all pages S points to
4. Let F be the set of all pages that point to S
5. Let $S = S + T +$ some or all of F (some if F is large)
6. Delete all links with the same domain name
7. This S is returned

Step 5 allows only some pages of F to be included if F is large since we do not wish to be swamped by a large number of pages that point to pages in S.

The set S is called the *base set* for the given query, it may contain perhaps 100–3000 pages and we assume all the authorities and the hubs for the given query are within these pages. We find the hubs and the authorities from the base set as follows.

One simple approach for finding hubs and authorities is ordering them by the count of their out-degree and the count of their in-degree. This works well in some situations but does not work well always. Kleinberg asserts that authoritative pages relevant to a query should not only have large in-degree they should also have considerable overlap in the sets of pages that point to them. Thus he suggests that hubs and authorities may be found together.

Before starting the hubs and authorities step of the algorithm, HITS removes all links between pages on the same website (or same domain) in step 6. The reasoning behind this step is that links between pages on the same site are for navigational purposes, not for conferring authority. Furthermore, if many links from a domain are pointing to a single page outside the domain then only a small number of these links are counted. This eliminates advertisements or some other type of "collusion" amongst the websites.

6.7.3 Step 2—Finding Hubs and Authorities

The algorithm for finding hubs and authorities now works as follows:

1. Let a page p have a non-negative authority weight x_p and a non-negative hub weight y_p. Pages with relatively large weights x_p will be classified to be the authorities (similarly for the hubs with large weights y_p).
2. The weights are normalised so their squared sum for each type of weight is 1 since we are only the relative weights are important.
3. For a page p, the value of x_p is updated to be the sum of y_q overall pages q that link to p.

4. For a page p, the value of y_p is updated to be the sum of x_q overall pages q that p links to.
5. Continue with step 2 unless a termination condition has been reached.
6. On termination, the output of the algorithm is a set of pages with the largest x_p weights that can be assumed to be authorities and those with the largest y_p weights that can be assumed to be the hubs.

Kleinberg provides examples of how the HITS algorithm works and it is shown to perform well.

Theorem: The sequences of weights x_p and y_p converge.

Proof: Let $G = (V, E)$. The graph can be represented by an adjacency matrix A where each element (i, j) is 1 if there is an edge between the two vertices and 0 otherwise.

The weights are modified according to simple operations $x = A^T y$ and $y = Ax$. Therefore, $x = A^T Ax$. Similarly, $y = AA^T y$. The iterations therefore converge to the principal eigenvectors of AA^T.

Example 6.2

Assume that a query has been specified. The first step has been carried out and a set of pages that contains most of the authorities has been found. Let the set be given by the following ten pages. Their out-links are listed below:

Page *A* (out-links to *G*, *H*, *I*, *J*)
Page *B* (out-links to *A*, *G*, *H*, *I*, *J*)
Page *C* (out-links to *B*, *G*, *H*, *I*, *J*)
Page *D* (out-links to *B*, *G*, *H*, *J*)
Page *E* (out-links to *B*, *H*, *I*, *J*)
Page *F* (out-links to *B*, *G*, *I*, *J*)
Page *G* (out-links to *H*, *I*)
Page *H* (out-links to *G*, *I*, *J*)
Page *I* (out-links to *H*)
Page *J* (out-links to *F*, *G*, *H*, *I*)

First we present the above information in the connection matrix in Table 6.3.

Table 6.3 Connection matrix for Example 2

Page \ Page	A	B	C	D	E	F	G	H	I	J
A	0	0	0	0	0	0	1	1	1	1
B	1	0	0	0	0	0	1	1	1	1
C	0	1	0	0	0	0	1	1	1	1
D	0	1	0	0	0	0	1	1	0	1
E	0	1	0	0	0	0	0	1	1	1
F	0	1	0	0	0	0	1	0	1	1
G	0	0	0	0	0	0	0	1	1	0
H	0	0	0	0	0	0	1	0	1	1
I	0	0	0	0	0	0	0	1	0	0
J	0	0	0	0	0	1	1	1	1	0

Every row in Table 6.3 matrix shows the out-links from the Web page that is identified in the first column. Every column shows the in-links from the Web page that is identified in the first row of the table. Another way to represent the information in the connection matrix is listing the out-links and the in-links from each Web page as shown in Table 6.4.

Table 6.4 In-links and out-links of the Web pages in Example 6.2

Web page	*In-links*	*Out-links*
A	*B*	*G, H, I, J*
B	*C, D, E, F*	*A, G, H, I, J*
C	None	*B, G, H, I, J*
D	None	*B, G, H, J*
E	None	*B, H, I, J*
F	*J*	*B, G, I, J*
G	*A, B, C, D, F, H, J*	*H, I*
H	*A, B, C, D, E, G, I, J*	*G, I, J*
I	*A, B, C, E, F, G, H, J*	*H*
J	*A, B, C, D, E, F, H*	*F, G, H, I*

The next step involves iterations to compute the hubs and authorities. Initially, for ease of understanding, we carry out the iterations without normalisation in Table 6.5. We assume all initial weights to be 1. Note that the x values are the authority weights (derived from the hub weights of the pages pointing to them) and y values are the hub weights (derived from the authority weights of pages that each page points to).

Table 6.5 Computing hubs and authorities without normalisation

Weight / *Page*	x_0	y_0	x_1	y_1	x_2	y_2
A	1	1	1	4	5	118
B	1	1	4	5	17	123
C	1	1	0	5	0	135
D	1	1	0	4	0	104
E	1	1	0	4	0	106
F	1	1	1	4	4	106
G	1	1	7	2	29	60
H	1	1	8	3	29	89
I	1	1	8	1	31	29
J	1	1	7	4	29	93

We can see that the hub and authority weight start growing in Table 6.5 without normalisation. The result of the same iterations with normalisations of the hubs and authorities weights so that the sum of squares of the hubs' weight as well as the authorities' weights is 1 is given in Table 6.6.

We have used the symbols x_i and y_i as the values that are not normalised while the symbols X_i and Y_i are used for the values that are normalised.

Table 6.6 Computing hubs and authorities with normalisation

Page \ Weight	x_0	X_0	y_0	Y_0	x_1	X_1	y_1	Y_1	x_2	X_2	y_2	Y_2
A	1	0.32	1	0.32	0.32	0.06	1.26	0.33	0.42	0.08	1.91	0.37
B	1	0.32	1	0.32	1.26	0.26	1.58	0.42	1.42	0.28	1.99	0.39
C	1	0.32	1	0.32	0	0	1.58	0.42	0	0	2.19	0.42
D	1	0.32	1	0.32	0	0	1.26	0.33	0	0	1.68	0.33
E	1	0.32	1	0.32	0	0	1.26	0.33	0	0	1.72	0.33
F	1	0.32	1	0.32	0.32	0.06	1.26	0.33	0.33	0.06	1.72	0.33
G	1	0.32	1	0.32	2.21	0.45	0.63	0.17	2.42	0.47	0.97	0.19
H	1	0.32	1	0.32	2.53	0.51	0.95	0.25	2.42	0.47	1.44	0.28
I	1	0.32	1	0.32	2.53	0.51	0.32	0.08	2.58	0.5	0.47	0.09
J	1	0.32	1	0.32	2.21	0.45	1.26	0.33	2.42	0.47	1.51	0.29
SSQ	10	1	10	1	24.4	1	14.4	1	26.5	1	26.6	1
SQRT	3.16		3.16	1	4.94	1	3.79	1	5.15	1	5.16	1

We note the following about this algorithm:

1. The last row of Table 6.6 is the square root of the sum of squares. We divide all the weights in that column by this number to obtain the normalised weights.
2. After two iterations it appears that *G*, *H*, *I* and *J* are the authorities and *A*, *B* and *C* are the hubs. The hub weights for *D*, *E*, *F*, *H* and *J* are also relatively large.

The above iterations may be written as the following equations for Web page *A*:

$$x_A = y_B$$

$$y_A = x_G + x_H + x_I + x_J$$

Similar equations may be written for *x* and *y* weights of all the nodes.

6.7.4 Problems with the HITS Algorithm

There has been much research done in evaluating the HITS algorithm and it has been shown that while the algorithm works well for most queries, it does not work well for some others. There are a number of reasons for this:

1. ***Hubs and authorities:*** A clear-cut distinction between hubs and authorities may not be appropriate since many sites are hubs as well as authorities.
2. **Topic drift:** Certain arrangements of tightly connected documents, perhaps due to mutually reinforcing relationships between hosts, can dominate the HITS computation. These documents in some instances may not be the most relevant to the query that was posed. It has been reported that in one case when the search item was “jaguar” the HITS algorithm converged to a football team called Jaguars. Other examples of topic drift have been found on topics like “gun control”, “abortion” and “movies”.

3. ***Automatically generated links:*** Some of the links are computer generated (for example, every page in my School has a link to the School homepage and to the copyright page. Many pages generated using the university template have links to the university homepage as well as some other links) and represent no human judgement but HITS still gives them equal importance.
4. ***Non-relevant documents:*** Some queries can return non-relevant documents in the highly ranked queries and this can then lead to erroneous results from the HITS algorithm. The problem is more common than it might appear.
5. ***Efficiency:*** The real-time performance of the algorithm is not good given the steps that involve finding sites that are pointed to by pages in the root pages.

A number of proposals have been made for modifying HITS. These include:

- More careful selection of the base set to reduce the possibility of topic drift. One possible approach might be to modify the HITS algorithm so that the hub and authority weights are modified only based on the best hubs and the best authorities.
- One may argue that the in-link information is more important than the out-link information. A hub can become important just by pointing to a lot of authorities.

6.7.5 Web Communities

Although the Web appears to have grown rapidly in all directions without any structure, an analysis of the Web graph provides a surprisingly structured view of the Web. One of the major structures is the hundreds of thousands of implicit Web communities that have sprung up because of the open nature of the Web and not by design.

A Web community is generated by a group of individuals that share a common interest. It manifests on the Web as a collection of Web pages with the common interest as the theme. These could for example be communities about a sub-discipline, a religious group, about a sport or a sports team, a hobby, an event, a country, a state, or whatever. The communities include in them newsgroups, portals and the large ones may include directories in sites like Yahoo! Web communities may be discovered by exploring the Web as a graph and identifying subgraphs that have strong link structure within them but weak associations with other parts of the graph. Such subgraphs may be called Web communities or cyber-communities.

The HITS algorithm finds authorities and hubs for a specified broad topic. The idea of cyber-communities is to find all Web communities on any topic by processing the whole Web graph. To formalise the concept of cyber-communities we first define a complete bipartite $G_{i,j}$ graph that consists of $i + j$ nodes and in which every one of the nodes has an edge directed to each of the j nodes. One possible definition of a cyber-community may be a collection of Web pages that include a bipartite graph $G_{i,j}$ consisting of $i + j$ nodes as defined above. Of course, such a tightly knit group of Web pages could well appear accidentally, but it has been found that such accidental communities are extremely unlikely.

The concept of cyber-communities may be related to the hubs and authorities of the HITS algorithm by labelling the i Web pages of the bipartite graph as the hubs and the j Web pages as the authorities, but other structures of communities are possible. It has been found that there are several hundred thousand cyber-communities devoted to a variety of topics as noted above.

How does one find the cyber-communities efficiently? One approach involves sorting all the Web pages by in-links and out-links. Now if we were insisting that each cyber-community must have a core of a bipartite graph $C_{4,5}$ then we can prune all the Web pages that do not have either at least five out-links or at least four in-links. Given that most Web pages have only one or two in-links and only one or two out-links, this pruning removes a very large number of Web pages from the list.

6.8 WEB MINING SOFTWARE

Many general purpose data mining software packages include some Web mining software. For example Clementine from SPSS includes Web mining modules. The list here includes a variety of Web mining software. It should be noted that the Web mining software market is new and not mature. New software vendors appear regularly and existing vendors disappear or get taken over by others.

More comprehensive lists of Web mining software are available at:

http://www.kdnuggets.com/software/web.html

http://www.terrylund.com/vendorListing.shtml

All software products listed below are commercial products unless noted otherwise.

- 123LogAnalyzer from a company with the same name is low-cost Web mining software that provides an overview of a website's performance, statistics about Web server activity including the number of visitors, the number of unique IPs, Web pages viewed, files downloaded, directories that were accessed, number of hits, broken down by day of the week and hour of the day and images that were accessed and more.
http://www.123loganalyzer.com/
- Azure Web Log Analyzer from Azure Desktop claims to find the usual Web information including the most popular pages, the number of visitors and where they are from, what browser and computer they used and site's traffic.
http://www.azuredesktop.com/
- LiveStats.NET and LiveStats.BIZ from DeepMetrix (Founded 1992) provide website analysis, data visualisation and statistics on distinct visitors, repeat visits, popular entry and exit pages, time spent on pages, geographic reports which break down visits by country and continent, click paths, keywords by search engine, and more.
http://www.deepmetrix.com/
- NetTracker Web Analytics from the Sane Solutions (Founded 1996) claims to analyse log files (from Web servers, proxy servers, and firewalls), data gathered by JavaScript page tags, or a hybrid of both. Comprehensive analysis of behaviour of visitors to Internet, intranet, and extranet sites.
http://www.sane.com/
- WebAnalyst from Megaputer (Founded 1997) is based on PolyAnalyst text mining software, WebAnalyst claims to find visitors' interests and preferences.
http://www.megaputer.com/
- WebLog Expert 3.5 from a company with the same name (Founded in—not known) produces reports that include the following information: activity statistics, accessed files, paths through the site, information about referring pages, search engines, browsers, operating systems, and more.
http://www.weblogexpert.com/

- WebTrends 7 from NetIQ (Founded 1995) is a collection of modules that provide a variety of Web data including navigation analysis and customer segmentation and more. http://www.webtrends.com/

SUMMARY

In a short time of not much more than 20 years, the Web revolution has had a profound impact on the lives of people that have access to the Internet. It has dramatically changed the way we search and find information at home and at work. From its beginning in the early 1990s the Web has grown to more than four billion Web pages in 2004 with millions of people from all over the world accessing it every day. Millions of Web pages are added every day and millions of others are modified or deleted. One of the most important features of the Web is the hyperlink by which one Web page may provide links to other pages allowing a user to traverse the Web following links of interest to him or her.

The Web is an open medium with no controls on who puts up what kind of material. The openness has meant that the Web has grown exponentially, which is its strength as well as its weakness. The strength is that one can find information on just about any topic however esoteric. The weakness of an open Web is the problem of abundance of information. For example, searching for the phrase "data mining" on Google found more than 2.5 million hits in early September 2004.

This chapter has defined some of the commonly used Web terminology and graph terminology. The nature of Web content mining, Web usage mining and Web structure mining has been presented. Web data mining is perhaps still in its infancy and much research is being carried out in the area.

REVIEW QUESTIONS

1. What is Web data mining? In what situations can Web data mining techniques be useful? (Section 6.1)
2. What are the aims of Web data mining? (Section 6.1)
3. Explain the differences between the three types of Web data mining. (Section 6.1)
4. Describe some of the Web terminology. (Section 6.2)
5. How can Lotka's inverse-square law apply to links from a Web page? (Section 6.2)
6. What is the Bow-tie structure of the Web? (Section 6.2)
7. What is DIPRE algorithm? (Section 6.2)
8. How can Web pages be clustered? What is the STC algorithm? (Section 6.4)
9. What is document fingerprinting and similarity? (Section 6.4)
10. How should one measure usage of a Web page? (Section 6.5)
11. What data mining techniques can be used for log data analysis? (Section 6.2)
12. What is HITS algorithm? What are its aims and how does it work? What are its weaknesses? (Section 6.7)
13. Explain how Web communities may be determined. (Section 6.7.5)

EXERCISES

1. What is Lotka's Inverse-Square Law regarding scholarly publications? What relation does it have to the power laws of distribution of in-links and out-links from Web pages?
2. Describe the "bow-tie" structure of the Web. What percentage of pages forms the Strongly Connected Core? What is the main property of the Core?
3. What is the difference between the deep and shallow Web? Why do we need the deep Web?
4. What is the aim of the algorithm presented by Brin? What is the most difficult part of the DIPRE algorithm? Why?
5. How can clustering be used in Web usage mining?
6. What is the basis of Kleinberg's HITS algorithm? Provide a step-by-step description of Kleinberg's HITS algorithm for finding authorities and hubs for topic "data mining". Discuss the advantages and disadvantages of the HITS algorithm.
7. What is a Web community? How do you discover them?
8. Describe the concept of similar pages on the Web. Give an algorithm for finding similar pages.
9. What is a bipartite graph? What role does a bipartite graph plays in discovering Web communities?
10. Use the HITS algorithm to find hubs and authorities from the following five Web pages:
    (a) Page *A* (out-links to *B*, *C*, *D*)
    (b) Page *B* (out-links to *A*, *C*, *D*)
    (c) Page *C* (out-links to *D*)
    (d) Page *D* (out-links to *C*, *E*)
    (e) Page *E* (out-links to *B*, *C*, *D*)
11. What are the major differences between classical information retrieval and Web search?
12. Make a brief literature review of two Web-mining methods: HITS and PageRank, and answer the following questions:
    (a) Briefly describe the fundamental ideas of both HITS and PageRank.
    (a) Respectively list some applications of HITS and PageRank.
13. Web Community (or Online Community) discovery has been a very hot research topic in the last few years and many methods have been proposed.
    (a) List the main properties of Web Community.
14. Briefly describe how to measure the similarity between Web pages.

MULTIPLE CHOICE QUESTIONS

1. Which of the following belongs to Web data mining
    (a) Discovering authority sites
    (b) Clustering Web pages

(c) Understanding Web users behaviour
(d) Web search
(e) All of the above

2. Which one of the following is a part of Web data mining?
(a) Crawler
(b) Indexer
(c) Structure mining
(d) Hyperlink mining

3. Which one of the following is not a simple principles in designing Web pages?
(a) Relevant linkage principle
(b) Topical unity principle
(c) Lexical affinity principle
(d) Uniform display principle

4. Which one of the following is not part of Web structure mining?
(a) Finding hubs
(b) Finding authorities
(c) Finding communities
(d) Finding most popular sites

5. Which one of the following is not an aim of clustering Web documents returned by a query?
(a) The clusters must be relevant to the user query
(b) The clusters must have a high level of precision
(c) Each cluster must be easy to understand
(d) The clustering algorithm must have high performance

6. Which one of the following steps is part of a fingerprinting algorithm to find similar Web pages?
(a) Each document is divided into all possible substrings of length L
(b) The substrings of two documents are compared
(c) The number of substrings that match provides an indication of similarity
(d) All of the above

7. Which one of the following is true?
(a) Web is growing exponentially
(b) Web mining involves finding interesting and useful knowledge from Web data
(c) Hyperlink and log data are used in Web mining
(d) All of the above

8. Which one of the following is not part of Web mining?
(a) Web content mining
(b) Web structure mining
(c) Web quality mining
(d) Web usage mining

9. Which of the following are the differences between conventional documents and Web documents?
   (a) Web documents are usually larger than conventional documents
   (b) Web documents have hyperlinks while conventional documents don't
   (c) Web documents are dynamic while conventional documents are not
   (d) Conventional large libraries have large document collections while the Web doesn't
10. Which one of the following is true?
   (a) The Web is the collection of all documents
   (b) A Web cookie is data sent from a client to a Web server
   (c) Web domain name server is a distributed database of name and address mappings
   (d) Web usage mining involves push and pull

BIBLIOGRAPHY

Recommended Reading for Students

As noted earlier, Web data mining is a very active area for research. We present a number of references including two books that are suitable for students.

Chakrabarti, S., *Mining the Web: Discovering Knowledge from Hypertext Data*, Morgan Kaufmann, 350 pp., 2002.

Kosala, R. and Blockeel, H., *Web Mining: A Survey*
http://maya.cs.depaul.edu/~classes/ect584/papers/kosala.pdf

Linoff, G.S. and Berry, M.J.A., *Mining the Web*, John Wiley & Sons, 352 pp., 2001.

Recommended Reading for Lecturers

The introduction to the chapter was based on a W3C document on Web terminology. A good discussion of graph terminology as it relates to the Web is given in the paper by Broder et al. (2000). Some of our discussion in this section is based on that paper.

The important papers for this chapter are Broder et al. (2000), Nanopoulos and Manolopoulos (2001) and Cooley, Srivastava and Mobasher (1997). Cooley, Mobasher and Srivastava (1999) discuss the data preparation needed for Web mining. The section on Web structure mining is mostly based on the classic paper by Kleinberg. Some of the discussion about merits of the HITS algorithm is based on Bharat and Henzinger (1998). The section on Web clustering is based on paper by Zamir and Etzioni (1998) who developed the STC algorithm.

Adamic, L., The Small World Web, *Proc. 3rd European Conf. Research and Advanced Technology for Digital Libraries* (*ECDL*), pp. 443–452, 1999.

Bharat, K. and Henzinger, M.R., Improved Algorithms for Topic Distillation in a Hyperlinked Environment, *Proc. Conf. on Research and Development in Information Retrieval* (*SIGIR '98*), Melbourne, Australia, pp. 104–111, 1998.

Borodin, A., Roberts, G., Rosenthal, J.S., and Tsaparas, P., Finding Authorities and Hubs from Link Structures on the World Wide Web. *Proc. 10th Int. World Wide Web Conf.* (*WWW10*), Hong Kong, pp. 415–429, 2001.

Brin, S., Extracting Patterns and Relations from the World Wide Web, *WEBDB Workshop at 6th International Conference on Extending Database Technology* (*EDBT '98*), Valencia, Spain, 1998.

Broder, A., Kumar, R., Maghoul, F., Raghvan, P., Rajagopalan, S., Stat, R., Tomkins A., and Wiener, J., Graph Structure in the Web: Experiments and Models, *Proc. 9th Int. World Wide Web Conf.* (*WWW9*), Amsterdam, Netherlands, pp. 309–320, 2000.

Chakrabarti, S., Dom, B.E., Gibson, D., Kleinberg, J.M., Raghavan, P., and Rajagopalan, S., Automatic Resource Compilation by Analyzing Hyperlink Structure and Associated Text, *Proc. 7th Int. World Wide Web Conf.* (*WWW '98*), Brisbane, Australia, pp. 65–74, 1998.

Cho, J. and Garcia-Molina, H., Estimating Frequency of Change, *ACM Trans. on Internet Technology*, Vol. 3, No. 3, pp. 256–290, 2003.

Cho, J., Garcia-Molina, H., and Page, L., Efficient Crawling Through URL Ordering, *Computer Networks and ISDN Systems*, Vol. 30, pp. 161–172, 1998.

Cooley, R., Mobasher, B., and Srivastava, J., Data Preparation for Mining World Wide Web Browsing Patterns, *Knowledge and Information Systems*, Vol. 1, No. 1, pp. 5–32, 1999.

Cooley, R., Srivastava, J., and Mobasher, B., Web Mining: Information and Pattern Discovery on The World Wide Web, *Proc. 9th IEEE Int. Conf. on Tools with Artificial Intelligence* (*ICTAI '97*), Newport Beach, CA, 1997.

Cooley, R., Tan, P.N., and Srivastava, J., Discovery of Interesting Usage Patterns from Web Data, *Advances in Web Usage Analysis and User Profiling, Lecture Notes in Computer Science*, Spiliopoulou, M. and Masand, B. (Eds.), Vol. 1836, Springer-Verlag, pp. 163–182, 2000.

Dean, J. and Henzinger, M., Finding Related Pages in the World Wide Web, *Computer Networks*, Vol. 31, No. 11–16, pp. 1467–1479, 1999.

Dhyani, D., Ng, W.K., and Bhowmick, S.V., A Survey of Web Metrics, *ACM Computing Surveys*, Vol. 34, No. 4, pp. 469–503, 2002.

Dill, S., Kumar, R., Mccurley, K., Rajagopalan, S., Sivakumar, D., and Tomkins, A., Self-Similarity in the Web, *ACM Trans. on Internet Technology*, Vol. 2, No. 3, pp. 205–223.

Flake, G.W., Lawrence, S., and Giles, C.L., Efficient Identification of Web Communities, *Proc. Int. Conf. on Knowledge Discovery and Data Mining* (*SIGKDD00*), Boston, MA, pp. 150–160, 2000.

Fu, Y., Sandhu, K., and Shih, M.Y., Clustering of Web Users Based on Access Patterns, *Int. Workshop on Web Usage Analysis and User Profiling* (*WEBKDD '99*), San Diego, CA, 1999.

Gibson, D., Kleinberg, J., and Raghavan, P., Inferring Web Communities from Link Topology, *Proc. 9th Conf. on Hypertext and Hypermedia* (*UK*), Pittsburgh, PA, pp. 225–234, 1998.

Kleinberg, J.M., Authoritative Sources in a Hyperlinked Environment, *Journal of the ACM*, Vol. 46, No. 5, pp. 604–632, 1999.

Kleinberg, J.M., Kumar, R., Raghvan, P., Rajagopalan, S., and Tomkins, A.S., The Web as a Graph: Measurements, Models and Methods, *Proc. Int. Conf. on Combinatorics and Computing*, No. 1627 in Lecture Notes in Computer Science, Springer, Berlin, pp. 1–18, 1999.

Kleinberg, J.M., The Small-World Phenomenon: An Algorithmic Perspective, *Proc. 32nd ACM Symposium on Theory of Computing*, pp. 163–170, 2000.

Kohavi, R. and Parekh, R., Ten Supplementary Analyses to Improve E-Commerce Websites, WEBKDD, Washington, DC, 2003.

Kohavi, R., Mason, L., Parekh, R., and Zheng, Z., Lessons and Challenges from Mining Retail E-Commerce Data, *Machine Learning*, Special Issue on Data Mining Lessons Learned, Vol. 57, No. 1–2, pp. 83–113, 2004.

Kumar, R., Raghavan, P., Rajagopalan, S., and Tomkins, A., 1999, Trawling the Web for Emerging Cyber-Communities, *Computer Networks*, Vol. 31, No. 11–16, pp. 1481–1493, 1999.

Levene, M. and Poulovassilis, A. (Eds.), *Web Dynamics*, Springer, 2004.

Liu, B., Web Data Mining: Exploring Hyperlinks, Contents, and Usage Data, 493 pp., Springer, 2007.

Mobasher, B., Cooley, R., and Srivastava, J., 2000, Automatic Personalization Based on Web Usage Mining, *Communications of the ACM*, Vol. 43, No. 8, pp. 142–151, 2000.

Nanopoulos, A. and Manolopoulos, Y., Mining Patterns from Graph Traversals, *Data and Knowledge Engineering*, Vol. 37, No. 3, pp. 243–266, 2001.

Pirolli, P., Pitkow, J., and Rao, R., 1996, Silk from A Sow's Ear: Extracting Usable Structures from the Web, *Proc. SIGCHI Conf. on Human Factors in Computing Systems,* Vancouver, Canada, pp. 118–125, 1996.

Pitkow, J.E., Summary of WWW Characterizations, *Computer Networks and ISDN Systems*, Vol. 30, No. 1–7, pp. 551–558, 1998.

Scieme, A. (Ed.), Web Mining: Applications and Techniques, Idea Group, 433 pp., 2005.

Srivastava, J., Cooley, R., Deshpande, M., and Tan, P.N., 2000, Web Usage Mining: Discovery and Applications of Usage Patterns from Web Data, *SIGKDD Explorations*, Vol. 1, Issue 2, pp. 12–23, 2000.

Srivastava, J., Web Mining: Accomplishments & Future Directions, University of Minnesota, 148 pp.

World Wide Web Committee on Web Usage Characterization Activity, http://www.w3.org/wca.

Zaiane, O.R., Xin, M., and Han, J., Discovering Web Access Patterns and Trends by Applying OLAP and Data Mining Technology on Web Logs, *Advances in Digital Libraries*, pp. 19–29, 1998.

Zamir, O. and Etzioni, O., Web Document Clustering: A Feasibility Demonstration, *Research and Development in Information Retrieval*, pp. 46–54, 1998.

Zhong, N, Liu, J., and Yao, Y. (Eds.), *Web Intelligence*, Springer, 2003.

TIM BERNERS-LEE—INVENTOR OF THE WORLD WIDE WEB

While working at the European Laboratory for Particle Physics, better known as CERN, Tim Berners-Lee proposed a new protocol which was based on a system called hypertext, where embedded links in a text can be used to link to other texts. This developed into something which we now know as the World Wide Web.

Currently, Tim Berners-Lee directs the World Wide Web Consortium (W3C), an open forum of companies and organisations with the mission to lead the Web to its full potential through the development of Web technical standards, which he founded in October 1994. He is a Distinguished Fellow of the British Computer Society, and an Honorary Fellow of the Institution of Electrical Engineers, a member of the American Academy of Arts and Sciences, and a Fellow of the Royal Society.

Tim Berners-Lee was made a Knight Commander of the Order of the British Empire (KBE) in 2004. He is a graduate of Oxford University and holds the 3Com Founders chair at MIT.

CASE STUDY 6

Lessons and Challenges from Mining Retail E-Commerce Data*

Reproduced with permission from Springer Verlag.

ABSTRACT

The architecture of Blue Martini Software's e-commerce suite has supported data collection, data transformation, and data mining since its inception. With clickstreams being collected at the application-server layer, high-level events being logged, and data automatically transformed into a data warehouse using metadata, common problems plaguing data mining using weblogs (e.g., sessionization and conflating multi-sourced data) were obviated, thus allowing us to concentrate on actual data mining goals. The paper briefly reviews the architecture and discusses many lessons learned over the last four years and the challenges that still need to be addressed. The lessons and challenges are presented across two dimensions: business-level vs. technical; and throughout the data mining lifecycle stages of data collection, data warehouse construction, business intelligence, and deployment. The lessons and challenges are also widely applicable to data mining domains outside retail e-commerce.

Keywords: data mining, data analysis, business intelligence, web analytics, web mining, OLAP, visualization, reporting, data transformations, retail, e-commerce, Simpson's paradox, sessionization, bot detection, clickstreams, application server, web logs, data cleansing, hierarchical attributes, business reporting, data warehousing.

1. INTRODUCTION

E-commerce is an important domain for data mining (Kohavi & Provost, 2001), with massive amounts of clickstream and transactional data that dwarf in size data warehouses from a few years ago (Kimball & Merz, 2000).

At Blue Martini Software, we had the opportunity to develop a data mining system for business users and data analysts from the ground up, including data collection, creation of a data warehouse, transformations, and associated business intelligence systems that include reporting, visualization, and data mining. The system was made available to clients in 1999 and has since been purchased for e-commerce by brand-name retailers, such as Bluefly, Canadian Tire, Debenhams, Harley Davidson, Gymboree, Kohl's, Mountain Equipment Co-op, Saks Fifth Avenue, Sainsbury, Sprint, and The Men's Wearhouse.

Focusing on the retail e-commerce domain allowed us to provide solutions to some tough problems. For example, Pfahringer (2002) wrote that one of his lessons from participating in the KDD Cup (an annual data mining competition) was that "Every problem is different! There is no such thing as a standard problem." Kohavi (1998) suggested that one way to

* Kohavi, R., L. Mason, R. Parekh, and Z. Zheng, Lessons and Challenges from Mining Retail E-commerce Data, Springer Verlag, *Machine Learning,* Vol. 57, No. 1–2, pp. 88–113, 2004.

ronnyk@cs.stanford.edu lmason@bluemartini.com rparekh@bluemartini.com zijianz@microsoft.com cross the chasm from academia to commercial data mining was to build a vertical solution and complete the chain around data mining from collection to cleaning, mining, acting, and verifying. The e-commerce and data mining architecture (Ansari et al., 2001) we built provided us with unique capabilities to collect more data than is usually available for data mining projects. From the very beginning, significant consideration was given to data transformations and analysis needs. This can be contrasted with one of the challenges facing business intelligence in situations where analysis is performed as an afterthought. In these cases, there is often a gap between the potential value of analytics and the actual value achieved because limited relevant data were collected or because data must go through complex transformations before they can be effectively mined (Kohavi, Rothleder, & Simoudis, 2002). We limit further discussion of the architecture to areas where the additional information provides context for sharing the lessons learned. More details about the architecture are available in Ansari et al. (2001).

The lessons described in this paper are based on data mining projects we completed during the past four years. Over this time we have analyzed data from more than twenty clients. The durations of each of these projects varied from a few person-weeks to several person-months. Results of some of these projects are available as case studies or white papers such as MEC Case Study (Blue Martini Software, 2003a), Debenhams Case Study (Blue Martini Software, 2003b), and eMetrics Study (Mason et al., 2001). Although all of the client data analyzed can be classified broadly as retail e-commerce, the clients' businesses were often significantly different from each other, coming from multiple industry verticals, with varying business models, and based in different geographic locations (including the US, Europe, Asia, and Africa). Sources of data included some or all of customer registration and demographic information, web clickstreams, response to direct-mail and email campaigns, and orders placed through a website, call center, or in-store POS (Point-Of-Sale) systems. Depending on the client, the quantity of data analyzed varied from a few thousand records to more than 100 million records, and the time period of the data varied from a few months to several years. Despite these differences, all the lessons we describe are general, in the sense that they are valid across many of the clients we have analyzed. In fact, we believe that many of the lessons we describe are also widely applicable to data mining domains outside of retail e-commerce.

The paper is organized as follows. Section 2 begins with high-level business lessons and challenges. Section 3 describes technical lessons and challenges on data definition, collection, and preparation. Section 4 presents technical lessons and challenges for analysis, including experi-mentation, deployment, and measurement. We conclude with a summary in Section 5.

2. BUSINESS LESSONS

Our goal in designing the software was to make it easy for an organization to utilize business intelligence capabilities, including reporting, visualizations, and data mining. We consider the data mining lifecycle stages in the following natural order: requirements gathering, data collection, data warehouse construction, business intelligence, and deployment (closing the loop). In each of the following subsections we describe our approach, the lessons learned and the challenges that merit further investigation. It should be noted that this section includes lessons and challenges from the perspective of the business user or the broader organizational unit that is the main sponsor of the data mining projects. Lessons that deal with the more technical aspects will be described in Sections 3 and 4.

Our clients, i.e., the "businesses," expect a seamless integration of business intelligence capabilities with the software for the channels we provide, namely the website, call center, and campaign management, while allowing relatively easy integration with their other sources of data.

2.1 Requirements Gathering

The process of gathering the requirements for data analysis is critical to the eventual success of any data mining project. Since all the clients we focused on are from the retail e-commerce domain, we have developed significant experience in this domain and a clear understanding of the business terminology. We learned the following lessons related to the requirements gathering phase.

1. *Clients are often reluctant to list specific business questions*. In quite a few of our engagements our clients did not give us any specific business questions. Sometimes, they do not even know what questions to ask because they do not understand the underlying technology. Even when we specifically asked them to give us questions, they simply asked us to find some interesting insights. The importance of involving the business users has been previously documented (Berry & Linoff, 2000). Our lesson here is the value of whetting the clients' appetite by presenting preliminary findings. After an interim meeting with basic findings, the clients often came up with quite a long list of business questions they wanted us to answer.

2. *Push clients to ask characterization and strategic questions*. Even when the clients did present us with business questions, they were basic reporting type questions. Clients had to be pushed to formulate deeper analytic questions. For example, the question asked initially would be something like "What is the distribution of males and females among people who spend more than $500?" or "What is the response rate of the last email campaign in each region?" instead of asking "What characterizes people who spend more than $500?" or "What distinguishes the people who responded to the last email campaign from those who did not?" This lesson is aligned with the CRISP-DM (Chapman et al., 2000) recommendations on business understanding and with Berry and Linoff (2000) who write, "Defining the business problem is the trickiest part of successful data mining because it is exclusively a communication problem."

It is worth mentioning that formulating questions through interacting with business experts is part of the data mining process. While providing example questions to business people and educating them on data mining could be useful in many cases, developing some methodology and best practices to help them define appropriate questions remains challenging.

2.2 Data Collection

Data collection at a website includes clickstreams (both page views and session information), customer registration attributes, and order transactions (both order lines and order headers). From a business perspective, the collection in the Blue Martini architecture is mostly transparent. Page views are tied (through database foreign keys) to sessions, which are determined by the application-server logic, obviating the need for sessionization (see Section 3). Transactions are automatically tied to sessions and to the customers. All the data are automatically recorded directly into the database, avoiding the need to collect web logs from multiple web servers, parse them, and load them. These are all possible because the architecture is "aware" of higher abstraction levels, unlike stateless http requests seen by web servers.

Many of the data preparation steps described by Cooley, Mobasher, and Srivastava (1999), which put significant burden on organizations that would like to mine their data, are unnecessary when using this collection architecture (or a similar architecture that collects data at the application-server layer). One of the reasons why we have seen so much research around web logs and sessionization is that the web logs were designed to debug web servers and not necessarily to provide useful data for data mining.

The architecture also records the following unique "business events":

1. Every search and the number of results returned. This allows us to produce often requested reports on searches that return too many results and hence need dedicated results pages and "failed searches" (zero results returned) that help improve the search thesaurus and merchandising (e.g., they

help identify early trends) for products the merchandisers are not aware of.

2. Shopping cart events (add to cart, change quantity, and delete). These are very hard to discern from web logs, yet are automatically handled by the architecture. The availability of these events makes it easy to track shopping cart abandonment.
3. Important events such as registration, initiation of checkout, and order confirmation. These provided data for computing micro-conversion metrics (Lee et al., 2001).
4. Any form field failure. The architecture supports a validation regular expression for every form field. Validation failures are recorded to help with usability testing. One example of the usefulness of this event happened with one of our clients. Two weeks after deployment of our system, we looked at form failures and found thousands of failures on the home page every day! There was only one form field on the home page: a place to enter your email address to join their mailing list. Thousands of visitors were typing search keywords into the box and because these search keywords failed to validate as email addresses, the architecture logged them. To fix the problem, the client simply added a clearly identified search box on the home page and set the default contents of the email box to the word "email."

The important observation is that the collection of these events is transparent. While website designers may not think about collecting form field failures as they concentrate on the aesthetics, the architecture automatically collects them because they are useful for analysis.

The architecture also collects additional attributes that are not commonly available, such as the user's local time zone, whether their browsers accept *gzip'ed* content (useful for robot detection), color depth, and screen resolution. Screen resolution and color depth help identify more technical users who are using advanced hardware and are potentially heavier spenders. These attributes were useful for customer segmentation. We have learned two important lessons with respect to data collection and management.

1. *Collect the right data, up front.* Changes to operational systems typically pass through multiple business processes, and the time taken for requested changes to actually appear in production is often lengthy. This means that the time taken to get data collection right the first time is typically dwarfed by the time taken to make changes later. In our framework, we often collect data that have no use within the transactional system itself, and are collected exclusively for analytical purposes.
2. *Integrate external events.* There are many external events that fall outside the realm of data collection per se, but can have a large impact on data analysis. For example, in the retail domain, marketing events like promotions or advertisements are often not directly captured within the transactional system, and are thus not found within the collected data. However, these marketing events can have dramatic effects in terms of patterns within the data. False conclusions can easily be drawn if these external events are not taken into account. In the KDD-Cup 2000 competition (Kohavi et al., 2000), we provided the Gazelle.com marketing calendar to contestants as many of the marketing events were correlated with patterns in the data. Yet several of the participants reached incorrect conclusions because they neglected to look at the marketing calendar.

In summary, the architecture has served us well and has solved many practical issues that would otherwise make data mining of e-commerce data extremely difficult.

2.3 Creation of the Data Warehouse

The creation of a data warehouse requires significant data transformations from an operational system, sometimes called On-Line Transaction Processing, or OLTP (Kimball, 1996). It is often quoted that 80% of the time to complete an analysis is spent in data transformation (Piatetsky-Shapiro et al., 1996). In our application, the analytics component and production component including the website and call center are well integrated and we control the data sources in the production subsystem, allowing us to automate the creation of the data warehouse for those channels.

A process that we call *DSSGen* generates the Decision Support System database automatically, based on the meta-data that we have available and specific operations, such as denormalizations and pivots that we coded.

Our clients have been able to use DSSGen successfully and get the transfer to work in a matter of days, compared to several months of work for common Extract-Transform-Load (ETL) tools. Custom changes to the production site are automatically reflected in the generated data warehouse thereby dramatically reducing the maintenance costs. For example, if in a client implementation, ten new customer attributes are added based on the client's unique registration form, these will automatically be transferred and made available in the data warehouse.

From a business intelligence perspective, the process of automatically creating the data warehouse was extremely successful. Here are some of the challenges we face:

1. *Firewalls*. Firewall issues continue to complicate the implementation because the website is usually in a demilitarized zone (DMZ) (Cheswick & Bellovin, 1994), which has restricted access. This means that on secure implementations that are now common, copying of files across firewalls must be customized.
2. *Integration*. Integration with other data sources still requires the "standard" significant effort. There is little we can do here, except to point to available ETL packages. This may have been an easier route had we used a standard ETL package for our own transfers, but we believe that, in such a case, we could not have provided the tight integration we provide today with DSSGen.

2.4 Business Intelligence

Business Intelligence includes reporting, visualizations, and data mining. In our architecture, we provided clients with an industry standard report writer (Crystal Reports), visualizations, and data mining algorithms that included rules induction, anomaly detection, entropy-based targeted statistics, and association rules. Since different activities require data transformations, we also developed a very powerful transformation engine with an accompanying graphical user interface (GUI).

On the positive side, we were able to derive very interesting insights from clients such as Mountain Equipment Co-op (Blue Martini Software, 2003a) and Debenhams (Blue Martini Software, 2003b). For example, we found that merchandisers were far from optimal in assigning cross-sells and that product associations using association rules (Agrawal & Srikant, 1994) were much better; we identified characteristics of customers who were low spenders but were likely to migrate to a higher tier of heavy spenders; we showed that for Mountain Equipment Co-op, flat-fee shipping was superior to free shipping for revenues and profits, at least in the short term, etc. We also learned several important lessons worth sharing:

1. *Expect the operational channels to be higher priority than decision support.* Insight will come later. When businesses were building their websites and call centers, they were typically backlogged with things that were urgent for these operational channels and that left little time for analysis. Sites went live, call centers were taking calls, but business intelligence was going to be done once things were more stable, often months later.
2. *Crawl, walk, run.* The most immediate need for our clients was basic reporting, not fancy analytics. The businesses were trying to understand basic metrics related to their website performance and needed more out-of-the-box reports such as dashboards of key performance indicators and summary reports, which we started to provide more and more with each release. We found that providing out-of-the-box reports is one way to jump-start the business intelligence process.
3. *Train data analysts.* There is clear recognition now that a large database requires a good Database Administrator (DBA). However, data mining has a "magical" aura surrounding it. Unrealistic expectations about "press

the button and insight will flow out" need to be reset. For people to do data mining effectively they need to be properly trained and this takes time and effort. Data mining methodologies like CRISP-DM (Chapman et al., 2000) can help here.

4. *Tell people the time, not how to build clocks.* In "Built to Last" (Collins & Porras, 1994), the authors suggested that building clocks to tell time is far more important than telling people in time. We found the opposite to be true—clients wanted interesting insights, and early on did not care how we found them. Because many of the insights we discovered generalized well across multiple clients, it was easy to show a graph that depicts how online spending correlates with distance from their physical stores (the farther you live from the nearest retailer's physical store, the more money you spend on the average purchase) than to explain how we found it. Over time we started to develop standard reports that are available out-of-the-box. These reports include interesting findings and highlight insights that make a difference to the business.
5. *Define the terminology.* Our clients often ask questions such as: What is the difference between a visit and a session? How do you define a customer? Did every customer purchase? Why does there appear to be a difference between the same metrics in different reports? Are orders from our Quality Assurance (QA) department included in the revenue, even though the shipping address for all these orders is specified as 555 Foobar Ave and we know not to ship to this address? Writing a good glossary and sharing the terms across reports was something we learned the hard way.

While we learned from the above lessons and believe they can be reasonably addressed, several significant challenges remain elusive:

1. *Make it easier to map business questions to data transformations.* Mapping business questions to data transformations is a complex task today. Can we make that easier? While we built a user interface that supports many useful transformations, fundamental operations like aggregations remain a complex concept to grasp. When System-R was initially conceived at IBM San Jose Research Lab (now Almaden Research Center) in the early 70s, they were designing a language (now SQL) for non-programmers. In a System-R reunion Don Chamberlin (1995) said "What we thought we were doing was making it possible for non-programmers to interact with databases." The SQL92 standard is now 600 pages and the SQL99 standard is 1,000 pages. Is it possible to build a transformation language and a user interface that is significantly easier to learn?
2. *Automate feature construction.* Feature construction requires a mix of domain knowledge and a data miner's expertise. While we are able to provide many features out-of-the-box for our domain, with every client we build hundreds of unique attributes as a customer signature against which to run. These include features specific to their site design, product mix, etc. Can these be easier to construct automatically?
3. *Build comprehensible models.* The goal of data mining is to provide business users with interesting insights. We have restricted ourselves to building models that are easily understood, such as decision trees, decision rules, and Naïve-Bayes. Are there other models that one can build, which are easy to understand by business users?
4. *Experiment because correlation does not imply causality.* When interpreting data mining results it is often the case that correlation is confused with causality. Business users need to be made aware that correlation does not necessarily imply causality. For example, when analyzing the benefits of online search functionality that is provided on our clients' sites, it is immediately apparent that visits with search on the site have a higher average session length than those that do not.

However, upon carefully examining the data, one can see that in order to perform a search on the site a session must have at least two page views, one to type in the search string, and the other to view the search results that are returned (if any). So to truly compare whether people who search on the site spend more time than those who do not, we must first filter out all visits of length one which can account for 50% of all visits. It turns out that even after excluding visits of length one there is still a strong correlation. To establish a causal relationship, one should conduct control/treatment experiments.

5. *Explain counter-intuitive insights.* On a few occasions it becomes difficult to present insights that are seemingly counter-intuitive. For instance, when analyzing a client's data we came across an example of Simpson's paradox (Simpson, 1951). Simpson's paradox occurs when the correlation between two variables is reversed when a third variable is controlled. We were comparing customers and looking at their channel preferences, i.e., where they purchased. Do people who shop from the web-channel only spend more on average as compared to people who shop from more than one channel, such as the web and physical retail stores? The line chart in Figure 1 shows that for each group of shoppers who shopped once, twice, three times, four times, five times, and more than five times respectively, the average spending per customer on the web-only channel is more than the average spending per customer on multiple channels. However, the bar chart in Figure 1 shows that the average spending per customer for multi-channel customers is more than that of the web-only channel. This reversal in the trend is happening because a weighted average is being computed and the number of customers who shopped more than five times on the web is much smaller than the number of customers who shopped more than five times across multiple channels. Such insights are often difficult to explain to business users.

6. *Assess the ROI of insights.* It is difficult to assign a quantitative value to determine the return on investment (ROI) of the insights that are obtained from data mining. In some cases, the insights are directly actionable in which case one can measure the impact of taking the recommended action. For example, in the case of one large automotive manufacturer, they managed to measure the effect of changes to their website that were suggested by our analysis. These changes directly

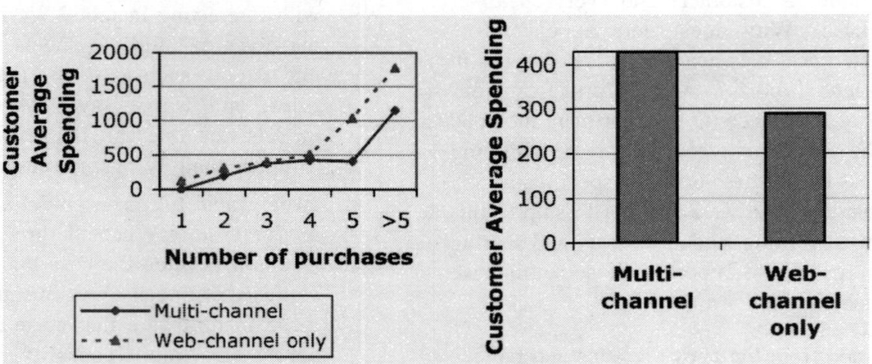

Figure 1: Average yearly spending per customer for multi-channel and web-only purchasers by number of purchases (left), and average yearly spending per customer for multi-channel and web-only purchasers (right). Web-only customers dominate multi-channel customers in their spending in all segments showing number of purchases (left), yet they spend less on average (Simpson's Paradox).

resulted in a 30% improvement in revenue. However, in other cases, the insights might be related to improved browsing experience or better customer satisfaction, the results of which are hard to measure quantitatively. It could make things even harder when they have different or opposite short term effects and long term effects.

2.5 Deployment and Closing the Loop

Insight is only useful if it is shared across the organization and utilized. There are two ways to utilize insights and models:

1. *Share insights*. Insights obtained by data mining should be shared across the organization. Our initial products required people to install client software. In later releases we converted to a browser-based "Analysis Center," where reports and data mining results can be viewed and shared. Users do not need to install anything, just enter a URL into the browser, which made the reports and analyses much more accessible.
2. *Take action*. Score visitors by their likelihood of response, implement a product recommender (e.g., based on associations), and improve the interface on the site based on events. All these things can be done if people see the value. Many of these things are not done often because it is hard to automate the deployment of results. Our experience showed that it is useful to have the architecture providing easy ways to implement product recommendations based on associations and to score customers based on models.

One of the challenges that we see in this area is:

- *Have transformed data available for scoring*. Scoring customers on something of interest implies that information needs to be collected at the touch point (point of interaction with the customer), data transferred to the warehouse, customers scored, and scores transferred back to the operational touch points to close the loop. This cycle with off-line analysis is good for coarse decisions, and developed models are useful for some types of real time choices such as showing different products and images when users return to the website later on. However it is not appropriate for dynamic actions (e.g., recommendation based on the purchase a few minutes ago). Conversely, building a model requires significant data transformations and only simple models can be built without access to transformed data. It is usually too expensive and complex to transform the data at the operational side. Is there a middle ground that is useful? Some companies, such as E. piphany (http://www.epiphany.com), provide real-time scoring and learning based on very simple models.

3. DATA DEFINITION, COLLECTION, AND PREPARATION

In Sections 3 and 4 we drill into the technical details and discuss the low-level lessons learned from data and analysis related issues. Business intelligence efforts must have clear metrics to evaluate success. Once these goals and metrics are defined, organizations must strive to collect the appropriate data, clean and transform them, and make them available for analysis. We divide our discussion of data-related lessons and challenges into three sub-sections: data collection and management, data cleansing, and data processing.

3.1 Data Collection and Management

For any organization, data collection should be driven by its business intelligence goals. As mentioned in Section 2, data collection is often an afterthought (Kohavi, Rothleder, & Simoudis, 2002) and this restricts the type and depth of analysis that can be performed.

1. *Collect data at the right abstraction levels*. Most web analytics are performed using web logs, collected by the web server. The web logs were generated mainly for the purpose of debugging the web server. As a result,

they are "information-poor" and also require significant pre-processing before they are a useful data source for analysis. Web servers are stateless, each page requested is served independently, but all of the pages viewed in a single visit to the website are logically grouped together in a session. Much effort has been expended on devising reliable methods for this process of "sessionizing" web logs (Spiliopoulou et al., 2003). We completely bypassed the issue by having the application server (where the application logic is executed) log the clickstreams and sessions, rather than the web server. The architecture uses cookies to track sessions, and if cookies are not available, it rewrites the URL for each hyperlink to keep track of the session for the visitor (ensuring that the next click belongs to the same session).

2. *Design forms with data mining in mind.* Significant time and effort is spent in designing forms that are aesthetically pleasing. The eventual use of the collected form data for the purpose of data mining must also be kept in mind when designing forms. Analysis of Gazelle.com data (Kohavi et al., 2000) revealed a very large number of female customers. Even customers with male names had their gender recorded as female. The registration form defaulted the gender field to "female" and many customers did not bother to change the default value. To collect unbiased data, the form design must not specify any default value and ask customers to select a value.
3. *Validate forms to ease data cleansing and analysis.* In the electronic world, form data is a big source of data errors. Appropriate form validation can save a lot of time needed for data cleansing and later data analysis. Some example data types that can be validated automatically include date, time, phone numbers, postal addresses, and age (check the value range). For domain data types, use drop down lists instead of free text fields. For example, use a drop down list containing "Decline", "Male", and "Female" for gender.
4. *Determine thresholds based on careful data analysis.* Session timeout duration is an important threshold for clickstream collection. It determines the duration of inactivity after which a session would be considered timed out. In prior work that characterized browsing strategies for users on the World-Wide Web it was determined that the mean time between two browser events across all users was 9.3 minutes and a session timeout threshold of 25.5 minutes (11/2 standard deviations from the mean) was recommended (Catledge & Pitkow, 1995). Analysis of clickstream data from a large clients' website revealed that several user sessions were experiencing a timeout as a result of a low timeout threshold. These users got an unpleasant timeout message and lost their active shopping cart. (More recent versions of the software save the shopping cart automatically at timeout and restore it when the visitor returns.) However, even if it were not for the loss of the shopping cart, identifying a session for analysis purposes is very important because breaking the session could result in an item added to the shopping cart and the checkout process being assigned to different sessions, even if the user experience was that of a single (long) session. Figure 2 shows the impact of different session timeout thresholds set at 10-minute intervals on two large clients. For this experiment we designate a visitor session as having timed out prematurely if the visitor does not make a page request for a duration longer than the timeout threshold, yet comes back (makes a request) in less than 3 hours. If the session timeout threshold were set to 25 minutes then for client A (left chart in Figure 2), 7.25% of all sessions would experience timeout and 8.6% of sessions with active shopping carts would lose their carts as a result. However, for client B (right chart in Figure 2), the numbers are 3.5%

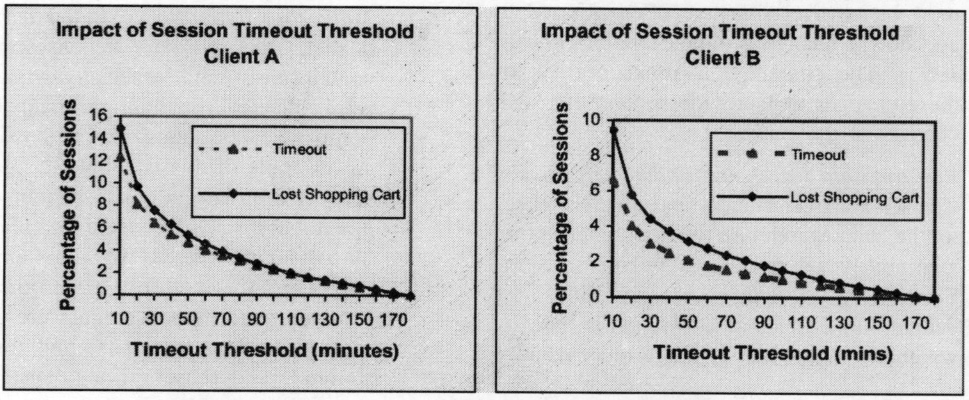

Figure 2: Setting a suitable session timeout threshold.

and 5.1% respectively. Thus, clients must determine the timeout threshold only after careful analysis of their own data. Further, the smooth curves in both the charts do not suggest any threshold beyond which the impact of session timeout would be minimal for either of the two clients. As a general rule, we recommend that the session timeout for e-commerce sites be set to no less than 60 minutes. That is more than double the sessionization time recommended in Catledge and Pitkow (1995). When sessionizing for analysis purposes (as opposed to operational concerns about keeping sessions in memory), the referrer field in the request can be used to further improve the process. If the referring page is another page on the site being analyzed, the allowed threshold could be large (e.g., 120 minutes) because the user has clearly clicked on a link in the current site, while a request with an external referrer could be used to initiate a new session when the gap is longer than 60 minutes.

The following challenges apply to data collection and management:

1. *Sample at collection*. Large e-commerce websites generate on the order of 10–100 million page views in a single day. Logging data for every single request and every session is very expensive in these cases both in terms of the load on the system that logs the data to the database and the space requirements for storing so much data. An obvious question to ask is whether or not to sample at the source (Domingos, 2002). We provided our clients with the ability to sample clickstream collection. Although sampling would effectively address the two issues mentioned above, it introduces new problems. Sampled data will not be able to accurately capture *rare* events such as searching for a particular term or credit card authorization failure. Further, business requirements, such as payment for advertising clickthrough referrals, require that exact (rather than approximate) statistics are available. Can we provide enough flexibility to apply sampling intelligently, while still capturing rare events or required statistics with full accuracy?

2. *Support "slowly changing dimensions."* Visitors' demographics change: people get married, their children grow, their salaries change, etc. With these changes, the visitors' needs, which are being modeled, change. Product attributes change: new choices (e.g., colors) may be available, packaging material or design change, and even quality may improve or degrade. These attributes

that change over time are often referred to as "slowly changing dimensions" (Kimball, 1996). The challenge is to keep track of these changes and provide support for such changes in the analyses.

3. *Perform data warehouse updates effectively.* Can we manage efficient and timely updates to the data warehouse without interrupting availability of results to business users? Further, what are good guidelines for deciding how much data to retain in the data warehouse and when to purge older data?

3.2 Data Cleansing

Data cleansing is a crucial prerequisite to any form of data analysis (Fayyad et al., 1996; English, 1999). Even when most (or all) of the data are collected electronically, as in the case of e-commerce, there can be serious data quality issues. Typical sources for these data quality issues include software bugs, customization mistakes, or plain oversights in (any or all of) the software, implementation, system configuration, data collection, or data transfer (Extract-Transform-Load, or ETL) process. In cleansing data collected by our clients, we have learned a valuable lesson:

- *Audit the data.* We've found serious data quality issues in data warehouses that should contain clean data, especially when the data were collected from multiple channels, archaic point-of-sale systems, and old mainframes. An example of this is shown in figure 3 that shows the orders and visits by hour-of-day for a real website. Orders seem to "follow" visits by five hours, whereas we would expect visits and orders to be close to each other in time. It turned out different servers were being used to log clickstream (visits) and transactions (orders), and these servers' system clocks were off by five hours. One was set to GMT and the other to EST.

There are several significant challenges related to data cleansing in the e-commerce domain:

1. *Detect bots.* Web robots, spiders, and crawlers, collectively called bots, are automated programs that visit websites (Heaton, 2002). Typical bots include web search engines (like Google), site monitoring software (like Keynote), shopping comparators (like mySimon), email harvesters (like Power Email Harvester), offline browsers, and computer science students' experiments. Due to the volume and type of traffic that

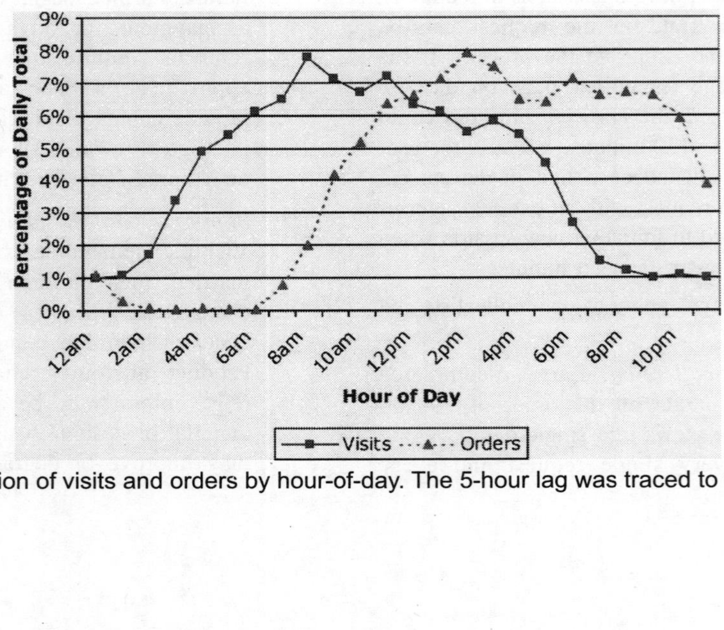

Figure 3: Distribution of visits and orders by hour-of-day. The 5-hour lag was traced to time-zone problems.

they generate, bots can dramatically change clickstream patterns at a website, in turn skewing any clickstream statistics. For example, on several of our client websites we observed that the average page views per visit when bot visits were excluded was 1.5 to 2 times the average page views per visit when bot visits were included. It must be pointed out that in the clickstream collection described here bots appear in short, mostly single request sessions instead of a single long session that can span several days. Even on high volume retail e-commerce sites, between 5% and 40% of visits are due to bots. Identifying bots in order to filter out their clickstreams is a difficult task since they often do not identify themselves adequately or pretend to be real visitors, and different bots can generate radically different traffic patterns. Current bot filtering is mostly based on a combination of a continuously tuned set of heuristics and manual labeling. It is worth mentioning that *page tagging* methods of clickstream collection (Madsen, 2002), which execute blocks of javascript at the client's browser and log the statistics returned by the javascript at a server, avoid bots because they require the execution of javascript, which bots rarely execute. However, people who do not have javascript turned on in their browsers or who click on a link before the javascript code can download and execute will not have their visits correctly logged by page tagging systems. These visits can amount to about 5% of all human visits, thereby resulting in inaccurate clickstream statistics.

2. *Perform regular de-duping of customers and accounts.* Transactional systems usually do not provide safeguards to stop the generation of duplicate customer records. Some businesses also have the notion of accounts, where the mapping between customers and accounts is a many-to-many relationship (one customer may have multiple accounts, or one account may be shared amongst multiple customers). Additional difficulties in identifying unique customers arise in e-commerce systems from the availability of kiosks that are used by multiple people to log on to the website. The fact that customer records might not have enough information to reliably distinguish unique customers poses significant challenges in reliably merging or "de-duping" customer records.

3.3 Data Processing

Most analytical algorithms, and software packages that implement these algorithms, provide limited support for many of the complex data types that occur commonly in retail e-commerce data. Examples of "complex" data types include attributes that are hierarchical, cyclical, or include multiple notions of "missing" values. Specialized data processing is often required to effectively mine this type of data. We will first discuss some lessons in dealing with these types of attributes, and then list some challenges.

1. *Support hierarchical attributes.* In retail, products are commonly organized into hierarchies in a product catalog: SKUs (Stock Keeping Units) represent the most fine-grained definition of a product (e.g., individual SKUs for different colors of the same product), and are derived from products, which are derived from product families, which are in turn derived from product categories. An example product hierarchy is shown in Figure 4. Hierarchies of SKUs, products, families, and categories are typically between three and eight levels deep, and contain between three and ten items at each level—meaning that the total number of unique SKUs could range from a few hundred to several million. A customer purchases SKU level items, but generalizations of purchasing behavior are likely to be found at higher levels (e.g., families or categories). Another example of a hierarchical attribute that occurs frequently in retail data is geography, where the hierarchy could be zip code, city, state, and country.

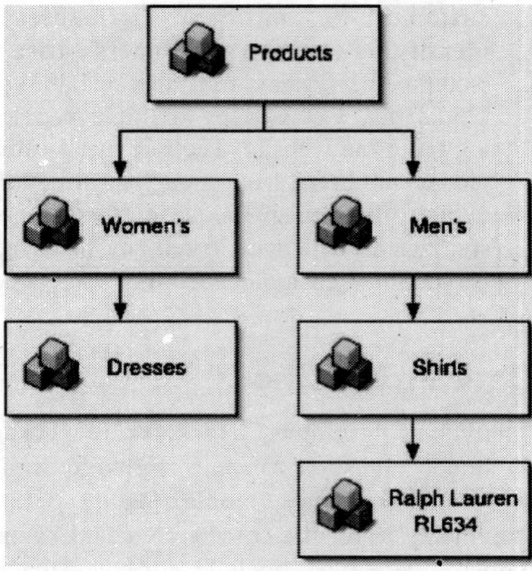

#	Women's	Men's	Shirts	Dresses
1	T	F	F	F
2	F	T	T	F

Figure 4: An example product hierarchy (left) and a pivot for a "Women's" item and a "Men's Shirt" item (right).

For learning algorithms that do not directly support hierarchical attributes, a product hierarchy could be exposed to the algorithms using attributes representing the product family and category. These attributes will often contain many distinct values. Some approaches have been proposed to deal with set-valued attributes (Cohen, 1996) and for improving the efficiency of algorithms that deal with hierarchical attributes (Aronis & Provost, 1997). An alternative, which works well in practice, is to perform what we call a hierarchy pivot. For each node in the product hierarchy that was identified as interesting by the business user, we create a boolean attribute in the purchased line item. The value of the boolean attribute indicates whether the SKU belongs to that node in the hierarchy. Figure 4 shows two example records, the first representing a SKU under the "Women's" node (but not under "Women's Dresses"), and the second representing a SKU under the "Men's Shirts" node.

2. *Handle cyclical attributes*. Due to the transactional nature of retail e-commerce systems, date and time attributes occur frequently (e.g., account creation date, order placement date, and web visit date). However, the common date/time format containing the year, month, day, hour, minute, and second is rarely supported directly by data mining algorithms. Even when it is supported, a date/time attribute is typically treated as a single continuous variable, which rules out the discovery of interesting date and time patterns that generalize to predicting future events. Patterns that generalize most often involve the time *delta* between two dates (e.g., order placement and shipment date), or are based on the *hierarchical* or *cyclical* nature of dates and times (e.g., hour-of-day). In order to effectively mine date and time attributes, data transformations are required to compute time intervals between dates, and to create new attributes taking into account the hierarchical and cyclical nature of dates and times. We found that transforming date-time attributes to multiple attributes, such as hour-of-day, day-of-week, week, day-of-month, month, and quarter is useful in supporting the discovery and visualization of cyclical patterns, such as "Saturday traffic is high." It is worth noting that businesses often define their own

date cycles based on marketing or financial processes, meaning that using standard calendar date cycles to build attributes may fail to uncover patterns.

3. *Support rich data transformations.* We found that it is necessary for a data analytics package to provide integrated transformations with a suitable user interface. Examples of transformations are aggregation, row filtering, column deletion, new column creation with an expression builder, and binning which is the process of mapping integers and real-values to discrete values. Working with these kinds of transformations saved us significant time in data processing.

Some challenges related to processing data include:

1. *Support hierarchical attributes.* Supporting hierarchical attributes is important in practice (see bullet point 1 above). A few algorithms have been designed to support hierarchical attributes directly (Almuallim, Akiba, & Kaneda, 1995; Aronis & Provost, 1997; Zhang, Silvescu, & Honavar, 2002), but they do not scale to large hierarchies. The process of automating the (now manual) process of utilizing hierarchies effectively still remains challenging.
2. *Handle "unknown" and "not applicable" attribute values.* The assignment of attributes, such as size, weight, or color to products is common in e-commerce, and they are often used for restricting search results ("show me all extra-large shirts"), or the grouping of products for display based on common attribute values. These product attributes are coincidentally also valuable for data mining, since generalizations can be found based on the attributes of products, rather than on just the particular type of product. However, some attributes may apply to some classes of products, but not to others. For example, size makes sense for clothes and shoes, but not for books. For books, the size attribute would have a NULL value. In this case, NULL means "not applicable", rather than "unknown", and needs to be treated differently (Quinlan, 1989). In fact, NULLs in database have multiple interpretations and semantics. The ANSI/SPARCinterim report (ANSI/X3/SPARC, 1975) lists 14 of them. We supported this distinction between our two interpretations for NULLs using meta-data. For every attribute, meta-data would determine whether a NULL value should be treated as either "not applicable" or "unknown." "Not applicable" is a distinct value for mining purposes, whereas "unknown" implies that the attribute is relevant but its value is unknown. For example, if a site adds a registration question that asks new customers registering for their gender, then all customers who registered prior to this addition should have a NULL value that implies "unknown." Our solution, while providing a step forward, does not address cases where an attribute may need both an "unknown" and a "not applicable." For example, a "mega-pixel" attribute is applicable only to digital cameras, hence a NULL should imply not applicable; however, for some digital cameras the value may be unknown because the manufacturer did not specify it. The need to have two types of NULLs is complicated by the fact that databases support only one NULL. For real-valued columns in a database, one must resort to special values (e.g., negative infinity) to denote the second semantic NULL, causing problems in aggregate functions like sums and averages. Very few data mining algorithms, with the notable exception of C5.0 (RuleQuest Research, 2003), can correctly accommodate this subtle difference.

4. ANALYSIS

This section presents the technical lessons and challenges based on our experience with analysis of data from our clients. We organize these lessons by the following phases of the data analysis process:

1. understanding and enriching the data,
2. building models and identifying insights,

3. deploying models, acting upon the insights, and closing the loop, and
4. empowering business users to conduct their own analyses.

4.1 Understanding and Enriching Data

The first step after getting the business questions from the client is to get a good overview of the data. We cannot emphasize how much value we have derived from just getting a feel for the data and getting to know what tables are available, what attributes belong to each table, what the different attributes mean, and how they relate to each other.

1. *Statistics*. Elementary statistics including the distribution of each attribute, the number of NULL and non-NULL values, the minimum, maximum, and mean value for each continuous valued attribute are useful in obtaining an overview of the data and for identifying anomalies. Further, in cases where we plan to build predictive models to predict a discrete target such as *campaign responder* or *heavy spender*, it is beneficial to run targeted statistics that give an idea about the degree of correlation between each attribute and the target. We found it extremely useful to order the columns by their information gain (an entropy-based metric) (Quinlan, 1986), highlighting the most critical columns first. Figure 5 shows a lift chart for the target that indicates whether there was a search in the visit in relation to *screen resolution*. Overall, 10.5% of all visits searched (i.e., had the target value true). The chart shows lift greater than one for the commonly used screen resolutions such as 1280 × 1024, 1024 × 768, and 800 × 600 implying that visits with these resolutions tended to search more than the average visit. The resolution 640 × 480 has lift less than one. The reason for this is interesting. We found that when the screen resolution was set to 640 × 480, the search button disappeared past the right edge of the browser screen. In order to access the search button, one would have to scroll to the right, which explains why so few visits with that resolution performed a search.
2. *Weighted averages.* Averaging is a common operation in aggregating data. Although the computation is simple, it is very easy to make mistakes in some situations. In a typical aggregation scenario, *Order Line* (individual line items) data is aggregated to the *Order Header* (a single purchase) level and then to the *Customer* level. Consider, for example, the need to calculate the average amount spent per order line by a customer. The average order line amount per order would be computed in the first aggregation from *Order Line* level to the *Order Header* level by dividing the total order line amount by the number of order lines in the order. However, in the next aggregation from the *Order Header* level to the *Customer* level, it is not correct to simply average the average order line amount per order that was computed previously. Instead, it is necessary to compute a weighted average taking into account the number of order lines in each order placed by the customer. Most transformational tools do not automatically compute averages of averages correctly. We found that by building this knowledge into the tool itself (by having average operations generate weighted numerical attributes rather than simple numerical attributes, and then accordingly taking these weights into account on following average calculations), the chance of user error is reduced.
3. *Visualization.* A picture is worth a thousand words. Visualization tools ranging from elementary *line* and *bar charts* to *scatter plots*, *heatmaps*, and *filter charts* are very useful in identifying interesting trends and patterns in the data.

   Bar charts are used to visualize attribute distributions and to study the degree of correlation between two attributes (see the lift chart in Figure 5).

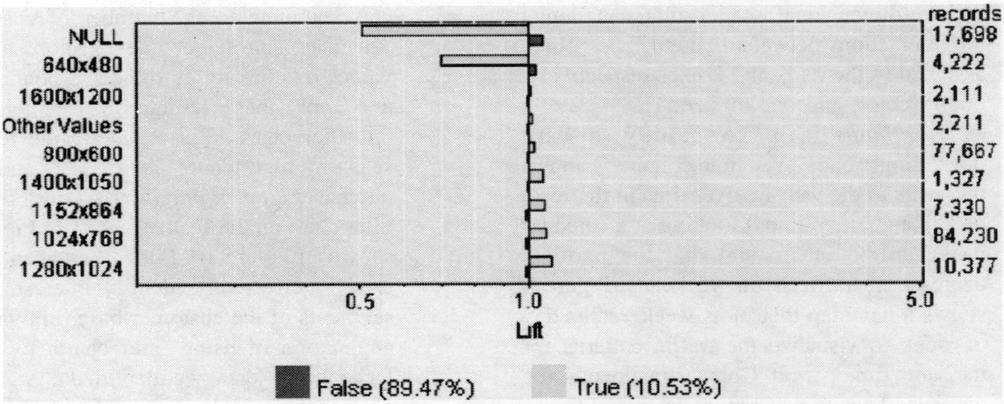

Figure 5: Lift chart showing relationship between screen resolution and search. NULL means the browser returned no information.

Scatter plots enable users to visualize the interaction between multiple attributes. Figure 6 shows a scatter plot where recency and frequency are mapped to the *X* and *Y*-axes respectively; the size of each square is mapped to the number of customers in that segment; and the color of each square is mapped to the average response spending which ranges from *light gray* (low) to *black* (high). Recency and frequency are ordered from one to five with one being the most recent and most frequent respectively and five being the least recent and least frequent respectively. The more recent and more frequent purchasers have a significantly better response in terms of higher average spending than those who have shopped less recently or infrequently. The scatter plot emphasizes the segment sizes due to attribute interactions. The squares are of different sizes indicating that there are a different number of customers in each segment. For instance, the square corresponding to recency = 1 and frequency = 1 is larger than its neighbors since it represents a larger segment of the customer base as compared to its neighbors. Similarly,

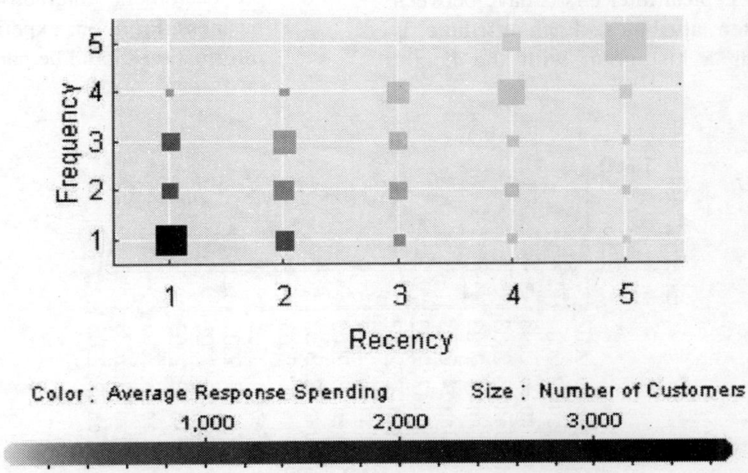

Figure 6: Scatter plot depicting customer segments by recency and frequency.

a three-dimensional scatter plot can depict the interactions between five attributes (three assigned to the *X*, *Y*, and *Z* axes respectively, one to color, and one to size).

Heatmaps help to readily discern interesting trends over time. Figure 7 shows the visits to the website over time in the form of a line chart. Without looking at a calendar it is hard to understand that the periodic decrease in traffic is on weekends. Figure 8 shows a heatmap that plots week versus day of week to visualize the traffic patterns for the same time period. Color is mapped to the number of visits that ranges from *light gray* (low) to *black* (high). The heatmap clearly shows that the website attracts fewer visitors during the weekends (Saturday and Sunday). Further, the entire week of December 30, 2002 had low traffic due to the New Year holidays. Monday, February 17, 2003 had lighter traffic compared to other Mondays in the graph owing to the US President's Day holiday. Such patterns are extremely hard to discern from the chart in Figure 7.

Filter charts allow users to interactively pick different attributes to filter the data on and immediately see the impact of the selected filter settings. Figure 9 shows a sample filter chart with two attributes: *repeat purchaser* and *tenure* (number of years as a customer). Typical filter charts have between five and ten attributes. Each attribute is depicted as a histogram with the height corresponding to the number of customers. The user can select one or more attribute values by clicking on the corresponding bars and apply these settings to see their effect on other charts. For example, the result of selecting high tenure (*tenure* = 3) and repeat purchaser (*repeat purchaser* = true) from the filter chart on the scatter plot from Figure 6 is shown in Figure 10. Filter charts can thus be used to effectively identify interesting sub-segments of the customer base. In a practical application of using filter charts to analyse Debenhams' data, we identified a large group of Debenhams' loyalty card members with very high average spending per order but who had not purchased very recently and were not frequent purchasers (Blue Martini Software, 2003b). Note that Debenhams has contact information for these customers since they are loyalty card members. Thus, customers in this group are good candidates for a marketing promotion encouraging them to purchase again.

4. *Enriched customer signatures.* Customers are the center of many data analysis projects in retail e-commerce. To generate good insights and effective models in customer-centric analyses, it is imperative to generate rich customer signatures covering all aspects of the customers' interactive history with the business. From our experience, the following information should be part of the signature in

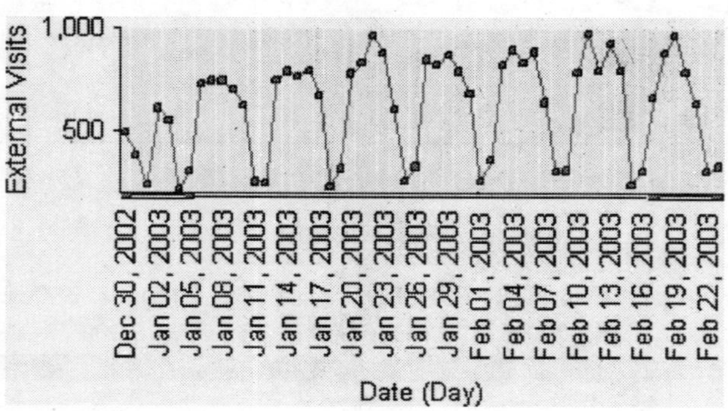

Figure 7: Line chart showing visits to the website over time.

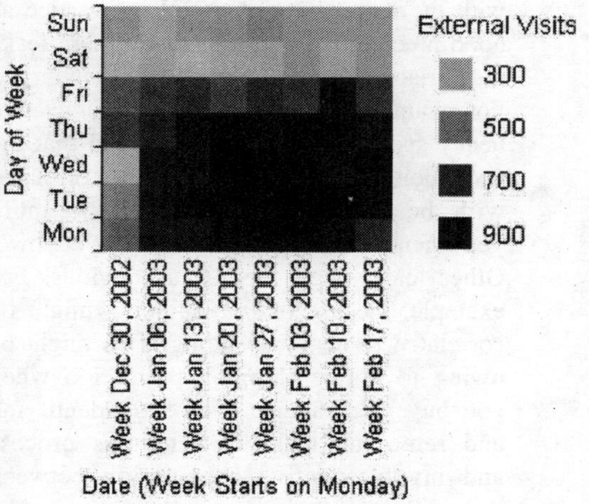

Figure 8: Heatmap showing trends in visits to the website over time.

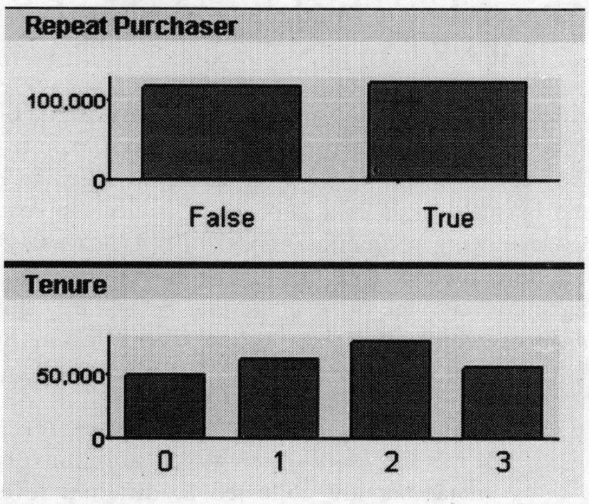

Figure 9: Filter chart depicting two attributes.

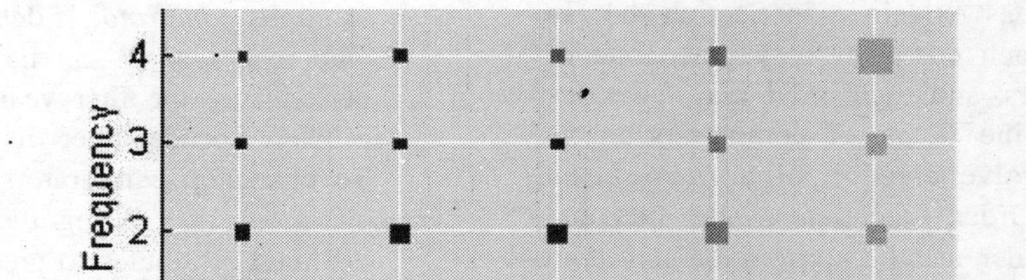

Figure 10: Scatter plot for customer segments filtered to high tenure, repeat purchasers.

general: (1) customer registration information, (2) agg-regated information from customer web visits including referrers, areas of the site visited, products viewed and purchased, average session length, visit frequency, searches, and abandoned shopping carts and their contents, (3) customer purchase information including Recency, Frequency, and Monetary (RFM) scores (Hughes, 2000), (4) campaign response, (5) performance and error-related logs, (6) bricks-and-mortar store shopping history if available, (7) demographic and socio-economic attributes such as those available from data providers such as Acxiom and Experian. Beyond these standard features, every client data has its own set of custom attributes. These attributes can be used to further enrich the customer signature. A rich customer signature can serve as the starting point for many interesting analyses such as *migrator* studies and RFM analysis (Blue Martini Software, 2003a).

4.2 Building Models and Identifying Insights

Analyzing data is a complex task (Berry & Linoff, 1997, 2000). It needs experience and expertise. Nevertheless, starting from the questions specified by the business users is a good and practical approach to developing appropriate models. To a data analyst, building models and identifying novel insights is almost always the more interesting part of the entire analysis project. We share below several lessons we have learned from our experiences in model building.

1. *Mine data at right granularity levels.* Practical data mining scenarios involve data that are collected at different levels of granularity. For example, in retail e-commerce we have *Order Line* level data, *Order Header* level data, and *Customer* level data as explained in Section 4.1. In general, each customer may place one or more orders, and each order may have one or more line items. A common scenario would involve creation of a *star-schema* with the Order Line data as the fact and Order Header and Customer data joined in as dimensions (Kimball, 1996; Kimball et al., 1998; Rosset et al., 1999). The resulting data contains one row per order line with the order header and customer level attributes joined. Computing the number of male and female customers from this data without regard to the granularity levels would give incorrect results because the customer attributes are repeated for each order line that is placed by the customer. The number of males and females must be computed at the correct granularity level (the customer level). Data at different levels of granularity must be suitably aggregated before using it for mining (Pyle, 1999). For instance, to determine the characteristics of heavy spenders the data must first be aggregated to the customer level (Kohavi et al., 2000).
2. *Handle leaks in predictive models.* When building predictive models one has to be careful about potential leaks in the data. Leaks are attributes that are highly correlated with the target but not useful in practice as good predictors. In several cases, these leaks are variables that are derived from the target. For example, in an analysis to characterize heavy spenders, it will be observed that the tax amount is very likely highly correlated with heavy spending in that, the more you spend, the higher is the tax you owe. Other leaks might not be as obvious. For example, the use of free shipping might be correlated to heavy spending. This might be owing to a free shipping promotion when you buy merchandise over $50. Identifying and removing leaks is a tedious process and involves active cooperation between the analyst and the business experts. The problem of leaks is ameliorated to some extent when targets of predictive models are defined based on time-based measures. For example, a *migrator* is defined as a customer who makes small purchases over one time period (say the first year) but migrates to a heavy spender over the next time period. To characterize migrators we identify their characteristics during the earlier year and use these attributes to predict their behavior the following year. A careful selection of attributes used for prediction in this case will reduce the likelihood of leaks. Thus, as opposed to heavy spender analysis that is fraught with potential leaks, it is worthwhile to perform a migrator analysis, which does not suffer as much from the problem of leaks.
3. *Improve scalability.* The need for fast, scalable data mining algorithms has been recognized since the early days of data mining research (Chan & Stolfo, 1997; Freitas, 1998; Freitas & Lavington, 1998; Provost & Kolluri, 1999). The tremendous advances in computing power and systems resources have been matched by the increase in the quantity of data being analyzed. Sites that have 30 million page views per day will need to house about 10 billion records each year. Pfahringer (2002) wrote "in [KDD Cup] 1999 for instance, I was never able to run learning algorithms on the full dataset.

Only sub-samples were practical in terms of processing time or main memory limits." Sampling has been used quite effectively as a way to address the data size problem (Domingos, 2002). It is worth mentioning that sampling should be performed at the correct granularity level. For example, in the retail e-commerce arena, sampling should be performed at the customer (or visitor) level. A certain portion of all customers must be selected at random along with all order data and all clickstream data corresponding to these customers. If sampling is performed at the clickstream level instead, then the resulting sample will include a random subset of all clicks (page requests) from which a clear picture of the customers purchasing behavior and navigational preferences cannot be constructed. Parallel and distributed processing is another effective way of reducing the computation time. While parallel versions of the popular data mining algorithms have received a lot of attention (Agrawal & Shafer, 1996; Maniatty & Zaki, 2000), several practical challenges still remain unsolved. One example is the inability of most data mining algorithms to scale to thousands of attributes. Pfahringer (2002) wrote "In [KDD Cup] 2001, none of the standard tools, not even the commercial ones, could directly deal with the training set of about 2000 examples comprised of approximately 140,000 attributes each."

4. *Build simple models first.* A common mistake often made by analysts involves beginning the analysis without establishing a baseline to compare the results of analysis. The temptation to build powerful models using the most sophisticated tools should be resisted at least until a clear need is established for these models. Business users tend to appreciate and accept models that are more under-standable. Further, the business might have some sort of model already in place. In order to convince the business user that the current model must be replaced, the analyst must start from the existing model as the baseline and work on approaches to improve upon it. Projects where the business users are not comfortable with the models that have been built stand the risk of not being implemented at all. It is therefore a good practice to start simple, earn the confidence of the business user, and then gradually develop more sophisticated models as necessary. In a recent analysis of a client's data, we were required to identify interesting segments within their customer base. The approach we took was to build a data cube based on recency, frequency, and monetary scores that could be easily visualized using simple visualizations. RFM analysis has been the workhorse of marketers for several decades and has been used extensively for customer segmentation (David Shepard Associates, 1998; Hughes, 2000). Additional customer attributes such as demographics, browsing behavior, and purchasing history were used to augment the cube. The business users at the client side who happened to be marketing experts were extremely pleased to see a representation of the data that they understood and could interactively explore using visualization tools such as filter charts described in Section 4.1. We found that the client was much more receptive to our recommendations and appreciative of the efforts we had put in.

5. *Use data mining suites.* There are several advantages of using data mining suites where comprehensive tools for data processing, transformation, cleansing, analysis, and reporting are available in a single package. Such suites simplify data processing, analysis, and closing the loop, as there is no need to transfer data between disparate systems. Further, the availability of different types of tools enables the analysts and business users to pick the tools that are most appropriate for the type of analysis they are performing. Designers of commercial data mining software claimed to have taken this approach from the very beginning. Often however, these suites have several data mining algorithms (Elder & Abbott, 1998) but lack capabilities

such as data transformations, or reporting, or visualization.

6. *Peel the onion and validate results.* Langley addressed the need to move beyond describing the data to providing explanations of the data (Langley, 2002). However, extreme care must be taken while providing explanations of the data. Often during analysis we are likely to come up with superficial correlations that seem interesting and also make perfect business sense. Careful investigation may reveal very different relationships hidden beneath. It is therefore imperative to peel the onion and ascertain the true merit of the proposed explanation of the data. A good example is from the KDD Cup 2000 competition question 3: "*Characterize heavy spenders at Gazalle.com web store*" (Kohavi et al., 2000). Several submissions contained the rule "*Customers who expressed willingness to receive emails from Gazalle.com are heavy spenders.*" At first sight, we found this makes sense as it reflects the customers' loyalty. However, this was primarily due to the correlation between time and the willingness to receive emails. Gazelle.com changed the default for the registration question about receiving emails from *yes* to *no* on 2/28 and back to *yes* on 3/16. The resulting changes in the percentage of customers who are willing to receive emails are evident in Figure 11. Independent of this change, a huge promotion was announced on 2/28 that offered a $10 discount off every purchase. This drove down the percentage of heavy spenders during the promotion period which happened by chance to coincide with the duration for which the default value for the regis-tration question regarding receiving emails was *no.*

4.3 Sharing Insights, Deploying Models, and Closing the Loop

The ultimate objective of most data analysis projects is to use the insights and the models to improve business. The analysis is incomplete until the results of the analysis are shared across the relevant departments in the organization and concrete actions have been taken based on the findings.

1. *Represent models visually for better insights.* Generated models and insights are much better understood when presented in visual format. Simple visual representations such as bar charts, line charts, and heatmaps can convey a lot of information in a concise yet effective manner. Business users do not want to deal with advanced statistical concepts. They want straightforward visualizations and task-

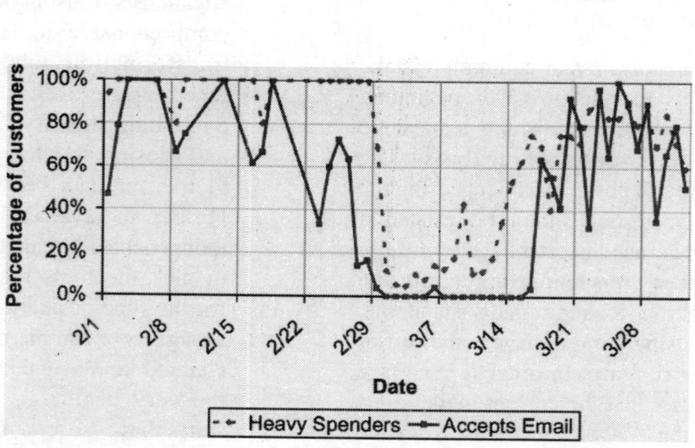

Figure 11: Correlation between heavy spending and willingness to receive emails.

relevant outputs. Consider Figure 12, which summarizes a Naïve-Bayes model for predicting which people earn more than $50,000 in yearly salary. Instead of the underlying log conditional probabilities that the model actually manipulates, the visualization uses bar height to represent evidence for each value of a contributing factor listed on the left of the figure and color saturation to signify confidence of that evidence (Becker, Kohavi, & Sommerfield, 2001). For example, evidence for higher salaries increases with age, until the last age bracket, where it drops off; evidence for higher salaries increases with years of education, with the number of hours worked, and with certain marital statuses (e.g., married to civilian spouse, but not married to a spouse in the armed forces) and occupations (e.g., professional specialty and executive managerial). Note also that the visualization shows only a few attributes that were determined by the mining algorithm to be the most important ones, highlighting to the business users the most critical attributes from a larger set.

2. *Understand the importance of the deployment context.* It is common in practice to have the analyst or data mining team develop the models and have the marketing or the IT team deploy these models (this often happens in an interactive and iterative fashion). In order to ensure a successful deployment of the designed models it is very important to understand the deployment context. For example, a product recommender model based on association rules might not be deployed in its entirety. The marketers responsible for manually picking up cross-sells and up-sells might only want to deploy those rules that make sense to them or might want to merge their hand crafted rules with the generated model. In this case, it is important that the generated model be editable. In another project, we came upon a physical limitation imposed by the mail house that is responsible for printing and mailing physical letters. The client performs segmentation of their customers based on purchase history and propensity to purchase. Multiple monthly campaigns are run based on this segmentation. Each campaign results in an insert for the monthly mailing sent to the customer. The mail house they use has a physical limitation that the different letters belonging to a segment could only be coded by a two-digit code. As a result, the above segmentation process was limited to finding at most 100 distinct segments. This poses a problem especially when the client wants to run up to 30 campaigns each month, which can potentially create 230 segments.

3. *Creating actionable models and closing the loop.* Insights and models that are directly actionable are usually more interesting and

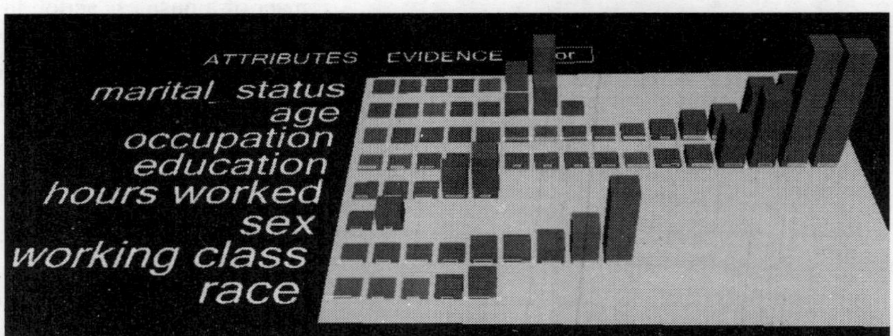

Figure 12: A visualization of Naïve-Bayes.

can directly impact the business. Consider the insight "*Heavy spenders tend to purchase blue shirts*." This might be a good insight but is not readily actionable because it is not clear whether a visitor to the website is a heavy spender or not. On the other hand, an insight like "*Visitors referred by Google tend to purchase blue shirts*." It is easy to determine in real-time whether the visitor to the site is referred from Google and take appropriate action such as promote the latest blue shirts to the visitor. Some models might be actionable but might require complex processing. As a result these models are not readily deployable for use in real-time say at the live website. Finally, it is preferable to develop systems whereby models can be automatically updated with little or no manual intervention. In our system, a product recommender or scoring model can be updated nightly or weekly based on the new data and deployed automatically to the website to help in targeting new visitors.

4.4 Empowering Business Users to Conduct Their Own Analyses

A big challenge for data mining is the need to reduce the time and analytical expertise required to analyze the data. Empowering business users to perform their own analysis would partly address this issue. At the same time, we must mention that expert analysts must perform the more involved analysis. This is to prevent misinterpretation of the results by a non-expert, which can prove to be more costly in the long run.

1. Share the results among business users via simple, easy to understand reports. A web browser accessible business intelligence portal is quickly becoming the method of choice for sharing the insights.
2. Provide canned reports that can be run by business users by simply specifying values for a few parameters such as date ranges. This provides a method to allow business users to change the behaviors of data mining analysis in controlled ways.
3. Technically savvy business users might be comfortable designing their own investigations if a simple graphical user interface is provided as part of the data mining tool.

A variety of challenges related to performing the analysis remain to be addressed:

1. *Visualize models.* More sophisticated models such as rules and associations are not easy to visualize. Despite some recent advances in this area (Zhang, 2000) a suitable visualization approach that will help business users clearly understand the model is yet to be designed.
2. *Prune rules and associations.* Often a product recommender model comes up with thousands or even millions of association rules (Zheng, Kohavi, & Mason, 2001). It is impossible for a human to manually go through even a small number of these rules. Further, scoring based on such complex models is an expensive operation and might slow down the operations at the website where the model is deployed. Some work on generating only top-N rules with respect to certain criterion (Webb, 2000) might help to some extent.
3. *Analyze and measure long-term impact of changes.* Business actions such as promotions, altered procedures, changes to the user experience, etc. have short and long term impact. Often, the short-term impact of an action is easy to measure. For example, test and control groups can be used to identify the impact of a business action in the short term. Long-term impact is much more difficult to analyze and measure. For instance, an email promotion might boost sales in the short term but in the long run frequent email blasts might encourage customers to opt-out from the email list. Frequent promotional campaigns might also result in an undesired effect. Customers who get used to receiving these frequent promotions hold off purchasing products until the next promotion is announced. Retailers have overcome this problem to some extent by not

pre-announcing promotions and designing promotions such that they have very short expiry durations.

5. SUMMARY

We reviewed the Blue Martini Software architecture, which provided us with powerful capabilities to collect additional clickstream data not usually available in web logs, while also obviating the need to solve problems usually bottlenecking analysis (and which are much less accurate when done as an afterthought), such as sessionization and conflating data from multiple sources. We believe that such architectures where clickstreams are logged by the application server layer are significantly superior and have proven themselves with our clients and at other sites like Amazon.com, which uses a proprietary application server.

Our focus on Business to Consumer (B2C) e-commerce for retailers allowed us to drill deeper into business needs to develop the required expertise and design out-of-the-box reports and analyses in this domain. Further, we believe that most lessons and challenges will generalize to other domains outside of retail e-commerce. We reviewed many lessons at differing levels of granularity. If we were to choose the top three, they would be:

1. Integrate data collection into operations to support analytics and experimentation, and make it easy to transfer the collected information to a data warehouse where it can be combined and conflated for a 360-degree view.
2. Do not confuse yourself with the target user. Provide as much insight out-of-the-box and make it easy to derive insight and take action. While this is certainly easier in a specific domain, we believe it is the only way to succeed in businesses that have little analytical expertise in-house. Business users have a daily job to perform and learning about data mining is not on the top of their agenda. However, insight that can impact their decisions and help them optimize the business is certainly ranked high.
3. Provide simple reports and visualizations before building more complex models. Many of the strongest insights are usually a side effect of a business process. If something looks too good to be true, or has too high a confidence, you must peel the onion and drill deeper keeping in mind that correlation does not imply causality.

For challenges, the top three would be:

1. The ability to translate business questions to the desired data transformations is especially hard.
2. Efficient algorithms whose output is comprehensible for business insight, and which can handle multiple data types (dates, hierarchical attributes, different granularity data) need to be designed.
3. Integrated workflow. Many business tasks require multiple people and processes (Chapman et al., 2000). More guidance and tracking of progress is necessary.

The web is an experimental laboratory (Kohavi, 2001) where hundreds of experiments can be performed easily and quickly, but data must be collected for reasons other than operational performance and debugging (the main reasons for standard web logs). E-commerce is still in its infancy, with less than a decade of experience. Best practices and important lessons are being learned every day. The Science of Shopping (Underhill, 2000) is well developed for bricks and mortar stores. Despite our success with the Blue Martini architecture, there is significant work remaining in understanding data mining in the context of retail e-commerce.

ACKNOWLEDGMENTS

We thank the members of the data mining team at Blue Martini Software for the numerous discussions and debates that have helped to shape the ideas in this paper. We are grateful to our clients for sharing their data with us. We thank the editors and the anonymous reviewers for their insightful comments and suggestions on improving the paper. We are also grateful to numerous people who helped us with feedback, including Jon Becher, Tom Breur,

Rob Cooley, Rob Gerritsen, David Liu, Brij Masand, Foster Provost, Ross Quinlan, Paat Rusmevichientong, David Selinger, Evangelos Simoudis, Jim Sterne, Kai Ming Ting, Noe Tuason, Alex Tuzhilin, Geoff Webb, Andreas Weigend, and Shenghuo Zhu.

REFERENCES

ANSI/X3/SPARC. (1975). Study group on data base management systems. Interim Report, ANSI.

Agrawal, R., & Srikant, R. (1994). Fast algorithms for mining association rules. In *Proceedings of the 20th International Conference on Very Large Data Bases* (*VLDB'94*) (pp. 487–499). Morgan Kauffmann.

Agrawal, R., & Shafer, J. (1996). Parallel mining of association rules. *IEEE Transactions of Knowledge and Data Engineering,* 8, 962–969. IEEE. http://www.almaden.ibm.com/cs/people/ragrawal/papers/parassoc96.ps.

Almuallim, H., Akiba, Y., & Kaneda, S. (1995). On handling tree-structured attributes. In *Proceedings of the Twelfth International Conference on Machine Learning* (*ICML'95*) (pp. 12–20). Morgan Kauffmann.

Ansari, S., Kohavi, R., Mason, L., & Zheng, Z. (2001). Integrating E-commerce and data mining: Architecture and challenges. In *Proceedings of the IEEE International Conference on Data Mining* (*ICDM'2001*). IEEE. http://www.lsmason.com/papers/ICDM01-eCommerceMining.pdf.

Aronis, J., & Provost, F. (1997). Increasing the efficiency of data mining algorithms with breadth-first marker propagation. In *Proceedings of Knowledge Discovery and Data Mining* (*KDD'97*) (pp. 119–122). AAAI Press.

Becker, B., Kohavi, R., & Sommerfield, D. (2001). Visualizing the simple Bayesian classifier. *Information Visualization in Data Mining and Knowledge Discovery, 18,* 237–249. Morgan Kaufmann. http://robotics.stanford.edu/users/ronnyk/ronnyk-bib.html.

Berry, M., & Linoff, G. (1997). *Data mining techniques: For marketing, sales, and customer support.* John Wiley & Sons.

Berry, M., & Linoff, G. (2000). *Mastering data mining: The art and science of customer relationship management.* John Wiley & Sons.

Blue Martini Software. (2003a). Blue Martini business intelligence at work: Charting the terrains of MECWebsite data.

http://robotics.stanford.edu/users/ronnyk/ronnyk-bib.html.

Blue Martini Software. (2003b). Blue Martini business intelligence delivers unparalleled insight into user behavior at the Debenhams Web site. http://robotics.stanford.edu/users/ronnyk/ronnyk-bib.html.

Catledge, L., & Pitkow, J. (1995). Characterizing browsing strategies in the World-Wide Web. *Computer Networks and ISDN Systems, 27:6,* 1065–1073. Elsevier Science. http://citeseer.ist.psu.edu/catledge95characterizing.html.

Chan, P., & Stolfo, S. (1997). On the accuracy of meta-learning for scalable data mining. *Journal of Intelligent Information Systems, 8:1,* 5–28. Kluwer Academic Publishers.

http://www1.cs.columbia.edu/~pkc/papers/jiis97.ps.

Chapman, P., Clinton, J., Kerber, R., Khabaza, T., Reinartz, T., Sherer, C., & Wirth, R. (2000). Cross industry standard process for data mining (CRISP-DM) 1.0. http://www.crisp-dm.org/.

Cheswick, W., & Bellovin, S. (1994). *Firewalls and internet security: Repelling the wily hacker.* Addison-Wesley Publishing Company.

Cohen, W. (1996). Learning trees and rules with set-valued features. In *Proceedings of the AAAI/IAAI Conference, 1,* 709–716. AAAI Press.

Collins, J., & Porras, J. (1994). *Built to last, successful habits of visionary companies.* Harper Collins Publishers.

Cooley, R., Mobasher, B., & Srivastava, J. (1999). Data preparation for mining world wide web browsing patterns. *Knowledge and Information Systems, 1:1.* Springer-Verlag. http://maya.cs.depaul.edu/~mobasher/papers/webminerkais. ps.

David Shepard Associates. (1998). *The newdirect marketing:How to implement a profit-driven database marketing strategy,* 3rd edition. McGraw-Hill.

Domingos, P. (2002). When and how to subsample: Report on the KDD-2001 panel. *SIGKDD Explorations, 3:2*, 74–76. ACM. http://www.acm.org/sigs/sigkdd/explorations/issue3-2/contents.htm#Domingos.

Elder, J., & Abbott, D. (1998). A comparison of leading data mining tools. *Tutorial at the Knowledge Discovery and Data Mining Conference (KDD'98)*. ACM. http://www.datamininglab.com/pubs/kdd98_elder abbott_nopics_bw.pdf.

English, L. (1999). *Improving data warehouse and business information quality: Methods for reducing costs and increasing profits*. John Wiley & Sons.

Fayyad, U., Piatetsky-Shapiro, G., Smyth, P., & Uthurusamy, R. (Eds.). (1996). *Advances in knowledge discovery and data mining*. MIT Press.

Freitas, A. (1998). Tutorial on scalable, high-performance data mining with parallel processing. In *Proceedings of the Principles and Practice of Knowledge Discovery in Databases (PKDD'98)*. Springer.

Freitas, A., & Lavington, S. (1998). *Mining very large databases with parallel processing*. Kluwer Academic Publishers.

Heaton, J. (2002). *Programming spiders, bots, and aggregators in Java*. Sybex Book.

Hughes, A. (2000). *Strategic database marketing*, 2nd edition. McGraw-Hill.

Kimball, R. (1996). *The data warehouse toolkit: Practical techniques for building dimensional data warehouses*. John Wiley & Sons.

Kimball, R., & Merz, R. (2000). *The data webhouse toolkit: Building the Web-enabled data warehouse*. John Wiley & Sons.

Kimball, R., Reeves, L., Ross, M., & Thornthwaite, W. (1998). *The data warehouse lifecycle toolkit: Expert methods for designing, developing, and deploying data warehouses*. John Wiley & Sons.

Kohavi, R. (1998). Crossing the Chasm: From academic machine learning to commercial data mining. *Invited talk at the Fifteenth International Conference on Machine Learning (ICML'98)*, Madison, WA. Morgan Kauffmann. http://robotics.stanford.edu/users/ronnyk/ronnyk-bib.html.

Kohavi, R. (2001). Mining e-commerce data: The good, the bad, and the ugly. In *Proceedings of the Seventh ACM SIGKDD International Conference on Knowledge Discovery and Data Mining (KDD 2001)* (pp. 8–13). ACM Press. http://robotics.stanford.edu/users/ronnyk/ronnyk-bib.html.

Kohavi, R., Brodley, C., Frasca, B., Mason, L., & Zheng, Z. (2000). KDD-Cup 2000 organizers' report: Peeling the onion. *SIGKDD Explorations, 2:2*, 86–98. ACM Press. http://robotics.stanford.edu/users/ronnyk/ronnykbib-html.

Kohavi, R., & Provost, F. (2001). Applications of data mining to electronic commerce. *Data Mining and Knowledge Discovery, 5:1/2*. Kluwer Academic. http://robotics.Stanford.EDU/users/ronnyk/ecommerce-dm.

Kohavi, R., Rothleder, N., & Simoudis, E. (2002). Emerging trends in business analytics. *Communications of the ACM, 45:8*, 45–48. ACM Press. http://robotics.stanford.edu/users/ronnyk/ronnyk-bib.html.

Langley, P. (2002). Lessons for the computational discovery of scientific knowledge. *Proceedings of the First International Workshop on Data Mining Lessons Learned (DMLL'2002)*. http://www.hpl.hp.com/personal/Tom_Fawcett/DMLL-2002/Langley.pdf.

Lee, J., Podlaseck, M., Schonberg, E., & Hoch, R. (2001). Visualization and analysis of clickstream data of online stores for under-standing Web merchandising. *Data Mining and Knowledge Discovery, 5:1/2*. Kluwer Academic.

Linoff, G., & Berry, M. (2002). *Mining the Web: Transforming customer data*. John Wiley Sons.

Madsen, M.R. (2002). Integrating Web-based clickstream data into the data warehouse. DM Review, August, 2002. http://www.dmreview.com/editorial/dmreview/print action.cfm?EdID=5565.

Maniatty, W., & Zaki, M. (2000). A requirements analysis for parallel (KDD) systems. In *Proceedings of the Data Mining Workshop at the International Parallel and Distributed Processing*

Symposium (*IPDPS'2000*). IEEE Computer Society.

Mason, L., Zheng, Z., Kohavi, R., & Frasca, B. (2001). Blue Martini eMetrics study. http://developer.bluemartini.com.

McJones, P. (1995). The 1995 SQL reunion: People, projects, and politics an informal but first-hand account of the birth of SQL, the history of System R, and the origins of a number of other relational systems inside and outside IBM. http://www.mcjones.org/System_R/SQL Reunion_95/sqlr95-System.html.

Pfahringer, B. (2002). Data mining challenge problems: Any lessons learned? In *Proceedings of the First International Workshop on Data Mining Lessons Learned* (*DMLL'2002*). http://www.hpl.hp.com/personal/Tom_Fawcett/DMLL-2002/Proceedings.html.

Piatetsky-Shapiro, G., Brachman, R., Khabaza, T., Kloesgen, W., & Simoudis, E. (1996). An overview of issues in developing industrial data mining and knowledge discovery applications. In *Proceedings of the Second International Conference on Knowledge Discovery and Data Mining* (*KDD'96*) (pp. 89–95). AAAI Press.

Provost, F., & Kolluri, V. (1999). A survey of methods for scaling up inductive algorithms. *Data Mining and Knowledge Discovery, 3:2*, 131–169. Kluwer Academic.

Pyle, D. (1999). *Data preparation for data mining*. Morgan Kauffmann.

Quinlan, R. (1986). Induction of decision trees. *Machine Learning, 1*, 81–106. Kluwer Academic.

Quinlan, R. (1989). Unknown attribute values in induction. In *Proceedings of the Sixth International Machine Learning Workshop* (*ICML'89*) (pp. 164–168). Morgan Kauffmann.

Rosset, S., Murad, U., Neumann, E., Idan, Y., & Pinkas, G. (1999). Discovery of fraud rules for telecommunications: Challenges and solutions. In *Proceedings of the Fifth ACM SIGKDD International Conference on Knowledge Discovery and Data Mining* (*KDD'99*) (pp. 409–413). ACM Press. http://www-stat.stanford.edu/%7Esaharon/papers/fraud.pdf.

RuleQuest Research. (2003). C5.0: An informal tutorial. http://www.rulequest.com/see5-unix.html.

Simpson, E. (1951). The interpretation of inter-action in contingency tables. *Journal of the Royal Statistical Society, Ser. B, 13*, 238–241.

Spiliopoulou, M., Mobasher, B., Berendt, B., & Nakagawa, M. (2003). A framework for the evaluation of session reconstruction heuristics in Web usage. *INFORMS Journal of Computing, Special Issue on Mining Web-Based Data for E-Business Applications, 15:2*. http://maya.cs.depaul.edu/~"mobasher/papers/SMBN03.pdf.

Tan, P., & Kumar, V. (2002). Discovery of Web Robot sessions based on their Navigational patterns. *Data Mining and Knowledge Discovery, 6:1*, 9–35. Kluwer Academic. http://www-users.cs.umn.edu/~ptan/Papers/DMKD. ps.gz.

Underhill, P. (2000). *Why we buy: The science of shopping*. Touchstone Books.

Webb, G. I. (2000). Efficient search for association rules. In *Proceedings of the Discovery and Data Mining Conference* (*KDD 2000*) (pp. 99–107). ACM Press. http://portal.acm.org/citation.cfm?id=347112&coll= portal&d= portal & CFID=8086514&CFTOKEN =81282849.

Zhang, H. (2000). Mining and visualization of association rules over relational DBMSs. PhD thesis, Department of Computer and Information Science and Engineering, The University of Florida. http://citeseer.ist.psu.edu/cache/papers/cs/20450/http:zSzzSzetd.fcla.eduzSzetdzSzufzSz2000zSzana7033zSzEtd.pdf/zhang00mining.pdf.

Zhang, J., Silvescu, A., & Honavar, V. (2002). Ontology-driven induction of decision trees at multiple levels of abstraction. In *Proceedings of Symposium on Abstraction, Reformulation, and Approximation. Lecture Notes in Arti-ficial Intelligence* (Vol. 2371), Springer-Verlag.

Zheng, Z., Kohavi, R., & Mason, L. (2001). Real world performance of association rule algorithms. In *Proceedings of the Knowledge Discovery and Data Mining Conference* (*KDD 2001*) (pp. 401–406). ACM Press. http://www.lsmason.com/papers/KDD01-Real AssocPerformance.pdf.

CASE STUDY 6 SUMMARY

This study discusses lessons learned from e-commerce projects completed by the authors over a period of four years at a company by the name Blue Martini Software. A data mining system was built for business users. The system included data collection, creation of a data warehouse, transformations as well as reporting, visualization and data mining. The system was made available to a number of users and data was analysed from more than twenty clients. The size and complexity of these projects varied from a few thousand records to 100 million records. The authors present a variety of very useful lessons learned in requirements gathering, data collection, creation of a data warehouse, extracting business intelligence, and system deployment. Furthermore a number of challenges that remain have been discussed. These include a need for more sophisticated tools for visualization, a need to prune rules and associations, and finally a need to be able to analyse and measure long-term impact of changes.

CASE STUDY 6 EXERCISES

1. What major lessons are described in this case study regarding data gathering and data cleaning?
2. What major lessons were learned regarding data mining analysis of data?
3. What challenges did the authors identify that still remain to be addressed?

CHAPTER

7 Search Engines and Query Mining

LEARNING OBJECTIVES

After completing this chapter, you will be able to:

- Understand the role of search engines and how they work
- Learn the characteristics of web search
- Understand a typical search engine architecture
- Explain the Page Rank algorithm
- Understand what query mining is how it may be useful, and
- Find other resources to learn further about search engines and about query mining

7.1 INTRODUCTION

Most libraries have a relatively small collection of documents and a catalogue to search the documents. The Web on the other hand is a very large collection of documents. In fact, perhaps more than ten billion pages were indexed by Google in 2013. A Google blog dated 25 July 2008 claims that there are more than one trillion (1000 Billion!) unique URLs on the Internet. The search engines, directories, portals and indexes are the Web's "catalogues" allowing a user to carry out the task of searching the Web for the information that he/she requires.

A number of websites provide a large amount of interesting information about search engines. In a recent study dated November 2013 it was found that Google dominates the search engine market accounting for about two-thirds of the searches carried out by users all over the world. This is in contrast to about 40% of the search engine visits in 2004. In 2013, Microsoft accounted for less than 20% while Yahoo! accounted for just over 10%.

A USA company comScore has indicated that almost 20 billion searches were conducted in October 2013 with Google ranking first with about 13 billion. Microsoft ranked second with 3.5 billion searches while Yahoo! accounted for over two billion. It has been reported that many users spend as much as 70% of their online time searching the Web.[1]

CHAPTER OVERVIEW

This chapter deals with search engines and what they consist of and how they produce the results that they do when a user poses a search query. In addition, the chapter deals with how the search terms may be mined to obtain interesting and useful information. The next section, Section 7.2, describes the differences between normal information retrieval and searching the Web. Section 7.3 describes a number of characteristics of search engines. This includes a discussion about searching using a search engine as well as users' goals when they search and the quality of search results. Section 7.4 explains search engine functionality. The main functions of any search engine are briefly explained. Section 7.5 presents architecture of a search engine. The components of this architecture are now described. These include the crawler as well as the indexer. Section 7.6 deals with the presentation of the results. This involves ranking of result Web pages using the Page Rank algorithm. An example of how the algorithm works is presented. The next section describes query mining. A number of applications of query mining are described.

7.2 DIFFERENCES BETWEEN WEB SEARCH AND INFORMATION RETRIEVAL

A Web search is very different than a normal information retrieval search of a document because of the following factors:

- ***Bulk:*** The Web is very large, much larger than any set of documents used in information retrieval applications. As noted above, the number of Web pages indexed by Google in 2013 was estimated to be more than ten billion. Furthermore, it has been estimated that there are perhaps one trillion documents on the Web.
- ***Diversity:*** The Web is very diverse. The Web pages differ widely in structure, quality and their usefulness. Web pages may consist of text, tables, diagrams, figures, images, movies, audio, animation and other multimedia content. The authors can be from anywhere with any background. The pages are built using a variety of software and are stored on a variety of machines all over the world.
- ***Growth:*** The Web continues to grow in size exponentially. The number of new pages added to the Web each day was some years ago estimated to be between one million and seven million. A more recent estimate is not available.
- ***Dynamic:*** A text document does not change unless a new version is produced while the Web changes significantly with time. One estimate suggests that about one third of the Web

[1] It is difficult to obtain reliable statistics about the Web. Different sources quote different statistics and it is difficult to precisely estimate even some basic statistics. For example, the number of new pages added each day is estimated anywhere between 1 million and 7 million depending on the source, the date and the definition of a new page.

changes each year while another estimate suggests that 40% of the .com pages change every day (every day!—perhaps a bit difficult to believe). The link structure of the Web itself changes quickly as new links are established and some current ones removed. In another study, 50% of pages were found to disappear within 50 days.

- ***Demanding Users:*** Users sitting at a computer are very impatient. They demand immediate results otherwise they abandon the search and move on to something else. They rarely read more than one or two screens of results returned by a search engine even when the query they have posed is short and ambiguous and is not carefully thought out. More and more users are looking to the search engines for all kinds of information including the latest news.
- ***Quality of Documents:*** Text documents are usually of high quality since they usually go through a quality control process because they are expensive to produce. In contrast, much of the information on the Web has no quality controls and much of it is of low quality. Some people claim that may be only 10% of the Web pages (or less) are of high quality. Furthermore, it has been estimated that as much as 30% of the content on the Web is duplicated.
- ***Hyperlinks:*** A normal text document contains citations but has no hyperlinks. On the other hand the hyperlinks are very important component of a Web document. They provide important information by linking to other Web documents. It has been estimated that about half of the traffic on the Web is users navigating using links. Some search results may return only index pages providing little content but many useful links.
- ***Queries:*** Generally search engine queries are short (1 to 3 words), quite ambiguous due to synonyms and homonyms (for example, windows and gates). The number of terms in queries appears to be growing somewhat.

It is therefore clear that Web search is very different than classical information retrieval given that the Web is a huge collection of documents of variable quality compared to say documents in a library which are a much smaller collection of documents of relatively high quality.

We now look at the characteristics of search engines given the task that they try to perform.

7.3 CHARACTERISTICS OF SEARCH ENGINES

Designing and building a good search engine is a challenging task because of the requirements of scalability and performance. A robust search engine must be distributed over thousands or even tens of thousands of machines. Given such a large number of machines, machine failure is a common occurrence, it is critical that the search engine deal with the integrity of data. In addition, in a large distributed database environment one must also deal with load distribution to ensure high levels of performance.

Search engines are huge databases of Web pages as well as software packages for indexing and retrieving the pages that enable users to find the information of interest to them. Normally the search engine databases of Web pages are built and updated automatically by Web crawlers. When one searches the Web using one of the search engines, one is not searching the entire Web. Instead one is only searching the database that has been compiled by the search engine and this database, it is claimed, is likely to contain only a small percentage of the pages available on the Web. Normally the huge database is searched using some kind of index that has been built. Although search engines try to update their databases by using Web crawlers to find pages that have changed, most pages in a search engine database can be some hours or even days old. Users increasingly demand up to date information from search engines, for example, users expect search engines to be able to find the latest news. The search engines are able to deal with such user demands by working with newswire services and refreshing newspaper pages frequently thus providing information about news stories as they happen.

It is worth noting that the search engine business is an advertising business. Every search engine provides advertising (sometimes called sponsored links). For example Google generated a profit in the last quarter of 2013 of about $15 Billion.

There are a variety of ways businesses advertise on the search engines. Most commonly, whenever a particular keyword is typed by the user, related sponsored links appear with the results of the search. Even the order of the sponsored links is important. The top link advertiser pays more than lower ranked links. An advertisement in position 6 or lower may not be even visible on the first page.

Given the importance of visibility of an enterprise's website on the major search engines, some new businesses that claim to improve a site's visibility and thus improve traffic have sprung up. These businesses are called 'search engine optimizers' or SEOs. The businesses use a variety of tricks in trying to improve visibility of a site including building a collection of Web pages on related and popular topics and have all of them pointing to the website whose visibility is to be improved. The sole purpose of these pages (called spam pages) is to improve visibility of the target website. No wonder millions of new pages are added to the Web each day. Perhaps a significant proportion of these are set up only to play the "site visibility game".

7.3.1 Problems with Searching Using a Search Engine

Querying a search engine involves the user specifying a number of keywords that are used by the search engine to search its indexes to find relevant documents. One of the major problems with this approach is that specifying query keywords can challenging. For example, if I wish to find what the search engines try to do, I could use many different keywords including the following:

- objectives of search engines
- goals of search engines
- what search engines try to do

I could also use phrases, for example, "what search engines try to do" although often such phrase queries face the problem of scarcity. All of the queries listed above produce a different set of results, although one would expect some common items in the results. Other problems can arise because of the nature of the English language in which the same word can have more than one meaning (homonyms). For example, the following words have more than one meaning and use of such words in a query is likely to result in a variety of documents[2]:

[2] Gates and Windows may refer to parts of a house or to Bill Gates and Windows operating system. Bush may refer to a small plant, area outside the populated areas in Australia or to George Bush (father or son!). Current may refer to electric current, current in a river or recent and so on.

Gates
Windows
Bush
Current
Screen
Slight
Muffler

Furthermore, it is difficult for a search engine to be certain what users want. Some users may be seeking destinations while others may want only a small number of highly relevant results and do not care if the recall is low. Recall essentially measures the proportion of relevant documents returned by the search engine. It is defined later. Also, users do not want to be served with a number of items that are duplicates of each other. This happens frequently if a user's keywords relate to a news story because it is quite likely that the same story is published in many newspapers given that the source of the story may be the same for them all, for example Reuters. An obvious way to improve the search process would be to remove duplicates and to introduce some good feedback mechanism. For example, a query can either be refined by the user or can be refined by the search engine by asking the user to provide feedback on the results displayed. The user could indicate which of the retrieved items are relevant and which are not. The refined query can then provide improved results, providing the user another opportunity to further refine the query. Considerable research is currently being done regarding some of these issues including using information about pages that users click when served with results of a query.

It is a diverse group of users who use the Web. Some users are as young as 5 years old, others over 80 or even 90 years old. It has been estimated that about 15% to 20% of users belong to each of the age groups under 21, 21–30, 31–40, 41–50 and over 50 years. In the USA some 20% had education only up to high school while 50% had some college education including about half of them having completed a bachelor's degree. Another 25% or so had completed either a Masters or PhD degree. About 20% of the user population were students. A search engine is therefore attempting to meet the needs of a diverse group of users.

7.3.2 The Goals of Web Search

There has been consideration research into nature of search engine queries. A 2002 study deals with the information needs of the user making a query. It has been suggested that the information needs of the user may be divided into three classes:

1. ***Navigational:*** The primary information need in these queries is to reach a website that the user has in mind. The user may know that such a site exists (for example, a user knows that there is a website for Air India) or may have visited the site earlier but does not know the site URL.
2. ***Informational:*** The primary information need in such queries is to find a website that provides useful information about a topic of interest. The user does not have a particular website in mind. For example, a user may wish to find out the difference between an

ordinary digital camera and a digital SLR camera or a user may be want to find about IT career prospects in Kolkata.

3. ***Transactional:*** The primary information need in such queries is to go to a website to perform some kind of transaction. The user may or may not know the target website. An obvious example is to buy a book. The user may wish to go to amazon.com or the user may want to go to a local website, for example, flipkart.com. Another user may be interested in downloading some images or some other multimedia content from a website.

The study estimated that the percentage of queries from each of these categories. The percentages were estimated to be in the following ranges:

Navigational queries	20–25%
Informational queries	40–50%
Transactional queries	30–35%

We assume these percentages have changed with the growth in online shopping over the last ten years.

7.3.3 The Quality of Search Results

The quality of results from a search engine ideally should satisfy the following requirements:

1. ***Precision:*** Only relevant documents should be returned.
2. ***Recall:*** All the relevant documents should be returned.
3. ***Ranking:*** A ranking of the documents providing some indication of the relative relevance of the results should be returned.
4. ***First screen:*** The first page of results should include the most relevant results.
5. ***Speed:*** Results should be provided quickly since users have little patience.

These kinds of considerations are not unique to search engines. In the information retrieval field the conventional concepts of precision and recall were designed in the early 1950s and have been used extensively. Often information retrieval evaluation uses test reference collections which consist of a collection of documents and a set of queries. The results of any retrieval set can then be compared with the set of relevant documents that is already known. A similar approach is not possible for the search engines.

Precision deals with questions like "what percentage of documents retrieved are relevant?" and "what rankings are the most relevant documents being given?"

Recall deals with the question "what percentage of relevant documents is returned by the search engine?" The requirement of a high level of recall is generally in conflict with precision and correct ranking. If we wish to improve recall, precision is almost always going to go down unless some user feedback mechanism is used which adds complexity and cost to the search process that is required to provide instant results to the user.

In the information retrieval field, it is known that precision and recall usually have a trade-off relationship that is often shown by a precision-recall graph (A good example of such a graph is given at http://www.searchtechnologies.com/precision-recall.html). It is well known that in this trade-off relationship:

1. Precision decreases faster than recall increase
2. It is much more difficult to improve precision than improve recall

It has been claimed that in a Web search users are often looking for one single document or a website. Users usually do not and do not wish to go through many documents. It is therefore important that a search engine provides the most relevant documents with high ranking so that they are visible generally in the first screen of information.

7.3.4 Definition—Precision and Recall

Brief definitions of the two concepts are given below.

Precision is the proportion of items retrieved that are relevant.

Recall is the proportion of relevant items retrieved.

Therefore

Precision = number of relevant retrieved/total retrieved
= {Total Retrieved ∩ Total Relevant}/Total Retrieved

Recall = number of relevant retrieved/total relevant items
= {Total Retrieved ∩ Total Relevant}/Total Relevant

Figure 7.1 illustrates the relationship between precision and recall.

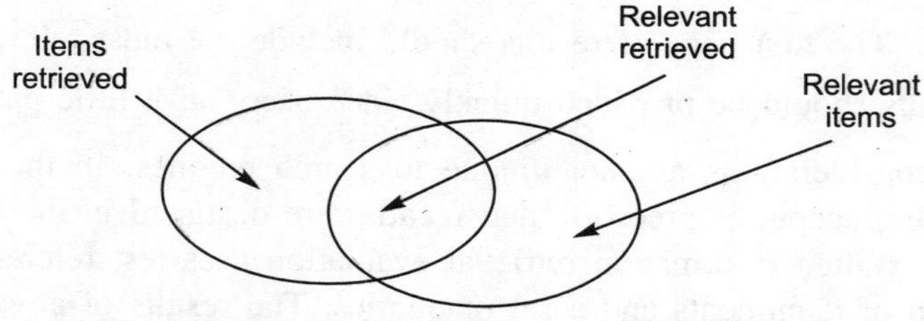

Figure 7.1 Recall and precision in information retrieval.

Although recall and precision are appropriate concepts for evaluating an information retrieval system, the major problem with using these two metrics for Web search is that recall is impossible to measure. We don't know and have no way of knowing how many relevant documents are there on the Web and thus cannot determine what proportion of relevant documents has been retrieved.

Furthermore, the recall and precision criteria require that each item be labelled either relevant or irrelevant. Often there are documents that cannot be put in either of these two categories.

7.4 SEARCH ENGINE FUNCTIONALITY

A search engine is a rather complex collection of software modules. We discuss a number of functional areas.

A search engine carries out a variety of tasks. Some of these tasks are similar to those described for CRISP in Chapter 1. These include:

1. ***Collecting information:*** A search engine would normally collect Web pages or information about them by Web crawling or, if allowed, by human submission of pages.
2. ***Evaluating and categorising information:*** In some cases, for example when Web pages are submitted to a directory, it may be necessary to evaluate and decide whether a submitted page should be selected. In addition it may be necessary to categorise information based on some ontology[3] used by the search engine.
3. ***Creating a database and creating indexes:*** The information collected needs to be stored either in a database or some kind of file system. Indexes must be created so that the information may be searched efficiently.
4. ***Computing ranks of the Web documents:*** A variety of methods are being used to determine the rank of each page retrieved in response to a user query. The information used may include frequency of keywords, value of in-links and out-links from the page and frequency of use of the page. In some cases human judgement may be used.
5. ***Checking queries and executing them:*** Queries posed by users need to be checked, for example, for spelling errors and whether words in the query are recognisable. Once checked (and perhaps corrected), a query is executed by searching the search engine database.
6. ***Presenting results:*** How the search engine presents the results to the user is important. The search engine must determine what results to present (not all the information that the search engine has about the resulting items needs to be presented) and how to display them.
7. ***Profiling the users:*** To improve search performance the search engines carry out user profiling that deals with the way users use search engines.

7.5 SEARCH ENGINE ARCHITECTURE

No two search engines are exactly the same in terms of size, indexing techniques, page ranking algorithms, or speed of search. It has been found that if the same query is posed to two search engines, the results are often different although both results usually contain some common items.

A typical search engine architecture as shown in Figure 7.2 consists of many components including the following three major components to carry out the functions that were listed in the last section:

1. ***The crawler* and the *indexer:*** Collects pages from the Web, creates and maintains the index.
2. ***The user interface:*** To allow users to submit queries and for result presentation.
3. ***The database* and the *query server:*** Stores information about the Web pages and processes the query and returns results.

[3] Ontology is a philosophical concept that has a number of definitions. Ontology is about studying being or existence as well as the basic categories thereof—trying to find out what entities and what types of entities exist. In computer science, ontologies help in representing knowledge. The aim of ontology is to create a shared understanding between humans and computers.

All search engines essentially include a crawler, an indexer and a query server although the algorithms used in these components and the quality of the algorithms vary significantly. We now discuss these components.

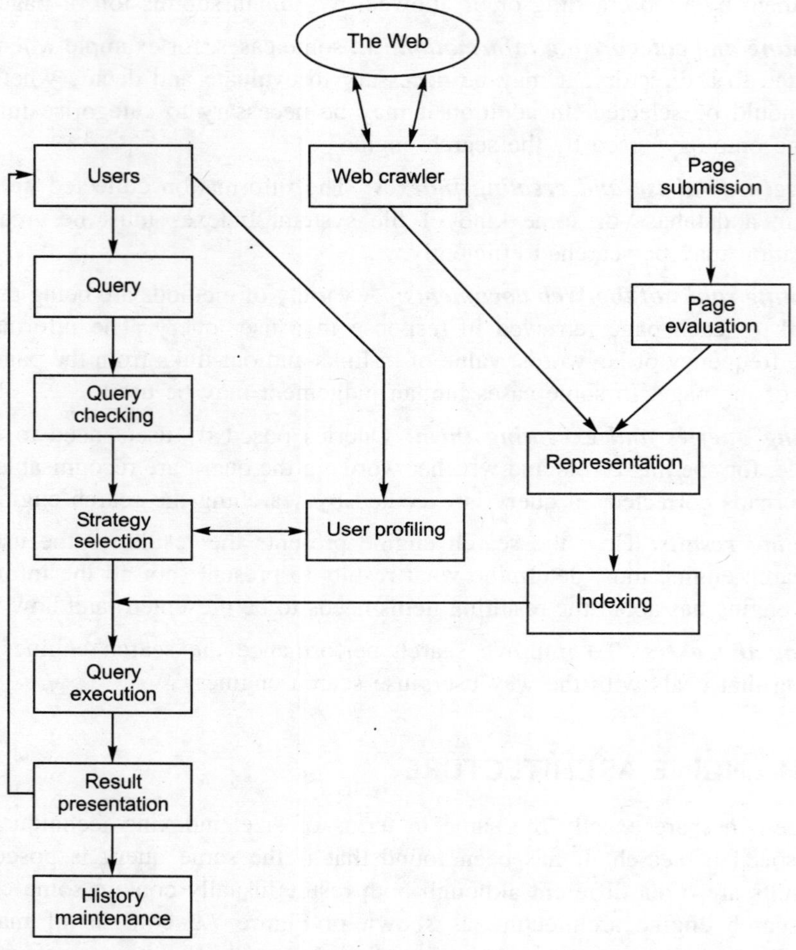

Figure 7.2 A typical search engine architecture.

7.5.1 The Crawler

The crawler (or spider or robot or bot) is an application program that carries out a task similar to graph traversal. It is given a set of starting URLs that it uses to automatically traverse the Web by retrieving a page, initially from the starting set. Some search engines use a number of distributed crawlers. Crawlers tend to return to each site on a regular basis, perhaps once in two months, to look for changes. Often search engines have a list of sites that change frequently, for example, newspaper sites, and visit them much more frequently, even every few hours.

Since a crawler has a relatively simple task, it is not CPU-bound. It is bandwidth bound. In crawling, bandwidth can become a bottleneck.

A Web crawler must take into account the load (bandwidth, storage) on the search engine machines and sometimes also on the machines being traversed in guiding its traversal. For example, when a crawler is being run, the resources used by it should not be so high that it disrupts the use of the Web by other users. It is expected that a crawler would not swamp the network and would not swamp the individual Web servers. There are a number of ways to reduce network traffic, for example avoid large pages, avoid .gif pages and avoid sites with large multimedia material.

As noted above, a Web crawler starts with a given set of URLs and fetches the pages that the URLs refer to. The crawler then reads the out-links of the pages so fetched and fetches those pages. This continues until no new pages are found or a threshold is reached. The number of new URLs found in the beginning grows quickly but as more and more pages are fetched and indexed the number of new pages found will reach a peak and then decline as much of the Web is traversed. Of course while the crawler is fetching pages, new pages are being put on the Web and old pages are being deleted or being modified. Therefore in some way a crawler could continue finding new or modified pages for ever. In practice however a threshold is often used to terminate a crawler session.

Each page found by the crawler is often not stored as a separate file otherwise four billion pages would require managing four billion files. Usually lots of pages are stuffed into one file.

Crawlers follow an algorithm like the following:

1. Find base URLs—a set of known and working hyperlinks are collected
2. Build a queue—put the base URLs in the queue and add new URLs to the queue as more are discovered
3. Retrieve the next page—retrieve the next page in the queue, process and store in the search engine database
4. Add to the queue—check if the out-links of the current page have already been processed. Add the unprocessed out-links to the queue of URLs
5. Continue the process until some stopping criteria are met

The above algorithm shows that if a page is not linked to any page, the crawler can never find it and therefore the search engines will not show it in response to any query. Some search engines allow users to submit their Web pages to them. If a page has been submitted in that way, it is more likely be indexed by the search engine.

The task of a crawler is rather large since as the crawler collects more pages it discovers more links and has even more work ahead of it. To understand the task, let us consider that a crawler was to collect one million pages a day (that is, 365 million pages a year). To do this task, a crawler needs to find 700 pages per minute! A search engine therefore cannot maintain up to date information even if it consists of more than one crawler. One expects a search engine crawler to at least manage to visit every site once a month.

A crawler would often have a traversal strategy. It may traverse the Web breadth first, depth first or the traversal may be priority based. Breadth first traversal is claimed to perform better than depth first traversal since it better spreads load. Priority based traversal has been found to perform better since priority based traversal is often based on frequency of change of pages and *PageRank* of pages. The crawl order is important since it also impacts the quality of the index because a crawler is only going to crawl part of the Web.

7.5.2 The Indexer

Given the size of the Web and the number of documents that current search engines have in their databases, an index is essential to ensure efficient query evaluation. Many researchers recommend an inverted file structure in which each document is essentially indexed on every word other than the most common words. Google uses this approach. These indexes may be built while the crawler is collecting the Web pages or this could be done later. Indexing can be a very resource intensive process and is often CPU-bound since it involves a lot of analysis of each page. The search engines have refined indexing approaches ensuring that indexes can be updated quickly.

As noted earlier, the Web has no catalogue although some directory-type search engines do exist. A search engine index is the closest thing to a giant Web catalogue although the user does not have direct access to it. For a search engine to answer queries efficiently from a collection of billions of pages, the search engine needs an efficient index. In addition, the indexer may be required to assist in page ranking.

Building an index requires document analysis and term extraction. Term extraction may involve extracting all the words from each page, elimination of stop words (common words like "the", "it", "and", "that") and stemming (transforming words like "computer", "computing" and "computation" into one word, say "computer", since there is little point in treating them as different words and similarly transforming "find" and "found" into one word) to help modify, for example, the inverted file structure. It may also involve analysis of hyperlinks. The Web, as we have noted earlier, poses particularly difficult information retrieval problems due to its rapid growth and its dynamic nature. The indexes therefore require major updates every time a cycle of crawling has been completed. These updates take time even after a page has been visited by a crawler.

In automatic indexing of Web documents, many parts of the documents are difficult to use for indexing. This for example applies to multimedia content. Keywords also need to be extracted from a wide variety of document formats including PDF, MS Excel and MS Word. In the early days of search engines, most search engines only extracted terms from the title and some other parts of the documents (e.g. meta-tags) while some search engines used the full documents. The recent trend has been to use the full documents and store them in the search engine database. The information is not updated every day and may be somewhat stale given the dynamic nature of the Web.

A good indexing approach is to create an index that will relate keywords to pages. Clearly every page has many keywords and an index should allow access to the pages based on any of these keywords efficiently. The overheads of maintaining such indexes can be high.

An inverted index, rather than listing keywords for each page, lists pages for each keyword. The roles of keywords and pages have therefore been "inverted". This description is not quite accurate because an inverted database normally still maintains a collection of pages including its content in some way. A good example of an inverted file is a review journal which has a list of article titles, their reviews and a keyword index which lists keywords and for each keyword, a reference to articles that contain the keyword for each keyword. This index however is far from being complete in that not all words in the article would have been used for indexing.

As an example of an inverted index consider the data structure shown in Table 7.1. This index specifies a number of keywords and the pages (the pages are stored elsewhere) that contain the keywords. If we were searching for "data mining" we look for pages for each keyword "data" and "mining" and then find the intersection of the two lists and obtain page numbers 26 and 41.

Table 7.1 A simple inverted index

Words	*Page ID*
data	10, 18, 26, 41
mining	26, 30, 31, 41
search	72, 74, 75, 76
engine	72, 74, 79, 82
google	72, 74, 90

The challenging part of such an exercise is when the two lists are large. For example, in Google "data" appears in more than 1.4 billion pages (on 10 March 2014) and "mining" appears in more than 70 million pages. Finding an intersection of these very large lists takes time. The usual approach is to split the lists across many machines to find the intersection quickly. The task becomes easier if one of the lists is relatively smaller than the others. Also, the speed is improved if much of the inverted index is main memory based. Since a search engine might be using a thousand or more machines and each machine could have perhaps a gigabyte of main memory, much of the index can in fact be stored in the main memory.

Another problem is to search for phrases like "data mining". The above intersection will provide us a list of documents that have "data" and "mining" in them. Looking for the phrase "data mining" requires that we find a subset of the list produced by the intersection found above. One possible solution is to store the position of the word in the inverted index as well and then it is possible to find if the words are next to each other.

Given that the number of unique keywords on the Web is several million (including proper names), this kind of index is huge. It can occupy almost as much storage as the Web pages do. As noted earlier, to deal with this problem the index may be distributed over many machines.

7.5.3 Updating the Index

Crawlers usually continuously crawl the Web and new content is discovered all the time. The inverted index must also be updated continuously. There are a number of options for index maintenance. Firstly it is not possible to regularly regenerate the whole index since this is quite expensive and a substantial amount of resources are used redoing what was already done. Another less expensive option is to incrementally update the index. Depending on how the index is stored, updating may be relatively easy but at some stage after many updates it may become necessary to rebuild the whole index which normally will take substantial resources. Yet another option is to create an auxiliary index which is used with the main index so the most recent pages are picked up from the auxiliary index. The auxiliary index continues to grow and use of both main and auxiliary index together then becomes inefficient. Eventually the two indexes are then merged.

7.5.4 Query Server

First of all, a search engine needs to receive the query and check the spelling of keywords that the user has typed. If the search engine cannot recognise the keywords as words in the language or proper nouns it is desirable to suggest alternative spellings to the user. Once the keywords are found to be acceptable, the query may need to be transformed. It is assumed that all queries are case insensitive so the keywords are transformed into lower case. Stemming is then carried out and stop words are removed unless they form part of a phrase that the user wants to search for.

7.5.5 Query Composition

Query composition is a major problem. Often a user has to submit a query a number of times using somewhat different keywords before more or less the "right" result is obtained. A search engine providing query refinement based on user feedback would be useful. Search engines often cache the results of a query and can then use the cached results if the refined query is a modification of a query that has already been processed.

Search engines are coming up with new features all the time. A feature that may be worth considering is that the user is able to choose from a number of different collections on the Web, e.g. the user could be given an option to search or not search articles in scholarly journals, newspapers, .com sites, .gov sites, .edu sites and so on.

Since a simple request may be formulated in a number of ways and the user is provided no indication of which one might be most suitable, providing a feedback cycle by which the user can refine the query may help the user obtain better results. Another approach might be to provide the user an overview of items so that the user develops a better understanding of the field that the information is about. Another possibility might be to provide user with a collection of keywords related to the keywords, as is done in Google Suggest, to assist in refining the query.

7.5.6 Query Processing

Search engine query processing is quite different than query processing and query optimisation in relational database systems. In database systems, query processing requires that attribute values match exactly the values provided in the query. In search engine query processing, an exact match is not always necessary. A partial match or a fuzzy match may be sufficient. Often search engines assign a weight to each document that has been retrieved to indicate the "goodness of fit". Some search engines provide an indication of how well the document matches the user query.

A major search engine will run a collection of machines, several replicating the index. A query may then be broadcast to all that are not heavily loaded. If the query consists of a number of keywords then the indexes will need to be searched a number of times and as discussed earlier an intersection of the results will need to be found. A search engine may put weights on different words in a query. For example, if a query has the words "going" "to" "Paris" then the search engine could well put greater weight on the word Paris than the word going. Also, search engines often give higher weights to results that have all the query words close to each other in the document.

7.5.7 Caching Query Results

Network traffic due to the Web has been growing strongly in the last few years. Although more and more bandwidth is becoming available and bandwidth is becoming cheaper, the delay in fetching pages from the Web continues to be one of the major complaints of the users. It is therefore natural to look for ways to reduce Web traffic and improve latency. The most common approach is to use Web caches and proxies as intermediaries between the client browser processes and the machines serving the Web pages. A Web cache or proxy essentially mediates access to the Web for improved efficiency. It is an intermediary that acts as server on behalf of some other server by supplying Web resources without contacting the server.

Essentially a cache is supposed to catch a user's or client's request, get the page that the user has requested if one is not available in the cache and then save a copy of it in the cache. It is assumed that if a page is saved, there is a strong likelihood that it will be requested again by the same user or some other user. Also, the Web has some very popular sites which are requested frequently. The proxy essentially satisfies such requests without going to the Web server.

Since even the largest cache cannot store everything that the users are requesting, a proxy cache must have algorithms to replace pages in the hope that the pages being stored in the cache are fresh and are likely to be pages that users are likely to request. The page replacement algorithm used in a proxy is the key to the efficiency of the proxy cache. Page replacement is an old problem, having been studied by operating system researchers since the 1960s for managing CPU cache. The Web cache page replacement problem is perhaps slightly different. The most common page replacement algorithms are least recently used (LRU), least frequently used (LFU) and remove the largest page. We will not discuss these algorithms here.

Proxy caching has many advantages. It reduces average latency in fetching Web pages, reduces network traffic and reduces load on busy Web servers. Also, since all user requests go through a cache, it is possible for site managers to monitor who is accessing what information and if necessary block some of the sites. This can be rather useful since most enterprises wish to block pornographic and hate sites which no employee should have any need to visit.

It is common practice for Web browsers to cache Web pages in a user's PC main memory or disk. A part of the user's hard disk is usually dedicated to the cache to store pages that the user has browsed. The browsers provide the user with some control on how large the cache should be by providing a setting for cache size. The browser cache is particularly useful when the user hits the back button since the most recently visited pages are likely to be in the cache and do not need to be fetched again.

Proxy caches are designed to provide a facility for an enterprise similar to that provided by the client cache for an individual user. Enterprise proxy caches are therefore shared caches and are often very large, even hundreds of gigabytes. Since they are caching a large number of pages that have been requested by employees, even a large proxy cache may not be very effective if the user community is diverse. In some experiments though, it has been shown that the hit rate of a well designed proxy cache can be as high as 50%.

7.5.8 Results Presentation

Before presentation of results to the user, the results must be ranked. Ranking is often based on page popularity in terms of number of other pages providing links to it.

How much of what has been found should be presented to the user and what is the best way to present it? Regarding how much, the number of items retrieved could be very large. Should all items retrieved be presented to the user? Would it be better to present only the 100 or 200 most relevant items given that users very rarely look beyond a screen or two of results? Most current search engines present the retrieved items as a list on the screen with some information for each item, for example, the type of document, its URL, perhaps the date of the document and a very brief extract from the document description. Other presentation styles are possible. One possibility might be to present the retrieved documents as clusters of documents with some common features.

7.6 RANKING OF WEB PAGES

As discussed in the last chapter, the Web consists of a huge number of documents that have been published without any quality control. It is therefore important to devise methods for determining the relative importance and quality of the pages given a topic of interest or given a query.

Search engines differ in size significantly and so the number of documents that they index may be quite different. Also, no two search engines will have exactly the same pages on a given topic even if they were of similar size.

Various search engines follow different algorithms for ranking pages although they may still return the same pages at the top of their lists. Even if search engines return good documents at the top of the rankings, it is not uncommon for irrelevant documents to make it to the high rankings and appear in the top one or two pages. For example, searching for "Computer Science Australia" in mid-2004 using Google, one of the computer science departments at a university in the USA was returned as a highly ranked document.

When ranking pages, some search engines pay considerable importance to location and frequency of keywords and phrases in the page and some may consider the meta-tags as well. Some search engines may give more importance to pages that have the required keywords close to the top of the page, or in the title. This may be based on the assumption that if a page is important to the topic, it will mention the topic from the beginning.

7.6.1 PageRank Algorithm

Google has the most well-known ranking algorithm, called the PageRank algorithm, that has been claimed to supply top ranking pages that are relevant. The PageRank algorithm is based on using the hyperlinks as indicators of a page's importance. It is almost like vote counting in an election. Every unique page is assigned a PageRank. If a lot of pages vote for a page by linking to it then the page that is being pointed to will be considered important. The voting is not fully democratic since votes cast by important pages are given more importance than votes cast by unimportant pages. Votes cast by a link farm (a page with many links) are given less importance than votes cast by an article that only links to a few pages. Internal site links also count in assessing PageRank. PageRank has no relationship with the content of the page, the PageRank stands on its own.

PageRank was originally developed based on a probability model of a random surfer visiting a Web page. The probability of a random surfer clicking on a link may be estimated based on the number of links on that page. The probability of the surfer clicking any link is assumed to be inversely proportional to the number of links on the page. The more links a page has the less chance that a surfer will click on a particular link. For example, if we assume that the Web has a total of 100 pages and a page had a PageRank value of 2, it is supposed to indicate that the random surfer would reach that page on an average twice if he/she surfs the Web separately 100 times.

Therefore the probability for the random surfer reaching one page is the sum of probabilities for the random surfer following links to that page. The probability model also introduces a damping factor to take into account that the random surfer sometimes does not click on any link and jumps to another page at random. If the damping factor is d (assumed to be between 0 and 1) then the probability of the surfer jumping off to some other page is assumed to be $1 - d$. The higher the value of d the more likely the surfer will follow one of the links. Given that the surfer has $1 - d$ probability of jumping to some random page; every page has a minimum PageRank of $1 - d$.

The algorithm essentially works as follows. Let A be the page whose PageRank PR(A) is required. Let page A be pointed to by pages T_1, T_2, etc. Let $C(T_1)$ be the number of links going out from page T_1. PageRank of A is then given by:

$$\text{PR}(A) = (1 - d) + d(\text{PR}(T_1)/C(T_1) + \text{PR}(T_2)/C(T_2) + \cdots)$$

The constant d is the damping factor. Therefore the PageRank is essentially a count of its votes as we noted earlier. The strength of a vote depends on the PageRank of the voting page and the number of out-links from the voting page. If a page has many out-links, each link has quite a low weight when compared to the weight of a link from a page of similar PageRank that had only one or two out-links.

To compute the PageRank of a page A we need to know the PageRank of each page that points to it (i.e. votes for it) and the number of out-links from each of those pages. Let us consider a simple example followed by a more complex one.

Example 7.1—A Simple Three Page Example

Let us consider a simple of only three pages. We are given the following information:

1. The damping factor is 0.8
2. The page A has an out-link to B
3. The page B has an out-link to A and another to C
4. The page C has an out-link to A
5. The starting PageRank for each page is 1.

We may show the links between the pages as in Figure 7.3.

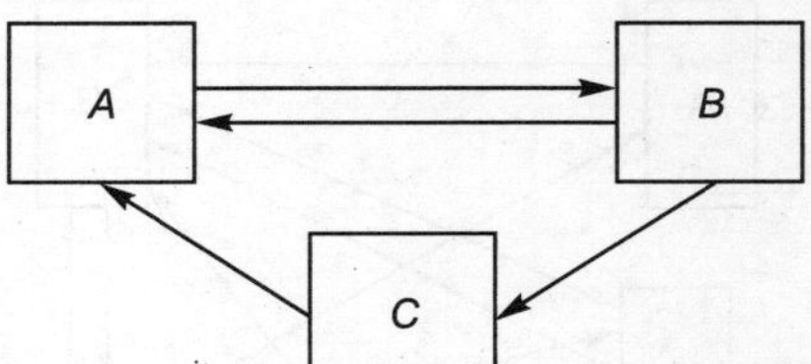

Figure 7.3 The three Web pages in Example 7.1.

The PageRank equations may be written as:

$$\text{PR}(A) = 0.2 + 0.4\text{PR}(B) + 0.8\text{PR}(C)$$

$$\text{PR}(B) = 0.2 + 0.8\text{PR}(A)$$

$$\text{PR}(C) = 0.2 + 0.4\text{PR}(B)$$

Since these are three linear equations in three unknowns, we may solve them. First we write them as follows if we replace PR(*A*) by *a* and others similarly:

$$a - 0.4b - 0.8c = 0.2$$

$$b - 0.8a = 0.2$$

$$c - 0.4b = 0.2$$

The solution of the above equations is given by

$$a = \text{PR}(A) = 1.19$$

$$b = \text{PR}(B) = 1.15$$

$$c = \text{PR}(C) = 0.66$$

Note that the total of the three PageRanks is 3.0. We will discuss this later. First we show a slightly more complex example that has five pages.

Example 7.2—A Five Page Example

Consider five pages *A*, *B*, *C*, *D*, and *E* whose PageRanks have been arbitrarily assigned and out-links are known. As we compute the PageRanks, we will find that the initial PageRanks don't have much influence on the final PageRanks. Starting from the initial PageRank allocations we will recompute the PageRanks at each iteration. We are given the following information about the pages:

1. Page *A* has PageRank of 1 and has one link to *B*
2. Page *B* has PageRank of 2 and has two links to *C* and *D*
3. Page *C* has PageRank of 3 and has three links to *B*, *D*, and *E*
4. Page *D* has PageRank of 2 and has four links, to *A*, *B*, *C*, and *E*
5. Page *E* has PageRank of 3 and has three links, to *B*, *C*, and *D*

The links are displayed in Figure 7.4. We are not asserting that these pages are not connected to the rest of the Web but to simplify our calculations of PageRank we assume as if these pages are an island.

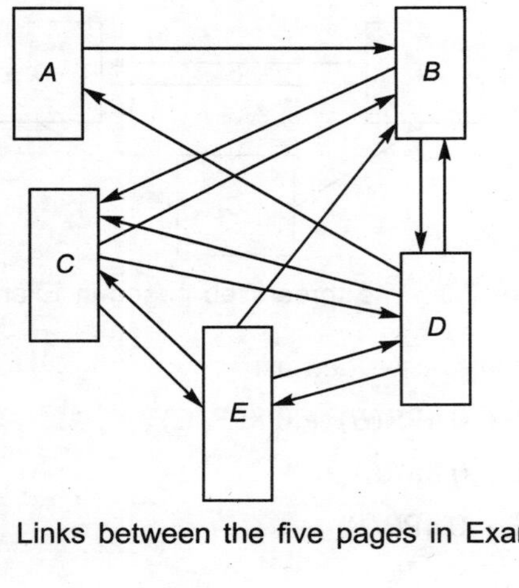

Figure 7.4 Links between the five pages in Example 7.2.

We first make a list of the in-links based on the above out-links. The list is shwon in Table 7.2.

Table 7.2 In-links of the pages in Example 7.2

Page name	*In-links*
A	*D*
B	*A, C, D* and *E*
C	*B, D* and *E*
D	*B, C* and *E*
E	*C* and *D*

We will assume a dampening factor of 0.9 which is essentially used to ensure that in most cases the PageRank will be slightly dampened given the chance that at every page the random surfer will not click on any link and go off to some random page. The result of this dampening factor is, for example, if a page was two links away from a very highly ranked page then the highly ranked page would not be able to pass all of its PageRank to a page that is two links away. We now find $d*PR(X)/C(X)$ which is what a page X can pass on to the page that X is pointing to:

1. Page A has one out-link to B, its PageRank is 1 and therefore $PR(A)/C(A)$ is 1. Since $d = 0.9$, A's vote is worth 0.9 and it will pass on 0.9 to page B.
2. Page B has two out-links to C and D, its PageRank is 2 and therefore $\text{PR}(B)/C(B)$ is 1. Therefore B will also pass on 0.9 to C and D.
3. Page C has three out-links to B, D, E, its PageRank is 3 and therefore $\text{PR}(B)/C(B)$ is again 1. C passes 0.9 to B, D and E.
4. Page D has four out-links, to A, B, C, E, its PageRank is 2, and therefore $\text{PR}(B)/C(B)$ is 0.5. D passes on 0.45 to A, B, C and E.
5. Page E has three out-links to B, C, D, its PageRank is 3, and therefore $\text{PR}(B)/C(B)$ is 1. E passes on 0.9 to B, C and D.

Now we can carry out an iteration and revise the PageRanks (Note the 0.1 in the calculations below relates to $1 - d$ in the formula given that $d = 0.9$)

$$\text{PR}(A) = (1 - d) + d\left(\frac{\text{PR}(D)}{C(D)}\right) = 0.1 + 0.45 = 0.55$$

$$\text{PR}(B) = (1 - d) + d\left(\frac{\text{PR}(A)}{C(A)} + \frac{\text{PR}(C)}{C(C)} + \frac{\text{PR}(D)}{C(D)} + \frac{\text{PR}(E)}{D(E)}\right)$$

$$= 0.1 + 0.9 + 0.9 + 0.45 + 0.9 = 3.25$$

$$\text{PR}(C) = (1 - d) + d\left(\frac{\text{PR}(B)}{C(B)} + \frac{\text{PR}(D)}{C(D)} + \frac{\text{PR}(E)}{D(E)}\right)$$

$$= 0.1 + 0.9 + 0.45 + 0.9 = 2.35$$

$$\text{PR}(D) = (1 - d) + d\left(\frac{\text{PR}(B)}{C(B)} + \frac{\text{PR}(C)}{C(C)} + \frac{\text{PR}(E)}{D(E)}\right)$$

$$= 0.1 + 0.9 + 0.9 + 0.9 = 2.80$$

$$PR(E) = (1-d) + d\left(\frac{PR(C)}{C(C)} + \frac{PR(D)}{C(D)}\right)$$
$$= 0.1 + 0.9 + 0.45 = 1.45$$

Although more iterations are required, on the basis of the first iteration we can say that Page *B* is the most important page amongst the five pages and page *A* is the least important. Pages *C* and *E* had higher PageRanks when we started.

If we continue the iterations we find that *B* continues to be the page with the highest PageRank. The information about these iterations is presented in Table 7.3.

Table 7.3 PageRank iterations for Example 7.2

Page	*PR*	*PR2*	*PR3*	*PR4*	*PR5*	*PR6*	*PR7*
A	1	0.55	0.73	0.71	0.64	0.63	0.60
B	2	3.25	2.37	2.58	2.38	2.27	2.19
C	3	2.35	2.63	2.20	2.25	2.10	2.02
D	2	2.8	2.70	2.38	2.37	2.24	2.14
E	3	1.45	1.44	1.50	1.30	1.31	1.23
Total	11.00	10.40	9.86	9.37	8.94	8.54	8.19

The sum of PageRanks of all the five pages is given in the last row of Table 7.3.

The sum is going down with every iteration. How far would it go down to? We explain this now.

Let us have a look at the PageRank calculations from a different point of view. PageRank of each page is given by (1 – *d*) plus the contributions of each page that links to it. This is summarized in Table 7.4.

Table 7.4 The sum of PageRanks of the five pages

Page	*Damping*	*Link from Page A*	*Link from Page B*	*Link from Page C*	*Link from Page D*	*Link from Page E*
A	1 – *d*	0	0	0	*d*(PR(*D*)/4)	0
B	1 – *d*	*d*(PR(*A*))	0	*d*(PR(*C*)/3)	*d*(PR(*D*)/4)	*d*(PR(*E*)/3)
C	1 – *d*	0	*d*(PR(*B*)/2)	0	*d*(PR(*D*)/4)	*d*(PR(*E*)/3)
D	1 – *d*	0	*d*(PR(*B*)/2)	*d*(PR(*C*)/3)	0	d(PR(*E*)/3)
E	1 – *d*	0	0	*d*(PR(*C*)/3)	*d*(PR(*D*)/4)	0
Total PageRank	5(1 – *d*)	*d*(PR(*A*))	*d*(PR(*B*))	*d*(PR(*C*))	*d*(PR(*D*))	*d*(PR(*E*)

The total PageRank of the five pages in the example is given in the last row of Table 7.4. It is 5(1 – *d*) plus *d* times the total PageRanks of all the pages in the example. This shows an interesting nature of the iterations. Let us assume that the total starting PageRanks of all pages is 100 then at each iteration the total PageRank is reduced by 100(1 – *d*) – 5(1 – *d*). Therefore as iterations continue the total PageRank will keep going down until the total PageRank becomes equal to the number of pages. The opposite happens if one starts with PageRank estimates that are too small.

7.6.2 Weaknesses of the PageRank Algorithm

As noted in the last chapter, the HITS algorithm has several weaknesses including the problem of topic drift. The PageRank algorithm also has similar weaknesses since a link cannot always be considered a recommendation and as noted earlier people are now trying to influence the links. Perhaps because of these, the influence of PageRank in ranking pages in Google has been reported to be decreasing in importance (The Black Box Group, 2002).

The major weakness of the PageRank algorithm arises because of PageRank's focus on the importance of a page rather than on its relevancy given the user query. PageRank is calculated independent of a user query so the result served on the first screen may not be the most relevant, it may be the one with the highest PageRank amongst the pages retrieved. The side effect of PageRank therefore can be something like this. For example, suppose *amazon.com* decides to get into real estate business. Obviously its real estate website will have links from all other *amazon.com* sites which have no relevance whatsoever with real estate. When a user then searches for real estate, the amazon.com real estate site is likely to be served high in the results because of its high PageRank (since it has links from very high PageRank *amazon.com* sites) while most other real estate businesses whatever their quality will appear further down the list.

Because of the nature of the algorithm, PageRank does not deal with new pages fairly since it makes high PageRank pages even more popular by serving them at the top of the results. Thus the rich get richer and the poor get poorer and a new page that wishes to improve its rank can do so only by advertising its existence on the web. It has been shown that if an algorithm like PageRank algorithm is used for ranking Web pages, it will take a very long time for a new page to become popular even if the new page was of high quality. Since rank of a page is closely related to the page's visibility on the Web, which in turn impacts the popularity of the business that the page is advertising, page ranking is likely to become a very controversial topic. In fact, in one or two cases companies have sued search engines claiming that their ranking algorithm is unfair to their business.

7.6.3 Other Issues in Page Ranking

Page ranking is still in some ways black magic (some call it martial arts in which there is a battle between search engines and people who want to manipulate the ranks of their pages). The algorithm given above is good but do the users interpret relevance and quality in the same way as the page ranking algorithm does? Some page ranking algorithms consider the following in determining page rank:

1. Page title including keywords
2. Page content including links, keywords, keywords in link text, spelling errors, length of the page
3. Out-links including relevance of links to the content
4. In-links and their importance (as in PageRank algorithm)
5. In-links text—keywords
6. In-linking page content
7. Traffic including number of unique visitors and time spent on the page

Some people claim that using some of this information works just as well or better than the PageRank algorithm does.

As noted earlier, a determined group of people can manipulate the PageRank of pages on the Web. For example, for some time in 2003 querying with a phrase "miserable failure" found a page at the White House. Then a number of other people got organised and the same query pointed to a variety of other people including former US presidents. Such PageRank manipulation is called "Google bombing". Similar games can be played with other search engines such as Yahoo! and MSN Search.

Since page rank algorithms are not perfect and there is a serious problem regarding visibility of high quality new pages, perhaps other approaches are needed. One possibility might be to introduce some randomness to the selection criteria so some new pages are displayed. Other option might be to let the user select if they are willing to look at some new sites that do not have high page rank.

7.7 SEARCH QUERY MINING

Considerable research has been carried out during the last few years in data mining the query terms that users pose to a search engine. Search engine users are individuals and they together pose hundreds of millions of queries to a search engine each day. The search engine traffic is huge and dynamic. Most searched queries change from day to day depending on local and world events.

Search engines store a lot of information in their logs about users and the queries they pose. There are a number of purposes for saving this information. For example, it can be used for determining what queries are frequent and what words are frequently misspelled. A query log, also contains information about users, queries issued, and results clicked,

The information in the query logs is being increasingly used by researchers. Aggregate trends for search terms have been used by them to make a variety of claims about public health and about users' opinions. These claims are based on the assumption that the trends in search data track those in the wider population.

Let us consider briefly the methodology used in a study that deals with one disease. First of all it is necessary to collect a number of terms that will be searched for. One approach might be to ask each participant or colleague to list queries they think are likely to be used for searching information about the disease of interest. Google search queries for these terms for every country are now counted and separate daily counts are computed for every country except those that are quite infrequent. The query counts are now normalized by dividing each daily query count by the total query count for that country for that day. This is called *search query fraction*. Data may also be analysed for each week and each month. Thus a time series of search query fraction data is produced.

As noted above, researchers have found that there is a close relationship between how many people search for a disease-related symptoms and how many people actually have that disease. It is worth noting that not every person who searches for the symptoms or the disease name is actually sick, but usually a pattern emerges when all the chosen disease-related search queries are added together. By counting how often the disease-related search queries are found, it is possible to estimate how much the disease is circulating in different countries and regions around the world.

7.7.1 Health

A new trend in query terms data mining in the health sector has emerged in the last few years. Perhaps it started when Google used query terms mining to predict trends in Influenza two weeks ahead of the US Government Centres for Disease Control (CDC) and Prevention Morbidity and Mortality Report. It essentially showed that as the incidence of influenza increases or decreases in a particular geographical region, the number of certain search query terms within the same geographical region changes with a high degree of correlation. Using a more up to date search query terms data, Google was able to predict the trend in the disease in a more timely fashion.

Researchers have now found that similar technique may be used in monitoring some other diseases, for example Dengue, which affects many Asian countries. Incidence of Dengue has been reported to vary from 15,000 cases to 175,000 cases annually in Bangkok. Furthermore, it has been reported that more than 500 million people are infected by Dengue each year.

One research used Dengue data available from Singapore and Bangkok over the years 2004–2011. Query data for the same period was obtained from Google search engine using a number of query terms that included signs, symptoms and treatment for the disease, for example, symptoms like fever, rash, headache, myalgia (muscle pain) and arthralgia (joint pain). Up to 16 terms were used in this research. It was found that there was strong correlation between the actual data obtained from Singapore and Bangkok and corresponding number of search query terms. It was concluded that the query search terms predicted quite accurately the incidence of dengue.

Another related research broadened the geographical area that was explored. It included Bolivia, Brazil, India, Indonesia and Singapore. It should be noted that such query mining is only likely to be successful for a high prevalence disease since there is likely to be sufficient search data available for it. In addition it was necessary to have access to official data sets so that results of search query mining may be compared with the official statistics. It was required that query data and official data be available for at least three years and there be fluctuation in the occurrence of the disease.

Google search engine log data between the years 2003 and 2010 was used. Daily counts were collected for a number of most common query terms for each country in any language. It was found that there were more than a million queries each month. That the number of search queries based on the model matched the official data quite well. The correlation between the two sets of data was found to be between 0.82 and 0.99.

We now look at another example. A number of French researchers investigated several diseases. In one study, they compared search trends based on a list of Google queries related to three infectious diseases (influenza-like illness ILL, gastroenteritis, and chickenpox) with clinical surveillance data from the French Sentinel Network. They constructed queries by asking each participant to list queries they think are likely to be used for searching information about these diseases. The query time series from January 2004 through February 2009 for France were downloaded from Google Trends. Correlations with weekly incidence rates (number of cases/100,000 inhabitants) of the three diseases provided by the Sentinel Network were calculated for different periods.

The highest correlation with influenza-like illness was obtained with the query terms grippe—aviaire—vaccin, the French words for influenza, avian, and vaccine respectively (correlation = 0.82). The minus signs removed queries that contained the terms avian or vaccine. Use of the query word grippe alone resulted in a lower correlation (correlation = 0.34).

The highest correlation with acute diarrhea was obtained when searched for the French word for gastroenteritis (correlation = 0.90). Various spellings were used to account for the presence/absence of an accent or a hyphen. The Google database was searched for gastro-enterite + gastro-entérite + gastroentérite + gastroenterite + (gastro enterite) + (gastro entérite).

The project involved crawling of 20,000 websites every hour, tracking about 75 infectious diseases. The diseases include malaria, cholera, ebola and others. About 300 reports are collected every day. Processing large amounts of information and sorting out the noise from the useful information is quite difficult but improved tools are helping.

This research became the foundation for what is now known as Google Flu Trends. Its algorithm however misfired during the 2013 season: "Google Flu Trends has continued to perform remarkably well, and researchers in many countries have confirmed that its ILI estimates are accurate. But the latest US flu season seems to have confounded its algorithms. Its estimate for the Christmas national peak of flu was almost double the CDC's, and some of its state data show even larger discrepancies. In 2009, Flu Trends had to tweak its algorithms after its models badly underestimated ILI (influenza like illnesses) in the United States at the start of the H1N1 (Swine Flu).

Query mining techniques have other applications, for example ecological monitoring, climate monitoring, fauna and flora monitoring. Even applications like how many students are likely to apply to which university and which course is possible. Furthermore, outbreak of rioting, shortage of some food items in some localities may be possible.

7.7.2 Mental Health and Depression

It is also possible to find the level of depression in a country using data from tens of millions of queries and measuring how many of them used the word "depression" and are categorized by Google's algorithms as health related on each day of the year, across the United States, over a period of nine years. (This method counts searches like "depression symptoms" and "depression treatment" but not searches like "The Great Depression."). It should be noted that not every health-related search using "depression" is a sign that someone is depressed, and not everyone who is depressed queries Google. But thanks to the incredibly large sample size, meaningful patterns emerge.

According to the data, depression is highest in the USA in April and is lowest in August. The state with the highest rate of depression is North Dakota; the one with the lowest, Virginia. Depression is, unsurprisingly, highest on Mondays and lowest on Saturdays.

The Global Financial Crisis (GFC) appears to have caused a significant increase in depression. In 2009 and 2010, there was a large increase in depression queries in states with large increases in unemployment, like Nevada, Florida and Alabama, compared with states that were little affected, like North Dakota and Arkansas. A 1 percentage point increase in the unemployment rate was associated with a 2 per cent increase in depression queries.

It was found that the colder the place, the higher the rate of depression, with the correlation concentrated in the colder months. Google searches, the biggest data source, clearly show that climate is important as far as people's mood is concerned. Besides temperature, the biggest predictors of "depression" searches were the sizes of the Hispanic population and the college-educated population. More Hispanic-Americans meant fewer searches (though this might have been a result of language factors). More college-educated people meant less depression.

Another study has found that that Google searches for symptoms of psychological distress are surpassing 1 million per month, 300,000 of which can be attributed to changes in the economy. The searches for psychological distress are also 40 per cent higher than they were just before the Great Financial Crisis (GFC).

A number of researchers have mapped the number of Google searches for symptoms of depression and anxiety with certain economic events, such as unemployment. They found that effects of trauma can last a long time.

7.7.3 Discovering Side Effects of Drugs

In an article in the New York Times in March 2013, it was reported that a number of researchers have for the first time been able to detect evidence of unreported prescription drug side effects before they were found by the USA Food and Drug Administration's warning system.

Using data from six million queries in 2010, the researchers looked for searches relating to an antidepressant, paroxetine, and a cholesterol lowering drug, pravastatin. They were able to find evidence that the combination of the two drugs caused high blood sugar.

The F.D.A. asks physicians to report side effects through a system known as the Adverse Event Reporting System. But its scope is limited by the fact that data is generated only when a physician notices something and reports it. This research explored whether it was possible to automate the process of discovering "drug-drug" interactions by using software to hunt through the data found in F.D.A. reports.

The researchers found that it was possible to detect the interaction between paroxetine and pravastatin using the query data. They first identified individual searches for the terms paroxetine and pravastatin, as well as searches for both terms. They then computed the likelihood that users in each group would also search for hyperglycemia as well as roughly 80 of its symptoms—words or phrases like "high blood sugar" or "blurry vision."

They determined that people who searched for both drugs during the 12-month period were significantly more likely to search for terms related to hyperglycemia (about 10%) than were those who searched for just one of the drugs. (About 5 per cent and 4 per cent).

It was noted that this kind of combination would be very hard to study given all the different drug pairs or combinations that are out there.

There are perhaps many drug-drug interactions but fortunately the query mining can assist in identifying side effects.

7.7.4 Crime

After declining for many years in the U.S., Google searches that seem to have come from child-abuse victims themselves rose as soon as the recession began. An economist found that on weeks that unemployment claims rose, these searches rose as well. Searches that appear to have originated with people who suspect abuse provide evidence that the increase is caused by the economic downturn. States that had comparatively suffered the most had increased search rates for child abuse and neglect. Each percentage point increase in the unemployment rate was associated with a 3 per cent increase in the search rate for "child abuse" or "child neglect."

An analysis of Google requests shows that "we should be sceptical of statistics based on official reports of crime in general, not just child abuse or neglect," Stephens-Davidowitz says. Google search data can fill holes in our understanding of crime generally. If your iPad was stolen, whom would you be more likely to tell: the police or Google? He contends that Google queries for "stolen iPad" and "stolen iPod" yield meaningful information about property crime rates.

7.8 INDIVIDUAL PRIVACY AND QUERY DATA MINING

It is interesting to discover that analysis of query logs, even without user identification, can lead to identification of some individuals that have posed queries. A famous example is the query logs released by AOL in 2006. The query log released was some twenty million queries posed to the search engine by 650,000 individuals. No user names were released. Instead AOL replaced the names by numbers. Although each users name was replaced by a unique number, the number provided a thread of queries posed by each user. This enabled researchers to find the names of some individuals who were posing queries.

The problem is somewhat similar to the issue of privacy violation in statistical databases. Similarly, privacy can be breached by combining data from a published query log with some other publicly available information.

One of the approaches used in privacy protection is the technique of *anonomisation*. It is discussed further in Chapter 10.

Some researchers suggest that there are two major types of privacy attacks that may be mounted against a query log. One of the two attacks is a trace attack and the second attack is a person attack. In the first attack the attacker looks at a sequence of searches made by a particular user. This usually allows the attacker to discover information about the user. It is shown how combination of simple classifiers can be used to discover gender, age, location, etc. of the posers of their queries to a search engine. In the second type of attack, the attacker is looking for query activity of a known user in the query log.

Query log researchers have found that commercially available classifiers may be used to classify large query logs into a much smaller number of classes. In one example, it was shown that 1428 users could be classified into classes of 10 to 100 users. The small classes then may be further analysed, perhaps manually, to identify at least some of the query makers.

Person attacks are shown to work very effectively if the attacker has reasonable knowledge of the person they are looking for. In most cases the attacker is able to find the individual they are looking for.

It is also shown that removing some personal information does not eliminate the threat from attackers. Privacy of query users may still be compromised.

Classification requires training data and a number of keywords may be used for training. It has been suggested that for users in India words like bridal, baby, pregnancy, sarees, jewellery, makeup, ecards, glitter, yoga, diet, movie and kitchen are good predictors of a female user. On the other hand espn, cricket, IIT, university, USA, hockey, wrestling, coffee, cars, motorcycle and holidays are may be good predictors of a male user. The user's age may be derived from keywords as well. For example Facebook, email, college, etc. may indicate a young user while holidays, apartment, jobs, investment, shares, etc. may suggest an older user.

Different techniques will be required for a person attack. We assume that the attacker knows the approximate age of the person, the gender, the location, what kind of food the person loves, etc. Given this knowledge the attacker may be able to identify the user from a query log.

A number of suggestions have been made to make it more difficult to derive personal information from query logs. To protect sensitivity or confidentiality of shared data, the query data may be sanitized. This approach involves anonymization, which is to remove all personal information from the log. It has been shown that this technique is not very effective. Another approach he involves combining a number of queries together in a bundle making it difficult to determine who posed which queries.

SUMMARY

In this chapter we have considered the differences between classical information retrieval and searching the Web and have described some of the characteristics of search engines. We have also outlines some problems that search engines face given short queries and diversity of users. Measuring the quality of results returned using precision and recall was discussed. We have then discussed the task search engines try to tackle. Search engine functionality and architecture was discussed and the roles of a crawler, indexer and query processor are described. Next we described the PageRank algorithm. Query mining was described and a number of areas of its applications explained.

REVIEW QUESTIONS

1. Why is the nature of Web document collection quite different than a library's document collection? (Section 7.1)
2. What are the characteristics of search engines including problems with searching, wide variety of users, and the quality of search results? (Section 7.2)
3. Explain the concepts of precision, recall, and ranking and their relationships. (Section 7.2)
4. Describe search engine functionality including collecting information, indexing it and storing it. (Section 7.3)
5. Explain the various components of a search engine architecture including the crawler, the indexer, database and the user interface. (Section 7.4)
6. What is the role of crawler and indexer? (Section 7.4)
7. Explain the PageRank algorithm using an example, its strengths and weaknesses. (Section 7.5)
8. Describe the nature of the search engine industry. (Section 7.6)
9. What is search engine query mining? (Section 7.1)
10. Describe the methodology used in search engine query mining. (Section 7.2)
11. Explain how query mining has been used in the health area. (Section 7.3)
12. Describe how query mining has been used in studying depression. (Section 7.4)
13. Explain two other applications of query mining. (Sections 7.5, 7.6, 7.7 and 7.8)
14. How some types of query mining are quite predictable? (Section 7.9)

EXERCISES

1. What are the primary goals of Web search?
2. Discuss some problems that arise when searching the Web.
3. What are precision and recall? How do they apply to Web search?
4. What are the different components of a search engine? Describe them briefly.

5. What is a crawler? Present a basic crawling algorithm.
6. Describe the PageRank algorithm. Using an example, show how it works.
7. What is the most important property of a Web page in determining its PageRank? Assume that we are calculating PageRanks of 100 pages. What will the total of all PageRanks converge to? Why? Would the results be different if we assumed starting PageRank of 0.1 for each page compared to the results if we assumed starting PageRank of 10 for each page? Consider the following four pages and their links in the context of the PageRank algorithm.

   Page *A* has PageRank of 1 and has one link to *B*

   Page *B* has PageRank of 2 and has two links to *C* and *D*

   Page *C* PageRank of 3 and has two links to *B* and *D*

   Page *D* PageRank of 2 and has three links to *A*, *B* and *C*

   Explain how the PageRank algorithm will work by showing one iteration of the algorithm. Do not describe the algorithm.
8. Discuss Kleinberg's HITS algorithm for finding Web authorities and hubs.
9. Describe the inverted file structure.
10. Build an inverted file structure for the following:
    - Document 1 Information technology is taught at Roorkee
    - Document 2 Data mining is taught at Roorkee
    - Document 3 Data base management is taught at Roorkee
    - Document 4 PhD studies are possible in the School
    - Document 5 Data structure using Java
11. How is Web search different than full-text retrieval?
12. Find a small query log and use unsupervised classification to classify the queries in the log. Discuss the results.
13. Is it possible to compare the above trend results with any polls that have been conducted in India? Can you in fact forecast the result of the next national poll? Can you even forecast the result of the next general election and how many seats each party is likely to win.
14. Using Google trends find out who is the most popular cricketer in India in years 2012–2014.
15. Compare the popularity of Anil Ambani, Mukesh Ambani, Ratan Tata, Narayan Murthy. Discuss the results.
16. Which car in India is the most popular according to the queries posed on Google?
17. List a number of major scams in India. Which one of these is the most frequently searched for during the three years 2010–2013. What search terms would you use. Explain why you have chosen them.
18. List ten query words each that are more commonly used by young females, young males, mothers, fathers and retired males. Check your list by talking to your friends and relatives.
19. Make a list of 20 query terms that indicate the location of the user.

20. Find a small query log and use unsupervised classification to classify the queries in the log. Discuss the results.
21. Use Google trend to find the frequency of search of political leaders "Narendra Modi", "L.K., Adwani", "Rahul Gandhi", "Manmohan Singh" and "Sonya Gandhi" over the last three years. What do the trends appear to show? Compare these trends with the results of the 2014 election.
22. Is it possible to compare the above trend results with results of any opinion polls that have been conducted in India?
23. Using Google trends find out who is the most popular cricketer in India in years 2012–2014.
24. Which car in India is the most popular according to the queries posed on Google?
25. List a number of major scams in India. Which one of these is the most frequently searched for during the three years 2010–2013. What search terms would you use. Explain why you have chosen them.
26. List ten query words each that are more commonly used by young females, young males, mothers, fathers and retired males. Check your list by talking to your friends and relatives.

MULTIPLE CHOICE QUESTIONS

1. Which one of the following is correct about the type of queries users pose to search engines?
   (a) Navigational
   (b) Informational
   (c) Transactional
   (d) All of the above
2. Which of the following are correct about the Web?
   (a) The Web is large
   (b) The Web is dynamic
   (c) The Web has diversity
   (d) All of the above
3. Which one of the following is not correct about a search engine?
   (a) A search engine needs a crawler to collect information
   (b) A search engine needs an indexer
   (c) A search engine needs a query language like SQL
   (d) A search engine needs a database
4. Which one of the following is not correct about search engines?
   (a) Search engines maintain very large databases
   (b) The search engine databases built and updated automatically
   (c) The search engines search the whole Web when a query is posed
   (d) PageRank is not the only way to rank search engine results

5. Which one of the following is correct?
   (a) Search engines results have high recall
   (b) Search engine results provide high precision
   (c) Precision decreases faster than recall increases
   (d) It is easy to improve precision of search engine results
6. Which of the following are correct about search engine functionality?
   (a) It must check queries and execute them
   (b) It must present the results of the search to the user
   (c) It must carry out user profiling to improve performance
   (d) All of the above
7. Which one of the following is not correct about the PageRank algorithm?
   (a) The idea behind PageRank is to find probability of a random surfer reaching that page
   (b) PageRank uses the outlinks and inlinks to a page to determine its PageRank
   (c) PageRank also considers the content of the page in determining its rank
   (d) To compute PageRank of page it is necessary to know the rank of each page that points to it
8. Which of the following should be used to assess quality of search results?
   (a) Recall
   (b) Ranking
   (c) Relevance of the first page results
   (d) All of the above
9. Which one of the following is not the role of the indexer?
   (a) Term extraction
   (b) Removing stop words
   (c) Building or updating user profiles
   (d) Building or updating the inverted index
10. Which one of the following is a problem in searching using a search engine?
   (a) There is too much data
   (b) There are synonyms
   (c) There are duplicates
   (d) There are homonyms

PROJECT

Study the following papers that analyse search engine query data:

- J. Ginsberg, M.H. Mohebbi, R.S. Patel, L. Brammer, M.S. Smolinski, and L. Brilliant, Detecting Influenza Epidemics using Search Engine Query Data, *Nature*, Vol. 457, 19 February 2009. cs.wellesley.edu/~cs315/papers/predicting%20flu%20epidemics.pdf

- N.M. Schuster, M.A.M. Rogers, and L.F. McMahon, Using Search Engine Query Data to Track Pharmaceutical Utilization: A study of statins, *The American Journal of Managed Care*, Vol. 16, No. 8, August 2010.
  http://www.ajmc.com/issue/managed-care/2010/2010-0vol16n08/ajmc_10aug_schusterwebx_e216
- T. Preis, D. Reith, and H.E. Stanley, Complex Dynamics of Our Economic Life on Different Scales: Insights from search engine query data, *Philosophical Transactions of the Royal Society A*, Vol. 368, pp. 5707–5719, 2010. http://rsta.royalsocietypublishing.org/content/368/1933/5707.full.pdf

Explain what is common in these research papers and explain how similar studies in India might be useful. Chose one possible application and describe how query data may be useful in investigating it for India. Discuss the limitations of this approach in India.

BIBLIOGRAPHY

The Web and various aspects of Web search are very active areas of research at the present time. Much of the discussion about search engine architecture is based on the work of Arasu, Cho, Garcia-Molina, Paepcke and Raghavan (2001) as well as on papers in the book Web Dynamics. Brin and Page describe the PageRank algorithm. They also provide a description of Google.

Recommended Reading for Students

We list a number of interesting tutorials and survey articles. The papers by Brin and Page and by Arasu, Cho and Garcia-Molina are the most important papers in the list.
http://www.searchengineshowdown.com/stats/

Arasu, A., Cho, J., Garcia-Molina, H., Paepcke, A., and Raghavan, S., Searching the web, *ACM Transactions on Internet Technology*, Vol. 1, No. 1, pp. 2–43, 2001.

Shimshoni, Y., Efron N., and Matias, Y., On the Predictability of Search Trends, Google, Israel Labs, 2009.

Recommended Reading for Lecturers

Abrol, M., Latarche, N., Mahadevan, U., Mao, J., Mukherjee, R., Raghavan, P., Tourn, M., Wang, J., and Zhang, G., Navigating Large-Scale Semi-Structured Data in Business Portals, *VLDB '01*, Rome, Italy, pp. 663–666, 2001.

Althouse, B.M., Ng, Y.Y., and Cummings, D.A.T., Prediction of Dengue Incidence using Search Query Surveillance, *PLoS Negl Trop Dis*, 5(8): 2011.

Ayers, J.W., Ribisi, K., and Brownstein, J.S., Using Search Query Surveillance to Monitor Tax Avoidance and Smoking Cessation Following the United States 2009 "SCHIP" Cigarette Tax Increase, *PLoS One*, 6(3): 2011.

Bayer, B.N. and Eisenberg, M.L., Use of Google in Study of Non-infectious Medical Conditions, Epidemiology, 21, pp. 584–585, 2009.

Berry, M.W. and Browne, M., Understanding Search Engines: Mathematical Modeling and Text Retrieval, *SIAM*, Philadelphia, PA, 116 pp., 1999.

Bharat, K., Web Information Retrieval, Tutorial Presented at COMAD 2005, Goa, India, 2005.

Brin, S. and Page, L., The Anatomy of a Large-Scale Hypertextual Web Search Engine, *Proc. 7th Int. World Wide Web Conf.* (WWW'98), Brisbane, Australia, pp. 107–117, 1998. Also in *Computer Networks and ISDN Systems*, Vol. 30, Issue 1–7 (April 1998), pp. 107–117.
http://www-db.stanford.edu/~backrub/google.html

Broder, A., A Taxonomy of Web search, *ACM SIGIR Forum*, Vol. 36, No. 2, pp. 3–10, 2002.
http://www.acm.org/sigir/forum/f2002/broder.pdf

Chan, E.H., Sahai, V., Conrad, C., and Brownstein, J.S., Using Web Search Query Data to Monitor Dengue Epidemics: A New Model for Neglected Tropical Disease Surveillance, *PLoS Negl Trop Dis*, 5(5): 2011.

Croft, B., Metzler, D., and Strohman, T., *Search Engines: Information Retrieval in Practice*, Pearson Education, 2009.

Ginsberg, J., Mohebbi, M.H., Patel, R.S., Brammer, L., et al., Detecting Influenza Epidemics Using Search Engine Query Data, *Nature*, 457, pp. 1012–1014, 2009.

Goel, S., Hoffman, M.H., Lahale, S., Pennock D.M., and Watts, D.M., Predicting Consumer Behaviour with Web Search, *Proc. of National Academy of Sciences of the USA*, 107, pp. 17486–17490, 2010.

Jones, R., Kumar, R., Pang, B., and Tomkins, A., I know What You Did Last Summer, *CIKM '07*, pp. 909–915, 2007.

Langville, A.N. and Meyer, C.D., A Survey of Eigenvector Methods for Web Information Retrieval, *SIAM Review*, Vol. 47, No. 1, pp. 135–161, 2005.

Langville, A.N., *Google's PageRank and Beyond: The Science of Search Engine*, Princeton University Press, 2006.

Levene, M. and Poulovassilis, A. (Eds.), *Web Dynamics*, Springer-Verlag, 2004.

Page, L., Brin, S., Motwani, R., and Winograd, T., 1998, The PageRank Citation Ranking: Bringing Order to The Web, 2008. Technical Report. http://dbpubs.stanford.edu:8090/pub/1999-66.

Preis, T., Reith, D., and Stanley, H.E., Complex Dynamics of our Economic Life on Different Scales: Insights from Search Engine Query Data, *Phil. Trans. R. Soc.*, 368, pp. 5707–5719, 2010.

Richardson, M. and Domingos, P., The Intelligent Surfer: Probabilistic Combination of Link and Content Information in PageRank, *Advances in Neural Information Processing Systems 14*, MIT Press, 2002.

Search Engine Genie, Google PageRank Explained, 2002. http://www.searchenginegenie.com/google-pagerankexplained.htm (long!)

Silvestri, F., Mining Query Logs: Turning Search Usage Data into Knowledge, *Foundations and Trends in Information Retrieval*, Vol. 4, Issue 1–2, pp. 1–174, 2010.

CASE STUDY 7

The Anatomy of a Large-Scale Hypertextual Web Search Engine*

Reproduced with permission from Elsevier

ABSTRACT

In this paper, we present Google, a prototype of a large-scale search engine which makes heavy use of the structure present in hypertext. Google is designed to crawl and index the Web efficiently and produce much more satisfying search results than existing systems. The prototype with a full text and hyperlink database of at least 24 million pages is available at http://google.stanford.edu/

To engineer a search engine is a challenging task. Search engines index tens to hundreds of millions of web pages involving a comparable number of distinct terms. They answer tens of millions of queries every day. Despite the importance of large-scale search engines on the web, very little academic research has been done on them. Furthermore, due to rapid advance in technology and web proliferation, creating a web search engine today is very different from three years ago. This paper provides an in-depth description of our large-scale web search engine—the first such detailed public description we know of to-date. Apart from the problems of scaling traditional search techniques to data of this magnitude, there are new technical challenges involved with using the additional information present in hypertext to produce better search results. This paper addresses this question of how to build a practical large-scale system which can exploit the additional information present in hypertext. Also we look at the problem of how to effectively deal with uncontrolled hypertext collections where anyone can publish anything they want.

Keywords: World Wide Web, Search Engines, Information Retrieval, PageRank, Google

1. INTRODUCTION

Note: There are two versions of this paper—a longer full version and a shorter printed version. The full version is available on the web.

The web creates new challenges for information retrieval. The amount of information on the web is growing rapidly, as well as the number of new users inexperienced in the art of web research. People are likely to surf the web using its link graph, often starting with high quality human maintained indices such as Yahoo! or with search engines. Human maintained lists cover popular topics effectively but are subjective, expensive to build and maintain, slow to improve, and cannot cover all esoteric topics. Automated search engines that rely on keyword matching usually return too many low quality matches. To make matters worse, some advertisers attempt to gain people's attention by taking measures meant to mislead automated search

---

* Brin, S. and L. Page, 1998, The anatomy of a large-scale hypertextual Web search engine, *Proc. 7th Int. World Wide Web Conf.* (*WWW'98*), Brisbane, Australia, pp. 107–117. Also in *Computer Networks and ISDN Systems*, Vol. 30, Issue 1–7, pp. 107–117.

http://www-db.stanford.edu/~backrub/google.html

engines. We have built a large-scale search engine which addresses many of the problems of existing systems. It makes especially heavy use of the additional structure present in hypertext to provide much higher quality search results. We chose our system name, Google, because it is a common spelling of googol, or 10^{100} and fits well with our goal of building very large-scale search engines.

1.1 Web Search Engines—Scaling Up: 1994-2000

Search engine technology has had to scale dramatically to keep up with the growth of the web. In 1994, one of the first web search engines, the World Wide Web Worm (WWWW) [McBryan 94] had an index of 110,000 web pages and web accessible documents. As of November, 1997, the top search engines claim to index from 2 million (WebCrawler) to 100 million web documents (from Search Engine Watch). It is foreseeable that by the year 2000, a comprehensive index of the Web will contain over a billion documents. At the same time, the number of queries search engines handle has grown incredibly too. In March and April 1994, the World Wide Web Worm received an average of about 1500 queries per day. In November 1997, Altavista claimed it handled roughly 20 million queries per day. With the increasing number of users on the web, and automated systems which query search engines, it is likely that top search engines will handle hundreds of millions of queries per day by the year 2000. The goal of our system is to address many of the problems, both in quality and scalability, introduced by scaling search engine technology to such extraordinary numbers.

1.2 Google: Scaling with the Web

Creating a search engine which scales even to today's web presents many challenges. Fast crawling technology is needed to gather the web documents and keep them up to date. Storage space must be used efficiently to store indices and, optionally, the documents themselves. The indexing system must process hundreds of gigabytes of data efficiently. Queries must be handled quickly, at a rate of hundreds to thousands per second.

These tasks are becoming increasingly difficult as the Web grows. However, hardware performance and cost have improved dramatically to partially offset the difficulty. There are, however, several notable exceptions to this progress such as disk seek time and operating system robustness. In designing Google, we have considered both the rate of growth of the Web and technological changes. Google is designed to scale well to extremely large data sets. It makes efficient use of storage space to store the index. Its data structures are optimized for fast and efficient access (see Section 4.2). Further, we expect that the cost to index and store text or HTML will eventually decline relative to the amount that will be available (see Appendix B). This will result in favorable scaling properties for centralized systems like Google.

1.3 Design Goals

1.3.1 Improved Search Quality

Our main goal is to improve the quality of web search engines. In 1994, some people believed that a complete search index would make it possible to find anything easily. According to *Best of the Web 1994—Navigators*, "The best navigation service should make it easy to find almost anything on the Web (once all the data is entered)." However, the Web of 1997 is quite different. Anyone who has used a search engine recently, can readily testify that the completeness of the index is not the only factor in the quality of search results. "Junk results" often wash out any results that a user is interested in. In fact, as of November 1997, only one of the top four commercial search engines finds itself (returns its own search page in response to its name in the top ten results). One of the main causes of this problem is that the number of documents in the indices has been increasing by many orders of magnitude, but the user's ability to look at documents has not. People are still only willing to look at the first few tens of results.

Because of this, as the collection size grows, we need tools that have very high precision (number of relevant documents returned, say in the top tens of results). Indeed, we want our notion of "relevant" to only include the very best documents since there may be tens of thousands of slightly relevant documents. This very high precision is important even at the expense of recall (the total number of relevant documents the system is able to return). There is quite a bit of recent optimism that the use of more hypertextual information can help improve search and other applications [Marchiori 97] [Spertus 97] [Weiss 96] [Kleinberg 98]. In particular, link structure [Page 98] and link text provide a lot of information for making relevance judgments and quality filtering. Google makes use of both link structure and anchor text (see Sections 2.1 and 2.2).

1.3.2 Academic Search Engine Research

Aside from tremendous growth, the Web has also become increasingly commercial over time. In 1993, 1.5% of web servers were on .com domains. This number grew to over 60% in 1997. At the same time, search engines have migrated from the academic domain to the commercial. Up until now most search engine development has gone on at companies with little publication of technical details. This causes search engine technology to remain largely a black art and to be advertising oriented (see Appendix A). With Google, we have a strong goal to push more development and understanding into the academic realm.

Another important design goal was to build systems that reasonable numbers of people can actually use. Usage was important to us because we think some of the most interesting research will involve leveraging the vast amount of usage data that is available from modern web systems. For example, there are many tens of millions of searches performed every day. However, it is very difficult to get this data, mainly because it is considered commercially valuable.

Our final design goal was to build an architecture that can support novel research activities on large-scale web data. To support novel research uses, Google stores all of the actual documents it crawls in compressed form. One of our main goals in designing Google was to set up an environment where other researchers can come in quickly, process large chunks of the web, and produce interesting results that would have been very difficult to produce otherwise. In the short time the system has been up, there have already been several papers using databases generated by Google, and many others are underway.

Another goal we have is to set up a Spacelab-like environment where researchers or even students can propose and do interesting experiments on our large-scale web data.

2. SYSTEM FEATURES

The Google search engine has two important features that help it produce high precision results. First, it makes use of the link structure of the Web to calculate a quality ranking for each web page. This ranking is called PageRank and is described in detail in [Page 98]. Second, Google utilizes link to improve search results.

2.1 PageRank: Bringing Order to the Web

The citation (link) graph of the web is an important resource that has largely gone unused in existing web search engines. We have created maps containing as many as 518 million of these hyperlinks, a significant sample of the total. These maps allow rapid calculation of a web page's "PageRank", an objective measure of its citation importance that corresponds well with people's subjective idea of importance. Because of this correspondence, PageRank is an excellent way to prioritize the results of web keyword searches. For most popular subjects, a simple text matching search that is restricted to web page titles performs admirably when PageRank prioritizes the results (demo available at google.stanford.edu). For the type of full text searches in the main Google system, PageRank also helps a great deal.

2.1.1 Description of PageRank Calculation

Academic citation literature has been applied to the web, largely by counting citations or backlinks to a given page. This gives some approximation of a page's importance or quality. PageRank extends this idea by not counting links from all pages equally, and by normalizing by the number of links on a page. PageRank is defined as follows:

We assume page A has pages T1...Tn which point to it (i.e., are citations). The parameter d is a damping factor which can be set between 0 and 1. We usually set d to 0.85. There are more details about d in the next section. Also C(A) *is defined as the number of links going out of page A. The PageRank of a page A is given as follows:*

$$PR(A) = (1 - d) + d(PR(T1)/C(T1) + \cdots + PR(Tn)/C(Tn))$$

Note that the PageRanks form a probability distribution over web pages, so the sum of all web pages' PageRanks will be one.

PageRank or PR(A) can be calculated using a simple iterative algorithm, and corresponds to the principal eigenvector of the normalized link matrix of the web. Also, a PageRank for 26 million web pages can be computed in a few hours on a medium size workstation. There are many other details which are beyond the scope of this paper.

2.1.2 Intuitive Justification

PageRank can be thought of as a model of user behavior. We assume there is a "random surfer" who is given a web page at random and keeps clicking on links, never hitting "back" but eventually gets bored and starts on another random page. The probability that the random surfer visits a page is its PageRank. And, the d damping factor is the probability at each page the "random surfer" will get bored and request another random page. One important variation is to only add the damping factor d to a single page, or a group of pages. This allows for personalization and can make it nearly impossible to deliberately mislead the system in order to get a higher ranking. We have several other extensions to PageRank, again see [Page 98].

Another intuitive justification is that a page can have a high PageRank if there are many pages that point to it, or if there are some pages that point to it and have a high PageRank. Intuitively, pages that are well cited from many places around the web are worth looking at. Also, pages that have perhaps only one citation from something like the Yahoo! homepage are also generally worth looking at. If a page was not high quality, or was a broken link, it is quite likely that Yahoo's homepage would not link to it. PageRank handles both these cases and everything in between by recursively propagating weights through the link structure of the web.

2.2 Anchor Text

The text of links is treated in a special way in our search engine. Most search engines associate the text of a link with the page that the link is on. In addition, we associate it with the page the link points to. This has several advantages. First, anchors often provide more accurate descriptions of web pages than the pages themselves. Second, anchors may exist for documents which cannot be indexed by a text-based search engine, such as images, programs, and databases. This makes it possible to return web pages which have not actually been crawled. Note that pages that have not been crawled can cause problems, since they are never checked for validity before being returned to the user. In this case, the search engine can even return a page that never actually existed, but had hyperlinks pointing to it.

However, it is possible to sort the results, so that this particular problem rarely happens. This idea of propagating anchor text to the page it refers to was implemented in the World Wide Web Worm [McBryan 94] especially because it helps search non-text information, and expands the search coverage with fewer downloaded documents. We use anchor propagation mostly because anchor text can help provide better quality results. Using anchor text efficiently is technically difficult because of the large amounts of data which must be processed. In our current crawl of 24 million pages, we had over 259 million anchors which we indexed.

2.3 Other Features

Aside from PageRank and the use of anchor text, Google has several other features. First, it has location information for all hits and so it makes extensive use of proximity in search. Second, Google keeps track of some visual presentation details such as font size of words. Words in a larger or bolder font are weighted higher than other words. Third, full raw HTML of pages is available in a repository.

3. RELATED WORK

Search research on the web has a short and concise history. The World Wide Web Worm (WWWW) [McBryan 94] was one of the first web search engines. It was subsequently followed by several other academic search engines, many of which are now public companies. Compared to the growth of the Web and the importance of search engines there are precious few documents about recent search engines [Pinkerton 94]. According to Michael Mauldin (chief scientist, Lycos Inc) [Mauldin], "the various services (including Lycos) closely guard the details of these databases". However, there has been a fair amount of work on specific features of search engines. Especially well represented is work which can get results by post-processing the results of existing commercial search engines, or produce small scale "individualized" search engines. Finally, there has been a lot of research on information retrieval systems, especially on well controlled collections. In the next two sections, we discuss some areas where this research needs to be extended to work better on the web.

3.1 Information Retrieval

Work in information retrieval systems goes back many years and is well developed [Witten 94]. However, most of the research on information retrieval systems is on small well controlled homogeneous collections such as collections of scientific papers or news stories on a related topic. Indeed, the primary benchmark for information retrieval, the Text Retrieval Conference [TREC 96], uses a fairly small, well controlled collection for their benchmarks. The "Very Large Corpus" benchmark is only 20GB compared to the 147GB from our crawl of 24 million web pages. Things that work well on TREC often do not produce good results on the web. For example, the standard vector space model tries to return the document that most closely approximates the query, given that both query and document are vectors defined by their word occurrence. On the web, this strategy often returns very short documents that are the query plus a few words. For example, we have seen a major search engine return a page containing only "Bill Clinton Sucks" and picture from a "Bill Clinton" query. Some argue that on the web, users should specify more accurately what they want and add more words to their query. We disagree vehemently with this position. If a user issues a query like "Bill Clinton" they should get reasonable results since there is a enormous amount of high quality information available on this topic. Given examples like these, we believe that the standard information retrieval work needs to be extended to deal effectively with the web.

3.2 Differences Between the Web and Well Controlled Collections

The web is a vast collection of completely uncontrolled heterogeneous documents. Documents on the web have extreme variation internal to the documents, and also in the external meta information that might be available. For example, documents differ internally in their language (both human and programming), vocabulary (email addresses, links, zip codes, phone numbers, product numbers), type or format (text, HTML, PDF, images, sounds), and may even be machine generated (log files or output from a database). On the other hand, we define external meta information as information that can be inferred about a document, but is not contained within it. Examples of external meta information include things like reputation of the source, update frequency, quality, popularity or usage, and citations. Not only are the possible sources of external meta information varied, but the things that are being measured vary many orders of magnitude as well. For example, compare the usage information from a major homepage, like Yahoo's which currently receives millions of page views every day with an obscure historical article which might receive one view every ten years. Clearly, these two items must be treated very differently by a search engine.

Another big difference between the web and traditional well controlled collections is that there is virtually no control over what people can put on the web. Couple this flexibility to publish anything with the enormous influence of search engines to route traffic and companies which deliberately manipulating search engines for profit become a serious problem. This problem that has not been addressed in traditional closed information retrieval systems. Also, it is interesting to note that metadata efforts have largely failed with web search engines, because any text on the page which is not directly represented to the user is abused to manipulate search engines. There are even numerous companies which specialize in manipulating search engines for profit.

4. SYSTEM ANATOMY

First, we will provide a high level discussion of the architecture. Then, there is some in-depth descriptions of important data structures. Finally, the major applications: crawling, indexing, and searching will be examined in depth.

4.1 Google Architecture Overview

In this section, we will give a high level overview of how the whole system works as pictured in Figure 1. Further sections will discuss the applications and data structures not mentioned in this section. Most of Google is implemented in C or C++ for efficiency and can run in either Solaris or Linux.

In Google, the web crawling (downloading of web pages) is done by several distributed crawlers. There is a URLserver that sends lists of URLs to be fetched to the crawlers. The web pages that are fetched are then sent to the storeserver. The storeserver then compresses and stores the web pages into a repository. Every web page has an associated ID number called a docID which is assigned whenever a new URL is parsed out of a web page. The indexing function is performed by the indexer and the sorter. The indexer performs a number of functions. It reads the repository, uncompresses the documents, and parses them. Each document is converted into a set of word occurrences called hits. The hits record the word, position in document, an approximation of font size, and capitalization. The indexer distributes these hits into a set of "barrels", creating a partially sorted forward index. The indexer performs another important function. It parses out all the links in every web page and stores important information about them in an anchors file. This file contains enough information to determine where each link points from and to, and the text of the link. The URLresolver reads the anchors file and converts relative URLs into absolute URLs and in turn into docIDs. It puts the anchor text into the forward index, associated with the docID that the anchor points to. It also generates a database of links which are pairs of docIDs. The links database is used to compute PageRanks for all the documents. The sorter takes the barrels, which are sorted by docID (this is a simplification, see Section 4.2.5), and resorts them by wordID to generate the inverted index. This is done in place so that little temporary space is needed for this operation. The sorter also produces a list of wordIDs and offsets into the inverted index. A program called DumpLexicon takes this list together

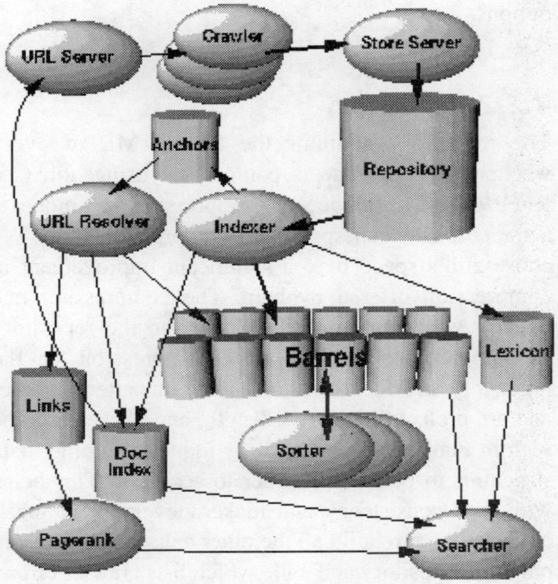

Figure 1: High Level Google Architecture.

with the lexicon produced by the indexer and generates a new lexicon to be used by the searcher. The searcher is run by a web server and uses the lexicon built by DumpLexicon together with the inverted index and the PageRanks to answer queries.

4.2 Major Data Structures

Google's data structures are optimized so that a large document collection can be crawled, indexed, and searched with little cost. Although, CPUs and bulk input output rates have improved dramatically over the years, a disk seek still requires about 10 ms to complete. Google is designed to avoid disk seeks whenever possible, and this has had a considerable influence on the design of the data structures.

4.2.1 Big Files

BigFiles are virtual files spanning multiple file systems and are addressable by 64 bit integers. The allocation among multiple file systems is handled automatically. The BigFiles package also handles allocation and deallocation of file descriptors, since the operating systems do not provide enough for our needs. BigFiles also support rudimentary compression options.

4.2.2 Repository

The repository contains the full HTML of every web page. Each page is compressed using zlib (see RFC1950). The choice of compression technique is a tradeoff between speed and compression ratio. We chose zlib's speed over a significant improvement in compression offered by bzip. The compression rate of bzip was approximately 4 to 1 on the repository as compared to zlib's 3 to 1 compression. In the repository, the documents are stored one after the other and are prefixed by docID, length, and URL as can be seen in Figure 2. The repository requires no other data structures to be used in order to access it. This helps with data consistency and makes development much easier; we can rebuild all the other data structures from only the repository and a file which lists crawler errors.

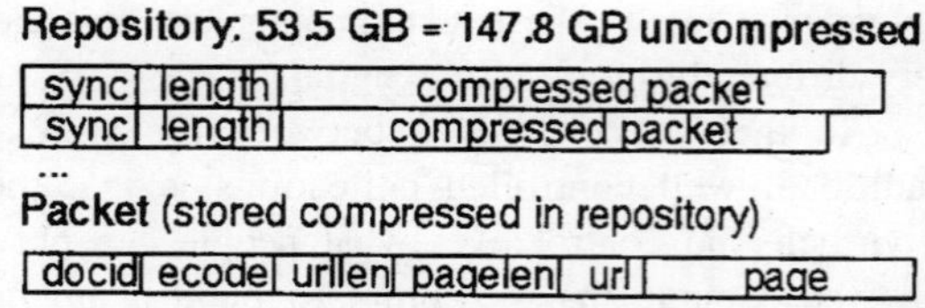

Figure 2: Repository Data Structure.

4.2.3 Document Index

The document index keeps information about each document. It is a fixed width ISAM (Index sequential access mode) index, ordered by docID. The information stored in each entry includes the current document status, a pointer into the repository, a document checksum, and various statistics. If the document has been crawled, it also contains a pointer into a variable width file called docinfo which contains its URL and title. Otherwise the pointer points into the URLlist which contains just the URL. This design decision was driven by the desire to have a reasonably compact data structure, and the ability to fetch a record in one disk seek during a search. Additionally, there is a file which is used to convert URLs into docIDs. It is a list of URL checksums with their corresponding docIDs and is sorted by checksum. In order to find the docID of a particular URL, the URL's checksum is computed and a binary search is performed on the checksums file to find its docID. URLs may be converted into docIDs in batch by doing a merge with this file. This is the technique the URLresolver uses to turn URLs into docIDs. This batch mode of update is crucial because otherwise we must perform one seek for every link which assuming one disk would take more than a month for our 322 million link dataset.

4.2.4 Lexicon

The lexicon has several different forms. One important change from earlier systems is that the lexicon can fit in memory for a reasonable price. In the current implementation we can keep the lexicon in memory on a machine with 256 MB of main memory. The current lexicon contains 14 million words (though some rare words were not added to the lexicon). It is implemented in two parts—a list of the words (concatenated together but separated by nulls) and a hash table of pointers. For various functions, the list of words has some auxiliary information which is beyond the scope of this paper to explain fully.

4.2.5 Hit Lists

A hit list corresponds to a list of occurrences of a particular word in a particular document including position, font, and capitalization information. Hit lists account for most of the space used in both the forward and the inverted indices. Because of this, it is important to represent them as efficiently as possible. We considered several alternatives for encoding position, font, and capitalization—simple encoding (a triple of integers), a compact encoding (a hand optimized allocation of bits), and Huffman coding. In the end we chose a hand optimized compact encoding since it required far less space than the simple encoding and far less bit manipulation than Huffman coding. The details of the hits are shown in Figure 3.

Our compact encoding uses two bytes for every hit. There are two types of hits: fancy hits and plain hits. Fancy hits include hits occurring in a URL, title,

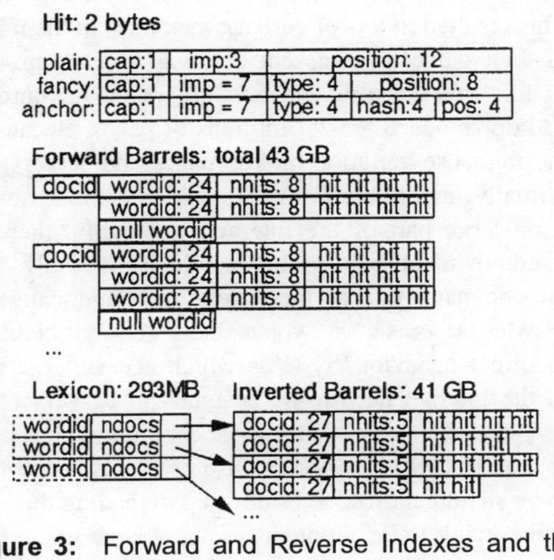

Figure 3: Forward and Reverse Indexes and the Lexicon.

anchor text, or meta tag. Plain hits include everything else. A plain hit consists of a capitalization bit, font size, and 12 bits of word position in a document (all positions higher than 4095 are labeled 4096). Font size is represented relative to the rest of the document using three bits (only 7 values are actually used because 111 is the flag that signals a fancy hit). A fancy hit consists of a capitalization bit, the font size set to 7 to indicate it is a fancy hit, 4 bits to encode the type of fancy hit, and 8 bits of position. For anchor hits, the 8 bits of position are split into 4 bits for position in anchor and 4 bits for a hash of the docID the anchor occurs in. This gives us some limited phrase searching as long as there are not that many anchors for a particular word. We expect to update the way that anchor hits are stored to allow for greater resolution in the position and docIDhash fields. We use font size relative to the rest of the document because when searching, you do not want to rank otherwise identical documents differently just because one of the documents is in a larger font.

The length of a hit list is stored before the hits themselves. To save space, the length of the hit list is combined with the wordID in the forward index and the docID in the inverted index. This limits it to 8 and 5 bits respectively (there are some tricks which allow 8 bits to be borrowed from the wordID). If the length is longer than would fit in that many bits, an escape code is used in those bits, and the next two bytes contain the actual length.

4.2.6 Forward Index

The forward index is actually already partially sorted. It is stored in a number of barrels (we used 64). Each barrel holds a range of wordID's. If a document contains words that fall into a particular barrel, the docID is recorded into the barrel, followed by a list of wordID's with hit lists which correspond to those words. This scheme requires slightly more storage because of duplicated docIDs but the difference is very small for a reasonable number of buckets and saves considerable time and coding complexity in the final indexing phase done by the sorter. Furthermore, instead of storing actual wordID's, we store each wordID as a relative difference from the minimum wordID that falls into the barrel the wordID is in. This way, we can use just 24 bits for the wordID's in the unsorted barrels, leaving 8 bits for the hit list length.

4.2.7 Inverted Index

The inverted index consists of the same barrels as the forward index, except that they have been processed by the sorter. For every valid wordID, the lexicon contains a pointer into the barrel that wordID falls into. It points to a doclist of docID's together with their corresponding hit lists. This doclist represents all the occurrences of that word in all documents. An important issue is in what order the docID's should appear in the doclist. One simple solution is to store them sorted by docID. This allows for quick merging of different doclists for multiple word queries. Another option is to store them sorted by a ranking of the occurrence of the word in each document. This makes answering one word queries trivial and makes it likely that the answers to multiple word queries are near the start. However, merging is much more difficult. Also, this makes development much more difficult in that a change to the ranking function requires a rebuild of the index. We chose a compromise between these options, keeping two sets of inverted barrels—one set for hit lists which include title or anchor hits and another set for all hit lists. This way, we check the first set of barrels first and if there are not enough matches within those barrels we check the larger ones.

4.3 Crawling the Web

Running a web crawler is a challenging task. There are tricky performance and reliability issues and even more importantly, there are social issues. Crawling is the most fragile application since it involves interacting with hundreds of thousands of web servers and various name servers which are all beyond the control of the system.

In order to scale to hundreds of millions of web pages, Google has a fast distributed crawling system. A single URLserver serves lists of URLs to a number of crawlers (we typically ran about 3). Both the URLserver and the crawlers are implemented in Python. Each crawler keeps roughly 300 connections open at once. This is necessary to retrieve web pages at a fast enough pace. At peak speeds, the system can crawl over 100 web pages per second using four crawlers. This amounts to roughly 600K per second of data. A major performance stress is DNS lookup. Each crawler maintains a its own DNS cache so it does not need to do a DNS lookup before crawling each document. Each of the hundreds of connections can be in a number of different states: looking up DNS, connecting to host, sending request, and receiving response. These factors make the crawler a complex component of the system. It uses asynchronous IO to manage events, and a number of queues to move page fetches from state to state.

It turns out that running a crawler which connects to more than half a million servers, and generates tens of millions of log entries generates a fair amount of email and phone calls. Because of the vast number of people coming on line, there are always those who do not know what a crawler is, because this is the first one they have seen. Almost daily, we receive an email something like, "Wow, you looked at a lot of pages from my web site. How did you like it?" There are also some people who do not know about the robots exclusion protocol, and think their page should be protected from indexing by a statement like, "This page is copyrighted and should not be indexed", which needless to say is difficult for web crawlers to understand. Also, because of the huge amount of data involved, unexpected things will happen. For example, our system tried to crawl an online game. This resulted in lots of garbage messages in the middle of their game! It turns out this was an easy problem to fix. But this problem had not come up until we had downloaded tens of millions of pages. Because of the immense variation in web pages and servers, it is virtually impossible to test a crawler without running it on large part of the Internet. Invariably, there are hundreds of obscure problems which may only occur on one page out of the whole web and cause the crawler to crash, or worse, cause unpredictable or incorrect behavior. Systems which access large parts of the Internet need to be designed to be very robust and carefully tested. Since large complex systems such as crawlers will invariably cause problems, there needs to be significant resources devoted to reading the email and solving these problems as they come up.

4.4 Indexing the Web

- **Parsing**—Any parser which is designed to run on the entire Web must handle a huge array of possible errors. These range from typos in HTML tags to kilobytes of zeros in the middle of a tag, non-ASCII characters, HTML tags nested hundreds deep, and a great variety of other errors that challenge anyone's imagination to come up with equally creative ones. For maximum speed, instead of using YACC to generate a CFG parser, we use flex to generate a lexical analyzer which we outfit with its own stack. Developing this parser which runs at a reasonable speed and is very robust involved a fair amount of work.

- **Indexing Documents into Barrels**—After each document is parsed, it is encoded into a number of barrels. Every word is converted into a wordID by using an in-memory hash table—the lexicon. New additions to the lexicon hash table are logged to a file. Once the words are converted into wordID's, their occurrences in the current document are translated into hit lists and are written into the forward barrels. The main difficulty with parallelization of the indexing phase is that the lexicon needs to be shared. Instead of sharing the lexicon, we took the approach of writing a log of all the extra words that were not in a base lexicon, which we fixed at 14 million words. That way multiple indexers can run in parallel and then the small log file of extra words can be processed by one final indexer.
- **Sorting**—In order to generate the inverted index, the sorter takes each of the forward barrels and sorts it by wordID to produce an inverted barrel for title and anchor hits and a full text inverted barrel. This process happens one barrel at a time, thus requiring little temporary storage. Also, we parallelize the sorting phase to use as many machines as we have simply by running multiple sorters, which can process different buckets at the same time. Since the barrels don't fit into main memory, the sorter further subdivides them into baskets which do fit into memory based on wordID and docID. Then the sorter, loads each basket into memory, sorts it and writes its contents into the short inverted barrel and the full inverted barrel.

4.5 Searching

The goal of searching is to provide quality search results efficiently. Many of the large commercial search engines seemed to have made great progress in terms of efficiency. Therefore, we have focused more on quality of search in our research, although we believe our solutions are scalable to commercial volumes with a bit more effort. The Google query evaluation process is shown in Figure 4.

1. Parse the query.
2. Convert words into wordIDs.
3. Seek to the start of the doclist in the short barrel for every word.
4. Scan through the doclists until there is a document that matches all the search terms.
5. Compute the rank of that document for the query.
6. If we are in the short barrels and at the end of any doclist, seek to the start of the doclist in the full barrel for every word and go to step 4.
7. If we are not at the end of any doclist go to step 4.

Sort the documents that have matched by rank and return the top k.

Figure 4: Google Query Evaluation.

To put a limit on response time, once a certain number (currently 40,000) of matching documents are found, the searcher automatically goes to step 8 in Figure 4. This means that it is possible that sub-optimal results would be returned. We are currently investigating other ways to solve this problem. In the past, we sorted the hits according to PageRank, which seemed to improve the situation.

4.5.1 The Ranking System

Google maintains much more information about web documents than typical search engines. Every hit list includes position, font, and capitalization information. Additionally, we factor in hits from anchor text and the PageRank of the document. Combining all of this information into a rank is difficult. We designed our ranking function so that no particular factor can have too much influence. First, consider the simplest case—a single word query. In order to rank a document with a single word query, Google looks at that document's hit list for that word. Google considers each hit to be one of several different types (title, anchor, URL, plain text large font, plain text small font, ...), each of which has its own type-weight. The type-weights make up a vector indexed by type. Google counts the number of hits of each type in the hit list. Then every count is converted into a count-weight. Count-weights increase linearly with counts at first but quickly taper off so that more than a certain count will not help. We take the dot product of the vector of count-weights with the vector of type-weights to compute an IR score for the document. Finally, the IR score is combined with PageRank to give a final rank to the document.

For a multi-word search, the situation is more complicated. Now multiple hit lists must be scanned through at once so that hits occurring close together in a document are weighted higher than hits occurring far apart. The hits from the multiple hit lists are matched up so that nearby hits are matched together. For every matched set of hits, a proximity is computed. The proximity is based on how far apart the hits are in the document (or anchor) but is classified into 10 different value "bins" ranging from a phrase match to "not even close". Counts are computed not only for every type of hit but for every type and proximity. Every type and proximity pair has a type-prox-weight. The counts are converted into count-weights and we take the dot product of the count-weights and the type-prox-weights to compute an IR score. All of these numbers and matrices can all be displayed with the search results using a special debug mode. These displays have been very helpful in developing the ranking system.

4.5.2 Feedback

The ranking function has many parameters like the type-weights and the type-prox-weights. Figuring out the right values for these parameters is something of a black art. In order to do this, we have a user feedback mechanism in the search engine. A trusted user may optionally evaluate all of the results that are returned. This feedback is saved. Then when we modify the ranking function, we can see the impact of this change on all previous searches which were ranked. Although far from perfect, this gives us some idea of how a change in the ranking function affects the search results.

5. RESULTS AND PERFORMANCE

The most important measure of a search engine is the quality of its search results. While a complete user evaluation is beyond the scope of this paper, our own experience with Google has shown it to produce better results than the major commercial search engines for most searches. As an example which illustrates the use of PageRank, anchor text, and proximity, Figure 5 shows Google's results for a search on "bill clinton". These results demon-strates some of Google's features. The results are clustered by server. This helps considerably when sifting through result sets. A number of results are from the whitehouse.gov domain which is what one may reasonably expect from such a search. Currently, most major commercial search engines do not return any results from whitehouse.gov, much less the right ones. Notice that there is no title for the first result. This is because it was not crawled. Instead, Google relied on anchor text to determine this was a good answer to the query. Similarly, the fifth result is an email address which, of course, is not crawlable. It is also a result of anchor text.

All of the results are reasonably high quality pages and, at last check, none were broken links. This is largely because they all have high PageRank. The PageRanks are the percentages in red along with bar graphs. Finally, there are no results about a Bill other than Clinton or about a Clinton other than Bill. This is because we place heavy importance on the proximity of word occurrences. Of course a true test of the quality of a search engine would involve an extensive user study or results analysis which we do not have room for here. Instead, we invite the reader to try Google for themselves at http://google.stanford.edu.

5.1 Storage Requirements

Aside from search quality, Google is designed to scale cost effectively to the size of the Web as it grows. One aspect of this is to use storage efficiently. Table 1 has a

Query: bill clinton

http://www.whitehouse.gov/
100.00% (no date) (0K)
http://www.whitehouse.gov/
Office of the President
99.67% (Dec 23 1996) (2K)
http://www.whitehouse.gov/WH/EOP/OP/html/OP_Home.html
Welcome To The White House
99.98% (Nov 09 1997) (5K)
http://www.whitehouse.gov/WH/Welcome.html
Send Electronic Mail to the President
99.86% (Jul 14 1997) (5K)
http://www.whitehouse.gov/WH/Mail/html/Mail_President.html

mailto:president@whitehouse.gov
99.98%
mailto:President@whitehouse.gov
99.27%
The "Unofficial" Bill Clinton
94.06% (Nov 11 1997) (14K)
http://zpub.com/un/un-bc.html
Bill Clinton Meets The Shrinks
86.27% (Jun 29 1997) (63K)
http://zpub.com/un/un-bc9.html
President Bill Clinton - The Dark Side
97.27% (Nov 10 1997) (15K)
http://www.realchange.org/clinton.htm
$3 Bill Clinton
94.73% (no date) (4K)
http://www.gatewy.net/~tjohnson/clinton1.html

Figure 5: ample Results from Google

Table 1: Statistics

Storage Statistics	
Total Size of Fetched Pages	147.8 GB
Compressed Repository	53.5 GB
Short Inverted Index	4.1 GB
Full Inverted Index	37.2 GB
Lexicon	293 MB
Temporary Anchor Data (not in total)	6.6 GB
Document Index Incl. Variable Width Data	9.7 GB
Links Database	3.9 GB
Total Without Repository	**55.2 GB**
Total With Repository	**108.7 GB**

Web Page Statistics	
Number of Web Pages Fetched	24 million
Number of Urls Seen	76.5 million
Number of Email Addresses	1.7 million
Number of 404's	1.6 million

breakdown of some statistics and storage requirements of Google. Due to compression the total size of the repository is about 53 GB, just over one third of the total data it stores. At current disk prices this makes the repository a relatively cheap source of useful data. More importantly, the total of all the data used by the search engine requires a comparable amount of storage, about 55 GB. Furthermore, most queries can be answered using just the short inverted index. With better encoding and compression of the Document Index, a high quality web search engine may fit onto a 7GB drive of a new PC.

5.2 System Performance

It is important for a search engine to crawl and index efficiently. This way information can be kept up to date and major changes to the system can be tested relatively quickly. For Google, the major operations are Crawling, Indexing, and Sorting. It is difficult to measure how long crawling took overall because disks filled up, name servers crashed, or any number of other problems which stopped the system. In total it took roughly 9 days to download the 26 million pages (including errors). However, once the system was running smoothly, it ran much faster, downloading the last 11 million pages in just 63 hours, averaging just over 4 million pages per day or 48.5 pages per second. We ran the indexer and the crawler simultaneously. The indexer ran just faster than the crawlers. This is largely because we spent just enough time optimizing the indexer so that it would not be a bottleneck. These optimizations included bulk updates to the document index and placement of critical data structures on the local disk. The indexer runs at roughly 54 pages per second. The sorters can be run completely in parallel; using four machines, the whole process of sorting takes about 24 hours.

5.3 Search Performance

Improving the performance of search was not the major focus of our research up to this point. The current version of Google answers most queries in between 1 and 10 seconds. This time is mostly dominated by disk IO over NFS (since disks are spread over a number of machines). Furthermore, Google does not have any optimizations such as query caching, subindices on common terms, and other common optimizations. We intend to speed up Google considerably through distribution and hardware, software, and algorithmic improvements. Our target is to be able to handle several hundred queries per second. Table 2 has some sample query times from the current version of Google. They are repeated to show the speedups resulting from cached IO.

Table 2: Search Times

	Initial Query		**Same Query Repeated (IO mostly cached)**	
Query	**CPU Time(s)**	**Total Time(s)**	**CPU Time(s)**	**Total Time(s)**
al gore	0.09	2.13	0.06	0.06
vice president	1.77	3.84	1.66	1.80
hard disks	0.25	4.86	0.20	0.24
search engines	1.31	9.63	1.16	1.16

6. CONCLUSIONS

Google is designed to be a scalable search engine. The primary goal is to provide high quality search results over a rapidly growing World Wide Web. Google employs a number of techniques to improve search quality including page rank, anchor text, and proximity information. Furthermore, Google is a complete architecture for gathering web pages, indexing them, and performing search queries over them.

6.1 Future Work

A large-scale web search engine is a complex system and much remains to be done. Our immediate goals are to improve search efficiency and to scale to approximately 100 million web pages. Some simple improvements to efficiency include query caching, smart disk allocation, and subindices. Another area which requires much research is updates. We must have smart algorithms to decide what old web pages should be recrawled and what new ones should be crawled. Work toward this goal has been done in [Cho 98]. One promising area of research is using proxy caches to build search databases, since they are demand driven. We are planning to add simple features supported by commercial search engines like boolean operators, negation, and stemming. However, other features are just starting to be explored such as relevance feedback and clustering (Google currently supports a simple hostname based clustering). We also plan to support user context (like the user's location), and result summarization. We are also working to extend the use of link structure and link text. Simple experiments indicate PageRank can be personalized by increasing the weight of a user's home page or bookmarks. As for link text, we are experimenting with using text surrounding links in addition to the link text itself. A Web search engine is a very rich environment for research ideas. We have far too many to list here so we do not expect this Future Work section to become much shorter in the near future.

6.2 High Quality Search

The biggest problem facing users of web search engines today is the quality of the results they get back. While the results are often amusing and expand users' horizons, they are often frustrating and consume precious time. For example, the top result for a search for "Bill Clinton" on one of the most popular commercial search engines was the Bill Clinton Joke of the Day: April 14, 1997. Google is designed to provide higher quality search so as the Web continues to grow rapidly, information can be found easily.

In order to accomplish this Google makes heavy use of hypertextual information consisting of link structure and link (anchor) text. Google also uses proximity and font information. While evaluation of a search engine is difficult, we have subjectively found that Google returns higher quality search results than current commercial search engines. The analysis of link structure via PageRank allows Google to evaluate the quality of web pages. The use of link text as a description of what the link points to helps the search engine return relevant (and to some degree high quality) results. Finally, the use of proximity information helps increase relevance a great deal for many queries.

6.3 Scalable Architecture

Aside from the quality of search, Google is designed to scale. It must be efficient in both space and time, and constant factors are very important when dealing with the entire Web. In implementing Google, we have seen bottlenecks in CPU, memory access, memory capacity, disk seeks, disk throughput, disk capacity, and network IO. Google has evolved to overcome a number of these bottlenecks during various operations. Google's major data structures make efficient use of available storage space. Furthermore, the crawling, indexing, and sorting operations are efficient enough to be able to build an index of a substantial portion of the web—24 million pages, in less than one week. We expect to be able to build an index of 100 million pages in less than a month.

6.4 A Research Tool

In addition to being a high quality search engine, Google is a research tool. The data Google has collected has already resulted in many other papers submitted to conferences and many more on the way. Recent research such as [Abiteboul 97] has shown a number of limitations to queries about the Web that may be answered without having the Web available locally. This means that Google (or a similar system) is not only a valuable research tool but a necessary one for a wide range of applications. We hope Google will be a resource for searchers and researchers all around the world and will spark the next generation of search engine technology.

ACKNOWLEDGMENTS

Scott Hassan and Alan Steremberg have been critical to the development of Google. Their talented contributions are irreplaceable, and the authors owe them much gratitude. We would also like to thank Hector Garcia-Molina, Rajeev Motwani, Jeff Ullman, and Terry Winograd and the whole WebBase group for their support and insightful discussions. Finally we would like to recognize the generous support of our equipment donors IBM, Intel, and Sun and our funders. The research described here was conducted as part of the Stanford Integrated Digital Library Project, supported by the National Science Foundation under Cooperative Agreement IRI-9411306. Funding for this cooperative agreement is also provided by DARPA and NASA, and by Interval Research, and the industrial partners of the Stanford Digital Libraries Project.

REFERENCES

- Best of the Web 1994—Navigators http://botw.org/1994/awards/navigators.html
- Bill Clinton Joke of the Day: April 14, 1997. http://www.io.com/~cjburke/clinton/970414.html.
- Bzip2 Homepage http://www.muraroa.demon.co.uk/
- Google Search Engine http://google.stanford.edu/
- Harvest http://harvest.transarc.com/
- Mauldin, Michael L. Lycos Design Choices in an Internet Search Service, IEEE Expert Interview http://www.computer.org/pubs/expert/ 1997/trends/x1008/mauldin.htm
- The Effect of Cellular Phone Use Upon Driver Attention http://www.webfirst.com/aaa/text/cell/cell0toc.htm
- Search Engine Watch http://www.searchenginewatch.com/
- RFC 1950 (zlib) ftp://ftp.uu.net/graphics/png/documents/zlib/zdoc-index.html
- Robots Exclusion Protocol: http://info.webcrawler. com/mak/projects/robots/exclusion.htm
- Web Growth Summary: http://www.mit.edu/people/mkgray/net/web-growth-summary.html
- Yahoo! http://www.yahoo.com/
- [Abiteboul 97] Serge Abiteboul and Victor Vianu, Queries and Computation on the Web. *Proceedings of the International Conference on Database Theory*. Delphi, Greece 1997.
- [Bagdikian 97] Ben H. Bagdikian. *The Media Monopoly*. 5th Edition. Publisher: Beacon, ISBN:0807061557
- [Cho 98] Junghoo Cho, Hector Garcia-Molina, Lawrence Page. Efficient Crawling Through URL Ordering. *Seventh International Web Conference* (*WWW 98*). Brisbane, Australia, April 14-18, 1998.
- [Gravano 94] Luis Gravano, Hector Garcia-Molina, and A. Tomasic. The Effectiveness of GlOSS for the Text-Database Discovery Problem. *Proc. of the 1994 ACM SIGMOD International Conference On Management Of Data,* 1994.
- [Kleinberg 98] Jon Kleinberg. Authoritative Sources in a Hyperlinked Environment, *Proc. ACM-SIAM Symposium on Discrete Algorithms*, 1998.
- [Marchiori 97] Massimo Marchiori. The Quest for Correct Information on the Web: Hyper Search Engines. *The Sixth International WWW Conference* (*WWW 97*). Santa Clara, USA, April 7–11, 1997.
- [McBryan 94] Oliver A. McBryan. GENVL and WWWW: Tools for Taming the web. *First International Conference on the World Wide Web.* CERN, Geneva (Switzerland), May 25–26–27, 1994. http://www.cs.colorado.edu/home/mcbryan/mypapers/www94.ps
- [Page 98] Lawrence Page, Sergey Brin, Rajeev Motwani, Terry Winograd. *The PageRank Citation Ranking: Bringing Order to the Web.* Manuscript in progress. http://google. stanford.edu/~backrub/pageranksub.ps
- [Pinkerton 94] Brian Pinkerton. Finding What People Want: Experiences with the WebCrawler. *The Second International WWW Conference Chicago,* USA, October 17-20, 1994. http://info.webcrawler.com/bp/WWW94. html
- [Spertus 97] Ellen Spertus. ParaSite: Mining Structural Information on the Web. *The Sixth International WWW Conference* (*WWW 97*). Santa Clara, USA, April 7–11, 1997.
- [TREC 96] *Proceedings of the fifth Text REtrieval Conference* (*TREC-5*). Gaithersburg, Maryland, November 20–22, 1996. Publisher: Department of Commerce, National Institute of Standards and Technology. Editors: D.K. Harman and E.M. Voorhees. Full text at: http://trec.nist.gov/
- [Witten 94] Ian H Witten, Alistair Moffat, and Timothy C. Bell. *Managing Gigabytes:*

Compressing and Indexing Documents and Images. New York: Van Nostrand Reinhold, 1994.

- [Weiss 96] Ron Weiss, Bienvenido Velez, Mark A. Sheldon, Chanathip Manprempre, Peter Szilagyi, Andrzej Duda, and David K. Gifford. HyPursuit: A Hierarchical Network Search Engine that Exploits Content-Link Hypertext Clustering. *Proceedings of the 7th ACM Conference on hypertext.* New York, 1996.

Sergey Brin received his B.S. degree in mathematics and computer science from the University of Maryland at College Park in 1993. Currently, he is a Ph.D. candidate in computer science at Stanford University where he received his M.S. in 1995. He is a recipient of a National Science Foundation Graduate Fellowship. His research interests include search engines, information extraction from unstructured sources, and data mining of large text collections and scientific data.

Lawrence Page was born in East Lansing, Michigan, and received a B.S.E. in Computer Engineering at the University of Michigan Ann Arbor in 1995. He is currently a Ph.D. candidate in Computer Science at Stanford University. Some of his research interests include the link structure of the web, human computer interaction, search engines, scalability of information access interfaces, and personal data mining.

APPENDIX A: ADVERTISING AND MIXED MOTIVES

Currently, the predominant business model for commercial search engines is advertising. The goals of the advertising business model do not always correspond to providing quality search to users. For example, in our prototype search engine one of the top results for cellular phone is "The Effect of Cellular Phone Use Upon Driver Attention", a study which explains in great detail the distractions and risk associated with conversing on a cell phone while driving. This search result came up first because of its high importance as judged by the PageRank algorithm, an approximation of citation importance on the web [Page 98]. It is clear that a search engine which was taking money for showing cellular phone ads would have difficulty justifying the page that our system returned to its paying advertisers. For this type of reason and historical experience with other media [Bagdikian 97], we expect that advertising funded search engines will be inherently biased towards the advertisers and away from the needs of the consumers.

Since it is very difficult even for experts to evaluate search engines, search engine bias is particularly insidious. A good example was OpenText, which was reported to be selling companies the right to be listed at the top of the search results for particular queries [Marchiori 97]. This type of bias is much more insidious than advertising, because it is not clear who "deserves" to be there, and who is willing to pay money to be listed. This business model resulted in an uproar, and OpenText has ceased to be a viable search engine. But less blatant bias are likely to be tolerated by the market. For example, a search engine could add a small factor to search results from "friendly" companies, and subtract a factor from results from competitors. This type of bias is very difficult to detect but could still have a significant effect on the market. Furthermore, advertising income often provides an incentive to provide poor quality search results. For example, we noticed a major search engine would not return a large airline's homepa ge when the airline's name was given as a query. It so happened that the airline had placed an expensive ad, linked to the query that was its name. A better search engine would not have required this ad, and possibly resulted in the loss of the revenue from the airline to the search engine. In general, it could be argued from the consumer point of view that the better the search engine is, the fewer advertisements will be needed for the consumer to find what they want. This of course erodes the advertising supported business model of the existing search engines. However, there will always be money from advertisers who want a customer to switch products, or have something that is genuinely new. But we believe the issue of advertising causes enough mixed incentives that it is crucial to have a competitive search engine that is transparent and in the academic realm.

APPENDIX B: SCALABILITY

Scalability of Google

We have designed Google to be scalable in the near term to a goal of 100 million web pages. We have just received disk and machines to handle roughly that amount. All of the time consuming parts of the system are parallelize and roughly linear time. These include things like the crawlers, indexers, and sorters. We also think that most of the data structures will deal gracefully with the expansion. However, at 100 million web pages we will be very close up against all sorts of operating system limits in the common operating systems (currently we run on both Solaris and Linux). These include things like addressable memory, number of open file descriptors, network sockets and bandwidth, and many others. We believe expanding to a lot more than 100 million pages would greatly increase the complexity of our system.

Scalability of Centralized Indexing Architectures

As the capabilities of computers increase, it becomes possible to index a very large amount of text for a reasonable cost. Of course, other more bandwidth intensive media such as video is likely to become more pervasive. But, because the cost of production of text is low compared to media like video, text is likely to remain very pervasive. Also, it is likely that soon we will have speech recognition that does a reasonable job converting speech into text, expanding the amount of text available. All of this provides amazing possibilities for centralized indexing. Here is an illustrative example. We assume we want to index everything everyone in the US has written for a year. We assume that there are 250 million people in the US and they write an average of 10k per day. That works out to be about 850 terabytes. Also assume that indexing a terabyte can be done now for a reasonable cost. We also assume that the indexing methods used over the text are linear, or nearly linear in their complexity. Given all these assumptions we can compute how long it would take before we could index our 850 terabytes for a reasonable cost assuming certain growth factors. Moore's Law was defined in 1965 as a doubling every 18 months in processor power. It has held remarkably true, not just for processors, but for other important system parameters such as disk as well. If we assume that Moore's law holds for the future, we need only 10 more doublings, or 15 years to reach our goal of indexing everything everyone in the US has written for a year for a price that a small company could afford. Of course, hardware experts are somewhat concerned Moore's Law may not continue to hold for the next 15 years, but there are certainly a lot of interesting centralized applications even if we only get part of the way to our hypothetical example.

Of course a distributed systems like *Gloss* [Gravano 94] or Harvest will often be the most efficient and elegant technical solution for indexing, but it seems difficult to convince the world to use these systems because of the high administration costs of setting up large numbers of installations. Of course, it is quite likely that reducing the administration cost drastically is possible. If that happens, and everyone starts running a distributed indexing system, searching would certainly improve drastically.

Because humans can only type or speak a finite amount, and as computers continue improving, text indexing will scale even better than it does now. Of course there could be an infinite amount of machine generated content, but just indexing huge amounts of human generated content seems tremendously useful. So we are optimistic that our centralized web search engine architecture will improve in its ability to cover the pertinent text information over time and that there is a bright future for search.

CASE STUDY 7 SUMMARY

The case study describes the architecture of Google in 1998 as Google was establishing itself in California. It provides good early history of search engines and it presents design goals of the search engine. Google's high level architecture is described, data structures used and storage requirements are discussed. The case study also describes how crawling, indexing and searching is carried out. The PageRank algorithm is briefly discussed. Finally, the case study concludes with a discussion of results of performance testing of the search engine.

CASE STUDY 7 EXERCISES

1. Describe the architecture of the search engine presented in the case study.
2. The case study presents some results of performance evaluations of the search engine. Briefly describe the performance evaluation and results.
3. How, in your opinion, is the present Google different than what is described in this 1998 case study?

CHAPTER

8 Data Warehousing

LEARNING OBJECTIVES

After completing this chapter, you will be able to:

- Learn why there is a need for a separate database for decision making
- Understand the role and architecture of an Operational Data Store
- Understand the role and architecture of a Data Warehouse
- Learn Data Warehouse modelling and implementation
- Describe differences between an Operational Data Store and a Data Warehouse
- Learn how to find additional resources that provide more information about Data Warehouses

8.1 INTRODUCTION

Major enterprises have many computers (other than PCs on staff desks) that run a variety of enterprise applications. For an enterprise with branches in many locations, the branches may have their own systems. For example, in a university with only one campus, the library may run its own catalogue and borrowing database system while the student administration may have own systems running on another machine. There might be a separate finance system, a property and facilities management system and another for human resources management. A large company on the other hand might have the following systems:

- Human Resources (HR)
- Financials
- Billing

- Sales leads
- Web sales
- Customer support

As discussed earlier, such OLTP systems are mostly relational database systems designed for transaction processing. The performance of OLTP systems is usually very important since such systems are used to support the users (i.e. staff) that provide service to the customers. The systems therefore must be able to deal with insert and update operations as well as answering simple queries quickly. OLTP systems are suitably indexed and designed to handle such transactions but they are not designed to handle management queries efficiently since management queries are often complex, requiring many joins and aggregations.

In addition to a number of OLTP systems which we assume are relational, perhaps built using different relational products, an enterprise may have old pre-relational systems that store valuable information but are too expensive to convert into relational database systems. These may include file systems using complex data structures. There might even be some old legacy systems that were built using different applications at different times and where the data semantics may not be even properly documented. Such systems may still be running since they have valuable historical information.

While proliferation of such systems may not create difficulties in meeting the operational needs of an enterprise and may be understandable given diverse needs of various sections of the enterprise, the proliferation can lead to a variety of problems. For example, generating some reports for operational managers (and even answering some user queries) becomes difficult involving intolerable delays. The management wants to view the whole enterprise as one but there is no unified view of the enterprise as far as computer systems are concerned.

It has been reported that several years ago Coca-Cola could not even quickly determine how many bottles their plants produced in a day since the information was distributed in more than 20 different computer systems in different locations. In some enterprises it may even be difficult to obtain a well maintained list of all the customers or all the suppliers since the customers and suppliers may be spread over more than one system. To communicate effectively with customers or suppliers an extraordinarily clean and accurate list of correct addresses, emails and telephone numbers is needed. Furthermore, when a customer calls to make an enquiry it is essential that the staff member who is handling the query is quickly able to find the customer in the enterprise OLTP systems.

Since OLTP systems are performance driven, many enterprises are deciding that another separate database is needed for decision making. Such databases are called *data warehouses*. A data warehouse does not duplicate an OLTP database since the aims of the two database systems are quite different. A data warehouse is designed to have summary information collected from one or more OLTP systems. It is long term storage to allow detection of patterns which have longer time frame. In addition, a data warehouse can support complex queries, report writing and analysis of information. It does not need detailed information about transactions of all customers. A data warehouse need not be updated every minute or even every day, although some updating of information is required to ensure that the information is current.

To some extent, the query and reporting tools of a OLTP system can assist in answering questions like "which state did the largest number of students come from last year?" but these tools cannot provide any intelligence about why it happened. If the manager had a series of hypotheses, the process of proving or disproving them using OLTP databases is likely to be time consuming and expensive.

The DW provides the infrastructure for decision support. It has all the detailed data that has been loaded from one, and usually a number, of operational and historical DBMS. This process of loading data in a DW is often quite complex. A process called ETL was presented in Chapter 2. A DW is usually quite large; it may have hundreds of millions of rows of data. Once a DW has been implemented, OLAP normally sits on top of it. OLAP may then be used to answer management queries quickly using the large amount of data in the DW. If these queries were posed using the operational DBMS, they would normally involve aggregations which are likely to use "Group By" function is the queries making them rather inefficient to process.

The focus of operational managers is on improving business management and processes across the various enterprise functions, for example customer support, inventory, marketing. To achieve this they require:

- a single sign-on path to the enterprise information
- a single version of the enterprise information
- high level of data accuracy
- a user-friendly interface to the information
- easy sharing of data across enterprise business units

Furthermore, some managers that are not involved in operational management are more interested in looking at overall trends and aggregations of the operational data. While the operational managers might be, for example in a university, more interested in finding out how many students are enrolled in the current semester and how many have dropped out, managers involved in university strategy may be more interested in knowing how these numbers are changing from year to year and other questions like what percentage of the top 5% of high school graduates enrolled in the university this year and what the trend is.

This chapter and the next chapter (OLAP, Online Analytical Processing) look at some solutions to meet the variety of needs of management staff in an enterprise.

One simple solution to meeting these needs is to allow managers to pose queries of interest to a mediator system that decomposes each query into appropriate subqueries for the systems that the query needs to access, obtains results from those systems and then combines and presents the result to the user. This is sometimes called *lazy* or *on-demand* query processing. There are some significant advantages of this approach since the user is provided up-to-date information if the information is changing rapidly. This approach however has some disadvantages, for example, the management queries may generate such a heavy load on some OLTP systems that the performance of the systems becomes unacceptable. Also, the OLTP systems have no historical data and so finding trends may not be possible.

Another approach is that one could collect the most common queries that the managers ask and run them regularly and have the results available when a manager poses one of these queries. This approach, called the *eager* approach, has the advantage of being quick but has obvious drawbacks since the information may not be up-to-date and managers may pose queries that have not been pre-computed which would again have to be run in the lazy mode.

The third approach is somewhere in between the two extremes. It involves creation of a separate database that only stores information that is of interest to the management staff and involves the following two steps:

1. The information needs of management staff are analysed and the enterprise systems that store some or all of the information are identified. A suitable data model is developed and the information is then extracted, transformed and loaded in the new database.
2. The new database is then used to answer management queries and the OLTP systems are not accessed for such queries.

We discuss two approaches of this type of database in this chapter, the *operational data store (ODS)* and the *data warehouse (DW)*. An ODS may be considered as a special simple type of DW.

8.2 OPERATIONAL DATA STORES

As noted above, to meet the information needs of management staff, one possible solution is to build a separate database. One such approach is called the *operational data store (ODS)* approach. An ODS is designed to provide a consolidated view of the enterprise's current operational information.

An ODS has been defined by Inmon and Imhoff (1996) as follows.

> **Operational Data Store**
> An Operational Data Store is a subject oriented, integrated, volatile, current valued data store, containing only corporate detailed data.

In contrast a data warehouse (discussed later in this chapter) does not have operational data in it. A data warehouse is a reporting database that contains relatively recent as well as historical data and may also contain aggregate data.

The ODS is *subject-oriented*. That is, it is organised around the major data subjects of an enterprise. In a university, the subjects might be students, lecturers and courses while in a company the subjects might be customers, salesmen and products.

The ODS is *integrated*. That is, it is a collection of subject-oriented data from a variety of systems to provide an enterprise-wide view of the data.

The ODS is *current valued*. That is, an ODS is up-to-date and reflects the current status of the information. An ODS does not include historical data. Since the OLTP systems data is changing all the time, data from underlying sources should refresh the ODS as regularly and frequently as possible.

The ODS is *volatile*. That is, the data in the ODS changes frequently as new information refreshes the ODS.

The ODS is *detailed*. That is, the ODS is detailed enough to serve the needs of the operational management staff in the enterprise. The granularity of the data in the ODS does not have to be exactly the same as in the source OLTP systems.

An ODS may also be used as an interim database for a data warehouse. Since the contents of an ODS are updated frequently, it may also be used to quickly perform relatively simple queries (such as finding the status of a customer order), rather than complex queries on large amounts of data typical of a data warehouse.

An ODS may be viewed as an enterprise's short term memory in that it stores only very recent information; in comparison, the data warehouse is more like an enterprise's long term memory in that it stores historical information relatively permanently.

As noted earlier, an ODS may be considered a type of data warehouse. An ODS itself may be of different types depending on the needs of an enterprise. For example, an ODS may be fairly simple that is essentially a reporting tool for administrative purposes. Such an ODS is usually updated daily. It provides reports about business transactions for that day, such as sales totals or orders filled. Another type of ODS may be designed to track more complex information such as product and location codes. This database is updated more frequently (perhaps hourly) to reflect changes. Yet another type of ODS may be designed to support customer relationship management (CRM). In these systems, synchronous or near-synchronous updates are used to provide customers with consistently valid and organised information.

An ODS can provide a number of benefits to an enterprise. For example, an ODS is the unified operational view of the enterprise that provides the operational managers improved access to important operational data. This view may assist in better understanding of the business and the customer. An ODS can be much more effective in generating current reports without having to access the OLTP or legacy systems. The ODS may also shorten the time required to implement and populate a data warehouse system because ODS already provides integrated enterprise data. An ODS may also become a source of reliable information for some other applications.

8.2.1 ODS Design and Implementation

A typical architecture of an ODS is shown in Figure 8.1.

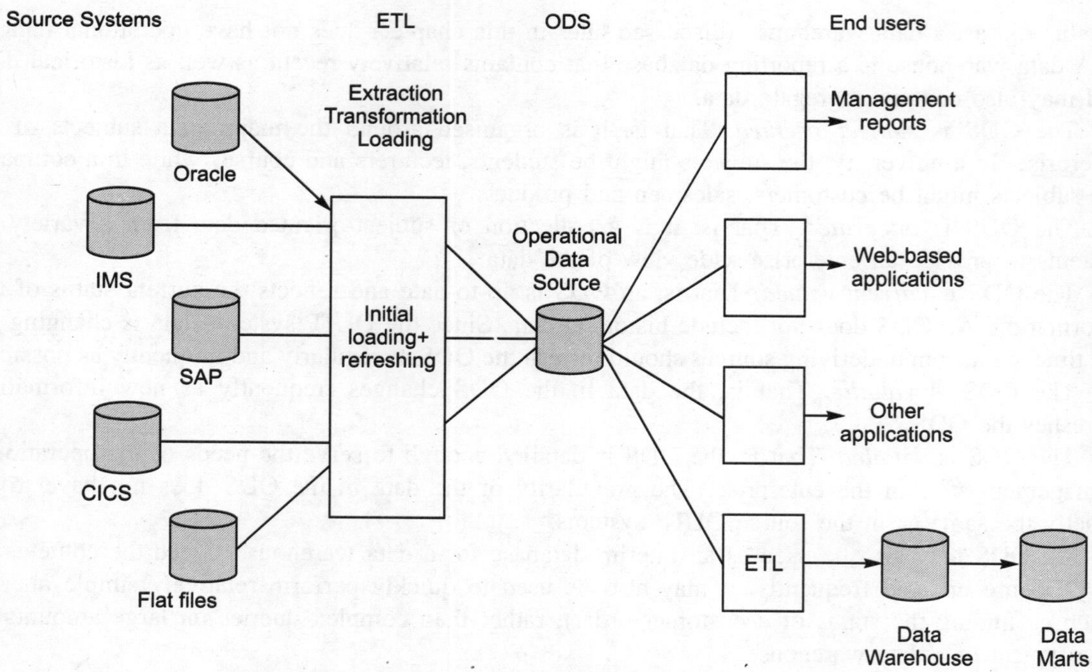

Figure 8.1 Possible operational data store structure.

To implement an ODS, just like implementing any database system, a data model should be developed. Often the Star Join model, discussed later in Section 8.5, has been found to be suitable.

The database model should match the structure of the enterprise. Although all the attributes included in the source databases do not need to be included in the ODS, all attributes that are likely to be needed by the operational management staff should be identified and included.

The extraction of information from source databases needs to be efficient and the quality of data needs to be maintained. Since the data is refreshed regularly and frequently, suitable checks are required to ensure quality of data after each refresh. An ODS would of course be required to satisfy normal integrity constraints, for example, existential integrity, referential integrity and appropriate action to deal with nulls. An ODS is a read only database other than regular refreshing by the OLTP systems. Users should not be allowed to update ODS information.

Populating an ODS involves an acquisition process of extracting, transforming and loading data from OLTP source systems. This process, called ETL, is discussed in detail in the next section. Completing populating the database, checking for anomalies and testing for performance are necessary before an ODS system can go on line.

8.2.2 Why a Separate Database?

There is no theoretical basis for justifying a separate ODS. It is always possible to carry out the ODS queries on the existing OLTP systems but as we have noted ODS makes query processing for operational managers much more efficient without loading the OLTP systems. It is therefore a question of trade-off. Shall we perhaps spend more money on the OLTP systems to improve their capacity so that they can also deal with operational management queries or shall we spend money on building and maintaining a separate ODS? One may also wonder why ODS cannot be combined with the data warehouse if the enterprise is building or already has a data warehouse. This issue is discussed later in this chapter.

Perhaps the most important reason why an ODS should be separate from the operational databases is that from time to time complex queries are likely to degrade the performance of the OLTP systems. The OLTP systems have to provide a quick response to operational users and businesses cannot afford to have response time suffer when a manager is running a complex query.

8.3 DATA WAREHOUSES

Data warehousing is a process for assembling and managing data from various sources for the purpose of gaining a single detailed view of an enterprise. Although there are several definitions of data warehouse, a widely accepted definition by Inmon (1992) is given below.

Data Warehouse
A Data Warehouse is an integrated subject oriented and time variant repository of information in support of management's decision making process.

The definition is similar to the definition of an ODS except that an ODS is a current-valued data store while a data warehouse is a time-variant repository of data.

In the early database systems, and the file systems before that, whenever the managers required information for decision making, a special application program had to be written to retrieve the information and print the reports that the managers required. The head office in most enterprises therefore needed a computing section that could carry out such tasks. More recently, it has been found that this is not an effective way of providing decision making information to the managers since the needs of decision makers change frequently in the competitive environment of today. One day the reports requested may be by region while the next day they might be by product.

The primary aims in building a data warehouse are to provide a single version of the truth about the enterprise information and to provide good performance for ad hoc management queries required for enterprise analysis to manipulate, animate and synthesise enterprise information.

As noted earlier, modern decision making requires strategic use of information. For example, the student recruitment department in a university would want to study the profiles of students that have been recruited over the last few years. The department may also want to study the trends in student performance and student numbers from different countries assuming that the university has international students. A sales department of a music store would want to study the buying profiles of its customers. A government department on the other hand may want to study how the use of services provided has been changing over the last few years.

In summary, the benefits of implementing a data warehouse are as follows:

- To provide a single version of truth about enterprise information.
- To speed up ad hoc reports and queries that involve aggregations across many attributes (that is, many GROUP BY's) which are resource intensive. The managers require trends, sums and aggregations that allow, for example, to compare this year's performance to last year's or prepare forecasts for next year.
- To provide a system in which managers who do not have a strong technical background are able to run complex queries.
- To provide a database that stores relatively clean data. By using a good ETL process, the data warehouse should have data of high quality.
- To provide a database that stores historical data that may have been deleted from the OLTP systems.

As noted for ODS, to achieve these benefits it is necessary to build a separate data warehouse. This database is very different than OLTP systems and different than an ODS. We first summarise the differences between OLTP and data warehouse systems in Table 8.1.

Table 8.1 Comparing OLTP and data warehouse systems (Based on Oracle, 2002)

Property	*OLTP*	*Data warehouse*
Nature of the database	3NF	Multidimensional
Indexes	Few	Many
Joins	Many	Some
Duplicated data	Normalised data	Denormalised data
Derived data and aggregates	Rare	Common
Queries	Mostly pre-defined	Mostly ad-hoc
Nature of queries	Mostly simple	Mostly complex
Updates	All the time	Not allowed, only refreshed
Historical data	Often not available	Essential

The term data warehouse was not coined until the late 1980s. It was only in the early 1990s that tools for implementing data warehouses became available and enterprises started implementing these technologies. It appears that there are now hundreds of vendors that supply some aspects of data warehouse technology.

As shown in Figure 8.2, a data warehouse is different than an ODS. The data warehouse, as noted earlier, is more like an enterprise's long-term memory. The objectives in building the two systems, ODS and data warehouse, are somewhat conflicting and therefore the two databases are likely to have different schemas.

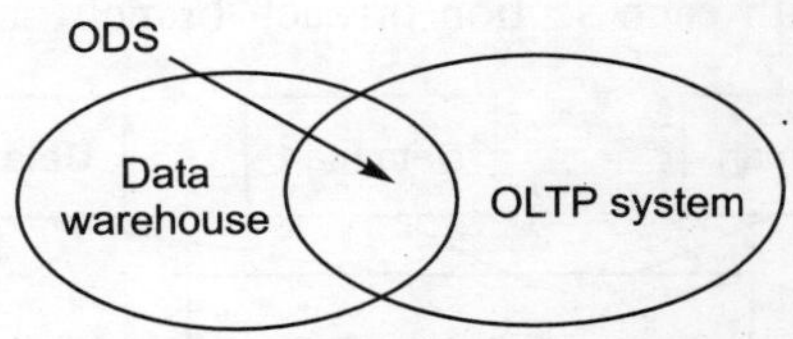

Figure 8.2 Relationship between OLTP, ODS and DW systems.

Conventionally, operational data does not need to deal with historical data. A data warehouse, as noted above, deals primarily with historical data and needs to include some of the legacy data as well as data from a number of current enterprise OLTP systems. Since much warehouse data is built around the time dimension, a data warehouse has to be separate from the OLTP systems and an ODS.

As discussed earlier in the case of an ODS, perhaps the most important reason why a data warehouse must be separate from OLTP systems is that complex queries involving a number of aggregations are likely to degrade the performance of the OLTP systems and may not even be possible since the OLTP systems may not include the needed historical data.

The data warehouse does not store real-time data and does not require real-time updates while the ODS does. The ODS does not have historical information but the data warehouse does. A data warehouse can be large but growing only slowly over time. Figure 8.2 shows the relationship between the OLTP systems, ODS and data warehouse. Table 8.2 outlines the differences between an ODS and a data warehouse.

Table 8.2 Comparison of the ODS and data warehouse (Based on IBM, 2001)

ODS	*DW*
Data of high quality at detailed level and assured availability	Data may not be perfect, but sufficient for strategic analysts; data does not have to be highly available
Contains current and near-current data	Contains historical data
Real-time and near real-time data loads	Normally batch data loads
Mostly updated at data field level (even if it may be appended)	Data is appended, not updated
Typically detailed data only	Contains summarised and detailed data
Modelled to support rapid data updates (3NF)	Variety of modelling techniques used, typically multidimensional for data marts to optimise query performance
Transactions similar to those in OLTP system	Complex queries processing larger volumes of data
Used for detailed decision making and operational reporting	Used for long-term decision making and management reporting
Used at the operational level	Used at the managerial level

A data warehouse not only takes the aggregate query load off the OLTP systems, it also provides the OLTP systems a facility to off-load data that the systems no longer require. If a data warehouse was not available, historical data may have to be downloaded to tapes or CDs, media that may not be available for online queries.

Just like in building an ODS, data warehousing is a process of integrating enterprise-wide data, originating from a variety of sources, into a single repository. As shown in Figure 8.3, the warehouse may be a central enterprise-wide data warehouse for use by all the decision makers in the enterprise or it may consist of a number of smaller data warehouses (often called *data marts* or *local data warehouses*) that deal perhaps with each section or each branch or each subject in the enterprise.

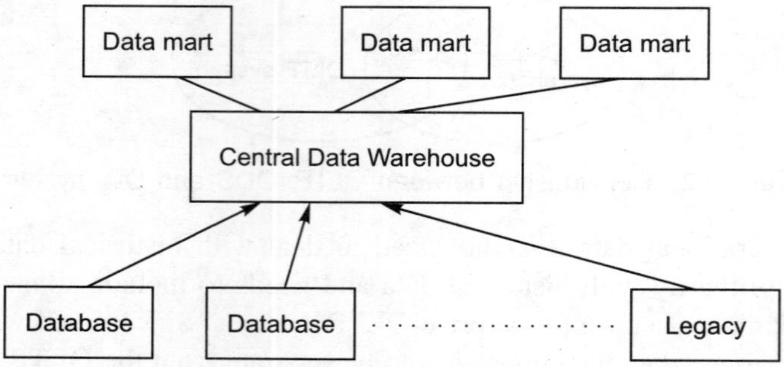

Figure 8.3 Simple structure of a data warehouse system.

A data mart stores information for a limited number of subject areas. For example, a company might have a data mart about marketing that supports marketing and sales. The data mart approach is attractive since beginning with a single data mart is relatively inexpensive and easier to implement. A data mart may be used as a proof of data warehouse concept. Data marts can also create difficulties by setting up "silos of information" although one may build dependent data marts which are populated from the central data warehouse.

Data marts are often the common approach for building data warehouse since the cost curve for data marts tends to be more linear. A centralised data warehouse project can be very resource intensive and requires significant investment at the beginning although overall costs over a number of years for a centralised data warehouse and for decentralised data marts are likely to be similar.

A centralised warehouse can provide better quality data and minimise data inconsistencies since the data quality is controlled centrally. The tools and procedures for putting data in the warehouse can then be better controlled. Controlling data quality with a decentralised approach is obviously more difficult. As with any centralised function, though, the units or branches of an enterprise may feel no ownership of the centralised warehouse and may in some cases not fully cooperate with the administration of the warehouse. Also, maintaining a centralised warehouse would require considerable coordination between the various units if the enterprise is large and this coordination may incur significant costs for the enterprise.

Although many companies appear to be implementing data warehouse systems, the challenges of such implementations are not yet fully understood since data warehousing is a relatively new technology that involves a number of major steps. First of all, aims of implementing a warehouse should be clearly identified. Once the decision to implement has been made, one needs to consider whether the enterprise is going to go to a vendor that provides a full data warehousing solution (expensive) or to other vendors who provide parts of the solution (cheaper but more risks). We provide some guidelines that can assist in successful data warehouse implementations later in this chapter.

As an example of a data warehouse application we consider the telecommunications industry which in most countries has become very competitive during the last few years. If a company is able to identify a market trend before its competitors do then that can lead to a competitive advantage. What is therefore needed is to analyse customer needs and behaviour in an attempt to better understand what the customers want and need. Such understanding might make it easier for a company to identify, develop and deliver some relevant new products or new pricing schemes to retain and attract customers. It can also help in improving profitability since it can help the company understand what type of customers are the most profitable.

8.3.1 ODS and DW Architecture

A typical ODS architecture was shown in Figure 8.1. It involved extracting information from source systems by using ETL processes and then storing it in the ODS. The ODS could then be used for producing a variety of reports for management.

The architecture shown in Figure 8.4 is more complex. It involves extracting information from source systems by using an ETL process and then storing the information in a staging database. The daily changes also come to the staging area. Another ETL process is used to transform information from the staging area to populate the ODS. The ODS is then used for supplying information via another ETL process to the data warehouse which in turn feeds a number of data marts that generate the reports required by management.

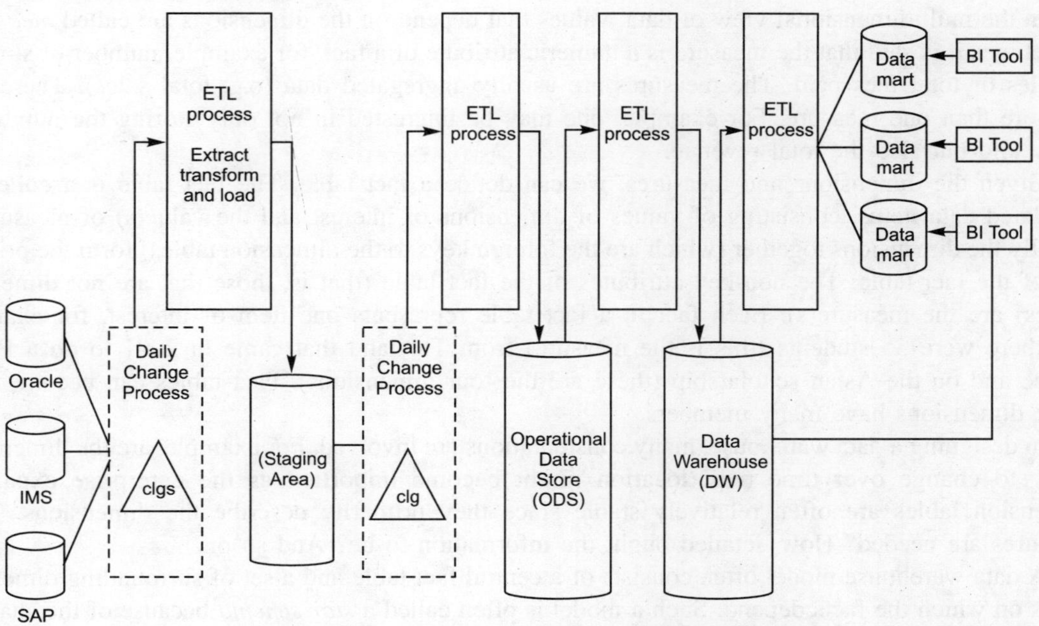

Figure 8.4 Another structure for ODS and DW.

8.4 DATA WAREHOUSE DESIGN

There are a number of ways of conceptualising a data warehouse. One approach is to view it as a three-level architecture. The lowest level consists of the OLTP and legacy systems, the middle level consists of the global or central data warehouse while the top level consists of local data warehouses or data marts. Another approach is possible if the enterprise has an ODS. The three levels then might consist of OLTP and legacy systems at the bottom, the ODS in the middle and the data warehouse at the top.

Whatever the architecture, a data warehouse needs to have a data model that can form the basis for implementing it. To develop a data model we view a data warehouse as a multidimensional structure consisting of dimensions, since that is an intuitive model that matches the types of OLAP queries posed by management. A dimension (essentially an attribute) is an ordinate within a multidimensional structure consisting of a list of ordered values (sometimes called *members*) just like the x-axis and y-axis values on a two-dimensional graph. A member is a distinct value (or name or identifier) for the dimension (e.g. degree dimension has a member BSc). Dimensions often have hierarchies that show parent/child relationships between the members of a dimension. For example, the dimension country may have a hierarchy that divides the world into continents and continents into regions followed by regions into countries if such a hierarchy is useful for the application. For example, Asia may be divided into South Asia, South East Asia, North Asia and possibly West Asia. Each of these regions may then be divided into countries. Thus we may have several levels in a hierarchy. A more commonly used hierarchy is time. Time may be divided into years which are divided into quarters and then in months. There may be more than one hierarchy for a dimension (e.g. degree may have a Faculty, Department hierarchy as well as a hierarchy that divides them in postgraduate and undergraduate degrees).

In the multidimensional view of data, values that depend on the dimensions are called *measures*. Sometimes it is said that the measure is a numeric attribute of a fact, for example, number of students or sales or total fees paid. The measures are usually aggregated data (e.g. total sales). There may be more than one measure. For example, one may be interested in not only storing the number of items sold but also the total revenue.

Given the dimensions and measures, we can define a fact table. The fact table is a collection of related data items, consisting of values of dimensions of interest and the value(s) of measure(s). Usually the dimensions together (which are the foreign keys to the dimension tables) form the primary key of the fact table. The non-key attributes of the fact table (that is, those that are not dimension values) are the measure(s). Each fact in a fact table represents one item of interest, for example, that there were 35 students (this is the measure) from Thailand that came in 2001 to do a BCom degree and on the Asian scholarship (these are the four dimensions). Fact tables can become large if the dimensions have many members.

In designing a data warehouse, many considerations are involved. For example, are the dimensions likely to change over time (e.g. location might become important as the enterprise expands)? Dimension tables are often relatively stable since they primarily describe the dimensions. What measures are needed? How detailed ought the information to be? And so on.

A data warehouse model often consists of a central fact table and a set of surrounding dimension tables on which the facts depend. Such a model is often called a *star schema* because of the shape of the model representation. A simple example of such a schema is shown in Figure 8.5 for a university where we assume that the number of students is given by the four dimensions, e.g. degree, year, country and scholarship.

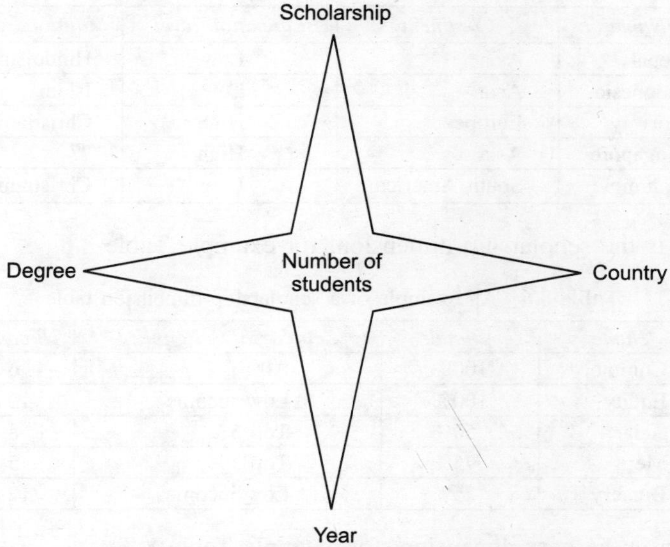

Figure 8.5 A simple example of star schema.

A characteristic of a star schema is that all the dimensions directly link to the fact table. The fact table and the dimension tables then look like Table 8.3.

Table 8.3 An example of a fact table

Year	*Degree name*	*Country name*	*Scholarship name*	*Number*
200301	BSc	Australia	Govt	35
199902	MBBS	Canada	None	50
200002	LLB	USA	ABC	22
199901	BCom	UK	Commonwealth	7
200102	LLB	Australia	Equity	2

We now present the dimension tables. The first dimension is the degree dimension, for example Table 8.4.

Table 8.4 An example of a degree dimension table

Name	*Faculty*	*Scholarship eligibility*	*Number of semesters*
BSc	Science	Yes	6
MBBS	Medicine	No	10
LLB	Law	Yes	8
BCom	Business	No	6
BA	Arts	No	6

We now present the second dimension, the country dimension, for example Table 8.5.

Table 8.5 An example of a country dimension table

Name	*Continent*	*Education level*	*Major religion*
Nepal	Asia	Low	Hinduism
Indonesia	Asia	Low	Islam
Norway	Europe	High	Christianity
Singapore	Asia	High	??
Columbia	South America	Low	Christianity

The third dimension is the scholarship dimension, for example Table 8.6.

Table 8.6 An example of a scholarship dimension table

Name	*Amount*	*Scholarship eligibility*	*Number*
Colombo	100%	All	6
Equity	100%	Low income	10
Asia	50%	Top 5%	8
Merit	75%	Top 5%	5
Bursary	25%	Low income	12

The fourth dimension is the year dimension, for example Table 8.7.

Table 8.7 An example of a year dimension table

Name	*New programs*
2001	Journalism
2002	Multimedia
2003	Biotechnology

We now present a star schema for two dimensions in Figure 8.6 and another for four dimensions in Figure 8.7.

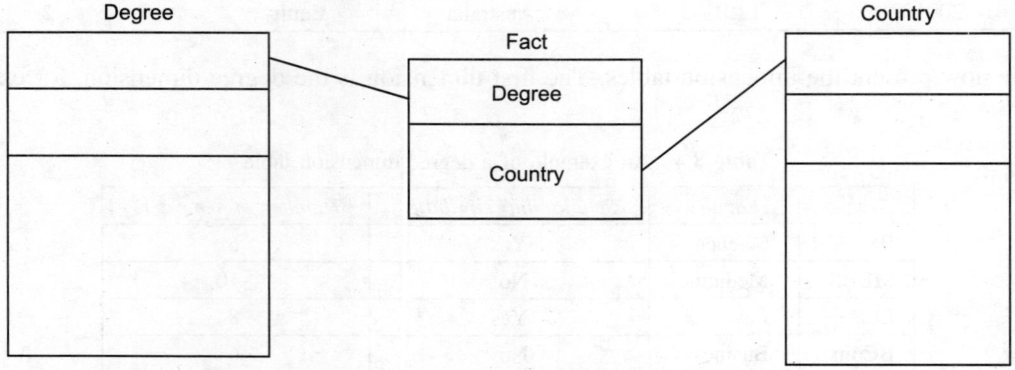

Figure 8.6 Star schema for a two-dimensional example.

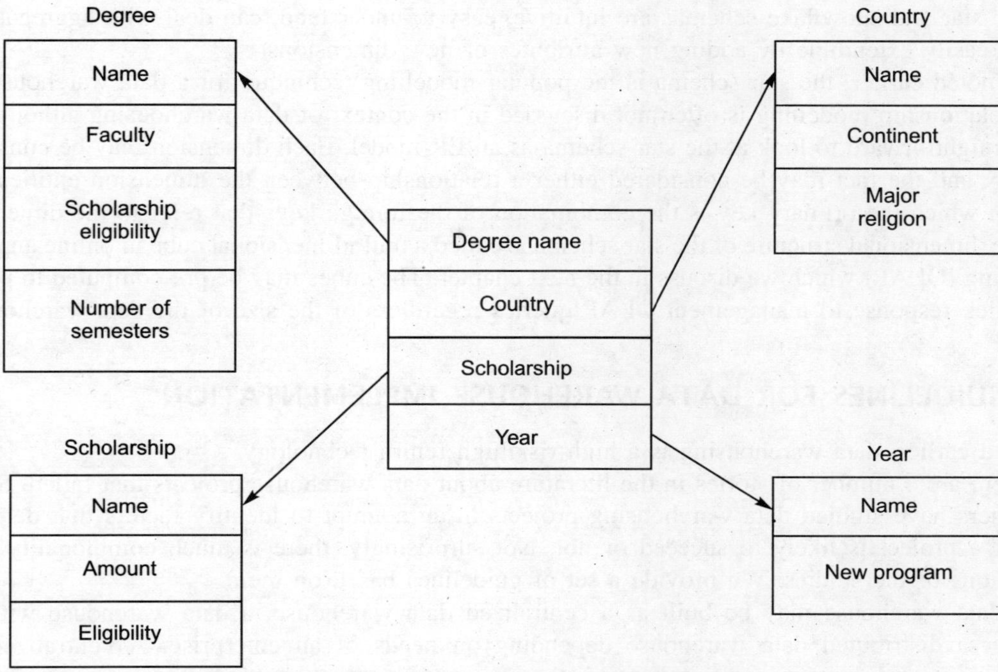

Figure 8.7 Star schema for a four-dimensional example.

Star schemas may be refined into *snowflake schemas* if we wish to provide support for dimension hierarchies by allowing the dimension tables to have subtables to represent the hierarchies. For example, Figure 8.8 shows a simple snowflake schema for a two-dimensional example.

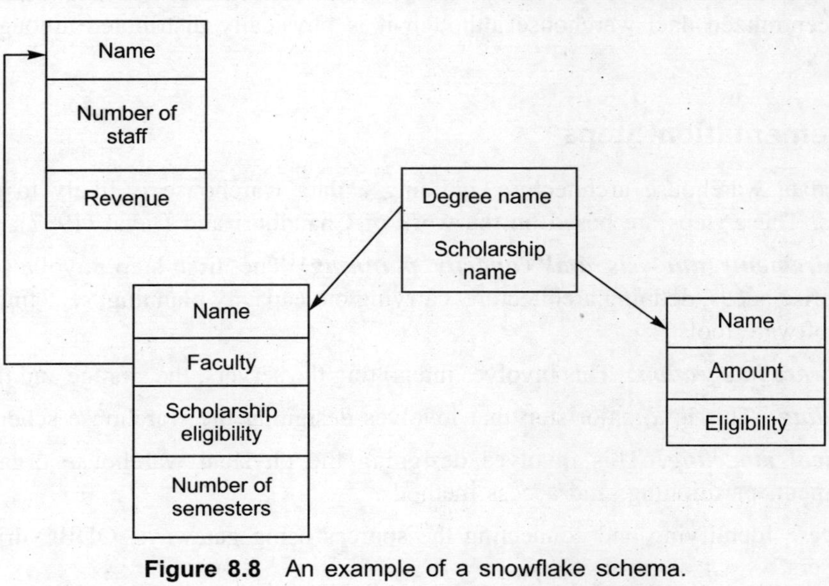

Figure 8.8 An example of a snowflake schema.

The star and snowflake schemas are intuitive, easy to understand, can deal with aggregate data and are easily extendible by adding new attributes or new dimensions.

As noted earlier, the star schema is the popular modelling technique for a data warehouse. The entity-relationship modelling is often not discussed in the context of data warehousing although it is quite straightforward to look at the star schema as an ER model. Each dimension may be considered an entity and the fact may be considered either a relationship between the dimension entities or an entity in which the primary key is the combination of the foreign keys that refer to the dimensions.

The dimensional structure of the star schema is called a multidimensional cube in online analytical processing (OLAP) which we discuss in the next chapter. The cubes may be pre-computed to provide very quick response to management OLAP queries regardless of the size of the data warehouse.

8.5 GUIDELINES FOR DATA WAREHOUSE IMPLEMENTATION

As noted earlier, data warehousing is a high risk/high return technology.

There are a number of stories in the literature about data warehouse projects that failed. Several researchers have studied data warehousing projects in an attempt to identify factors that determine whether a project is likely to succeed or not. Not surprisingly, there is much commonality in the conclusions of the studies. We provide a set of guidelines based on them.

A data warehouse may be built as a centralized data warehouse, a data warehouse with data marts or a distributed data warehouse depending on needs of an enterprise. A centralized data warehouse perhaps is relatively simple and is therefore a common choice for most large organisations. In the data warehouse with data marts architecture, it is best to have the data marts extracting information from the central data warehouse to maintain integrity of data in all of them. The benefit of this approach is that each data mart can have a local view of the data and much processing can be carried out in the local data mart. Distributed data warehouse on the other is suitable for a large international organisation with offices in several countries. The distributed data warehouse should appear like a centralized data warehouse although it is physically distributed among a number of data warehouses.

8.5.1 Implementation Steps

Whatever the data warehouse architecture, building a data warehouse is likely to consist of the following steps. These steps are based on the work of Chaudhuri and Dayal (1997).

1. ***Requirements analysis and capacity planning:*** The first step involves defining the enterprise needs, defining architecture, carrying out capacity planning, selecting the hardware and software tools.
2. ***Hardware integration*:** This involves integrating the servers, the storage and the client tools.
3. ***Modeling:*** This is a major step that involves designing the warehouse schema and views.
4. ***Physical modeling:*** This involves designing the physical warehouse organisation, data placement, partitioning, and access methods.
5. ***Sources:*** Identifying and connecting the sources using gateways, ODBC drivers, or other wrappers.

6. ***ETL (extraction, transformation and loading):*** Designing and implementing the ETL process. This may involve identifying a suitable ETL tool vendor and purchasing and implementing the tool.
7. ***Populate the data warehouse:*** After ETL, populating the warehouse with the schema and view definitions.
8. ***User application:*** This step involves designing and implementing end-user applications since for the data warehouse to be useful there must be end-user applications.
9. ***Roll-out the warehouse and applications:*** Once the data warehouse has been populated and the end-user applications tested, the warehouse system and the applications may be rolled out for the user community to use.

We now present some guidelines for successfully implementing a data warehouse. These are general guidelines, not each of them will be applicable to every data warehouse project.

8.5.2 Implementation Guidelines

- **Build incrementally:** Data warehouse must be built incrementally. Generally it is recommended that a data mart may first be built with one particular project in mind and once it is implemented a number of other sections of the enterprise may also wish to implement similar systems. An enterprise data warehouse can then be implemented in an iterative manner allowing all data marts to extract information from the data warehouse. Data warehousing modelling itself is an iterative methodology as users become familiar with the technology and are then able to understand and express their requirements more clearly.
- **Need a champion:** A data warehouse project must have a champion who is willing to carry out considerable research into expected costs and benefits of the project. Data warehousing projects require an input from many units in an enterprise and therefore need to be driven by someone who is capable of interacting with people in the enterprise and can actively persuade colleagues. Without the cooperation of other units, the data model for the warehouse and the data required to populate the warehouse may be more complicated than they need to be. Studies have shown that having a champion can help adoption and success of data warehousing projects.
- **Senior management support:** A data warehouse project must be fully supported by the senior management. Given the resource intensive nature of such projects and the time they can take to implement, a warehouse project calls for a sustained commitment from senior management. This can sometime be difficult since it may be hard to quantify the benefits of data warehouse technology and the managers may consider it as a cost without any explicit return on investment. Data warehousing projects studies show that top management support is essential for the success of a data warehousing project.
- **Ensure quality:** Only data that has been cleaned and is of a quality that is understood by the organization should be loaded in the data warehouse.
- **Corporate strategy:** A data warehouse project must fit with corporate strategy and business objectives. The objectives of the project must be clearly defined before the start of the project.

- **Business plan:** The financial costs (hardware, software, peopleware), expected benefits and a project plan (including an ETL plan) for a data warehouse project must be clearly outlined and understood by all stake holders.
- **Training:** A data warehouse project must not overlook data warehouse training requirements. For a data warehouse project to be successful the users must be trained to use the warehouse and to understand its capabilities. The training and professional development of the project team may also be required since data warehousing is a complex task and the skills of the project team are critical in the success of the project.
- **Adaptability:** The project should build in adaptability so changes may be made to the data warehouse if required. Like any system, a data warehouse will need to change, as an enterprise's needs change. Furthermore, once the data warehouse is operational, new applications using the data warehouse may be required. The system should be able to support such new applications.
- **Joint management:** The project must be managed by both IT and business professionals. Only technical professionals must not manage a data warehouse project for the project to be successful. The business professionals must also be involved in its management.

8.6 DATA WAREHOUSE METADATA

Given the complexity of information in an ODS and a data warehouse, it is essential that there be a mechanism for users to easily find out what data is there and how it can be used to meet their needs. Providing *metadata* about the ODS or the data warehouse achieves this. Metadata is data about data or documentation about the data that is needed by the users. It is stored in the system itself and can be queried using tools that are available on the system. Simple examples of metadata are tables and figures in a document like this book. A table (which is data) has a name (e.g. table titles in this chapter) and there are column names of the table which may also be considered metadata. The figures also have titles or names. In the context of a data warehouse, metadata has been defined as "all of the information in the data warehouse environment that is not the actual data itself".

In a database, metadata usually consists of table (relation) lists, schemas, record counts and perhaps a list of the most common queries. Additional information may be provided including logical and physical data structures and when and what data was loaded.

In a data warehouse, metadata may be much more comprehensive. It may be classified as back room metadata and front room metadata. Much important information is included in the back room metadata. For example, information about the ETL process should be stored there. This could include dates on which ETL process was carried out and names of data that were extracted. It could also include information on what source systems the ETL process uses and what their schemas are. What parameters are needed when ETL is run manually? When and how often an automatic ETL process is run? What ETL and DW logs are there? The front room metadata could include information needed by the users, for example, user security privileges, various statistics about usage, information on network security, etc.

Just like any other data, metadata needs to satisfy the needs of experienced as well as inexperienced users. Metadata needs to be complete, correct and current and should be easily accessible, perhaps via the Web using secure access, to all users. The metadata should also include definitions of terms used.

8.7 SOFTWARE FOR ODS AND DATA WAREHOUSING

There is a large variety of software available for ODS, ETL and data warehousing. Most of the major database vendors have products in these areas. A number of smaller companies are operating in niche markets, e.g. ETL or data warehousing. It is difficult to judge the quality of software when there are so many vendors in the market, many of them relatively new. One must therefore be careful in selecting software and should ensure sufficient evidence is available to support the case that a particular software will meet the needs of the user.

We present relatively small lists of available software. The lists are not intended to suggest that the software included in them is better than that which are not listed. The lists have been prepared almost by random selection from much larger lists that are available on the Web. The only filtering we undertook was that if the website of a software vendor did not even explain what the software did then we did not include that software on the list.

ODS Software

- IQ Solutions: Dynamic ODS from Sybase offloads data from OLTP systems and makes it available on a Sybase IQ platform for queries and analysis.
  http://www.sybase.com/products/informationmanagement/sybaseiq
- Virtual ODS from CenterBoard supplies CenterBoard Integrator, a network-based Virtual ODS that provides access to information across the enterprise as if it were a single database, without copying data.
  http://www.centerboard.com/
- ADH Active Data Hub from Glenridge Solutions is a real-time data integration and reporting solution for PeopleSoft, Oracle and SAP databases. ADH includes an ODS, an enterprise data warehouse, a workflow initiator and a metadata library.
  http://www.glenridgesolutions.com/
- Teradata provides ODS facilities within the enterprise data warehouse, eliminating the need to create new copies of data. Teradata claims that the creation of separate ODS components is primarily a response to technological limitations of database products rather than an architectural necessity.
  http://www.teradata.com/t/page/115926/

Data Warehousing Software

- Aardvark Knowledge Builder from D2K provides solution to identifying, tagging/extracting and structuring key data into custom relational database schemas and proprietary taxonomies.
  http://www.d2k.com/
- BusinessObjects Warehouse from BusinessObjects is based on Ralph Kimball's data warehouse design techniques. It has a modular approach that allows an incremental implementation of a data warehouse that provides data access, integration, and optimization for cross-departmental reporting and analysis. It includes tool for data sourcing and metadata management as well as for end user querying, reporting, and analysis.
  http://www.businessobjects.com/

- Informatica Data Integration Software from 3Com is a suite of software that provides data integration from enterprise data stored in a wide variety of transactional systems and applications, data warehouses, operational data stores, legacy systems, and flat files.
http://www.informatica.com/
- mySAP Business Intelligence provides facilities for ETL, data warehouse management and business modeling to help build data warehouses, model information architecture and manage data from multiple sources.
http://www.sap.com/solutions/netweaver/businessintelligence/featuresfunctions/index.epx
- Oracle Warehouse Builder 10g is a design tool that provides an easy to use, graphical environment to rapidly design, deploy, and manage a data warehouse.
http://www.oracle.com/technology/products/warehouse/index.html
- SAS/Warehouse Administrator is designed for setup and management of multiple data warehouses and data marts. It includes ETL tools and provides a framework for effective warehouse management through a metadata-driven architecture.
http://www.sas.com/technologies/dw/management/wadmin/
- SQL Server 2005 from Microsoft provides ETL tools as well as tools for building a relational data warehouse and a multidimensional database.
http://www.microsoft.com/sql/2005/default.asp
- Sybase IQ is designed for reporting, data warehousing, and analytics. It claims to deliver high query performance and storage efficiency for structured and unstructured data. Sybase has partnered with Sun in providing data warehousing solutions.
http://www.sybase.com/
- WhereScape Red from WhereSpace is a tool for rapid design, prototype, test and deployment of Oracle-based and SQL-Server based data warehouses. The company is primarily involved in data warehousing software.
http://www.wherescape.com/Home.asp

SUMMARY

In this chapter we have discussed the need for an enterprise to have separate databases to support the needs of management. Two such databases have been discussed. One is the operational data store (ODS) that stores current-valued operational data from a number of operational systems. The other is the data warehouse (DW) that does not store operational data but stores historical data to assist in efficiently computing aggregates and trends. Both are important technologies and can only be implemented by using an effective technique for extracting, transforming and loading data from operational and legacy systems. We have discussed some aspects of ETL.

A full-blown management support environment (sometimes called an enterprise's information factory) could well consist of an ODS, an ETL tool, some staging area for copying information from OLTP and legacy systems, a data warehouse, a metadata repository, some data marts and OLAP tools.

Implementing an ODS and a data warehouse may involve considerable research regarding requirements, tools available in the market and trial and error but once implemented the benefits can be significant. It has been found that often when an ODS and a data warehouse have been set up, the importance and usage of these systems grows as management discovers new uses for the systems.

It has been found that in certain situations it is useful to send some information available in a data warehouse back to one or more OLTP systems to help serve the customers better.

Implementing systems like an ODS and a data warehouse requires considerable cooperation within the organisation. Implementing such systems must not be taken without the full support of top management and without appropriate consultation processes including all stake holders.

As noted earlier, data warehouse is often a high risk/high return technology and is not suitable for all enterprises. The technology has inherent risks that need to be understood before embarking on an implementation. We have earlier identified critical factors that should be in place for a data warehouse project to be successful. In some businesses, the market may be so volatile that historical data is of little use. In others, an enterprise has been or is being restructured, merged with another business or being taken over and therefore historical information may be of little relevance to it at such time. In some businesses, reporting needed may be possible with the OLTP systems since the reporting may be relatively simple. In other businesses the company may have only one or two OLTP systems. There may be situations in which the cost of capturing data, implementing a data warehouse and training the employees to use the warehouse effectively are so high that the overall benefits of a data warehouse are likely to be relatively small.

REVIEW QUESTIONS

1. Why do many enterprises need a data warehouse? (Section 8.1)
2. What are OLTP and OLAP database systems. (Section 8.1)
3. What is ODS and what is it used for? (Section 8.2)
4. Explain why ETL must deal with dirty data when extracting information from the source systems. (Section 8.3)
5. List the major steps involved in the ETL process. (Section 8.3)
6. The need for a separate database for decision makers. (Section 8.4)
7. What is a data warehouse and how it might be defined? (Section 8.4)
8. What are the likely benefits of building an enterprise data warehouse? (Section 8.4)
9. What is the major difference in the star schema and the snowflake schema. (Section 8.4)
10. List some differences between a OLTP system and a data warehouse system. (Section 8.4)
11. Describe the features of a data warehouse. (Section 8.5)
12. Explain the star schema technique of modelling a data warehouse. (Section 8.5)
13. List guidelines for implementing a data warehouse. What is the most important step in implementing a data warehouse? (Section 8.6)
14. What types of queries do managers need to pose to the enterprise's database systems. (Section 8.2)
15. List reasons when implementing a data warehouse is not recommended. (Section 8.6)
16. Describe the type of metadata that is maintained in a data warehouse. (Section 8.7)

EXERCISES

1. How is data warehouse different from a database? How are they similar?
2. Select a large enterprise in your city. How many different database systems does it have? Try to investigate and make a list. If you are able to contact one of the managers, ask the person if there is a problem of errors in data in their company. Write a one-page report.
3. Describe how a data warehouse is modelled and implemented using the star schema and the snowflake schema. Explain using an example. Are there any other modelling techniques for data warehouse? Could E-R model be used? Discuss.
4. What is ETL? List some of the major issues in the ETL process and list and discuss the steps that are required in the ETL process. Illustrate the issues using examples.
5. Discuss the following data cleaning issues:
   - Missing data
   - Duplication removal
   - Instance identity problems
   - Matching codes
   - Keyboard entry errors
6. What are the benefits of implementing a data warehouse? What are the risks? Explain each of them.
7. Present a list of guidelines that may assist in the success of a data warehouse project implementation? Discuss the importance of each of these guidelines.
8. What is the role of metadata for a data warehouse? Give some examples of data warehouse metadata and explain how it differs from metadata for OLTP systems.

MULTIPLE CHOICE QUESTIONS

1. Which one of the following is true about OLTP systems?
   (a) OLTP systems run day-to-day business of the enterprise
   (b) OLTP systems are primarily for senior managers
   (c) OLTP systems cannot be accessed by enterprise call centres
   (d) OLTP systems never delete any historical data
2. Which one of the following is true?
   (a) A separate enterprise database is needed to provide additional computing power
   (b) An ODS is a special type of data warehouse
   (c) A DW only has current values
   (d) A data warehouse cannot be implemented without implementing an ODS first
3. Which of the following information is needed by managers?
   (a) A single version of enterprise information
   (b) A high level of data accuracy
   (c) A small number of OLTP systems
   (d) All of the above

4. Which one of the following is required for an ODS?
   (a) It should be subject-oriented
   (b) It should be current valued
   (c) It should be detailed
   (d) All of the above
5. Which one of the following features a data warehouse must have?
   (a) Allow updates by the users
   (b) Allow retrieval through the Web
   (c) Data is organized around subject areas important to management
   (d) Is refreshed as soon as data in OLTP systems is updated
6. Which one is not true?
   (a) ETL is essential to implement an ODS or a DW
   (b) ETS involves extraction, transformation and loading
   (c) ETL can be done after loading OLTP data in a DW
   (d) ETL deals with dummy codes, multipurpose fields and cryptic data
7. Which one of the following is not required in building a data warehouse?
   (a) Testing
   (b) Requirements analysis
   (c) Data Modelling
   (d) Data recovery
8. Which one of the following is part of the extraction process in ETL?
   (a) Extracting all the data available in the enterprise
   (b) Extracting all the data required in building a data warehouse
   (c) Extracting data that has been loaded in the data warehouse
   (d) Extracting data from the MOLAP system
9. Which one of the following is not true?
   (a) OLTP is usually 3NF and DW is multidimensional
   (b) DW has few indexes while OLTP has many
   (c) OLTP mostly deals with simple queries while DW deals mostly with complex queries
   (d) OLTP does not retain historical data while DW does
10. Which two of the following are correct regarding data warehouse metadata?
    (a) It may be classified into front room metadata and back room metadata
    (b) Metadata does not include information about the ETL process
    (c) The front room metadata includes information on security privileges
    (d) Data warehouse metadata is usually not very large
11. Which two of the following are good guidelines for data warehouse implementations?
    (a) A data warehouse should be implemented incrementally
    (b) A data warehouse needs a technical person as a champion
    (c) The data warehouse should be managed by the technical IT staff
    (d) Training should be provided to the users of a data warehouse

12. Which of the following are steps in building a data warehouse?
    (a) Requirements analysis
    (b) Modelling
    (c) Identifying data sources
    (d) All of the above
13. Which of the following problems must be dealt by an ETL system?
    (a) Instance identity problem
    (b) Record linkage problem
    (c) Semantic integration problem
    (d) All of the above
14. Which one of the following is **not** an ETL step?
    (a) Compiling
    (b) Combining
    (c) Matching
    (d) Standardizing

PROJECTS

Consider an airline booking system and assume that the following database system has been implemented. Clearly the database schema is rather primitive.

Customer(CustomerID, Title, First name, Last name, Gender, Age, Address1, Address2, Address3, Moble, TelephoneBH, TelephoneAH, Email, FrequentFlyerNumber)

Flight(FlightNUM, DepartureDate, DepartureTime, ArrivalDate, ArrivalTime, PlaneType, Capacity)

Seat(FlightNUM, CustomerID, DepartureDate, SeatNUM, Class)

Ticket(SerialNUM, FlightNUM, DepartureDate, SeatNUM, CustomerID, CreditCardType, CreditCardNumber)

- What, in your opinion, are the dimensions of interest for the management?
- What types of queries would the airline managers like to pose to this system? Make a list of at least 10 aggregation queries.
- What information should be included in the airline data warehouse from these tables?
- Select three most important dimensions and show them in a data cube using some artificial data.

Laboratory Exercises

1. List some aggregation queries that may be made to the above database.
2. Does it make sense to build a data warehouse for the above database perhaps based on more information than is in the database given above? Consult an airline website and look at the types of information that is available there.
3. How frequently would you need to refresh the airline data warehouse?

BIBLIOGRAPHY

The concept of a data warehouse was introduced by Inmon and the concept of ODS was introduced by Inmon and Imhoff. Codd et al. suggested the need for OLAP.

Much of the ODS discussion in this chapter is based on the Microsoft SQL Server Resource Guide and IBM Red Book on building ODS. The data warehouse discussion is based on Chapter 17 of the Microsoft SQL Resource Guide. The section on ETL is based on Chapter 19 of the SQL Server Resource Guide. Data warehouse modelling has benefited from a number of references that are listed below. The brief description of ZLE is based on two white papers from HP.

Recommended Reading for Students

The IBM Red Book, the Oracle Data Warehouse Guide and the SQL Resource Kit Chapters 17 and 19 are easy to read. They should be consulted for a much more thorough discussion of these topics. The Data Warehousing Information Center is also a good source of information about data warehousing.

The Data Warehousing Information Center
http://www.dwinfocenter.org/

IBM, IBM Red Book on ODS, Building the Operational Data Store on DB2 UDB Using IBM Data Replication, WebSphere MQ Family, and DB2 Warehouse Manager, 2001
http://www.redbooks.ibm.com
/redbooks.nsf/0/8e25ee50fda6951b85256aac0003c546?opendocument

Oracle9i Data Warehousing Guide, Release 2(9.2), March 2002
http://www.lc.leidenuniv.nl/awcourse/oracle/server.920/a96520/toc.htm

SQL Server 2000 Resource Kit, Data Extraction, Transformation, and Loading, Chapter 19
http://www.microsoft.com/resources/documentation/sql/2000/all/reskit/en-us/default.mspx

SQL Server 2000 Resource Kit—Data Warehouse Design Considerations, Chapters 17
http://www.microsoft.com/resources/documentation/sql/2000/all/reskit/en-us/default.mspx

Recommended Reading for Lecturers

The classical references on data warehouse are by Inmon and Kimball. The paper by Widom has been highly cited.

Agrawal, D., El Abbadi, A., Singh A., and Yurek, T., Efficient View Maintenance at Data Warehouses, *ACM SIGMOD Management of Data*, pp. 417–427, 1997.

Ariyachandra, T. and Watson, H., Key Organizational Factors in Data Warehouse Architecture Selection, *Decision Support Systems*, Vol. 49, pp. 200–212, 2010.

Chaudhuri, S. and Dayal, U., An Overview of Data Warehousing and OLAP Technology. *SIGMOD Record*, 26(1), March 1997.

Chute, C.G., Beck, S.A., Fisk T.B., and Mohr, D.N., The Enterprise Data Trust at Mayo Clinic: A Semantically Integrated Warehouse of Biomedical Data, *Journal of the American Medical Informatics Association*, Vol. 17, No. 2, pp. 131–135, 2010.

Codd, E.F., Codd, S.B., and Salley. C.T., Providing OLAP (on-line analytical processing) to user-analysts: an IT mandate, 1993 http://dev.hyperion.com/download_files/resource_library/white_papers/providing_olap_to_user_analysts.pdf.

Goldfarelli, M., From User Requirements to Conceptual Design in Data Warehouse Design—A Survey, in *Data Warehousing Design and Advanced Engineering Applications: Methods for Complex Construction*, 2010.

Golfarelli M. and Rizzi, S., *Data Warehouse Design: Modern Principles and Methodologies*, Tata McGraw-Hill Education, 445 pp., 2009.

Golfarelli, M. and Rizzi, S., *Data Warehouse Design: Modern Principles and Methodologies*, McGraw-Hill, Osborne Media, 480 pp., 2009.

Gupta, H., Selection of Views to Materialize in a Data Warehouse, *6th ICDT*, pp. 98–112, 1997.

Inmon W.H. and Imhoff, C., *Building the Operational Data Store*, John Wiley, 1996.

Inmon, W.H., *Building the Data Warehouse*, John Wiley, 1992.

Inmon, W.H., Imhoff, C., and Sousa, R., *Corporate Information Factory*, John Wiley, 2001.

Kimball, R. and Ross, M., *The Data Warehouse Toolkit: The Complete Guide to Dimensional Modeling*, 2nd ed., Wiley, 464 pp., 2002.

Kimball, R., Thornthwaite, W., Mundy, J., and Becker, W., *The Data Warehouse Lifecycle Toolkit*, 2nd ed., Wiley, 672 pp., 2008.

Maté, A., Trujillo, J., de Gregorio, E., and Song, I.Y., Improving the Maintainability of Data Warehouse Designs: Modeling Relationships between Sources and User Concepts, Data Warehousing and OLAP, 2012.

Mundy, J. and Thornthwaite, W., The Microsoft Data Warehouse Toolkit: With SQL Server 2008 R2 and the Microsoft Business Intelligence Toolset, 2011.

Ross, M. and Kimball, R., *The Data Warehouse Toolkit: The Complete Guide to Dimensional Modeling*, Wiley, 2013.

Schuff, D., Corral, K., and Turetken, O., Comparing the Understandability of Alternative Data Warehouse Schemas: An Empirical Study, Decision Support Systems, 2011.

Theodoratos, D. and Sellis, T., Data Warehouse Configuration, *The VLDB Journal*, pp. 126–135, 1997.

Thusoo, A., Sarma, J.S., Jain, N., and Shao, Z., et al., Hive-A Petabyte Scale Data Warehouse Using Hadoop, International Conference on Data Engineering, pp. 996–1005, 2010.

Weir, R., Peng, T., and Kerridge, J., Best Practice for Implementing a Data Warehouse: A Review for Strategic Alignment, in Data Warehousing and Data Mining Workshop, *VLDB*, Berlin, 2003.

Widom, J., Research Problems in Data Warehousing, *4th International Conference on Information and Knowledge Management*, pp. 25–30, 1995.

Zhuge, Y., Garcia-Molina, H., Hammer, J., and Widom, J., View Maintenance in a Warehousing Environment, *ACM SIGMOD Management of Data*, pp. 316–327, 1995.

BILL INMON—INVENTOR OF DATA WAREHOUSE

William Inmon is sometimes called the father of Data Warehousing. He is the creator of the Corporate Information Factory and more recently, creator of the Government Information Factory.

He has many years of experience in database technology management and data warehouse design.

Inmon has written a large number of articles on a variety of topics about building, using, and maintaining the data warehouse and the Corporate Information Factory. These articles have been published in major computing journals. He has also written many books. Bill Inmon also established a number of companies.

Inmon received his Bachelor of Science degree in Mathematics from Yale University and his Master of Science degree in Computer Science from New Mexico State University.

CASE STUDY 8

Data Warehouse Governance: Best Practices at Blue Cross and Blue Shield of North Carolina*

Reproduced with permission
from Elsevier

ABSTRACT

Effective governance is a key to data warehousing success. An example of a company that has excelled in data warehouse governance is Blue Cross and Blue Shield of North Carolina (BCBSNC). The data warehouse has resulted in many organizational benefits, including providing "a single version of the truth," better data analysis and time savings for users, reductions in head count, facilitation of the development of new applications, better data, and support for customer-focused business strategies. The structures and processes used by BCBSNC for data warehouse governance represent best practices for other companies to follow. For researchers, the experiences at BCBSNC support and add to the body of knowledge about IT governance, in general, and data warehousing governance, in particular.

Keywords: Blue Cross and Blue Shield of North Carolina; Data warehouse; Data warehousing; Governance; Staffing; Decision support; Training; Benefits

1. INTRODUCTION

Data warehouses (and smaller scale data marts) have become the focal point for decision support in organizations today. They provide a repository of data that can be used to support queries, reporting, online analytical processing (OLAP), DSS/EIS, and data mining [11]. They are also integral components of strategic business initiatives such as customer relationship management (CRM), electronic commerce, and supply chain integration [9]. Data warehouses resolve a long-standing decision support problem—the need for accurate, clean, well-organized, and accessible data.

Data warehouses are high risk/high return endeavors [15,25]. They offer benefits such as cost savings from the consolidation of multiple, disparate decision support platforms; improvements in the quantity and quality of data used to support decision making; productivity improvements resulting from redesigned work and business processes; and significant organizational transformation enabled by data warehousing [23]. Data warehouses are challenging technical undertakings, however, because of the disparate source systems that must be accessed; new technology that must be selected, implemented, and learned; and the vast quantities of data that must be managed and made available to users [24]. There are also organizational issues that must be addressed, such as maintaining sponsorship, managing expectations, avoiding scope creep, and handling political issues [2,7,12]. For these reasons, data warehousing projects are often over budget and behind schedule, do not meet expectations, or fail completely [27].

*Watson, H.J., Fuller, C., and Ariyachandra, T., Data Warehouse Governance: Best Practices at Blue Cross and Blue Shield of North Carolina, Elsevier, *Decision Support Systems*, Vol. 38, pp. 435–450, 2004.

Watson et al. [27] studied eight companies that had experienced a data warehousing failure. There were common reasons for failure across many of the companies—weak sponsorship and/or management support, insufficient funding, inadequate user involvement, and organizational politics. With few exceptions, the reasons for failure were organizational rather than technical. As with most IT projects, organizational issues are usually more daunting and critical to success than technical ones [1,7,29].

Effective data warehousing governance is required in order to successfully address both technical and organizational issues. Governance requires creating committees that have the authority and responsibility to carry out their assigned missions. The committees should have the appropriate composition (e.g., size), characteristics (e.g., experience), and structure (e.g., reporting and information flows), and use appropriate processes (e.g., frequency and length of meetings) [18]. When an enterprise data warehouse is built, multiple stakeholders should be involved in the organizational structures that are created and the processes that are followed.

The authors have personally seen the importance and interest in data warehousing governance in their work with The Data Warehousing Institute (TDWI), the leading organization for data warehousing professionals (www.dw-institute.com). Participants in TDWI's conferences express great interest in data warehousing committee structures and the staffing of the data warehousing team. TDWI also includes data warehousing governance as one of the categories in its annual Best Practices competition, which recognizes the best data warehousing work around the world.

In the following sections, we discuss IT and data warehousing governance. This discussion provides the perspectives needed for understanding and appreciating the case study that is presented next, which describes the data warehousing initiative at Blue Cross and Blue Shield of North Carolina (BCBSNC). BCBSNC is a TDWI Best Practices winner in the data warehousing governance category. Their work can be used as a model by other companies that are seeking insights about how to best govern their data warehouse. It also provides researchers with another company that can be used to develop and validate the emerging conceptualizations and understandings about IT and data warehousing governance [31].

2. IT AND DATA WAREHOUSING GOVERNANCE

Organizational investments in IT have become increasingly large as companies become more information intensive. It is imperative that these investments be used effectively and efficiently. To ensure this, organizations must put IT governance structures (e.g., committees) and processes in place [18].

Over the past two decades, the IS literature has discussed the IT governance activities that must be performed and who might best perform them, examined the various IT governance arrangements or forms that organizations can use, provided frameworks for understanding the various governance forms, and presented research findings on why organizations select particular governance forms [4,30,31].

The scope of IT governance activities ranges from strategic to operational. In many firms, IT is strategic to how, and how well, the firm competes in the marketplace. It is critical that there is alignment between the business and the IT strategies [13]. On the other hand, IT governance must also address operational issues, such as what end user data access tools to support and what data definitions to use. The scope of IT governance activities requires that there is broad participation in performing them. Multiple stakeholders (e.g., senior management, business unit managers, users, IT, and consultants) must work together in a coordinated manner [3].

A major focus of IS researchers is whether key IT-related activities should be delegated to and governed by the business units or performed by a central (usually corporate) IS organization [4,19]. The key activities include developing and maintaining the IT infrastructure, deciding on the use of the technology (including systems development), and managing projects [5,8,20,23]. Researchers have identified three primary IT governance forms or modes—centralized, decentralized, or hybrid—for handling the key activities [23]. They differ in regard to whether central IS, divisional IS, or line management is responsible for performing them. With centralized IS, all key activities are performed by a central IS organization. With divisional IS, the activities are performed by the business units. With a hybrid mode, some activities are performed by central IS (e.g., maintaining the IT infrastructure) while others are performed by the business units (e.g., project management). The literature suggests that many large, divisionalized firms adopt a hybrid governance mode where central IT maintains the infrastructure and the business units plan, build, and use their own applications. Zmud et al. [31] refers to this as a "federal government role" for IS.

IS research has concluded that there is no "universal" governance mode that is best for all organizations [17,20,30]. The best governance solution for an organization depends on its organizational context. For example, Brown [4] has studied a multidivisional firm where a subset of key IT activities, including systems development, is decentralized in some business units, but not in others, and concluded that contextual variables (e.g., business unit autonomy, competitive strategy) can be used to predict the governance arrangements that are made.

Data warehousing governance is a subset of IT governance. It requires that appropriate organization structures and processes are in place, with coordinated inputs from all stakeholder groups. It must cover infrastructure, use, and project manage-ment [23]. It is different from IT governance in that it deals with a more limited domain—only those activities and issues related to data warehousing.

Data warehousing governance must address many, varied areas:

- Identifying business needs. There are many potential reasons for developing a data warehouse. The most overarching one is to improve the quality of information in an organization: make it more accurate, better integrated, and accessible from a single source [26]. There are often specific applications that are the drivers behind a data warehousing initiative, such as to support a CRM initiative [6].
- Achieving alignment with company goals. It is well understood that a system that supports business needs is more likely to be successful than one that provides less support [10]. For this reason, there needs to be alignment between warehouse and company goals. Maintaining alignment is an ongoing process. It is not unusual for the goals for a warehouse to become more strategic over time as management becomes more aware of the potential of the warehouse for supporting business strategy.
- Determining information requirements. Users' information requirements drive what data are stored in the warehouse, the granularity of the data, how much historical data are maintained, and the data model that is used [14]. The greatest challenge is when the data warehouse is designed to support new, cross-organizational infor-mation needs. The needs must be identified and agreed upon, the source systems that best meet the needs must be selected, and the reports and queries (to the extent that is possible) must be identified.
- Setting priorities. A data warehouse should be developed in an evolutionary manner [15]. The initial version contains data for one or a few subject areas, and supports applications and users that access the initial data. Often with a 3-month cycle time, additional subject areas, users, and applications are brought on board. A data warehouse is never "completed." As is frequently heard, "data warehousing is a journey, not a destination." Priorities for implementing the various subject areas and applications must be set. It is common for multiple business units to want the initial or an early version of the data warehouse to meet their needs. High-level, cross-organizational committees are needed to set the priorities and develop the overall warehouse implementation plan. The committees must select criteria for establishing the priorities (e.g., strength of sponsorship, the readiness of source data, and business need) and then evaluate the implementation alternatives using the criteria.

- Establishing data definitions and models. Two design issues that must be addressed are: (1) what data definitions to use and (2) what data model will allow users to effectively and efficiently run queries across subject areas. Organizations have hundreds of terms (e.g., customer, sale) that have slightly different meanings (such as when a sale is recognized) that vary with the business units. This is a natural consequence of business units defining terms in ways that best serve their purposes. For the warehouse, it is important to agree on data definitions, make sure the definitions are understood, and utilize source systems that are consistent with the definitions. Warehouses provide users with a dimensional view of the data (e.g., product, place, time), and each of the dimensions has measures (e.g., the time dimension may have hour, day, and month as measures). To query across subject areas, it is necessary for the data model to have consistent dimensions and measures. This is referred to as creating "conformed dimensions" [16]. It is necessary for users to identify and agree upon the dimensions and measures that will be used in the warehouse's data model.
- Maintaining data quality. Ensuring that the data warehouse contains high quality data is an ongoing concern [22]. Most organizations find that the data in their source systems is even worse than imagined. The combined efforts of the data warehousing staff and business units are required to assess the quality of the data and to put data cleansing processes in place. Initially, the data in the source systems most likely must be accepted as is, with the data being cleansed before it is loaded into the warehouse. In the longer term, there should be initiatives to improve the quality of the data in the source systems, so that there is less downstream cleansing.

Even when the warehouse is operational, data quality issues will continue to arise and require attention. For example, new subject areas will be added with all of the attendant problems of adding new source systems to the extraction, transformation, and loading processes. Changes will be made to existing source systems and these changes have rippling effects on the data warehouse and must be accommodated.

There is only limited research on data warehousing governance [23,28]. However, the existing research is consistent with IT governance research in that it considers the activities that must be performed, who should perform the activities, what the governance alternatives are, frameworks for understanding governance, and what governance alternatives are or should be used. For example, Winter and Meyer [28] discuss the activities that data warehousing governance must address, develop a concept of data ownership that is related to data warehousing governance, and illustrate the application of this concept for data warehousing governance in a large Swiss bank. Based on six case studies, Sujitparapitaya et al. [23] show how the data warehouse architecture used (e.g., enterprise data warehouse, divisional data marts) impacts how companies practise data warehousing governance. For example, companies with enterprise data warehouses are more likely to have centralized IT authority than firms with divisional data marts. This finding shows that data warehousing architecture is a contextual variable for predicting data warehousing governance.

This discussion of IT and data warehousing governance allows the case study of Blue Cross and Blue Shield of North Carolina to be put in perspective. The case discusses the development of BCBSNC's data warehouse and the governance committees and processes that are used. The development activities (e.g., determining information requirements) are common to data warehousing projects, but how they were performed (e.g., the opportunity analysis) is probably unique to BCBSNC. Likewise, the governance committees and processes used at BCBSNC are consistent with high-level "conventional wisdom" (e.g., include multiple stakeholders working together in a coordinated manner), but the details of BCBSNC's practices are noteworthy. As mentioned before, BCBSNC has been recognized by TDWI for best practices in data warehousing governance. Some of the most interesting insights learned at BCBSNC are provided in Section 3.10. Sujitparapitaya et al. [23] have shown that data warehousing architecture is a contextual variable that affects data warehousing governance. BCBSNC implemented an enterprise data warehouse, and the governance practices used are most appropriate for that kind of architecture.

3. ABOUT BLUE CROSS AND BLUE SHIELD OF NORTH CAROLINA

3.1 Company Background

Blue Cross and Blue Shield of North Carolina (www.bcbsnc.com), based in Chapel Hill, NC, is North Carolina's largest health insurer, serving 2.8 million members, including 470,000 served on behalf of other Blue plans. BCBSNC's HMO and POS products have earned excellent accreditation from the National Committee for Quality Assurance (NCQA), an independent, not-for-profit organization dedicated to measuring the quality of America's health care. Blue Cross and Blue Shield of North Carolina is an independent licensee of the Blue Cross and Blue Shield Association. As an organization in the highly competitive health care industry, BCBSNC views being customer-focused as an important element of its strategy for organizational success. The company strives to provide its members effective services such as high quality health care information in order to improve their health.

3.2 The Business Drivers for the CDW

Fundamental deficiencies in the information access and reporting capabilities within BCBSNC were the key drivers that led to the creation of the corporate data warehouse (CDW) in 1997. Prior to its implementation, organizational personnel, including top management, had a general lack of confidence in data quality and information reporting within the organization. Insufficient data definitions, redundancy in data, multiple data extract and transformation processes, lack of accountability, absence of data documentation, and poor communications on data usage were some of the contributing factors underlying the lack of credibility of existing data management systems.

The ever-changing health care regulatory environment further supported the need for consistent and effective data management practices across the organization. In order to ensure that the organization's practices were in compliance with health insurance regulations such as Health Insurance Portability and Accountability Act (HIPAA), an integrated single repository of corporate data became essential. The warehouse would be the focal point for ensuring that BCBSNC was compliant with HIPAA's (1) transaction processing, (2) security, (3) code sets, and (4) identifier requirements. Any data included in the warehouse would satisfy HIPAA requirements [21].

In addition, areas within the organization requiring strong decision support capabilities were experiencing great difficulty in accessing and manipulating data to meet their daily needs. As a result, an information management oversight team, with representatives from the business units and IS, was established to investigate these issues and develop a set of recommendations that addressed them. The final recommendations included esta-blishing a corporate data glossary, working on source data quality initiatives, and creating a corporate data warehouse.

The original mission of the warehouse was to establish a system of record for decision support in the organization, but this mission has evolved over time to be better aligned with the company's strategic focus and direction. The current mission is to be an "engine that powers a customer-focused, information driven company."

3.3 Getting Started

The CDW project began with the formation of a cross-functional team, composed of members of IS and representatives from the business areas. This team conducted an extensive opportunity analysis of four primary decision support areas: (1) actuarial and underwriting, (2) market analysis, (3) financial analysis, and (4) health services analysis. The opportunity analysis revealed the following business requirements for the data warehouse: (1) establish consistent, timely, and easily accessible data; (2) address data quality issues; (3) develop and document common data definitions and business rules for using data; (4) provide ease of use for nontechnical users; and (5) support sophisticated analytical processes.

The cross-functional team identified the business areas that required decision support capabilities and prioritized the timing of the implementation of eight key subject areas. Figure 1 shows a sample of the two dozen information opportunities that were discovered (the rows), their priority level (reflected by the shading of the cells), and the eight subject areas (the columns) that were identified to support the opportunities. Joint application development (JAD) sessions conducted during this phase led to the creation of common data definitions with cross-functional consensus.

In the months that followed, a series of workshops with operational and decision support areas were held to help build a logical data model around the subject areas. These long, arduous logical modeling sessions enabled the team to clearly understand the business processes, information processes, and data needs. The result was a comprehensive data model that has enabled the team to design, implement, and make continuous improvements to the CDW. Figure 2 presents a sample of the high-level logical data model for the CDW.

3.4 The Current Data Warehouse

Since 1997, the data warehousing initiative has evolved and delivered data and functionality in phases as identified and prioritized by the business areas. The current CDW supports a broad set of applications for more than 200 users in the business areas of sales and marketing, financial services, corporate analysis and risk assessment, corporate audit, and health quality improvement. It draws data from 12 source systems, including 5 legacy claims processing systems, 6 external and third-party data sources, and a new managed care claims processing system introduced by the company. Figure 3 presents the detail tables in the eight subject areas identified in the logical model as well as five summary tables and two clinical constructs. Clinical constructs are complex tables for inpatient and outpatient cases and the associated professional health services. For example, a patient case might include the initial visit to a physician, the tests run at a diagnostic center, and the follow up appointment with the physician to review the test results and develop a treatment plan.

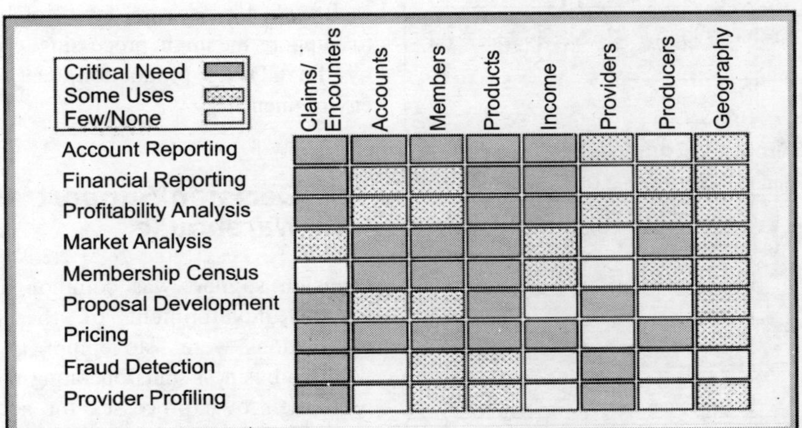

Figure 1: Opportunity analysis.

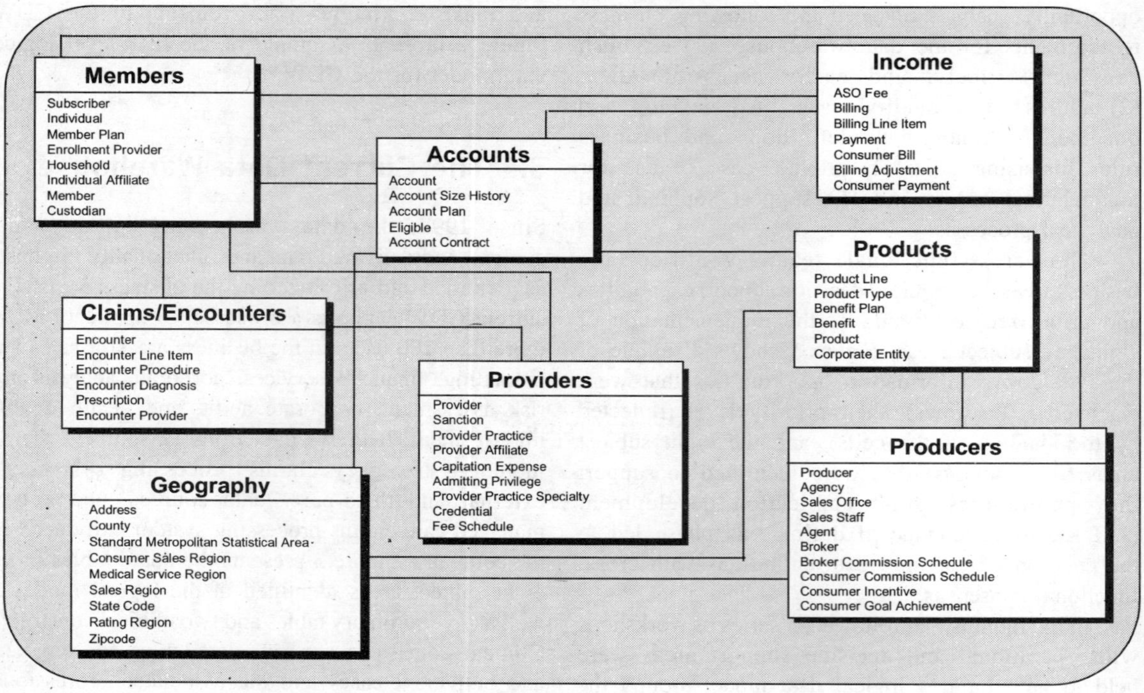

Figure 2: The logical data model.

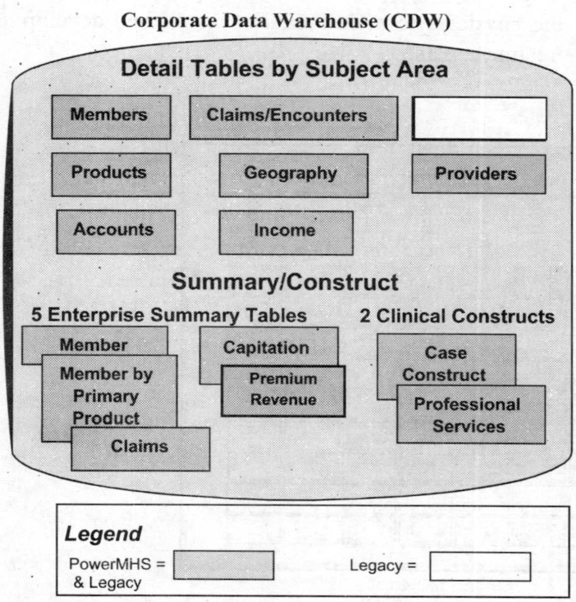

Figure 3: The corporate data warehouse.

At present, the CDW environment has more than 200 tables, 1500 data elements, and 2.5 terabytes of data storage. The hardware architecture is massively parallel processing (MPP) with 17 nodes each with 4 processors for a total of 68 pro-cessors to support the high processing capabilities required by the CDW's production, test, and development environments.

3.5 Decision Support and the Data Warehouse

Decision support was common at BCBSNC prior to the development of the warehouse. The applications were "stovepipe" in nature, however, with the business units operating independently. They used their own processes for accessing data from operational systems; employed their own data definitions, business rules, and analytical processes; and presented and interpreted output in ways that best served their unit's purposes. Not surprisingly, the different units had inconsistencies in their analyses (i.e., "dueling spreadsheets"), and there was limited ability to do cross-organizational analyses. These problems sparked interest in the data warehouse.

The data warehouse provides the data infrastructure that is needed for decision support. Most applications are customer built. Both (in-house) decision support consultants and end users build applications using the warehouse. The consultants do not build applications on their own; rather, they act as facilitators, provide technical expertise, and work with end users in all phases of the development process. Some end users develop applications using access, SAS, or Business Objects as the data Access tools.

There are five full-time decision support consultants. They write SQL queries, know how to use the various data access tools (e.g., Business Objects), and understand the data in the warehouse. Most have MBAs and several of them worked in the business units before becoming consultants.

The most sophisticated analytical applications (e.g., statistical analyses, simulations) are in the actuarial area. BCBSNC has recently filed to become a for profit organization. If approved, advanced analytics in marketing, health care services, and finance will become critical.

Most of the decision support applications reside within the business units but the warehouse has facilitated the development of cross-organizational applications. As an example of the latter, BCBSNC is currently working on a system called the Management Report. It will provide executive level information on key financial and other measures. It will automate a manual effort that currently is performed every month by multiple people who collaborate to create a spreadsheet in order to provide the needed information. Also "on the radar" is the building of a more formal executive information system that will use the warehouse.

The warehouse is affecting how BCBSNC is managed. Over the past few years, there has been a dramatic increase in more fact-based decision making. At the executive level, there is the expectation that when assertions are made, there will be numbers to back them up.

3.6 Data Warehouse Governance

From the inception of the warehouse project, the data warehouse governance structure has played a key role in the CDW's ability to meet business needs and to adapt to organizational change. This is due to the cross-functional, multi-level nature of the governance structure that supports the data warehousing effort. Figure 4 shows the current governance structure, its composition, and major activities. The governance structure has gradually evolved over the years to include three groups that correspond with the three different levels of the organizational hierarchy. The groups are: the Vice President Data Oversight Team, the Data Development Oversight Team, and the Business Requirements Group. To ensure effective communication between the CDW team (i.e., the data warehouse staff) and the different levels of organizational hierarchy, a member of the CDW team chairs and facilitates the activities of each of the governance groups (the CDW team structure is described in greater detail in Section 3.7). The manager of the Business Information Design and Architecture group of the CDW team is accountable for facilitating the Business Requirements Group (BRG), the director of the CDW team chairs the Data Development Oversight Team (DDOT), and the Vice President of Decision Support chairs the Vice President Data Oversight Team (VPDOT).

3.6.1 VPDOT: The Vice President Data Oversight Team

This officer level, cross-functional team includes a business leader from each of the major divisions within the organization. They meet as needed and provide high-level direction for the entire warehouse initiative. For instance, they provide prioritization criteria and strategic guidance for the CDW project and deal with resource management and prioritization issues when

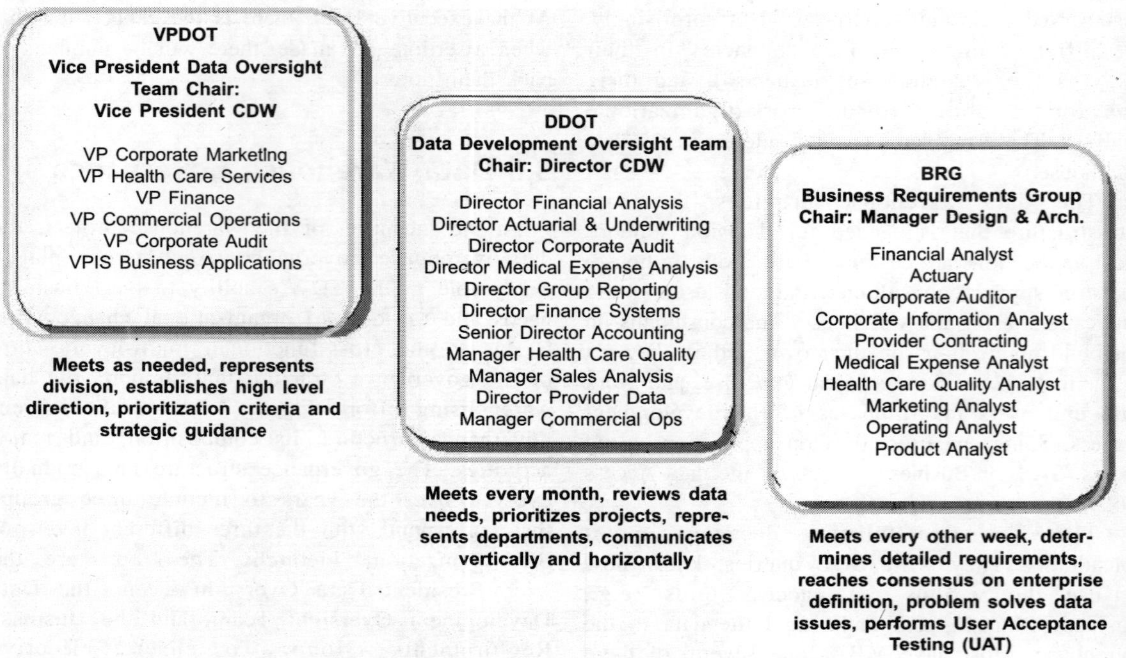

Figure 4: Current governance structure.

the DDOT cannot resolve them. The VPDOT focuses on ensuring the alignment of the direction of the CDW with the corporate direction.

3.6.2 DDOT: The Data Development Oversight Team

This director/manager level team performs most of the project and resource prioritization tasks. It establishes the schedules and priorities for development phases, enhancements, and functionality of the warehouse within budgeted resources. Additionally, it helps resolve cross-functional issues. The DDOT initially met bi-monthly, but due to the high volume of planning and prioritization required, the meetings are currently conducted on a monthly basis.

3.6.3 BRG: The Business Requirements Group

This group has been involved in the development of the warehouse almost since the inception of the warehouse project and is composed of CDW power users as well as representatives from the primary decision support areas that were involved in the initial opportunity analysis. The purpose of this group is to discuss and communicate CDW development and use issues with CDW team members and users. Much of their focus is on the development of data. For example, they develop the rules for populating the CDW and cross-functional data definitions.

The Business Requirements Group meets biweekly in order to make day-to-day decisions on data quality problems, production data fixes, data stewardship issues, and other daily project management decisions.

Since 1997, there has been turnover in BCBSNC's CEO, CIO, and most of the Senior Vice President positions. Despite these changes in the upper management of the company, where the main source of sponsorship and direction for the CDW project lies, the original requirements and priorities described in the initial opportunity analysis have not changed.

Although requirements that drive the direction of the CDW are owned by the leadership of the business areas, any changes in direction and enhancements are quickly and effectively communicated to the CDW team via the VPDOT, DDOT, and the BRG. As a result, CDW awareness of needed changes in direction occurs early in the process. The frequency of meetings with these groups and the buy-in these groups have to the data warehouse development process support good communications, healthy debate, and a commitment to consensus on the vision and direction for the CDW.

3.7 The CDW Team

In addition to the cross-functional, multiple level governance structure, a strong warehouse team is critical to the successful execution and continued development of a data warehouse in a business environment that is changing rapidly. Since the introduction of the data warehouse, the data warehousing team has undergone continuous restructuring and evolution in order to serve the changing needs of the different stakeholders within the organization, including upper management, regulatory bodies, the governance groups, and the user community in different business areas.

In 2001, the CDW team was restructured to four groups to better adapt to the changing business environment: the Decision Support Consulting Team, the Business Information and Design and Architecture Team, the DW Project Management and Development Team, and the DW Operations and Quality Control Team. Figure 5 provides a detailed listing of the roles and responsibilities of each of the four teams.

The Business Information Design and Architecture team is responsible for the identification of high-level needs and requirements of new development projects, design and data analysis, logical data modeling and business rules, and meta-data specification. The Project Management and Development group manages the technical design and ETL tool development and testing. The Data Warehouse Operations and Quality Control team is responsible for the operation of the data warehouse. Finally, the Decision Support Consulting team manages training and educating the users on the current functionality of the data warehouse. This team interacts with users in the field and provides one-on-one mentoring and training where required. They also work closely with users in various business areas to identify new needs, functionality, and business areas to be served. It is interesting to note that the Decision Support Consulting team does not produce reports or do analyses; rather, their role is to support these functions which happen in business areas.

3.8 Training Users

Along with the recent restructuring of the CDW team, training practices have also evolved. As a result of the close working relationship between the decision support consultants and the business areas, a new approach to training has been implemented. Previously, users were given computer-based training (CBT) designed to provide skills on specific tools (e.g., Business Objects, SQL*Plus). In addition, the CDW staff conducted classes on data warehousing concepts and the data in the warehouse. With this approach, users found it difficult to apply the skills learned to their daily work. In response, the decision support consultants designed a training program that targets the users' specific job functions (i.e., the reports and analyses they need to perform). Users bring a specific work-related project to the training course, and in the course of 1 day per week over 4 weeks, complete the project using skills learned during the course. At the end of the training program, the users make a presentation of their project accomplishments and leave the training session with a better understanding of how to utilize the data warehouse in their work. The user project presentations also serve as a means of educating other users on the potential uses of the warehouse. The training sessions at BCBSNC have been met with great enthusiasm by the user groups and have proven to be an effective strategy for educating the user community. The ongoing user support provided by the CDW staff is an additional source of assistance and exposure of the data warehouse to current and potential users. The Reporter/User Group Meetings provide a bi-weekly open forum for users of all levels to discuss topics of interest and cover all methods of accessing the warehouse. Consequently, on alternate weeks, users have access to training laboratories that present in-depth presentations on business cases and

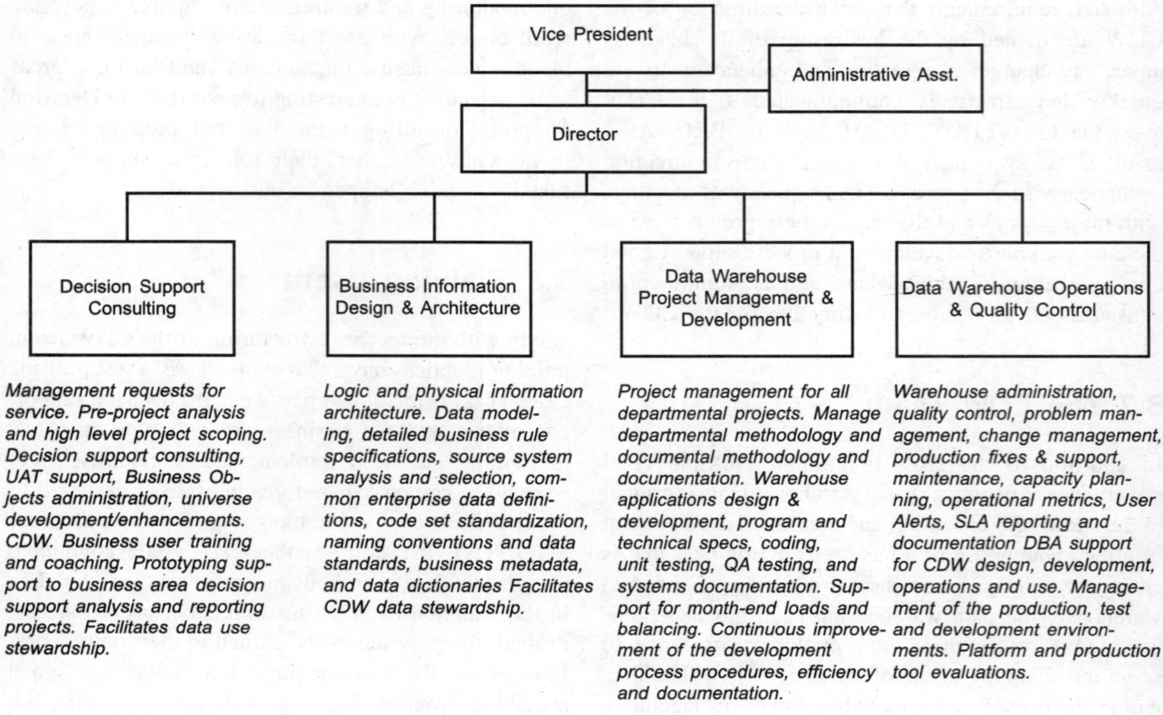

Figure 5: CDW team structure.

advanced query concepts as well as provide one-on-one coaching.

3.9 Benefits

BCBSNC has gained a wide range of benefits from its data warehouse. The most obvious benefit has been the creation of a "single view of the truth;" that is, a single source of organization-wide data. The cross-functional team approach to CDW development led to consensus in data definitions, identification of the best source systems to use for reporting and analysis purposes, and greater data accuracy. This resulted in valid and consistent reporting across the organization, which was the primary requirement of the CDW.

In addition, the warehouse has led to numerous other tangible and intangible benefits. Its introduction has promoted a better understanding of the use and efficiencies that can be gained through relational databases. The comprehension and ability to conduct better technical cost analyses has led to the retirement of a marketing information system. It also allowed the actuarial and underwriting areas to attain head count savings by reassigning and eliminating programming staff.

The use of the warehouse has also contributed to better data analysis and time savings by users. Corporate analysts spend less time compiling data and more time analyzing data. Figure 6 presents a sample of some of the benefits and savings in reporting and processes that BCBSNC is currently reaping from the CDW. The cost savings also extend to costs associated with accessing data from external sources. For instance, the CDW eliminated a cost of US$20,000 associated with obtaining data from a vendor to support legislative activities.

Report/Process	Description	Savings/Benefit
Renewal Reports—Large Groups	Automated download of data into rating model as well as an application specific Business Objects Universe for ad hoc reporting.	• Available within 2 hours of request (before 4–5 day process) • Data retained for 30 days • Data entry eliminated • Drill down capability • Improved reporting
Renewal Reports—Small/Medium Groups	Streamlined, working report designed to capture underwriting decisions	• Eliminated end-user job (19 hour process) • Reduced end-user working days from 12 to 5 • Provides better documentation of underwriting decisions
Policy Year Loss Ratios	Applications specific Business Objects Universe	• Information not available previously • End-user designs own reports as needed
Active Life Reserves	Scheduled download of data	• Overnight plus mainframe job reduced to 20 minute query • Eliminated end user job scheduling and maintenance
Quarterly Rate Reviews Factor Model and Stop Loss	Data Mart designed to contain data for Benefit Adjustment Analysis in addition to Quarterly Rate Reviews	• Macro-driven procedures utilized to create data mart (intimated by end-user as needed) • Dates and logs are in sync within all the tables • Eliminated programmer dependent jobs
Ad Hoc Requests	Corporate Analysis Production Business Objects Universe	• Corporate Analysis trained to go directly to CDW • Ability to analyse claims data
Facility/Professional Duplicate Billing	Analysis with Corporate Audit for procedure codes billed for both facility/prof.	• Increasing trend over the last several years (approx. $1 million) • Working with hospitals to correct

Figure 6: Example uses of the CDW.

The warehouse also eased the establishment of the new claims system, which introduced new products, benefits, and a new way of providing service to BCBSNC customers. The new system was an unexpected addition to the original requirements for the CDW team. As BCBSNC customers were gradually migrated to the new products and benefits, the consolidation of data from the existing systems and the new system was critical. The data warehouse became the means of data consolidation from both core systems and a key component in the transition.

An organization-wide effort to improve data quality is another initiative that was driven by the development of the CDW. As part of the monthly CDW load process, source data are evaluated and reports documenting differences are broadcast to the business areas. This has enabled the warehouse team to drive operational business areas to correctly capture data in the source systems, resulting in greater data accuracy and cost savings through more efficient data loading to the CDW.

In addition to satisfying its primary goal of improving reporting, the data warehousing effort has enabled BCBSNC to effectively pursue its customer-focused corporate information management strategy. For example, there are future plans to capture and store data from additional customer touchpoints, such as the call center and the corporate website, in order to better understand customer behavior and improve customer service. Visitors to the corporate website who are known (such as BCBSNC members) will be able to experience dialogs that are customized to best meet their needs and support BCBSNC's marketing efforts. Knowledge of a customer's projected lifetime value will be made available to operational personnel, such as customer service representatives. All of these customer relationship management-oriented applications will be enabled by the enhanced CDW.

Despite being subject to a competitive, dynamic business environment, a difficult regulatory environment, and a changing corporate management, the effective governance practices at BCBSNC have helped the company establish a successful CDW. It enabled the organization to change from a one-dimensional mindset in different business areas to a cross-functional consensus on data and processes critical to the overall operation of the organization.

3.10 Lessons Learned

The experiences at BCBSNC substantiate and enhance the emerging understandings of effective data warehouse governance. Some of the experiences, such as the importance of having cross-functional committees, are part of the emerging "conventional wisdom" for data warehousing. There are other experiences at BCBSNC, however, that provide richer insights into data warehouse governance. These are presented and discussed as lessons learned.

3.10.1 Lesson #1: senior management participation is necessary but not sufficient—management needs to be passionately involved

Even though the Vice President Data Oversight Team has the responsibility for setting the strategic direction for the data warehouse, some of the members of the committee are not as passionate about the warehouse and are comfortable delegating decision making to others. Cross-functional participation is important, but active participation is what is really needed. The committee members need to be a "passionate advocate" for information. Rather than having all of the business units represented on the committee, only senior managers who have a strong interest in the warehouse, want to link the warehouse closely to business strategy, and use the warehouse heavily in their business units, are critical to the composition of the committee. As a result, the vice-president level committee may be smaller, but more interested and dedicated to the warehouse.

3.10.2 Lesson #2: data quality should be a strategic issue

It is easy and tempting to treat data quality as a tactical issue. With this approach, data are extracted from source systems and data cleansing processes are used to improve the data's quality. Little effort and few resources are used to improve the quality of the data in the source systems themselves. Also, limited attention is devoted to improving the quality of data that are external to the warehouse. When the warehouse becomes of strategic importance to the company and the company's data warehouse experience grows, data quality becomes more of a strategic issue. Consequently, data quality should draw the attention and support of senior management, resources must be devoted to improving data quality at the source system level, and everyone in the organization must be more cognizant of the importance of data quality. The data warehouse must also become the official, "single version of the truth" for decision support data.

3.10.3 Lesson #3: multiple committees are needed, some with a business focus, others with a technical focus

Initially at BCBSNC, there were fewer data warehouse governance committees, and the committees had mixed memberships. Some committee members had a business focus, while others had a technical focus. This arrangement did not work well. The business members were not interested in the technical discussions, and the technical members were only slightly more interested in the business issues. Over time, attendance at meetings dropped off.

With the current arrangements, the VPDOT and DDOT deal primarily with the business issues, while the Business Requirements Group works with the CDW team on technical matters. However, business and technical issues are shared with all of the committee members. Emailing and posting on a website the agendas, minutes, documents, and actions associated with the various committee meetings accomplishes this. It has been BCBSNC's experience that without aggressive communications, important business and technical issues are not adequately shared.

3.10.4 Lesson #4: do not underestimate the need for educating committee members

It is important for the warehouse staff to recognize that many committee members do not fully understand data warehousing and especially the technical complexity that is involved. A good understanding of warehousing is critical to creating realistic expectations of what can be done, the timeframe for doing it, and resources that are needed. Part of each committee meeting should be spent on educating committee members about data warehousing.

4. CONCLUSION

BCBSNC has achieved great success with data warehousing, and a major reason for the success is the strong data warehousing governance that is in place. Let us reconsider the critical areas for data warehousing governance and how BCBSNC has addressed them. The starting point for a data warehousing initiative is the clear identification of business needs. BCBSNC recognized that it had fundamental deficiencies in its information access and reporting capabilities, which were being manifested in multiple ways. In response, senior management formed an information oversight committee with representatives from the business units and IS to investigate the problems and develop a recommended course of action. One of the recommendations was the building of a data warehouse.

The business needs for the warehouse have evolved over time. The Vice President Data Oversight Team, which includes business leaders from each of the major divisions of the company, ensures that the direction for the CDW is aligned with company goals. The current focus is on helping BCBSNC become a more customer-focused, information-driven company.

The CDW team and representatives from the business areas conducted an opportunity analysis to determine the information requirements that were used in building the initial version of the warehouse.

On an ongoing basis, the Business Requirements Group is responsible for handling information requirements. This is a very "nuts and bolts" oriented group that receives suggestions for change, reviews them carefully, and identifies those that should be implemented. When an information requirement warrants a project rather than a minor change (i.e., more than 10 days of effort), it goes on the list of projects that are reviewed by the Data Development Oversight Team for approval.

The group that identified the information requirements for the initial version of the warehouse also prioritized the implementation of the eight subject areas. Since then, the business areas have prioritized how changes and enhancements to the warehouse should be made. At the highest level, the Vice President Data Oversight Team sets priorities. At the project level, the Data Development Oversight Team sets priorities and schedules for the projects.

The cross-functional team that conducted the opportunity analysis also came to a consensus on common data definitions. Then in a series of workshops with the operational and decision support areas, a logical data model was developed. This initial data model continues to serve BCBSNC well and has required only minor fine-tuning. The Business Requirements Group has the ongoing responsibilities for cross-functional data definitions and making sure that the data model meets emerging needs.

Maintaining data quality is an ongoing concern. Data problems are often identified by the Reporter/User Group, which meets every other week. Depending on the nature and severity of the problem, it may be addressed by the CDW staff directly, the Business

Requirements Group, or the Data Development Oversight Team.

BCBSNC has experienced turnover in the CEO, CIO, and most of the Senior Vice President positions. Despite these changes in upper management, the CDW has continued to thrive. Effective data warehouse governance has provided the continuity and ongoing direction that has been required. The structures and processes used by BCBSNC for data warehouse governance can be considered to be best practices for other companies to follow. Of particular note, BCBSNC uses multi-level, cross-functional committees. At the highest level, the Vice President Data Oversight Committee has senior management representatives from all of the major divisions within the organization. It provides strategic direction for the warehouse and handles resource acquisition and allocation. Next, the Data Development Oversight Team is comprised of cross-functional managers who set the priorities for the warehouse, manage the resources allocated to the warehouse, and resolve cross-functional conflicts. Finally, the Business Requirements Group is made up of power users and representatives from the various decision support areas in the company. This group communicates and discusses data warehouse development and use issues with the data warehouse staff. It also deals with data management issues. Collectively, these three committees handle all of the critical areas of data warehouse governance.

There is no single way to organize for and execute data warehouse governance. The approach used at BCBSNC has been recognized for best practices, but there is a need to study additional organizations that excel in data warehousing governance. Such a study would likely find additional best practices. It would also allow a comparison across companies in order to identify a core of best practices. Based on previous data warehousing governance research, one would expect several different best practices in companies implementing departmental data marts [23].

Research has examined factors associated with data warehousing success [11,29]. Data warehouse governance has not been used as a predictor variable in this research, even though some of the factors (e.g., management support, user participation) are related to data warehouse governance (e.g., alignment with company goals, identifying information requirements). It would be useful to restudy data warehousing success using a research model that more directly incorporates the factors associated with effective data warehouse governance.

The experience at BCBSNC suggests that there are multiple factors associated with effective data warehouse governance—cross-functional committees, which serve different yet complimentary roles; coverage of the areas associated with data warehouse governance, such as establishing data definitions and models. It would be useful to validate the data warehouse governance findings at BCBSNC in an empirical study of a large sample of firms.

REFERENCES

[1] L. Agosta, Planning a data warehouse? Assemble a crossfunctional team, *DM Review* (2002 March) 50.

[2] J. Ang, S.H. Teo Thompson, Management issues in data warehousing: insights from the housing and development board, *Decision Support Systems* 29(1) (2000) 11–20.

[3] A.C. Boynton, R.W. Zmud, G. Jacobs, The influence of IT management practice on IT use in large organizations, *MIS Quarterly* 18(3) (1994) 299–318.

[4] C.V. Brown, Examining the emergence of hybrid IS governance solutions: evidence from a single case site, *Information Systems Research* 8(1) (1997) 69–94.

[5] C.E. Clark, N.C. Cavanaugh, C.V. Brown, V. Sambamurthy, Building change-readiness capabilities in the IS organization: insights from the Bell Atlantic experience, *MIS Quarterly* 21(4) (1997) 425–455.

[6] B.L. Cooper, H.J. Watson, B.H. Wixom, D.L. Goodhue, Data warehousing supports corporate strategy at First American, *MIS Quarterly* 24(4) (2000 December) 547–567.

[7] S. Crofts, Twenty steps to data warehousing success, *Journal of Data Warehousing* 3(2) (1998 Summer) 19–23.

[8] J. Cross, M. Earl, J. Sampler, Transformation of the IT function at British Petroleum, *MIS Quarterly* 21(4) (1997) 401–424.

[9] W.W. Eckerson, Evolution of data warehousing: the trend toward analytical applications, *The Patricia Seybold Group* (1999 April) 1–8.

[10] M. Ginzberg, Steps toward more effective implementation of MS and MIS, *Interfaces* 8(3) (1978 May) 57–63.

[11] P. Gray, H.J. Watson, *Decision Support in the Data Warehouse*, Prentice-Hall, Upper Saddle River, NJ, 1998.

[12] B. Haley, Implementing successful data warehouses, *Journal of Data Warehousing* 3(2) (1998 Summer) 48–51.

[13] J.C. Henderson, N. Vankatraman, Strategic alignment: leveraging information technology for transforming organizations, *IBM Systems Journal* 32(1) (1993) 4–16.

[14] W.H. Inmon, *Building the Data Warehouse*, 2nd ed., Wiley, New York, 1996.

[15] S. Kelly, *Data Warehousing in Action*, Wiley, New York, 1997.

[16] R. Kimball, *The Data Warehouse Toolkit*, Wiley, New York, 1992.

[17] J.L. King, Centralized versus decentralized computing: organizational considerations and management options, *Computing Surveys* 15(4) (1983 December) 320–349.

[18] N. Korac-Kakabadse, A. Kakabadse, IS/IT governance: need for an integrated model, *Corporate Governance* 1(4) (2001) 9–11.

[19] J.F. Rockart, L. Ball, C.V. Bullen, Future role of the information systems executive, *MIS Quarterly* 13(2) (1992) 119–134 (special issue).

[20] V. Sambamurthy, R.W. Zmud, Arrangements for information technology governance: a theory of multiple contingencies, *MIS Quarterly* 23(2) (1999) 261–290.

[21] J. Schwartz, HIPAA Compliance, *CRN*, 2003 March 24, pp. 6A–8A.

[22] G. Shanks, P.A. Darke, Framework for understanding data quality, *Journal of Data Warehousing* 3(3) (1998 Summer) 46–51.

[23] S. Sujitparapitaya, B. Janz, M. Gillenson, The contributions of IT governance solutions to the implementation of data warehouse practice, *Journal of Database Management* 14(2) (2003 April–June) 52–69.

[24] B. Vatanasombut, P. Gray, Factors for success in data warehousing: what the literature tells us, *Journal of Data Warehousing* 4(3) (1999 Summer) 25–33.

[25] H.J. Watson, B.J. Haley, Data warehousing: a framework and survey of current practices, *Journal of Data Warehousing* 2(1) (1997 January) 10–17.

[26] H.J. Watson, B.J. Haley, Managerial considerations with data warehousing, *Communications of the ACM* 41(9) (1998 September) 32–37.

[27] H.J. Watson, J.G. Gerard, L.E. Gonzalez, M.E. Haywood, D. Fenton, Data warehousing failures: case studies and findings, *Journal of Data Warehousing* 4(1) (1999 Spring) 44–55.

[28] R. Winter, M. Meyer, Organization of data warehousing in large service organizations: a matrix approach based on data ownership and competence centers, *Journal of Data Warehousing* 6(4) (2001 Fall) 23–29.

[29] B.H. Wixom, H.J. Watson, An empirical investigation of the factors affecting data warehousing success, *MIS Quarterly* 25(1) (2001 March) 17–41.

[30] R.W. Zmud, Design alternatives for organizing information systems activities, *MIS Quarterly* 8(2) (1984 June) 79–93.

[31] R.W. Zmud, A.C. Boynton, G.C. Jacobs, The information economy: a new perspective for effective information systems management, *Data Base* 18(1) (1986) 17–23.

Hugh J. Watson is a Professor of MIS and holder of a C. Herman and Mary Virginia Terry Chair of Business Administration in the Terry College of Business at the University of Georgia. He is the author of 22 books and over 100 scholarly journal articles. He is the Senior Editor of the Business Intelligence Journal and the Senior Director of the Teradata University Network.

Celia Fuller is Director of the Corporate Data Warehouse at Blue Cross and Blue Shield of North Carolina. She has over 20 years of experience in business intelligence, data warehousing, decision support systems, data management, analysis, evaluation, and physician profiling in healthcare, insurance, and government sectors. The BCBSNC data warehouse has won two best practices awards from The Data Warehousing Institute. She has published the results of her projects and is a regular speaker at conferences and symposia.

Thilini Ariyachandra is a doctoral candidate in MIS in the Terry College of Business at the University of Georgia. Her research is focused on the selection, design, implementation and success evaluation of decision support systems in organizations. Her research has been published in Information Systems Management and in national and international conference proceedings.

CASE STUDY 8 SUMMARY

This case study described implementation of a data warehouse (DW) in a relatively large healthcare organization of 2.8 million members supporting 200 users in the areas of sales and marketing, financial services, corporate analysis and risk assessment, corporate audit and health quality improvement. The DW described drew data from 12 source systems, including 5 legacy systems, 6 external and third party systems and a new claims system. The system consisted of 200 tables, 1500 data elements and 2.5 terabytes of storage running on a system with 17 nodes each with 4 processors.

The focus of the paper however is on governance, not technology. The quality of governance can make or break a high risk/high return data warehouse project. It has been shown that the primary reason for most DW project failures is organizational rather than technical. Although the idea of data warehousing is simple, implementing a DW is complex since it involves quite challenging technical undertakings and significant organizational issues. The paper presents a discussion of issues that DW governance needs to deal with before the project starts. These include the usual: identifying the need, setting up project priorities, aligning them with company goals, and so on. The role of governance after the DW is operational is also discussed. The need for a data warehouse in Blue Cross and Blue Shield of North Carolina is presented and the implementation of the DW project is described. A team headed by a Vice-President manages the operations of the DW. The team consists of four groups (Decision Support Consulting, Business Information and Design and Architecture, Project Management and Development, and Operations and Quality Control). The governance structure consists of three strategic and operational committees each chaired by staff of the data warehouse group. These are the Vice-President Data Oversight Team (VPDOT), the Data Development Oversight Team (DDOT) and the Business Requirements Group (BRG). VPDOT provides high-level direction to the entire DW project and is a cross-functional team that includes a business leader from each of the major divisions of the organization. DDOT deals with resource prioritization tasks while BRG deals with communicating DW developments and issues with the users. Both the DW operational structure and the governance structure have evolved over time. In spite of changes at the senior management level of the organization, the role and support for DW has remained unchanged.

The DW project was started in 1997, and the paper describes a number of years of experience in building, maintaining and refining the DW.

The paper concludes with the benefits of building a DW and the lessons learned. The most important benefit of course was that the organization had a "single view" of truth. The lessons learned include that the senior management must be passionately involved in the project to be successful, committees are needed to deal with business and technical DW issues and finally the importance of educating committee members about what the DW project is supposed to achieve.

CASE STUDY 8 EXERCISES

1. Briefly describe the governance structure used in the case study.
2. What lessons were learned in implementing the data warehouse in the case study?
3. Who are the stakeholders in an enterprise data warehouse project?

CHAPTER

9 Online Analytical Processing (OLAP)

LEARNING OBJECTIVES

After completing this chapter, you will be able to:

- Learn what OLAP is
- Understand the characteristics of OLAP systems
- Describe the concept of a data cube
- Provide examples to show how data cubes are used
- Find resources to learn further about OLAP

9.1 INTRODUCTION

Before discussing OLAP, we recap some of the concepts and terminology from Chapter 8 that are required in this chapter.

A *dimension* is an attribute or an ordinate within a multidimensional structure[1] consisting of a list of values (sometimes called *members*). For example, the degree, the country, the scholarship and the year were the four dimensions used in the student database example in Chapter 8. Dimensions are used for selecting and aggregating data at the desired level of detail. A dimension often does not include ordering of values, for example there is no ordering associated with values of each of the four dimensions listed above, but a dimension may have one or more hierarchies that show parent/child relationships between the members of a dimension. For example, the dimension country may have a hierarchy that divides the world into continents and continents into regions followed by regions into countries if such a hierarchy is useful for the application. Multiple hierarchies may be

[1] The term multidimensional appears to have been borrowed from multidimensional matrix algebra.

defined on a dimension. For example, countries may be defined to have a geographical hierarchy as described above and may have another hierarchy defined on the basis of their wealth or per capita income (e.g. high, medium, low) or some other basis of interest to the enterprise.

A fact is defined or determined by a combination of dimension values for which a non-null value exists. For example, the dimension values (BSc, India, Merit, 2001) for dimensions (degree, country, scholarship, year) describe a fact. Let us assume that the value of this fact is 10. The non-null values of facts are the numerical values stored in each data cube cell. They are called *measures*. A measure is a non-key attribute in a fact table and the value of the measure is dependent on the values of the dimensions. Each unique combination of members in the Cartesian product of the cube's dimensions identifies precisely one data cell within the cube and that cell stores the value(s) of the measure(s). The fact table is multidimensional and is a nice way to flatten a cube of any dimension. A cube may have more than one measure. For example, we may be interested in not only storing the number of students but also the total fees paid by them.

The SQL command GROUP BY is a somewhat unusual aggregation operator in that a table is divided into sub-tables based on the attributes' values in the GROUP BY clause so that each sub-table has the same values for the(se) attribute(s) and then aggregations over each sub-table are carried out. SQL has a variety of aggregation functions including max, min, average, count which are used widely by employing the GROUP BY facility. In spite of these functions, SQL does not provide sufficient facilities for a variety of aggregations. For example, the standard deviation function is not available. One cannot construct histograms using SQL or build a cross tabulation. Also, GROUP BY on several dimensions can become a performance bottleneck for OLTP systems.

A data cube computes aggregates over all subsets of dimensions specified in the cube. A cube may therefore be looked at as the union of a (large) number of SQL GROUP-BY operations. Generally all or some of the aggregates are pre-computed to improve query response time. A decision has to be made as to what and how much should be pre-computed since pre-computed queries require storage and time to compute them.

A data cube is often implemented as a database in which there are dimension tables each of which provides details of a dimension. This database may be the enterprise data warehouse.

9.2 OLAP

There is considerable confusion about the terms OLAP, data warehouse and data mining. We have discussed data warehousing in Chapter 8 and data mining in Chapters 1 to 7. OLAP is different from both; it is primarily a software technology concerned with fast analysis of enterprise information. Often OLAP systems are data warehouse front-end software tools to make aggregate data available efficiently, for advanced analysis, to an enterprise's managers. As noted in Chapter 8, the analysis often requires resource intensive aggregations processing and therefore it becomes necessary to implement a special database (e.g. a data warehouse) to improve OLAP response time. It is essential that an OLAP system provides facilities for a manager to pose ad hoc complex queries to obtain the information that he/she requires.

Another term that is being used increasingly is *business intelligence*. It is sometimes used to mean both data warehousing and OLAP. Other times, it has been defined as a user-centred process of exploring data, data relationships and trends, thereby helping to improve overall decision making.

Normally, this involves a process of accessing data (usually stored within the data warehouse) and analysing it to draw conclusions and derive insights with the purpose of effecting positive change within an enterprise. Business intelligence therefore is closely related to OLAP.

As discussed in Chapter 8, a data warehouse and OLAP are based on a multidimensional conceptual view of the enterprise data. Any enterprise data may be viewed as multidimensional, for example, in a university one may view the student data as multidimensional consisting of dimensions degree, country, scholarship, and year. Data that is arranged by the dimensions is like a spreadsheet, although a spreadsheet presents only two-dimensional data with each cell containing an aggregation. As an example, Table 9.1 shows one such two-dimensional spreadsheet with dimensions Degree and Country, where the measure is the number of students joining a university in a particular year or semester.

Table 9.1 A multidimensional view of data for two dimensions

Degree / *Countary*	BSc	LLB	MBBS	BCom	BIT	ALL
Australia	5	20	15	50	11	101
India	10	0	15	25	17	67
Malaysia	5	1	10	12	23	51
Singapore	2	2	10	10	31	55
Sweden	5	0	5	25	7	42
UK	5	15	20	20	13	73
USA	0	2	20	15	19	56
ALL	32	40	95	157	121	445

Let Table 9.1 be the information for the year 2001. We will use this table in an example later in the chapter. Similar spreadsheet views would be available for other years. Three-dimensional data can also be organized in a spreadsheet using a number of sheets or by using a number of two-dimensional tables in the same sheet.

Although it is useful to think of OLAP systems as a generalization of spreadsheets, spreadsheets are not really suitable for OLAP in spite of the nice user-friendly interface that they provide. Spreadsheets tie data storage too tightly to the presentation. It is therefore difficult to obtain other desirable views of the information. Furthermore it is not possible to query spreadsheets. Also, spreadsheets become unwieldy when more than three dimensions are to be represented, as often is the case with OLAP. There is also a significant scalability problem with spreadsheets. It is difficult to imagine a spreadsheet with millions of rows or with thousands of formulas. Even with small spreadsheets, formulas often have errors. An error-free spreadsheet with thousands of formulas would therefore be very difficult to build. Data cubes essentially generalize spreadsheets to any number of dimensions.

In 1993, E.F. Codd presented this somewhat difficult to understand definition of OLAP:

> *OLAP is the dynamic enterprise analysis required to create, manipulate, animate and synthesise information from exegetical, contemplative and formulaic data analysis models.*

Essentially what this definition means is that the information is manipulated from the point of view of a manager (exegetical), from the point of view of someone who has thought about it (contemplative) and according to some formula (formulaic).

Another definition of OLAP is that OLAP is software technology that enables analysts, managers and executives to gain insight into data through fast, consistent, interactive access to a wide variety of possible views of information that has been transformed from raw data to reflect the real dimensionality of the enterprise as understood by the user.

An even simpler definition is that OLAP is fast analysis of shared multidimensional information for advanced analysis. This definition (sometimes called FASMI) implies that most OLAP queries should be answered within seconds. Furthermore, it is expected that most OLAP queries can be answered without any programming.

In summary, a manager would want even the most complex query to be answered quickly. OLAP is usually a multi-user system that may be run on a separate server using specialized OLAP software. The major OLAP applications are trend analysis over a number of time periods, slicing, dicing, drill-down and roll-up to look at the data at different levels of detail and pivoting or rotating to obtain a new multidimensional view. We will discuss these operations later in the chapter.

9.3 CHARACTERISTICS OF OLAP SYSTEMS

Before discussing the characteristics of OLAP systems, let us compare OLTP and OLAP systems. In Chapter 8 we compared OLTP systems with data warehouses. We now compare OLTP systems with OLAP systems. The differences between the two types of systems may be summarized as follows:

1. ***Users:*** OLTP systems are designed for office workers while the OLAP systems are designed for decision makers. Therefore while an OLTP system may be accessed by hundreds or even thousands of users in a large enterprise, an OLAP system is likely to be accessed only by a select group of managers and may be used only by dozens of users.
2. ***Functions:*** OLTP systems are mission-critical. They support an enterprise's day-to-day operations and are mostly performance and availability driven. These systems carry out simple repetitive operations. OLAP systems on the other hand are management-critical to support an enterprise's decision-support functions using analytical investigations. They are more functionality driven. These are ad hoc and often much more complex operations.
3. ***Nature:*** Although SQL queries often return a set of records, OLTP systems are designed to process one record at a time, for example a record related to the customer who might be on the phone or in the store. OLAP systems are not designed to deal with individual customer records. Instead they involve queries that deal with many records at a time and provide summary or aggregate data to a manager. OLAP applications often involve data stored in a data warehouse that has been extracted from many tables and perhaps from more than one enterprise database.
4. ***Design:*** OLTP database systems are designed to be application-oriented while OLAP systems are designed to be subject-oriented. OLTP systems view the enterprise data as a collection of tables (perhaps based on an entity-relationship model). OLAP systems view enterprise information as multidimensional.

5. ***Data:*** OLTP systems normally deal only with the current status of information. For example, information about an employee who left three years ago may not be available on the Human Resources system. The old information may have been archived on some type of stable storage media and may not be accessible online. On the other hand, OLAP systems require historical data over several years since trends are often important in decision making.
6. ***Kind of use:*** OLTP systems are used for read and write operations while OLAP systems normally do not update the data.

The differences between OLTP and OLAP systems are summarized in Table 9.2.

Table 9.2 Comparison of OLTP and OLAP systems

Property	*OLTP*	*OLAP*
Nature of users	Operations workers	Decision makers
Functions	Mission-critical	Management-critical
Nature of queries	Mostly simple	Mostly complex
Nature of usage	Mostly repetitive	Mostly ad hoc
Nature of design	Application oriented	Subject oriented
Number of users	Thousands	Dozens
Nature of data	Current, detailed, relational	Historical, summarized, multidimensional
Updates	All the time	Usually not allowed

The above comparison highlights some of the characteristics of OLAP systems. There are a number of other characteristics that we now discuss. There are two main views about OLAP that are based on two different definitions of OLAP presented earlier. One view is by Codd and the other is by publishers of "The OLAP Report". We discuss the second one first followed by Codd's list of characteristics.

FASMI Characteristics

The FASMI characteristics of OLAP systems, the name derived from the first letters of the characteristics, are:

Fast: As noted earlier, most OLAP queries should be answered very quickly, perhaps within seconds. The performance of an OLAP system has to be like that of a search engine. If the response takes more than say 20 seconds, the user is likely to move away to something else assuming there is a problem with the query. Achieving such performance is difficult. The data structures must be efficient. The hardware must be powerful enough for the amount of data and the number of users. Full pre-computation of aggregates helps but is often not practical due to the large number of aggregates. One approach is to pre-compute the most commonly queried aggregates and compute the remaining on-the-fly.

Analytic: An OLAP system must provide rich analytic functionality and it is expected that most OLAP queries can be answered without any programming. The system should be able to cope with any relevant queries for the application and the user. Often the analysis will be done using the vendor's own tools although OLAP software capabilities differ widely between products in the market.

Shared: An OLAP system is a shared resource although it is unlikely to be shared by hundreds of users. An OLAP system is likely to be accessed only by a select group of managers and may be used by mere dozens of users. Being a shared system, an OLAP system should provide adequate security for confidentiality as well as integrity. It is often assumed that users do not update data in the database although this is not always true. Concurrency control is obviously required if users are writing or updating data in the database.

Multidimensional: This is the basic requirement. Whatever OLAP software is being used, it must provide a multidimensional conceptual view of the data. It is because of the multidimensional view of data that we often refer to the data as a cube. A dimension often has hierarchies that show parent/child relationships between the members of a dimension. The multidimensional structure should allow such hierarchies.

Information: OLAP systems usually obtain information from a data warehouse. The system should be able to handle a large amount of input data. The capacity of an OLAP system to handle information and its integration with the data warehouse may be critical.

Codd's OLAP Characteristics

Codd et al's 1993 paper listed 12 characteristics (or rules) of OLAP systems. Another six in 1995 followed these. Codd restructured the 18 rules into four groups. These rules provide another point of view on what constitutes an OLAP system.

All the 18 rules are available at http://www.olapreport.com/fasmi.htm. We will not discuss them all. Instead we will consider 10 characteristics that we consider the most important.

1. ***Multidimensional conceptual view:*** As noted above, this is the central characteristic of an OLAP system. By requiring a multidimensional view, it is possible to carry out operations like slice and dice.
2. ***Accessibility (OLAP as a mediator):*** The OLAP software should be sitting between data sources (e.g. a data warehouse) and an OLAP front-end.
3. ***Batch extraction vs interpretive:*** An OLAP system should provide multidimensional data staging plus partial precalculation of aggregates in large multidimensional databases.
4. ***Multi-user support:*** Since the OLAP system is shared, the OLAP software should provide many normal database operations including retrieval, update, concurrency control, integrity and security.
5. ***Storing OLAP results:*** OLAP results data should be kept separate from source data. Read-write OLAP applications should not be implemented directly on live transaction data if OLTP source systems are supplying information to the OLAP system directly.
6. ***Extraction of missing values:*** The OLAP system should distinguish missing values from zero values. A large data cube may have a large number of zeros as well as some missing values. If a distinction is not made between zero values and missing values, the aggregates are likely to be computed incorrectly.

7. ***Treatment of missing values:*** An OLAP system should ignore all missing values regardless of their source. Correct aggregate values will be computed once the missing values are ignored.

8. ***Uniform reporting performance:*** Increasing the number of dimensions or database size should not significantly degrade the reporting performance of the OLAP system. This is a good objective although it may be difficult to achieve in practice.

9. ***Generic dimensionality:*** An OLAP system should treat each dimension as equivalent in both its structure and operational capabilities. Additional operational capabilities may be granted to selected dimensions but such additional functions should be grantable to any dimension.

10. ***Unlimited dimensions and aggregation levels:*** An OLAP system should allow unlimited dimensions and aggregation levels. In practice, the number of dimensions is rarely more than 10 and the number of hierarchies rarely more than six.

These rules provide one point of view about the desirable characteristics of an OLAP system. Arbor Software (now Hyperion Solutions) commissioned the study by Codd that outlined the above characteristics and it is their product Essbase that generally follows the rules specified. Most other OLAP products lack some of the 18 characteristics that include the 10 listed above.

9.4 MOTIVATIONS FOR USING OLAP

As noted earlier, enterprise executives need to obtain accurate knowledge from the glut of information that most enterprises now generate. The growth of the Web has only compounded the problem of information glut. ODS and data warehouses, discussed in Chapter 8, help in collecting relevant business data into a single database. OLAP presents the tools for query and analysis of the data so collected. We give two examples to illustrate the types of information that OLAP tools can help in discovering.

1. ***Understanding and improving sales:*** For an enterprise that has many products and uses a number of channels for selling the products, OLAP can assist in finding the most popular products and the most popular channels. In some cases it may be possible to find the most profitable customers. For example, considering the telecommunications industry and only considering one product, communication minutes, there is a large amount of data if a company wanted to analyse the sales of product for every hour of the day (24 hours), differentiate between weekdays and weekends (2 values) and divide regions to which calls are made into 50 regions. One is therefore looking at a three-dimensional cube with $24 \times 2 \times 50 = 2400$ cells. OLAP analysis of such information can assist in improving the enterprise business.

2. ***Understanding and reducing costs of doing business:*** Improving sales is one aspect of improving a business, the other aspect is to analyse costs and to control them as much as possible without affecting sales. OLAP can assist in analysing the costs associated with sales. In some cases, it may also be possible to identify expenditures that produce a high return on investment (ROI). For example, recruiting a top salesperson may involve significant costs, but the revenue generated by the salesperson may justify the investment.

Many successful applications of OLAP have been reported including use of OLAP at well known companies like Wal-mart, AT&T and Borders Group (booksellers). A case study at the end of this chapter also shows how OLAP may be useful in an application area.

9.5 MULTIDIMENSIONAL VIEW AND DATA CUBE

The multidimensional view of data is in some ways a natural view of any enterprise for managers. The triangle diagram in Figure 9.1 shows that as we go higher in the triangle hierarchy the managers' need for detailed information declines.

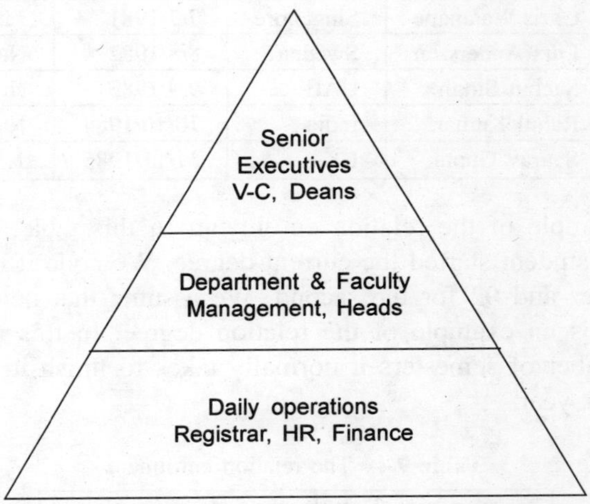

Figure 9.1 A typical university management hierarchy.

We illustrate the multidimensional view of data by using an example of a simple OLTP database consisting of three tables. Much of the literature on OLAP uses examples of a shoe store selling different colour shoes of different styles. We will resist the temptation of using the same example! Instead our example deals with student data that has only three dimensions. The first relation (student) provides information about students. The second relation (enrolment) provides information about the students' degree enrolment and the semester of their first enrolment. The third relation (degree) provides information about the degrees in the university and the departments that offer them.

It should be noted that the relation enrolment would normally not be required since the degree a student is enrolled in could be included in the relation student but some students are enrolled in double degrees and so the relation between the student and the degree is many-to-many and hence the need for the relation enrolment.

student(Student_id, Student_name, Country, DOB, Address)

enrolment(Student_id, Degree_id, SSemester)

degree(Degree_id, Degree_name, Degree_length, Fee, Department)

An example of the first relation, i.e. student, is given in Table 9.3.

Table 9.3 The relation student

Student_id	*Student_name*	*Country*	*DOB*	*Address*
8656789	Peta Williams	Australia	1/1/1980	Davis Hall
8700020	John Smith	Canada	2/2/1981	9 Davis Hall
8900020	Arun Krishna	USA	3/3/1983	90 Second Hall
8801234	Peter Chew	UK	4/4/1983	88 Long Hall
8654321	Reena Rani	Australia	5/5/1984	88 Long Hall
8712374	Kathy Garcia	Malaysia	6/6/1980	88 Long Hall
8612345	Chris Watanabe	Singapore	7/7/1981	11 Main Street
8744223	Lars Anderssen	Sweden	8/8/1982	Null
8977665	Sachin Singh	UAE	9/9/1983	Null
9234567	Rahul Kumar	India	10/10/1984	Null
9176543	Saurav Gupta	UK	11/11/1985	1, Captain Drive

Table 9.4 presents an example of the relation enrolment. In this table, the attribute SSemester is the semester in which the student started the current degree. We code it by using the year followed by 01 for the first semester and 02 for the second. We assume that new students are admitted in each semester. Table 9.5 is an example of the relation degree. In this table, the degree length is given in terms of the number of semesters it normally takes to finish it. The fee is assumed to be in thousands of dollars per year.

Table 9.4 The relation enrolment

Student_id	*Degree_id*	*SSemester*
8900020	1256	2002–01
8700074	3271	2002–01
8700074	3321	2002–02
8900020	4444	2000–01
8801234	1256	2001–01
8801234	3321	1999–02
8801234	3333	1999–02
8977665	3333	2000–02

Table 9.5 The relation degree

Degree_id	*Degree_name*	*Degree_length*	*Fee*	*Department*
1256	BIT	6	18	Computer Science
2345	BSc	6	20	Computer Science
4325	BSc	6	20	Chemistry
3271	BSc	6	20	Physics
3321	BCom	6	16	Business
4444	MBBS	12	30	Medicine
3333	LLB	8	22	Law

It is clear that the information given in Tables 9.3, 9.4 and 9.5, although suitable for a student enrolment OLTP system, is not suitable for efficient management decision making. The managers do not need information about the individual students, the degree they are enrolled in, and the semester they joined the university. What the managers need is the trends in student numbers in different degree programs and from different countries.

We first consider only two dimensions. Let us say we are primarily interested in finding out how many students from each country came to do a particular degree. Therefore we may visualize the data as two-dimensional, i.e.

Country × Degree

A table that summarizes this type of information may be represented by a two-dimensional spreadsheet given in Table 9.6 (the numbers in Table 9.6 do not relate to the numbers in Table 9.4).

We may call this table that gives the number of students admitted (in, say, 2000–01) a two-dimensional "cube".

Table 9.6 A two-dimensional table of aggregates for semester 2000–01

Degree / *Country*	BSc	LLB	MBBS	BCom	BIT	ALL
Australia	5	20	15	50	11	101
India	10	0	15	25	17	67
Malaysia	5	1	10	12	23	51
Singapore	2	2	10	10	31	55
Sweden	5	0	5	25	7	42
UK	5	15	20	20	13	73
USA	0	2	20	15	19	56
ALL	32	40	95	157	121	445

Using this two-dimensional view we are able to find the number of students joining any degree from any country (only for semester 2000–01). Other queries that we are quickly able to answer are:

- How many students started BIT in 2000–01?
- How many students joined from Singapore in 2000–01?

The data given in Table 9.6 is for a particular semester, 2000–01. A similar table would be available for other semesters. Let us assume that the data for 2001–01 is given in Table 9.7.

Table 9.7 Two-dimensional table of aggregates for semester 2001–01

Country \ *Degree*	BSc	LLB	MBBS	BCom	BIT	ALL
Australia	7	10	16	53	10	96
India	9	0	17	22	13	61
Malaysia	5	1	19	19	20	64
Singapore	2	2	10	12	23	49
Sweden	8	0	5	16	7	36
UK	4	13	20	26	11	74
USA	4	2	10	10	12	38
ALL	39	28	97	158	96	418

Let us now imagine that Table 9.7 is put on top of Table 9.6. We now have a three-dimensional cube with SSemester as the vertical dimension. We now put on top of these two tables another table that gives the vertical sums, as shown in Table 9.8.

Table 9.8 Two-dimensional table of aggregates for both semesters

Country \ *Degree*	BSc	LLB	MBBS	BCom	BIT	ALL
Australia	12	30	31	103	21	197
India	19	0	32	47	30	128
Malaysia	10	2	29	31	43	115
Singapore	4	4	20	22	54	104
Sweden	13	0	10	41	14	78
UK	9	28	40	46	24	147
USA	4	4	30	25	31	94
ALL	71	68	192	315	217	863

Tables 9.6, 9.7 and 9.8 together now form a three-dimensional cube as shown in Figure 9.2. The top table, Table 9.8, provides totals for the two semesters and we are able to "drill-down" to find numbers in individual semesters. Note that a cube does not need to have an equal number of members in each dimension. Putting the three tables together gives a cube of 8 × 6 × 3 (= 144) cells including the totals along every dimension.

A cube such as we have described could be represented by:

Country × Degree × Semester

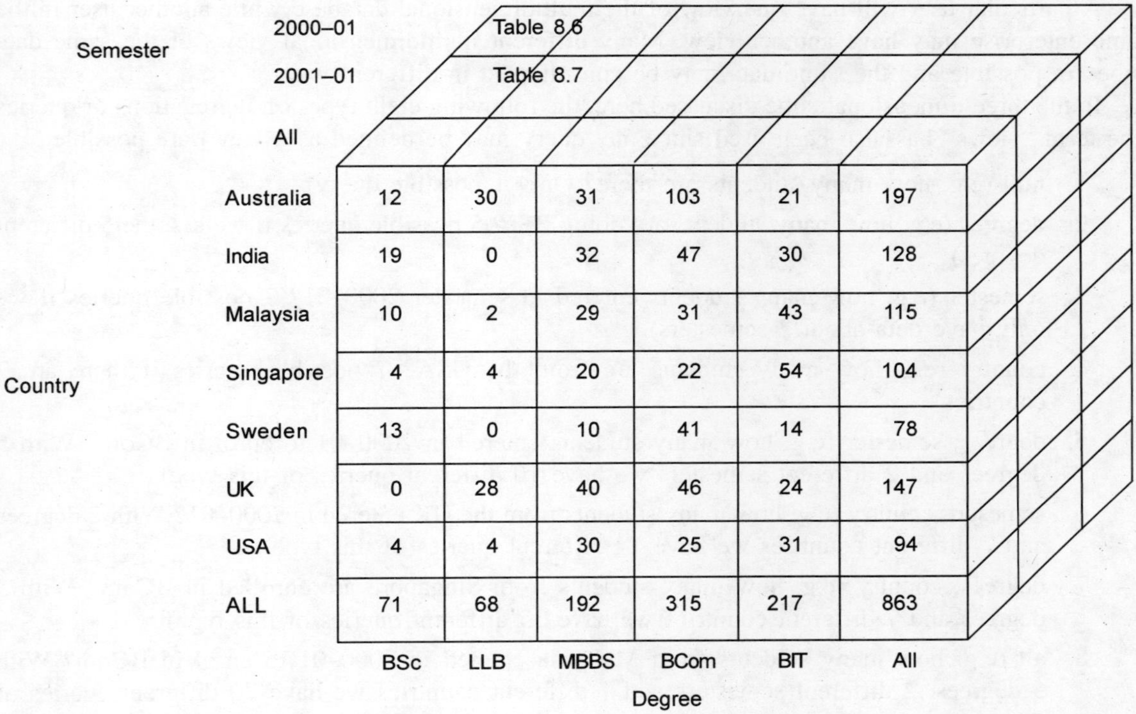

Figure 9.2 The cube formed by Tables 9.6, 9.7 and 9.8.

Each of the edges in the cube represents a dimension. Each dimension has a number of members, for example, the dimension Degree has members BSc, LLB, MBBS, BCom and BIT. Similarly the dimensions Country and SSemester have members. We have not defined any hierarchies on the dimensions but hierarchies are possible. Each of the dimensions may have attributes (for example, population of each country) that are not given in the cube. All the cells in the cube represent measures or aggregations. For example, a cell may provide the number of students from Malaysia admitted to BCom in semester 2001–01.

Different types of measures may behave differently in computations. For example, the measures in this example are the number of students and we may further add them up to obtain the total number of students from Malaysia or the total number of students doing BIT. We can also add the number of students who were admitted in 2000–01 and 2001–01 to obtain the total number of students in the two semesters. Such measures are called *additive*. Some measures cannot be so added. For example, if the number of students in semester 2000–01 was the total number of students enrolled in the university rather than the number of students admitted it may not make much sense to sum those numbers along the SSemester dimension although summing them along Country and Degree dimensions is fine. Such measures are called *semi-additive*. Some measures, called *nonadditive*, cannot be combined along any dimensions.

A particular user will have one view of the multidimensional database while another user in the same enterprise may have another view. Many different multidimensional views of the same data cube are possible and the same data may be consolidated in different ways.

In the three-dimensional cube discussed here, the following eight types of aggregations or queries (the term "views" has also been used since any query may be defined as a view) are possible:

1. null (e.g. how many students are there? Only 1 possible query)
2. degrees (e.g. how many students are doing BSc? 5 possible queries if we assume 5 different degrees)
3. semester (e.g. how many students entered in semester 2000–01? 2 possible queries if we only have data about 2 semesters)
4. country (e.g. how many students are from the USA? 7 possible queries if there are 7 countries)
5. degrees, semester (e.g. how many students entered in 2000–01 to enrol in BCom? With 5 degrees and 2 different semesters we have 10 different queries of this type)
6. semester, country (e.g. how many students from the UK entered in 2000–01? With 2 degrees and 7 different countries we have 14 different queries of this type)
7. degrees, country (e.g. how many students from Singapore are enrolled in BCom? With 5 degrees and 7 different countries we have 35 different queries of this type)
8. all (e.g. how many students from Malaysia entered in 2000–01 to enrol in BCom? With 5 degrees, 2 different semesters and 7 different countries we have 70 different queries of this type)

Therefore eight different types of aggregations are possible for three dimensions. In general, 2^n types of aggregations are possible for n dimensions.

Assuming that we have 20 different semesters, 50 different degrees and 10 different countries, there are 20 × 50 × 10 or 10,000 possible different combinations of the three attributes without including the totals. Aggregates for all these combinations as well as those of two attributes and single attributes will need to be pre-computed if we want to have every possible aggregate. The numbers given in the above list add to 144 different aggregations as we discussed earlier.

Once we have all the pre-computed aggregates not only for semesters 2000–01 and 2001–01 but for many other semesters, we are able to quickly answer any of the following queries:

- How many students from the UK started degree BCom in semester 1999–01?
- How many Swedish students joined the university in 2001–01?
- How many students started the BSc degree each semester?

It is clear that SQL can be used for all such queries although the OLTP system may not have all the historical data. For example, all of the aggregations in the list above can be built by queries like:

```
SELECT Degree_id, count(*)
FROM enrolment
GROUP BY Degree_id
```

This query returns the total number of enrolments in each degree. To obtain the aggregations for any one entry semester, a WHERE clause may be used. A one-dimensional cube represents this aggregation as shown in Table 9.9. Note that the first row is just labels and is not part of the "cube".

Table 9.9 A one-dimensional table of aggregates

BSc	LLB	MBBS	BCom	BIT
71	68	192	315	217

or

```
SELECT Degree_id, Country, count(*)
FROM degree, enrolment, student
WHERE degree.Degree_id = enrolment.Degree_id
AND student.Student_id = enrolment.Student_id
AND SSemester = "2000-01"
GROUP BY Degree_id, Country
```

These aggregations have already been shown in a two-dimensional "cube" in Table 9.6.

or

```
SELECT SSemester, Degree_name, Country, count(*)
FROM student, enrolment, degree
WHERE degree.Degree_id = enrolment.Degree_id
WHERE student.Student_id = enrolment.Student_id
GROUP BY Degree_id, SSemester, Country
```

Aggregates generated by this query essentially are a fact table representation of a three-dimensional cube.

9.6 DATA CUBE IMPLEMENTATIONS

Given that we have already identified 10,000 aggregates for a very simple example, the number of aggregates can be very large for a real example. Many universities in Australia have decided to offer so many named degrees that a large university like Monash could well be offering 200 degrees or more. Also, students come from many countries and one could conceivably be interested in almost 100 countries. Some universities run three semesters a year and thus the last ten years data would have 30 semester dates. Therefore one could well have 200 × 100 × 30 (i.e. 600,000) aggregates with only three dimensions. Million of aggregates are likely in a large enterprise when there are more than three dimensions. Should all these aggregates be pre-computed? Many of the aggregates will be zero. How should they be stored? How should sparsity be managed? Some possible solutions are:

1. ***Pre-compute and store all:*** This means that perhaps millions of aggregates will need to be computed and stored. Although this is the best solution as far as query response time is concerned, the solution is impractical since resources required to compute the aggregates and to store them will be prohibitively large for a large data cube. Indexing large amounts of data is also expensive.

2. ***Pre-compute (and store) none:*** This means that the aggregates are computed on-the-fly using the raw data whenever a query is posed. This approach does not require additional space for storing the cube but the query response time is likely to be very poor for large data cubes.
3. ***Pre-compute and store some:*** This means that we pre-compute and store the most frequently queried aggregates and compute others as the need arises. We may also be able to derive some of the remaining aggregates using the aggregates that have already been computed. It may therefore be worthwhile to also pre-compute some aggregates that are not most frequently queried but help in deriving many other aggregates. It will of course not be possible to derive all the aggregates from the pre-computed aggregates and it will be necessary to access the source database (e.g. the data warehouse) to compute the remaining aggregates. The more aggregates we are able to pre-compute the better the query performance.

Each cell of a data cube may be identified by the values of its dimensions. For example, (BSc, India, 2001–01) for dimensions (degree, country and entry semester) describes a cell. It has been suggested that an additional value of dimension "ALL" be added to identify cells like (BSc, ALL, 2001–01). This gives the number of all students who entered the university in 2001–01 to do a BSc. Such aggregates do not need to be materialized since one could obtain the aggregate on-the-fly by summing all cells like (BSc, ?, 2001–01) for all the countries. If a cell's dimension values do not contain an "ALL" value then the aggregate must be computed from raw data since there is no way to derive that aggregate but if they do contain ALL then they can always be derived from other aggregates.

It can be shown that large numbers of cells do have an "ALL" value and may therefore be derived from other aggregates. Let us reproduce the list of queries we had in the last section and define them as (*a*, *b*, *c*) where *a* stands for a value of the degree dimension, *b* for country and *c* for starting semester:

1. (ALL, ALL, ALL) null (e.g. how many students are there? Only 1 query)
2. (*a*, ALL, ALL) degrees (e.g. how many students are doing BSc? 5 queries)
3. (ALL, ALL, *c*) semester (e.g. how many students entered in semester 2000–01? 2 queries)
4. (ALL, *b*, ALL) country (e.g. how many students are from the USA? 7 queries)
5. (*a*, ALL, *c*) degrees, semester (e.g. how many students entered in 2000–01 to enrol in BCom? 10 queries)
6. (ALL, *b*, *c*) semester, country (e.g. how many students from the UK entered in 2000–01? 14 queries)
7. (*a*, *b*, ALL) degrees, country (e.g. how many students from Singapore are enrolled in BCom? 35 queries)
8. (*a*, *b*, *c*) all (e.g. how many students from Malaysia entered in 2000–01 to enrol in BCom? 70 queries)

It is therefore possible to derive the other 74 of the 144 queries from the last 70 queries of type (*a*, *b*, *c*). Of course in a very large data cube, it may not be practical to even pre-compute all the (*a*, *b*, *c*) queries and decisions will need to be made which ones should be pre-computed given that storage availability may be limited and it may be required to minimize the average query cost.

In Figure 9.3 we show how the aggregates above are related and how an aggregate at a higher level may be computed from the aggregates below. For example, aggregates (ALL, ALL, *c*) may be derived from either (*a*, ALL, *c*) by summing over all *a* values or from (ALL, *b*, *c*) by summing over all *b* values.

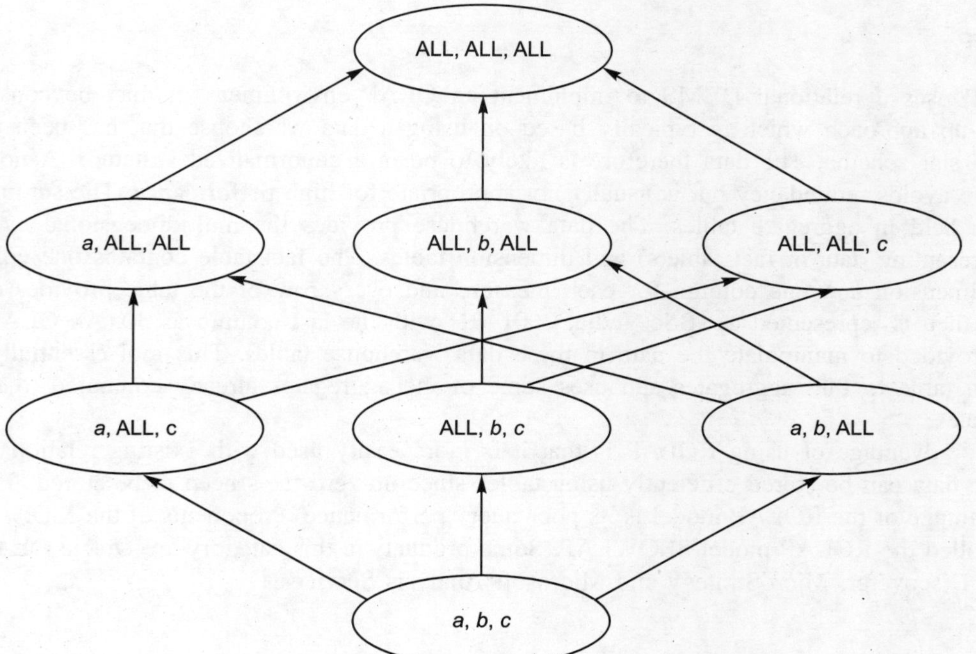

Figure 9.3 Relationships between aggregations of a three-dimensional cube.

Another related issue is where the data used by OLAP will reside. We assume that the data is stored in a data warehouse or in one or more data marts. As we noted in Chapter 8, it is not appropriate to use data directly from OLTP systems because OLAP applications are often large and use complex aggregate analysis. Also, OLAP often uses data from more than one OLTP system and the process of merging these multiple systems can be complex. Data may also need to be transformed if a company is operating in many locations, including a number of countries since different states and countries are likely to have different record-keeping conventions.

Data cube products use different techniques for pre-computing aggregates and storing them. They are generally based on one of two implementation models. The first model, supported by vendors of traditional relational model databases, is called the ROLAP model or the Relational OLAP model. The second model is called the MOLAP model for multidimensional OLAP. The MOLAP model provides a direct multidimensional view of the data whereas the ROLAP model provides a relational view of the multidimensional data in the form of a fact table.

Often however it is not necessary to pre-compute all the cube aggregations since most cubes have many empty cells. For example, if we consider the university example involving degrees and countries and if we find that only business and information technology degrees were popular amongst the Asian students then a large percentage of cells in the cube are likely to be empty. In a, say, four-dimensional large cube of many millions of cells it is possible that more than 99% of cells are empty. Various storage techniques are available to maximize storage utilization of a sparse data cube.

ROLAP

ROLAP uses a relational DBMS to implement an OLAP environment. It may be considered a bottom-up approach which is typically based on using a data warehouse that has been designed using a star schema. The data therefore is likely to be in a denormalized structure. A normalized database avoids redundancy but is usually not appropriate for high performance. The summary data will be held in aggregate tables. The data warehouse provides the multidimensional capabilities by representing data in fact table(s) and dimension tables. The fact table contains one column for each dimension and one column for each measure and every row of the table provides one fact. A fact then is represented as (BSc, India, 2001–01) with the last column as 30. An OLAP tool is then provided to manipulate the data in these data warehouse tables. This tool essentially groups the fact table to find aggregates and uses some of the aggregates already computed to find new aggregates.

The advantage of using ROLAP is that it is more easily used with existing relational DBMS and the data can be stored efficiently using tables since no zero facts need to be stored. The major disadvantage of the ROLAP model is its poor query performance. Proponents of the MOLAP model have called the ROLAP model SLOWLAP. Some products in this category are Oracle OLAP mode, OLAP Discoverer, MicroStrategy and Microsoft Analysis Services.

MOLAP

MOLAP is based on using a multidimensional DBMS rather than a data warehouse to store and access data. It may be considered as a top-down approach to OLAP. The multidimensional database systems do not have a standard approach to storing and maintaining their data. They often use special-purpose file systems or indexes that store pre-computation of all aggregations in the cube. For example, in ROLAP a cell was represented as (BSc, India, 2001–01) with a value 30 stored in the last column. In MOLAP, the same information is stored as just 30 and the storage location implicitly gives the values of the dimensions. The dimension values do not need to be stored since all the values of the cube could be stored in an array in a predefined way. For example, the cube in Figure 9.2 may be represented as an array like the following:

12	30	31	103	21	197	19	0	32	47	30	128	10	2	29	31	43	...

If the values of the dimensions are known, we can infer the cell location in the array. If the cell location is known, the values of the dimension may be inferred. This is obviously a very compact notation for storing a multidimensional data cube although a couple of problems remain. Firstly, the array is likely to be too large to be stored in the main memory. Secondly, this representation does not solve the problem of efficiently representing sparse cubes. To overcome the problem of the array being too large for the main memory, the array may be split into pieces called "chunks", each of which is small enough to fit in the main memory. To overcome the problem of sparseness, the "chunks" may be compressed.

Since MOLAP does not use a relational data warehouse as its basis, it is necessary to use proprietary software tools. These tools try to optimize storage usage and query execution times. The data for pre-computation has to come from source systems and could come from a data warehouse. The multidimensional DBMS is normally stored on disk but storing data in main memory can further boost the performance of the system. The pre-computed aggregates are often stored in some form of array structure.

MOLAP systems have to deal with sparsity since a very high percentage of the cells can be empty in some applications. The MOLAP implementation is usually exceptionally efficient. The disadvantage of using MOLAP is that it is likely to be more expensive than ROLAP, the data is not always current, and it may be more difficult to scale a MOLAP system for very large OLAP problems. Some MOLAP products are Hyperion Essbase and Applix iTM1. Oracle and Microsoft are also competing in this segment of the OLAP market.

It has been suggested that MOLAP is easier to use and therefore may be more suitable for inexperienced users. Users who need a tool that they can use for frequently changing query requirements may be better advised to use ROLAP. The differences between ROLAP and MOLAP are summarized in Table 9.10.

Table 9.10 Comparison of MOLAP and ROLAP

Property	*MOLAP*	*ROLAP*
Data structure	Multidimensional database using sparse arrays	Relational tables (each cell is a row)
Disk space	Separate database for data cube; large for large data cubes	May not require any space other than that available in the data warehouse
Retrieval	Fast (pre-computed)	Slow (computes on-the-fly)
Scalability	Limited (cubes can be very large)	Excellent
Best suited for	Inexperienced users, limited set of queries	Experienced users, queries change frequently
DBMS facilities	Usually weak	Usually very strong

9.7 DATA CUBE OPERATIONS

A number of operations may be applied to data cubes. The common ones are:

- Roll-up
- Drill-down
- Slice and dice
- Pivot

We describe these operations now.

Roll-up

Roll-up is like zooming out on the data cube. It is required when the user needs further abstraction or less detail. This operation performs further aggregations on the data, for example, from single degree programs to all programs offered by a School or department, from single countries to a collection of countries, and from individual semesters to academic years. Often a hierarchy defined on a dimension is useful in the roll-up operation as suggested by the example of countries and regions.

We provide an example of roll-up based on Tables 9.6, 9.7 and 9.8. We first define hierarchies on two dimensions. Amongst countries, let us define:

1. Asia (India, Malaysia, Singapore)
2. Europe (Sweden, UK)
3. Rest (Australia, USA)

Another hierarchy is defined on the dimension degree:

1. Science (BSc, BIT)
2. Medicine (MBBS)
3. Business and Law (BCom, LLB)

The result of a roll-up for both semesters together from Table 9.8 then is given in Table 9.11.

Table 9.11 Result of a roll-up operation using Table 9.8

Degree / *Country*	*Science*	*Medicine*	*Business and Law*
Asia	160	81	106
Europe	60	50	115
Rest	68	61	162

Drill-down

Drill-down is like zooming in on the data and is therefore the reverse of roll-up. It is an appropriate operation when the user needs further details or when the user wants to partition more finely or wants to focus on some particular values of certain dimensions. Drill-down adds more details to the data. Hierarchy defined on a dimension may be involved in drill-down. For example, a higher level view of student data, for example in Table 9.11, gives student numbers for the two semesters for groups of countries and groups of degrees. If one is interested in more detail then it is possible to drill-down to Tables 9.6 and 9.7 for student numbers in each of the semesters for each country and for each degree.

Slice and Dice

Slice and dice are operations for browsing the data in the cube. The terms refer to the ability to look at information from different viewpoints.

A slice is a subset of the cube corresponding to a single value for one or more members of the dimensions. For example, a slice operation is performed when the user wants a selection on one dimension of a three-dimensional cube resulting in a two-dimensional slice. Let the degree dimension be fixed as degree = BIT. The slice will not include any information about other degrees. The information retrieved therefore is more like a two-dimensional cube for degree = BIT as shown in Table 9.12.

Table 9.12 Result of a slice when degree value is 'BIT'

Country \ *Semester*	2000–01	2000–02	2001–01	2001–02
Australia	11	5	10	2
India	17	0	13	5
Malaysia	23	2	20	1
Singapore	31	4	23	2
Sweden	7	0	7	4
UK	13	8	11	6
USA	19	4	12	5

It should be noted that Table 9.7 also is a slice (with SSemester = '2000–01') from the cube built by piling several tables like Tables 9.7 and 9.8 about different semesters on top of each other. It is shown in Figure 9.4.

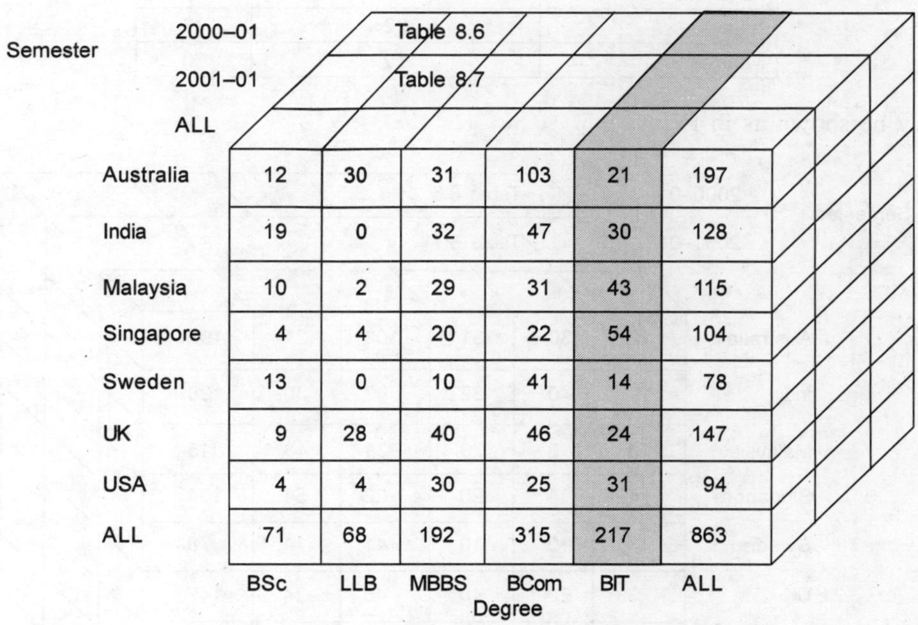

Figure 9.4 A slice from the cube in Figure 9.2.

The dice operation is similar to slice but dicing does not involve reducing the number of dimensions. A dice is obtained by performing a selection on two or more dimensions. For example, one may only be interested in degrees BIT and BCom and countries Australia, India and Malaysia for semesters 2000–01 and 2000–01. The result is a three-dimensional cube and we show it by Tables 9.13 and 9.14 placed on top of each other. For example one may only be interested in the degrees BIT and BCom and the countries Australia, India and Malaysia for semesters 2000–01 and 2001–01. The result is a three-dimensional cube as shown in Figure 9.4 and we show it by Tables 9.13 and 9.14 for the two semesters placed on top of each other. We have left out the table that shows the totals from these tables.

Table 9.13 A three-dimensional dice from a three-dimensional cube (SSemester 2000–01)

Degree / *Country*	BCom	BIT
Australia	50	11
India	25	17
Malaysia	12	23

Table 9.14 A three-dimensional dice from a three-dimensional cube (SSemester 2001–01)

Degree / *Country*	BCom	BIT
Australia	53	10
India	22	13
Malaysia	19	20

A dice may be shown as in Figure 9.5.

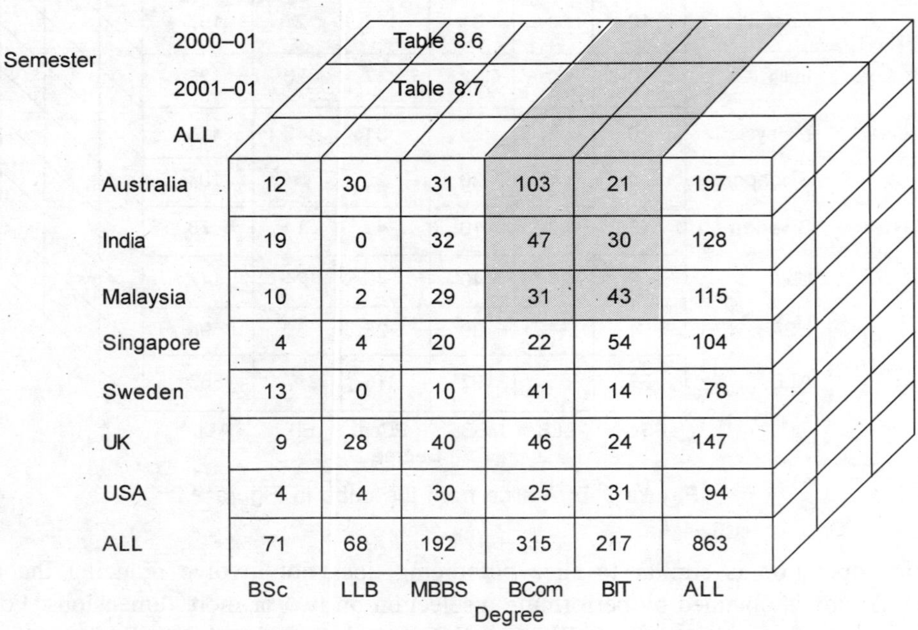

Figure 9.5 A dice from the cube in Figure 9.2.

Slice and dice often figure in interactive use of an OLAP system in which the user can navigate through the cube by specifying either one or two dimensions or values of all three dimensions that are of interest.

Pivot or Rotate

The pivot operation is used when the user wishes to re-orient the view of the data cube. It may involve swapping the rows and columns, or moving one of the row dimensions into the column dimension. For example, the cube consisting of Tables 9.6, 9.7 and 9.8 gives the dimension degree along the *x*-axis, country along the *y*-axis and starting semester along the *z*-axis (or the vertical axis). One may want to swap the dimensions country and starting semester. The cube will then consist of several tables like those given in Tables 9.15 and 9.16 on top of each other.

Table 9.15 One table on which other similar tables are piled up in a rotated cube (Country dimension value = Australia)

Degree / *Semester*	BSc	LLB	MBBS	BCom	BIT	ALL
2000–01	5	20	15	50	11	101
2001–01	7	10	16	53	10	96
ALL	12	30	31	103	21	197

Table 9.16 Another table that is part of a rotated cube (Country dimension value = India)

Degree / *Semester*	BSc	LLB	MBBS	BCom	BIT	ALL
2000–01	10	0	15	22	17	67
2001–01	9	0	17	22	13	61
ALL	19	0	32	47	30	128

Clearly this rotated cube gives a different view of the same data. Such views can be particularly useful if the number of dimensions is greater than three.

9.8 GUIDELINES FOR OLAP IMPLEMENTATION

In this section we present a number of guidelines for successful implementation of OLAP. The guidelines are, perhaps not surprisingly, somewhat similar to those presented for data warehouse implementation in the last chapter.

1. ***Vision:*** The OLAP team must, in consultation with the users, develop a clear vision for the OLAP system. This vision including the business objectives should be clearly defined, understood, and shared by the stakeholders.
2. ***Senior management support:*** The OLAP project should be fully supported by the senior managers. Since a data warehouse may have been developed already, this should not be difficult.
3. ***Selecting an OLAP tool:*** The OLAP team should familiarize themselves with the ROLAP and MOLAP tools available in the market. Since tools are quite different, careful planning

may be required in selecting a tool that is appropriate for the enterprise. In some situations, a combination of ROLAP and MOLAP may be most effective.

4. ***Corporate strategy:*** The OLAP strategy should fit with the enterprise strategy and business objectives. A good fit will result in the OLAP tools being used more widely.
5. ***Focus on the users:*** The OLAP project should be focused on the users. Users should, in consultation with the technical professionals, decide what tasks will be done first and what will be done later. Attempts should be made to provide each user with a tool suitable for that person's skill level and information needs. A good GUI user interface should be provided to non-technical users. The project can only be successful with the full support of the users.
6. ***Joint management:*** The OLAP project must be managed by both the IT and business professionals. Many other people should be involved in supplying ideas. An appropriate committee structure may be necessary to channel these ideas.
7. ***Review and adapt:*** As noted in the last chapter, organizations evolve and so must the OLAP system. Regular reviews of the project may be required to ensure that the project is meeting the current needs of the enterprise.

9.9 OLAP SOFTWARE

There is much OLAP software available in the market. A list is available at http://www.kdnuggets.com/software/dbolap.html. Another is available at http://www.olapreport.com/market.htm. This site provides 2005 market ranking for top ten OLAP software. Yet another list is http://dmoz.org/Computers/Software/Databases/OLAP/. The list below provides some major OLAP software.

- BI2M (Business Intelligence to Marketing and Management) from B&M Services has three modules one of which is for OLAP. The OLAP module allows database exploring including slice and dice, roll-up, drill-down and displays results as 2D charts, 3D charts and tables.
  http://www.bandmservices.com/
- Business Objects OLAP Intelligence from BusinessObjects allows access to OLAP servers from Microsoft, Hyperion, IBM and SAP. Usual operations like slice and dice, and drill directly on multidimensional sources are possible. BusinessObjects also has widely used Crystal Analysis and Reports. Its 2005 market rating was 4.
  http://www.businessobjects.com/
- ContourCube from Contour Components is an OLAP product that enables users to slice and dice, roll-up, drill-down and pivot efficiently.
  http://www.contourcomponents.com/
- DB2 Cube Views from IBM includes features and functions for managing and deploying multidimensional data. It is claimed that OLAP solutions can be deployed quickly.
  http://www-306.ibm.com/software/data/db2/db2md/
- Essbase Integration Services from Hyperion Solutions is a widely used suite of tools. The company's Web sites make it difficult to understand what the software does. It 2005 market ranking was 2.
  http://www.hyperion.com/

- Everest from OutlookSoft is a Microsoft-based single application and database that provides operational reporting and analysis including OLAP and multidimensional slice and dice and other analysis operations.
  http://www.outlooksoft.com/
- Executive Suite from CIP-Global is an integrated corporate planning, forecasting, consolidation and reporting solution based on Microsoft's SQL Server 2000 and Analysis Services platform.
  http://www.microsoft.com/uk/windowsserversystem/bi/CIP-Global.mspx
- Executive Viewer from Temtec provides users real-time Web access to OLAP databases such as Microsoft Analysis Services and Hyperion Essbase for advanced ad hoc analysis as well as reporting.
  http://www.temtec.com/
- Express and the Oracle OLAP Option—Express is a multidimensional database and application development environment for building OLAP applications. It is MOLAP. OLAP Analytic Workspaces is a porting of the Oracle Express analytic engine to the Oracle RDBMS kernel which now runs as an OLAP virtual machine. Its 2005 market ranking was 7.
  www.oracle.com/olap
- MicroStrategy 8 from MicroStrategy provides facilities for query, reporting and advanced analytical needs. It 205 market ranking was 5.
  http://www.microstrategy.com/
- NovaView from Panorama extends the Microsoft platform that integrates analysis, reporting and performance measurement information into a single solution.
  http://www.panorama.com/
- PowerPlay from Cognos is widely used OLAP software that allows users to analyze large volumes of data with fast response times. Its 2005 market ranking was 3.
- SQL Server 2000 Analysis Services from Microsoft. SQL Server 2000 Analysis Services is the OLAP Services component in SQL Server 7.0. There is a large amount of information available at this site. Its 2005 market ranking was 1.
  http://www.microsoft.com/sql/evaluation/bi/bianalysis.asp
- TM1 from Applix is a multidimensional business planning, reporting and analytics platform. Its 2005 market ranking was 8.

SUMMARY

In this chapter we discussed OLAP terminology and defined OLAP. A comparison of OLAP and OLTP systems has been presented and two sets of characteristics of OLAP systems have been described. The concept of the data cube has been discussed in detail. Two different OLAP implementations, ROLAP and MOLAP, have been briefly discussed. Data cube operations, roll-up, drill-down, slice and dice and pivoting have been described. Some guidelines for successful implementation of OLAP have been suggested and a list of some OLAP software has been presented.

REVIEW QUESTIONS

1. What are dimension, members, measure and fact table? (Section 9.1)
2. What is OLAP? (Section 9.2)
3. List the characteristics of OLAP systems. (Section 9.3)
4. List some of the motivations for using OLAP. (Section 9.4)
5. Explain multidimensional view and a data cube. (Section 9.5)
6. What are the different implementations of a data cube? (Section 9.6)
7. Explain the differences between ROLAP and MOLAP. (Section 9.6)
8. Describe the operations roll-up, drill-down, slice and dice and pivot. (Section 9.7)
9. List some guidelines for implementing OLAP. (Section 9.8)
10. What OLAP software is available in the market? (Section 9.9)

EXERCISES

1. Define OLAP. Give two definitions.
2. What is a data cube? Define the terminology used in it. Use an example to illustrate the use of data cube.
3. List the major differences between OLTP systems and OLAP systems.
4. Discuss the problem of sparsity in a data cube.
5. What is the purpose of OLAP?
6. Discuss the FASMI characteristics of OLAP.
7. Present five major rules or characteristics from Codd's 18 rules.
8. What is the purpose of a data cube?
9. What are ROLAP and MOLAP? Describe the two approaches and list their advantages and disadvantages.
10. Describe the operations roll-up, drill-down and slice and dice.
11. A company is using OLAP to provide monthly summary information about its products and branch sales to the company managers. How many different aggregates would be required to fill a data cube on product, branches and dates if there are 20 products, 10 branches and five years of monthly data?

MULTIPLE CHOICE QUESTIONS

1. Which one of the following is true?
   (a) Dimension is an attribute.
   (b) A measure is numeric attribute of a fact.

(c) A fact table has dimensions and measures.
(d) All of the above.

2. Which one of the following is correct?
(a) OLAP is essentially the same as data warehousing.
(b) ODS is essentially the same as an OLTP system.
(c) ROLAP and MOLAP are the same.
(d) ETL is an essential part of implementing DW.

3. Which of the following is not a use of a data warehouse?
(a) Managers' queries
(b) Customer enquiries
(c) OLAP
(d) Data mining

4. Which one of the following is not true?
(a) OLTP systems are for office workers while OLAP is for managers.
(b) OLTP systems are mission critical while OLAP is not.
(c) OLTP systems process aggregation queries efficiently.
(d) OLTP systems are used for updating information while OLAP systems are not.

5. Which one of the following is included in the guidelines for OLAP?
(a) OLAP implementation must have support of technical staff.
(b) OLAP software should normally be built in-house.
(c) OLAP system must focus on needs of operational staff.
(d) OLAP must be managed both by technical and business professionals.

6. Given the cardinality of tables of players, match, batting and bowling (each 100), which one of the following is the true number of rows in the fact table?
(a) 100
(b) 1000
(c) 10000
(d) 100000000

7. Which one of the following is not an option in data cube implementation?
(a) Find the aggregations that are zero and store them.
(b) Precompute and store all aggregations.
(c) Precompute and store no aggregations.
(d) Precompute and store some aggregations.

8. Which one of the following is correct?
(a) OLTP system usage is mostly repetitive while OLAP is more ad hoc.
(b) OLTP system is application oriented while OLAP is subject oriented.
(c) OLTP system may have thousands of users but OLAP does not.
(d) All of the above.

9. Which one of the following is correct?
(a) OLAP and Business Intelligence are the same.
(b) Dimension and measure are the same.

(c) MOLAP and ROLAP are the same.
(d) None of the above.

10. Which one of the following is true?
    (a) Roll-up is looking at more data than is available in the data cube.
    (b) Drill-down is looking at more detail than is available in the data cube.
    (c) Slice is a subset of a data cube corresponding to a single value of a dimension.
    (d) Dicing involves reducing the number of dimensions in the data cube.

BIBLIOGRAPHY

The papers by Gray et al. and Codd et al. are the classical papers on the data cube and OLAP respectively. They have been highly cited. Gray et al.'s two papers have together been cited more than 500 times. The paper by Harinarayan, Rajaraman and Ullman on implementing data cubes efficiently has been cited more than 200 times.

Recommended Reading for Students

The references from Microsoft, IBM and Oracle are very useful. Much useful information is available at www.olapreport.com.

IBM, DB2 Cube Views: A Primer.
http://www.redbooks.ibm.com/abstracts/sg247002.html (very long, 760 pages)

SQL Server 2000 Resource Kit, Cubes in the Real World, Chapter 22.
http://www.microsoft.com/resources/documentation/sql/2000/all/reskit/en-us/default.mspx (long)

Recommended Reading for Teachers

Data Warehousing and OLAP: A Research-Oriented Bibliography
http://www.ondelette.com/OLAP/dwbib.html#4_3

Agarwal, S., Agrawal, R., Deshpande, P.M., Gupta, A., Naughton, J.F., Ramakrishnan, R., and Sarawagi, S., 1996, On the Computation of Multidimensional Aggregates, *Proc. Int. Conf. on Very Large Data Bases* (*VLDB'96*), Bombay, India, pp. 506–521.

Agrawal, R., Gupta, A., and Sarawagi S., 1997, Modeling Multidimensional Databases, *Proc. 13th ICDE*, pp. 232–243.

Beyer, K. and Ramakrishnan, R., 1999, Bottom-up Computation of Sparse and Iceberg Cubes, *Proc. ACM SIGMOD Int. Conf. on Management of Data*, Philadelphia, Pennsylvania, pp. 359–370.

Codd, E.F., Codd, S.B., and Salley, C.T., 1993, Providing OLAP (on-line analytical processing) to User-analysts: An IT mandate, 1993.
http://dev.hyperion.com/download_files/resource_library/white_papers/providing_olap_to_ user_analysts.pdf.

Gray, J., Bosworth, A., Layman, A., and Pirahesh, H., 1996, Data Cube: A relational aggregation operator generalizing group-by, cross-tab, and sub-totals, *Proc. 12th ICDE*, New Orleans, pp. 152–159.

Gray, J., Chaudhuri, S., Bosworth, A., Layman, A., Reichart, D., Venkatrao, M., Pellow, F., and Pirahesh, H., 1997, Data Cube: A relational aggregation operator generalizing group-by, cross-tab and sub-totals, *Data Mining and Knowledge Discovery*, Vol. 1, No. 1, pp. 29–53.

Gupta, H., Harinarayan, V., Rajaraman, A., and Ullman, J.D., 1997, Index Selection for OLAP, *Proc. 13th ICDE*, Birmingham, UK, pp. 208–219.

Harinarayan, V., Rajaraman, A., and Ullman, J.D., 1996, Implementing Data Cubes Efficiently, *Proc. ACM SIGMOD Int. Conf. on Management of Data*, Montreal, Canada, pp. 205–216.

Russo, M., Ferrari, A., and Webb, C., *Expert Cube Development with Microsoft SQL Server 2008 Analysis Services*, Packt Publishing, pp. 360, 2009.

Sarawagi, S., Agrawal, R., and Megiddo, N., 1998, Discovery Driven Exploration of OLAP Data Cubes, *Proc. Int. Conf. on Extending Database Technology* (*EDBT'98*), pp. 168–182.

Thomsen, E., *OLAP Solutions: Building Multidimensional Information Systems*, Wiley, pp. 696, 2002.

JIM GRAY (1944–2007)—PIONEER IN DATABASES AND OLAP

Gray's work led to the definition of the desired key transaction properties: atomicity, consistency, isolation and durability; and his locking and recovery work demonstrated how to build database systems that exhibit these properties. The work he did on data cubes with a number of colleagues at Microsoft is very important.

Jim Gray worked at IBM and AT&T on database and transaction processing systems. He co-authored the book *Transaction Processing Concepts and Techniques*. He was a Member of the National Academy of Engineering, Fellow of the ACM, a member of the National Research Council's Computer Science and Telecommunications Board, and President's Information Technology Advisor Committee. Jim Gray was awarded the ACM Turing Award in 1998 for contributions to database systems and transaction processing research and technical leadership in system implementation.

Jim Gray mysteriously disappeared at sea in 2007 when he went to scatter his mother's ashes in his yacht.

CASE STUDY 9

Discovering Web Access Patterns and Trends by Applying OLAP and Data Mining Technology on Web Logs*

ABSTRACT

As a confluence of data mining and WWW technologies, it is now possible to perform data mining on web log records collected from the Internet web page access history. The behavior of the web page readers is imprinted in the web server log files. Analyzing and exploring regularities in this behavior can improve system performance, enhance the quality and delivery of Internet information services to the end user, and identify populations of potential customers for electronic commerce. Thus, by observing people using collections of data, data mining can bring considerable contributions to digital library designers.

In a joint effort between the TeleLearning-NCE project on Virtual University and NCE-IRIS project on data mining, we have been developing the knowledge discovery tool, WebLogMiner, for mining web server log files. This paper presents the design of the WebLogMiner, reports the current progress, and outlines the future work in this direction.

1. INTRODUCTION

Web servers register a (web) log entry for every single access they get in which they save the URL requested, the IP address from which the request originated, and a timestamp. With the rapid progress of World-Wide Web (WWW) technology, and the ever growing popularity of the WWW, a huge number of Web access log records are being collected. Popular web sites can see their web log growing by hundreds of megabytes every day. Condensing these colossal files of raw web log data in order to retrieve significant and useful information is a nontrivial task. It is not easy to perform systematic analysis on such a huge amount of data and therefore, most institutions have not been able to make effective use of web access history for server performance enhancement, system design improvement, or customer targeting in electronic commerce. However, many people have realized the potential usage of such data.

Using web log files, studies have been conducted on analyzing system performance, improving system design, understanding the nature of web traffic, and understanding user reaction and motivation [7, 9, 18, 19]. One innovative study has proposed adaptive sites: web sites that improve themselves by learning from user access patterns [14]. While it is encouraging and exciting to see the various potential applications of web log file analysis, it is important to know that the success of such applications depends on what and how much valid and reliable knowledge one can discover from the large raw log data.

Currently, there are more than 30 commercially available applications for web log analysis and

* Zaïane, O.R., M., Xin, and J. Han, Discovering Web access patterns and trends by applying OLAP and data mining technology on Web logs, in *Proc. ADL'98* (Advances in Digital Libraries), Santa Barbara, April, 1998.
{zaiane, cxin, han}@cis.sfu.ca

many more are available free on the Internet (The University of Illinois maintains a list of web access analyzers on a HyperNews page accessible at http://union.ncsa.uiuc.edu/HyperNews/get/www/log-analyzers.html). Regardless of their price, most of them are disliked by their users and considered too slow, inflexible and difficult to maintain [17]. We can even argue that most of these web log analysis tools are very limited in the results they can provide. After reviewing over twenty such analysis tools, including Getstats, Analog, Microsoft Intersé Market Focus, and WebTrends, we found that most of the reports of these tools reveal only frequency count and/or low conceptual descriptive level. While these types of report are valuable, they are certainly not enough. The most frequent reports pre-defined by web log analysis tools are: a summary report of hits and bytes transferred, a list of top requested URLs, a list of top referrers, a list of the most common browsers used, hits per hour/day/week/month reports, hits per domain report, an error report, a directory tree report, etc. Despite the fact that some of the reports can be customized with some of these tools, the majority of the currently available web log analysis tools have rigid pre-defined reports. Most if not all of these web log analysis tools have limitations with regard to the size of the web log files, whether it is physical in size or practical in time because of the low speed of the analysis. To reduce the size of the log files to analyze, web log analysis tools make assumptions in order to filter out some data like failed requests (i.e. errors) or page graphic requests, or to round off the log entries by combining similar requests. Different assumptions are made for each of the web log analysis tools resulting in the prospect of different statistics with the same log file. It has been reported in [2] that the analysis of the same web log with different web log analysis tools ended up with different statistic results.

Overall, the current web log analysis tools are still limited in their performance, the comprehensiveness and depth of their analyses, and the validity and reliability of their results.

The recent progress and development of data mining and data warehousing has made available powerful data mining and data warehousing systems [6, 4]. Many successful data mining systems can handle very large data files like the web log files. However, we have not seen a systematic study and development of data warehousing and mining systems for mining knowledge from web access log records. Recent research and development of data mining technology have promoted some studies on efficient data mining for user access patterns in distributed systems, referred to as mining path traversal patterns [5]. Understanding user access patterns in a web site using these mining techniques not only helps improve web system design, but also leads to wise marketing decisions (e.g. putting advertisements in proper places, classifying users, etc.). However, as mentioned in [4], mining path traversal patterns is still in its infancy.

In this paper we propose to use data mining and data warehousing techniques to analyze web log records. Based on our experience on the development of relational database and data warehouse-based data mining system, DBMiner [10], by the Intelligent Database Systems Research Laboratory at Simon Fraser University, and on the development of a Web-based collaborative teaching and learning environment, Virtual-U, by the Virtual-U Research Laboratory at Simon Fraser University, we jointly study the challenging issues on data mining in web log databases, and propose the WebLogMiner system which performs data mining on web log records collected from web page access history.

The remainder of this paper is organized as follows. In Section 2, we describe the design of a data mining system for web log records. Our implementation efforts and experiments are presented in Section 3. Finally, Section 4 summarizes our conclusions and future enhancements.

2. DESIGN OF A WEB LOG MINER

The most commonly used method to evaluate access to web resources or user interest in resources is by counting page accesses or "hits". As we will see, this is not sufficient and often not correct. Web server log files of current common web servers contain insufficient data upon which thorough analysis can be performed. However, they contain useful data from which a well designed data mining system can discover beneficial information.

Web server log files customarily contain: the domain name (or IP address) of the request; the user name of the user who generated the request (if applicable); the date and time of the request; the method of the request (GET or POST); the name of the file requested; the result of the request (success, failure, error, etc.); the size of the data sent back; the URL of the referring page; and the identification of the client agent.

A log entry is automatically added each time a request for a resource reaches the web server. While this may reflect the actual use of the resources on a site, it does not record reader behaviors like frequent backtracking or frequent reloading of the same resource when the resource is cached by the browser or a proxy. A cache would store resources and hand them to a client requesting them without leaving a trace in the log files. Frequent backtracking and reload may suggest a deficient design of the site navigation, which can be very informative for a site designer, however, this cannot be measured solely from the server logs. Many have suggested other means of data gathering like client-site log files collected by the browser, or a Java Applet. While these techniques solve problems created by page backtracking and proxy caching, they necessitate the user's collaboration, which is not always available. Until the web server log files are enriched with more collected data, our data mining process is solely based on the information currently gathered by the web servers.

Researchers working on web log analysis discredit the use of web access counts as indicators of user interest or measures of the interestingness of a web page. Indeed as described by Fuller and deGraaff in [7], access counts, when considered alone, can be misleading metrics. For example, if one must go through a sequence of documents to reach a desired document, all documents leading to the final one get their counters incremented even if the user is not interested in them at all. The access counters alone do not account for the user's ability to access the information and the appropriateness of the information to the user. Nonetheless, when access counts are used in conjunction with other metrics, they can help infer interesting findings.

Despite the impoverished state of the server logs, much useful information can be discovered when using data mining techniques. The date and time collected for each successive request can give interesting clues regarding the user interest by evaluating the time spent by users on each resource, and can allow time sequence analysis using different time values: minutes, hours, days, months, years, etc. The domain name collected can allow practical classification of the resources based on countries or type of domain (commercial, education, government, etc.). The sequence of requests can help predict next requests or popular requests for given days, and thus help improve the network traffic by caching those resources, or by allowing clustering of resources in a site based on user motivation. Notwithstanding, the server logs cannot be used as recorded by the web server and need to be filtered before data mining can be applied.

In the WebLogMiner project, the data collected in the web logs goes through four stages. In the first stage, the data is filtered to remove irrelevant information and a relational database is created containing the meaningful remaining data. This database facilitates information extraction and data summarization based on individual attributes like user, resource, user's locality, day, etc. In the second stage, a data cube is constructed using the available dimensions. Online analytical processing (OLAP) is used in the third stage to drill-down, roll-up, slice and dice in the web log data cube. Finally, in the fourth stage, data mining techniques are put to use with the data cube to predict, classify, and discover interesting correlations.

2.1 Database Construction from Server Log Files: Data Cleaning and Data Transformation

The data filtering step is a typical step adopted by many web log analysis tools. While typically web log analysis tools may filter out requests for page graphics (as well as sound and video) in order to concentrate on data pertaining to actual page hits, we tend to keep these entries because we believe they can give us interesting clues regarding web site structure, traffic performance, as well as user motivation. Moreover, one user action can generate multiple server requests, and some of them are requests for page media. Some of these requests are important to deduce the intended action of the user. Another typical cleaning process consists of eliminating log entries generated by web agents like web spiders, indexers, link checkers, or other intelligent agents that pre-fetch pages for caching purposes. We chose not to screen out these requests generated by the web agents. It is often interesting and useful to analyze web agents' behaviour on a site and compare the traffic generated by these automated agents with the rest of the traffic. The data filtering we adopted mainly transforms the data into a more meaningful representation. We tend to consider most of the data are relevant and eliminate a minimal amount of data.

There are two types of data cleaning and data transformation, one that does not necessitate knowledge about the resources at the site and one that does. Cleaning the date and time field of the log entry, for instance, does not need any knowledge about the site itself. The date and time field is simply restructured in a set of fields to specify the day, month, year, hour, minute and seconds. Filtering out server requests that failed or transforming server error codes is also generic. Transforming IP addresses to domain names is independent from the site content as well. However, associating a server request or a set of server requests to an intended action or event clearly necessitates knowledge about the site structure. Moreover, different dynamically generated web pages can be the result of a single script, thus, an identical server request. Knowledge about the parameters provided to the script to generate the dynamic page, or knowledge about the necessary sequence in the request history before a request for a script, can be essential in disambiguating a server request and associating it to an event.

Metadata provided by the site designers is required for the knowledge-based data cleaning and transformation. The metadata consists of a mapping table between a server request (URL) with parameters, if available, or a sequence of requests (URLs) and an event with a representative URL. The transformation process replaces the request sequence by the representative URL and adds the event tag to the log entry.

After the cleaning and transformation of the web log entries, the web log is loaded into a relational database and new implicit data, like the time spent by event, is calculated. The time spent by event (or page) is approximated from the difference between the time the page for the current event is requested and the time the next page is requested with an upper-bound threshold for the case when the user does not come back to the same server. This notion of time spent is an approximation of the actual perusal duration since it intrinsically includes the time for network transfer, navigation inside the page, etc. It may seem a biased metric but can be very useful comparing pages with the same design.

2.2 Multi-dimensional Web Log Data Cube Construction and Manipulation

After the data has been cleaned and transformed, a multi-dimensional array structure, called a data cube, is built to aggregate the hit counts. The multi-dimensional data cube has numerous dimensions (i.e. generally more than 3), each dimension representing a field with all possible values described by attributes. For example, the dimension URL may have the attributes: server domain, directory, file name and extension, or the dimension time may have the attributes: second, minute, hour, day, week, month, quarter, year. Attributes of a dimension may be related by partial order indicating a hierarchical relationship among the dimension attributes. Hierarchies are generally pre-defined, but in some cases partitioning the dimension in ranges automatically generates these hierarchies. For example the dimension file size can be partitioned into size ranges and later grouped into categories like: *tiny, small, medium, large, huge.*

An n-dimensional data cube $C[A_1, \ldots, A_n]$, is an n-D database where $A_1, \ldots, A_n$ are n dimensions. Each dimension of the cube, A_i, represents an attribute and contains $|A_i| + 1$ rows where $|A_i|$ is the number of distinct values in the dimension A_i. The first $|A_i|$ rows are *data rows*. Each distinct value of A_i takes one data row. The last row, the *sum* row, is used to store the summation of the counts of the corresponding columns of the above rows. A `data cell` in the cube, $C[a_1, i_1, \ldots, a_n, i_n]$, stores the count of the corresponding (generalized) tuple of the initial relation, $r(A_1 = a_1,i_1, \ldots, A_n = a_n,i_n, count)$. In the case of the web log cube, count is for resource hits. A sum cell in the cube, such as $C[sum, a_2,i_2, \ldots, a_n,i_n]$, where *sum* is often represented by * or a keyword `all`, stores sum_1, the *sum of the counts* of the generalized tuples which share the same values for all the second to the *n*th columns, i.e., $r(*, A_2 = a_2,i_2, \ldots, A_n = a_n,i_n, sum_1)$. Conceptually, a data cube can be viewed as a lattice of *cuboids*. The *n-D space* (i.e., *base cuboid*) consists of all data cells (i.e, no *'s in any dimension). The $(n-1)$-*D space* consists of all the cells with a single * in any dimension, such as $r(*, a_2,i_2, \ldots, a_n,i_n, sum_1)$, and so on. Finally, the *0-D space* consists of one cell with n*'s in all the n dimensions, i.e., $r(*, *, \ldots,*, sum_n)$.

A 3-D data cube is shown in Figure 1. Notice since a large number of the cells in the cube can be empty, to handle sparse cubes efficiently, sparse matrix technology should be applied in data cube construction [13, 20]. There have been many methods proposed recently for efficient computation of data cubes, such as [1, 20], which is beyond the scope of this study.

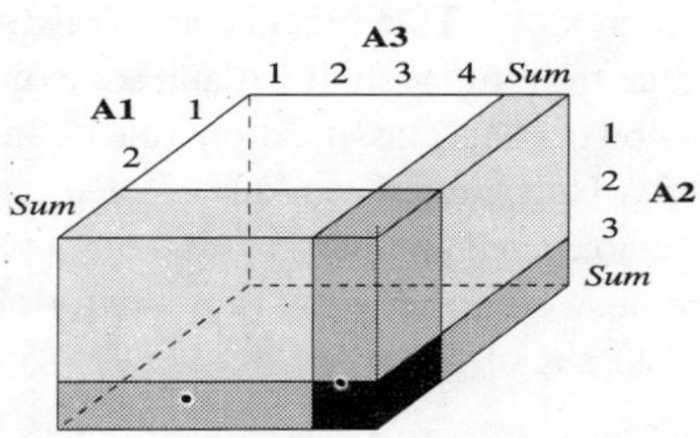

Figure 1: A 3-D data cube with summary layers.

Examples of dimensions in our web log data cube include the following. Notice that each dimension is defined on a concept hierarchy to facilitate generalization and specialization along the dimension.

- URL of the resource, where the concept hierarchy used is defined on the server directory structure;
- type of resource, defined on a pre-built file type hierarchy;
- size of the resource, defined on a range hierarchy;
- time at which the resource was requested, defined on a time hierarchy;
- time spent in page, defined on a range hierarchy of seconds;
- domain name from which the request originated, defined on a pre-built domain hierarchy;
- agent that made the request, defined on a pre-built hierarchy of known web agents and browsers;
- user, defined on a pre-built user hierarchy;
- server status, defined on an error code hierarchy.

The multi-dimensional structure of the data cube provides remarkable flexibility to manipulate the data and view it from different perspectives. The sum cells allow quick summarization at different levels of the concept hierarchies defined on the dimension attributes.

Building this web log data cube allows the application of OLAP (On-Line Analytical Processing) operations, such as drill-down, roll-up, slice and dice, to view and analyze the web log data from different angles, derive ratios and compute measures across many dimensions.

The drill-down operation navigates from generalized data to more details, or specializes an attribute by stepping down the aggregation hierarchy. For example, presenting the number of hits grouped by day from the number of hits grouped by month, is a drill-down along the hierarchy time. The roll-up is the reverse operation of the drill-down. It navigates from specific to general, or generalizes an attribute by climbing up the aggregation hierarchy. For example, the *aggregation of total requests from group-by organization by day to group-by country by day* is a roll-up by summarization over the server domain hierarchy.

The slice operation defines a sub-cube by performing a selection on one dimension by selecting one or some values in a dimension. It is a literal cut of a slice (or slices) on the same dimension. For example, the selection domain = ".edu" on the dimension server domain, is a slice on the educational internet domain. The dice operation is a set of consecutive slice operations on several dimensions. It defines a sub-cube by performing selections on several dimensions. For example, a sub-cube can be derived by dicing the web log data cube on four dimensions using the following clause, country = "Canada" and month = 11/97 and agent = "Mozila" and file type = "cgi". These OLAP operations assist in interactive and quick retrieval of 2D and 3D cross-tables and chartable data from the web log data cube which allow quick querying and analysis of very large web access history files.

2.3 Data Mining on Web Log Data Cube and Web Log Database

On-line analytical processing and the data cube structure offer analytical modeling capabilities, including a calculation engine for deriving various statistics, and a highly interactive and powerful data retrieval and analysis environment. It is possible to use this environment to discover implicit knowledge in the web log database by implementing data mining techniques on the web log data cube. The knowledge that can be discovered is represented in the form of rules, tables, charts, graphs, and other visual presentation forms for characterizing, comparing, associating, predicting, or classifying data from the web access log. These data mining functions are briefly explained as follows.

Data characterization: This function characterizes data in the web log. It consists of finding rules that summarize general characteristics of a set of user-defined data. The rules are generated from a generalized data cube produced using the web log data cube and the OLAP operations. For example, the traffic on a web server for a given type of media in a particular time of day can be summarized by a characteristic rule.

Class comparison: Comparison plays the role of examining the Web log data to discover discriminant rules, which summarize the features that distinguish the data in the target class from that in the contrasting classes. For example, to compare requests from two different web browsers (or two web robots), a discriminant rule summarizes the features that discriminate one agent from the other, like time, file type, etc.

Association: This function mines association rules (in the form of "$A_1 \wedge \ldots \wedge A_i \ldots B_1 \wedge \ldots \wedge B_j$") at multiple-levels of abstraction. For example, one may discover the patterns with accesses to different resources occurring consistently together, or accesses from a particular place occurring at regular times.

Prediction: Prediction involves predicting values or value distributions of an attribute of interest based on its relevance to other attributes. Both relevance analysis and predictive model construction need statistical analysis techniques. This helps prediction of possible values of missing data or the value distribution of certain attributes in a set of objects. For example, the access to a new resource on a given day can be predicted based on accesses to similar old resources on similar days, or the traffic for a given page can be predicted based on the distribution of traffic on other pages in the server directory.

Classification: Classification consists of building a model for each given class based upon features in the web log data and generating classification rules from such models. The models are constructed by analyzing a training web log data set whose class label is known. The classification rules can be used to develop a better understanding of each class in the web log database, and perhaps restructure a web site or customize answers to requests (i.e. quality of service) based on classes of requests.

Time-series analysis: Time-series analysis is to analyze data collected along time sequences to discover time-related interesting patterns, characteristics, trends, similarities, differences, periodicity, and so on. It may also involve attribute relevance analysis, model construction, classification, and prediction. Thus time-series analysis explores most of the techniques developed in the above (data mining functions) plus its own techniques for time-sequence search, similarity analysis, periodicity analysis, and so on. For example, time-series analysis of the web log data may disclose the patterns and trends of web page accesses in the last year and suggest the improvement of services of the web server.

Since most data mining functions other than time-series analysis share many commonalities with the work in traditional data mining systems, such as IBM Intelligent Miner (Quest) [1], Silicon Graphics Mine Set [3], DBMiner [10], this paper will not discuss the application of these data mining functions to web log mining in detail. Our focus will be on time-series analysis because web log records are highly time-related, and the goals of data mining with web log records are largely aimed at mining time-related patterns.

Our time-series analysis includes *network traffic analysis, event sequence and user behavior pattern analysis, transition analysis, and trend analysis.* With the availability of data cube technology, such analysis can be performed systematically in the sense that analysis can be performed on multiple dimensions and at multiple granularities. Moreover, there are major differences in time-series analysis of web log mining in comparison with other traditional data mining processes.

We take trend analysis as an example to illustrate such a process. In the analysis of the trend of web accessing in the Virtual-U environment, we would like to see how a user changes his/her web navigation behavior and focuses his/her attention to interested topics. The analysis takes the following steps.

1. **Data/user selection.** Since a Virtual-U user accesses the Virtual-U web pages regularly, those who access the Virtual-U web page only occasionally for curiosity will not be included in the analysis. That is, access regularity will be taken as a standard (or threshold) to filter out scattered accesses.

2. **Cycle detection.** For web accessing, a regular Virtual-U user usually starts a Virtual-U session, traverses a set of pages with possible inputs to some pages, and then leaves the Virtual-U sessions for a while or for a long time before coming back to start another session. Thus the starting or restarting of a Virtual-U web page, followed by a sequence of other local web page accesses forms a cycle. A data mining task needs to detect such cycles effectively for meaningful analysis. We have developed techniques on how to find such cycles and detect periodicity efficiently using data cube structure and OLAP techniques [8].

3. **Trend analysis.** With the accumulation of the discovered sequences and periods, analysis can be performed on them to discover patterns and trends with different interests. One kind of pattern which can be easily discovered is the repetition of similar web page accesses. For the same set of web pages, many users will access such pages repeatedly in a similar pattern. Number of accesses will be associated with each page node to register such access frequency.

Moreover, with data cube technology, one can rollup the access history to get general web page accessing statistics. Such access statistics form a group of web access trees/graphs. These access trees demonstrate some clear trend along the time axis: taking the structural complexity of the access tree as a focus, one can easily see the trend is the gradually reduced structural complexity of the access tree, which shows more experienced users are more focused on specific topics with reduced number of random searches to other scattered topics.

Notice with the data cube technology, such a trend can be demonstrated with different time granularities, such as by week, bi-week, month, bi-month, quarter, etc. by simply clicking the button of time axis. However, the trend will be "discovered" by a human with the help of visualization tools instead of a fully automated process. The detailed process of this web page access trend analysis is presented in Example 3.5.

3. EXPERIMENTS WITH THE WEB LOG MINER DESIGN

Based on our design elaborated in Section 2, experiments have been carried out to analyze a server-based online teaching/learning system, Virtual-U, which is developed by the Virtual-U Research Laboratory at Simon Fraser University. The system enables customized design, delivery, and enhancement of education and training courses delivered over the World Wide Web (WWW). Virtual-U is a collaborative teaching and learning environment which accumulates large collections of multimedia resources.

Virtual-U consists of six different major components as follows: (1) V-Groups which is a web-based conferencing system, (2) course structuring tools, (3) system administration tools, (4) a grade book, (5) upload and submission tools, and (6) a virtual workspace.

V-Groups is a predominant component in which the on-line discussion and collaboration take place. It holds and organizes sets of conferences for different courses. The instructors and students read and write messages in conferences. This amasses a large number of messages and generates heavy access traffic. Thus, we will base our examples in this paper primarily on V-Groups events.

SFU-based Virtual-U server currently hosts different fieldsites ranging from academic institutions to industries across Canada.

The goal of the analysis of the server log files is to understand how the system is used in terms of the usage patterns and user behavior patterns, which will give us insights of the system design, user interface design, and the characteristics of different user populations.

3.1 Data Cleaning and Transformation

Before we could feed the information from the log file into a relational database, we had to first clean and transform the raw data.

The original log file entries include the following information: the domain name (or IP address) of the request, the user login id, the date and time of the request, the method of the request (GET or POST), the location and the name of the file requested, the result of the request (success, failure, error, etc.) and the size of the data transferred. An example entry is shown as in Table 1, where the user_id is masked by a faked id, such as user_1.

There were two processes we went through in the data cleaning and transformation. First, all entries of the log files were mapped one on one into a relational database. In other words, no information was lost in this process. Entries that recorded server request failures, authentication failures, page graphics, etc. were all kept in the database. We believe all entries have potential useful information depending on the purpose of one's analysis and the kind of questions one wants to answer. Once we get the maximum information into the relational database, we can always draw the relevant information and leave out the rest according to the analysis needs.

The transformed data entries had one additional field, the *fieldsite*, indicating which one of the seven fieldsites hosted by Virtual-U server the request was from. This field was derived from the path of the file requested. Example entries are given as shown in Table 2.

The second process was to infer user actions (events) from patterns of requests. In this process, we combined, eliminated and/or directly mapped the same set of log entries and translated them into a set of user actions. As Virtual-U is an interactive environment, most pages were generated dynamically by a user's requests of certain cgi scripts. After a page was generated, there were a number of options available for the user to choose from. Once the user made his/her choice, new cgi script(s) were called and a new page was generated possibly with another set of options. To infer user actions from the requested cgi scripts and corresponding parameters and then tag them with plain English was the fundamental step for further in-depth analysis of user behavior.

There were several general problems associated with this data process which would occur in the similar interactive online system. These problems and their solutions are described as follows.

First, extraneous information was mixed with useful information. Log entries that recorded the request failures, page graphics, etc. were irrelevant to our current analysis. To solve this problem we simply defined those entries and then eliminated them.

Second, multiple server requests were generated by the same user action. Two cases were associated with this problem. First, the user action could be identified by a single entry of the entry set. In this case, we simply tagged that entry and discarded the

Table 1: A fragment of the original log file

vanc01m03-115.bctel.ca - user1 [10/Apr/1997:19:06:44 -0700]	"GET /SFU/cgi-bin/VG/dspcnf.cgi?ci=40050&fp=MLIST&query= HTTP/1.0" 200 3927
cnts4p14.uwaterloo.ca - user2 [10/Apr/1997:19:09:43 -0700]	"GET /Waterloo/cgi-bin/UI/UI_welcome.cgi HTTP/1.0" 200 1288

Table 2: OLAP analysis of Web log database

requester IP address	user_id	date	time	request	fieldsite	files requested	result	size received
vanc01m03-115.bctel.ca	user1	10/Apr/1997	19:06:21	GET	SFU	/SFU/cgi-bin/VG/vgstart.cgi	200	386
vanc01m03-115.bctel.ca	user1	10/Apr/1997	19:06:34	GET	SFU	/SFU/cgi-bin/VG/VGTP_ListConfs.cgi?st=all_joined	200	9294
cnts4p14.uwaterloo.ca	user2	10/Apr/1997	19:09:43	GET	Waterloo	/Waterloo/cgi-bin/UI/UI_welcome.cgi	200	1288

rest. Second, the user action had to be identified by multiple entries of the entry set. In this case, we had to infer the user action by processing multiple entries.

Third, multiple user actions may generate the same server request. For example, in the case where a user adds a new message to a conference, or previews a to-be-added message, or cancels addition of a message, all the three actions call the same cgi script (VG addmsg.cgi) and generate the same entries in the log except the time stamps. Fortunately, for most cases like these in this study, we managed to solve the problem by examining the context in which the entry occurred. In the case we could not identify clearly, we translated the entry with multiple tags. In association with such problems, a suggestion made to the system developers is to use different scripts for different user actions or use the same script with parameter(s) signed with different values.

Fourth, local activities (browser functions, such as backing and forwarding) were not recorded. While there is no easy and quick solution to this problem at the present stage, certain backtracking can be inferred in some cases from the user behavior sequences. Frequent backtracking in the same context can indicate certain user interface problem(s).

After the second process, the transformed data entries had one more attribute—user action (event). Example entries are given as in Table 3.

One point of interest was the duration of the event. It gives additional information on the interaction between events. However, time-based metrics are subject to a fair amount of noise because of reasons such as time spent on file transfer, increasing use of offline browsers and unknown user behavior between events [18]. Nevertheless, when such metrics are used selectively on certain events and with valid sample size, they can still reveal very useful information [15].

To get the duration of the event, we used the time stamp of the current entry as the (event) *on-time* and the time stamp of the next entry as the (event) *off-time*.

3.2 Multi-dimensional Data Cube Construction and Manipulation

After data cleaning and transformation, a relational database was constructed with the processed data, and a multi-dimensional data cube was constructed. In addition to the dimensions given in Section 2.2, two more dimensions were added to the data cube for this experiment: one is the *fieldsite* dimension defined on a pre-built education and industry institution hierarchy, and the other is the event dimension defined by a set of user actions that could take place in the system environment, organized in a partial order.

Once the multi-dimensional data cube is constructed, various OLAP techniques are applied to provide further insight to any target data set from different perspectives and at different conceptual levels. This counts as a summarization function in data mining as well.

Some typical summarization includes the following:

- *request summary* to give request statistics for all pages/files;
- *domain summary* to give request statistics from different domains;
- *event summary* to give statistics of the occurring of all events;
- *session summary* to give statistics of session;
- *bandwidth summary* to give statistics of generated network traffic;
- *error summary* to give statistics of all the error messages;

Table 3: A fragment of the log file with user action added

...	fieldsite	files requested	user action	result	size received
...	SFU	/SFU/cgi-bin/VG/vgstart.cgi	start V-Groups	200	386
...	SFU	/SFU/cgi-bin/VG/VGTP_ListConfs.cgi?st=all_joined	list all joined conferences	200	9294
...	Waterloo	UI_welcome.cgi	load welcome page	200	1288

- *referring organization summary* to give statistics of where the users were from;
- *browser summary* to give statistics of the use of different browsers.

Such summaries could be applied to any given user population, conference(s), course(s) or fieldsite(s) and for any given length of time, hourly, daily, weekly, monthly and semesterwise. From the relational database and data warehouse point of view, these summaries correspond to *group-bys* on different dimensions, multiple abstraction levels, and their arbitrary combinations. Dicing, slicing, and drilling can be performed on the Web log data cube to examine request statistics, network traffic information, user information, etc. conveniently. From such results, we could gain insights of the system usability, accessibility and general perfor-mance as well as insights of the behavior characteristics of different user populations.

Example 3.1 (OLAP analysis of Web log)

Web log databases as shown in Figure 2 can be analyzed by OLAP analysis techniques.

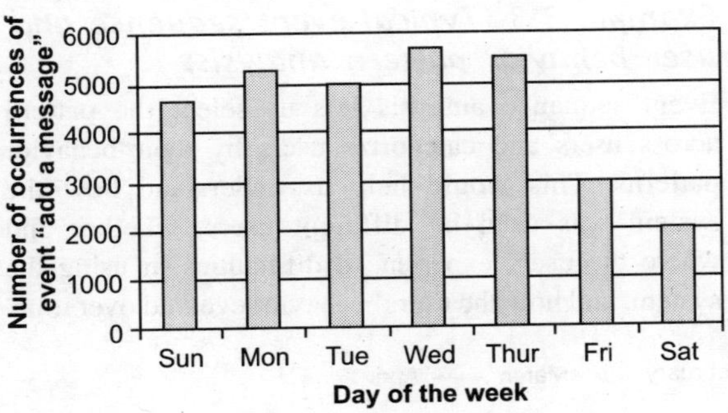

Figure 2: OLAP analysis of Web log database.

Here we illustrate a simple yet typical example of summarization using OLAP techniques. For example, we were interested in finding out how many new messages were created on each day of the week over a whole semester for a particular fieldsite. In this analysis, we chose a particular value of interest (i.e. slice) on the *event* dimension, example "Use V-Groups", then focused on a particular level (i.e. drill-down in the same dimension) ("add a message"), and chose a particular value of interest on the *fieldsite* dimension, we then projected the intersect of both dimensions on the *time* dimension to locate the cells we wanted. Figure 3 shows the result. Using OLAP techniques, such results can be generated interactively using the data cube structure.

From Figure 2 one can see the distribution of messages created on days of the week. When similar analyses are performed on other events and/or other fieldsites using the same time dimension, we could do interesting comparisons among the results to gain further knowledge of the analysis domain.

From these summarizations one can ask questions such as:

- Which components or features are the most/ least used?
- Which events are the most frequent?
- What is the distribution of network traffic over time (hour of the day, day of the week, month of the year, etc.)?
- What is the user distribution over different domain areas?
- Are there and what are the differences in access for users from different geographic areas?

For further analysis, more questions need to be answered, such as:

- In what context are the components or features used?

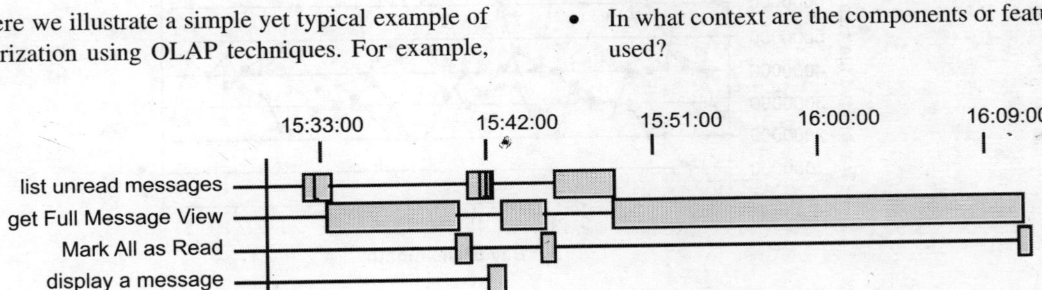

Figure 3: Usage pattern.

- What are the typical event sequences?
- Are there any general behavior patterns across all users, and what are they?
- What are the differences in usage and behavior for different user populations?
- Whether user behaviors change over time, and how?

Some of these questions can be answered by OLAP analysis. Others, however, will require more sophisticated data mining techniques, which will be examined in the following subsection.

3.3 Data Mining on Web Log Data Cube and Web Log Database

As discussed in Section 2, the WebLogMiner can perform various kinds of data mining tasks, including summarization, comparison, association, classification, prediction and time-series analysis. The first several kinds of data mining tasks have been discussed in our previous data mining research papers, such as [10, 11, 12]. Due to the limited space, the examples analyzed here are all related to the last data mining task: *time-series analysis*.

Time-series analysis is also the most important data mining task in the Web log analysis because all Web log records register time stamps, and most of the analyses are focused on time-related Web access behaviors.

Example 3.2 (Web traffic analysis)

Web traffic analysis identifies the network load and traffic patterns in relevance to time. It helps us monitor system performance, overlook the trends of the amount of users activities, and determine the optimal server size. This analysis is performed by generalization of some attributes, such as traffic volume, along the time dimension. Drilling can be performed along the time dimension to obtain more detailed charts of the traffic fluctuation patterns along time.

Figure 4 shows the network traffic generated by a particular fieldsite over a four month period (January to April 1997). The chart in Figure 4 shows that the traffic had a general increasing trend over the four months, while within each month there are cycles of peaks and valleys indicating the traffic generally went up at the beginning of the week (Sunday) and during the week days (Monday to Thursday) and came down during the weekend (Friday and Saturday), as expected by our own experience.

Example 3.3 (Typical event sequence and user behavior pattern analysis)

Event sequence analysis lets us select the pattern across users and categorize users by their behavior patterns. This would help us understand how the system was used by different users, whether and where the users experienced difficulties in using the system, and how the users' behavior evolved over time.

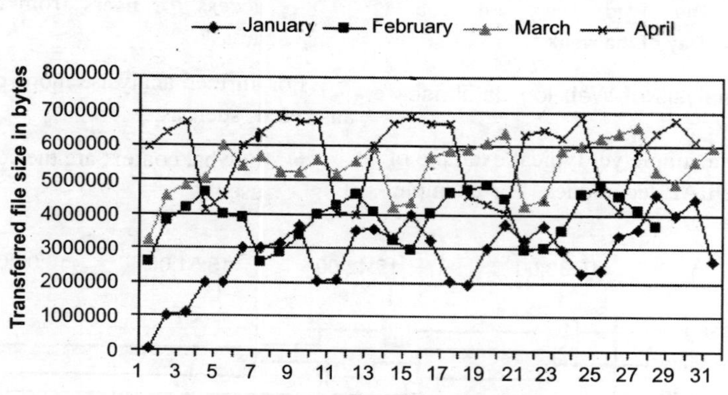

Figure 4: Network traffic generated by a particular fieldsite over a four month period.

Event sequence can be plotted into timeline charts as outputs or be used for further analysis. From our analysis, we have formed different behavior patterns emerging from different groups. Figure 3 shows a typical behavior pattern for one use group. A set of events is listed on the left-hand side.

The time intervals on the top are in the format of hour:minute:second. The bars running from left to right indicate the event sequence. The length of the bar indicates the duration of the event.

One phenomenon we have discovered is that at the beginning of a course the users tended to explore many different system features. However, they become more and more focused over time.

While this phenomenon is intuitively understandable, it is interesting to find out what are the features that are consistently being used over time, what are the features that are being less used or not being used at all over time, and what are features that are being used more over time.

By incorporation of data cube techniques, all these features can be plotted into the time-related data flow charts and be examined in the context of multiple dimensions and multiple granularities. For example, usage patterns can be analyzed in the data cube not only based on one particular message view, but also based on a repeated time framework. Drill-down and roll-up can be performed in such a framework to demonstrate regularities with different time attributes.

Example 3.4 (Transition analysis)

Transition analysis is similar to time-related association analysis, such as sequence analysis, studied in the literature [16]. Figure 5 shows a transition metric for a given group of users over a certain period of time, which indicates the probability one event follows another. This probability is calculated based on the event frequency and event sequence. For example, the probability that one would re-start V-Groups after listing all messages is 0.2 for this group of users. This actually indicates a problem in the navigation which was not foreseen by V-Groups designers. Such metrics can be used to do further Markov Chain analysis which may give us insights to the access paths, starting and ending points, etc.

Example 3.5 (Trend analysis)

Trend analysis helps us examine the patterns between key events and tells us what the trend is between the two events. This allows us to detect whether there is any consistent pattern and whether an established pattern changes over time.

Figure 6 shows the event trees of a particular user's behavior from the first to the fourth month of using the system. All branches were started with one key event, "start V-Groups" and ended with the other key event, "display a message". The numbers in the parentheses are frequencies. The figures indicate that while the event patterns diverged frequently in the first month, they became much more convergent over time. The figure indicates a strong event pattern of "start V-Groups", "list conferences", "list unread messages" and "display a message".

4. DISCUSSION AND CONCLUSIONS

The World-Wide Web is continuously growing and "collecting" all kinds of resources, text, multimedia, applications, etc. Despite the anarchy in which it is growing, the Web is one of the biggest repositories ever built. Analyzing the web access logs of different web sites can help understand the user behavior and the Web structure, thereby improving the design of this colossal collection of resources. Therefore, it is important to build tools to analyze the web access patterns.

Currently available web log analysis tools report interesting statistics, but are limited by the huge sizes of the log files continuously expanding, the type of data collected in the web logs, and the techniques used to analyze this data. Consequently, it is imperative to design a good web log analysis tool that would overcome the current limitations of the web log and recommend directives for new web log standards that would help better analyze the web access trends and discover useful knowledge from the access records.

In this paper, we have outlined the design of our system `WebLogMiner`, which benefits from OLAP and data mining techniques, and multi-dimensional data cube, to interactively extract implicit knowledge

	display VU campus map	start V-Groups	List conf	list unread messages	load VU Welcome Page	display a message	initiate Add a message	list all messages	preview /add/cancel a message	Total
display VU campus map		1.000								1.000
start V-Groups			.988	.012						1.000
List conference				.823	.177					1.000
list unread messages		.150		.017	.017	.732	.042	.042		1.000
load VU Welcome Page	1.000									1.000
display a message		.304		.467	.163	.012			.054	1.000
initiate Add a message									1.000	1.000
list all messages		.200		.200	.200	.400				1.000
preview /add/cancel a message				.382	.048	.048			.524	1.000

Figure 5: A transition metrics.

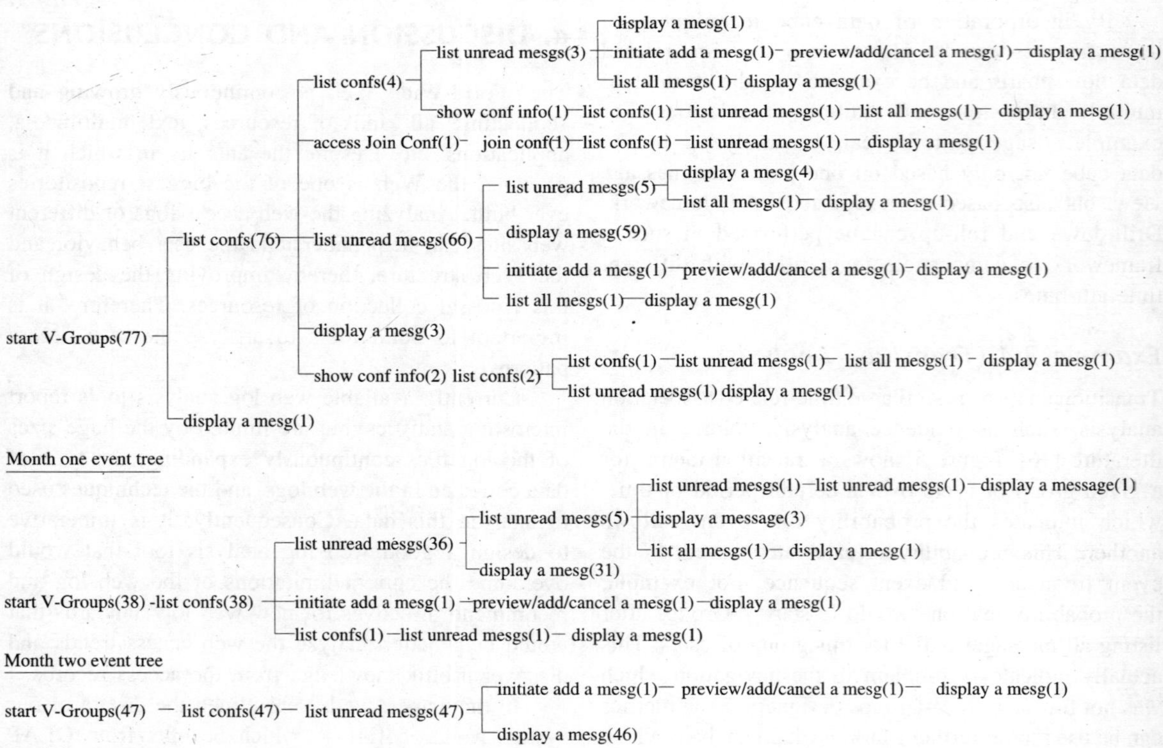

Figure 6: Event trees of months one to four.

from very large web log files. Concrete examples using these techniques were given for time-series pattern analysis. The major strengths of this design are its scalability, interactivity, and the variety and flexibility of the analyses possible to perform. Despite these strengths, the discovery potential of such a design is still limited due to the current impoverished web log files.

The web log file structure is still the same for most of the web servers as the structure of the first NCSA httpd server log. It is evident now that web servers should collect and enter more information in their logs. It is urgent to study specific needs in web access pattern analysis and recommend a new structure for web access logs. This new structure would significantly simplify the data cleaning and data transformation stage. Our experience showed us that the data cleaning and data transformation step is not only crucial, but also is the most time consuming. A good data filtering process needs metadata provided by web site designers to help interpret the access records and make effective assumption with regard to filtering irrelevant records and mapping the others to significant labels. We think there is a need for a web site metadata specification standard that would help designers to specify the structure of the resources delivered, and the web log analysis tools to interpret the web log entries. Such metadata specification standards could lead to the construction of generic tools for data cleaning and data transformation.

We are still in the implementation process of a `WebLogMiner` prototype. We plan to integrate the technology developed for our data mining system `DBMiner`[10] in `WebLogMiner` and use DBMiner's sparse data cube capabilities, and develop additional modules for time-series pattern analysis. Due to the important size and the ever exploding nature of the web log files, the construction of the multi-dimensional data cube necessary for the on-line analytical processing and knowledge discovery, is very demanding and time consuming. To reduce the data cube construction time, we plan to build a bridge between the web server and a data cube that would propagate access information directly to the aggregated cells of the data cube. The incrementally updated web log data cube would allow real time web access analysis and data mining.

Further development and experiments with `WebLogMiner` will be reported in the future.

REFERENCES

[1] S. Agarwal, R. Agrawal, P.M. Deshpande, A. Gupta, J.F. Naughton, R. Ramakrishnan, and S. Sarawagi. On the computation of multidimensional aggregates. In *Proc. 1996 Int. Conf. Very Large Data Bases*, pages 506–521, Bombay, India, Sept. 1996.

[2] D. Backman and J. Rubbin. Web log analysis: Finding a recipe for success. In *http://techweb.comp.com/nc/811/811cn2.html,* 1997.

[3] C. Brunk, J. Kelly, and R. Kohavi. MineSet: An integrated system for data mining. In *Proc. 3rd Int. Conf. Knowledge Discovery and Data Mining* (*KDD'97*), pages 135–138, Newport Beach, California, August 1997.

[4] M.S. Chen, J. Han, and P.S. Yu. Data mining: An overview from a database perspective. *IEEE Trans. Knowledge and Data Engineering,* 8:866–883, 1996.

[5] M.S. Chen, J.S. Park, and P.S. Yu. Data mining for path traversal patterns in a web environment. In *Proc. 16th Int'l Conf. Distributed Computing Systems*, pages 385–392, May 1996.

[6] U.M. Fayyad, G. Piatetsky-Shapiro, P. Smyth, and R. Uthurusamy. *Advances in Knowledge Discovery and Data Mining*. AAAI/MIT Press, 1996.

[7] R. Fuller and J. de Graaff. Measuring user motivation from server log files. In *http://www.microsoft.com/usability/webconf/fuller/ fuller.htm,* 1997.

[8] W. Gong. Periodic pattern search in time-related data sets. In *M.Sc. Thesis, Simon Fraser University*, Burnaby, B.C., Canada, November 1997.

[9] J. Graham-Cumming. Hits and misses: A year watching the web. In *Proc. 6th Int. World Wide Web Conf.*, Santa Clara, California, April 1997.

[10] J. Han, J. Chiang, S. Chee, J. Chen, Q. Chen, S. Cheng, W. Gong, M. Kamber, G. Liu, K. Koperski, Y. Lu, N. Stefanovic, L. Winstone, B. Xia, O. R. Zafiane, S. Zhang, and H. Zhu. DBMiner: A system for data mining in relational databases and data warehouses. In *Proc. CASCON'97: Meeting of Minds*, pages 249–260, Toronto, Canada, November 1997.

[11] J. Han and Y. Fu. Discovery of multiple-level association rules from large databases. In *Proc. 1995 Int. Conf. Very Large Data Bases*, pages 420–431, Zurich, Switzerland, Sept. 1995.

[12] M. Kamber, J. Han, and J.Y. Chiang. Metarule-guided mining of multi-dimensional association rules using data cubes. In *Proc. 3rd Int. Conf. Knowledge Discovery and Data Mining (KDD'97)*, pages 207–210, Newport Beach, California, August 1997.

[13] R. Kimball. *The Data Warehouse Toolkit*, John Wiley & Sons, New York, 1996.

[14] M. Perkowitz and O. Etzioni. Adaptive sites: Automatically learning from user access patterns. In *Proc. 6th Int. World Wide Web Conf.,* Santa Clara, California, April 1997.

[15] J. Pitkow. In search of reliable usage data on the www. In *Proc. 6th Int. World Wide Web Conf.*, Santa Clara, California, April 1997.

[16] R. Srikant and R. Agrawal. Mining generalized association rules. In *Proc. 1995 Int. Conf. Very Large Data Bases*, pages 407–419, Zurich, Switzerland, Sept. 1995.

[17] T. Stabin and C.E. Glasson. First impression: 7 commercial log processing tools slice & dice logs your way. In *http://www.netscapeworld.com/netscapeworld/nw-08-1997/nw-08-loganalysis.html,* 1997.

[18] T. Sullivan. Reading reader reaction: A proposal for inferential analysis of web server log files. In *Proc. 3rd Conf. Human Factors & the Web*, Denver, Colorado, June 1997.

[19] L. Tauscher and S. Greenberg. How people revisit web pages: Empirical findings and implications for the design of history systems. *International Journal of Human Computer Studies, Special issue on World Wide Web Usability*, 47:97–138, 1997.

[20] Y. Zhao, P.M. Deshpande, and J.F. Naughton. An array-based algorithm for simultaneous multidimensional aggregates. In *Proc. 1997 ACM-SIGMOD Int. Conf. Management of Data*, pages 159–170, Tucson, Arizona, May 1997.

CASE STUDY 9 SUMMARY

This case described the work done in analysing Web log data collected from Web page access history from Virtual-U at Simon Fraser University. The case study described the cleaning and transformation of data from the Web log. Once this was done, the data cube was built using the data. The OLAP analysis was next carried out using the data cube. Data mining of the information stored in the data cube was also carried out.

CASE STUDY 9 EXERCISES

1. What cleaning and transformation of Web logs was carried out in this case study? Why was this required?
2. What OLAP analysis of the data was carried out? What were the benefits of this analysis?
3. Why was it necessary to analyse the data using data mining techniques? Was data mining useful for Web log data analysis?

CHAPTER

10 Information Privacy and Data Mining

LEARNING OBJECTIVES

After completing this chapter, you will be able to:

- Understand the concept of information privacy
- Describe basic privacy protection principles
- Explain briefly information privacy legislative developments in india
- Discuss information privacy dangers of data mining
- Understand some examples of data mining and its impact on privacy
- Discuss basic privacy protection principles in the context of data mining
- Find further resources about information privacy in data mining

10.1 INTRODUCTION

In the last nine chapters we have discussed a number of data mining techniques. In this chapter we briefly look at one major social implication of data mining. In particular we look at how data mining can impact an individual's privacy.

The complexity of modern society coupled with growing competition due to trade globalisation has fuelled demand for data mining. As discussed earlier, most enterprises have collected information over at least the last 30 years and they are keen to discover business intelligence that might be buried in it. Business intelligence may be in the form of customer profiles which may result in better targeted marketing and other business actions.

During the 1970s and the 1980s, most Western societies developed a similar set of privacy principles and most of them enacted legislation to ensure that the governments and the private sector were following good privacy principles. Data mining is a relatively new technology and privacy principles developed some 30–40 years ago are not particularly effective in dealing with privacy concerns that are being raised about data mining. These concerns have been heightened by the dramatically increased use of data mining by governments as a result of the 9/11 terrorist attacks. A number of groups all over the world are trying to wrestle with the issues raised by widespread use of data mining techniques. This chapter briefly discusses these issues.

CHAPTER OVERVIEW

This chapter first provides an introduction to information privacy and defines it. Section 10.3 also describes the basic principles of information privacy protection. Section 10.4 deals with information privacy protection legislation in India starting from the first legislation in 2000. Key provisions of the 2011 Rules are described. Section 10.5 outlines some uses and abuses of data mining followed by a brief discussion of primary aims of data mining in Section 10.6. The following section, Section 10.7, presents a number of pitfalls of data mining that may result in violation of an individual's privacy. Section 10.8 lists why the current privacy protection is ineffective for data mining applications followed by a recommended revised set of privacy principles for data mining. Section 10.10 looks at some technological solution for protecting data mining. The chapter concludes with a number of examples of use of data mining by the USA government.

10.2 WHAT IS INFORMATION PRIVACY?

The daily use of the word privacy about information sharing and analysis is often vague and may be misleading. We will therefore provide a definition (or two). Discussions about the concept of information privacy started in the 1960s when a number of researchers recognised the dangers of privacy violations by large collections of personal information in computer systems. Over the years a number of definitions of information privacy have emerged. One of them defines information privacy as

> **Information Privacy**
> Information privacy is the individual's ability to control the circulation of information relating to him/her.

Another widely used definition is

> **Information Privacy**
> It is the claim of individuals groups or institutions to determine for themselves when how and to what extent information about them is communicated to others.

Sometimes privacy is confused with confidentiality and at other times with security. Privacy does involve confidentiality and security but it involves more than the two.

10.3 BASIC PRINCIPLES TO PROTECT INFORMATION PRIVACY

As noted earlier, during the 1970s and 1980s many countries and organisations (e.g. OECD, 1980) developed similar basic information privacy principles which were then enshrined in legislation by many nations. These principles are interrelated and partly overlapping and should therefore be treated together. The OECD principles, that celebrated its 30 years in 2010, are given below. Each subsection lists the principle first and then a brief description is included.

It should be noted that OECD member countries were recommended to exercise their discretion regarding the implementation of the guidelines.

10.3.1 Collection Limitation

There should be limits to the collection of personal data and any such data should be obtained by lawful and fair means and, where appropriate, with the knowledge or consent of the data subject.

This principle deals with two issues. Firstly it limits the collection of personal data that puts an end to indiscriminate collection of personal data. Secondly, deals with practices used in data collection. The knowledge or consent of the data subject is essential although the principle accepts that consent of the data subject may not always be possible.

10.3.2 Data Quality

Personal data should be relevant to the purposes for which they are to be used, and, to the extent necessary for those purposes, should be accurate, complete and kept up-to-date.

This principle in essence states that data should be related to the purpose for which it is to be used. For example, data including opinions may not always be useful to collect since it may not be relevant for the purposes for which the data is to be used.

10.3.3 Purpose Specification

The purposes for which personal data are collected should be specified not later than at the time of data collection and the subsequent use limited to the fulfilment of those purposes or such others as are not incompatible with those purposes and as are specified on each occasion of change of purpose.

The first three principles are interrelated. The purpose of data collection should be identified before data collection and any changes afterwards must be specified. Also, when data no longer serves a purpose, it may be necessary to destroy the data if practicable.

10.3.4 Use Limitation

Personal data should not be disclosed, made available or otherwise used for purposes other than those specified in accordance with Principle 3 except with the consent of the data subject or by the authority of law.

The earlier principles were more dealing with data collection. This principle deals with data use and data disclosure. Data should only be used for specified purposes.

10.3.5 Security Safeguards

Personal data should be protected by reasonable security safeguards against such risks as loss or unauthorised access, destruction, use, modification or disclosure of data.

To enforce the principle of use limitation, it is required that there be appropriate safeguards. The safeguards should include physical safeguards as well as safeguards for the computer systems.

10.3.6 Openness

There should be a general policy of openness about developments, practices and policies with respect to personal data. Means should be readily available of establishing the existence and nature of personal data, and the main purposes of their use, as well as the identity and usual residence of the data controller.

The openness principle is closely related to the next principle of individual participation.

10.3.7 Individual Participation

An individual should have the right:

(a) to obtain from a data controller, or otherwise, confirmation of whether or not the data controller has data relating to him;

(b) to have communicated to him, data relating to him

within a reasonable time;

at a charge, if any, that is not excessive;

in a reasonable manner; and

in a form that is readily intelligible to him;

(c) to be given reasons if a request made under subparagraphs(a) and (b) is denied, and to be able to challenge such denial; and

(d) to challenge data relating to him and, if the challenge is successful to have the data erased, rectified, completed or amended.

This is perhaps the most important principle. It involves the rights of the individuals to acquire information about the collection, storage and use of their personal data. The right of access should be simple to exercise.

10.3.8 Accountability

A data controller should be accountable for complying with measures which give effect to the principles stated above.

This principle requires that the data collector comply with the privacy protection principles. Accountability should be supported by legal sanctions and perhaps a code of conduct.

10.3.9 International Application

There are a number of principles; we do not list them here, which apply to international transfer of personal data. Flow of data between members of the OECD is admitted. The principles attempt to balance transborder flows of personal data against the need to ensure privacy protection.

These privacy protection principles were developed for on-line transaction processing (OLTP) systems before technologies like data mining became available. In OLTP systems, the purpose of the system is quite clearly defined since the system is used for a particular operational purpose of an enterprise (e.g. student enrolment). Given a clear purpose of the system, it is then possible to adhere to the above principles. We will show that this is not always so with data mining systems.

10.4 PRIVACY LEGISLATION IN INDIA

The Indian Government for the first time recognised electronic documents as legal documents in 2000 (Information Technology Act, 2000). This Act however did not address the issue of information privacy.

Other countries had already enacted data protection legislations and some legislation stated that the member states must cease to send personal data to any third country that did not have similar data protection laws. This forced India to pass amendments to the IT Act 2000. As a result IT Amendment Act 2008 (*ITAA 2008*) was enacted. Essentially this was the beginning of data protection laws in India. ITAA 2008 inserted new clauses in the IT Act 200. Section 43A required that compensation be provided by a person in possession of sensitive personal data who was negligent in maintaining and implementing reasonable security practices and procedures. There was considerable confusion about the 2008 Act. For example, distinction between "Personal Data" and "Sensitive Personal Data" was not clear. Such ambiguities made it difficult to compare ITAA 2008 with European data protection legislations.

To remove such ambiguities, in April 2011, India adopted further rules regarding information privacy protection. These regulations are known as the Information Technology (Reasonable Security Practices and Procedures and Sensitive Personal Data or Information) Rules, 2011 (sometime just called the *Rules*). The Rules impose wide-ranging obligations on any company that *collects, receives, possesses, stores, deals or handles* personal information. It is required that the companies provide privacy policies, restrict the processing of sensitive personal data, and restrict international data transfers. Additional security measures are also required. The Rules finally introduce an omnibus privacy law that is similar in many respects to existing EU data protection law. The Rules therefore raise some fundamental challenges for the outsourcing vendors and their customers.

10.4.1 Key Provisions of the 2011 Rules

We briefly describe the additional obligations on organizations. They are as summarized below:

- **Privacy policy:** As noted above, a company dealing with personal information must provide a privacy policy that clearly sets out its practices and policies. It is also required to identify any sensitive personal data collected and processed. The purposes of data collection and its uses need to be explained. The company must also provide reasonable security practices and procedures.
- **Definition of sensitive personal data:** The Rules define the term *Sensitive Personal Data*. It includes physical, physiological and mental health conditions, medical records and history, and sexual orientation. Furthermore, it also includes biometric data, passwords and financial information such as bank account details, credit and debit card details.

- **Restrictions on data collection and processing:** A data collector, at the point of collection of any data, must make individuals aware of the fact that their data is being collected, the purpose for which it is being collected, and the intended recipients of the data. Data must be used only for the purposes for which it was collected and must not be used for any secondary purposes.
- **Additional restrictions for sensitive personal data:** Consent of the individual in writing (by letter, fax or email) is required before their sensitive personal data may be processed. The individual is allowed not to provide data and may withdraw their consent to the processing at any time.
- **Rights of access and correction:** Individuals have the right to review the information about them and to ensure that inaccurate or deficient data is corrected or amended, as feasible.
- **Disclosure to third parties:** Personal information (including sensitive personal data) may only be provided to a third party with the consent of the provider of the information unless required for legal compliance purposes.
- **International data transfers:** The data collector may transfer, if necessary for performance of a lawful contract, sensitive personal data to another body corporate in India or abroad where the same level of data protection is assured.
- **Security:** The body corporate must have a comprehensive documented information security program and policies that contain managerial, technical, operational and physical control measures commensurate with the information assets and nature of the business.

Some confusion still remains about how the Rules will apply in practice.

Another area of concern is data surveillance by the Indian government. According to some reports, the Indian government uses a system called the Centralized Monitoring System (CMS) to monitor telecommunications in the country.

There is often very little transparency in India when it comes to surveillance and intelligence. No intelligence agency in India has been created under an act of Parliament and there are no clearly established roles and limitations on powers for them. The government has been reported to have been working on the CMS since 2006, which will integrate with another system that intercepts telephone calls. It appears that all Internet service providers and telecom providers are required to provide the government direct access to all communications passing through them. Furthermore it has been reported that the government uses equipment to gain access to vast quantities of raw data traversing the Internet across multiple cities.

In July 2013, the Indian government released a policy called *National Cyber Security Policy 2013 (NCSP 2013).* It appears that this policy was a result of increasing number of cyber-attacks on India's computer and communications infrastructure. This policy recommends that a national agency to coordinate all cyber security matters be established in India and it be headed by a Chief Information Security Officer.

10.5 USES AND MISUSES OF DATA MINING

Data mining involves the extraction of implicit, previously unknown and potentially useful knowledge from large databases. Data mining is a very challenging task since it involves building and using software that will manage, explore, summarise, model, analyse and interpret large datasets in order to identify patterns and abnormalities.

As noted in Chapter 1, data mining techniques are being used increasingly in a wide variety of applications. The applications include fraud prevention, catching tax avoidance, catching drug smugglers, reducing customer churn and learning more about customers' behaviour. There are also some (mis)uses of data mining that have little to do with any of these applications. For example, a number of newspapers in early 2005 have reported results of analysing associations between the political party that a person votes for and the car the person drives. A number of car models have been listed in the USA for each of the two major political parties.

In the wake of the 9/11 terrorism attacks, considerable use of personal information, provided by individuals for other purposes as well as information collected by governments including intercepted emails and telephone conversations, is being made in the belief that such information processing (including data mining) can assist in identifying persons who are likely to be involved in terrorist networks or individuals who might be in contact with such persons or other individuals involved in illegal activities (e.g. drug smuggling). Under legislation enacted since 9/11, many governments are able to demand access to most private sector data. This data can include records on travel, shopping, housing, utilities, credit, telecommunications and so on. Such data can then be mined in the belief that patterns can be found that will help identifying terrorists or drug smugglers.

Consider a very simple artificial example of data being analysed using a data mining technique like the decision tree:

Birth Country	*Age*	*Religion*	*Visited X*	*Studied in West*	*Risk Class*
A	<30	*P*	Yes	Yes	*B*
B	>60	*Q*	Yes	Yes	*A*
A	<30	*R*	Yes	No	*C*
X	30–45	*R*	No	No	*B*
Y	46–60	*S*	Yes	No	*C*
X	>60	*P*	Yes	Yes	*A*
Z	<25	*P*	No	Yes	*B*
A	<25	*Q*	Yes	No	*A*
B	<25	*Q*	Yes	No	*C*
B	30–45	*S*	Yes	No	*C*

Using the decision tree to analyse this data may result in rules like the following:

If Age = 30–45 and Birth Country = *A* and Visited *X* = Yes and Studied in West = Yes and Religion = *R* then Risk Class = *A*

User profiles are built based on relevant user characteristics. The number of characteristics may be large and may include all kinds of information including telephone zones phoned, travelling on the same flight as a person on a watch list and much more. User profiling is used in a variety of other areas, for example authorship analysis, plagiarism detection.

Once a user profile is formed, the basic action of the detection system is to compare incoming personal data to the profile and make a decision if the data fit any of the profiles. The comparison can in fact be quite complex because not all of the large number of characteristics in the profile are likely to match but a majority might.

Such profile matching can lead to faulty inferences. As an example, it was reported that a person was wrongly arrested just because the person had an Arab name and obtained a driver licence at the same motor vehicle office soon after one of the 9/11 hijackers did. Although this incident was not a result of data mining, it does show that an innocent person can be mistaken for a terrorist or a drug smuggler as a result of some matching characteristics.

10.6 PRIMARY AIMS OF DATA MINING

Essentially most data mining techniques that we are concerned about are designed to discover and match profiles. The aims of majority of such data mining are laudable but the techniques are not always perfect. What happens if a person matches the profile but does not belong to the category?

Perhaps it is not a matter of great concern if a telecommunications company labels a person as one that is likely to switch and then decide to target that person with a special campaign designed to encourage the person to stay. On the other hand, if the Customs department identifies a person as fitting the profile of a drug smuggler then that person is likely to undergo a special search whenever he/she returns home from overseas and perhaps at other airports if the customs department of one country shares information with other countries. This would be a matter of much more concern.

Knowledge about the classification or profile of an individual who has been so classified or profiled may lead to disclosure of personal information with some given probability. The characteristics that someone may be able to deduce about a person with some possibility may include sensitive information, for example race, religion, travel history and level of credit card expenditure.

This chapter does not suggest that all data mining applications are invasive or violate the individual's civil liberties. Data mining is used for many purposes that are beneficial to society, as the list of some of the common aims of data mining shows.

- The primary aim of many data mining applications is to better understand the customer and improve customer services.
- Some applications aim to discover anomalous patterns in order to help identify, for example, fraud, abuse, waste, terrorist suspects or drug smugglers.
- In many applications in private enterprises, the primary aim is to improve the profitability of an enterprise.
- As shown in case studies described in Chapter 1, in a number of data mining applications the primary purpose is to improve human judgement, for example, in making diagnoses, in resolving crime, in sorting out manufacturing problems, in predicting share prices or currency movements or commodity prices.
- In some government applications, one of the aims of data mining is to identify criminal activities.
- In some situations, data mining is used to find patterns that are simply not possible without the help of data mining, given the huge amounts of data that must be processed. As an example, as mentioned in Chapter 1, this is true in processing large amounts of astronomical data which cannot be easily processed in other ways.

Many data mining systems designed to achieve one or more of these aims do not lead to personal privacy violations, but some do. In particular, applications that aim to discover anomalous behaviour can lead to significant violations of individual privacy.

10.7 PITFALLS OF DATA MINING

Dempsey and Rosenzweig (2004) identify five pitfalls of data mining when personally identifiable information is used in data mining applications like identifying terrorist suspects. These five categories are:

10.7.1 Unintentional Mistake—Mistaken Identity

This kind of problem arises when an innocent person shares some identifier information with one or more persons that have been identified as having a profile of interest in a data mining application. A number of such incidents have been found to have taken place in the last year or two, for example, in the airline passenger screening system.

10.7.2 Unintentional Mistake—Faulty Inference

This kind of problem arises when profiles are matched and the data mining users misinterpret the result of the match. Faulty inferences then may be derived resulting, for example, in an innocent person becoming a suspect and leading to further investigation about the person. A number of such incidents have been found to have taken place in the last year or two when security people, for example, seized a Canadian citizen who was transiting through JFK airport in New York. This person was then flown to a number of middle-eastern countries for torture. He spent many months in captivity in these countries before he was released. Although not a result of data mining, such case could conceivably false positive result from profile matching.

10.7.3 Intentional Abuse

People employed in running a data mining system and security organisations have access to sensitive personal information and not all of them are trustworthy. This sensitive information may be used for unauthorised purposes for personal financial gain. For example, an employee of an intelligence or law enforcement agency may provide a profile checking service for a private company for a fee.

10.7.4 Security Breach

Given that data mining systems using personal information have sensitive information, information may be stolen or carelessly disclosed without strict security measures. In February 2004, a magnetic tape with information on about 120,000 Japanese customers of Citibank disappeared while being shipped by truck from a data management centre in Singapore. The tape held names, addresses, account numbers and balances. In June 2005, an entire box of Citibank tapes in the care of the United Parcel Service, with personal information on nearly four million American customers disappeared.

In February 2005, a US company ChoicePoint announced that personal data of 145,000 persons was accessed by an unauthorized person[1]. These cases highlight the dangers of security breach.

10.7.5 Mission Creep

Once a data mining system, for example for a national security application, has been established and personal information from a variety of sources collected, there is likely to be a temptation to use the information for other applications. Such mission creep has been reported in data mining applications.

The reliability of profile matching is often not high. If in an application, a very rare pattern is being sought for in a huge mountain of information about millions of individuals then mining is very likely to be ineffective. It is most likely to find either nothing or a relatively large number of suspects most of whom would have nothing at all to do with what the profile match is supposed to discover.

Searching for patterns or matching profiles is somewhat similar to searching the Web although a profile is likely to be much more complex than a search query. The Web had more than four billion pages in 2004. If the query is even slightly general then there is the problem of abundance. If the query is very specific, for example the phrase "when not to use data mining", then there is the problem of scarcity. No match was found for this simple query. A minor change to the query phrase to "when to use data mining" found a large number of matches.

In some data mining techniques, for example supervised classification, the training data available may not be sufficient or may not be sufficiently typical of the population at large. Data mining is then unlikely to be highly effective.

10.8 WHY CURRENT PRIVACY PRINCIPLES ARE INEFFECTIVE FOR DATA MINING?

We have noted earlier that the privacy principles of the 1970s and the 1980s were designed for OLTP systems. These principles are not fully effective for data mining applications for the following reasons.

10.8.1 Collection Limitation

In most current data mining applications, data used are normally not collected for the primary purpose of data mining, although in some cases additional information may be collected, for example through loyalty cards. Often data have been collected for another purpose and data mining is a secondary use of the data. For example, in market basket analysis the data are collected at the checkout counters for determining what the customer needs to pay for the purchase and perhaps inventory control. The secondary purpose of the data then could be market basket analysis to which the customer is likely to be totally oblivious.

---

[1] An article "Breach Points up Flaws in Privacy Laws" by Tom Zeller Jr in New York Times dated February 24, 2005 provides details of how some con artists gained access to the Social Security Numbers, addresses and other personal data of nearly 145,000 ChoicePoint's customers. The article also notes that ChoicePoint had 19 billion records and had revenue of US$919 million. Another article by the same reporter "The Scramble to Protect Personal Information" dated June 9, 2005 provides information on the Citibank cases.

Furthermore, data mining may involve collection of information from a number of the organisation's OLTP systems to build a data warehouse. The data subject would have no idea about such consolidation.

10.8.2 Data Quality

Data mining is often used only when there is a large amount of information available. It may be historical information as well as current information collected from a variety of sources. Data extraction, transformation and loading (ETL) often precedes data mining. An ETL process should ensure that the quality of data is high, but studies suggest that error levels in such data are significant in spite of ETL. Given that individuals generally do not know about data mining activities, they are not able to request access to their personal information and make corrections, erasures or deletions which could improve the quality of data.

10.8.3 Purpose Specification and Use Limitation

As noted above, data for data mining are usually not collected directly from the data subjects. Even when information is directly collected, the individuals are usually not informed of all the purposes of data collection and thus they are not aware of data mining uses of the data. For example, when a person visits a Web site, at which he might have registered and hence his/her identity is known, and navigates through the site, data may be collected about his/her visit and navigation. Data mining techniques may then be used to analyse the personal data, perhaps from several visits to the site, without the individual being aware of such analysis.

Data mining of personal information where data subjects' consent has not been obtained is a violation of privacy principles.

The problem of purpose specification and use limitation may be overcome by obtaining data subjects' consent which should be done in a transparent way rather than just including the words "data mining" in the fine print.

10.8.4 Security of Storage

As noted earlier, data mining often involves collection of information from a number of OLTP systems to build a data warehouse. This makes security even more critical since it can allow an intruder to access much more personal information than the intruder could access from a single OLTP system. It is therefore important that a system used for data mining (e.g. a data warehouse) be provided with tight security controls. Strict security procedures should be followed when it is required to transfer information to another site either through the network or by transporting magnetic media physically.

10.8.5 Openness, Individual Participation and Accountability

The openness principle requires that if data mining is being carried out on personal information then the data subjects should know that their information is being used for such processing. Because the data mining is often so far removed from the primary uses of the information, it is not an open and transparent activity and therefore an individual usually cannot participate.

Accountability may also not be possible since data mining is invisible and the data subjects do not know that the information they supplied for one purpose is being used for other purposes as well. To make the process open and accountable, it is essential that data subjects know about all uses of their data so that they are in a position to ask questions about the uses.

10.9 A REVISED SET OF PRIVACY PRINCIPLES FOR DATA MINING OF PERSONAL INFORMATION

Given the above discussion regarding the reasons for OLTP privacy principles being mostly ineffective for data mining, we suggest that a set of revised privacy principles for data mining of personal information are required. We present such a set in this section. These principles are based on the OECD privacy principles outlined earlier, a number of privacy reports published since 1970, and, most importantly, the May 2004 report of the US Technology and Privacy Advisory Committee and the data mining checklist provided in it.

TAPAC has noted that data mining of personal information runs the risk of becoming the 21st century equivalent of general searches.

Although the revised principles below are similar to the OECD principles, we move the purpose specification principle to be the first principle given its importance. A new principle on impact definition has been included following the purpose specification principle.

1. **Purpose specification:** An organisation planning to implement a data mining system that uses personal information must establish procedures to rigorously scrutinise the purposes, necessity, benefits, impacts and legality of the proposed system. If approved, the purposes of each data mining system should be clearly specified and the subsequent use limited to the fulfilment of those purposes or such others as are compatible with those purposes and as are specified on each occasion of change of purpose.
2. **Impact definition:** The impact of a data mining system and processing should be clearly defined. The impact definition should include a clear explanation of what happens when a person is identified to fit a profile. It should also provide information on the estimated or expected false positive rate of the technique being used. The impact statement should include a justification of the reasons why the false positive rate is acceptable. Furthermore, there should be a clear explanation of whether individuals could suffer adverse action as a result of data mining and the impact definition should outline the procedures that would be used to deal with such situations.
3. **Collection limitation:** There should be limits to the collection of personal data and any such data should be obtained by lawful and fair means and, where appropriate, with the knowledge or consent of the data subject. Data collected for other purposes should not be used for data mining without the consent of data subjects. When data are collected directly from data subjects, the individuals should be provided with appropriate notice explaining the proposed use of the information. Personal information from a number of OLTP systems of an organisation should not be collected in a data warehouse if it violates current privacy principles.

4. **Data quality:** Any organisation creating, maintaining, using or disseminating identifiable personal data in a data mining system must ensure the accuracy and completeness of the data for their intended use and should ensure that the data are kept up-to-date.
5. **Use limitation:** A data mining system should only be used for the purpose defined under Principle 1 above and not used for other purposes. Personal data should not be disclosed, made available or otherwise used for purposes other than those specified in accordance with Principle 1 except with the consent of the data subjects or by the authority of law.
6. **Security safeguards:** Personal data collected for data mining should be protected by reasonable security safeguards against such risks as loss or unauthorised access, destruction, use, modification or disclosure of data.
7. **Openness:** Organisations using data mining should ensure that the data subjects are informed of its existence, developments, practices and policies with respect to data mining of personal information. Means should be readily available for establishing the existence and nature of data mining, and the main purposes of their use, as well as the identity and usual residence of the data controller.
8. **Individual participation:** Whenever an individual may be affected by the results of data mining, every attempt should be made to immediately inform the individual about the data mining process and the information used. There must also be a simple way for individuals to obtain confirmation of whether or not data relating to them is being used in data mining. If a false positive has been found, the data subject should be able to challenge the finding and, if the challenge is successful, to have the data erased, rectified, completed or amended.
9. **Oversight and accountability:** Each organisation using data mining of personal information must establish procedures to provide oversight of the data mining system and to regularly monitor and review the organisation's data mining activities. The review should include a review of any complaints from data subjects, any problems arising because of false positives and any other problems that might have been identified with the system. A data controller should be accountable for complying with measures which give effect to the principles stated above.

10.10 TECHNOLOGICAL SOLUTIONS

In this section we look at some technological solutions that can in some cases assist in protection of individual privacy by data mining systems while still allowing some data mining uses of the data.

10.10.1 Anonymization

Anonymization is removal of identifying information from data in order to protect privacy of the data subjects while allowing the data so modified to be used for secondary purposes like data mining. For example, Anonymization may be used by a Web user to prevent collection of his/her information by hiding personal information like cookies and IP addresses.

Anonymization may be based on one-way hashing technique. Hashing allows different people to share information because when a hash function is applied to any information the resulting hashed value will always be the same if the same hash function is applied to the same information. It therefore allows sharing and matching of information without disclosing personal information about a person. Although Anonymization is usually safe, in some extreme cases identity of the person may be discovered.

Let us look at an example of some transaction data for an individual.

Name: Suresh Kumar
Identifier: 87652468
Non-sensitive information: whatever

Using hashing we assume that we obtain the following

Name: hashed value of (Suresh Kumar) = 297632139
Identifier: hashed value of (87652468) = 333765889

Now when information is being shared, someone receiving two transaction records that have been hashed is able to conclude by comparing the hashed values whether the two records belong to the same individual or not. This could be useful, for example government departments like customs and immigration and airlines that carry a watch list of names and other information do not need to have a list of actual names. They could carry a list of hashed values for matching.

There are however some difficulties. Firstly if the name has been misspelled or Suresh Kumar in some records is written as Suresh C Kumar then the hashed values of the two names are unlikely to be the same and will not match. The second problem is that if a person receiving the hashed record has some other data that is plaintext then the receiver can hash the plaintext information and find out which of the anonymized data is about the person that he/she already knows about. Furthermore, a receiver may compile a list of common names, date of births, identifier values etc and hash them all and compare the anonymized data so obtained with anonymized values received. It is very likely that some of the hashed data will match some of the hashed values of common names and other information.

The first problem can be overcome by standardisation of information. For example, standardisation may involve every name to consist of full first and last name only.

K-Anonymization

The idea of k-Anonymization is related to the problem of compromising a statistical database, e.g. census database. Although no personal information is included in statistical databases, it is possible to derive personal information if a number of attribute values together help identify a person or a small number of people in the database.

We do not discuss k-Anonymization in detail since it is not particularly relevant to data mining personal privacy violation. We define the concept of quasi-identifier as the set of attributes that together can be used to identify an individual. It might be something like {date of birth, suburb, number of children}.

The main idea in k-Anonymization is to modify the data in the database to ensure that each set of quasi-identifier value in it appears at least *k* times so that a person using the quasi-identifier to retrieve information will retrieve at least *k* records.

10.10.2 Privacy-Preserving Data Mining

Privacy-preserving data mining techniques usually involve randomising the data subjects' personal data. An enterprise wishing to carry out data mining obtains randomised user information which may be used for data mining but randomisation ensures that the personal information is not disclosed. This may involve use of client-side software that randomises the data. For example, the date of birth 1/1/81 may be randomised as 2/2/82 and 2/2/82 may be randomised as 3/4/81. The true date of birth then cannot be determined by analysing the randomised date of birth. The randomisation may be based on some parameters and approximations to the true distributions may be determined knowing the randomisation parameters.

Although technology based solutions can prevent some types of individual privacy violations in data mining, technology cannot address some other privacy concerns, e.g. concerns when governments carry out data mining to build profiles of individuals who might be potential drug smuggler or terrorist suspects. In such cases suitable legislative safeguards are required to control data mining uses and to prevent individual personal privacy violations. No technology solution can help overcome the concerns regarding false matches in profiles matching.

10.11 EXAMPLES OF USE OF DATA MINING BY THE US GOVERNMENT

There are many data mining activities conducted by the US Government[2]. A General Accounts Office study reported in May 2004 that US Government agencies had some 131 operational data mining efforts and 68 projects were planned. Most of these efforts however do not pose any threats to individuals' personal privacy.

It has been reported that the US Government has developed a number of data mining projects in response to the 9/11 attacks. Some of these programs seek to sift through large data repositories to identify threatening patterns and people. It appears that most of these projects do not pay sufficient attention to concerns of individual privacy.

We briefly discuss three US Government data mining projects:

- Terrorist Information Awareness (TIA)
- Multistate Anti-Terrorism Information Exchange (Matrix)
- Flying Passenger Screening Systems

In the frantic efforts following 9/11 the US Government was persuaded that technology could be better used in fighting terrorism. Some people claimed that technology like data mining could be used to predict and pre-empt terrorist attacks. The US Government's task may be described as akin to finding dangerous groups of needles hidden in stacks of needle pieces and it has been claimed by some technology enthusiasts that technology can help track all the dangerous needle pieces all of the time. Unfortunately no data mining technique or collection of techniques can achieve such an ambitious objective. Some researchers advising the government claim that they can quickly analyse multiple Petabytes of data. One Petabyte would hold 40 pages of text for each of the more than six

[2] The US Congress mandated in the Homeland Security Act that DHS "establish and utilize ...information technology... including data mining and other advanced analytical tools to access, receive and analyze data to detect and identify threats of terrorism against the United States."

billion humans on Earth! How such large amounts of data could be analysed quickly has not been explained.

In an attempt to demonstrate the effectiveness of data mining techniques, one of the projects used two online databases, the Internet Movie Database and the Physics Preprint Archive, to develop tools that would predict whether a movie would gross more than $2 million on its opening weekend and would identify authoritative physics authors. Based on such trivial test results, some technology enthusiastic people claim that data mining can help the nation avoid strategic surprise, events critical to national security, such as 9/11.

10.11.1 Terrorist Information Awareness (TIA)

As noted earlier, new legislations enacted in many countries after 9/11 have given governments access to records held by a variety of private companies including bank records, driver's licence information, credit card purchases, medical data, phone and email records, airline and other travel company data. Governments are now in a position to collect this data in real-time and store it into a giant centralised database(s).

The US Defense Advanced Research Projects Agency (DARPA) started developing a system called Total (later Terrorist) Information Awareness (TIA), to detect terrorists through analyzing large amounts of information listed above as well as new sources of information including intelligence data. TIA planned to build profiles of people so that the government could track potential terrorists and criminals. The goal was to track individuals through collecting as much information about them as possible and using data mining to detect suspects.

The data-mining tools were to sort through the massive amounts of information to find patterns and associations. TIA aimed to fund the development of more data-mining technology to help analysts understand and even pre-empt future action.

The plan was to build profiles that established norms based on a person's spending and travel habits. Then the system was to look for patterns that break from the norms, such as purchases of materials that are considered likely for terrorist activity, travel to specific areas or a change in spending habits. Patterns that fit pre-defined criteria result in an investigative alert and the individual becomes a "person of interest" who is referred relevant authorities. Some industries, for example the telecommunications, have been experimenting with use of profiles in an attempt to detect fraud and they have found that it is difficult to identify with some certainty unusual behaviour by comparing incoming data with a person's profile.

The primary reason for concern with a system like TIA is that although the system may eventually find some useful information, in finding that it might involve a thousand wrong hits. Does the cost of the wrong hits and the pain the hits might cause to innocent people justify one or two correct hits which perhaps would have been more easily obtained by other means?

In September 2003, the US Congress eliminated funding for the controversial project and closed the Pentagon's Information Awareness Office, which had developed TIA. Although TIA is now defunct, other similar data mining projects techniques have been rumoured to be continuing.

The Technology and Privacy Advisory Committee (TAPAC) in its report in March 2004 concluded that TIA was a flawed effort, flawed by its perceived insensitivity to critical privacy issues, and the manner in which it was presented to the public. TAPAC also concluded that data mining is a vital tool in the fight against terrorism, but when used in connection with personal data concerning US persons, data mining can present significant privacy issues.

10.11.2 Multistate Anti-Terrorism Information Exchange (Matrix)

The US Government launched a database system called Matrix in 2002 which stores more than four billion records and is suspected of using data mining to find the likelihood of a person being a terrorist. The private company that was given the contract for this system and for development of the "terrorism quotient" was reported to have prepared a list of 120,000 people based on intelligence data that was made available to them that they thought were suspect. Of the people with the 80 highest scores, five were among the September 11 hijackers. It has been reported that the terrorist quotient idea was abandoned. Because the system includes information on people with no criminal record as well as known criminals, Utah and at least eight other states were reported to have pulled out, leaving only five states in the scheme.

It has been reported that the private company used reverse engineering of an unnamed "Terrorist Handbook". The scoring used incorporated such factors as age, gender, ethnicity, credit history, information about pilot and driver licences, and connections to addresses known to have been used by other suspects.

10.11.3 Flying Passenger Screening Systems

It has been reported that the TSA administers two lists: a "no-fly" list and a "selectee" list. A passenger who is on one of those lists goes through additional security measures. The names on the lists are provided to air carriers and are stored in their computer systems so that an individual with a name that matches the list can be flagged when getting a boarding pass. A "no-fly" match requires the agent to call a law enforcement officer to detain and question the passenger. In the case of a Selectee, a special mark is printed on their boarding pass and the person receives additional screening at security. The number of names on each of the lists has not been made public.

It is not clear if safeguards are in place to ensure the accuracy of the information in the lists. At one time it was reported that Senator Edward Kennedy was having difficulty boarding planes because his name was similar to a name on the "no-fly" list. A nine-term congressman by the name of John Lewis has been reported to have been stopped at least 35 times over one year.

A new airline passenger pre-screening system, called Secure Flight, is currently under development. It has been reported that in November 2004, the TSA ordered the commercial airlines to turn over their passenger records from the month of June 2004 in order to test the new system. Another system called the Computer Assisted Passenger Prescreening System (CAPPS II) has now been abandoned. CAPPS II was scheduled for a test run in the spring of 2003 using passenger data provided by Delta Airlines. Delta refused to provide the data. Later the TSA abandoned the system.

The Government Accountability Office has raised many concerns about the Secure Flight system. The concerns included the accuracy of intelligence data that is to be used and the adequacy of redress for passengers who are improperly flagged by the system.

Need for transparency

For the systems discussed above to be successful, it is essential that information about them be made available to the public. What kind of data and from what sources it will be compiled? Will it include sensitive personal information? With whom will the data be shared? Will it be shared with foreign governments who are US allies? What security mechanisms will be there to protect unauthorised sharing and access?

How will the data quality be guaranteed? Data errors may lead to false matches that may have unintended consequences for individuals. How will such cases be dealt with? Will individuals be able to check their data and correct errors? If individuals were harmed by any such system, would they be able to take specific legal recourse against the government?

SUMMARY

In this chapter we have explained the concept of information privacy and have presented the 1980 OECD privacy principles. We have discussed applications of data mining and have shown why some applications pose serious threats to individual privacy. We discussed why the 1980 OECD guidelines designed for OLTP systems are not adequate to deal with privacy threats of data mining. A revised set of privacy principles has been presented.

It is useful to note two cases of wrong arrests in the USA. An Oregon lawyer Brandon Mayfield was arrested in May 2002. He had attended a local mosque, he advertised his law practice in a publication owned by a man with terrorism ties, and he represented in a child-custody case Jeffrey Battle, who had pleaded guilty to conspiring to help al-Qaida and the Taliban fight US forces in Afghanistan. His finger prints were claimed to match a set of finder prints found in the Madrid bombing. The case of Maher Arar, a Canadian born in Syria, has already been described in Section 10.6. It has been reported that this was not an isolated case. Other individuals have suffered similar treatment, which is called extraordinary rendition.

The two cases presented above were not arrested as a result of data mining. They were identified and arrested by security officials. However, the security officials can only look through only so much data. If data mining tools were used to sift through large amounts of data then it is likely that the number of hits for people similar to those described above could well be much larger. That is where the dangers of data mining personal privacy violations come from.

A brief discussion of data mining used by the US Government concluded the chapter.

REVIEW QUESTIONS

1. What is information privacy? (Section 10.2)
2. What are basic OECD information privacy protection principles? (Section 10.3)
3. What does “openness” principle require? (Section 10.3.6)
4. Briefly describe the history of privacy legislation in India (Section 10.4)
5. What is “sensitive personal data”? (Section 10.4)
6. List two important uses of data mining (Section 10.5)

7. List two important misuses of data mining. (Section 10.5)
8. What are the primary aims of data mining? (Section 10.6)
9. List the five pitfalls of data mining. (Section 10.7)
10. What is "mission creep"? (Section 10.7.5)
11. Give three reasons why the current privacy principles are ineffective for data mining. (Section 10.8)
12. Give three important revised privacy principles for data mining. (Section 10.9)
13. Give an example of data anonymization. (Section 10.10.1)
14. What is privacy preserving data mining? (Section 10.10.2)
15. Describe one important use of data mining by the US Government (Section 10.11)

EXERCISES

1. What is information privacy? When did the concept of information privacy originate? Using the Web research the topic and write a brief report of less than 1000 words. You must not cut and paste.
2. List the OECD privacy principles and discuss them.
3. Explain why some applications of data mining pose threats to personal privacy.
4. Discuss how the OECD privacy principles may be revised to deal with data mining privacy threats.
5. Compare the revised set of privacy protection principles presented in Section 10.9 and those in Section 10.3. Discuss the major differences and why these are important.
6. Discuss some of the dangers posed by data mining systems being developed in the USA in response to the 9/11 terrorist attacks.

MULTIPLE CHOICE QUESTIONS

1. Which one of the following is a good definition of information privacy?
   (a) Information privacy is same as information security
   (b) It is individual's ability to control the circulation of information about him/her
   (c) It is an individual's ability to determine for themselves when, how and what information about them is communicated to other
   (d) It is an individual's ability to ensure that his/her computer is fully protected against intruders
2. Which one of the following is not part of the OECD privacy protection principles?
   (a) Openness
   (b) Security safeguards
   (c) No collection of personal information
   (d) Accountability

3. Which one of the following is true about IT legislation in India?
   (a) The latest legislation was enacted in 2013
   (b) The first IT legislation was enacted in 2000
   (c) The current legislation only protects sensitive personal information
   (d) The new legislation does not apply to the call centres
4. Which one of the following is true about the Rules adapted in India in 2011?
   (a) The Rules are identical to the OECD privacy principles
   (b) The security of personal information is not considered in the Rules
   (c) The Rules include restrictions on data collection
   (d) The Rules include restriction on data surveillance
5. Which one of the following is true?
   (a) Most data mining applications involve finding the personal identification of an individual
   (b) There is no data surveillance is being carried out by the government in India
   (c) Data mining operations usually do not involves unintentional mistakes
   (d) Matching of profiles can lead to false inferences
6. Which one of the following is not a pitfall of data mining?
   (a) Poor data collection
   (b) Faulty inference
   (c) Mission creep
   (d) Intentional abuse
7. Which one of the following makes the data protection principles ineffective for data mining?
   (a) Poor data collection
   (b) Faulty inference
   (c) Mission creep
   (d) Intentional abuse
8. Which one of the following is a technological solution for privacy protection?
   (a) Anonymization
   (b) Randomness
   (c) Adding noise to all data
   (d) Banning all international data transfers

BIBLIOGRAPHY

Recommended Reading for Students

A number of sites provide good information about information privacy. One such site is www.epic.or. We list some references to information on this site.

Clarke, R., Annotated Bibliography: Papers on Data Surveillance: Theory, Practice & Policy. http://www.anu.edu.au/people/roger.clarke/dv/annbibl.html

Terrorism Information Awareness (TIA), Electronic Privacy Information Center, http://www.epic.org/privacy/profiling/tia/

Privacy and Consumer Profiling, Electronic Privacy Information Center, http://www.epic.org/privacy/profiling/

Secure Flight, Electronic Privacy Information Center, http://www.epic.org/privacy/airtravel/secureflight.html

Recommended Reading for Lecturers

Ananthapur, R., India's New Data Protection Legislation, Scripted, 2011.

Berndt, D.J., Fisher, J.W., Hevner, A.R., and Studnicki, J., Healthcare Data Warehousing and Quality Assurance, *IEEE Computer*, pp. 33–42, December 2001.

Cavoukian, A., Data Mining: Staking a Claim on Your Privacy, Information and Privacy Commissioner, Ontario, Canada, January 1998.
http://www.ipc.on.ca/docs/datamine.pdf

Cavoukian, A., National Security in a Post-9/11 World: The Rise of Surveillance. The Demise of Privacy? Information and Privacy Commissioner, Ontario, Canada, May 2003.
www.ipc.on.ca/userfiles/page_attachments/nat-sec.pdf

Dempsey, J.X. and Rosenzweig, R., Technologies that can Protect Privacy as Information is Shared to Combat Terrorism, Center for Democracy & Technology, 2004.
http://www.heritage.org/research/homelanddefense/lm11.cfm

Dempsey, J.X., Privacy's Gap: The Largely Non-Existent Legal Framework for Government Mining of Commercial Data, Center for Democracy & Technology, May 2004.

GAO, Data Mining: Federal Efforts Cover a Wide Range of Uses, US General Accounts Office, May 2004.
www.gao.gov/new.items/d04548.pdf

Hunton & Williams, India Drafts New Privacy Regulations, Posted on May 18, 2011.
http://www.huntonprivacyblog.com/2011/05/articles/india-drafts-new-privacy-regulations/

Impact of Data Mining on Privacy and ISAT, 2001, 74 pp.
http://www.pet-pisa.nl/dscgi/ds.py/get/file-216/wp41-d16_impact_of_datamining_matching_on_privacy_and_isats.pdf

OECD, Guidelines on the Protection of Privacy and Transborder Flows of Personal Data, Recommendation of the Council Concerning Guidelines Governing the Protection of Privacy and Transborder Flows of Personal Data, 23rd September 1980.
http://www.oecd.org/document/18/0,2340,en_2649_34255_1815186_1_1_1_1,00.html

OECD Guidelines on the Protection of Privacy and Transborder Flows of Personal Data,
http://www.oecd.org/internet/ieconomy/
oecdguidelinesontheprotectionofprivacyandtransborderflowsofpersonaldata.htm#memorandum

Prakash, P., How Surveillance Works in India, *New York Times*, July 10, 2013.

Privacy and Information Security Law Blog—Global Privacy and Information Security Law Updates and Analysis, Hunton and Williams LLP, 2014 (accessed on 1 July 2014).

Raghavan, R. and Ramchandran, R., Data Protection Law in India: An Overview, *The Lex-Warrier Online Law Journal*, January 29, 2013.

Safeguarding Privacy in the Fight against Terrorism, the Report of the Technology and Privacy Advisory Committee, March 2004, 140 pp.
http://www.sainc.com/tapac/finalReport.htm

Slane, B.H., Data Mining and Fair Information Practices Good Business Sense,
http://www.privacy.org.nz/media/data_min.html

Sweeney, L., k-anonymity: A Model for Protecting Privacy, *International Journal on Uncertainty, Fuzziness and Knowledge-based Systems*, 10(5), 2002; 557–570.
http://privacy.cs.cmu.edu/people/sweeney/kanonymity.html

Taipale, K.A., Data Mining and Domestic Security: Connecting the Dots to Make Sense of Data, *The Columbia Science and Technology Law Review*, Vol. 2, December 2003.
http://www.stlr.org/html/volume5/taipaleintro.html

Westin, A.F., Legal Safeguards to Insure Privacy in a Computer Society, *Communications of the ACM*, Vol. 10, No. 9, pp. 533–537, September 1967.

CASE STUDY 10

Privacy Conflicts in CRM Services for Online Shops: A Case Study*

Reproduced with permission
from the Australian Computer Society

ABSTRACT

Sophisticated Data Mining tools are able to provide valuable information for online retailers. But especially when an external data mining service provider is contracted, important questions arise concerning the privacy preservation of the shop customers. This paper discusses the specific case of an online retailer who aims at usefully analysing customers' data for product and capacity planning while still preserving its users' privacy. We expose several privacy-sensitive areas and propose protection measures in order to face these problems.

Keywords: Online Retailer, Metrics, Privacy levels

1. INTRODUCTION

The fast progress in networking technologies has led to an enormous amount of digital information stored all over the world. This process has been accompanied by a rise of tools that are able to collect data, add them to databases and find information that could not be discovered in an obvious way. The analysis of huge data amounts is of particular relevance in online commerce, where companies are given the opportunity to learn more about their customer profitability and customer segmentation. While yielding benefits to the companies (marketing, etc.), these analyses of customer behaviour, preferences and interests may provoke the fear of privacy breaches (Kobsa 2002).

Individuals often transmit personal information to their online retailer, either actively by sending customer data (e.g. a shipping address for books), or passively, by leaving traces that are registered at the server site (in the so-called web log). A service provider who wants to mine its transaction and web log data, is confronted with a twofold privacy problem. First, with regard to customers' privacy: Can the mining of data disclose sensitive information about a client's identity or behaviour? Second, with regard to the company's own confidential information: If the service of data mining is outsourced to a third party, how can it be guaranteed that the mining company is not misusing the received information for analyses that exceed the agreed purposes?

We will not discuss the strengths and weaknesses of privacy regulations in different countries. A lot of related work has been contributed to this issue (e.g. Bellman et al. 2001). Instead, we want to describe and analyse potential threats that occur when interacting with a typical online retailer: What kind of data is revealed and what part of it is potentially privacy-critical? What purposes do online shops pursue when analysing client data and are they achievable without compromising customer privacy? Which technical measures can be employed to guarantee a maximum

---

* Boyens, C., O. Günther, and M. Teltzrow, 2001, Privacy conflicts in CRM services for online shops: a case study, Workshop on Privacy, Security, and Data Mining. This paper appeared in *Conferences in Research and Practice in Information Technology,* Vol 1. J. Weckert, Ed. Copyright (C) 2001, Australian Computer Society Inc. {boyens,gunther,teltzrow}@wiwi.hu-berlin.de

of privacy to the customers and to still allow the shop to obtain valuable results on the other hand?

Chapter 2 gives an overview of threats to user privacy in online shops. After explaining the users' priorities on different kinds of data, we examine when and how this customer information is collected and processed. We outline possibilities of abuse and discuss some technical countermeasures.

Chapter 3 is dedicated to an extensive case study. We analyse the data revelations of an online retailer who is outsourcing the analysis of his product and customer profitabilities to an external data mining service provider. We examine in how far different types of measures compromise different levels of privacy. We conclude with a couple of new research ideas.

2. THREATS TO PRIVACY IN ONLINE SHOPS

2.1 Privacy Awareness

The privacy awareness of web users has grown significantly: They often leave web sites that require registration and even renounce shopping online due to privacy concerns (Kobsa 2002). Ackerman et al. (1999) report 87% of their web users being at least somewhat concerned about threats to their personal privacy when online. Hoffman et al. (1999) found that this is due to the fact that users perceive a lack of control over their data while interacting online. This lack of control even increases when more than two parties (customer and retailer) are involved. This may be the case when an additional service is invoked that requires data input, e.g. when the coverage of a credit card is verified at a remote system during the purchase process, or when the transactional data is analysed by a third party using data mining tools in order to indicate customer and product profitability. This frameset raises several questions: As the retailer is obliged by law not to forward customer-related data to a third party, how can one modify his database in a way that all requirements are met while still allowing the external data mining company to perform useful analyses?

In the following, we will examine what kind of data revelation is perceived as dangerous by the users. In a second step, we will discuss how this sensitive information is collected and finally, we will give an overview of current techniques in use that enable the retailer to minimize the risk of sensitive information revelation to a third party.

2.2 User Perception of Sensitive Data

The importance of particular personal information differs tremendously among users. Ackerman et al. (2001) report that only 1% (resp. 3%) of their sample felt comfortable with giving away their social security number (resp. their credit card number), whereas 69% would divulge their age and even 76% their email address. Spiekermann et al. (2001) point out that individuals differentiate between profile- and identity-revealing data when transmitting personal information. Identity-related data potentially points to a single person via key attributes such as first name, second name, social security number or address. Profile-related information refers to attributes such as profession, age, hobbies, interests, preferences, etc. The most sensitive profile-related attributes, nevertheless, are income and medical information (Ackerman et al. 1999).

People who want neither their identity nor their profile to be revealed are called privacy fundamentalists, who correspond to 17% to 30% of all web users, following Ackerman et al. (1999) and Spiekermann et al. (2001). We will focus on this most sensitive type of user and assume that she will give the shop no more data than what is absolutely essential to fulfil the transaction at hand.

2.3 Collecting Customer-related Information

After discussing different types of data and their significance to the customers, it is interesting to know how this information may be collected by the retailer. Basically, an online shop customer can divulge information in two ways. First, he may transmit personal data actively to the remote site by filling fields with text and pressing the "submit" button. This may be the case when indicating the shipping address for a product bought online or when registering as a new client. Indeed, some common attributes such as name, billing address, shipping address and payment and delivery preferences are necessary to finalize online transactions between customer and online shop. Furthermore, additional attributes can be necessary such as password entry for registration, or credit card number or date of birth to conclude the sale. On most retail sites this data is sufficient to place an order.

A second source for customer-related data is web log data. A user who interacts with a remote computer (passively) leaves traces that describe his behaviour pattern. An online book store may not only gather information about products bought but also about books that were just looked up by the customer. The connection between the (anonymous) browsing behaviour and the specific person is achieved via required log-ins, session ID's or via cookies (Srivastava et al. 2000). Once a specific user is recognized, the service can look up the cookie on the client's computer, link the information to the user's profile and draw conclusions about her preferences. This may result in a purchase recommendation e.g. about football books when some related articles have been looked up during the last online session. One can easily imagine more critical examples dealing with books about particular medical diseases.

Table 1 summarizes the basic differences in the collection of customer-related data.

Table 1: Transactional Data vs. Web Log Data

Transactional Data	*Weg Log Data*
Actively divulged	Passively recorded
Registration and transaction purposes	Personalization purposes
Rather identity-revealing	Rather profile-revealing
Insecurity about correctness	Deterministic data

Attributes of web log data alone can not reveal an individual's identity. By analysing them, however, companies often obtain a more precise image of their customers and products. The linking of user profiles and log files bears risks of abuse which will be discussed in the following.

2.4 Data Mining: Benefits and Risks

Purposes and methods of data mining for online shops are manifold and often help the shop to analyse business-critical data including person-related information. The knowledge about customers is a valuable asset for the company in a competitive landscape. However, data protection regulations rightfully limit the use of person-related data. Nevertheless, the potential for privacy breaches is a risk to customers, especially if highly user-sensitive data such as medical, financial or transaction data are involved.

Meanwhile, advances in data mining have allowed to search for patterns in large databases more efficiently, while data sources such as the Internet have increased the amount of person-related information. External data from surveys, geographical demographics or from an individual's financial and purchase history have contributed to a better picture of customers.

This has put companies in to a position to segment customers according to demographic profiles and rank segments according to their profitability for the shop. Thus, marketing campaigns can be improved to better target customer preferences.

Of course, the abundance of personal data is an incentive for abuse. This is just a sample of what could happen to a shop client:

- The shop could enrich its customer data sets with additional demographic information about the residence area of its clients. This could lead to an even more detailed user profile.
- If the user accepts cookies, the browsing behaviour on the shop site could be tracked every time the customer is entering the shop. Besides the referrer that indicates the site from which the user comes, a long-term profile about his preferred products and services is easy to produce.
- Payment failures and demographics often lead to a credit history that can be used to expulse potentially insolvent customers.

In the European Union (EU), critical profile aggregation in shops starts when data about individual customers are used for other purposes than transaction fulfilment or if the customer has not explicitly agreed to the usage of her data for other purposes (European Union 1995).

Due to the risk of losing reputation, most online shops handle person-related data securely. Nevertheless, sharing data and outsourcing data mining will increase in the future as companies increasingly rely on external service providers. Thus, methods for handling transaction and log data from an online shop need to be considered. This will be addressed in the following section.

2.5 Technical Approaches

The online service provider may take several steps to avoid privacy breaches when transferring customer data to an external data mining company. The basic idea is to turn the entire, "sensitive" database into a modified, "clean" database that can then be sent to the data miner. There are different approaches to realizing such a modification:

(1) *Limit access to the data*, i.e. hide attributes that potentially identify data subjects. In an online shop, this could be the *customer number*, the *name* or the *email address*. The differentiation between sensitive data and necessary data for useful mining is not an obvious task because of the so-called *inference problem*.

Even though identity keys are not given, other attributes may doubtlessly point to a single person (Denning 1982). Sweeney (2001), e.g., found that for 69% of all data records in a partially anonymized table the combination of the given birth date and zip code were unique identifiers that pointed to a specific person.

(2) *Aggregate the data*, i.e. to summarize the data in a way that no conclusions can be drawn for a single subject. For an online shop, this could mean to transfer the revenue figures of a whole day instead of single customer purchase volume. This would still allow for trend analysis but not for the assignment of single purchases to specific customers.

Nevertheless, this method is facing the so-called *aggregation problem*: In order to protect individual sensitive information, data has been aggregated so extensively that no reasonable mining is possible anymore.

(3) *Assign unique identifiers randomly*, i.e. to deploy primary keys that do not contain additional information about the subject they are pointing to. E.g., keys should not contain initials as it often happens in student computer IDs. A user called Bob Miller often is assigned an ID like "bm259@...". Even if no direct information can be drawn from the keys, the same attribute values from a number of subjects with similar ID's pròvoke further investigation.

A more elaborate summary of related work can be found in (Agrawal 2000, Adam and Wortmann 1989), who classify statistical privacy techniques in query restriction and data perturbation. For example, query restriction can include techniques such as restricting the size of query results (Fellegi 1972, Denning, Denning and Schwartz 1979), controlling the overlap amongst successive queries (Dobkin, Jones and Lipton 1979), suppression of data cells of small size (Cox 1980), and clustering entities into mutually exclusive atomic populations (Yu and Chin 1977). Perturbation techniques include swapping values between records (Denning 1982), replacing the original database by a sample from the same distribution (Lefons, Silvestri and Tangorra 1983, Liew, Choi, Liew 1985), adding noise to the results of a query (Beck 1980), and sampling the result of a query (Denning 1982). The perturbation family also includes a more recent proposal for privacy in association rule mining (Estivill-Castro and Brankovic 1999).

Of course this listing is not complete, but gives a good overview of existing modification methods. In the following chapter, we will apply these methods to a specific case and we will verify their suitability in concrete application scenarios.

3. CASE STUDY

3.1 Data Sample and Analysis Objectives

The case in this paper is based on a data sample from a click-and-mortar retailer with affiliated branch offices across Europe.

The company's overall goal is to identify the impact of their recently launched Internet presence on overall business performance. More specifically, the company was interested in information that would allow segmentation of its online customers to improve its marketing efforts. Thus, the company wanted to know who their customers are and what purchase behaviour they exhibit.

The company consulted the Institute of Information Systems at Humboldt University for support on data mining tasks. In order to protect customer privacy, we looked at the data model of the transaction and log data and proposed methods to anonymise the data. The data that had to be anonymised included a sample from transaction data of approximately 14,000 online customers. Moreover, log data was cleaned, sessionized and stored in a separate table for analysis with OLAP techniques (Zaiane 1998).

In addition the company acquired data from external service providers to determine geographic characteristics of online customers.

For our declared goal to disclose potential privacy breaches, one of the most interesting aspects was the data model of the company. The company's database consists of more than 30 tables from which we identified 7 as privacy-relevant. Each relation consisted of a set of attributes. In order to anonymise the data, we identified those attributes that were necessary to calculate relevant CRM measures on the one hand and that could induce privacy breaches on the other hand. The following table represents an overview of the selected tables and attributes:

customer (customer_id, credit_rating, second_name, first_name, gender, date_of_birth)

address (address_id, customer_id, country_code, street_name, street_number, street_number_supplement, zip_code, town, p.o.b., recipient)

order (order_id, customer_id, position_id, status, number, order_date, delivery_type, payment_method, delivery_date, status_change, currency)

position (position_id, order_id, product_id, quantity, price, currency)

retour (retour_id, order_id, retour_date, retour_value)

logdata (session_id, customer_id, geography, pages_visited, browser type, access_time, status_code)

external data (geo_id, customer_id, longitude_customer, latitude_customer, zip_code_shop, longitude_shop, latitude_shop, street_name, product_preferences, survey_data)

3.2 Sample CRM Measures

The company's specific analysis needs focused on a variety of metrics. However, in this paper we only present a sample of customer-related metrics that might infer privacy-concerns and demonstrate different levels of privacy criticality. Methods are proposed to prevent an invasion of one's individual privacy on the one hand and to allow the company to mine business-critical information on the other hand.

Important measures of CRM have been summarized in (Cutler and Sterne 2000). We selected a set of customer-related metrics and checked their criticality concerning privacy invasion.

Attributes affected by this analysis included the tables customers, address, order, position and external data.

The queries on the transaction data were conducted with OLAP methods (Codd et al. 1993). Further analysis of web log data was conducted with advanced statistical analysis methods including association rule mining, clustering and decision trees. In this context,

Table 2: Overview measures, attributes, privacy levels and protection techniques

Privacy Level	*Measure*	*Tables Used*	*Data Type*	*Privacy Protection Technique in Use*
1	Revenue Concentration (RC)	`Customer, order, position`	`Identity`	Access limitation
2	Revenue partition	`Customer, order, position`	`Identity`	Access limitation, aggregation
3A	Customers geographical distance from local shop	`Customer, external data`	`Identity, Profile`	Access limitation, aggregation
3B	Geo-marketing	`Customer, order, position, external data`	`Identity, Profile`	Access limitation, aggregation

related work has been published focusing on privacy protection (Evfimievski et al. 2002).

A sample of four core measures is summarized in the following table. It points out attributes and tables used and differentiates between identity and profile data. Furthermore, it proposes protection techniques to address privacy concerns.

The proposed measures all include attributes directly related to individual customers. We explain the relevance of the measures for the company, differentiate three privacy levels and propose techniques to calculate the measures without violating an individual's privacy.

3.2.1 Level 1: Little Impact on Privacy

Identifying the most profitable customers and binding them to the company is a declared goal in CRM. Therefore, a typical measure is the revenue concentration which points out the contribution of a smaller percentage of customers to the overall revenue of the company. A typical conclusion drawn from a revenue concentration analysis would be: *10% of the customers generate 63% of all revenues*. The results are often depicted in a *Lorenz-Curve*, a graphical device which allows for the direct interpretation of concentration in subsets.

The following table attributes are necessary to calculate the metric (potentially privacy-compromising attributes in *italics*).

`customer` *`customer_id`*

`order` `order_id`, *`customer_id`*

`position` `position_id, order_id, revenue`

This is a relatively simple case for privacy protection measures: First, there is only one attribute (`customer_id`) that points to the customer in question. Second, the total number of tables and attributes is comparatively low.

Assuming that the `customer_id` primary key is randomly assigned (cf. section 2.5) and contains no information by itself, limiting the access to all other critical attributes such as `name`, `gender`, `dateofbirth`, `address`, etc. should be a solid way to prevent privacy violations.

Nevertheless, this assumes that all other calculated measures require as little sensitive information. This might not necessarily be true. Other metrics may well require some of the sensitive data mentioned above, and once a link between a specific customer and his customer_ID is established, the protected revenue figures would be exposed. That means that the criticality of the Lorenz curve also depends on the other methods employed.

3.2.2 Level 2: Significant Impact on Privacy

In order to refine the revenue analysis of the last section, marketers often partition their customers according to their age or their gender. The aim is to discover specific target groups or segments with high revenue potential. The results of these analyses are often represented as bar diagrams: The abscissa is partitioned into classes who are assigned the total of all revenues of customers that belong to this class.

The following table attributes are necessary to calculate the bar chart:

customer *customer_id, gender, date_of_birth*

order order_id, *customer_id*

position position_id, order_id, revenue

This kind of analysis requires more attributes than the calculation of the Lorenz curve described above which especially increases the inference problem. In her sample, Sweeney (2001) was able to identify 29% of all persons by combining gender and date_of_birth. The shop can now employ various of the security mechanisms discussed in section 2.5. First, it may limit the access to attributes such as name or credit_rating.

Second, it can employ the method of aggregation: For the histogram, it is sufficient to know the age of a customer, the entire date of birth is not necessary. The shop can either transmit the age or the year of birth, which fully meets the requirements.

Third, the shop can alter the denomination of the attribute gender to, say, premium_customer and regular customer, in order to prevent misuse.

3.2.3 Level 3: Huge Impact on Privacy

A third level with a severe potential of privacy impacts is represented by geographical marketing (*geo-marketing*), where external data is combined with customer data from a company.

A variety of tools can link proprietary customer data to demographic, geographic, segmentation, business location and survey data (see e.g. www.mapinfo.com). Therefore, zip codes and address data are often used to combine customer profiles to external data.

The granularity of third party data often includes household levels within a country. The availability of such data may vary in different countries depending on the existing privacy regulations.

Nevertheless, the dilemma of potential privacy breaches on the one hand and the rightful interest of companies to utilize hidden business knowledge on the other hand, is particularly high for geo-marketing.

If data mining tasks are outsourced, the company has to provide the data miner with extensive insights into its customer profiles. Customer attributes such as gender, data_of_birth, credit_rating, zip_code, street_name, street_number, pages_visited, product_name represent valuable input for geo-marketing to search for potential new customers, to identify cross-selling opportunities or to offer loyalty incentives.

According to the attribute zip_code, detailed profile data can be derived for that region. Samples for population profiles according to US zip_codes can be found at [http://www.demographics.caci.com/free_samples/zip_code_searches.htm].

This data is also available on household levels as far as it complies with existing regional privacy regulations. Demographic data can be purchased for different industries or products, [http://www.esribis. com]. Often companies want to estimate the potential market in different regions in comparison with the actual penetration rate of their exiting customers.

In the following, we discuss two important geo-marketing measures: The correlation between shop and customer density in specific regions and product marketing at street level.

Correlation between shop and customer density

An interesting measure for geo-marketing is the physical distance of online customers to the next shop. The correlation between shop density and customer density in specific regions (e.g. the zip code areas) gives valuable insight into the impact of a small-meshed branch network as an additional distribution channel. A possible finding could indicate the need for shop openings in densely populated regions with a relatively small customer share. Enriched with data from other sources such as demographic data, this gives valuable input for determining optimal shop placements and product assortment.

Further conclusions would include recommendations for serving customers across multiple sales channels.

In order to compare the relation between shop and customer density in different regions, the following attributes are necessary:

customer customer_id

address *address_id, customer_id, country_code, zip_code,* town

external data `geo_id, customer_id, longitude_customer, latitude_customer, zip_code_shop, longitude_shop, latitude_shop`

As long as just the pure number of customers in a specific region is relevant to calculate this measure, no sensitive data beyond the `customer_id` and the `zip code` is necessary. This is not critical as long as no additional information can be assigned to the data set. But once the `customer_id` can be linked to orders and products, conclusions can be drawn from the customer's preferences and residence. E.g. a researcher who orders specialized books in his field of interest is likely to be identified by the zip code that indicates the location of his university or research institution.

Our sample was comprised of 14,000 customers spread over an area of approximately 80,000 square kilometers. In order to find clues about new shop placements, the correlation of customer density and shop location had to be measured. Therefore, data was available that linked a zip code area to a longitude/latitude value in a format such as (*ZipCode; Longitude; Latitude*) = (01234;12.1234; 56.7654). With this data, a calculation error had to be taken into account because the customers' and the shops' locations were matched with the geographical center of each zip code area. The zip codes included an area of x_{av} = 43 km^2 on average with values ranging from 2–200 km^2. In densely populated areas—which were most interesting for the retailer—the areas were rather small.

Thereupon minimal distances between customer zip code and shop zip code were calculated. The average distance was x_{min} = 14.3 km with s_{min} = 10.5 km. Apparently, the initial calculation error could already reduce the precise-ness of determining optimal shop placements.

While the maximum error for the distance between customer and shop is acceptable for two zip code areas[1] with an average of x_{av} = 43 km^2 where the maximum error could reach ε_{av} = 7.4 km, larger zip code areas of 200 km^2 could already induce a maximum distance error of ε_{max} = 16 km.

For fine-tuning shop placements, the error might be yet too high, especially if the retailer wants to establish a small-meshed network of stores within a densely populated area.

Thus, geographical values as granular as street coordinates are desirable to achieve better results for shop placements. Having the exact geographical location of a customer, however, infers more severe privacy impacts because precise coordinates could clearly reveal identities of many households.

Furthermore, it has been found that the number of customers per zip code area was x_{cus} = 2.5. The population density for zip code areas was about x_{pop} = 12,500 with s_{pop} = 58,900. This could already represent a potential impact on privacy. The mining service provider would know that there were 2.5 customers per zip code area who bought from the specific retailer. Especially for sparsely populated zip code areas—the smallest data cell included 12 residents—the data miner could possibly find out who the customers are. Information about the products bought represents an additional factor for concluding customer identities.

Nevertheless, in this case, the analysis on the zip code level already helped the company identifying densely populated areas offering only remote access to a physical shop.

As described in this case, aggregation is not the best solution to this problem of optimal store placement as it results in a lack of precision. Extensive research has been conducted to determine statistical query results (*sum*, *count*, *average* etc.) without compromising sensitive information about individuals. Adam et al. (1989) have suggested techniques such as query restriction and data perturbation for obtaining high quality point estimates. However, Adam also indicated that the proposed techniques do not completely prevent exact or partial disclosure of individual infor-mation. A summary of references for protecting privacy in queries on statistical databases has been given in (Agrawal, Srikant 2000). Proposed techniques such as suppression of data cells of small size (Cox 1980), could contribute some solution to our case. For example, excluding zip code areas with small sizes such as in data cells below a threshold of 100 residents

[1] For simplification reasons the zip code areas were assumed to be round.

would already help in preserving privacy to some extent.

More recent privacy protection techniques have been proposed in (Agrawal, Srikant 2000, Estivill-Castro, Brankovic 1999). If the company was just interested in the analysis of the distribution of their actual customers—for example the number of customers in zip code areas—*discretization* and *value distortion* as well as *value dissociation* could deliver valuable results under the premise of privacy preservation. The basic values in a user's record such as identity and profile data would be perturbed using a randomization function based on Gaussian or Uniform perturbation. It has been found that the reconstruction of the distribution would cause only a small drop in accuracy compared to the original distribution (Agrawal, Srikant 2000).

Nevertheless, geographical mining still remains a problem as far as the calculation of distances with geographical data as granular as street and household levels are concerned. Even if longitude/latitude values and other attributes are sufficiently perturbed, an external miner could easily find out who the original customer was as long as longitude/latitude values are given.

A solution that is often pursued in practice is to allocate customers to so-called micro-cells containing a specific threshold number of households. The cells are characterized by attributes such as geographical coordinates, income or purchase preferences. Geographical cell infor-mation is not detailed enough to reveal an individual's identity. It would be an interesting research problem to determine the optimal size of a micro-cell that provides both the highest privacy as well as accuracy.

Product marketing at street level

Another measure in this category is product marketing on street level. It is of special interest to the company to spend marketing budgets optimally by targeting customers only with services, product offers and promotion mailings that would most likely catch their interest. For product campaigns companies might want to know for which streets in a town it would be most beneficial to conduct direct marketing. According to information about customers' previous purchases, companies may predict what the customer might buy next and provide her with targeted product information. Therefore, the following attributes would be necessary:

```
customer customer_id
address address_id, customer_id,
country_code, street_name, street_number,
street_number_supplement, zip_code, town)
order (order_id, customer_id)
position (position_id, order_id, product_id,
quantity, price)
```

For product marketing, sophisticated algorithms have been developed such as collaborative filtering (Yu et al. 2001, Aggarwal et al. 1999) and association rule mining (Agrawal et al. 1993; Sarawagi et al. 1998) to predict what a customer might buy next based on her own and others' previous purchases. Association rules are often represented with a confidence and a support factor in a format such as $Bread \Rightarrow_{s=0.5,\ c=0.8} Butter$. For product marketing at street level, a company could pick an area, look at the products and volumes that have been bought and find matching products with a high support level in order to optimally target that region. Often external, demographic data about product preferences can be added. In this case, the company was also interested in transaction services and delivery options preferred by customers. For example, it wanted to know preferred payment methods (*P=online payment*, *D=Payment on Delivery*) of repeat customers (*R*) in comparison to one-time-shoppers (*O*) such as $R \Rightarrow_{s=0.5,\ c=0.8} P$ without violating privacy regulations.

Recent approaches to maintaining privacy in association rule mining have been published in (Rizvi, Haritsa 2002). They propose an approach based on probabilistic distortion providing both a high degree of privacy to the user as well as a high level of accuracy in the mining results. The database model in our case would consist of columns containing the online shop's products or delivery and service options. Each row would contain a sequence of boolean operators representing a customer who purchased the product or not. Similarly, the service and delivery options would be mapped for each customer. This problem could be solved with the probabilistic randomization approach proposed in (Rizvi, Haritsa 2002). For the example with loyal customers a previous query has to identify repeat buyers first.

For the example of marketing at street level, a similar problem as in the first example of section 3.2 occurs. From the attributes `street_name` and `street_number` an external data miner could easily conclude the real names of the customers. With regard to the level 2 measure of customer discrimination regarding gender and age, the `customer_ID` grants the link to the profile and is another opportunity for abuse. If executed to this large extent, an almost complete picture of the customers can be drawn.

The EU's privacy directive forbids this kind of data forwarding to third parties if no explicit compliance was given by the customer. The extent of collected data cannot be justified by its direct relevance for the completion of the transaction.

However, the shop might address those privacy breaches by employing a couple of technical measures. The most important one is to reduce the precision of the geographical information. In the zip code case, the aggregation of several zip code areas to bigger regions could reduce the threat of re-identification, which of course complicates the task to place shop openings precisely.

In the street level case, limiting the access to the street number already reduces the identification risk while still granting reasonable results. Nevertheless, the shop has to undergo a clear trade-off between the preservation of their users' privacy and the preciseness of the data mining results. If the aggregation is continued to *town* and *zip code* level, significant losses in the precision of the results cannot be avoided.

To sum up, the threat of geo-marketing to customer privacy depends very much on the specific measure in use. Whereas zip-code based analyses may not automatically be harmful, the revelation of complete addresses often suffices to identify persons. If the related profiles can be linked, the idea of the "transparent customer" is not far from realization.

4. CONCLUSIONS AND FURTHER RESEARCH

The analysis of the present case reveals that an online retailer who contracts an external data mining service provider has to consider a couple of delicate issues when the shop users' privacy shall be guaranteed.

As forwarding the entire customer database to the service provider does neither conform to current privacy regulations nor to the very own interest of the shop itself, some technical measures as access limitation or aggregation techniques help to reduce the potential of consequent privacy breaches. Nevertheless, a remaining risk consists of inference opportunities from the restricted data. In the case of geo-marketing, the shop obviously needs to undergo a trade-off between the preciseness of its results and the potential privacy violation of its users.

From a legal viewpoint, it would be interesting to know if the mentioned technical measures suffice to meet the requirements of current privacy regulations in different countries, especially as forwarding sensitive data to third parties is commonly prohibited.

From a technical point of view, the design of a "bullet-proof" geo-marketing data system represents an attractive research problem. This gains even more momentum since data mining tasks are increasingly outsourced to external service providers. Developing encryption techniques for a data mining web service that guarantees anonymised transfer of data back and forth from a company to a service provider is a desirable research goal. Finally, an interesting question is in how far the lax handling of these privacy issues actually harms the general reputation of an online shop or any other online company.

REFERENCES

ACKERMAN, M.S., CRANOR, L.F., REAGLE, J. (1999): Privacy in E-Commerce: Examining User Scenarios and Privacy Preferences. *Proceedings of the first ACM conference on Electronic Commerce*, Denver.

AGGARWAL, C.C., WOLF, J., WU. K.-L., YU, P.S. (1999): Horting hatches an egg: a new graph-theoretic approach to collaborative filtering. *Proceedings of the fifth ACM SIGKDD International Conference on Knowledge Discovery and Data Mining*, San Diego.

AGRAWAL, R., IMIELINSKI, T., SWAMI, A. (1993): Mining associations between sets of items in massive databases. *ACM SIGMOD International Conference on Management of Data*, Washington, D.C.

AGRAWAL, R., SRIKANT, R. (2000): Privacy-Preserving Data Mining. *Proceeding of the ACM SIGMOD Conference on Management of Data*, Dallas.

BECK, L.L. (1980): A security mechanism for statistical databases. *ACM TODS*, 5(3): 316–328.

BELLMAN, S., JOHNSON, E.J., LOHSE, G.L. (2001): To Opt-In or Opt-Out? It Depends on the Question. *Communications of the ACM*, Vol. 44, No. 2.

BOYENS, C., GÜNTHER, O. (2002): Trust is not enough: Privacy and Security in ASP and Web Service Environments. *Proceedings of Advances in Database and Information Systems* (*ADBIS 2002*), Bratislava.

CLIFTON, C., MARKS, D. (1996): Security and Privacy Implications of Data Mining. *Proceedings of the ACM SIGMOD workshop on Data Mining and Knowledge Discovery,* Montreal, Canada.

CODD, E.F., CODD, S.B., SALLEY, C.T. (1993): Providing OLAP (On-Line Analytical Processing) to User-Analysts: An IT Mandate. White Paper, E.F. Codd & Associates, Sunnyvale.

COX, L.H. (1980): Suppression methodology and statistical disclosure control, *Journal of the American Statistical Association,* 75(370).

CUTLER, M., STERNE J. (2001): E-metrics — business metrics for the new economy. *Technical report*, NetGenesis Corp., [http://www.netgen.com/emetrics], access date: July 22, 2001.

DENNING, D. (1982), *Cryptography and Data Security*, Addison-Wesley.

DENNING, D.E., DENNING, P.J., SCHWARTZ, M.D. (1979): The tracker: A threat to statistical database security. *ACM TODS*, 4(1):76–79.

DOBKIN, D., JONES, A.K., LIPTON, R.J. (1979): Secure databases: Protection against user influence. *ACM TODS*, 4(1):97–106.

ESTIVILL-CASTRO, V., BRANKOVIC, L. (1999): Data Swapping: Balancing Privacy against Precision in Mining for Logic Rules. *First International Conference on Data Warehousing and Knowledge Discovery*, Florence, Italy.

EUROPEAN UNION (1995): Directive 95/46/EC on the protection of individuals with regard to the processing of personal data and on the free movement of such data. July 1995.

EVFIMIEVSKI, A., SRIKANT, R., AGRAWAL, R., GEHRKE, J. (2002): Privacy Preserving Mining of Association Rules. *Proceedings of ACM SIGKDD*, Edmonton, Alberta.

FAYYAD, U.M., PIATETSKY-SHAPIRO, G., SMYTH, P. (1996): From Data Mining to Knowledge Discovery: An Overview. In *Advances in Knowledge Discovery and Data Mining*. 1–34. FAYYAD, U.M., PIATETSKY-SHAPIRO, G., SMYTH, P. (eds). AAAI Press/MIT Press.

FEIGENBAUM, J., FREEDMAN, M.J., SANDER, T. SHOSTACK, A. (2001): Privacy Engineering for Digital Rights Management Systems. In *Proceedings of the ACM Workshop in Security and Privacy in Digital Rights Management.*

FELLEGI, I.P. (1972): On the question of statistical confidentiality. *Journal of American Statistical Association,* 67(337):7–18.

HACIGUMUS, H., MEHROTRA, S., IYER, B., LI, C. (2002): Executing SQL over Encrypted Data in the Database Service Provider Model. *Proceedings of the SIGMOD International Conference on the Management of Data*, Madison.

HOFFMAN, D.L., NOVAK, T.P., PERALTA, M. (1999): Building Consumer Trust Online. *Communications of the ACM*, Vol. 42, No. 4.

KOBSA, A. (2002): Personalized Hypermedia and International Privacy. *Communications of the ACM, Special Issue on Adaptive Web-based Systems and Adaptive Hypermedia*. 45(5): 64–67.

LEFONS, E., SILVESTRI, A., TANGORRA, F. (1983): An analytical approach to statistical databases. *Procceedings of the 9th International Conference on Very Large Databases* (VLDB). 260–274.

RIVEST, R., ADLEMAN, L., DERTOUZOS, M.L. (1978): On Data Banks and Privacy Homomorphisms. In *Foundations of Secure Computations*. Academic Press, New York.

RIZVI, S.J., HARITSA, J.R. (2002): Maintaining Data privacy in Association Rule Mining. *Proceedings of the 28th VLDB Conference*, Hong Kong, China.

SARAWAGI, S., THOMAS, S., AGRAWAL, R. (1998): Integrating association rule mining with relational database systems: alternatives and implications. *ACM SIGMOD International Conference on Management of Data*, Washington.

SPIEKERMANN, S., GROßKLAGS, J., BERENDT, B. (2001): E-privacy in 2nd generation E-commerce: privacy preferences versus actual behavior. *Proceedings of the 3rd ACM conference on Electronic Commerce*, Tampa, Florida.

SRIVASTAVA, J., COOLEY, R., DESHPANDE, M., TAN, P.-N. (2000): Web Usage Mining: Discovery and Applications of Usage Patterns from Web Data, *ACM SIGKDD Explorations* 1(2):12–23.

SWEENEY, L. (2001): Computational Disclosure Control: A Primer on Data Privacy Protection, Ph.D. thesis. MIT, Cambridge [http://www.swiss.ai.mit.edu/classes/6.805/articles/privacy/sweeney-thesis-draft.pdf]

YU, C.T., CHIN, F.Y. (1977): A study on the protection of statistical databases. *Proceedings ACM SIGMOD, International Conference of the Management of Data*, Toronto, Canada.

YU, K., XU, X., ESTER, M., KRIEGEL, H.-P. (2001): Collaborative Filtering and Algorithms: Selecting relevant instances for efficient and accurate collaborative filtering, *Proceedings of the 10th international conference on information and knowledge management,* New York.

ZAIANE, O.R. (1998): Discovering Web Access Patterns and Trends by Applying OLAP and Data Mining Technology on Web Logs. In *Proceedings of the IEEE Advances in Digital Libaries Conference*, Santa Barbara.

CASE STUDY 10 SUMMARY

This study was published in a workshop in 2001:

Boyens, C., Gunther, O., and Telzrow, M., Privacy conflicts in CRM services for online shops: A case study, Workshop on Privacy, Security, and Data Mining, 2001.

The case study deals with privacy of customers of an online shop and looks at what type of information is considered sensitive by customers. The data of several thousand customers was looked at and the data was divided as

- Little impact on privacy
- Significant impact on privacy
- Huge impact on privacy

Recommendations are then made how the company should deal with various classes of data when contacting an external company for data mining.

CASE STUDY 10 EXERCISES

1. What were the primary aims of the case study?
2. How was the data divided into the three categories?
3. Describe the recommendations that were made to the company regarding privacy.

Answers to Multiple Choice Questions

Chapter 1

1. (a) and (b)	**2.** (c)	**3.** (c)	**4.** (d)	**5.** (e)	**6.** (a)
7. (d)	**8.** (b)	**9.** (c)	**10.** (a)	**11.** (b)	**12.** (b)

Chapter 2

1. (a)	**2.** (e)	**3.** (d)	**4.** (d)	**5.** (b)	**6.** (d)
7. (e)	**8.** (e)	**9.** (c)	**10.** (b)	**11.** (d)	**12** (d)

Chapter 3

1. (c)	**2.** (a)	**3.** (c)	**4.** (a)	**5.** (c)	**6.** (a)
7. (c)	**8.** (a)	**9.** (e)	**10.** (b)		

Chapter 4

1. (a)	**2.** (d)	**3.** (b)	**4.** (c) and (d)	**5.** (a) and (d)	**6.** (c)
7. (a)	**8.** (a)	**9.** (d)	**10.** (e)		

Chapter 5

1. (d)	**2.** (b)	**3.** (c)	**4.** (d)	**5.** (d)	**6.** (b)
7. (a)	**8.** (a)	**9.** (b)	**10.** (d)	**11.** (b) and (c)	**12.** (d)

Chapter 6

1. (e)	**2.** (c)	**3.** (d)	**4.** (d)	**5.** (b)	**6.** (d)
7. (d)	**8.** (c)	**9.** (b) and (c)	**10.** (c)		

Chapter 7

1. (d) **2.** (d) **3.** (c) **4.** (c) **5.** (c) **6.** (a) and (b)
7. (c) **8.** (d) **9.** (c) **10.** (a)

Chapter 8

1. (a) **2.** (b) **3.** (a) and (b) **4.** (d) **5.** (c) **6.** (c)
7. (d) **8.** (b) **9.** (b) **10.** (a) and (c) **11.** (a) and (d) **12.** (d)
13. (d) **14.** (a)

Chapter 9

1. (a) **2.** (d) **3.** (b) **4.** (c) **5.** (d) **6.** (d)
7. (a) **8.** (d) **9.** (a) **10.** (c)

Chapter 10

1. (c) **2.** (c) **3.** (d) **4.** (a) **5.** (d) **6.** (a)
7. (c) **8.** (a)

Index